STATE GEOLOGICAL S[...]
J.D. WHITN[...]

TOPOGR[...]

# CENTRAL CALIFORNIA

C.F. HOFFMANN, Principal Topographer.
V. WACKENREUDER, J.T. GARDNER, A. CRAVEN, A.D. WILSON,
Field Assistants.
1873.

# Fresno County—The Pioneer Years

Sponsored by the
Fresno City and County Historical Society

# Fresno County— The Pioneer Years

## From the Beginning to 1900

by Charles W. Clough
and
William B. Secrest, Jr.

Editor
Bobbye Sisk Temple

Fresno Panorama West Books Fresno, California 1984

Library of Congress Catalog Card Number 84-061577
ISBN 0-914330-70-5

Published by
Panorama West Books
2002 North Gateway, Suite 102
Fresno, California 93727
Manufactured in the United States of America

# Contents

## Maps

# Preface and Acknowledgments

This book makes up the first part of a projected two-volume Fresno County history; even though the county's formal history spans but 128 years, it is now impossible to relate it between two covers. Here, then, is a record—as complete as we could make it—of the county's past up to 1900. Important events since then will be detailed in the second volume.

To date, nine books have been published overviewing Fresno County history either wholly or in large part. Each had its own editorial or commercial goals. Space does not permit a critique of each and generalizations are risky, but a few comments seem appropriate.

Of the nine, five were "mug books"; they were subsidized by biographies and pictures (mug shots) of those who were willing to pay for one or both of these privileges. Two others were partially subsidized by payment for the inclusion of persons' homes or businesses. This does not mean that the books were bad, per se—three of them were quite good. The major objection is that the subsidies guaranteed underwriting only a limited printing so most people never had a chance to buy a book and they are in short supply today. The libraries fortunate enough to have a copy of the better books are obliged to keep them under lock and key—this does not encourage the reading of history just for the pure enjoyment of it.

Wallace W. Elliott published his *History of Fresno County*—the first book-length treatise on the subject—in 1882, and it was well received. The same cannot be said for the second, which followed in less than ten years. The *Memorial and Biographical History of Fresno, Tulare and Kern Counties* brought the following comments in the November 13, 1891, *Fresno Daily Evening Expositor*:

> A few days ago the volumes arrived in Fresno and were delivered to subscribers. A roar at once went up . . . It was said that the book was to contain maps, diagrams and pictures, which it did not contain . . . Instead of a history of Fresno, Tulare and Kern there was a sort of chronicle of events, without much regard to time, place or relationship. There were no maps at all; and much of the space that might have been given to historical matter was taken up with dry statistics.

One is obligated to agree with the above comments after reading the book today. It had been sold for eighteen dollars and that in a period when sugar was selling for six cents a pound.

Also in 1891, Thomas H. Thompson published the *Official Atlas of Fresno County* with a brief history by C. O. Ziegenfuss. The next entry in this field, Paul A. Vandor's *History of Fresno County* appeared in 1919 in two volumes. Lilbourne A. Winchell's history in 1930 was the best of all. Ben R. Walker followed it with two books, the *Fresno Blue Book* and *Fresno Community History* in 1941 and 1946 respectively. (See bibliography for all these books.)

The other two were Wallace Smith's *Garden of the Sun* and the *Fresno County Almanac*. The former concerned itself with the history of the San Joaquin Valley with Fresno County getting preferential attention. The *Almanac* is admirable for its scope—all Fresno County towns of any significance are covered—a feature missing in large part from all other histories.

As we researched and wrote this volume we were always appreciative of the efforts of our predecessors while remaining ever mindful of their weaknesses and strengths. This work, it is hoped, accentuates the latter and eludes the former, but we have surely made a few errors and unwittingly omitted some important data. For these transgressions we apologize, and trust that alert readers will set us aright for the sake of future editions.

In this volume, our major aim had been simple: to make the Fresno County of yesteryear live again. To do this, we have employed three integral features: a narrative that provides a basic historical account, the reprinting of important historical documents, reminiscences and other items to help supply the narrative with depth, and the extensive use of illustrations and maps. We hope that these materials, considered together, will enthrall, enlighten and inform the reader. If they make the past come alive, we are satisfied.

We have deliberately written this book for the layman, while endeavoring to keep its quality and accuracy in the scholarly tradition. Since this is the first county history to appear in many a year, we felt it more important to speak to the general public, rather than the specialist. For these reasons, the book has not been weighted down with footnotes. Instead, we have provided an extensive annotated bibliography, so that readers can (1) find out more about historical subjects that pique their interest, and (2) know the difference— at least in our opinion—between reliable and unreliable sources, and the vast majority that fall in-between and must be used with caution. No qualitative guide to the literature of Fresno County history has been offered before, and we hope that this list will inspire more evaluative treatises of its kind.

The arrangement of this book is a nervous compromise between chronology and subject matter. We trust it will provide adequate continuity for the reader; few, if any, historical works are perfect in this regard. We begin with a brief introduction to the county's geology, geography, flora and fauna, and follow that with an account of its first inhabitants—the Indians. Early explorations, the gold rush and later mining activities are then considered. The county's first military outpost and first county seat (Fort Miller and Millerton, respectively) are then described at length, and after that the early cattle, lumber and agricultural industries are taken up. At this point, the 1872–1885 history of the county's hub and second seat, Fresno, is described, followed by a discussion of agriculture in the 1875–1887 period. The book then shifts to thematic concerns for five chapters: miniature histories of towns in four county regions (the west side, central flatlands, east side and Sierra) and a long dissertation on nineteenth-century crime. Rounding out the book are chapters on Fresno in 1885–1900 and agriculture in 1888–1900.

Anyone familiar with previous county histories will recognize that this scheme differs radically from all of them, and considers county towns and crime at greater length than ever before. Many familiar stories will be found, but we have taken pains to unearth new information and present it wherever appropriate. Thanks to a detailed survey of selected official records, period newspapers and local archival material, 50 percent or better of this book's material is new and cannot be found in the common historical sources.

In the three years it has taken to produce this volume, we have been assisted by many, but three institutions and their staffs deserve special mention. Director Sharon Hiigel and Archivist Maria Ortiz of the Fresno City and County Historical Society endured many months of pestering from us, braving summer heat and winter cold so we could dig through their extensive holdings in an unheated and uncooled building. It was an arduous, but historically profitable, process. We shall always remain grateful for their indulgence.

The late Dr. Samuel Suhler, head of the Fresno County Free Library's reference department, and his successor, Linda Goff, have advanced many helpful suggestions over the years and provided us with a host of helpful materials—in particular, a file of the first county newspaper, the *Fresno Times*. Our thanks to them, and to library staff members Ed Plummer, John Jewell and Charles Griggs.

We are also indebted to Ronald J. Mahoney, head of Special Collections at the Henry Madden Library, California State University Fresno; his assistant, Jean Coffey; and University Librarian Lillie S. Parker for many favors. Ron's eye for unusual and obscure source material is phenomenal, and he has pointed us toward a host of items we might have missed otherwise in our search for information.

Not long ago William B. Secrest, Sr. mentioned to the younger of us, "I want a big fat credit line for doing the maps and dust jacket for this book, for helping to proof the chapters and for the use of Fort Miller, Millerton, mining and crime dope from my files." There it is; we trust he will be satisfied. (For moral support during the term of this project, thanks go to a more modest contributor—Shirley Secrest, wife of W.B.S., Sr. and mother of W.B.S., Jr.)

It is difficult to define the help given by Carmen P. Clough because it was a daily sacrifice of time and activities over a long period while her most grateful husband pored over maps and writings, pounded the typewriter or otherwise separated himself from the daily routine of living. She also did yeoman service as a proofreader and gave expert assistance in solving some problems resulting from the use of Spanish in early land grants and writings. Thank you, Carmen, thank you many times over.

This manuscript has benefited immeasurably from suggestions and advice given by June English, Fresno County's dedicated historian. Her articles on early-day people and events, published in the *Ash Tree Echo* and other places, have been most enlightening to us, and have shed light on many dark subjects.

Assistance was received from scores of individuals including several who loaned us pictures. Credit lines on the pictures identify them and say "thank you for helping." In the course of three years we interviewed many people—probably two hundred or more—most of whom supplied valuable information, although others were limited to information of the period after 1900 which will be helpful for volume two. Their spirit of cooperation was unanimous, and we hope the readers of this book will join us in appreciation of the enrichment of this history by all these contributors.

There is a special group that are to be commended not only for their help in this project but for their ongoing work in preserving the histories of their own communities. In mentioning the following historical societies and museums we acknowledge the contributions of every member of each; and in naming the individuals we express our thanks for their special help for this book: Mickey Wells, Clovis-Big Dry Creek Historical Soceity; Audrey B. Acebedo, curator, R. C. Baker Memorial Museum, Coalinga; Norman Zech, curator, Reedley Museum; John Watson, president, Sanger Historical Society, and the volunteers in that attractive and growing museum; Dr. Dudley Varner and staff, California Agricultural Museum; staff of the Selma Library, custodian of the photographic collection of the Selma Historical Society and Pioneer Village; and, of course, the staff members and volunteers of the Fresno City and County Historical Society.

Throughout the county we received valuable assistance from the librarians in the libraries we called upon—Coalinga, Selma, Kingsburg, Fowler, Mendota, Huron, Clovis and, again, Fresno. In addition to the public libraries, we appreciate the help given us by Marjorie Arnold and staff of the *Fresno Bee* library, and Noal Collura, public relations director of the *Bee*, in supplying pictures from their library to enrich many chapters of the book.

Another group of people who deserve an emphatic expression of appreciation are those who have written articles or manuscripts about the past of their area. First and foremost in this group are Lilbourne A. and Ernestine M. Winchell. For over fifty years they compiled, talked and lived the history of the county to which he came in 1859, when five years old, and to which she came in 1883 after their marriage in Oakland, California. His original manuscript for the history of the county is about three times longer than the portion finally published in 1933 (see bibliography), a monumental undertaking that offers a wealth of information for the researcher of the early period. A contemporary historian wrote that Lil Winchell "in the opinion of those most competent to judge, is the best-posted man on early days in this locality . . . " He said of Mrs. Winchell that she was "of literary inclinations, [who] has written widely for magazines . . . " This was before she started a series of articles for the *Fresno Republican* and *Fresno Bee*—historical vignettes which give valuable insights into the private lives of people in all walks of life. These articles numbered nearly 500 and we are sorry that we could not use more in the preparation of this book. We acknowledge and thank the Winchells for the heritage they have left the county.

The list of others who have written on the history of their local areas is long and therefore prevents our discussing the contribution of each, but we hope that local readers join us in appreciation of their varied works. Prominent among them are: Robert M. Wash, Fresno;

Ivadelle D. Garrison, Tranquillity (Jefferson James); Donald W. Wells, compiler of the C. B. Wooten papers about the Kerman area (prehistory, as Kerman is a twentieth century town); Viola Kreyenhagen Van Dyke, Coalinga; Joseph Mouren, Huron; Anne F. Catlin, Kingsburg; Forest and Helen Clingan, Dunlap/mountain area; Louis Keintz, Auberry; Katherine Nickel, John C. McCubbin and various contributors to the annual tabloid of the Reedley Historical Society; William L. Chedister, Clovis; and J. Randall McFarland and George B. Otis, Selma. Special mention should be made of Lula Grigsby, who compiled three scrapbooks of pictures, news articles and historical papers for the Coalinga Public Library. We regret that we cannot give credit to all contributors to *Past and Present*, the quarterly of the Fresno City and County Historical Society, or to writers and editors for other historical publications, because their contributions have been valuable and will continue to be through the years.

We also acknowledge with thanks the help and courteous service given us by various public offices including those of the Fresno County clerk, recorder, tax collector and coroner; the Sierra National Forest offices in Fresno and Shaver Lake; and the office of Kings Canyon National Park.

We must acknowledge our considerable debt to Bobbye Temple, copy editor at the *Fresno Bee*. As editor of this volume, she has kept a wary eye out for faulty grammar, factual glitches and a multitude of other difficulties. She has saved us from a number of embarrassing errors, and has strapped wings to our frequently leaden prose and made it soar. Our book is richer for her help but, of course, she takes no responsibility for whatever shortcomings remain. We hope that the reader will not find many and will be generally pleased in spite of them.

The Honorable Wallace D. Henderson participated in the production of this book until his untimely death. He gave freely of his time and knowledge gained as a past president of the Fresno City and County Historical Society, a legislator, mayor of Fresno and a longtime resident in the area. He also supplied material gathered by his late wife, Esther, for a history planned several years ago. We express our sincere thanks for his help and suggestions.

Of course, no book is complete without an efficient publisher and staff. We are especially indebted to Doris Hall who as typesetter and coordinator of that phase of production kept her experienced eye open for any omissions or commissions that would have been embarrassing. We credit Steve Emanuels, owner of Panorama West Books, and Keith Bennett for all the remaining good production and coordination.

Charles W. Clough and William B. Secrest, Jr.
Labor Day 1984

# Chapter 1
# Beginnings

There is a time and a season for everything, said the wise man Solomon in Ecclesiastes. Everything in its own time and everything in its own season—and so it was with the geologic formation of the San Joaquin Valley and that part of it that is Fresno County.

Time—the eons that passed as this great valley was being formed and shaped.

Seasons—the passing of the centuries of blooming and fruiting and harvesting and resting that have produced the agricultural wealth the valley offers.

We who live in this great golden fruitful valley—the Garden of the Sun an early chamber of commerce campaign called it—cannot help but be aware of the seasons as they pass, and measure our lives and much of our material wealth by the passage of springtime and harvest. But it is easy to accept the bounty of the valley without giving much thought to what went into making it.

The story of the forces which shaped Fresno County and the San Joaquin Valley can best be told within the context of a discussion of the formation of the Great Central Valley of California. The Central Valley, bounded by the Coast Range on the west and the Sierra Nevada on the east, and extending from the Cascades on the north to the Tehachapi Mountains on the south, is some 450 miles long and 50 to 60 miles wide. The division of the Central Valley into the Sacramento Valley on the north and the San Joaquin Valley on the south is determined by the drainage areas of the valley's two major rivers, of the same names.

But how did the valley come to be in the first place? What forces combined over the millions of years to create this flat fruitful plain?

The evolution of the valley can best be explained by the geologic theory of plate tectonics. According to this current theory, the earth's outer layer, the crust, is divided into plates which move independently of each other, powered by the force of the molten magma deep within the earth. Both oceans and land masses ride on these slowly moving plates. The theory is that all of the earth's land masses were initially joined into one super continent, but that some 300 million years ago, the plates on which the land masses rested broke apart and drifted gradually into the continent placements as we know them today.

Some 185 million years ago, the plate holding the Pacific Ocean was thrust beneath the plate supporting the North American continent, a process known as subduction. Subduction is the principal cause for the formation of many of the earth's mountain ranges, and it was the major factor in the shaping of the San Joaquin Valley. Volcanic activity along the various fault lines of the West Coast indicates that the plates are still in motion.

When the Pacific and North American plates converged, what was to become the San Joaquin Valley—in fact, what was to become California—was inundated by the ocean. The mountain ranges of the continent and higher land areas eroded and the sediment from that erosion was deposited to form what we know as the Pacific continental shelf and continental slope. Forces of wind, water and ice all contributed to the erosion process, and the sediment was deposited by the sea. These sediments of the ancient continental shelf and slope which were eroded, deposited and consolidated millions of years ago comprise the deepest sedimentary rocks underlying the San Joaquin Valley today.

All of California lay beneath the seas, but over the eons, upthrusting from beneath the crust caused expanses of granite and a few volcanoes to emerge from the ocean bottom, in a line that ran roughly north and south. This was the birth of the Sierra Nevada mountain range—today the most distinctive and magnificent part of Fresno County's landscape. Emerging with the mountains were sizable deposits of gold and copper, two minerals whose presence would become increasingly significant during the nineteenth century—and, because of the great numbers of men who came to seek the precious minerals, would contribute to California being granted statehood in 1849.

After a long period of upthrusting, the Sierra Nevada subsided, shifting rocks and sediments westward. This allowed the floor of the Great Valley to start building up, out of the submerged muck. Sierra Nevada debris continued to move to the west, resting in another area where a new mountain range was in the making—the Coast Range. Uplifting, folding and faulting of land in this area eventually produced a combination coastline and high-altitude shield to keep the ocean from lapping at California's interior.

Within the past 70 million years, another period of major upthrusts and volcanic activity roughly tripled the height of the Sierra Nevada, from 4,000 to 15,000 feet. Erosion—caused by the elements, or by several large glaciers moving through the area—exposed the copper and gold deposits, carved the mountain peaks into their present shapes, and created wondrous canyons throughout eastern Fresno County. Glacier dissipation and additional erosion helped the county's two main rivers, the San Joaquin and Kings, to assume their present form. They replaced a succession of drainage channels that had wended through the Sierra for millions of years.

There also was much activity in the Coast Range. Compared to the Sierra its development was slow, for many of its peaks did not rise until a few million years ago—which, geologically speaking, is recent. Once the range was in place, though, it started to deposit alluvial and floodplain soils into the still-submerged Great Valley, just as the Sierra was doing on the east. This trapped large patches of organic material under shifting sands and sediments. That organic material was fully metamorphosized and became the oil and gas which are pumped out of the ground north of Coalinga. Over the next few million years the deposited sediment from both mountain ranges continued to mount. In time, the Great Valley's floor was raised several hundred feet above sea level, and the oceans could no longer intrude.

The valley then, in essence, was formed. But while the ocean could no longer wield an influence, the valley floor was still being molded and changed by the multitude of streams and creeks and rivers which flowed from the mountains, creating the great alluvial fan that is the valley floor. This alluvial plain, some 20,000 square miles, is actually the result of a combination of a great number of smaller alluvial fans.

Because of the various types of sediment being deposited on the valley floor over the many years, the soils in the valley vary considerably. Along the eastern side are a number of low terraces which may contain dense layers of hardpan—a hard, clay-like substance which underlies soft workable soil. Hardpan is a geologic reminder of the times when the climate in the valley was much wetter than it is today. As the water soaked into the soil and moved deeper into the earth, it carried with it particles of iron and sand from the sediment left by the glaciers that covered the area. Then the climate gradually changed and became drier and the ground water stored in the soil was needed to sustain plant life. Gradually that underground water was used, generally by being carried by the roots of plants to their leaves and being transpired into the atmosphere. The spaces in the soil, where the water had been, were filled in with clay and sand. Eventually the layer became a solid mass, so solid that no water could drain through it, and no plant roots could penetrate it—as any homeowner or farmer knows whose land sits on hardpan. Holes through the hardpan must be either drilled or blasted to provide tree roots access to stable soil and a water supply and drainage for shallow-rooted plants.

There are different kinds of hardpan, the differences being in the elements which make up the hardpan—the iron and sand under much of the Old Fig Garden area in Fresno, for instance, and the calcium carbonate in the area east of Clovis. In some places it is as close as nine or ten inches from the surface.

At a slightly lower level are extensive areas of fine deep alluvium. This zone once had a cover of trees and

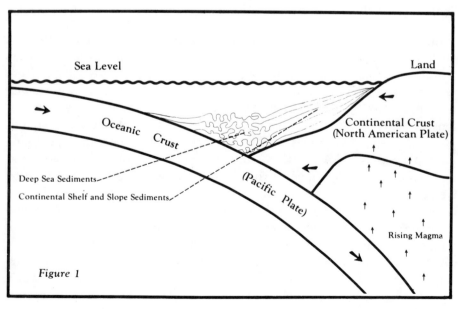

Figure 1

The phenomenon known as subduction.

Valley Magazine

grass. It is fertile, easy to cultivate and makes good farm land. In the lower part of the valley the soils are poorly drained and often contain salt or alkali. Flushing these areas with water or treating them with chemicals can make them usable, as evidenced by many of the West Side farming operations.

One topographic feature of the valley in the early days—the hog wallows—is seldom seen today, largely because most of the wallows have been leveled off for farming lands or housing developments. Hog wallows were mounds in the valley floor, mostly near the foothills, which ranged from one to five feet high and ten to over fifty feet across.

There probably are as many theories to explain the hog wallows as there are people studying them, but no one has as yet come up with a totally satisfactory or scientifically acceptable answer for the hog wallows being there.

One theory is that the hog wallows date from glacial times. The areas where the hog wallows exist were at the toe of the glaciers. The soil was frozen, much as the permafrost of Alaska freezes the ground for several feet below the surface. As the glaciers moved across the valley floor, the ground was frozen and thawed in rapid succession, causing the soil to crack as it contracted and expanded, and thus the mounds were formed.

One geologist, who has studied the mounds for forty years, is convinced that they represent the work of successive generations of pocket gophers, building up the mounds as their territory. The author also notes that the mounds are found only where the topsoil is shallow, as over hardpan, so that the animal has to build up his burrow, rather than digging deep into the ground where the soil is more pliable. He also supplies the information that the mounds—called mima mounds in general geologic terms, the term hog wallow being apparently only a Fresno County or Central California appellation—occur in areas in nineteen western states, northern Baja California and Saskatchewan.

Still another theory is that plants, probably large bushes or trees, acted as obstructions as soil was blown across the plains, and the mounds are the accumulation of soil around trees which have long since disappeared.

Some good hog wallows still are evident above the San Joaquin River between Willow Avenue and Friant Road. An interesting aspect of the mounds or wallows is that often they are lined up in rows, or are arranged in some type of discernible pattern.

Although reference is often made to the San Joaquin Valley as a desert, the valley was once part of a great wooded prairie. It was covered with a tall grass, and where water was close to the surface, valley oaks grew. These trees, many of which may reach a height of 100 feet, still are numerous, especially on the alluvial fans of the eastern side of the valley.

The outstanding development in plant life in the area encompassed by Fresno County was the *Sequoia gigantea*, which could grow up to 400 feet tall at higher elevations. Other trees which developed in the valley and mountain regions were the yellow, sugar and digger pines, tamarack, Douglas spruce, red and white fir, cedar, juniper, yew, foothill and burr oak, willow, poplar, sycamore, dogwood, maple, buckeye, manzanita, birch, and the ash tree whose Spanish designation gave rise to the name Fresno.

Flowers of many kinds covered the hills and plains—poppies, cream-cups, buttercups, honeysuckle, lupine, redbud, yuccas, sunflowers and goldenrods. Among smaller plants were wild gooseberry, elderberry and blackberry bushes, wild grape vines, wild cabbage and many different kinds of grasses. In the swamps around the San Joaquin and Kings rivers, several different tule varieties and cattails could be found.

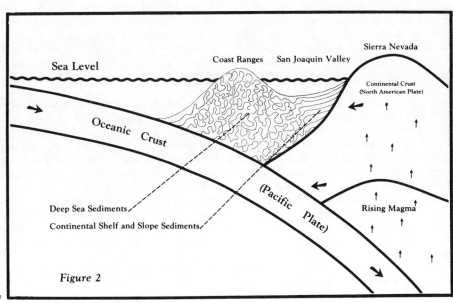

*The assembly that evolved into the Coast Ranges after further convergence of the plates.*

Figure 2

Valley Magazine

Early animal life in the valley area included some familiar types, and some not so familiar—mastodons (see 1:1), deer, rabbits, large cats, wolves, coyotes, horses and even camels roamed about in the area some ten million or so years ago. Eventually they were joined by grizzly bears, elk, squirrels, gophers, mountain sheep, otters, badgers, weasels, mink, skunks, woodchucks, raccoons, moles, mice and rats. Birds, also present for the past ten million years in the valley and mountain regions, came to include the vulture, turkey vulture, owls, woodpeckers, thrushes, pigeons, warblers, scrub jays, finches, doves, grouses, pheasants, quail, ducks, geese, cranes, ravens, mockingbirds, pelicans and several varieties of hummingbirds. Among fish were salmon, trout and pike; reptile life was dominated by snakes, lizards, toads and frogs.

Fresno County's land surface, once a combination of molten metals and boiling ocean, had been transformed into flat plains, rolling hills and jagged mountain peaks. There were mighty rivers flowing out from the highlands and numerous sloughs and swamps, all teeming with plant and animal life. Compared to the jungles, deserts and steppes that covered most of the rest of the earth, this area was a paradise.

One thing has become obvious as we have detailed the formation and evolution of the valley. The key element in the story is water—water which covered the whole of California in earlier geologic times, accepting the sediment which eroded the mountain peaks to the east and the west and formed the floor of the valley; the glaciers, frozen water, which moved over the surface of the valley and carved and shaped and molded the mountain canyons and left their deposits on the valley floor. And as we continue the story of the history of Fresno County as man finds his way into the valley—Indians, Spaniards, Mexican Army units and gold-seekers, American explorers, United States Army units, the forty-niners and finally, settlers—we will see

Reference 1:1

# THE BALEY MASTODON
## ERNESTINE WINCHELL

A natural phenomenon more or less was of but passing interest to Gillum Baley and Robert Parks, mining for gold in the early summer of 1864 . . . on the Fresno River . . . A ditch brought from higher up on the south side of the stream carried ample water freely to wash the dirt through the sluice boxes that collected the yellow substance of their search.

Through an alluvial deposit ten feet deep they tore with pick and shovel, and the fact that there happened to be an old burial ground of the native tribes made no difference at all except for the extra work of casting out the bones. Most of these shattered at a blow, but the skulls, blackened and full of soil, were as troublesome as so many rocks and as lightly regarded. Even a live Indian was of little importance and quite consistently a long-dead one was nothing to be sentimental about. Tossed into the rushing tide or up on the shore as was most convenient, the skulls were removed from the path of progress and soon a hundred or more were collected by little Charley Baley who unconcernedly played games with them, rolling them about or marshalling them in ranks and rows as fancy prompted.

Underlying this alluvial stratum was one of cemented lava ash or hardpan, and beneath was gravelly subsoil some five or six feet thick. In this Mr. Baley and his partner were presently surprised to observe that instead of human remains the sluice stream was uncovering bones of strange proportions, some of great size. They gave but casual attention, however, for it was gold they wanted, not phosphate and carbonate of lime.

One day the wash disclosed such an astonishing arc of smooth surface that their interest was held, and quite carefully they dug and sluiced around the object until, little by little, a gigantic skeleton was revealed lying intact as the prehistoric brute had fallen to die. Resting on its side, the head was so flung backward that the great tusks lay approximately in line with the vertebrae strung in massive units along the bed. Scarcely believing their eyes, they measured it off roughly with a shovel, that implement being about five feet long and four lengths being required, it was a stirring tale that Robert Parks eventually carried to Millerton.

E. C. Winchell, then judge of the county court, listened to the story as to one of the astonishing bits of news so casually passed from man to man, but he hitched his gray Billy to his buggy and made his way to the Baley mine on the Fresno to see for himself what truth there might be in the report. A thoughtful and methodical man, he went prepared to make accurate measurements should there prove to be anything worth measuring. Unfortunately his record has been lost and only such dimensions can now be set down as the boys of that day recall in agreement.

The tusks, blunted at the ends as of an old animal, were 6 feet 4 inches long, six inches at the base, and two inches at the worn tips. The total length of the skeleton was 16 feet. It was complete and sound, and the lawyer-naturalist was embarrassed by the richness of the find, its distance from transportation line, and the great weight of the immense bones. Into his buggy he loaded a number of the molars and several sections of vertebra; he sawed the tusks into pieces that could be lifted, and then took the precious freight to the county seat.

Together with Dr. Leach Judge Winchell classified the specimens, then part of them were sent to the State museum and others to the St. Louis University. Those remaining Dr. Leach set out on the porch of his office which was then in one of the brick buildings still indicated by the side of the road to Fort Miller, that the curious might examine them at will. For a long time they were as familiar as the gray rocks, and when in 1867 he removed to a new office on the main road west of the old courthouse the doctor unceremoniously tumbled them off the steep bluff into the river.

The parts of the frame left on the Fresno were displaced and scattered by Mr. Baley's continued mining operations and again covered with gravel wash. Before he left the location he buried the pathetic Indian skulls, too, and now not even the boy who played there can find the spot.

The wet winter of '67 flood waters uncovered a mastodon skeleton in the bank of Big Dry Creek on the old Simpson place near Academy. Boys at play threw portions out on the high land and for many years they could be observed by any passer-by, though few were interested enough to go to see.

Sixty years more or less should not matter to bones so old as these Fresno River and Big Dry Creek remains were upon discovery, so it is strange that those recently found on the San Joaquin in a similar soil formation at almost the identical depth should be so nearly at the point of disintegration. Someone with a paleontological turn of mind may eventually figure out the relation between these several Fresno County prehistoric pachyderms.

SOURCE: Ernestine Winchell columns.

that water continued to play the pre-eminent role in the development of the valley, even beyond the fertile soil and the nourishing sun.

Man learned to seek out and to use the water—tapping the underground reservoirs, catching the rain which falls in its short season, using the water which flows from the mountain streams into the rivers which are the lifeblood of the valley, and welcoming the snow in the high Sierra which melts and flows down into the rivers.

In the early days, water could be as destructive as it was valuable—the rivers often flooding and rampaging across the countryside, destroying crops and homes in their paths. But man learned to control the water,

and to save it behind storage dams so he could have it available when he needed it.

The value of water to the agricultural development of the area often resulted in conflict, and sometimes violence, as men fought to have their share of the life-giving water.

And the mountain streams and valley rivers hid for centuries the gold which lay just beneath the surface. Once discovered, the gold drew fortune seekers by the thousands, and the rivers and streams teemed with men seeking their share of the wealth.

All this, and much more, will be detailed as the story of Fresno County continues, but at every turn, water will be the focal point for much of what happens.

*Located about twenty miles northeast of Fresno, these mima mounds or hog wallows are some of the few left in Fresno County. In the early years much of the land north of Fresno was covered with them but cultivation, transportation and building have leveled most of them.*

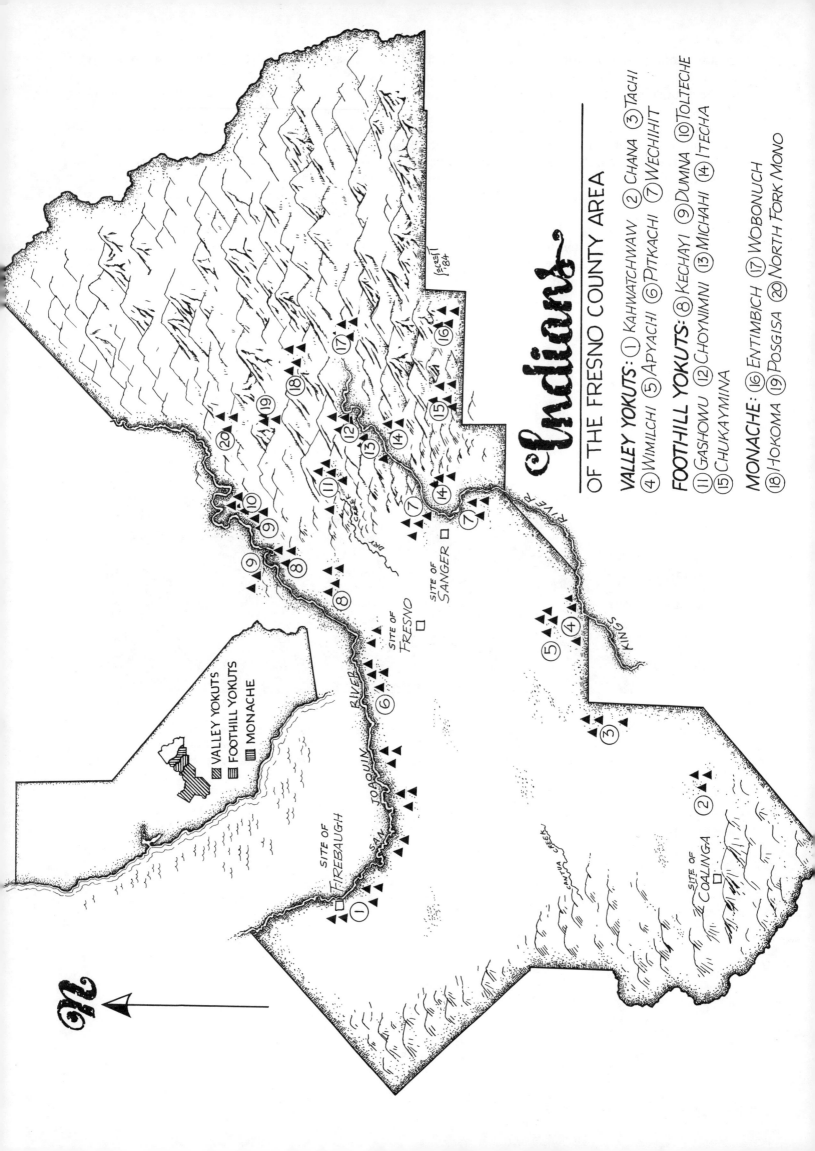

# Indians

## OF THE FRESNO COUNTY AREA

**VALLEY YOKUTS:** ① KAHWATCHWAW ② CHANA ③ TACHI
④ WIMILCHI ⑤ APYACHI ⑥ PITKACHI ⑦ WECHIHIT

**FOOTHILL YOKUTS:** ⑧ KECHAYI ⑨ DUMNA ⑩ TOLTECHE
⑪ GASHOWU ⑫ CHOYNIMNI ⑬ MICHAHI ⑭ ITECHA
⑮ CHUKAYMINA

**MONACHE:** ⑯ ENTIMBICH ⑰ WOBONUCH
⑱ HOKOMA ⑲ POSGISA ⑳ NORTH FORK MONO

VALLEY YOKUTS
FOOTHILL YOKUTS
MONACHE

SITE OF FIREBAUGH

SITE OF FRESNO

SITE OF SANGER

SITE OF COALINGA

SAN JOAQUIN RIVER

KINGS RIVER

CANTUA CREEK

DRY CREEK

N

# Chapter 2

# Native Fresnans: The Tragedy of the Indians

Long after glaciers, geological forces and floods created what is now Fresno County, the area's first inhabitants arrived. No date has been established for their coming, although it probably happened between 50,000 and 7,000 years ago. There is even greater uncertainty as to where they came from, by what route, and how long their journey took. But it is known that they were dark-complexioned, broad-faced, medium in build and height, and strong physically. They were Indians, the masters of the Americas until three centuries of outside invasions destroyed their extensive civilizations.

Like other Indian groups who migrated to California, the first found many inducements to settle in the central region. Its climate, despite the summer heat, was favorable for a good life. Game animals, fish, berries, nuts and other foodstuffs were readily available. And the setting itself—towering mountain peaks, wild rivers, boundless plains—must have held an aesthetic allure as well.

So the Indians stayed, with two major tribal groups ultimately occupying what became Fresno County. The Yokuts tribe settled on the valley floor and in the foothills, basing itself in "tribelets" on the San Joaquin and Kings rivers. On the upper reaches of these rivers lived the other tribe, known as the Monache.

Years of cultural contact, prompted by geographical closeness, caused the Yokuts and Monaches to live in similar ways. (Anthropologists are still unable to classify one in-between tribelet, the Entimbich, as Yokuts, Monache or both.) To simplify discussing these tribes, they will be treated as a unit. Cultural variations or discrepancies will be noted where appropriate.

In terms of personal appearance, native Fresnans adorned themselves in ways that remain familiar. Tattooing was practiced by both tribes. Surprisingly, it was more common among women than men! It was accomplished by cutting patterns, usually straight or zigzag lines, into a person's chin and/or upper chest, then rubbing ashes into the incisions. Ear and nose piercing, another decorative custom, was common to both sexes. Simple plugs made of animal bone were used to fill the opening thus made, along with more elaborate bead, shell and feather inserts. Hair was worn simply by everyone—grown long, parted in the middle, and tied back with a thong. Cosmetics, in the form of blue, black, white and red body paint, were popular and used principally on ceremonial occasions.

Dress styles were functional and quite casual. The valley climate allowed men to wear deerskin loincloths for most of the year. Women wore one- or two-piece skirts of deerskin, tule grass or willow bark; they frequently went bare to the waist. Children went naked, as did men during summer or when they became old.

Residents of the foothills and mountains dressed similarly, except that they used animal-hide blankets to withstand the cooler mountain temperatures. The presence of hard ground and rock also required the highland dwellers to wear deerskin or elk skin moccasins, an unnecessary item in the flat valley.

Fresno County's first inhabitants knew nothing of agriculture. This made constant hunting and gathering necessary—a process that involved all Indians except the very young and elderly. The search for food was dictated by sex. Men hunted and fished while women gathered, and both developed a large array of techniques for accomplishing these tasks.

Armed with wooden, sinew-backed bows and arrows usually made of cane shafts and stone points, men hunted in parties year-round. The only exceptions occurred when a village chief, like the governments of today, declared a limited hunting season on a particular animal. Deer, elk, antelope and bears were most often shot with arrows, although other methods could be used as well: chasing the animals until they were exhausted, driving them into nets by making loud noises or running them off cliffs.

Birds were either shot with arrows or trapped. In the latter instance noose-like devices were set up on the ground, equipped with a trigger to snare a bird who poked its head through. A hand version of this device could be used by stealthy hunters concealed in underbrush.

Methods of catching other game and fish were basic. Squirrels and rabbits were smoked out of their holes, and fish were caught with wicker-like dip nets, large weighted nets, harpoons, and weirs. (Angling was unknown to the Indians.) King salmon, lake trout, perch, chubs and suckers were so plentiful that they could be scooped out of the water at times.

Among gathered food items, the acorn was most important. Although difficult to prepare (they had to be pulverized, placed in a basket and repeatedly leached with hot water to eliminate poisonous tannic acid), acorns were sought after because they doubled for flour and meal. They were used to make cakes, bread, rolls, a hot or cold mush, and as a food additive.

Other important gathered foods were tule and yucca roots dug out of the ground. This practice gave rise to the derisive term for Indians, "root diggers" or just "diggers." Buckeye, laurel and pine nuts also were sought, as were manzanita berries, wild oats, tule seeds, wild plums, wild grapes, birds' eggs and insects. Since the natives ate almost anything that was not harmful, a full inventory of their diet would run to hundreds of items. The plentitude and variety of foods garnered by the Indians made them both well-nourished and healthy.

With neither stoves nor ovens available, Indian cooking was unsophisticated. Most food items were simply thrown on fires, in hot ashes or inside earth ovens to cook. Yet Indian women did have pots and pans of a sort—baskets and earthenware. Baskets, woven out of tule fibers, manzanita, redbud and other materials, were tight enough to hold water. (Larger versions were actually used as rafts.) They were ideal for cooking purposes, when liquids were placed inside and stirred with heated rocks.

Earthenware vessels, made by the foothill Yokuts and Monache, were used in the same fashion. Less sophisticated in design than the baskets—which possessed beautiful geometric patterns—the earthenware was made by the use of a crude coiling technique, and was dumped on a handy fire for hardening.

Food supplies in the Fresno County area were inevitably found near rivers and lakes, so the Indians built their villages near the water. A village could contain up to 100 single-family homes, plus several communal structures. Construction of family homes varied according to locale and the building materials readily available. Valley Yokuts built such dwellings by sticking wooden poles upright in a circle, tying the poles together to form a crude half-sphere, and thatching this frame with tules taken from a nearby river or swamp. Foothill Yokuts and Monaches modified this design, leaning poles against a center pole, tying them together, and covering the frame with pine slabs, cedar bark or tarweed. In both types of structures, two holes were made. One allowed people in or out, and the other let smoke escape. Indians always kept fires going in their homes—for cooking, heating or both.

Larger structures followed the basic dwelling designs outlined above, the main difference being occasional subterranean construction. In the latter instance the buildings consisted of little more than a large hole covered by a roof, along with the two necessary openings. If these structures were not used as community meeting halls, they served as sweathouses—combination men's clubs and saunas kept warm by perennial fires. The sweathouse was a place for relaxation, telling jokes, preparing for hunts, cleansing one's pores, lodging young unmarried men and initiating boys into manhood (of which more later). It was unique among Indian social institutions.

Tribelets were made up of two or three villages ruled by a hereditary chief. He was assisted in his duties by a messenger who usually inherited his office as well. Chiefs were responsible for hosting ceremonial feasts and dances (expensive even then, which kept them in precarious financial situations), making laws and decrees, lending money, punishing wrongdoers and performing other functions. Messengers, in addition to carrying out the chief's orders, acted as medicine men (shamans) and as primitive news services. If an Indian wanted to hear the latest local gossip, the messenger gladly recited it—for a fee.

External relations among the Fresno County Indians were peaceable. Only one tribelet, the Chukchansi Yokut, is said to have been aggressive. Hostilities broke out usually when one tribelet member murdered a person from a different tribelet, or was suspected of having caused a death through sorcery. Little is known of these conflicts, except that they appear to have been short in duration. There are no records of protracted blood feuds or wars.

Friendliness prevailed among the native Fresnans for an important reason: the necessity of maintaining trade networks. Indians from all over central California bartered items with each other. They traveled on foot to reach distant villages, carrying baskets loaded with goods on their backs, or paddled their way along rivers in bundled tule rafts. They mostly exchanged items hard to find in specific geographical locations. Tachi Yokuts had no access to the prized acorn, so they had to obtain it from foothill and mountain tribelets. Valley Indians were fond of seafood (mussels and abalone); they obtained it through trade with their Salinan and Costanoan neighbors to the west. In return, the coastal-dwelling Indians received items scarce in their own territory: pine nuts, obsidian (used to make arrow and knife points) and rabbit skins.

Birth, coming of age, marriage and death—the so-called "life crisis" events—were important to the Indians, just as they are important today.

The beginning of life involved several sensitive procedures. Pregnant women were generally forbidden to eat meat or to engage in difficult physical activities. When labor pains came the women were attended by midwives during a normal delivery, or by a tribal shaman if complications developed. Yokuts shamans had what they considered a clever device for inducing birth: they placed a bear's claw on the mother's abdomen, believing it would frighten the infant out.

During and after birth, the *couvade* often took place. This meant that the father went into sympathetic pains and subsequent exhaustion with the mother. A period of convalescence for both parents was necessary when this happened! Yet even in this circumstance they mustered enough energy to name their child, sometimes after a parent or grandparent, though never after a dead person. Uttering or commemorating the name of anyone deceased broke a grave Indian taboo.

For boys and girls, puberty signaled distinctive ceremonies that marked thier initiation into adulthood. Under adult supervision boys were taken to the village sweathouse and given jimson weed in a pipe to smoke. Partaking in this ceremony produced visions, trances and encounters with spiritual beings. Other-worldly contacts made at this ceremony could lead to more weed-smoking and communication with spirits, who taught the men they favored how to become shamans.

Initiation of the girls, which began with their first menstruation, was far less dramatic. They were simply required to stay indoors, eat no meat, drink cold water and scratch themselves with a special stick. Touching themselves or others at this time was thought to transmit uncleanliness.

Courtship and marriage took two common forms: prearrangement (especially by the Yokuts) or the winning of a woman's affections by a man. Trial-basis marriages were sometimes arranged, whereby a man and woman would return to their family homes if they proved to be incompatible. If the marriage survived this test a celebratory feast was held (which was the common way of solemnizing any marriage).

Once mutually bound, a couple would settle permanently, raise a family, and grow old together— unless personal conflicts developed. Divorces could take place, with the wife going back to her family and the children (if pre-adolescent) farmed out to both sets of grandparents. The remarriage of husband or wife was possible, and it lacked any social stigma.

When a person sank into a terminal illness, women would cluster around the dying party and wail. The village messenger would begin spreading the grim news, and family and friends would begin gathering for the inevitable funeral. Once death occurred the body was given to a professional undertaker. Transvestites, for some unspecified reason, were given this job among the Yokuts—and allowed to keep anything that came with the corpse. It was their responsibility to dig the grave, prepare the body, join in the wailing and possibly build a funeral pyre. Cremation was often practiced, especially if a person died away from home, for returning bodies was difficult.

After the funeral was held, ceremonial dances took place to help relieve the participants' anguish. Ethnographer Stephen Powers observed one of these ceremonies in the early 1870s, in what was then Fresno County, and wrote a remarkable account of it later (see 2:1.)

The lives of the Indians were not devoted solely to hunting, gathering and participating in set ceremonies and rituals. They devoted much of their time to recreational pursuits and played games that are recognizable today. A type of football played with a wooden ball was a favorite men's pastime. Shinny—a sort of field hockey played with wooden clubs and a puck— also was popular. Additionally, a "shell game" had great appeal among the Indians. It consisted of a person concealing sticks, bones or shells in his hands, mixing them up and asking another player which hand held a pre-selected item. Yokuts women were fond of various dice games; their dice were made of acorn or walnut shells filled with asphaltum and inlaid with shell chips to simulate dots.

Reference 2:1
## The Yokuts Dance for the Dead
### STEPHEN POWERS

While in Coarse Gulch it was my good fortune to witness the great dance for the dead ... which was one of the most extraordinary human spectacles I ever beheld. It was not the regular annual dance, but a special one, held by request of Kolomusnim, a subchief of the Chukchansi; but it was in all respects as awful, as strange, as imposing an exhibition of barbaric superstition and barbaric affection as is afforded by the formal anniversary. Not to my dying hour will the recollection of that frightful midnight pageant be effaced ...

When Tueh, the Indian interpreter, and myself entered the camp it was already an hour after nightfall, but there were yet no

indications of a beginning of the dark orgies that were to be enacted. We found about three hundred Indians assembled, in a place remote from any American habitations, and encamped in light, open booths of brushwood, running around three sides of a spacious quadrangle. This quadrangle had been swept and beaten smooth for a dancing-floor, and near one of the inside corners there was a small, circular enbankment[sic], like a circus-ring, with the sacred fire brightly burning in the center. Kolomusnim and his relatives, the chief mourners, occupied the corner-booths near this ring, and near by was Sloknich, the head-chief of the Chukchansi, by whose authority this assembly

had been convened. Here and there a fire burned with a staggering, sleepy blaze just outside the quadrangle, faintly glimmering through the booths; at intervals an Indian moved stealthily across the half-illuminated space within; while every few minutes the atmosphere was rendered discordant and hideous, as indeed the whole night was, during the most solemn passages, by the yelping, snarling, and fighting of the hordes of dogs.

For fully half an hour we slowly sauntered and loitered about the quadrangle, conversing in undertones, but still nothing occurred to break the somber silence, save the ever-recurring flurries of yelps from the accursed dogs. Now and then an Indian slowly passed across and sat down on the circular enbankment, while others in silence occasionally fed the sacred fire. But at last, from Kolumusnim's quarter, there came up a long, wild, haunting wail, in a woman's voice. After a few minutes it was repeated. Soon another joined in, then another, and another, slowly, very slowly, until the whole quarter was united in an eldritch, dirge-like, dismal chorus. After about half an hour it ceased, as slowly as it began; and again there was profound, death-like silence; and again it was broken by the ever-renewed janglings of the dogs.

Some time again elapsed before any further movement was made, and then Sloknich, a little, old man, but straight as an arrow, with a sharp face and keen, little, basilisk eyes, stepped forth into the quadrangle and began to walk slowly to and fro around its three sides, making the opening proclamation. He spoke in extremely short, jerky sentences, with much repetition, substantially as follows:

"Make ready for the mourning. Let all make ready. Everybody make ready. Prepare your offerings. Your offerings to the dead. Have them all ready. Show them to the mourners. Let them see your sympathy. the mourning comes on. It hastens. Everybody make ready."

He continued in this manner for about twenty minutes, then ceased and entered his booth; after which silence, funereal and profound, again brooded over the encampment. By this proclamation he had formally opened the proceedings, and he took no further part in them, except in a short speech of condolence. By this time the Indians had collected in considerable numbers on the enbankment, and they kept slowly coming forward until the circle was nearly completed, and the fire was only visible shooting up above their heads. A low hum of conversation began to buzz around it, as of slowly awakening activity. The slow piston-rod of aboriginal dignity was beginning to ply; the clatter and whizzing of the machinery were swelling gradually up. No women had yet come out, for they took no part in the earlier proceedings. It was now quite ten o'clock, and we were getting impatient.

Presently the herald, a short, stout Indian, with a most voluble tongue, came out into the quadrangle with a very long staff in his hand, and paced slowly up and down the lines of booths, proclaiming:

"Prepare for the dance. Let all make ready. We are all friends. We are all one people. We were a great tribe once. We are little now. All our hearts are as one. We have one heart. Make ready your offerings. The women have the most money. The women have the most offerings. They give the most. Get ready the tobacco. Let us chew the tobacco." . . .

He spoke fully as long as Sloknich had done, and while he was speaking they were preparing a decoction of Indian tobacco by

the fire. When he ceased he took his place in the circle, and all of them now began to sip and taste the tobacco, which seemed to be intended as a kind of mortification of the flesh. Sitting along on the embankment, while the nauseous mess was passing around in a basket, and others were tasting the boiled leaves, they sought to mitigate the bitter dose with jokes and laughter. One said, "Did you ever see the women gather tobacco for themselves?" This was intended as a jest, for no woman ever touches the weed, but nobody laughed at it. As the powerful emetic began to work out its inevitable effect, one Indian after another rose from the circle and passed slowly and silently into the outer darkness, whence there presently came up to our ears certain doleful and portentious sounds, painfully familiar to people who have been at sea. After all the Indians in the circle, except a few tough stomachs, had issued forth into the darkness and returned to their places, about eleven o'clock, the herald went around as before, making a third proclamation:

"Let all mourn and weep. O, weep for the dead. Think of the dead body lying in the grave. We shall all die soon. We were a great people once. We are weak and little now. Be sorrowful in your hearts. Let your tears flow fast. We are all one people. We are all friends. All our hearts are one heart."

For the last hour or so the mourners and their more intimate friends and sympathizers, mostly women, had been collecting in Kolomusnim's quarter, close behind the circle, and preparing their offerings. Occasionally a long, solitary wail came up, trembling on the cold night-wind. At the close of the third proclamation they began a death-dance, and the mourners crowded promiscuously in a great, open booth, and held aloft in their hands or on their heads, as they danced, the articles they intended to offer to the memory of the departed. It was a splendid exhibition of barbaric geegaws. Glittering necklaces of *Haliotis* and other rare marine shells; bits of American tapestry; baskets of the finest workmanship, on which they had toiled for months, perhaps for years, circled and furred with hundreds of little quail-plumes, bespangled, scalloped, festooned and embroidered with beadery until there was scarcely place for the handling; plumes, shawls, etc. Kolomusnim had a pretty plume of metallic-glistening ravens' feathers in his hand. But the most remarkable article was a great plume, nearly six feet long, shaped like a parasol slightly opened, mostly of ravens' feathers, but containing rare and brilliant plumage from many birds of the forest, topped with a smaller plume or kind of coronet, and lavishly bedecked through all its length with bulbs, shell-clusters, circlets of feathers, dangling festoons—a magnificent bauble, towering far above all, with its glittering spangles and nodding plume on plume contrasting it strangely with the tattered and howling savages over whom it gorgeously swayed and

flaunted. Another woman had an image, rudely constructed of shawls and clothing, to represent the dead woman, sister to Kolomusnim.

The beholding of all these things, some of which had belonged to the departed, and the strong contagion of human sorrow, wrought the Indians into a frenzy. Wildly they leaped and wailed; some flung themselves upon the earth and beat their breasts. There were constant exhortations to grief. Sloknich, sitting on the ground, poured forth burning and piercing words: "We have all one heart. All our hearts bleed with yours. Our eyes weep tears like a living spring. O, think of the poor, dead women in the grave." Kolomusnim, a savage of a majestic presence, bating his garb, through a hesitating orator, was so broken with grief that his few sobbing words moved the listeners like a funeral knell. Beholding now and then a special friend in the circle, he would run and fall upon his knees before him, bow down his head to the earth, and give way to uncontrollable sorrow. Others of the mourners would do the same, presenting to the friend's gaze some object which had belonged to the lamented woman. The friends, if a man, would pour forth long condolences; if a woman, she would receive the mourner's head in her hands, tenderly stroke down her hair, and unite her tears and lamentations with hers. Many an eye, both of men and women, both of mourners and strangers, glistened in the flickering firelight with copious and genuine tears . . .

These demonstrations continued a long time, a very long time, and I began to be impatient again, believing that the principal occasion had passed. It appeared afterward that they are compelled by their creed and custom to prolong the proceedings until daylight; hence this extreme deliberation.

But now, at last, about one o'clock in the morning, upon some preconcerted signal, there was a sudden and tumultuous rushing from all quarters of the quadrangle, amid which the interpreter and myself were almost borne down. For the first time during the night the women appeared conspicuously on the scene, thronged into the sacred circle, and quickly formed a ring close around the fire—a single circle of maidens, facing inward. The whole multitude of the populous camp crowded about them in confusion, jostling and struggling. A choir of male singers took their position hard by and commenced the death-song, though they were not audible except to the nearest listeners.

At the same instant the young women began their frightful dance, which consisted of two leaps on each foot alternately, causing the body to rock to and fro; and either hand was thrust out with the swaying, as if the offering it held were about to be consigned to the flames, while the breath was forced out with violence between the teeth, in regular cadence, with a harsh and grinding sound of *heh*! The blaze of the sacred fire

When the Indians tired of games, they entertained themselves in other ways. Grand feasts, accompanied by much singing and dancing, were frequent events in tribelet villages. Shamans often would compete in public contests to out-hex each other through casting verbal spells Each tribe also had a large store of mythological stories to draw upon and tell. These tales were usually based on the creation of the world and its early days. Young and old delighted in them, and these stories were passed on and embellished through many generations. (A sample of Yokuts mythology is given in 2:2.)

Such was the lifestyle of the native Fresnans— idyllic, peaceful and unhurried. It persisted for untold millenia, untouched by the encroachments of foreign cultures. Then the white invasions came, begun by the Spaniards in 1769 (see Chapter 3) and concluding with the American onslaught, virtually complete in Fresno County a century later. The intervening years saw Indians kidnapped from their homes, sold into slavery, robbed, beaten, maimed, raped, starved and killed— all to advance the interests of different conquerors at different times. No part of Fresno County's history has been so sordid, nor so sad.

For fifty years, two Spanish institutions decimated the ranks of the natives: the military and the missions. The former institution, albeit unofficially, began its dastardly task not long after the Spanish arrived in California. Soldiers from the garrisons at Monterey and Santa Barbara sometimes fled to the San Joaquin Valley, settling among the Indians and treating them badly. The Indians contracted venereal diseases from these soldiers. An early visiting priest, Father Juan Martín, suggested that such afflictions were epidemic by 1804.

The Indians obtained only one dubious advantage from the soldiers' presence: the knowledge that Spanish settlements were on the coast, ripe for raiding. Guns, livestock, horses and food began disappearing from the settlements, which provoked semi-regular military actions against the San Joaquin Valley Indians after 1805. In the Fresno County area it is known that the Nopchinchi, Pitkachi and Tachi Yokuts suffered serious losses from these incursions. Survivors

flamed redly out between the bodies of the dancers, swaying in accord, while the disheveled locks of the leaping hags wildly snapping in the night wind, and the frightful ululations and writhings of the mourners, conspired to produce a terrible effect. At the sight of this weird, awful, and lurid spectacle, which was swung into motion so suddenly, I felt all the blood creep and tingle in my veins, and my eyes moisten with the tears of a nameless awe and terror. We were beholding now, at last, the great dance for the dead . . .

About four o'clock, wearied, dinned, and benumbed with the cold of the mountains, I crept away to a friendly blanket and sought to sleep. But it was in vain, for still through the night-air were borne up to my ears the far-off crooning, the ululations, and that slow-pulsing, horrid *heh!* of the leaping witches, with all the distant voices, each more distinct than when heard nearer, of the mourning camp. The morning star drew itself far up into the blue reaches of heaven, blinking in the cold, dry California air, and still all the mournful riot of that Walpurgis-night went on.

Then slowly there was drawn over everything a soft curtain of oblivion; the distant voices blended into one undistinguishable murmur, then died away and were still; the mourning was ended; the dancers ceased because they were weary.

For half an hour, perhaps, I slept. Then awaking suddenly I stood up in my blankets and looked down upon the camp, now broadly flooded by the level sun. It was silent as the grave. Even the unresting dogs slept at last, and the Indian ponies ceased from browsing, and stood still between the manzanita bushes to let the first sunshine warm and mellow up their hides, on which the hair stood out straight. All that wonderful night seemed like the phantasmagoria of a fevered dream. But before the sun was three-quarters of an hour high that tireless herald was out again, and going the rounds with a loud voice, to waken the heavy sleepers. In a few minutes the whole camp was in motion; not one remained, though many an eyelid moved like lead. The choir of singers took their places promptly, squatting on the ground; and a great company of men and women, bearing their offerings aloft, as before, joined in the same dance as described, with the

same hissing *heh!* only it was performed in a disorderly rush-round, raising a great cloud of dust. Every five minutes, upon the ceasing of the singers, all faced suddenly to the west, ran forward a few paces, with a great clamor of mourning, and those in the front prostrated themselves, and bowed down their faces to the earth, while others stretched out their arms to the west, and piteously wrung them, with imploring cries, as if beckoning the departed spirits to return, or waving them a last farewell. This is in accordance with their belief in a Happy Western Land. Soon, upon the singers resuming, they all rose and joined again in the tumultuous rush-round. This lasted about an hour; then all was ended for that day, and the weary mourners betook themselves to their booths and to sleep.

SOURCE: Pp. 384–91 of Stephen Powers, *Tribes of California* with an introduction and notes [by] Robert F. Heizer. Berkeley, Los Angeles and London: University of California Press, c. 1976. [Reprinted from *Contributions to North American Ethnology*, Volume III. Washington: GPO, 1877.]

Reference 2:2

## A YOKUTS MYTH: THE MAN AND THE OWLS

A man and his wife were traveling. They camped overnight in a cave. They had a fire burning. Then they heard a horned owl (hutulu) hoot. The woman said to her husband: "Call in the same way. He will come and you can shoot him. Then we will eat him for supper." The man got his bow and arrows ready and called. The owl answered, coming nearer. At last it sat on a tree near the fire. The man shot. He killed it. Then his wife told him: "Do it again. Another one will come." Again he called and brought an owl and shot it. He said: "It is enough now." But his wife said: "No. Call again. If you call them in the morning they will not come. We have had no meat for a long time. We shall want something to eat tomorrow as well as now." Then the man called. More owls came. There were more and more of them. He shot, but more came. The air was full of owls. All his arrows were gone. The owls came closer and attacked them. The man took sticks from the fire and fought them off. He covered the woman with a basket and kept on fighting. More and more owls came. At last they killed both the man and the woman.

SOURCE: [Ed. with commentary by] Margolin, Malcolm. *The Way We Lived: California Indian Reminiscences Stories and Songs*. Berkeley, California: Heyday Books, c. 1981, p. 84.

were frequently taken prisoner and trundled off to the coastal missions.

In November–December of 1815 two expeditions left the coast to look for escaped Indians and stolen cattle in the Fresno County area. One left Mission San Juan Bautista under Master Sergeant Don Juan de Ortega; the other, Monterey under Sergeant José Dolores Pico. Judging from his expedition diary, Ortega and his men entered the valley northwest of Tulare Lake; a preliminary inspection by his corporal, Juan Arroyo, and a guide confirmed they were near the Kings River. Ortega soon decided to attack a nearby Indian village he called "Tache"—probably the Telwiyit or Chi settlement of the Tachi Yokuts.

While hidden in a river bend for a day, waiting to pounce on the Indians, Ortega blundered badly. His men captured two old Indians who told them Tache's location and were let go, probably to warn the others. Later spotting two other Indians on horseback, with four pack animals, Ortega's party commenced an unsuccessful chase. The Indians abandoned their animals, jumped into a nearby stream and swam away from the soldiers. Their intimate knowledge of the territory allowed them to outwit the soldiers easily. "In the darkness of the night, along the river and in the tule swamps and thickets it was impossible to catch them," Ortega later wrote.

The soldiers attacked Tache the next day and found it deserted. Making their way through the surrounding tule swamps, they found three armed Indians, to whom they talked at a distance through an interpreter. They refused to surrender when asked, dove into a convenient waterway, and made a clean escape. It was several hours before any other Indians were encountered. Using the marshes as cover, they talked to Ortega's men but would not come forth. "They said that all the people were scared and were hiding in the lake because the fugitive Indians and other Christian runaways from [Mission] Soledad had told them we were coming to kill them at the point of the lance," wrote Ortega.

Trekking eastward and then reversing course, Ortega's party talked to many Indians and learned where some hostile elements lay, but made no further raids. Near the Kings River they met Pico's party, which had captured sixty-three Indians and killed three in battle somewhere in the San Joaquin River-Fresno Slough region. After giving a lecture on horse-stealing to some Wimilchi Yokuts, the combined parties headed northwest to attack some villages named Tape, Malim and Cheneche. (They were probably inhabited by Nopchinchi and/or Coconoon Yokuts.) All were found deserted. "Not lacking in competent leadership, it [the Ortega-Pico expedition] nevertheless floundered for nearly two weeks through rain and mud, lost its horses, was led on repeated goose-chases by native guides and accomplished nothing in the military sense," wrote historian Sherburne F. Cook.

Pico returned to the Fresno County area in 1825 with two corporals and twenty-seven soldiers. Leaving Monterey on December 27, 1825, they were joined by three neophyte guides from Mission San Juan Bautista. The party's objectives were to capture escaped Indians needed as workers (in truth, slaves) and to find and return stolen cattle and horses. Some horses could not be brought back. The Indians considered them a delicacy and would butcher and eat them. To punish the Indians, soldiers would burn the carcasses or render them inedible.

Soon after reaching the San Joaquin River, the party captured some escaped neophytes. No time was lost in returning them to San Juan Bautista with an *alcalde*, a trusted Indian whom the military considered of "superior" ability. The neophytes mentioned that two of the Indian leaders that Pico's men sought had gone to a Yokuts village between the site of Herndon and the foothills.

Continuing eastward, the party reached and searched through Monte Redondo, an outstanding landmark on the Fresno River about six miles west of Madera's site. A thicket of brush and trees, as its Spanish name signified, Monte Redondo could be seen for miles on the valley floor.

When the soldiers reached the village, they attacked without delay. "I executed the assault and took by surprise as many as possible . . . none of the malefactors being sought were captured," Pico reported. Forty "natives" and one Christian Indian from San Juan Bautista were captured. The "natives" were later released and the escaped neophyte returned to his mission. He was not permitted to bring his heathen wife of four years with him because "she had a small daughter." Presumably they wanted only workers with no distractive influences such as children.

Pico lectured the Indians with considerable zeal when he discovered that they possessed partially-eaten horse remains. The Indians, as always when they were upbraided like this, seemed unimpressed, professed ignorance and had an excuse. Their usual claims were that a visiting traveler, or neighbors in other villages, had given them the carcasses.

The only reported killings were on January 24, when Pico and his men were camped on the Kings River. Five of the party's horses had disappeared the previous day. Pico scattered his men to search for the horses, telling them to start firing if an Indian "showed fight." The soldiers raided a nearby village, but found no trace of the stolen animals. "According to what the soldiers told me they killed seven Indians and caught six alive, among them a chief," he reported.

During this period, many expeditions like Pico's came to central California (see 2:3). Details of the expeditions, which were held on an almost-monthly basis, are always sketchy. It is certain, though, that they thinned the Indians' ranks and made them increasingly fearful of the white interlopers in their hallowed lands.

The mission system in California was established in 1769 with the founding of Mission San Diego. Franciscan fathers proceeded to set up a chain of establishments dotting the California coast, intending to convert the Indians who lived there to Christianity. After 1804 they became interested in securing Indians from the interior, and the Spanish troops—anxious to stop the incessant raiding parties—obliged the fathers' wishes.

Once at the missions, the Indians fared badly. They succumbed to many diseases imported by the white man, notably measles, scarlet fever and pneumonia. Malnutrition also caused many Indians to sicken and die. They were forced to raise crops and livestock at the missions, an enterprise they considered sheer drudgery. Their agricultural efforts were rarely successful, and access to foods they formerly hunted and gathered was minimal. As a consequence their daily food intake was an average 2,000 calories, inadequate to sustain their hard-working regimen at the missions.

To complicate matters, diseased Indians were escaping from the missions, returning to the interior and infecting others. What is thought to have been a malaria epidemic spread in this fashion during the early 1830s. "From the head of the Sacramento, to the great bend and slough of the San Joaquin, we did not see more than six or eight live Indians, while large numbers of their skulls and dead bodies were to be seen under every shade tree," wrote Colonel John J. Warner, a member of the Ewing Young trapping expedition of 1832–33. "On the San Joaquin river, in the immediate neighborhood of the larger class of villages, we found not only graves, but the vestiges of a funeral pyre."

As more Americans filtered into California, the Indians regarded their presence with trepidation and outright hostility. A party led by explorer John C. Fremont (see Chapter 3) discovered this on December 19, 1845. Traveling near what is now Los Banos, Fremont and his men spotted a sign of Indians—scattered horse bones. (Since mission times, Indians had become fond of horsemeat.) An advance party was sent out to find the local natives. They were surprised by a band of whooping Chawchila Yokuts that quickly dispersed when the rest of Fremont's party came into view. Fremont then decided to withdraw to a nearby campsite, "whence they [the Indians] harangued us, bestowing on us liberally all the epithets they could use, telling us what they would do with us," he wrote later.

The next day, a troublesome Chawchila was spotted riding northward on a horse for reinforcements. One of Fremont's men, also mounted, shot at the Indian with his pistol; the man retaliated with his bow and arrow. Hot lead won out, the Indian fell from his horse dead, and Fremont's party continued down the valley unmolested.

After war broke out between the United States and

Reference 2:3

## RAID ON A YOKUTS VILLAGE

[April 25, 1828.] This day I set out for the place called El Potrero, which I reached at about 11:00 o'clock at night. I established myself there until the soldier Norberto Garcia should return, whom I had sent out with four men to scout the village of the Joyimas [Hoyima Yokuts]...

This Garcia got back about 2:00 o'clock in the morning [of the 26th]. I immediately started out, leaving Corporal José Avila with four soldiers and four Indian auxiliaries to guard the horses and baggage. At about one eighth of a league before reaching the village I ordered Corporal Simeon Castro with 10 soldiers and 15 Indian auxiliaries to cross to the north side of the [San Joaquin] River, while I remained on the south side. However only five men on horseback, with Corporal Castro were able to get across because it was extremely muddy. We continued to approach the village which was between the two channels of the river in a willow thicket very difficult to penetrate. The party which was on the south side, before reaching the village, bogged down in some very miry tule swamps. Corporal Simeon got as close as 80 yards, more or less, from the village when the neighing of a horse gave the alarm to the heathen. They instant-

ly seized their weapons and fired several arrows. Seeing this, Corporal Simeon opened fire and killed two Indians. The party on the south entered the village, part on foot, part on horseback, killed 3 Indians, and captured 8 men and 7 women together with some boys and girls, the total being 26 souls. We found 27 horses, of the herd belonging to the Soberanes, the flesh of which the Indians had been eating for three days, after the animals had been killed with arrows. In the brush there may have been 60 to 80 more horses ...

...I had all the horse meat burned, not leaving the Indians as much as a quarter to eat. Then, after those who were wet had dried out, I retired and made camp at about 1:00 o'clock in the afternoon...We captured a Christian woman from [Mission] Soledad and another from [Mission] San Juan [Bautista] who had a small boy likewise Christian.

*April 27.* I started out about 1:00 o'clock in the morning toward the mountains in pursuit of those who had fled. I went about 8 leagues into the mountains to the place where they are accustomed to camp when they run away. When we found nobody, the guide, who was actually one of the prisoners,

told me that the Indians must be still behind us. So I went back, as the guide told me, and came upon two women, whom we caught. They gave us the information where the rest of the people were. The soldiers whose horses were least tired went out and captured 5 men, 19 women and 13 boys and girls. I lost the interpreter and 5 Christian auxiliaries. When I arrived at the village where the dead men were, I came upon 8 men including 2 chiefs who came out fighting and captured one chief, a Christian from San Juan and 3 women. Of those who got away seven encountered our troops while we were leaving the mountains. They were captured, among them a Christian from San Juan and two ... horse thieves, heathen, one named Selli, and the other Salmi. As soon as we had all reunited I retired to the camp, which we reached at about 7:00 o'clock in the evening ...

SOURCE: Diary of Sergeant Sebastian Rodriguez, pp. 184–85 of UC Anthropological Records 20:5, *Expeditions to the Interior of California, Central Valley, 1830–1840* by Sherburne F. Cook. Berkeley and Los Angeles: University of California Press, 1962.

Mexico in 1846, a regiment of New York volunteers under Colonel Jonathan Stevenson was mustered in and sent to California. Members of the regiment's Company D ventured into the San Joaquin Valley twice the following year to quell Indian troubles, horse thievery being widespread there. On the first expedition, there were no unpleasant encounters. The men even managed to conclude a non-aggression treaty with some Indians, probably Miwoks, who were farming corn and melons on the upper Merced River. While returning to the coast, though, George Henry Ashton, an Englishman attached to the expedition, disappeared. Indians were thought to be responsible, which led the expedition back to the valley two months later, in July. The detachment soon learned that a Yokuts band had killed Ashton. "We went to their village and found them 300 strong in warriors, while our party numbered only twenty-five men," recalled an expedition member in 1889. "Captain Naglee [the expedition commander] gave orders to have a detail of six men in readiness, with loaded muskets. A pow wow was had, and at last . . . three chiefs were discovered, seized, and bound to trees, and the order to fire given. Quick as a flash the volley rang out in the mountain stillness, and echoed from crag to peak far away, and three Indian corpses lay upon the sand beneath the glittering midsummer's sun." The company volunteers were forced to retreat hastily, with Indians pursuing them on horseback. After a day-long chase, the Indians gave up and the expedition returned to Monterey safely.

Soon after Stevenson's men left the Fresno County area local Indian affairs changed dramatically. A man named James D. Savage came down from San Francisco from a tour of duty with Fremont and established himself as a trader among the San Joaquin Valley Indians. Wiry, muscular, long-haired, a canny frontiersman and observant student of human nature, Savage quickly found ways to dominate the tribes around him and become their white king.

When Savage played the Indian "shell game," he never lost—thanks to sleight-of-hand. To make the natives think he was invincible, he loaded his pistol with blanks before a group of them one day, concealing real bullets in his hand as he proceeded. He then asked a bystander to shoot him. Six shots rang out; Savage pretended to catch the bullets and then showed the hidden ammunition to his audience. Awestruck by demonstrations like these, valley Indians soon revered Savage as a sort of god. He set them to work mining gold, acquired Indian concubines—estimates range from three to thirty-three—and became a wealthy man.

Early in 1850 the Indians of the mid-San Joaquin Valley region became restless. The gold discovery in California (see Chapter 4), now common knowledge, was bringing in miners who staked claims and drove Indians off their lands. The Indians became under-standably angry. When one B. Oscar Field tried to set up a ferry on the Kings River in early 1850, local Yokuts Indians invaded his property and carried away everything they could. There were hints that more serious reprisals were in the offing. Savage's concubines told him that the Indians were planning to drive white men out of the valley for good.

Savage set his mind to work and devised a plan to defuse Indian tensions. He took an important Chawchila chief, José Juarez, with him on a visit to San Francisco. The purpose of the trip was to show the influential chief that white men were massed close to the valley, and any Indian hostilities would be promptly quashed. José Juarez, unfortunately, was unimpressed. He got drunk and obnoxious while on his holiday, and Savage found it necessary to strike him on one occasion. When the two men returned to the valley, the Chawchila chief convened a tribal council and called for war.

At this point all hopes for peace were lost. Actual hostilities began on December 17, 1850, when Savage's trading post on the Fresno River was attacked. Three men in the crude wooden structure were asked by some Indians to come outside and were killed. A fourth, Anthony Brown, escaped by darting outside, grabbing a nearby chief, holding a gun to his head and running toward Mariposa with him. At a safe distance, Brown abandoned the chief and continued his flight.

Savage, in Mariposa when the attack occurred, hurried back to the store and found a scene of desolation awaiting him. Federal Indian agent Adam Johnston, who accompanied Savage, wrote that "the store was stripped of blankets, clothing, flour and everything of value; the safe broken open and rifled of its contents; the cattle, horses and mules had been run into the mountains; the murdered men had been stripped of their clothing and lay before us filled with arrows; one of them had yet twenty perfect arrows sticking in him."

Rumors soon flew about that miners along the Chowchilla, Fresno and San Joaquin rivers had been attacked or killed by Indians. Savage, knowing that action had to be taken, helped form a volunteer group at Agua Fria (the Mariposa County seat) on January 7, 1851. Three days after the group's creation, it saw action at a Miwok village where Chukchansis and Chawchilas had gathered to discuss war plans. Savage's men struck at daybreak, killing forty or fifty Indians and sustaining several casualties. Since the area had abundant cover where Indians could hide, Savage's group broke off its fighting and retreated to a camp on a Fresno River branch.

Leaving his men in the mountains, Savage scurried back to Agua Fria and returned with newly recruited reinforcements. The strengthened group inched its way toward a suspected encampment on the San Joaquin River, with Indians jeering and taunting them from the

*Left, transporting seeds and water in baskets for which the Yokuts were famous. Right, gathering seeds, a major source of food before arrival of the white man.*

Schoolcraft 1865

*Monache Indian grinding stone, near Huntington Lake.*

*Indian grinding stones, used primarily for preparing acorns.*

# Games Indians Played

Annual Report of the Bureau of American Ethnology to the Secretary of the Smithsonian Institution, 1902-1903
By W. H. Holmes, Chief

## Games of the North American Indians
### Introduction
by Stewart Culin

[This is a small sampling of the games of Central California Indians. The total report presents 809 pages of games followed by a 36-page index. Obviously life was not devoted to hunting, work and pow-wows. Portions of the introduction follow.]

The games of the American Indians may be divided into two general classes: I, games of chance; II, games of dexterity. Games of pure skill and calculation, such as chess, are entirely absent. The Indian games of chance fall into two categories: 1, games in which implements of the nature of dice are thrown at random to determine a number or numbers, and the sum of the counts is kept by means of sticks, pebbles, etc., or upon an abacus, or counting board, or circuit; 2, games in which one or more of the players guess in which of two or more places an odd or particularly marked lot is concealed, success or failure resulting in the gain or loss of counters.

The games of dexterity may be enumerated as: 1, archery in various modifications; 2, a game of sliding javelins or darts upon the hard ground or ice; 3, a game of shooting at a moving target consisting of a netted wheel or a ring; 4, the game of ball in several highly specialized forms; 5, the racing games, more or less related to and complicated with the ball games. In addition, there is a subclass related to the games of shooting at a moving target, of which it is a miniature and solitaire form, corresponding to the European game of cup and ball.

Games of all the classes designated are found among all the Indian tribes of North America and constitute the games par excellence of the Indians. Children have a variety of other amusements, such as top spinning, mimic fights, and similar imitative sports, but the games first described are played only by men and women, or youths and maidens, not be children, and usually at fixed seasons as the accompaniment of certain festivals or religious rites.

There is no evidence that any of the games described were imported into America at any time either before or after the Conquest. On the other hand, they appear to be the direct and natural outgrowth of aboriginal institutions in America. They show no modifications due to white influence other than the decay which characterizes all Indian institutions under existing conditions.

YOKUTS. Mouth of Mill creek, Fresno county, California. (Cat. no. 70671, 70672, Field Columbian Museum.)
Eight walnut-shell dice (figure 161); basket plaque, 23½ inches in diameter. Collected by Dr J. W. Hudson.

Mr Stephen Powers [b] gives the following account:

The Yokuts have a sort of gambling which pertains exclusively to women. It is a kind of dice throwing, and is called u-chu'-us. For dice they take half of a large acorn or walnut shell, fill it level with pitch and pounded charcoal, and inlay it with bits of bright colored abalone shells. For a dice table they weave a very large fine basket tray, almost flat, and ornamented with devices woven in black or brown, mostly rude imitations of trees and geometrical figures. Four squaws sit around it to play, and a fifth keeps tally with fifteen sticks. There are eight dice, and they scoop them up in their hands and dash them into the basket, counting 1 when two or five flat surfaces turn up. The rapidity with which the game goes forward is wonderful, and the players seem totally oblivious to all things in the world beside. After each throw that a player makes she exclaims, yet'-ni or wi-a-tak or ko-mai-éh, which are simply a kind of sing-song or chanting.

YOKUTS. Tule River agency, Tulare county, California. (Cat. no. 70392, Field Columbian Museum.)
Two willow saplings (figure 767), 50 inches in length, with an oak loop lashed on the lower end with sinew; accompanied by two small mistletoe-root balls coated with pitch and painted red.

These are implements for a ball game, collected by Dr J. W. Hudson.

The two balls are laid side by side on the ground at the end of the course, and at a word the captains dip them up with their spoon sticks and cast them forward to their mates, who send them on to the nearest pair of opponents. The course is about 1,200 yards—around a tree and back to the first goal. There are usually eight players, three and a captain on each side.

Fig. 767. Ball and racket; length of racket, 50 inches. Yokuts Indians, Tule River Agency, Tulare County, California.

YOKUTS. Tule River reservation, Tulare county, California. (Cat. no. 70402, 70403, Field Columbian Museum.)
Hoop of fiber, wrapped with buckskin, 4½ inches in diameter; and maple-wood lance (figure 633), about 8 feet long, sharpened at the point and marked with red stripes at the end. Collected by Dr J. W. Hudson, who thus describes the game under the name of hotush:

Fig. 633. Ring and pole; diameter of ring, 4½ inches; length of pole, 8 feet.

Played by four players, two on a side. One player casts the hoop, to-ko-in hotush, and his partner casts his lance so that the hoop will fall on it. If he is successful, and the hoop rests entirely on the lance, not touching the ground, he wins the game. If the hoop rests half on the ground, it counts 1. The game is also won at a throw by impaling the ring. Twelve counters are used. The lance, hoat, is thrown underhand with both hands. The ring is covered either with buckskin or bark.

*Group of Monache Indians seated in front of platform granaries. The granaries, used to store acorns and other seeds, were elevated to protect the food supply from moisture and rodents. A large cone-shaped basket for gathering food lies on the ground next to the cedar bark dwelling.*

*Indian cedar bark dwelling (note baby and metal cooking utensils).*

*Monache Indian papoose, photographed by A. W. Peters, circa 1896.*

*Mono Indian woman panning for gold.*

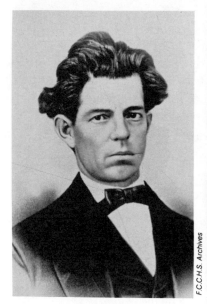

*Captain John Boling, one of the Mariposa Battalion volunteers during the Mariposa Indian War of 1850–51.*

*Monument to Major James D. Savage erected by his business partners at the site of one of his trading posts at the Fresno River. Hensley Lake now covers the original gravesite so it has been moved to roads 603 and 400.*

*In the latter nineteenth century, Fresno County Indians were employed as sheep shearers, grape pickers and domestics. These North Fork Monache Indians were employed as agricultural laborers by the Sherman family.*

underbrush all along the way. The Indians were found at "Battle Mountain" on January 18 and a daybreak raid was planned. At least twenty-three Indians were killed in the subsequent melee and another Chawchila chief, José Rey, was seriously wounded.

These conflicts and others to follow, later known collectively as the Mariposa Indian War, motivated Governor John McDougal to authorize formation of the Mariposa Battalion on January 24. (Most of these events took place in what later became Fresno County, but was then part of Mariposa County.) Word of the order reached Agua Fria the following month. The battalion, with Savage as its leader, was mustered in and divided into three companies on February 12.

In the interim, marauding Indians had moved into the San Joaquin Valley, raiding Wiley B. Cassity's ferry on the San Joaquin River (see Chapter 4). Although Cassity had been warned of the local Indian troubles by Savage, he scoffed at taking precautions. Cassity's body was later found some distance below the ferry. He had been disemboweled, his legs cut off and his tongue torn out, placed on his chest and stuck there with an arrow.

A month later, while the battalion was looking for Indians, four white men were reportedly killed in an Indian ambush near Fine Gold. Shortly afterward, Company A of the battalion, under Captain John Kuykendall, fought a band of Indians on the upper San Joaquin River. Thirteen Indians were killed and the rest pushed into retreat.

Making their way south, Kuykendall and his men marched up the Kings River and attacked the main Choinumni Yokuts village. At the same time the two other companies ventured into the high Sierra, coming upon the Yosemite region and quickly beating Indian tribes there into submission. By late April the Mariposa Indian War was over and the tribes involved were ready for a peace settlement. Even the fierce Chawchilas were now subdued, their spirits broken after José Rey succumbed to the wounds he had received at "Battle Mountain."

Through Indian messengers the word went out that a peace parley would be held at Camp Barbour on the San Joaquin River. (Its location is submerged under Millerton Lake today.) A group of federal Indian commissioners—Redick McKee, George W. Barbour (hence the camp's name) and Oliver W. Wozencraft—established the camp on April 14. Appointed previously to make treaties with California Indians, the commissioners hastened to that site after the Mariposa Indian War concluded.

After a short negotiation period "A Treaty of Peace and Friendship" was drawn up by the commissioners and approved by sixteen tribal representatives on April 29, 1851. Under its conditions the tribes agreed to stop fighting, give up their lands and relocate to the Fresno River Reservation, a tract of land established for them by the treaty. Allotments of food and clothing were promised to the Indians, whose welfare was to be looked after by a reservation agent. Nowhere was it mentioned that a military post would soon be founded near Camp Barbour, ready to deal with any problems the Indians might create. By the summer of 1851 both reservation and post were functioning.

A detachment of soldiers under the command of Lieutenant Tredwell Moore established the military installation—Fort Miller—on May 26, 1851 (see Chapter 5). An Indian village stood on the proposed site of the fort, only a small obstacle to the military's plans; Moore and his men burned it to the ground. Ironically the local Dumna Yokuts and their chief, Tom Kit, were ordered to help build this complex that sat atop their ancestral lands. They received no payment for their labor and were lashed with whips at the slightest sign of loafing. Particularly harsh whippings caused some to die.

Meanwhile, the Indians tried to fend for themselves in their new, white-dominated world. They were markedly unsuccessful. Some took up mining, only to be cheated by traders who weighed their gold with false lead counterweights. Unsuspecting and illiterate, the Indians received minimal trading value as a result. Young Indian women were repeatedly seduced by Fort Miller's finest or local undesirables. Most were raped outright.

Nor was this the sole form of exploitation, as William Faymonville noted in his *Reminiscences of Fresno County*:

> In the Summer of 1856 [Jefferson Milam] Shannon and Jim Roan made up a foot race between two squaws. Jeff trained a young squaw known by the euphonious name of Mustang, and Roan trained another named Chutaluya. Quite an interest was manifested in this race, and considerable money was bet. On the day appointed for the race, a great crowd assembled to witness the speed of the contestants, and when the squaws appeared upon the track, Mustang dressed in red, and the other in blue, a deafening cheer rent the air, and both the squaws looked eager for the fray, and when the word "go" was given, away they went, each doing her level best. The result was, Mustang came out a few feet ahead, and was declared the winner, and Jeff won about $150 on the race. L. A. Holmes, then editor of the Mariposa Gazette, in commenting on the race, observed that "if Roan had kept his squaw in as good training as Jeff kept his, the result of the race would have been different."

The Indians were not even safe from slavery, a practice which may have started in earnest a few years after the Mariposa Indian War. A March 5, 1859 report in the *Marysville Weekly Express* said that "they have a singular way of dispensing justice to Indians in Fresno County. An Indian sentenced for any delinquency, to be imprisoned for a certain time, is sold for that time, to the highest bidder . . . we do not know of [this system] being practiced in any other country." Indentures also were permissible, as the document given in 2:4 shows.

Liquor became the most pervasive problem of the Fresno County Indians. The white advance made whiskey (or "pyanna," as the Indians called it) readily available. It caused many drunken fights, beatings and slashings. When laws were later passed forbidding liquor sales to Indians, they went to any length to obtain it. In the *Fresno Daily Evening Expositor* of August 4, 1890, it was reported that a storekeeper on Whiskey Creek, near the San Joaquin River, was beaten senseless when he refused to sell an Indian gang some "pyanna." Many merchants, however, sold whiskey to Indians in spite of the law, and at excessive prices.

On the Fresno River Reservation there were more difficulties. Indians were being crowded into it from all over the mid-San Joaquin Valley. Many had had their belongings and stored food destroyed in the war, and the increased reservation population caused allocated food resources to shrink. The Indians were being taught to farm, as stipulated in the 1851 treaty, but not fast enough—starvation was widespread.

Problems were caused by simple white greed, too. The traders charged with supplying the reservation with food (one of whom was Savage) double-billed the government and provided fewer provisions than their contracts called for. The Indians' outlook was bleak. It seemed inevitable they would become restive again.

The summer of 1852 demonstrated how uneasy the Indian-white truce was on all fronts. In retribution for an Indian attack on some prospectors in the Yosemite Valley, Lieutenant Moore and most of his Fort Miller command went on several punitive expeditions into the mountains. They burned all the Indian dwellings and caches they could find. On July 4 they discovered a small Indian village, attacked it by surprise and took its twenty residents prisoner; all were relocated to the Fresno River Reservation.

On the San Joaquin River, matters became sticky when the "Jenny Lind" mining claim was being staked out and two Indians, Chawchila chief Federico and Puebla, began nosing around. An annoyed prospector fired two shots in the air to scare away the Indians, which apparently was taken as a threat. Three days later a large contingent of Indians, wearing war paint and toting weapons, visited the miners near the claim site, which lay on an island in the river. The frightened miners jumped into the water and swam to the island, expecting to defend themselves. Tom Kit, the leader of the Indian band, circled around the miners' position and demanded through an interpreter that one of them be surrendered to him. When it became clear that the miners were not taking Tom Kit's threats seriously, he and his forces slinked back to the river bluffs.

The most serious Indian troubles of 1852 occurred on the Kings River. On July 1 some Choinumni

Reference 2:4

## AN INDIAN INDENTURE

THIS INDENTURE made and entered into by the parties hereinafter named, Witnesseth: That James Sayles, Jr., County Judge of Fresno County . . . on behalf of the Indian boy "Jack" of the supposed age of Twelve Years, and at the special instance and request of Ira McCray of said County, does hereby bind and put out the said Indian boy "Jack" as an apprentice to the aforesaid Ira McCray . . .

And the said Indian boy "Jack" . . . does hereby fully and voluntarily bind himself as an apprentice to the said Ira McCray in the capacity of Domestic Servant and general laborer, until he, the said "Jack" shall have attained the full age of Twenty-five Years, and agress [sic] that the said McCray shall have the care, custody, control and earning of him, the said "Jack" during the whole of said term, and hereby provises and agrees to serve the said McCray honestly and faithfully in all things,—his lawful command everywhere readily obey,—to take charge of all property entrusted to his care, and not suffer the same to be lost, wasted, injured or destroyed,—not to absent himself from his said master's service, day or night, without his permission, and in all things conduct himself as a faithful and good servant ought to do, until he shall attain the full age of Twenty-five years aforesaid.

And the said Ira McCray . . . agress [sic] and promises with and to the said "Jack" that he will treat said "Jack" with kindness,—will furnish him a sufficient and suitable supply of food, clothing, medicine, bedding, and other necessaries of life, both in sickness and in health, during the whole of the term aforesaid . . . and that at the end of said term he will pay to said "Jack" the sum of Fifty Dollars and give him a horse.

In Testimony whereof this Indenture is executed in duplicate, and signed and sealed by all the parties hereinbefore named this 11th day of October, A.D. 1862.

James Sayles, Jr., County Judge
HIS
Jack          Indian
MARK
Ira McCray

Witness: E. C. Winchell

SOURCE: Fresno City and County Historical Society Archives.

F.C.C.H.S. Archives

*La-Ache, Centerville Indian, known as Jack, was indentured in 1862.*

Yokuts and their chief, Watoka, told a superintendent at Pool's Ferry (see Chapter 4) that his operation was on Indian land. They even brandished a scrap of paper from their chief of chiefs, Savage, confirming this. Unwilling to tolerate what they saw as insubordination, the ferry operators and a hastily assembled volunteer group struck out for a Choinumni village. When the whites arrived—or so they later claimed—the Indians refused to return to the valley and discuss a settlement. The armed men then fired on the Choinumnis present, wounding or killing eight or nine of them. Only one of the party's members was slightly wounded, suggesting that what really happened was a massacre.

When word of the attack reached army headquarters at Benecia, Brevet Major George W. Patton was sent south to help calm the situation. He learned soon after his arrival that 10,000 Indians were planning to meet on August 15, demand the arrest of the Choinumni murderers, and perhaps commence a new war. Patton quickly saw a way out of this debacle. In a letter to the assistant adjutant general at Benecia, he said that "the tribes have *still* confidence in the troops," and that if they marched conspicuously near the Indian encampment "it [would] save blood." Patton also induced Savage to journey south and assure the Indians there that no further hostilities were necessary.

The plan worked. Between Savage's glib talking and Patton's grand show of mounted troops and howitzers, the Indians were convinced that reprisals would be useless. One belligerent chief, Francisco, was so impressed that he delivered his twelve-year-old daughter to Patton as a guarantee against future conflict.

Helping to defuse tensions along the Kings River was Savage's final triumph. When he visited Pool's Ferry and met a ringleader of the Choinumni raid, Judge Walter Harvey of Tulare County, Savage could

not help voicing his disgust with the action. Harvey took umbrage at Savage, scuffled with him, then drew his pistol and fired. Several shots from a revolver thus ended the life of James D. Savage, a man the Indians, and perhaps some whites, had thought unconquerable.

Back at the Fresno River Reservation, conditions continued to deteriorate. Crop failures bedeviled the agricultural enterprises there, and many Indians died when they ate unripe corn and melons. Late in 1852 a correspondent for the *San Joaquin Republican*, a Stockton newspaper, wrote that the reservation Indians were "dissatisfied, discontented, and seemed to have no resting place; they are all in motion . . . the beef ration has been withheld at a season too late for them to provide a sufficient supply of acorns, &c., for the winter . . . they cannot supply half their wants at this late season. The rain has already set in; the winter is upon them; hunger will drive them to desperation at an early day." Indications are that the winter season was difficult for the Indians, but their weaknesses—physical and numerical—kept them from acting rashly against the whites.

Between 1852 and 1858, Indian affairs in the Fresno County area quieted down considerably. The forces of corruption, alcoholism, disease and malnutrition continued to act in unison, killing more Indians and reducing those left to a miserable existence. Just how badly the situation had degenerated was emphasized by army officer Erasmus D. Keyes in his 1884 memoirs, *Fifty Years' Observation of Men and Events.*

It was on the very site of Fort Miller, in the . . . month of May [1851], that I saw assembled above 1,200 aborigines, natives of the adjacent plains and mountains, many of whom had never seen a white man till they came to treat with us . . . As all these Indians had been assigned to a reservation of which Fort Miller was a central point, I inquired [upon returning to Fort

Reference 2:5
## "AS ABIDE WITH US THEY SHALL NOT"

Fresno Indian Sub Agency
November 14th 1858

Judge M. B. Lewis
Ind Sub Agent
Fresno

Dear Sir

We, the undersigned citizens of Fresno and Tulare counties having removed a numerous body (say 200) of the Na-tu-nu-too [Nutunutu], A-ta-chee [Tachi], and We-mel-chy's [Wimilchi] Indians from their homes and hunting grounds of King's River and the margins of Tulare Lake to this reservation would respectfully state the reasons that have induced us to this course.

First: Ever since the settlement of that region by the whites these Indians have been in the habit of killing great numbers of hogs and cattle and stealing provisions and other articles of value from the houses and camps

of the whites. And recently these depredations have been so frequent and of such agrevating [sic] character that further forbearance became impossible.

Second: The presence of these Indians in a region so densely populated by whites whose exclusive business is stock raising is prejudicial to their interests in many ways. These Indians and a community of stock growing people cannot inhabit the same country. No violence was used in capturing these Indians. They have been kindly treated, and have been subsisted at our expense from the place of capture. We would also state that this is the last time their peaceable removal will be attempted and that should they return they will surely be harshly dealt with. *As abide with us they shall not.* We have warned those who still remain in the vicinity from whence these came of the consequences that will fall upon them if they persist remaining where

they now are. We have advised them to depart in peace. Among these, there are probably thirty mission Indians who are all daring and expert marauders and who will be summarily treated should they not peaceably retire, or be removed from their present haunts.

Respectfully submitted by yours etc.
Justin Esney [Esrey]
B. A. Andrews
W. G. M. Kinney
A. M. Net
B. J. Hickell
W. A. Tull

SOURCE: Heizer, Robert F., ed. *The Destruction of California Indians.* Santa Barbara and Salt Lake City: Peregrine Smith, Inc., 1974. Pp. 130–31.

Miller in 1858] for several individuals whom I remembered. I was told that they were nearly all dead, victims to drunkenness, and that of the number I saw not above fifty remained. I took pains to see the wretched survivors, and was shocked with the spectacle of degradation and self-abandonment they presented.

Grave problems developed on the Fresno River Reservation in November 1858. Settlers along the Kings River began rounding up local Indians, burning their houses and belongings, and transporting them under guard to the reservation. The reasons for this round-up, begun as winter descended, are best described in a petition drafted by the settlers (see 2:5). It took more than two months to collect the Indians. Any resistance was met with beating, whipping, or the outright murder of the protesters.

When Sub Agent Martin B. Lewis of the Fresno River Reservation learned what was taking place, he urged the whites to treat the Indians "with humanity and moderation," a plea that went ignored. From Whitmore's Ferry on the Kings River (a point where the captured Indians were first gathered—see Chapter 4), the Indians trudged under guard toward the reservation, foraging for what food they could—their white captors provided none.

As the Indians began arriving at the reservation Lewis was faced with the problem of accommodating them. The declining reservation population and repeated crop failures made it hard to provide for new residents. Emergency supplies were ordered, and Lewis transported hundreds of Indians to another site on the San Joaquin River. Undoubtedly most of these people shared the fate of the earlier reservation Indians. Deprived of freedom, food and humane treatment, it is amazing that any survived.

Although the Fresno River Reservation was officially abandoned on November 9, 1859, its obituary had been written almost a year before by J. Ross Browne (see 2:6). A United States Treasury agent investigating the spending of federal funds in California, Browne was disgusted by the chicanery, bad management and failed ventures he saw on Indian reservations throughout the state. Profiteers operated from within and without; government Indian officials collected large salaries and ignored their administrative duties while traders and storekeepers abused supply contracts. A few men, like Savage, were officials and suppliers both, playing this dual role for its full value. These circumstances combined to make the Fresno River Reservation a grotesque failure. Even Sub Agent Lewis recognized this as he wrote his last annual report:

These people continue to enjoy the confidence and kind treatment of the white settlers [!], and have been blessed with good health; but owing to a want of success in the raising of subsistence on this farm for the past three years, after having labored hard and faithfully, and the loss of a larger portion of the crop raised on this place this season by smut; after having irrigated the land and having fine prospects, they have, in mass, become discouraged and dissatisfied with this place, and are now anxious to take their chances for success elsewhere within the bounds of their own country, where good land may be found and the seasons more reliable . . .

The land was good and the seasons reliable, but the Fresno County Indians failed to achieve the success Lewis wished for them. As the mission system had proved, they were exceedingly poor farmers. With the reservation gone they clustered in the foothill and mountain areas. Some tried to live in traditional ways; most found that impossible. Too many new customs, conveniences and vices were around. Indian life could never return to its former, idyllic standards.

During and after the reservation period, a fair number of Indian women became the wives of white men. Fresno County pioneers Joseph Kinsman, James

Reference 2:6

## ONE MAN'S VERDICT ON THE FRESNO RIVER RESERVATION

(Excerpt from a letter by J. Ross Browne, Special Agent Treasury Department, to Hon. John W. Denver, Commissioner of Indian Affairs, dated January 18, 1859.)

. . . The next serious difficulty to which I would invite your attention is that existing at the Fresno in the San Joaquin Valley. During several years past, as the Department is aware, two Indian farms have been conducted by Sub Agents in the San Joaquin Valley—one at the Fresno under M. B. Lewis, and the other at Kings River in charge of Mr. Campbell.

The results at both of these places, as shown by me in official reports dating as far back as 1856, have been a continued and almost entire failure of crops—especially at the Fresno—and an absolute waste of public money, without the least practical benefit to the Indians in that vicinity. So far from any encouragement being given to them to come on these farms and work, they have been kept away by positive orders, on the plea that there was nothing there upon which to feed them; and during my last visit to the Fresno (a few months since) Judge Lewis alleged as a reason for the informality of certain vouchers for articles purchased at Roane's Store, 30 miles distant in the mountains, and at Fort Miller, 16 miles distant—all of which were certified to in the Abstracts of Issues as having been delivered on the reservation—that he was forced to let the Indians get the articles there upon written orders, sent up by the Chiefs, in order to prevent them from coming upon the reservation, where he had nothing to give them . . .

These facts are well established, and the Department must perceive that they present a most pitiable condition of affairs. If, instead of the large and useless expenditure of means devoted to the payment of white employees at the places referred to, direct purchases of clothing and provisions had been made, or a better location chosen for a farm, where some return in the way of crops could have been obtained, much of this suffering might have been avoided. The facts are submitted for your consideration; but as everything now seems to be in an unsettled condition, as far as the future policy of the Department is concerned, I am unable to suggest a remedy . . .

SOURCE: Heizer, Robert F., ed. *The Destruction of California Indians.* Santa Barbara and Salt Lake City: Peregrine Smith, Inc., 1974. Pp. 135–36.

Bethel and Joseph Medley followed this practice early and it was common for many years. (See 2:7 for a biography of "Mrs. Medley.") A December 1857 *Mariposa Gazette* article commented on this phenomenon in Fresno County, noting that "they [the women] are said to make excellent wives, are neat, and tidy, and industrious, and soon learn to discharge domestic duties properly and creditably."

Indian men seemed to have more trouble adjusting to the white world. Some of them became trusted retainers of white families living in the foothills and mountains. Ernestine Winchell wrote that "the Yanceys of Tollhouse had Old Alec, the McCardles of Rush Creek had Indian Dan, the Firebaughs of the Sycamore had Applejack, and the Humphreys of Pine Ridge and the Cornstalk Ranch had McCray." These men performed all the necessary frontier tasks—felling trees, chopping wood, putting up houses and building fences. Most were industrious and adjusted well to their roles. One notable exception was Old Alec. He discovered the pleasures of "pyanna" and gradually stopped working for the Yanceys, though he tried to live off them anyway. "Whitemen heap damfool!" he exclaimed on one occasion during the 1870s. "All time wuck, wuck, wuck!" He died of acute alcoholism not long after.

Liquor bedeviled some Indian men to the point of violence. One of these, named John Bug, apparently believed that drunkenness gave him the right to raise hell—and he raised it well. An account of his exploits, presented in the September 7, 1893 *Fresno Daily Evening Expositor*, said that

When drunk he always felt like war; and he usually won his battles. But even Napoleon and Gustavus Adolphus sometimes got licked, and so did John Bug. But he was like truth—when crushed to earth he would rise again.

Reference 2:7
## "MRS. MEDLEY"
### ERNESTINE WINCHELL

When, about 1861, a soft-eyed Indian girl named Suze stole into a young miner's cabin on the bank of the San Joaquin and there set to rights the wild disorder she found, it was simply the way of a maid with a man. She had marked Joe Medley from amongst his fellows by reason of the height and strength and big black beard of him. And when Joe, noticing the youthful grace of her, her neatness and her wistful desire to please and accepted her devotion, it was the not-at-all complicated way of a white man with a native damsel.

In the summer of 1863 Medley varied his occupations of mining and hunting with occasional jobs of farm work. Young Suze, with a girl baby in its Indian cradle, made a home for him wherever it was convenient to stop—the shade of an oak tree near a spring or creek being all that was necessary in the warm months.

While there was but one baby it was easy enough for Suze to follow her man from one oak tree to another, but a family requires a home. The young mother was, therefore, made the proud mistress of a board house. The dwelling was similar to that of the white settlers, having three small rooms and a rock fireplace at one end. Household goods gradually accumulated, including a cooking stove, table and other simple furnishings. An eight-day clock was kept covered with mosquito bar to protect it from the flies, and eventually a sewing machine took an honored place in the cabin.

The Indian woman's pride was to keep her house like those of her white neighbors, and it was the boast of Joe Medley that no white woman was a better or cleaner cook than his brown Suze.

In the care of her babies, however, the Indian followed the practice of her tribe. She well knew the folly of leaving wee, tender bodies unsupported, and she bound them carefully into the native cradle-baskets.

It was on the edge of Big Sandy Valley that this first home was built, and there the babies continued to come—ten of them. On a little rise not far from the house Suze saw one after another buried. Five grew to maturity, and three survived her when, in the spring of 1913, she was laid there with her children.

No woman could have been more faithful to her home and her man and her babies than this Indian woman. At a time when, owing to a crisis in race affairs, every squaw-man between the San Joaquin and Kings rivers awoke one morning to find his breakfast fires deserted, Joe Medley's Suze remained calmly at her post though she thought any moment might be her last.

In 1880 a government survey was made in this region, and Joe Medley obtained a patent to 160 acres in his chosen valley. By some financial misadventure he finally lost it, and there was nothing to do but move to the claim of his daughter Mandy, leaving the old home and the little graves on the knoll. A new house was built about two and a half miles from Pleasant Vale Schoolhouse, and the household goods reinstalled. In this school and in that of the Big Sandy district the half-white children learned to read and write and "figger."

The time arrived when legal marriage or separation was required of the squaw-men of California. Joe Medley elected to marry the mother of his children, and Indian Suze became Mrs. Medley. The rite made the brown woman proud, but to the neighbors who had known her through the many years, who had always respected her womanly honesty and goodness, who had so often experienced her knowledge and generosity in sickness and trouble, she was still Aunt Suze.

A most friendly and sociable person, she loved to visit in a very few white homes where she was understood, but she never forgot race distinctions. For these occasions she made herself cleaner and neater than ever. Her hair was arranged in white-woman fashion and her hard black feet were painfully crowded into stockings and shoes. Her print sunbonnet and gingham dress, her white apron and petticoats were as beautifully starched and ironed as any in the hills.

Somehow Aunt Suze knew everything that went on in the neighborhood, but she never carried tales. A startling general statement, or a shrewdly expressed opinion would surprise her hearer with hints of knowledge her impassive face and controlled tongue would never betray. Her sense of humor, too, was as keen as her sense of justice.

As Suze Medley grew older she felt a stronger call of race, and each year she paid a visit to a sister at Coarsegold, forty miles away, going alone and on foot. In this she was all Indian, and yet one can imagine something of her quiet happiness in the return to the scenes and ways of her girlhood.

Deprived of her recreations of basket patchwork by failing eyesight, her body no longer fit for hard work and long journeys, Aunt Suze rapidly aged. Before she was 70 she passed away and received at her burial both Christian and Indian rites. She was long remembered by many friends of both races as a brave brown woman whose heart was big with true humanity.

SOURCE: Ernestine Winchell columns.

No man has ever tried to count the scars on his tough hide. In the first place, the smallpox gave him a pretty vigorous tustle and tried to subdue him, but he came off conqueror.

Once he attended an Indian funeral at Temperance Flat, and in order to mourn with appropriate gusto he filled himself with Indian whisky, made of liquid protoxide of nitrogen and oil of vitriol, a combination which raises an Indian's courage to the sticking point.

John Bug tried to break the enemy's center, but he was knocked down in the melee, had one eye gouged out, was hacked in the face with an ax, had his throat cut from ear to ear and gashes cut of several inches in length all over his head. He went to the Indian hospital under the manzanita brush for a day or two, and came out smiling.

The next year he started out to conquer the world, and began at Fresno Flats. Drunk and glorious, he fired a shot into an Indian camp. They swarmed out and returned the fire. He was shot two or three times in the body, but that failed to floor him. Then a half breed ran up behind him and shot him in the back of the head. Still he stood his ground. But an Indian with a horse pistol stuck it to John Bug's ear and fired. The bullet made a hole in his neck as big as a broom handle, and he fell as if dead. But he revived, and that night walked 25 miles to Hildreth, where he recovered, and now he has come to the surface again, and is in jail for biting a man's thumb off. Some dime museum ought to buy him and exhibit him as the toughest human being on earth.

Other than the occasional outbursts of a John Bug, the Fresno County Indians were rather unobtrusive after the 1850s. Problems of a sort occurred in 1870, although they were not as significant as the Mariposa Indian War. That was the year when Ghost Dance hysteria seized Indian tribes across America, including the Fresno County Monaches. Prophecies began circulating that the Indians would turn the tables on the whites (see 2:8), and orgies of dancing and singing would bring this to pass. Paiute Indians from the eastern Sierra passed this knowledge on to their Monache relatives (the two tribes are part of a larger group called the Shoshoneans). Soon large Monache encampments were established to hold Ghost Dances, and their villages were left uninhabited.

Contemporary accounts confirm that Fresno County's white population was alarmed by the Indian movements. "The Indians are certainly acting strangely," said an August 31, 1870, report in the *Fresno Weekly Expositor*. "They have abandoned their camps at all points, and with their women and children have gone back into the mountains. The course usually pursued, we learn from those versed in Indian matters, is, when they contemplate an uprising, to send their squaws and children out of the way of danger before commencing hostilities."

The resulting excitement caused a volunteer party to be raised and forts to be built at Humphrey's Mill and Tollhouse. An encampment in the mountains was raided and the participants driven back to Stephenson Meadows; otherwise, there were no hostile Indian-white encounters. It is unlikely that any physical harm was intended for the whites. The Ghost Dance was supposed to work through ceremony, not force. When a local Indian, Cow-whopper, was asked his opinion of the "difficulties," he summed it up best: "What for white man want to fight Injin? Injin no want to fight. You think Injun damn fool?"

Just as Cow-whopper said, the Indians were no "damn fools." They had produced governments, literatures, material cultures and a world outlook that remain unique in recorded history. Why the white invaders were unable to appreciate these achievements and pursue a policy of coexistence seems strange—yet, in another sense, it is unsurprising. As Armenia, Auschwitz and Cambodia have proven, humanitarianism remains a too-frequently rejected ideal.

Still, that offers no justification for the tragedy of the Indians, and apologetics at this stage seem futile. All our generation can do is remain aware of this, the blackest page in Fresno County's history, and ensure it never happens again, anywhere. That would be the most fitting memorial anyone could offer to the native Fresnans.

Reference 2:8
## WHAT THE GHOST DANCE WOULD BRING

We learn that the Indian uprising, mention of which we have made elsewhere, was instigated by an old witch, or "medicine man" . . . who . . . reported to the rest of the Indians—who were assembled at a fandango—that he had discovered the "Great Spirit," and that being had informed him that at the appearance of the new moon the whites were all to die, together with their cattle, sheep and hogs, and all the Indians in the service of the whites also. The horses, however, were to remain for the sole uses and benefits of "Lo." A good time was to come upon them. The witch was to furnish each and every Indian with a sack of flour, which, like the famous measure of meal of the widow, mentioned in the Old Testament, was never failing. A piece of bread of very small size, placed upon a piece of board, though attacked by a hundred hungry Indians, would constantly increase in size. The antelope and deer were again to return, and game of all kinds was to abound as in days of yore . . . The price of these blessings [was] that the Indians, after the whites were disposed of, were to be peaceable and orderly, and refrain from drinking . . . The witch is a Pah Ute [Paiute], and they seem to be the principal instigators of the affair.

SOURCE: Fresno County Scrapbook 1870-1899, p. 1399, taken from *Fresno Weekly Expositor*, August 20, 1870, p. 3, c. 1.

24

# Chapter 3
# Days of Discovery

The exploration and settlement of Fresno County by groups other than Indians was part of a process that took not just months and years; it took centuries. In effect it began when Hernan Cortes conquered Mexico in 1519–21 and the Spanish began pushing up North America's western edge, staking numerous land claims as they passed through. This investigative thrust eventually brought Juan Rodriguez Cabrillo's ship to the California coast in 1542–43.

Numerous expeditions to this new land followed in the next two centuries, culminating in Father Junipero Serra's establishment of a Franciscan mission for Indians—the first permanent settlement—at San Diego in 1769. With this foothold, more intensive explorations to California's interior began. Lieutenant Gabriel Moraga's party made it to present-day Fresno County in 1805.

It seems strange that forty-six years would elapse between Serra's arrival and Moraga's explorations in the valley, but there were valid reasons for not penetrating the interior. Preliminary expeditions, such as those led by Don Pedro Fages in 1772 and Father Francisco Garces in 1776, indicated that the central valley was a bleak, arid expanse of land punctuated by incidental marshlands, rivers, grass patches and oak groves.

Travel and communications between this area and the better-populated coast were slow. There were few roads and trails to the great valley, no maps, and no supply stations, all of which made travel difficult. On the coast, the Spanish enjoyed a good life and had Indian neophytes (converts) to support them agriculturally and otherwise. There was no need for them to move on, at least in the early years.

By the early nineteenth century, the situation had changed. The coast was becoming more populated and the Spanish needed new regions for settlement—perhaps even breathing space, for there were many landholders with thousands of acres apiece in the familiar areas. There was talk of establishing a new inland chain of missions to speed the process of inland colonization. Other complicating factors were the escape of neophytes and the desertion of soldiers, from

Los Angeles, Santa Barbara, Monterey, San Francisco and elsewhere. Personnel, civilian and military, were necessary for Spain to keep its grip on California, and out of the clutches of the Russians and British who lurked in Alaska, Fort Ross (in present-day Mendocino County) and British Columbia. Any manpower loss had to be taken seriously.

Moraga might have visited Fresno County for any of these reasons, but it is said that his trip—with a small party—was really made to satisfy his curiosity about the interior. Regrettably, no written record of this trip has been preserved. Later reports claim that, on this expedition, Moraga was the first to sight and name the Rio de los Santos Reyes (River of the Holy Kings, now Kings) and San Joaquin rivers. (San Joaquin was derived from Saint Joachim, father of the Virgin Mary.) Conjecturally, these rivers gained their names because of the days on which the Spanish encountered them. The feast day for the Holy Kings—the Biblical Wise Men—is January 6, and Saint Joachim's is March 20.

The following year, 1806, Governor Arrillaga ordered Moraga to head another expedition into the valley. Its purpose was to look for new mission sites, seek stolen livestock and capture escaped neophytes. Moraga, described as a handsome, eager young man, had by then been promoted to Alférez (officer in charge) of the San Francisco company. In September 1806 his party was assembled at Mission San Juan Bautista—a sergeant, a corporal, eight men from San Francisco and fifteen from Monterey. They started for the plains on the twenty-first, with Pedro Muñoz as chaplain and diarist for the group.

They reached the San Joaquin River a few miles north of present-day Firebaugh. Muñoz recorded there "was much good land to the south, but some alkali; plenty of beaver and salmon." From here they set off to the northeast, across the Merced County landscape. In this area they encountered swarms of yellow butterflies—in Spanish, *mariposas.* Their abundance led to the naming of Mariposa County, which initially included almost all of the San Joaquin Valley.

When Moraga's party reached the Sierra foothills, it

headed north, going almost to the Sacramento River. The men then turned south and returned down the eastern side of the valley, reaching the San Joaquin River again on October 11. After resting for a day, the party explored the river. Muñoz reported that:

> One party went down the river, and found nothing but bad land; the other went upstream into the mountains, finding plenty of pine and redwood, and having an interesting interview with the old chief Sujoyocomu at the rancheria of Pizcache [Pitkachi Yokuts village]. He said a band of soldiers like these came from across the Sierra [from New Mexico?] 20 years ago and killed some of the Indians.

There were other reports from the Indians of such a visit, but no record has been located identifying the early visitors or disclosing their fate.

Hubert Howe Bancroft's *History of California* assumes that the Moraga party camped near Millerton, the best-known early landmark on the river. Subsequent writers have unquestioningly accepted this assumption. However, a careful reading of Muñoz's diary indicates that the men probably camped several miles west of Millerton. It reports that on the fourteenth they traveled "5 leagues east to the Rio de los Santos Reyes." Going east from Millerton would have taken them into the foothills; the most direct route to the Kings River would have been due south. A more likely campsite for the party, then, would have been near Herndon or Gravelly Ford, a favorite crossing of the Spanish about nine miles west of Herndon. From there they could have gone eastward, as the diary says, and would have reached the Kings near Sanger. Such a campsite also would explain why the downstream exploration party found "nothing but bad lands," as the prairie would have been extremely dry in October.

Moraga's party considered the Kings River "an excellent location for a mission," according to Muñoz. A few days later they found an oak-covered region they adjudged the "best place seen for a mission." Although the exact location was not given, it may have been in present-day Tulare County. Continuing south, the expedition reached Mission San Fernando in early November. Moraga made several other trips to the San Joaquin Valley, but never again passed through Fresno County's eventual borders.

After Mexico declared its independence from Spain in 1810, and won that independence in 1822 following much political and military struggle, the character of the inland expeditions changed. The padres no longer came, for differences between them and the Mexican military government had caused the end of the expansion of the chain of twenty-one coastal missions. By 1834 the missions had been secularized by the government, heralding the end of an era in California history.

The languishing Spanish and unstable Mexican governments were more interested in consolidating their hold on California than anything else. Soldiers came almost exclusively to capture and punish runaway neophytes and military deserters. Their cruelty to the Indians could be extreme at times—beating-to-death and bodily mutilation were common. No padres were around to act as a stabilizing influence. The men—hastily recruited and poorly trained, to prop up the prevailing governments—were not as gentlemanly as their *conquistador* predecessors.

Other explorers entered the valley from the south but none reported reaching farther north than the Kings River. Father Juan Martín from San Miguél mission in 1804 led what is considered the earliest organized search for a mission site in the Tulare Valley. (Note that the 1873 map on the endpapers identifies much of southern Fresno County as being part of the Tulare Valley.)

In a report of his visit to the *gentiles Tulareños* he said the Indians "have shown good will toward the

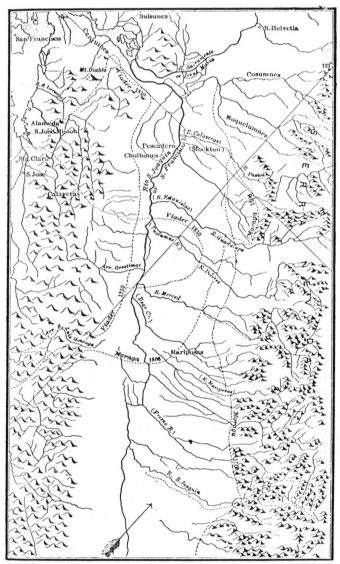

*This map, taken from Bancroft's* History of California, *gives approximate routes for Gabriel Moraga's 1806 foray into the San Joaquin Valley (Moraga 1806) and two other journeys he made ten years later, accompanied by Father José Viader. (Viader 1810).*

soldiers who have visited the Tulare region . . . Their good will would probably be constant if it were not that runaway Indians from the north make them hostile . . . Indians on horseback arrived telling them that the fathers do nothing but kill Indians." Father Martín preferred mission sites along the rivers but Governor Arrillaga thought they should be near the lake. None was ever chosen.

Writings indicate there were innumerable expeditions into the valley that left no record of what were probably very routine search and capture missions.

As the 1820s progressed, Americans involved in the burgeoning fur trapping and trading business began filtering into California. The first among them to enter Fresno County's area, a band of trappers led by Jedediah Strong Smith, arrived in February or March of 1827. Unlike most fur traders, Smith could read and write, was a devout Christian and led a clean life.

In 1826 Smith, then only twenty-seven, and his two partners had a crew of forty-five trappers. From the Great Salt Lake area, Smith led eighteen of his men on an expedition through the uncharted Southwest. He wrote that he "wanted to be the first to view a country on which the eyes of a white man had never gazed and to follow the course of rivers that run through a new land."

The men eventually reached San Gabriel Mission near Los Angeles, where the purpose of Smith's trip was questioned by Mexican authorities. (They were fearful of any foreigners who ventured onto California's soil, as mentioned before.) Smith finally obtained permission to leave by a northern route, which resulted in his visit to the Fresno County area.

Smith kept a record of his California sojourn in diary form. From it he prepared a detailed manuscript for a book about his trip. Lost for many years, it was uncovered and published in 1977. It provides a fascinating glimpse of his days in the middle San Joaquin Valley (see 3-1).

A series of events prevented most of Smith's trappers from leaving California on schedule. They continued working the previously untrapped streams of the San Joaquin Valley for several months. Their efforts were rewarded by a large pelt harvest, later sold for $20,000 at Fort Vancouver on the Columbia River. This was a princely sum for the time and attested to the quality and quantity of beaver and otter in California.

Before Smith could publish a personal account of his travels, fate intervened. In 1831, when he was only thirty-three, he was killed on the Santa Fe Trail by Comanche Indians. His death was an especially tragic loss, for he was a great leader of men and contributed much to the early knowledge and exploration of the far west.

Had Smith lived longer, California might have experienced its gold rush twenty years earlier. He found traces of gold in the northern streams and had planned to return and work the gold. Instead, the hundreds of trappers and venturesome travelers who visited the interior in the 1830s and 1840s did little except deplete the area's wildlife and contributed nothing to its permanent development.

News of the Smith party's success in California spread quickly. It has been estimated that, between 1827 and 1837, as many as 400 English, French and American trappers swarmed along California's rivers—depleting them of beaver and otter. At the same time, the Russians at Fort Ross were doing much the

Reference 3:1

## TRAVELS OF THE FIRST AMERICAN IN FRESNO COUNTY

### JEDEDIAH S. SMITH

Having remained two days at the last mentioned encampment I moved on N Westwardly 25 miles crossing in the course of the day 2 small streams and encamping near a large indian village on the bank of a river 80 yds wide where found some Beaver sign. These Indians called themselves Wim-milche and this name I applied to the river [Kings] which comes from E N E. In the vicinity was considerable timber (Oak) and a plenty of grass. The game of the country was principally Elk and Antelope. On the 28th of February I commenced trapping on the Wimmilche and during 10 days I moved up the river 25 or 30 miles. I was then near the foot of the Mt and finding no further inducement for trapping and the indians telling me of a river they called the Peticutry [San Joaquin] in which there was beaver I traveled north along near the foot of the Mt about 15 miles and encamped on the bank of the Peticutry* (*at the place where I first struck the Peticutry were a great number of

small artificial mounds.) running at this place west and not quite as large as the Wim mil che. In this vicinity the plains are generally clothed with grass and were at that time covered withe Blossoms. Along the river there is some timber. At the foot of the Mt the timber is Oak and far up the Mt Pine.

The Peticutry runs west 10 miles and then turns N N W. I continued trapping down this river about 35 miles after it turned N W . . . Since passing the Wimmilch there had been an abundance of Elk and some Antelope and on the West side of the Peticutry plenty of wild horses. Birds of the larger kinds were numerous and particularly birds of passage as this was their season. I saw wild Geese White and Grey Brant Blue and White Heron Cormorant many kinds of Ducks and common Buzzard. Hawk of all Colors. Magpyes. A kind of Pigeon resembling the tame Blue Pigeon, 2 or three kinds of Eagles and a verry [sic] large Bird which I supposed to be the Vulture or the Condor. Small birds were

quite scarce and I saw very few snakes. The Peticutry would be navigable for large boats as far up as the bend near the Mt. The country Generally is a most excellent grazing country . . . the soil is such as to admit of many fine farms. There might be in places a want of timber but the neighboring Mountain would afford an ample supply which could be easily floated down the streams almost to any desired point.

[The editor assumed Smith meant the bend near Firebaugh, but his reference to "near the Mt" seems to indicate he meant the bend near Herndon. In either case his prophecy came true for a few years.]

SOURCE: *The Southwest Expedition of Jedediah S. Smith, His Personal Account of the Journey to California 1826–27.* Reprinted by permission of the publishers, The Arthur H. Clark Co.

same on the north coast. There, the sea otter was trapped nearly to extinction.

Included in this onrush were two parties led by Ewing Young, a man (like Smith) interested in exploring the west's nether-regions and turning a nice profit in pelts simultaneously. Young's first expedition started from Taos, New Mexico—then a fur trade hub—and arrived in California, following the southern trails, in the spring of 1829. By making their way north from Mission San Gabriel, near Los Angeles, and the Tejon Pass area, the men reached the San Joaquin Valley. They soon appreciated, and took advantage of, the boundless fur and game reserves there. The next party, which took a similar route, made its visit in the winter of 1832–33.

Both expeditions entered Fresno County's eventual borders, according to the later recollections of their members. One of these, who was on the 1829 trip, was famed mountain man Christopher ("Kit") Carson. He said that

> We had plenty to eat and found grass in abundance for our animals. We found signs of trappers in the San Joaquin [River]. We followed their trail and, in a few days, overtook the party and found them to be of the Hudson's Bay Company [a large fur-trapping and trading enterprise based in Canada]. They were sixty men strong, commanded by Peter [Skene] Ogden. We trapped down the San Joaquin and its tributaries and found but little beaver, but game plenty: elk, deer and antelope in thousands... We remained during the summer. Not being the season for trapping, we passed our time in hunting.

The second expedition's memoirist was John J. Warner, later a large-scale rancher in southern California, who offered these comments:

> Ewing Young, with his small party of trappers... trapped [the Kings River] up to and some distance into the mountains and then passed on to the San Joaquin River, trapped that river down to canoe navigation in the foothills, where a canoe was made, and three men were detached from the party to trap that river by means of the canoe. The main body continued on northwesterly until they struck a tributary of the San Joaquin, now called the Fresno River, which was trapped down through the foothills to the plains, where it was discovered that the river had been recently trapped.

More Hudson's Bay men were found to be responsible for the Fresno's being "recently trapped." After venturing into northern California and Oregon, Warner tells that the party backtracked into their old haunts

> and then crossed the country to the San Joaquin River, up which [the men] traveled to the great bend

and then to the mouth of Kings River, where, striking the trail of the preceding year, he followed it southerly...

Meanwhile, another fur entrepreneur had become entranced with interior California's possibilities and decided to send a band of trappers there. He was Captain Benjamin L. E. Bonneville, a United States Army officer on extended leave, whose career was later commemorated in a biography by Washington Irving. Meeting with his trappers on the headwaters of Wyoming's Green River in the summer of 1833, Bonneville had seventy of his men strike out for California on a southwesterly course.

The group's leader was Joseph Reddeford Walker. Soldier, explorer, sheriff and trapper in various parts of the west before this time, and "strong built, dark complexioned, brave in spirit though mild in manners," according to Irving, Walker was an able guide for this trek into the unknown. White men had not yet ventured down the Green to Nevada's Humboldt River, across the Sierra and thence into California—as did this party.

"Tribulation from this time on, for many days, was their unceasing concomitant," wrote Lilbourne A. Winchell of Walker's expedition. "Grass for the animals was wanting, except at rare intervals; their own supply of provisions had practically been exhausted... They lost twenty-five horses, seventeen of which they ate the best parts—they had no other food."

On October 13 the men stumbled across a series of precipices that appeared to be more than a mile high, punctuated by waterfalls, according to party diarist Zenas Leonard. Given this description, the men seem to have been the first white discoverers of Yosemite Valley. Making their way south and west, the men feasted on acorns, deer and bear and encountered "some trees of the Redwood species incredibly large—some of which would measure 16 to 18 fathom around the trunk," wrote Leonard. This was another momentous discovery; white men had never glimpsed the mighty redwoods before, either.

Descending into the plains, within or near the Fresno County borders, Leonard reported that "these prairies are... swarming with wild horses, some of which are quite docile. They are all very fat, and can be seen of all colors; from spotted, to white, to jet black." They secured some of these animals at a friendly Indian village before plodding, in a westerly direction, along the "deep, clear and smooth" San Joaquin River and on to the Coast Range.

Before leaving the San Joaquin Valley, Walker's men encountered two strange sights. They found four dead Indians in a tule marsh, two of them "well wrapped up in beaver skins" and two "partly consumed by grizzly bears." A more intriguing incident happened on November 12, when, said Leonard, "soon after dark the air appeared to be completely thickened

*John C. Fremont.*

*Joseph Reddeford Walker.*

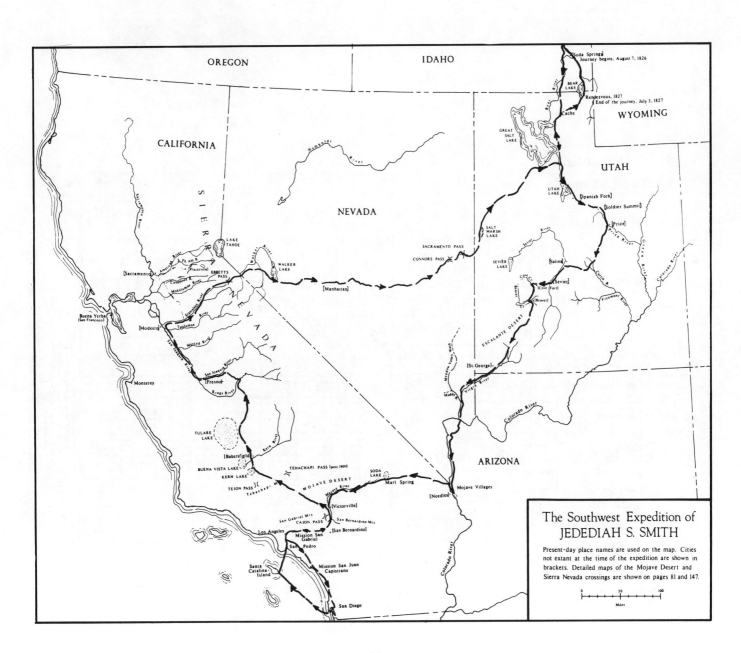

The Southwest Expedition of
JEDEDIAH S. SMITH

Present-day place names are used on the map. Cities
not extant at the time of the expedition are shown in
brackets. Detailed maps of the Mojave Desert and
Sierra Nevada crossings are shown on pages 81 and 147.

Surveyor's Map of
Rancho Rio del San Joaquin
(No *diseño* was ever filed)

*General José Castro*

Plat of the
Rancho Laguna de Tache

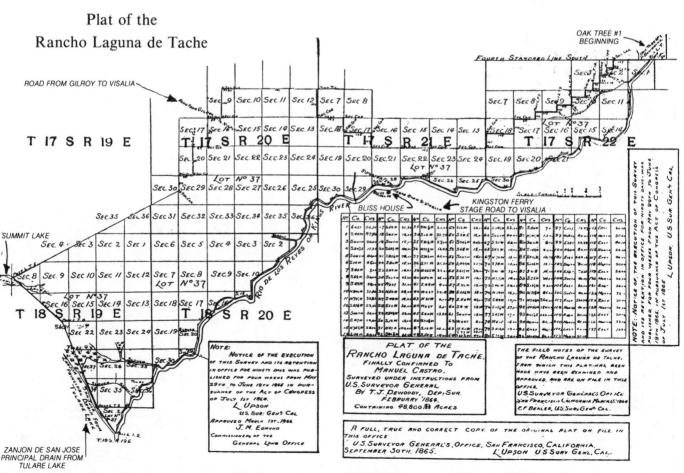

with meteors falling toward the earth, some of which would explode in the air and others would be dashed to pieces on the ground, frightening our horses so much that it required the most active vigilance of the whole company to keep them together." It was part of a gigantic meteor shower that blanketed the whole continent that night.

Walker and his men journeyed to San Juan Bautista, Monterey and elsewhere during November, December and January of 1834. They seemed to spend little time trapping and more time talking to sailors, settlers, Indians and Mexican government officials about general living conditions. They started on their return trip by mid-January, establishing camp on a river Leonard called the Sulphur. It may have been the San Joaquin. Here they hunted elk, deer and bear and joined some soldiers in a punitive expedition against some horse-stealing Indians on January 28. The Indians had been driving 300 or more horses across the plains, and the soldiers were getting ready to close in on them. Despite protests from the Americans, the soldiers killed the young, elderly and Indian women, cutting off their ears to "show the priests and Alcaldes that they had used every effort to regain the stolen property," said Leonard.

The party was stalled on the "Sulphur" banks until February 14, when Walker returned from Monterey with additional provisions for the return trip. Traveling along the river's south banks, they bought twenty-five horses from two deserting soldiers who subsequently accompanied the party as guides. Along the foothills Leonard noted that "game if very scarce owing to the numerous swarms of Indians scattered along in every direction." A plague of some kind, perhaps malaria spread by other trappers, had been afflicting the Indians. Many had removed, for reasons that are unclear, from the valley flatlands to the hills.

Continuing down the valley's eastern side, the party trudged up the Kern River and went through the mountain pass that has borne Walker's name ever since. Wending their way through the eastern Sierra slopes, the men reached their 1833 trail in the central mountain region. Along the way, they made another remarkable discovery—the Mono Hot Springs. After weeks of a northeasterly trek that took them into Idaho, the men finally met with Bonneville, still in that region, on July 12.

Other trappers, escaped soldiers and explorers ventured far up the eastern valley streams, but none left written records of their trips until 1845. In the winter of that year, American government explorer John C. Fremont led the first expedition to visit Fresno Coun-

Reference 3:2

## FIRST REPORTED VISIT TO THE MOUNTAINS OF FRESNO COUNTY

John C. Fremont left Sutter's *New Helvetia* of December 14, 1845 with 16 men headed south keeping to the lower foothills along the edge of the San Joaquin Valley. They reached the San Joaquin River on the 21st after some skirmishes with Indians. Fremont's report continued: December 22d. Temperature at sunrise was 39°. During the night there had been heavy rain, with high wind, and there was a thick fog this morning, but it began to go off at 8 o'clock when the sun broke through. We crossed the plain still in a southeasterly direction, reaching in about twenty miles the *Tulare Lake* river. This is the Lake Fork; one of the largest and handsomest streams in the valley, being about one hundred yards broad and having perhaps a larger body of fertile lands than any one of the others. It is called by the Mexicans the *Rio de los Reyes*. The broad alluvial bottoms were well wooded with several species of oaks. . . .

According to the appointment made when I left my party under Talbot, it was a valley upon the Lake Fork to which the guide Walker was to conduct him. Here I expected to find him. The position (camp) was good in the open ground among the oaks, there being no brush for cover to the Indians, and grass and water were abundant [probably just above Centerville]. Accordingly we remained here a day and on the 24th entered the mountain, keeping as nearly as possible the valley ground of the river.

While in the oak belt the travelling was easy and pleasant, but necessarily slow in the search for our people . . . Several days were spent here. At the elevation of 3500 feet the ridges were covered with oaks and pines intermixed, and the bottom lands with oaks, cottonwoods, and sycamores. . . . I began to be surprised at not finding my party, but continued on, thinking that perhaps in some spread of the river branches I was to find a beautiful mountain valley. Small varieties of evergreen oaks were found at the observed height of 9840 feet above the sea, at which elevation *Pinus Lambertiani* [*sic*] (sugar pine) and other varieties of pine, fir, and cypress (juniper) were large and lofty trees.

Indians were still around the camp at night. . . . I usually made the day's journey short, I found the mountains extremely rocky in the upper parts, the streams breaking through canyons, but wooded up to the granite ridges which compose its rocky eminences. We forced our way up among the head springs of the river and finally stood upon the flat ridge of naked granite which made the division of the waters and was 11,000 feet above the sea. . . . Lying immediately below, perhaps 1000 feet, at the foot of a precipitous descent was a small lake, which I judged to be one of the sources of the main San Joaquin. As I said, this bed of summit granite was naked. Here and there a pine or two, stunted and twisted, and worried out of shape by the winds, and clamping itself to the rock. But immediately below we encamped in the sheltering pine woods which now were needed, for towards evening the weather threatened a change.

The next day, December 31st, I made a short camp, the cattle being tender-footed and scarcely able to travel . . . The old year went out and the new year came in, rough as the country. Towards nightfall the snow began to come down thickly, and by morning all lay under a heavy fall. This was the end of the few remaining cattle. It was impossible to drive them over the treacherous ground . . . Left to themselves cattle could easily work their way to the lower grounds of the mountain if not killed by Indians. We had great trouble getting out from the snow region . . . There were three ridges to surmount, but we succeeded in crossing them, and by sunset when the storm ceased we made a safe camp between 9000 and 10,000 feet above the sea. The temperature at sunset was between eight and ten degrees.

(They continued into the valley without finding the other part of their party, but they were united when they both met at Sacramento.)

SOURCE: Excerpted from *The Expedition of John Charles Fremont*, v. 2. *The Bear Flag Revolt and the Court Martial*, edited by Donald Jackson and Mary Lee Spence.

ty's eastern mountains. Joseph Walker, now an experienced California trail guide, was with the party as a trusted lieutenant.

Entering California from the east, Fremont decided to travel over the northern mountains while a detachment under Theodore Talbot came in through the southern desert. They agreed to meet in a secluded valley near a river Fremont called "Lake Fork"—his name for the Kings. Talbot mistakenly believed "Lake Fork" was the Kern River and waited there more than a month for Fremont's contingent.

Fremont rested a day on the plains after reaching the Kings River and then turned into the foothills, looking for the meeting place Talbot had described as a "higher secluded valley." This trip is described in the accompanying excerpts from Fremont's later report (see 3:2).

The first settlers in Fresno County came here under Mexican land grant regulations, extended to include California in 1828. Such regulations did not automatically grant title to an applicant. He was required to meet certain residency and improvement requirements for gaining ownership (see 3:3).

Records of the grants are incomplete and confusing. Testimony in support of the claims was self-serving at best, and outright perjury at worst. Although the Fresno County land grants were allegedly made in 1841, 1843 and 1846, evidence fails to confirm any permanent residence established until 1849 or early 1850.

After California became a state in 1850, a California Land Commission was established to determine grant validity and performance of the grantees. In the Treaty of Guadalupe Hidalgo, signed at the end of the Mexican War, the United States had agreed to respect the grants so long as they complied with Mexican colonization laws. While the commission was formed to uphold that provision, its members were accused of wrongdoing and reports of the hectic proceedings have often been at variance. Its decisions could be appealed to the courts and frequently were.

The earliest Fresno County grant was issued September 7, 1841, to Francisco Soberanes. Only a few acres of the grant—which totaled 48,823—were in Fresno County, in the northwestern area, where its boundary with Merced County crosses the San Joaquin River. Historically it has been considered a Merced County grant. It was named *Sanjon de Santa Rita* for the Santa Rita Creek that ran through its borders. The name was later transferred to the headquarters ranch of the Miller and Lux cattle empire (see Chapter 6). The Santa Rita Ranch is still operated by Miller's descendants in the same location.

Indian harassment kept Soberanes from settling on the land for several years. The Indians' harsh treatment at the hands of white men had made them hostile toward any white man who ventured near them. Soberanes later was able to comply with the Mexican residency requirement, and on May 30, 1865, his title was confirmed by the United States.

Considerable confusion has existed through the years about the next grant because two adjacent grants were called by the same name, *Laguna de Tache*. Indefinite boundaries, misrepresentations and lack of adequate records also have clouded the grants' backgrounds.

Don José Y. Limantour claimed to have received the first of the two grants in 1843 from Governor Manuel Micheltorena. It consisted of eleven square leagues of land, lying mostly south of the Kings River in what is now Kings County. Limantour also filed claims for several other grants, including some to nearly three-quarters of the city of San Francisco.

The U.S. District Court denied Limantour's claims in a decision which reveals some of the tactics Mexican citizens used to regain lands the Mexican-American War took from their country. In a paper delivered

Reference 3:3

# RANCHO LAGUNA DE TACHE GRANT
## GEORGE COSGRAVE

(Excerpts from a paper read before the Fresno County Historical Society and published in the Fresno Morning Republican May 2, 1920.)

As is well known the title to the Laguna de Tache is based upon a Mexican grant and its history is quite characteristic of the early days of California. It was the custom both under the Spanish governors of California until the independence of Mexico was declared and then under the Mexican governors to grant individuals large tracts of land in consideration of money loaned, services rendered, promised settlements or other reasons. The entire country outside the mission settlement and pueblos being then almost entirely uninhabited, the Mexican government desired to encourage settlers. The governors were therefore quite generous with their grants and not always accurate in their descriptions. Immense tracts of this lordly domain then untouched and scarcely visited by civilized man, were granted by a single instrument and oftentimes with little formality attending its execution.

After the acquisition of California by the Americans in 1848, it was the policy of the United States, sanctioned both by the law of nations and the treaty closing the Mexican War, to recognize private rights in the ceded territory, including of course, the grants. This was done whether the grant had been entirely perfected or not, so long as a vested interest was created. After the first excitement attending the discovery of gold had subsided, the wiser heads recognized that California was destined on account of its soil and climate to become a land of promise. The value of the land was recognized and controversies between settlers on the public domain and claimants under the Mexican grants, especially where the possession under the grant had not been perfected, became numerous and serious. To such an extent was this the case in 1851 when Congress established a commission with authority to determine the validity of all grants in California. Beginning with the year 1853, numerous applications were filed before this commission. (Decisions by the commission could be appealed to the courts.)

before the Fresno County Historical Society in 1920, George Cosgrave condensed the decision of Judge Ogden Hoffman as follows:

> In this opinion the machinations of the enterprising Don José are described at length. It was shown that the peculiar kind of official paper upon which his grant was written was not in existence at the time it bore date, nor until two years thereafter. That the seal affixed to the instrument was not genuine. Also it was quite clearly demonstrated that in the year 1852, Don José Y. Limantour, ex-Governor Micheltorena, who was supposed to have executed the grant, and an expert penman were closeted in closed conference in the City of Mexico for some considerable time, having various quantities of official paper, maps, etc., in their possession, all of which convinced Judge Hoffman that the grant was not made until 1852 . . . Limantour was later indicted for the fraud, but at the time set for his trial he failed to appear.

Limantour filed his application for confirmation of the Laguna de Tache y Limantour grant, as it is called in most references, with the California Land Commission on February 3, 1853. He later abandoned this effort, and the fraudulence of the grant was never determined.

Just fifteen days later, on February 18, Manuel Castro filed an application for confirmation of the second Laguna de Tache grant. To distinguish it from Limantour's, it is usually called Rancho Laguna de Tache.

Castro was active in politics during the last years of Mexican rule in California and was prefect of Northern California in 1846. His claim was based on two grants. The first was from Micheltorena, dated December 12, 1843, and the second from Governor Pio Pico on January 10, 1846. Both were for eleven square leagues of land extending about twenty-five miles west from Kingsburg's site, and from two to six miles north of the Kings River. As originally described it was "Bounded on the South by the Laguna de Tache y Limantour, on the North by the Rancheria de los Notantos [Yokuts Indian Village], on the West by the Sanjon de San Jose and on the East by the Plains."

Castro claimed he sent Ysidro Villa with servants (*vaqueros*) to settle the land in February 1845. He said they built houses and corrals and planted a garden. Many writers have reported this story as established fact, but Villa's own testimony to the land commission proved this incorrect. On July 25, 1854, he told the commission that he went to the grant in 1845 and built a small house where he spent fifteen to twenty days with some men. They started to dig a canal but never finished it because friendly Indians warned them of an imminent attack some of their tribesmen were planning. No cattle accompanied the men, but Castro intended to send 600 head at the time.

Ramon Mesa of Santa Clara County testified differently some two weeks later. He claimed to have been at the Rancho in 1845 "and met Ysidro Villa who was tending cattle there . . . There was a small wooden house there in which lived said Villa" and manservants of Castro. "There was a canal, which they were finishing when I was there." He also mentioned that melons and vegetables were being planted in a small enclosed field, and there was a considerable number of cattle and horses on the property.

The land commission was not impressed favorably by the witnesses and held the testimony "insufficient to show any actual performance" to comply with Mexican colonization law. Accordingly, it rejected the claim on October 17, 1854. Castro followed with an appeal to

Reference 3:4

# ABSTRACT OF THE LAGUNA DE TACHE RANCHO

**Preface**

In the search of the records of Fresno County, for the purpose of compiling this Abstract of Title, the Searcher has encountered matters that make it necessary for this preliminary explanation.

One of the matters referred to is that fact, that it is evident that the State Authorities claimed title to the premises covered by this Abstract of Title, or, at least, to some parts of the same, as Swamp and Overflowed Land; that some parts of said premises were actually sold by the State as such Swamp and Overflowed Land and in some cases Patents were issued for the same.

The other matter referred to is the conflict between the owners of the Rancho Laguna de Tache, on the one side of the issue, and the owners of lands situate on the South bank of Kings River, on the other side of the issue, as to the true course of said Kings River.

The U.S. Patent for the Rancho Laguna de Tache described the Southeasterly boundary line of said Rancho by courses and distances (supposedly the North bank of Kings River, or Rio Reyes). But, in two separate Actions in the Superior Court of Fresno County to determine said boundary line and involving separate pieces of property the judgments and decrees therein do not agree, and in neither action does the boundary line determined by the Court agree with the boundary line as described in the U.S. Patent.

In one of said Actions the judgment is adverse to and in the other Action in favor of the contention of the owners of the Rancho Laguna de Tache.

Because of the matters above referred to it has become necessary to include in this Abstract of Title a large number of matters and instruments that could have been otherwise eliminated.

And in order to facilitate the examination of this Abstract of Title, we have compiled the same in three subdivisions and designated the same as "Subdivision 1," "Subdivision 2" and "Subdivision 3."

Subdivision 1 consisting of matters and instruments relating to the main title to the Rancho Laguna de Tache.

Subdivision 2 consisting of matters and instruments dealing with portions of said Rancho Laguna de Tache as Swamp and Overflowed Land hereinabove referred to, and also such instruments erroneously describing portions of said Rancho de Tache.

Subdivision 3 consisting of matters and instruments dealing with land on the South bank of Kings River and conflicting with the Southeasterly boundary of the Rancho de Tache.

THE SEARCHER
Fresno County Abstract Company

the Southern District Federal Court of California. To support his claim, former governor Juan B. Alvarado testified that Indian difficulties made it impossible or impractical to live on the rancho. Vincent Perfecto Gomes, a former clerk of Micheltorena and witness of several land litigations, confirmed this, and the court reversed the land commission on February 10, 1858.

The land was surveyed and legal boundaries determined according to law. On March 6, 1866, patent was issued to Castro for the 48,801-acre grant. Shortly thereafter, however, he was on the verge of losing his newly-won grant through foreclosures because of debts he was unable to pay. In 1863, needing money, Castro had borrowed $2,000 from Andrew Himmelman with a 5 percent compounded monthly interest, considerably more than the 3 percent compounded quarterly interest rates common at the time. The land grant, although not yet patented at the time of the loan, was given as security. Within six months the mortgage was sold to Dr. Edward Kane.

By 1867 the loan principal and interest amounted to $17,124. Castro could not meet the obligation and on June 18 the 12th District Court issued a decree of foreclosure for that amount plus $3,451.45 for attorney's fees, costs and taxes. Negotiations apparently took place at that time as it was eighteen months before the property was put up for sale. Nine square leagues (43,920 acres) were involved as Castro had deeded two leagues to his attorneys in 1852.

Notices were posted by Frenso County Sheriff J. N. Walker announcing that the sale would be held in front of the Millerton Courthouse on December 24, 1868. The high bidder was Jeremiah Clarke "for the sum of $20,000 cash, in gold coin," or somewhat less than fifty cents an acre. This is about ten times the amount Castro realized per acre from the loan he had made. What a pittance for the struggle to get the grant, the stories told to obtain its patent, and all the time and money spent in court trying to keep it. Yet it was not an unusual series of events, and some historians have described it as a history in microcosm of the Spanish and Mexican land grantees in California.

Rancho Laguna de Tache retained an important role in Fresno County's history for many years. For the most part it was farmed as a single unit by a series of owners and lessees. During the time Castro's rights were in dispute, many moved onto the grant, knowingly or unknowingly, as squatters. Some obtained title to land within the rancho under state law.

The complexity of these problems is best evidenced by a book, *Abstract to the Title of Rancho Laguna de Tache*. Published by the Fresno Abstract Company for Laguna Lands Limited, *circa* 1902, the book consists of 240 legal-sized pages, 250 documents and numerous plates. Its preface gives a useful summary of the controversies surrounding the grant (see 3:4 and 3:5).

Duplicate names and grants have caused historians considerable trouble through the years.

First there was the matter of the two grants bearing the same name—Laguna de Tache.

Then two different grants were issued to men who were not closely related but who had the same last name of Castro—Manuel and José.

Last, two almost identical grants were issued to José Castro on the same day—April 4, 1846. The first paragraph of each read:

> Pio Pico, Constitutional Governor of the Department of the Californias: Whereas the Lieutenant Colonel of Cavalry, Don José Castro, a Mexican Citizen, has petitioned for his personal benefit and that of his family a tract of land for the purpose of stock raising, situated on the San Joaquin River, containing eleven Square leagues, commencing at the skirt of the Sierra Nevada and running down the river . . .

The continuing texts were identical but the identifying titles on the grants were different. One read:

> José Castro, Six Square Leagues. [Note that the grant says eleven.]

The other read:

> B. I. Lippmont 11 Leagues in San Joaquin County. [The county was non-existent at that time, the location didn't match the text and the name was probably a misspelling of Benjamin L. Lippincott, a well known land speculator.]

Reference 3:5
## SQUATTERS
### GEORGE COSGRAVE

The patent [to Laguna de Tache grant] was issued in 1866, and at the time the survey was made quite a number of squatters had located on the land. They were all engaged in stock raising. Taking them in the order of their location from east to west, the first is William T. Cole, who gave his name to Cole Slough, a respected citizen of Fresno County for many years and the father of a numerous family; Daniel Murphy, who gave his name to Murphy Slough; Rube Reynolds; Lewis Waggoner; Ben Atwell; Lyall; Elisha Harlan; Elijah Wimmer; Enoch Lee and Daniel Lee, brothers who were located just west of Kingston; George Woods, whose location was where the home ranch of the grant was afterwards located; Oliver Childers; Silas Draper, and James X. Y. Sutherland (the Sutherland family were numerous, including several named James and these initials were adopted to prevent confusion). Steve Garcia; James (Four Trees) Moore (at his camp four trees were growing); Oliver H. Bliss. [No further mention was made of the squatters but it is to be assumed that they lost use of the land in the grant or bought it from Clark.]

SOURCE: May 2, 1920, paper. (See 3:3.)

Later events indicate that these errors did not cause Castro any problem, but the agent who filed on the "Lippmont" grant in San Joaquin County never prosecuted his claim—probably realizing it would be impossible to explain the discrepancies.

Lippincott eventually purchased one league of the Castro grant for $1,000. On May 28, 1853, he filed a deed in Mariposa from James H. Gleason of Monterey, who said he had purchased the land from Castro on September 4, 1849.

José Castro may very well have chosen his land grant site in 1844, when he was sent to the valley to stop Indians from stealing horses. In May 1844 it was suggested that the only way to cope with these disruptive activities would be to establish a permanent outpost in the *tulares*, as Fresno County's flatlands were then called. Within a few weeks Governor Micheltorena sent a detachment of twenty-five men under Castro's command. Since priests were no longer accompanying these expeditions, and it was they who customarily kept diaries of such journeys, no written record was kept of the trip.

Reports have persisted that Castro and a party of soldiers camped near Fort Miller's eventual site. Historians have generally concluded that this occurred after he received his grant, but it seems more likely the encampment took place in 1844. Castro still had troops under his command, and the San Joaquin River would have been a logical central location for their bivouac.

In November Micheltorena dispatched a courier to recall Castro. He needed him for assistance in Monterey, the state capital, where the political situation had become more unsettled. The governor's days were numbered, however, and on February 15, 1845, Pio Pico succeeded him. Later Pico named Castro commanding general of the Northern California Mexican forces. Pico served only seventeen months, but issued more land grants than the four previous governors combined during that short, unsettled period. One or two of these went to José Castro on April 4, 1846.

Castro's grant was for eleven square leagues or 48,801 acres. When surveyed in 1850 it was considered to be one league (about two and a half miles) wide and eleven leagues long. The survey made the San Joaquin River the grant's center, extending approximately an equal distance on either side, from just above Millerton's site to near Herndon's.

Following Mexico's signing of the treaty in 1848 ending the Mexican-American War, Castro lived in Monterey and San Juan Bautista. Although his grant was not confirmed under Mexican or United States laws, he soon began selling portions of the loosely-defined Rancho del Rio San Joaquin.

On June 8, 1849, Castro and his wife, Modesta, deeded six square leagues to Benjamin McKenzie and Robert C. Neligh for $1,000. On the same day McKen-

zie filed Castro's land grant claim with American authorities. This was more than three years after the grant was dated. The delay proved expensive to all parties involved.

McKenzie and Neligh were apparently performing services for Castro, partially accounting for the small amounts they paid for more than 26,000 acres. It must be remembered, however, that little was known of the area. Indians were still preventing settlement and gold had not yet been discovered on the San Joaquin—so far as is known.

McKenzie died before further action on the grant was taken. His widow, June, sold half of the six leagues to Neligh for $2,000 on April 8, 1852. June McKenzie was identified as a New York resident, and Neligh was living in Santa Clara County.

After selling seven of his eleven leagues in 1849, Castro became Fresno County's first subdivider. He had William Sharpe of Mariposa survey the remaining four leagues in 1850 and divide them into twenty-eight equal parcels of nearly 640 acres each. A copy of the survey has never been found, so the exact dimensions remain unknown.

To add to the stature of his project, Castro created the City of Washington. The first recorded deed in this subdivision was dated April 22, 1850, the approximate time J. M. Cassity and Major Lane established their trading station at or near the same location. This outpost became known as Fort Washington, a name still used for a golf course in the area.

Early settler Lorenzo D. Vinsonhaler (see Chapter 2) played a leading role in this project, as records reveal he was the agent for several sales of the Rancho del Rio San Joaquin tract.

Castro's first sale was to José Francisco León of San Francisco, who paid $5,000 for seven of the twenty-eight parcels, some 4,480 acres (about $1.10 per acre). Although signed on April 22, 1850, the deed was not recorded until July 9, 1855, at the request of Thomas J. Alsbury. Six weeks after the León sale Castro sold sixteen of the twenty-eight units to Alsbury "of the City of Washington" and Henri Cambuston of Soledad, Monterey County. For more than twice as much land they too paid $5,000 in a deed dated June 10, 1850, by Castro but not signed by his wife, Modesta, until January 11, 1853. On April 2, 1853, Alsbury bought two more parcels, just a month after Castro applied to the California Land Commission for a patent on his grant. He paid $1,000 for the two, or about seventy-five cents an acre.

Alsbury's name has not been prominent in previous Fresno County histories, but he played an important role on the San Joaquin from 1850 to at least 1855, when he filed the deed from Castro to León. Mariposa County records for 1850 show him as the licensed operator of the Fort Washington ferry.

On March 1, 1853, several men who had purchased

land in the tract petitioned the California Land Commission to confirm Castro's grant. James Wilson and Elisha O. Crosby, the latter representing Neligh, asserted that "said land was occupied and improved by the original grantee soon after the date of said grant." At later hearings it was recognized that the four leagues had been sold in small units with "José Castro... owning but a small interest in said claims." Only three of the twenty-eight parcels were not accounted for.

Vinsonhaler was the principal witness for Neligh. He testified on March 13, 1853, that Castro took possession of the land in the latter part of August or September 1849. He said a corral was built and cattle were there in the early part of 1850. "It would have been unsafe in consequence of the hostility of the wild Indians to have attempted to occupy it earlier," he said.

Later an attempt was made to show that Micheltorena, while governor, had promised in writing to issue Castro an eleven-league grant so long as he (Castro) determined what he wanted on the 1844 expedition. Castro was unable to locate the letter. Former Governor Juan B. Alvarado testified that, when Castro was traveling to the valley at that time, he stopped at Alvarado's ranch near Martinez. He showed Alvarado his military instructions, which included the letter promising the land grant. Alvarado further testified that he subsequently heard of Castro locating on the San Joaquin River and building a house and corral, ceasing residence only when recalled by Micheltorena.

Antonio Maria Pico of San Jose testified, "I was there in 1844 and José Castro, the General, told me the boundaries... Castro then had on it a house which he occupied himself with his servants. He had cattle and horses. I knew of 400 head of cattle he had there which were sent from Mission San Jose. He also had corrals on the land." The house was said to have been on the river banks, slightly below the mountains. It would appear that Vinsonhaler's testimony and other evidence are at odds with Castro's alleged 1844 development of the grant.

While these conflicting testimonies were being heard, Vinsonhaler was stripped of his capacity as a sales agent. On May 10, 1855, his power of attorney for such transactions was revoked by James L. Stewart and Elisha O. Crosby, the former being another landholder in the Castro grant. The revocation noted that these men, together with Neligh, had in "1853 or 1854" given Vinsonhaler permission "to let or lease any and all of the Rancho of the River San Joaquin."

The land commission finally decided to confirm Castro's grant on November 21, 1855, and a federal district court concurred on August 10, 1857, after an appeal. The case then went to the United States Supreme Court on November 30, a fact not generally known by historians. There the claim was rejected. The court's decision, handed down in the December 1860 term (see 3:6).

The court cited as other shortcomings "no petition from Castro; no *informe*, or decree, as required by the laws of Mexico... no trace of anything in relation to it is to be found in the archives of the Mexican authorities..." Castro was in Mexico when his claim went before the land commission and the federal district court, and not available to testify as to the validity of the evidence. By the time the Supreme Court's decision was announced he was dead, "killed in a drunken brawl—or as some say, assassinated—by one Manuel Marquez," in Santa Clara, according to Hubert Howe Bancroft.

Early writers and county histories are surprisingly silent about the José Castro grant. Millerton, then the Fresno County seat, was in fact Castro's property until the 1860 Supreme Court decision. Even the usually alert Lilbourne A. Winchell failed to mention this fact in his Fresno County history. He mistakenly believed there were only two land grants in the county—the Rancho Laguna de Tache and Sanjon de Santa Rita. Perhaps they were the only ones confirmed by the land commission, but Castro, the City of Washington and its investors deserve some recognition.

The preceding is a comprehensive survey of the

Reference 3:6

## THE END OF GENERAL CASTRO'S LAND GRANT

The United States, Appellants,
v.
Jose Castro and Others

It appears that the paper purporting to be the original grant was deposited in the Government archives of the United States, on the 8th of June, 1849, more than three years after its date, and two years after the cession of the territory. It was deposited not by Castro, but by Bernard McKenzie, whose representatives claim a portion of the land under a conveyance from Castro....

But no testimony was offered to show when or where this paper was executed, nor ...who had custody of it, nor any reason

for keeping it out of the public office for so long a time....

Here the difficulty is, whether there is legal evidence to prove that this alleged grant was ever made by the Mexican authorities. And the fact that it was so made must be established by competent evidence, before any of the questions which arose and were decided in Fremont's case can arise in this.

The authenticity of the grant must first be established before any question can arise upon the conditions annexed by law to such grants, or concerning the certainty or uncertainty of the boundaries specified in it. And

in the case before us, the grant itself not being maintained by competent testimony, we need not inquire whether the conditions were complied with, or the description of place and boundaries sufficiently certain.

And for the reasons above stated the judgment of the circuit Court must be reversed, and the same remanded in the District Court, with directions to dismiss the petition.

United States Supreme Court,
December term, 1860.

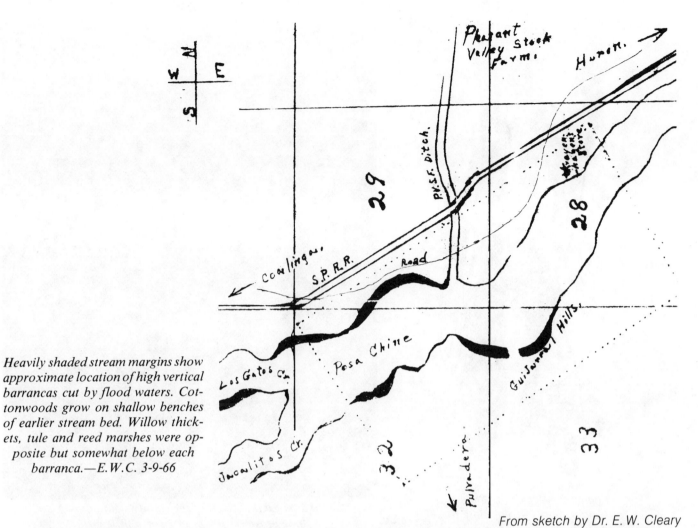

*Heavily shaded stream margins show approximate location of high vertical barrancas cut by flood waters. Cottonwoods grow on shallow benches of earlier stream bed. Willow thickets, tule and reed marshes were opposite but somewhat below each barranca.—E.W.C. 3-9-66*

*From sketch by Dr. E. W. Cleary*

*Brush house as used by Hispanics and vaqueros on the plains.*

Vaqueros—Mexican, Chilean or Californianos—were more fond of their horse and lasso than of gold digging.

Las Juntas. All that is left of the county's oldest town is a lone grave on the prairie for a little girl.

Native Californians racing—a way of life in the saddle as described by J. M. Hutchings: "... as horses are their (Californians') particular pride (even while they excessively abuse them when in passion), skill in riding is the most esteemed of all accomplishments. A native Californian will, therefore, invest his last real (and go hungry) rather than forego the indulgence of expensive ornaments for his saddle, bridle and spurs. And as horse-racing strikingly provides him with the opportunity for exhibiting these to the best advantage before the fair sex, and his envious companions, he indulges it to infatuation." (Drawing attributed to Charles Nahl)

Mexican land grant period in Fresno County's history, yet it has been necessary to admit that unanswered questions linger about the subject. There are even more questions regarding the first communities established within the county's eventual borders.

A much neglected chapter of early Fresno County history is the role of the early Hispanics—Spanish, Mexican and Chilean—who settled in the western portion of Fresno County in the first fifty to seventy years of the nineteenth century. For brevity we will refer to them as Hispanics, and the English-speaking people who arrived later as Anglos, although we must admit that the latter included many Germans, Italians, French and other Europeans (see 3:7).

The Hispanic communities were established along El Camino Viejo a Los Angeles (The Old Road to Los Angeles) (see 3:8) which had two branches running through the western part of the county. Settlements included Posa Chiné, La Libertad, Las Juntas, and Rancho de Los Californianos. The route of El Camino Viejo was best traced by historian Frank F. Latta. It began at San Pedro and ran to the San Fernando mission, over the Tejon Pass and keeping west of Tulare Lake continued to northern settlements. Just south of Fresno County's present boundary, it divided and the main route continued northwest to Posa Chiné (see 3:9), six miles east of Coalinga, and along the edge of the foothills to Arroyo de Panoche Grande (Big Sugar Loaf Canyon) near Mendota. The eastern route went through the sinks of Huron to La Libertad (Liberty), near Riverdale. From there it turned northwest along a high ridge of ground (that was later used by the railroad and for a major diagonal road in the county) to El

Rancho de Los Californianos (California Ranch) and Las Juntas (the meeting place or junction). It then turned west and joined the other road.

The Old Road was used extensively by Hispanics for many purposes, including the driving of cattle from one area to another. As the population of wild horses increased they attracted vaqueros who caught the horses, kept them in brush corrals (which still dotted the area when early Anglos arrived) and, after accumulating sufficient numbers, drove them to the Los Angeles area or to Sonora, Mexico, to sell at a substantial profit.

The Old Road was considerably more than a trail probably as early as 1800. A story by Frank Latta about a runaway Chilean bride and groom tells how in 1804 they traveled the road in an ox cart from San Pedro to Fort Ross north of San Francisco.

There is no evidence to determine which community was established first, so it is best to consider the Hispanic settlements on a geographic basis starting in the south with Posa Chiné.

Posa Chiné has had so many spellings and pronunciations that it seems worthwhile to discuss them. "Poso" means a large well or pond of water, while "Posa" indicates a small waterhole. The words have been used interchangeably in California place names, probably justifiably so as conditions changed. "Chine" has been spelled "Chana," "Chene," "Chena," "China," "Chine," and in 1815, possibly "Chenem." This last was the name of a campsite of Father Juan Ortega in the general area, but his diary is silent as to its exact location.

The best derivation of the name would seem to be

Reference 3:7
## EARLIEST SETTLERS
### L. A. WINCHELL

No settlers appeared in the early Fifties on the San Joaquin west of Cassady and Lane's ferry and trader's camp, except the groups of native Californians who gradually collected at Las Juntas and the California Ranch (properly, El Rancho de los Californianos), where they were chiefly engaged in capturing wild horses (mustenos). In explanation of the term "Californian," it is desirable to know that when the Americans came to this territory, they found a white people, mostly natives, who spoke the Spanish language. These were soon popularly alluded to as "Californians." The term "Mexicans" was applied to those who were known to have come from Mexico to dig for gold, though "Sonoranian" equally distinguished them. It is regrettable that in modern times all speaking the Spanish tongue, without recognition of nativity or caste, are inexcusably, and without discrimination, called Mexicans.

SOURCE: *History of Fresno County 1933* by L. A. Winchell.

Reference 3:8
## EL CAMINO VIEJO A LOS ANGELES

Statement of José Antonio Aguila to Frank F. Latta in the 1920s about El Camino Viejo.

"I was born on the 13th day of June, 1848, at Aromas Station, now in San Benito County. Since 1865 I have lived along the west side of the San Joaquin Valley. My father, Vicente Aguila, was born in 1810 in old Monterey. My mother, Pavala Cantua, was also born in Monterey. Both of my parents were born at the old Presidio of Monterey of parents who were members of the cavalry which established the presidio at that place.

"My mother's father, Guadalupe Cantua, was at the head of the party which first explored the Cantua Creek. It was named after him. This is where Joaquin Murrieta, who was well known to my parents, was wrongly said to have been killed. My father helped take the Indians from many of the west side creeks, including the Orestimba, to the missions of San Juan Bautista, Monterey and San Jose.

"My people have been well acquainted with the old west side road for more than 100 years. I have heard them talk about it since I was a little boy. It is the first road used in the San Joaquin Valley. In 1865 and '66 I knew old Spanish vaqueros working on the Santa Rita ranch east of Los Banos who had used the road when they were children."

SOURCE: Frank F. Latta, *El Camino Viejo a Los Angeles*. Kern County Historical Society, 1933.

the explanation that historian Frank Latta gave in an article in the *Tulare Daily Times* of March 29, 1932, following a conversation with a T. S. Larios, whose grandfather had helped build the San Juan Mission. The Larios family was well known in San Juan for passing down historical information from father to son. The grandfather told the family that he had visited the Poso many times in order to capture Indians to bring to the mission. The name of the Indian tribe was Chanet (Shaw-ney), so the name meant Watering Hole of the Chanet Indians. He also said that few if any of the Indians returned from the mission which would explain why the tribal name does not appear in early Anglo records. Now, however, most California Indian specialists recognize the Chana Indians as part of the Tache Indians whose central home was around Tulare Lake. The Poso was used by the Taches as a trading place with coastal Indians. (They feared the coastal tribes would attack or rob them if they saw their homes on the lake.)

At the confluence of three creeks—the Jacalitos, Los Gatos and Warthan (also known as Alcalde)—Posa Chiné was lush with tules, willows, wild flowers and many forms of wildlife. The swamp land was surrounded by many acres of fertile bottom land which were cultivated by early Hispanic farmers. Although the floods of 1862–63 destroyed much of the lushness of the area, it did not immediately become as barren as it is today (see 3:10).

When Hugo Kreyenhagen arrived in Pleasant Valley in 1874, he reported that there still were "several"

Spanish-speaking families living there and many more "in the mountains," probably along the three creeks.

It has been said that the Higueras and their compatriots chased away the Indians and took the land, and that the Anglos chased away the Hispanics. This is probably an oversimplification, but it is obvious that they did leave. They did not get land grants from the Spanish or Mexican governments, and later, possibly because of the language barriers, neither did they file for homesteads under United States law. Without title to the land and faced with general animosity from the Anglos, they left for other towns or their homeland.

There is not a well defined identification of where La Libertad actually was, but its location has been defined as being five miles east and a half mile south of the present town of Burrell. As late as 1870 the place was reported to have been occupied by a few Mexicans, with Amigo Garcia running a cantina. Of its early history there is little known. It probably was associated with the 25 Ranch, which was between the above site and the small community of Hub on the Kings River, southeast of present-day Riverdale. The 25 Ranch has been described as being little more than an Indian rancheria of about twenty brush and mud plaster houses with tule-thatched roofs.

Reports were made of early efforts to build a Mission del Rio de los Santos Rey on the Kings River, somewhat farther southeast of the site of La Libertad, near present-day Laton. Early Anglo settlers report that as late as 1852 there was a large pile of adobe bricks near the river banks. Later settlers report that in

Reference 3:9

## EARLY POSA CHANET (SHAW-NAY)

It appears that the first Spanish settlements in the San Joaquin Valley remained a desirable village site of which the Indians had been dispossessed. This was probably true of San Emigidio [an early mission site south of Fresno County]. All Spanish residents say that it was the case at Las Juntas and Rancho de los Californianos.

Concerning Posa Chanet, another very old settlement, we have a definite story of such occupation. About the year 1800, the Spanish calvary and priests came to Posa Chanet to take the Indians to the mission at San Juan Bautista. These Indians were known to the Spanish as the Chanet Indians. Their name was given to the site at which there was a large swamp and a poso—or deep pool of water. As such the place has since been known.

Posa Chiné [current usage] is mentioned many times in the earliest San Joaquin Valley press accounts. It was for many years the only settlement in that country which now surrounds Coalinga. At one time there were perhaps a dozen Spanish and Mexican families living at the old Posa. They ranged cattle and horses and a few goats. The swamp

area was cultivated and planted to trees, vines and garden truck.

At that time, Posa Chiné was known to American settlers as Curley's Springs. In the early 50s an old Irishman lived there. He had curly hair which appears to have been oddity enough to suggest the name of Curley's Wells or Curley's Springs. But the name Posa Chiné was well known long before and long after the time of the Irishman.

In 1854 Narcisso Higuera and family settled in Posa Chiné. They came from San Jose. There were three boys in the family: Narcisso, Jesus and Leandro. The Higueras were the first stock men of consequence to occupy the place. Their horses and cattle used to roam as far east as Tulare Lake. They used an old adobe dugout with tully roof for a vaquero headquarters while tending their stock at the lake. The old adobe was about three miles northeast of the present Kettleman City. The flood season of 1862 made a great change in Posa Chiné: the waters cut a deep channel through the swamp area and obliterated the old Posa. The water from the swamp drained into the sand of the new channel and all of the trees

and vines died. Drinking water had to be developed by digging. It is difficult for the visitor today to visualize the desert-like Posa Chiné as a swamp with a great pool of water and surrounded by trees and vines, but such we are assured was the case.

### Tollhouse — Posa Chiné

Maps in the 1860s and 1870s of property in the Big Dry Creek area showed the Tollhouse Road as the Tollhouse-Posa Chiné Road. Surprising but understandable. Reference to a map shows that the old stage road that struck out across the plains to the original Fresno City might well have turned south to where Huron was later established. From there the road went west to Posa Chiné and then to other areas where no settlements existed in those days. There was no better known point within fifty miles and at that time the name probably referred to a far greater area than the Posa actually covered. It also was the westernmost point in the county.

SOURCE: "San Joaquin Primeval," *Tulare Daily Times*, February 5, 1932, p. 4.

the sixties there was still a rounded, bare mound of earth at that site. One pioneer dug into the mound and was surprised to find evidence under the surface that it had consisted of rectangular sun-dried mud bricks. The exact date of this effort is not known, but it was probably prior to 1830, although one report does set it

at a later date (see 3:11). Much of this territory was included in the Laguna de Tache Land Grant of 1845. All three locations are within a radius of ten miles so the name La Libertad may have been attached to all at varying times.

The name of Liberty was adopted by early settlers

Reference 3:10

# POSA CHINE IN THE 1890s
## DR. E. W. CLEARY

[These observations were made about 30 years after the disastrous floods of 1862–63 destroyed much of the value and beauty of Posa Chiné.]

Even before I began my adventures of the Posa Chiné, at the age of ten, my grandfather, Robert Bruce Cooper, had inducted me in the ways and lore of a woodsman. On walks through the woods and fields and along the streams of Calaveras, he had taught me how to move noiselessly, when to remain motionless for an interval in places favorable for concealment, to use both eyes and ears well and, as he expressed it, "To read the country like a book."

My main concern [job] was to keep the stock within reasonable bounds and not to let them stray beyond the Posa Chiné. As there were two miles of sagebrush plain between our place and the Posa, and, because there were only a few places where they could pass the barriers of the high barrancas, the stock needed only occasional attention. I had many carefree hours to explore the wilderness and to come to intimate terms with many of its teeming population of animals, birds, reptiles and insects.

It would take many words to convey an adequate picture of life in Pleasant Valley in the early days. Especially of life near the great oasis. One would have to comment upon the extraordinary size of such creatures as badgers, bob cats, lizards, snakes, scorpions, tarantulas, and centipedes and many other species before the rising tide of ruthless humanity killed off all of the "old he ones" leaving the young no time to grow to full size even if in the changing environment former size could be attained.

Abundant living water in the deep ravine between the earthen cliffs that Mexicans call "barrancas" was the vital heart of this wilderness. Its power of attraction was a striking example of how necessary water is to all living things. The dense willow thickets and reed marshes bordering the water were sanctuary for an amazing variety of wild life. Water loving birds, ducks, coots, grebes, rail, snipe, curlew, herons and bitterns were often there, but its vulnerability to many varieties of predators, both bird and animal, made it an unfavorable nesting place for waterfowl. At certain seasons great flocks of curlew and golden plover frequented the adjacent plains and huge flocks of Canada geese came to grain fields. In early morning and late afternoon flocks of quail came to

water and often there was a tremendous flight of doves shortly before sunset. I often watched the birds and animals that came to drink while I was concealed nearby.

I practiced imitating bird calls and tried to speak bird language but bird-watching was only a modest part of my adventuring, though it went much beyond the nesting birds in the cottonwoods. One would occasionally hear a loud roaring in the sky and perhaps see a golden eagle diving like bullet upon some hapless rabbit in the sagebrush. Often the ragged blunt tipped pinions of California condors circled in the sky. These huge birds when perched upon a cottonwood sometimes would let me come near enough to see their angry red eyes, their great horny beaks and the intense yellow of their bare necks spotted with black and rising, like a stem, from a huge ruff of black feathers.

Using a cottonwood leaf, I imitated the cry of a rabbit in distress well enough so that predators, desert fox, bobcat or even coyote, sometimes came to investigate. Badgers can make a very nasty snarl and will, if closely pressed, sometimes charge at a man. Slinky little yellow weasels made me laugh when they poked their little black faces out of a burrow and put on their fiercest snarl but if they had been as big as their notorious northern cousin, the wolverine, it would not have been a laughing matter. Nothing can portray complete joyous abandon like a pair of playful skunks. They seem to count upon their peculiar odor or the waving plumes of graceful black and white tails to guarantee them immunity from all aggressors and they are about 100 percent right.

In the desert environment each part of the twenty-four hours tends to call forth particular actors and activities. Mid day is a good time to hide in some selected vantage spot in a willow thicket. Many birds take shelter in the branches and, on the floor beneath, many of the predatory animals seem to favor this time and environment in which to be relaxed and playful. So, if one is fortunate in the choice of a hiding place, one may see the "grown-ups" playing with their offspring. Badgers, no, but coons and bob cats, foxes and coyotes, yes, and how different their behavior when they have, for a short time, cast off the fear of man.

Among the sagebrush, dawn is a time of special interest and activity because many night-loving species have been caught by

daybreak, belated in their return to daytime hiding places. Quite a variety of four-footed predators may be spotted making their stealthy way to chosen spots or areas of daytime security. It is a good time to see snakes, lizards, horned toads and the like. One may even spot a big trapdoor spider outside his gauze-lined pit. Tarantulas, centipedes, scorpions and vinagaroons are likely to be out in the open.

Litters of dainty desert fox pups would gambol like kittens about the mouth of their burrow home while the mother fox looked on them fondly. A swift traveling shadow betokened an owl passing overhead. There was an incessant murmur and medley of sounds mostly minor and muted. At infrequent intervals the general milder motive was punctuated by sound of swoop or pounce, followed by the agonized cry of the victim, reminding that "Nature in the raw is seldom mild." How graceful a coyote would be, pausing with forefoot lifted to listen to the rustle of a kangaroo rat in the dry grass—and, a moment after, what a swift and ruthless hunter!

On a hummock beside the burrow, fledgling ground owls would stand in straight line like a corporal's guard, while the old owl looked on. Like magic a big bob cat would appear in a spot that was vacant a moment before. After a brief survey of the area, the cat would disappear as mysteriously as he came. Bob cats are rarely beautiful and interesting animals.

When winter rains have been sufficient, the short intense spring in the desert is a time of almost heavenly beauty. Hills and plain [not just the Posa] put on a coat of many colors. Many exquisite flowers bloom in a kaleidoscopic mingling of colors over large areas but there are also patches of a single variety massed in a blanket of solid color, blue lupine here, red princess feather (Owls clover) next to it, then perhaps a bed of cream cups or of colinsia, pink predominating. Of course, the California poppy (escholtzia, copa de oro) often takes the first place. Rare patches of thistle sage are discovered and, on miniature sand dune hummocks, evening primrose and sand verbena are most gorgeous in late afternoon.

SOURCE: Excerpts from letters by Dr. E. W. Cleary. Letters in R. C. Baker Memorial Museum, Coalinga.

for the district which in 1880 was defined as six square miles northeast of Riverdale. Included was the Liberty School, and newspapers attributed news items in the 1870s and 1880s to the Liberty District rather than to a town in that area.

Las Juntas and California Ranch were on the San Joaquin River and the latter is reportedly an outgrowth of the former.

There are no exact dates as to the founding of Las Juntas (see 3:12) but it was probably shortly after 1800 when soldiers and padres from Mission San Juan Bautista came to the valley to capture Indians. Some of the soldiers in the party were reportedly impressed by the Indian village and returned, possibly as deserters, after returning to San Juan Bautista. They intermarried with the Indians and the population grew to about two hundred fifty in the 1870s. At that time inhabitants were obliged to leave because the owner, Henry Miller, wished to fence his land in compliance with recently passed legislation. By the early 1890s, most of them had moved to Firebaugh.

The Spanish-speaking people born in California were inclined to distinguish themselves from the Mexican-born immigrants by calling themselves "Californianos." This gave rise to the name of Rancho de los Californianos for the new refuge outpost on the south bank of the San Joaquin River about six miles up from its junction with Fresno Slough. Here the people felt secure because approaching horsemen could be seen for many miles from the east, south and west, and to the north was a dense thicket of willows. The thick brush was a secure hiding place as pursuers would have taken their lives into their own hands to have tried to follow anyone into it.

Although it has generally been considered a hangout or rendezvous for horse thieves, robbers and murderers in the San Joaquin Valley, the rancho also was used as a recreation area by many of the vaqueros who made a living capturing wild horses in the valley.

After the floods of 1862, the country surrounding the old rancho was covered with logs of pine and redwood with which the residents converted the place into a fortress (a ditch was dug around the buildings and logs were placed in it forming a wall about twelve feet high). There they planned many of the robberies committed for miles in every direction, among them the Vasquez gang's raid on Kingston. It also was where they later took refuge. The old stockade was known to have been in existence as late as 1883, and some of the ruins of the other buildings were there in the 1920s.

The rancho was on the old stage road from Gilroy to Millerton via Panoche Valley. The stage crossed at Watson's Ferry or later White's Bridge and passed near the rancho, but it was not a regular stop. The stage would pick up or drop off mail or passengers when requested.

The houses were in the same style, brush and mud covered with tule-thatched roofs, that were used in Las Juntas. One of the houses was described as being of logs, chinked and plastered with mud, and in it were stored the barrels of liquor sold at the saloon and other supplies needed for the store.

It was said that during the 1870s the population of the rancho was about three hundred, which is more than had ever lived at the county seat of Millerton. Pedro Aguirre was the leading businessman, running both the store and saloon for several years. He reportedly had considerable trouble with the outlaw Vasquez and his gang and was forced to remove his family for a while until after Vasquez was captured.

The men of the town devoted much of their time to horse racing, gambling and fighting, and heavy consumption of liquor. Rodeos were often held and sometimes as many as one hundred vaqueros or stockmen

Reference 3:11

## A MISSION ON THE KINGS RIVER

The most definite information concerning Mission del Río de los Santos Rey comes from a grandson of one of the members of the original expedition. The man is not a Spaniard but an American who according to his descendants came to the Pacific Coast in the early '30s. His name was Caleb Strong Merrill. He was a stone mason by trade and about 1831 he came to San Diego around Cape Horn on the Boston Hide Drougher. At San Diego his services were in demand at the mission so he left the ship.

After completing repairs and additions to the buildings at the mission, Merrill was taken to Monterey where he completed similar work. At this time the San Joaquin mission attempt was to be made and he accompanied the friars and military on their expedition to the Kings River. In the early summer the party traveled by way of San Juan Bautista and Pacheco Pass to the Kings River. There a temporary camp was made under the oaks.

The work of making friends with the Indians was begun. It was seen the Indians had stored great granaries full of acorns— much more than they could consume in several years. When asked why they had done this they replied that a few years previously they had suffered a severe drought and that for seven years the Kings River had failed to flow into their locality. By the time the drought was over the oak trees had ceased to bear acorns and the Indians were afraid of a famine.

From the outset the Spaniards were doomed to defeat at the Kings River. The locality was pitted with the mess of grizzly bears. In the soft alluvial soil of the river banks these fierce animals dug holes and nested underground much like the squirrels. Merrill stated that the Indians and mission-aries took refuge in the trees and spent most of their time there.

The whole valley area near Laton was described as a vast jungle and swamp. The party was never able to approach Tulare Lake. After climbing the highest trees all they could see in that direction was more trees and a sea of tules. After about three months of unsuccessful work among the Indians, during which time the large pile of adobe bricks was made, the entire party returned to Monterey. Mr. Merrill reembarked for the American coast where he stayed until 1848. When gold was discovered in California he returned here and in later years was quite proud of having constructed some of the first stone and brick buildings in San Francisco.

SOURCE: "San Joaquin Primeval," *Tulare Daily Times*, January 19, 1932, p. 5.

participated. For these the saloon had a special wagon which followed the rodeo so the participants need not go thirsty.

As the large ranches of James, Miller and Lux, and Herminghaus expanded and engulfed all the land around them, the rancho's residents were deprived of the ample food supply from the hundreds of elk and thousands of antelope that previously had run near the river. As fences went up around some of the ranches, activities of the people at the rancho were greatly hampered, and the ever-increasing population of law-abiding citizens on the west side brought heavy pressures on the lawmen to keep the outlaws under more constant surveillance.

The official county map of 1891 shows no settlements around the elbow of the San Joaquin River, and the road that had previously passed by the rancho had been replaced by Whitesbridge Road two to three miles south of the river.

The last killing at the rancho was reported in March 1911, and soon after that the entire area was vacated.

It is unfortunate that the majority of details of the Californianos or Hispanics is about the outlaw element, as they were outnumbered many times over by constructive settlers who made a positive contribution to the development of the county. It is hoped that additional information about their work is to be found somewhere in written form and that it will eventually be made available to future generations.

Reference 3:12
# PUEBLO DE LAS JUNTAS

Rivaling if not exceeding Pueblo de San Emigdio in age, Las Juntas was one of the very first settlements in the San Joaquin Valley. In contrast with San Emigidio, Las Juntas was not a mission outpost but was a rendezvous for adverturers and pioneers and refugees from the Spanish settlements in the west.

Among the early settlers of American extraction, Pueblo de las Juntas had a bad name. They describe it as one of the oldest and the worst towns in the entire San Joaquin Valley. They said that American officers never went there after bad men. There was a Mexican peace officer on duty in Las Juntas. This man had a hard time handling the tough characters that congregated there. The bad reputation of Las Juntas was more or less borne out by the old Spanish and Mexican residents.

About 1874 a Mexican named Ciatano Robles killed a man in Las Juntas. He fled west into the Coast Range Mountains and took refuge in Arroyo de la Plata (Silver Creek) just about where it empties into Arroyo de Panoche Grande (Big Sugar Loaf Creek). Cavael, a Las Juntas constable, found Robles while he was asleep and killed him. Tying his riata on the dead body, he dragged it under a steep bank of the creek and caved the soil down upon it. This incident is given by old residents of Las Juntas as an example of the summary way in which law was enforced at the old pueblo.

Theodore Moreno, a member of the Vasquez gang of outlaws, killed Nocha Morales, a Mexican woman in Las Juntas. He came into the house swearing that he was going to kill Henry Miller. Nocha tried to tell him that Mr. Miller was a good friend to them. Moreno shot her. He later died at San Quentin prison after having been convicted of the killings at Piacines when the Vasquez gang raided that place.

Las Juntas was the point at which both the Murrieta and Vasquez gangs obtained their supplies. There they were safe from pursuit by the American officers. Murrieta was at Las Juntas a few days before the battle at the Cantua with Harry Love and the posse.

Among the Spanish and Mexican families who lived at Las Juntas were those of Juliano Higuera, Pedro Aguirre, Gregorio Yñigo, Francisco Cariponto, Juan López, Ambrosio Arias, Juan Mendez, Juan Liviano, Juan Salazar and Don Jesús Santamarta.

### Statement of Theodora Arredondo of Madera

"In 1850 my husband brought me to Las Juntas where Firebaugh is now. We came from San Pedro over the old road. We came horseback, but just about a year before we came a party came in with a carreta. About ten people who lived at Las Juntas claimed to have come in with carretas over the old road. One of these carretas stayed at Las Juntas. It was washed away in the big flood in 1862 when the steamboat came along and saved many people.

"While we were living at Las Juntas my husband took me to Contra Costa. We went horseback along the foothills. The old Los Angeles Road went that way. A trail led from Las Juntas to Panoche Creek and joined the Los Angeles trail there. It was a real old road. I believe it was in 1852 that we went that way.

"The old men and women at Las Juntas and along the foothills had known the old road and had traveled over it many years. There was a man at Las Juntas with grandchildren in 1850. He claimed to have come in over the road before he was married. I believe it had been used at least 50 years when I first came over it."

*This statement was taken in 1930.*

SOURCE: By Frank F. Latta and appeared in his book, *El Camino Viejo a Los Angeles*, Kern County Historical Society, 1933.

*Carreta—old fashioned Spanish ox-cart.*

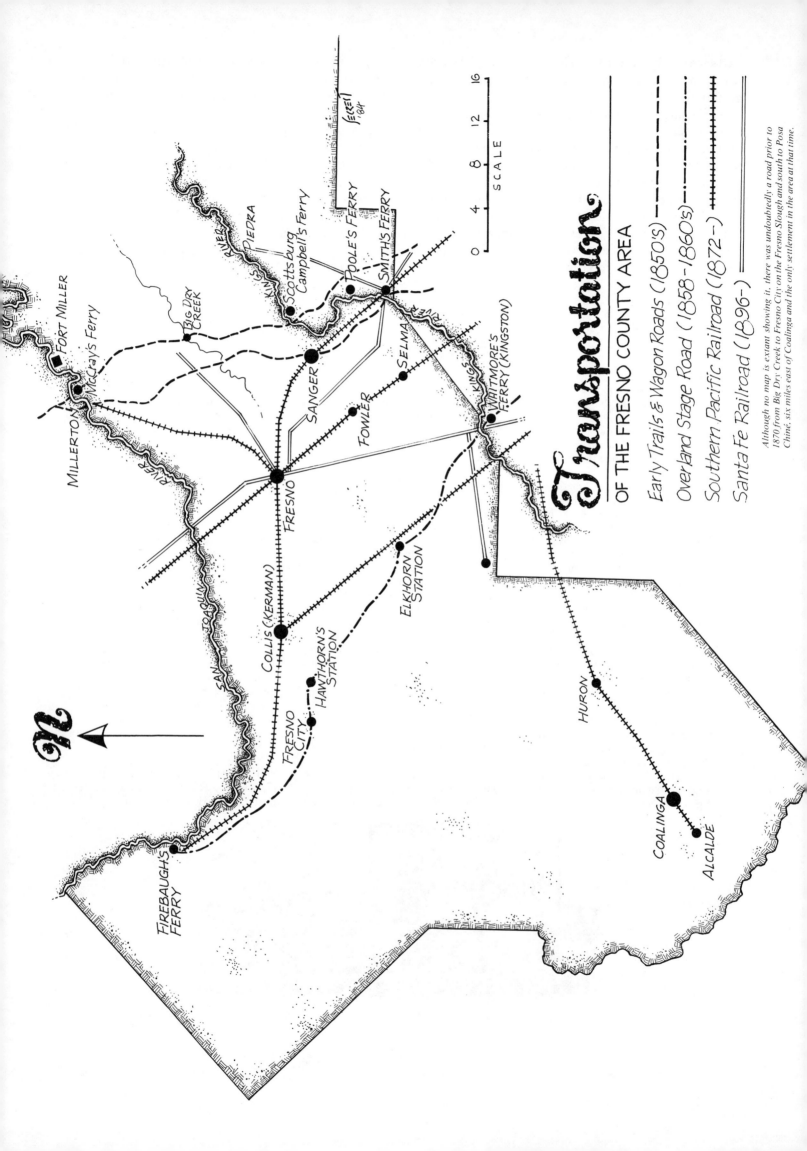

# Transportation
## OF THE FRESNO COUNTY AREA

Early Trails & Wagon Roads (1850's) — — —
Overland Stage Road (1858-1860's) —·—·—
Southern Pacific Railroad (1872- ) ┼┼┼┼
Santa Fe Railroad (1896- ) ━━━━

Although no map is extant showing it, there was undoubtedly a road prior to 1870 from Big Dry Creek to Fresno City on the Fresno Slough and south to Posa Chiné, six miles east of Coalinga and the only settlement in the area at that time.

SCALE
0   4   8   12   16

N

FORT MILLER
McCRAY'S FERRY
MILLERTON
SAN JOAQUIN RIVER
BIG DRY CREEK
KINGS RIVER
LA PIEDRA
SCOTTSBURG
CAMPBELL'S FERRY
POOLE'S FERRY
SMITH'S FERRY
FERREL BAR
SANGER
SELMA
FOWLER
WHITMORE'S FERRY (KINGSTON)
KINGS RIVER
FRESNO
COLLIS (KERMAN)
HAWTHORN'S STATION
FRESNO CITY
ELKHORN STATION
FIREBAUGH'S FERRY
HURON
COALINGA
ALCALDE

# Chapter 4
# Stampede to the Mines

To understand how Fresno County entered modern times and Western civilization, one should take a map of California and look northeast of the county's center. As the eye moves just beyond 200 miles in that direction, a place called Coloma comes into view. On today's maps nothing seems special about this hamlet, nestled on the slopes of the western Sierra Nevada. But it was here, on January 24, 1848, that California's destiny—and Fresno County's—was transformed, in a way that brought progress and sophistication to one of the least developed regions of North America.

The date, as the history-conscious will know, marks the discovery of gold in California. It happened, like many other momentous events, through a chain of random circumstances. Captain John Sutter, a Swiss immigrant building an agricultural and commercial empire in northern California, needed lumber for his varied enterprises. He dispatched a crew of men under James Wilson Marshall to seek a suitable timbering and sawmill site. Coloma was chosen as the best location, and work on the buildings was begun. It was then that Marshall noticed strange yellow flecks in the sawmill's tailrace.

"Marshall was no metallurgist, yet he had practical sense enough to know that gold is heavy and malleable," wrote Hubert Howe Bancroft in his *History of California*. "[So] he turned it over, and weighed it with his hand; then he bit it; and then he hammered it between two stones. It must be gold! And the mighty secret of the Sierra stood revealed!"

Marshall raced to Sutter's headquarters at New Helvetia (today, Sacramento). The men tried to keep the secret while filing new land claims around Coloma. It was useless. The sawmill crew had learned what had happened, and word was fast leaking to others. By May the famed California Gold Rush was on, and it lasted for better than a decade.

As word of the gold discovery spread, miners from all over the world streamed into California. The ports of San Diego, Monterey, San Francisco and other coastal towns saw arrivals from most of Latin America, principally Chile and Peru; Mexicans tended to take one of several overland routes to California. From across the Pacific Ocean, Chinese and Australians filtered in. And arrivals from New England, the eastern United States and Europe had their choice of three routes to California.

The easiest trip was around South America, past Cape Horn, in a ship—there being no Panama Canal. It was a fairly comfortable journey, but it took four to eight months. Treks overland, starting from places such as Saint Louis or Independence, Missouri, were of middling difficulty (see Chapter 5). The worst, albeit most efficient, route was to board a boat in the East, take it to the Panamanian isthmus, and cross overland there. If tropical diseases, exhaustion from crawling through the jungle, or thugs did not intervene, the gold seekers reached the Pacific side and took a boat bound for California.

While it is impossible to say when the first foreign miners penetrated Fresno County's landscape, the first Americans can be tentatively identified. James H. Carson's *Recollections of the Mines*, published in 1852, contains this intriguing information:

The first exploring parties for the discovery of gold to the South of where the discovery of '48 rested, was in the month of March, 1849. The Mission Indians of San Miguel had brought into Monterey large specimens of gold and reported it to have come from King's River and vicinity. Mr. William R. Gardner [sometimes spelled Garnier or Garner], who had been in California for some fifteen years, and was acquainted with some of these Indians, determined to fit out a trading expedition for that region; the writer of this was importuned to accompany him, but owing to the indefensive manner in which he persisted in going, the offers were declined. Gardner left Monterey the 1st of March with five or six ox wagons, with Indian drivers and four Spaniards as companions; he passed through the coast range at the pass of San Miguel, crossed the lake slough near the Tulare Lake, and then passed up the north side of King's River to the foot of the Sierra Nevada; here he was met by Indians in large numbers from the mountains, who displayed large quantities of gold; they refused to trade with him unless he came to

45

their settlements; they having every mark, apparently, of friendship for him, he travelled two days to the mountains, where the Indians attacked him, killing him and all his party with the exception of a Sonoranian [sic] who was accompanying them . . . The Indians who murdered Gardner & party, were the Chowchillas, Chowochicimnies [Choinimnis?], & Kaweeahs—the most thieving, treacherous and bloodthirsty tribes of the Tulares.

Bancroft's *History of California* states that William Robert Garner was a native of London, England, who deserted a whaling ship [circa 1826] at Santa Barbara, and worked as a lumberman, clerk, policeman, translator, auctioneer and alcalde's secretary at different times. The casualty figure for his expedition is given as seven men, including himself.

Confirmation of the Gardner massacre was later offered by French journalist Etienne Derbec, who noted in an October 27, 1850, letter from "Oro Grosso" [Coarse Gold, today Coarsegold] this information: "Last year fifty miners, who had been up there [on the Kings River] working a rich *cagnade*, were hacked to pieces; only seven returned, stripped of everything, and yet they considered themselves very lucky to have their lives spared." This account is obviously not in agreement with Carson's or Bancroft's, and at this date it is impossible to say which one is the more truthful.

A journalist for the Paris newspaper *Journal des Débats*, Derbec wrote a lucid description of life in the southern mines during 1850 (see 4:1). Together with Lilbourne A. Winchell's narrative on mining methods (see 4:2), an accurate picture of early mining activities in the Fresno County region can be reconstructed. Derbec's account is also significant because he was the first to visit—and write about—what were apparently the area's first two mining camps, Coarse Gold and Oro Fino (Fine Gold). His notes concerning these places are too valuable to be edited, and are given in full below.

*Oro Grosso* are two very significant words describing perfectly the type of placer it is. In Castilian they mean "coarse gold." This arroyo was thus named by the Mexicans because one finds gold there in grains which are worth several dollars and even several ounces. Fine gold is rare there, and although small, it is round and thick, quite different in that [respect] from the gold of other placers. Moreover, when we passed through here the first time, the miners were not searching for this small gold; they disdained it because the earth does not contain enough of it to pay them for the time it takes to wash it. They were digging until the rock was uncovered; that done, they scraped carefully in the crevices of the rocks with their knives, at the very bottom of the bed of the arroyo, or they broke it with their picks and gathered the gold by hand, for those good grains struck their sight in the midst of the dark

Reference 4:1

# THE MINING LIFE
### ETIENNE DERBEC

Oro-Grosso [Coarse Gold]
on the San Joaquin
October 23, 1850

Sir,

It will soon be a month that we have been traveling through the mountains south of Mariposa, looking for new placers. We are making a stop of several days here to rest a little from our fatigues and to cease a moment from that wandering life to which miners are condemned. It is in fact a strange existence, especially when compared to the usual life of a civilized man. Without a home, without any other shelter than the heavens, the miner goes from place to place, from stream to stream, searching for a good mine, everywhere testing the earth to determine its richness. In his peregrinations he carries his entire fortune with him: his pick, his shovel, his pan, his cradle, with which he gathers the gold; to that must be added his kitchen utensils, his blankets, a powder bag at his side, a double barrel shotgun or a *rifle*, one or two pistols hung from his leather belt, which even holds the special knife which the miner uses to dig with at the bottom of the holes and in the clefts of the rocks; finally, a sack containing his provisions completes his burden. All that makes a heavy load, and it is not the least of his troubles to drag that with him everywhere in these mountains. Always

on the go, always searching, he camps where night overtakes him and leaves the next day on some new excursions. When he has found a placer rich enough to reward his efforts, he stops, settles himself at the foot of a neighboring tree, carries his tools to the place which he has marked out by means of four stakes placed in the four corners, and according to the law of the placers, he prepares to exploit it.

The next day the miner is up before dawn; he begins by eating a modest breakfast, which usually consists of tea or black coffee in which he dips the bread which he baked himself. He roasts his coffee in the same vessel in which he bakes his bread, and lacking a coffee grinder, he pulverizes it between two rocks; tea and coffee are the usual drinks of the miner, and one might even say that they are the basis of his diet, for he uses them in great quantities, digesting with difficulty the food which he takes with revulsion and which, for lack of others, he cannot do without. Made without leavening, poorly cooked, scarcely kneaded, the bread of the miner is of poor quality and as heavy as lead. All cannot stand it; some make *tortillas* . . . [which have] the advantage of cooking almost instantly, of tasting better than miserable bread, and can be eaten [alone]. Unfortunately the salty grease with which they

season it eventually produces scurvy, and so they must not use it constantly.

The normal diet of the miner is, therefore, not very elegant and cannot be. For a long time he had no choice and had to eat bacon and flour, glad that he could even get that. Gradually they began to get dried vegetables. At first there were only beans; then lentils and rice came later to give a little variety to that monotonous and repulsive diet, always cooked in the grease of melted bacon. Since this past August the miner has been able to eat potatoes, and he consumes a great number of them. Thus, they are sold almost as soon as they are brought in. In addition, the miner can today obtain some small cans of sardines which are sold for $2.00 (10 fr.), vinegar, olive oil from the South of France and which costs $3.00 for a bottle containing less than three demi-setiers.

No miner works on Sundays; it is, in fact, the hardest day for the miners from our country. He puts off until Sunday all the work not connected with the mine itself. For him, the most difficult task is going to the nearest "city" . . . to buy his provisions for the week. He is often several leagues away from it. In such an instance, he leaves very early in the morning to avoid as much as possible the heat of the day, which is oppressive. He bravely returns with an enormous

depths in which they were buried. The miners call that "working with the knife." At that time there was a certain [amount of] enthusiasm among the few miners who were newly arrived at that place. A sailor from our country [France], after having dug a hole about five feet square and about nine or ten feet deep, had found in the crevices at the bottom eleven ounces in a single morning of magnificent gold, perfectly smooth and pure; the most perfect piece weighed more than six ounces. Joy spread throughout the camp; that lucky find seemed a good omen to the miners, and all worked with courage around that privileged terrain, hoping with good reason [to get] a share of the vein. But the vein ended in the hole where it was born, and we could see their disappointment! their work was not rewarded, or very little; then they began the quest again. They found a plateau, with which they must not have been dissatisfied, for on our return [from prospecting] we found it turned upside down, which proves that it was worth the trouble. A hundred attempts scattered throughout the extent of the arroyo caused us to suppose that they searched after that for places even slightly rich, without finding any, and they moved once again to seek their fortune elsewhere. Thus, we were greatly surprised to find no one here. . . .

The southern placer where the miners were complaining the least is the Oro Fino that is "fine gold"; the few miners who were there, for the placer is still unknown and we were quite astonished in coming across it, always made more than their subsistence and sometimes withdrew as much as an ounce [of gold] during a day; but that is an exception which we must be careful not to take for a general thing. The Oro Fino is half way between the Oro Grosso and the San Joaquin, but more to the left in the mountains; it is about a day's walk from either of them. The gold is scattered throughout the whole thickness of the stream bed; but that small placer is not habitable; no merchant had come to establish himself there, and in order to live, the miners were forced to go to *ranchos (fermes)* on the plain, several days' walk, to buy deer meat dried in the sun, the only food which they could obtain, along with some salmon, also dried in the sun, which was supplied by the Indians of the San Joaquin.

As for the San Joaquin itself, it is certainly the poorest of the placers; the best days yield four dollars there; at every step one finds abandoned quicksilver machines, and it is entirely deserted today. However, the time will come when the miner will be very glad to come back to it. Thus, already this year they are working the terrain they disdained last year [1849], and it is certain that next spring they will begin working the other lands which are scorned today, unless, however, they make some new and important discoveries, which is not impossible.

Derbec was proved right; miners always were loath to give up on the San Joaquin, hopeful it might yield a deposit everyone else had missed. When Kentuckian William Mayfield and his family arrived in the summer of 1850, they set up a flume and sluice box near Fort Miller's eventual site. There they found two men readying a ferry (Laroine's? See Chapter 5) for opera-

load on his back through the mountain passes which would often be considered inaccessible if he did not succeed in getting through them. Ordinarily, the higher they are, the more auriferous they are: it is in such places that he prefers to establish his camp. If he is well off, he owns a mule or a horse on which he loads his supplies; he had paid from a minimum of . . . $100 to a maximum of $300 . . . according to their scarcity and to the placer. But he does not often keep them. It is rare for a night to pass without the Indians stealing several of these animals . . .

The miner's diet is gradually improving everywhere, and now he brings back from the city, with his other provisions, a little fresh meat, beef or mutton, which is a real treat for him. Unfortunately, the heat does not allow him to keep it and he can use it only at the beginning of the week. If the week has been fairly good, the miner adds to his supplies some fresh bread, a bottle of brandy, a bottle of wine, and some dried fruit for which he pays a dollar a pound (5 fr.). If, on the contrary, it has been a poor week, he limits himself to the strict necessities and feeds on flour and beans cooked in the grease of salt pork. . . .

Returning from the city, the miner uses the rest of Sunday to repair his tools, to mend, and to do his small washing. For this last operation, he uses one of the numerous bulbs which grow in the ground and which have the properties of soap; the Mexicans make great use of them.

The Americans have maintained their northern customs in the mines; they stop work around two or three in the afternoon on Saturday and prepare for the next day. Some of them get together in one of the cabins and sing in chorus religious songs; others read from the Holy Bible; still others sit around the gambling tables, losing or winning with the most apathetic manner in the world. Generally, they play for small stakes with wooden tokens for lack of small change; these tokens are worth ten cents or ten sous. . . .

When night falls, our miners get together around a frugal supper and do honor to the modest Sunday feast. Appetites are voracious, for the mountain air is stimulating and the days are filled with hard work: consequently hunger always gives a zest to the meal; nothing ever remains for the next day except sometimes from Sunday night, for that is the day chosen for the feast. Our miners go hunting. If they have had any luck on the hunt, there is a feast; if they have been unsuccessful, they content themselves with the usual, and gaiety prevails nonetheless after supper. Sometimes some unhoped-for game animal comes to spread joy among the guests. Turtle doves, partridges, blue birds, squirrels, a hare or a rabbit appear fairly often in these meals; as for large game, such as deer, elk, stag, even bear, it is not so easy to obtain them, and they drink a double portion in honor of the conqueror, especially when he has killed a bear, that troublesome neighbor of the miner. . . .

The sedentary life of the miner who is not too far from the settlement is still bearable, despite the hard work. But when he goes "prospecting," that is, when he goes at random in unknown regions to discover mines, where there are no roads and no possible guides, laden down with tools and provisions, fighting the Indians and ferocious animals, always on guard against their surprises or their traps, lacking first food and then water, sometimes feeding on acorns or herbs to keep from dying, and sleeping between two stones to avoid the arrows of the Indian who is following his trail, that is the existence which quickly makes or breaks a man. So, it can be said that in the mines many children have become men, while many men have returned children once more.

SOURCE: *A French Journalist in the California Gold Rush: The Letters of Etienne Derbec*, ed. by A. P. Nasatir. Georgetown, California: The Talisman Press, 1964.

tion across the San Joaquin. This was a significant development; no ferry would have been in place unless there was a substantial flow of travelers up and down the valley.

In reading of Mayfield's experiences—reported by his son, "Uncle Jeff," in Frank F. Latta's *Tailholt Tales*—one gathers that his mining success was minimal or nonexistent. When a flood raced down the San Joaquin's banks, washing out his mining equipment, Mayfield unhesitatingly retreated to the Kings River area. There he settled near Centerville's site and began raising horses and cattle.

Concerning the flood, Uncle Jeff recalled that it struck at night. He remembered that he had left a prized bow-and-arrow set outside, and scrambled out of the family's tent, frantically searching for the items, while his equally frantic family searched for him. "I soon appeared and they were glad to see me but made me stay with our pile of equipment high up on the river bank," he said. "The next morning we were a discouraged family. We had lost part of our supplies, and the flume and sluice box were entirely gone." Interestingly, Uncle Jeff mentioned that twenty miners, apparently undiscouraged, were working around the ferry at the time of his family's departure.

While details on the ferry Uncle Jeff mentions are sketchy, the history of one operating in the area as early—or earlier—is better known. It was approximately ten miles down river from the Fort Miller site and founded, perhaps, in the spring of 1850. At that time, Mariposa County authorities (for Fresno County's land surface lay within that county, mostly, until 1856) granted Thomas J. Alsbury a license to run a ferry at "Fort Washington." Traffic to and from the

Reference 4:2

## GOLD MINING: METHODS, TOOLS AND IMPLEMENTS

When the thousands of young, American fortune seekers thronged the western trails and crowded the ocean vessels in their haste to get to California and pick up the gold of the canyons and gulches, few had any knowledge of mining methods, and but vague ideas of how to obtain the coveted treasures. . . .

The American, or others, used a pan, and at first some frantic miners employed any utensil that would possibly serve—even skillets and piggins [wooden pails]. . . . Having found a "prospect" the miner filled his pan with the gravelly soil, which often contained clay, and at the water's edge dipped his pan full, then stirring the softening mass with his fingers, and as the mud flowed from the pan, he continued dipping and gently whirling the pan. . . . By the repeated dipping and outflow all the lighter particles were carried off, and finally the last clear water left only the gold mixed with a fine black sand. These last elements, of nearly equal gravity when wet, could not be separated until the sand was thoroughly dried out, when it could be gently blown away by the breath. . . .

The rocker or cradle, was next employed. . . . [To manufacture it] sections of hollow logs, with thin walls, were split in half, and one end of this semi-circular trough was closed by a fitted block. A sieve, or coarse strainer, was made by weaving and stretching criss-cross strips of rawhide, fastened securely over the top of the trough. A rough cleat in the log caught some of the gold. Another invention was made of willow branches woven loosely which answered as a strainer, suspended above a mat or bed of fine twigs, upon which much of the coarser gold was caught. . . .

With the rocker gold could be much more rapidly accumulated. The basis of a [more sophisticated] rocker was a box-like arrangement . . . with a tight bottom, and with sides and one end. . . . On the bottom of the box were fixed two rockers (as in an old-fashioned baby cradle). When in use these rested on two flat rocks. On one side of the box, at the top, was nailed an upright handle to be grasped—generally by the left hand. This gold extractor was now ready for expectant fortune making. . . .

Bucketfuls of soil were deposited until the hopper was full enough to suit. Then, while sitting on his soft rock he continuously dipped and poured water into the hopper, while rocking simultaneously with the other hand. . . . The water flowed towards the open end of the box—the gold and black sand being held by tight cleats fastened across the bottom. A "cleanup" was made as often as necessary—depending on the quantity of gold collected. . . .

The next development in gold mining machines or appliances was that of the "long-tom." This was a grown-up rocker (without the rockers). [The soil was shoveled through an iron sieve into a cleated box] of desired length, similar to a rocker's bottom. Water was turned in at the head of the "tom" from a ditch or flume. (Sometimes water was poured in from buckets; but only where the claim was small.) The miners then continuously shoveled the gravels into the "tom," and all material was washed, separated and deposited by the regular flow of the water . . . Where much fine flaked gold was mingled with the coarser particles, quicksilver was placed above the cleats to catch and retain it. The resulting amalgam was purified by heating in any convenient utensil—pot, frying-pan, or on a shovel blade. The mercury evaporated, leaving the gold. . . .

Flume or sluice mining was a method used at *placeres* of considerable extent. . . . Lines of long, three-sided boxes were used like the "long tom. . . . "

"Coyoteing" was chiefly a Mexican practice. Finding promising indications, the prospector would sink a shallow shaft to reach the bedrock—not often over six or eight feet beneath the surface. He would then scrape up the gravel and clay in his pan; take it to the water and wash it. If the "prospect" was favorable he re-entered the shaft and began driving a hole or tunnel as small in diameter as he could work in with a short crowbar—often lying on his side in the narrow opening. In this way he worked in all directions along the "leads" till the claim was worked out. The similarity of these channels to a coyote's burrough [sic] suggests the reason for the designation.

Ground-sluicing [hydraulic mining] involved turning a strong current of water against a bank along a stream, or a flat. As the miners cut away the soil with their picks, the swift water disintegrated the mass, carrying everything away except the gold, which was left collected in the crevices of the bed rock. When the water was diverted the gold was cleaned up. Thus tons of rock and gravel were quickly and cheaply handled [with great damage to the landscape, streams and rivers].

Quartz mining differed from all placer operations. Quartz carries gold; it has been called the "mother of gold." When an outcropping of this rock contained the golden specks, the discoverer proceeded to sink on it—otherwise, he started a shaft, tunnel or incline. This initial work was continued if the ore was rich enough. . . . [The gold had to be separated from the quartz. The Hispanic method used by many was in an arrastra, a circular compound in which the ore was crushed by large stones dragged around by a horse hitched to an arm from a center post. Later stamp mills were used of various size and powered by horse, water, steam or internal combustion engines.]

SOURCE: Lilbourne A. Winchell, *History of Fresno County*. Original manuscript in possession of Fresno City and County Historical Society.

*A miner's hut served as a one-room kitchen, dining room, parlor, bedroom and storeroom.*

L'Illustration, Journal Universel, Paris, August 6, 1853

Frost's Pictorial History of California. 1854.

Wooden bowls made out of the roots of trees were used by the Mexicans from Sonora for "panning" gold as well as for "dry-washing" gold. The latter process was described in *Personal Adventures in Upper and Lower California* by William Redmond Ryan as reprinted in *Frost's Pictorial History of California* of 1854 as follows:

"These men were actively pursuing a process that is termed 'dry-washing.' One was shovelling up the sand into a large cloth, stretched out upon the ground, and which, when it was tolerable well covered, he took up by the corners, and shook until the pebbles and larger particles of stone and dirt came to the surface. These he brushed away carefully with his hand, repeating the process of shaking and clearing until the residue was sufficiently fine for the next operation. This was performed by the other men, who, depositing the sand in large bowls hewn out of a solid block of wood, which they held in the hands, dextrously cast the contents up before them, about four feet into the air, catching the sand again very cleverly, and blowing at it as it descended. This process being repeated, the sand gradually disappeared, and from two to three ounces of pure gold remained at the bottom of the bowl . . . They work in this fashion at the mines in their own country; but I doubt if any other than a native constitution could very long bear up against the peculiar labor of 'dry-washing' in such a climate and under such difficult circumstances."

*Frost's History of California—1854.*

49

*The three most common mining procedures:* center foreground, *panning;* left, *a horse-powered arrastra (Spanish arrastre) for breaking up gold bearing rock;* right, *a miner operates a rocker with one hand while pouring in water or gravel with the other.*

*The arrastra was replaced by the stamp mill, a method used in Europe, as more miners turned to quartz mining. By 1861, rock breakers were developed to prepare large rocks for the mill. Stamps were first made of wood, but by the middle sixties they were supplemented by cylindrical stamp stems made of iron fitted with tappets which, when engaged with cams on the horizontal power shaft, lifted and rotated the stamp. They were horse-, steam- or water-powered. Gold was then extracted from the amalgam in sluices or by various advanced techniques with minerals or chemicals. (This stamp mill is a working mill at the Mariposa County Museum and History Center, Mariposa. Information is excerpted from State Division of Mines Bulletin 141.)*

*An artist's concept of an early Chinese man going to the mines where he was recognized as frugal, industrious and temperate.*

mines had made this ferry, and others like it in succeeding years, necessary. The "Fort" designation derived from the fact that Indians, and Indian attacks, were common in the area, and this outpost had to be protected with rough defense works. "Washington" unquestionably was applied because of the "City of Washington" José Castro had earlier subdivided (see Chapter 3). On an old emigrant trail, it seemed like a good place for business. A trading post and hotel eventually were established to complement the ferry.

Little is known of how Fort Washington looked. Contemporary mentions of it always lack detail, and an archaeological or topographical survey conducted today would probably yield little. The best description available was given by Lilbourne A. Winchell, who said there was "a ferry boat constructed of logs of sycamore, willow and cottonwood lashed together with the light raft foundation, upon which a wagon body was fastened. Ropes stretched from each bank of the river were used to haul the ferry across. Live stock [sic] forded or swam across, according to the volumes of water."

Who owned and/or managed Fort Washington in this era is debatable. Alsbury got the first license, but historians usually credit Mississippian Wiley B. Cassity and Major (his first name, not a title) Lane as its founders. This may not be a contradiction. Alsbury could have established the ferry, with Cassity and Lane purchasing it later, or Alsbury may have been the operation's manager and the other men investors. Exact circumstances often went unrecorded in those days.

Cassity and Lane arrived in the upper San Joaquin River area around the time of Fort Washington's founding, and became successful miners. At a place called Cassity's Bar, eight miles upstream from Fort Washington, the men were said to have taken out $250,000 when gold was valued at fourteen to eighteen dollars an ounce. A current estimated value of this yield would be in the $7 to $8 million range. The men hired white miners and Indians to dive for gold-laden sand on the river bottom, while Indians on the banks panned for whatever surface gold was available.

Lane eventually left the partnership with Cassity and was replaced by Charles Drayton Gibbes. The ferry, trading post and hotel seem to have prospered until Cassity—said to have mistreated his hired Indians—was murdered by them in January 1851, at the start of the Mariposa Indian War (see Chapter 2). Gibbes left Fort Washington in turn; he became a mapmaker and produced the first detailed charts of the central San Joaquin Valley and southern mines. After his departure, Mariposa County supervisors granted James D. Savage (see Chapter 2 and below), John G. Marvin and Walter Harvey a license to operate a ferry at "Cassidy's [sic] Crossing"—presumably the same location—on August 2, 1852. Alsbury apparently remained in the area, running the "Cassidy's Crossing"

ferry or a competing service. On October 6, 1853, he was allowed to pay his license for the ferry at Washington for a period commencing the previous September 1. Another ferry operator of this era, and a neighbor of Alsbury, was Tennessean Berry Typpett.

While Fort Washington was being established, B. Oscar Field attempted to set up a similar operation on the Kings River's banks (see Chapter 2). Field's outpost was probably the one described by a United States Army mapmaker, Lieutenant George H. Derby, who was visiting the area in May 1850. "I was informed by Colonel Hampton at the upper ferry [on the Kings River] . . . [that] a party of armed Indians had dropped by at the ferryman's hut and told the occupants they must leave that part of the country in four days . . ." Field later testified that he was driven away by the Indians. The "upper ferry" comment suggests that a "lower ferry," run by a person or persons unknown, was in place.

A respectable amount of mining must have taken place in 1851, when David Bice James began working on the Fine Gold and San Joaquin River diggings (see 4:3). Not all enjoyed the success he reported.

Robert Eccleston, who prospected the Fine Gold and Coarse Gold areas at the same time, alternated between encouragement and discouragement in his diary. On July 11, he wrote that a bar on Fine Gold Gulch "did not turn out to be as rich as by the prospecting the boys [his mining party] anticipated." His July 14 entry mentioned that he "spent the day in prospecting with machines, found nothing would pay," but the next day he mentioned that his party "moved up the River crossing the mountain & came down near what is called the Coarse Gold Bar, found quite a number to work among us. Prospected in the afternoon, tolerable success."

Eccleston said little about his luck in the following weeks, while working in the same area, but a late August entry displayed unmistakable chagrin: "This week was broken by the Several occurrences one of which [was] being the getting of provision. Mr. Adams left for the Friseno [Fresno River]. We bought out another claim tools &c $54.00. The news from the Friseno discouraging—our provisions cost some $58.00 Which nearly covered the Amount we made."

The mining party decreased in size, from seven to five members, and Eccleston's comments became increasingly mundane. "Our diggings gave out this week and we Spent considerable time in prospecting . . . Continued prospecting and got back to the [Fine Gold?] Gulch on Tues evening. We found nothing very rich on our trip. Miners were daming [sic] and working in the bed of Stream generally, the bed has been found tolerable rich . . . This week was badly broken by the necessity of getting further supplies of provision, it taking 3 days, having to go down to the [San Joaquin?] River for them some 30 miles or more."

Despite Eccleston's varied fortunes, the Coarse Gold area had entered into a boom. William Faymonville's *Reminiscences of Fresno County* describe the place as "a prominent mining camp" by the summer of 1851. The town of Rootville, later Millerton, was founded at this time (see Chapter 5), and other mining communities were prospering—Grub Gulch, seven miles north of Coarse Gold, and Texas Flat, one and a half miles to the west. At the latter location, there was a store owned by two men named Roney and Thornburg and a sizable population. Faymonville reported that, in the 1851 Mariposa County election, 150 votes were cast at the precinct there. He mentioned also that an Indian scare in October left Coarse Gold Gulch deserted, "only four or five miners remaining, among whom was William Abbie, but before December many returned, amongst whom were C[harles] P[orter] Converse and T[heodore] C. Stallo, who opened a store about one and a half miles below Texas Flat, which was placed in the hands of Samuel H. P. Ross (nicknamed Alphabet Ross)."

Along the southern San Joaquin River banks, ten miles above Rootville, another mining settlement was born in 1851. David Bice James made some significant discoveries of gold at a bend in the river, and eager miners followed. Among them was Billy Martin, a Vermonter who staked a large claim and developed a mine that kept producing well into the twentieth century. Later worked by Henry and John L. Sullivan, the mine's output reached $100,000 after a half-century

Reference 4:3

## THE FRESNO COUNTY DIGGINGS IN '51
### DAVID BICE JAMES

[When arriving on the San Joaquin River in 1851] I found only two men mining [there]—Crumbly and Jameson; they were rocking and they told me they were making about $5.00 per day each out of the gravel upon the bars. The gold was in thin scales. I found there was no store there and I had to hit the steep trail, twelve miles, in July, to Fine Gold Gulch for supplies. I bought from [storekeeper] Larry Cowen a shovel for $5., pick $5., pan $2.50, and flour $.25 per lb., tea $1. per lb., onions $.50 per lb., tobacco $1. a plug and other things in proportion. I had a load of about 60 pounds to carry.

I had located a site for my hotel,—it was roomy, the sky for a roof and one single blanket was all my household furniture. I did not get back to the river, opposite my camp, until nearly dark and as the ford was quite deep and the boulders large in the bottom I made several trips before I got supplies across to camp. As I had no stove or cooking utensils I utilized an old shovel blade to fry bacon upon; baked my bread upon a stick in the ashes and used an oyster can to make tea and coffee in. It is surprising what a few things are necessary to do cooking with.

I had seen one of the men pan out and I thought that was easy. I commenced panning and I found little, infinitessimally [sic] small, specks of gold in the crease of the pan and picked them out with a splint and deposited them in a rag. My fingers got sore and the blood came to the ends and I had to do them up in rags. The second day a ghost of a long, lanky being hailed me with "Good luck to you and the top of the morning to ye, and have ye got any tobacco about ye?" I handed him my plug and [he] decreased the size of it wonderfully; he came again next day and said the same, and I did not hand him the plug, but cut off a piece and gave him. I asked him if he was mining, but he said no he was just "looking around." His name was Mike Finnegan.

Mike hit me every day for tobacco until I got tired and told him I had no more. In three weeks my supplies were consumed and I took my load of dust to buy more, but, to make a long story short, Larry Cowen weighed my dust and said there was just 75 cents in the lot. Now this was a damper on my dreams of wealth to be obtained from mining. After suffering the bites of the "que-dow," an insect like a woolly ant, red in color, but Oh My! they always bite twice for fear one would not wake a fellow up. I always had to jump into the river to kill the pain. Then there was a rattlesnake snuggled up to me in the night and I found him asleep next morning. But Cowen told me to try it again and he would let me have all the provisions I wanted.

In returning over the trail from Fine Gold Gulch to my camp, loaded down with supplies, the thought occurred to me that there must have been something wrong in my panning and I would try to find out what it was. The next day I went to Jameson and Crumbly Camp and told the boys my experience and the wealth I had extracted from the gravel in three weeks panning, and they both laughed until I thought they would have a fit; but I could not see anything to laugh at. However, they told me if I wanted to pan I had better let the bars alone and go crevic-ing. . . .

Further up the river there was a canyon [Arnold's Bar, near the mouth of Fine Gold Gulch] cut through the solid rock, with very precipitous sides, and the river came thundering through. Upon investigation of this canyon I discovered that there were some places like shelves above the water, that gravel had lodged in, and at last I found a place where I could see the gold in the black sand and gravel and got a little excited, as I suppose most everyone does when they see the actual stuff in the dirt. This kind of mining has a tendency to keep a person's cuticle moderately clean, as I could not follow the river without swimming, carrying what little clothes I wore in a bundle on my head, the pick over my shoulder and the pan fastened around my neck with a string and doing my swimming with my free hand and feet.

At last I struck it rich in a small spot of bedrock and pot holes; holes made in the bedrock perfectly round by the swirl of the water. The gravel it carried around with it had cut down into the bedrock, all sizes and depths.

Right here I may say that the largest and most remarkable pothole I ever saw, or worked in, is located in the bottom of a granite gorge about a quarter of a mile below the town of Fine Gold Gulch. It was twelve feet across, after taking out about four feet of sand I came to gravel that averaged $2. per pan or bucket; the gold was coarse and like grains of wheat; the gravel was round as billiard balls. I worked this pothole down seventeen feet and the bottom was not reached yet, the gravel still paying, but not so well; about seventy-five cents a bucket. A rain storm one night filled it to the top again with sand and I abandoned it. I found the dirt, using a common term among miners, just "lousy"; in fact, I got some dirt, which if I could have saved all the gold, would have netted fifty dollars to the pan, but the black sand with the gold was so heavy and the gold in such thin light scales it would go out of the pan in spite of all my efforts to avoid it, and some pans of dirt took me hours to get it panned down. Such tiresome work I never experienced before. But, knocking off a long story, in about two weeks time I had lots of dust and paid Larry Cowen my bill and had nearly five hundred dollars left.

SOURCE: "Reminiscences of Early Days in the Southern Mines." Manuscript, Fresno City and County Historical Society and Fresno County Free Library.

of work. Martin also gained renown for agricultural experiments near his mine property (see Chapter 6).

In time this district became known, jokingly, as Temperance Flat. James Urquhart, another early miner and resident there, operated a saloon and trading post there in 1857–61. "Not only the bars at the water's edge, but the lateral gullies, as well, gave occupation to many miners," wrote Lilbourne A. Winchell. "The gold yield from this populous community and contiguous *placeres* [placers], steadily contributed to individual and cooperative labors. It was a rich camp."

On the Fresno River, roughly six miles below its junction with Coarse Gold Gulch, another trading post was founded in the summer of 1851. The first partners in this enterprise were James D. Savage, Dr. Lewis Leach (see Chapter 5), Lorenzo D. Vinsonhaler and Samuel A. Bishop. It was established for two reasons—Savage had contracted to furnish the nearby Fresno River Indian Reservation (see Chapter 2) with supplies and needed a distribution point, and there also was money to be made in servicing the needs of miners on the Fresno and Chowchilla rivers.

The jointly-operated trading post apparently was successful, for Bishop soon set up a similar operation several miles below. "For protection he had built up a wall of rocks, portions of which capped a natural, circular ledge or rim of granite," wrote Lilbourne A. Winchell. "This fortification enclosed his tent and lent a degree of security from stealthy [Indian] attack. The structure was known as Fort Bishop." Miners and occasional travelers thronged to this location. It also served reservation Indians, who enjoyed panning for gold in the river and trading for foodstuffs and other supplies. (As noted in Chapter 2, the government failed to support the Indians properly—though it had promised by treaty to do so—because Savage and other traders routinely shortchanged their supply contracts. Since the Indians traded directly with some of the reservation suppliers to make up the difference, immense profiteering was taking place.)

Roughly ten miles east of present-day Madera, close to Fort Bishop and also on the Fresno River, Vinsonhaler created another early-day landmark. Dubbed the Adobe House, it was designated a Mariposa County polling place in 1853, with Vinsonhaler in charge of balloting. In 1854 he leased his land to the Fresno River Reservation, left the trading post partnership and moved to Los Angeles, where he died on March 10, 1857. That same year, he and a Thomas Vinsonhaler were named in a list of Fresno County property owners. Thomas has not been further identified, and descendants of either Vinsonhaler are unknown today.

After Savage's death in 1852, the jointly-held trading post—at what was known as the Fresno River's Lower Crossing—was renamed Leach and Company. Bishop departed the next year, heading for Kern County, where he became a large landowner and early-

day supervisor. Later he moved to the Owens Valley, where the town of Bishop was named after him.

When a transcontinental railroad survey team, under Lieutenant R. S. Williamson, forded the Fresno in 1853, its geologist, William P. Blake, offered some comments on "Leach and Company." "Drs. Haller [Vinsonhaler] and Leech [*sic*] have a farm on the banks, where they have raised thousands of bushels of barley; the spontaneous or second crop averaging thirty bushels to the acre."

The above reference was undoubtedly to the Adobe Ranch, successor to the Adobe House. Its acreage expanded in later years; Wallace W. Elliott's *History of Fresno County*, published in 1882, said it contained 6,800 acres and was owned by J. G. Still (John G. Stitt), with its title based on a United States patent. By 1887, when the property was sold to a group of San Francisco-based investors, it made up 20,922.15 acres. Though reduced in size, the Adobe Ranch remains today. The present ranch house includes the remains of an adobe building in its entrance way, but it is not part of the original Vinsonhaler house.

When the Fresno River Reservation shut down in 1859, gold excitement was wearing thin. Leach had no reason to keep his store going, so he closed it in the 1860–61 winter. For years, however, the spot was marked by Savage's grave. Leach had removed Savage's remains to that location in 1855, placing a Connecticut granite shaft over them inscribed "to the memory of Maj. James D. Savage." The monument cost $800 and the lettering on it was inlaid with gold. The gold was stolen later, and when the marker and grave were moved to a new location in 1971 (a dam-created lake now covers the site), Savage's body was discovered out of its coffin and without its head!

In the hectic year of 1851, another ferry was established in the Fresno County area to service miners and travelers. William Campbell, previously a sub agent at a Kings River Indian reservation, began operating a ferry on the Kings ten miles above Reedley's eventual location. Early the next year, Campbell took John Pool (often misspelled Poole) in as a partner. The men suffered through disastrous flooding in 1852–53 and shortly afterward moved the ferry to a location two miles above Reedley's site.

By now situated in the part of Tulare County that became Fresno County, the Campbell and Pool ferry was not licensed formally until April 2, 1855. On the same day Pool resigned his position as a Tulare County supervisor, a post he had held since the county's formation. Perhaps he considered the right to operate a ferry a part of his compensation as supervisor, since other ferries paid a seventy-five-dollar yearly license fee prior to 1855. After that year ferry fees were changed to five dollars a month.

Campbell eventually left the ferry business to become a Tulare County cattle raiser. Pool announced plans to open a new ferry, five miles downstream from his first operation, but never proceeded with the scheme. Some supplies were carted to the site and were stolen by Indians, thieves or both. Pool was still working on a ferry on the Kings River as late as June 20, 1857, when he signed a receipt for "ferriage, drinks and board" for $11.50, but he reportedly moved to Mendocino County. W. W. Hill, a justice of the peace at Centerville and later Fresno County treasurer (see Chapter 11), was operating the upper ferry in the mid-1850s.

In 1852 the mining regions along the Chowchilla, Fresno and San Joaquin rivers had a population of perhaps 1,500, scattered through camps and places such as Sulphur Spring Bar, Arnold's Bar, Red Banks, Clark's Bar, Soldier's Bar, Italian Bar, Mitchell's Riffle, Mechanics Bar, Sharp's Riffle, Brown Bar Riffle and Poorman's Bar. Some of the claims proved exceedingly worthwhile. That June, Jesse Morrow, William Bowers, David Bice James and Theodore Thule ("Swede Bill") Strombeck located perhaps the most famous claim. Inspecting a slatey reef on the San Joaquin River, one and a half miles south of Rootville, they found some gold and decided to see if the river bottom would yield more. Since the river separated into upper and lower channels at this point, divided by an island, the men dammed the lower to expose any gold.

"This claim proved to be very rich," wrote James later. "Some of the dirt ran as high as fifty dollars to the bucket, and I have seen pieces of gold, worth three or four dollars, composed of scales that looked like white nuggets; the scales held together with white clay. Even when the claim was worked in the back water, four feet deep, the dirt paid two dollars a bucket, and there is lots of it left." After the easiest extractions were made, this "Jenny Lind" claim—named after the Swedish singer idolized by Americans—was abandoned, although much gold remained on the site. The channel was said to be too rough and narrow to permit anything but superficial mining.

The *San Francisco Daily Herald* of August 8, 1852, had the following to say about mining conditions in the Fresno County area: "There are about a thousand miners on the San Joaquin [River] at present, who are, as a general thing, averaging moderate wages. The bank diggings are all that can be worked at present, during the high state of the water, and they pay an average from $2 to $5 a day. On the Fresno, where the bars can be worked, men earn from $10 to $16 a day, but they have been roughly worked over, and when the river falls, it is not expected that they will yield anything like this amount as an average."

General prosperity resulted from these conditions, which allowed more supply stores and ferries to open up throughout the year. Near the junction of Coarse Gold Creek and the Fresno River, known as the

"Fresno Crossing," John Letford and a man named Carson opened a store that year. It was sold shortly afterward to J. L. Hunt and J. R. Nichols. Hunt left the partnership soon after the purchase and was replaced by James M. Roan, a Mariposa County supervisor and a deputy sheriff, at different times. The store eventually became Roan's sole property, with Thomas J. Allen leasing a saloon and restaurant concession from Roan. Since Allen was a justice of the peace, "meat, drink and Justice were dealt out in the same room," according to William Faymonville. Roan later sold the store to local rancher S. B. Coffee (see Chapter 6).

The brothers James Null and Charles F. Walker opened a store on Coarse Gold Gulch in the spring of 1852, replacing the Converse-Stallo concern mentioned previously. The new business lasted until 1859. Ten miles due south of the Walkers' store, and half a year later, Ira Stroud commenced another new business venture. "Stroud first engaged in mining, but later concluded that there was easier and more certain profit in aiding the miners to keep up their enthusiasm and fortify them for their arduous labors," wrote Lilbourne A. Winchell, "so he opened an institution in a tent,—generally called a saloon by modern chroniclers—but referred to as a 'grocery' or 'doggery' by the common custom of that era. Stroud flourished, and kept a popular open house for several years."

Ferries opened during 1852 included one built by Walter Harvey, Francis M. Davenport and their relatives from Georgia. It was probably located near a rival enterprise kept by Robert Fagan on the San Joaquin River, just below Fort Miller (see Chapter 5). The Harvey-Davenport business was known as the "H. & D. Ferry," and its license was granted by Mariposa County on April 9.

The following June, one Thomas Payne gained a license from Tulare County supervisors to build a ferry on the Kings River "at a point known as the Lower Ferry on the direct road from the San Joaquin River, to Los Angeles." Given without charge, the license was to expire on March 1, 1853. This man may have been Theodore J. Payne, who owned a store on Fine Gold Gulch in 1854, sold that business to J. Scott Ashman in 1856 or before, and met a violent death at Toll House in 1873 (see Chapter 11).

Southerly traffic to and from the mines continued to make Kings River ferries necessary. Two licenses for such operations were approved by the Tulare County Board of Supervisors on October 5, 1852. The first went to J. M. Ball, whose ferry was "at or near where the road to Four Creeks [in Tulare County] strikes said river on the south side . . . " According to later maps, this could have been synonymous with the Campbell-Pool ferry site, yet there is no evidence that Ball was representing anyone other than himself.

The second license was granted to B. F. Edmonds,

for a ferry "on the Kings River below Pasqual Indian Rancheria [village], where the road to Campbell & Co. ferry to Four Creeks strikes said river the first time." The rough distance given, and uncertainty as to the Indian village's location, make it difficult to determine this ferry's location. John C. McCubbin pinpointed the village's location between Centerville and Reedley, so it must have been close to Campbell and Pool's second ferry site. Rates for both the Ball and Edmonds ferries were fifty cents for footmen and local horses, one dollar for men on horses and loaded pack animals, and one dollar per wheel for wagons.

Back on the San Joaquin River, two more ferries were started in 1853. One was twenty-five miles above Fort Miller, past the Patterson Bend where many mining claims were being worked. Here Stephen A. Gaster and Joe Royal built a two-story adobe store, with an accompanying ferry. The store's trade was brisk, for the nearby granite ledges were jammed with gold and local miners had much money to spend. Gaster and Royal were flush enough to afford a promotional gesture—no tolls on their ferry—and (perhaps) because of this, no license for that operation was obtained until August 11, 1856, from the new Fresno County government. When the local mines were exhausted in the early 1860s, the store and ferry were abandoned, and the disastrous winter floods of 1867–68 removed all traces of both. Today the Gaster-Royal business site can be found on the extreme northern edge of Kerckhoff Lake, on the Fresno County side of the river.

At a place three miles below Fort Miller, on or near the site of the Harvey-Davenport operation, Charles Porter Converse started a new ferry in the fall of 1853. He soon took in W. W. Worland as his partner, and they obtained their first ferry license on August 16, 1854. After Fresno County's formation, a replacement license was granted on November 22, 1856. Converse's ferry and nearby adobe house soon became popular wayside landmarks. They were augmented in 1863 when Colonel James Richardson Jones built a two-story hotel/store/saloon on the river's opposite bank. Four years later, after the December 1867 floods wrecked the ferry boat—a substitute pontoon ferry was used—Converse sold out to Jones. Years passed and a community, variously known as Jones' Store, Hamptonville, Pollasky and now Friant, grew up at the site (see Chapter 13).

Converse's Ferry and the Jones businesses were popular because they were on a stage route running from Stockton to Los Angeles. The road's opening, in the mid-1850s, marked the introduction of stages to

Reference 4:4

# SMITH'S FERRY

### JOHN C. McCUBBIN

James Smith, the owner and operator of Smith's Ferry, was born in Pennsylvania November 26, 1821 and died at Smith's Ferry on December 17, 1862. He was an intelligent, energetic and progressive man. He was studious and acquired more education than the usual young man of his day. He taught school for several years in Ohio and Illinois. In 1846 he married Miss Martha Lucinda Hamilton of Findlay, Ohio. To Mr. and Mrs. Smith were born four children—three sons and a daughter. . . .

Following the reported discovery of gold in California in 1848, Mr. Smith left his wife and one-year-old child with relatives in Ohio and joined a party to cross the plains and mountains to California. On this trip and a following one, Smith served as leader and captain to the company of pioneers with whom he traveled.

His first field of mining activity was near the Feather River, but later he went south where he took up a claim and pitched the first tent in the place that later became the town of Columbia, Tuolumne County. . . . Smith was very successful in his mining operations in Columbia. . . .

When Smith came down from Columbia, he brought with him seventeen yoke of oxen, besides other cattle. His oxen were divided into three teams as follows: two teams of six yoke each, and one team of five yoke.

In 1851 Mr. Smith returned to his home in Ohio via boat, by way of Cape Horn. The following year he moved his family to California. Early in 1855, Smith came down the San Joaquin Valley with his family in search of a suitable place to live. . . .

In 1855 he established his ferry near the southwest corner of the present town of Reedley and near the northwest corner of the present Reedley Cemetery. [The Tulare County Board of Supervisors granted a ferry license on August 8, 1855, to Crumbly and Smith at this location. Three months before, S. B. Campbell had been issued a license to operate a ferry at the same location; why he retired from the business is unknown.] It was located on the lower detour of the old Stockton-Los Angeles stage road. At no other place on the Kings River could a crossing be made during high water. For that reason, the ferry remained open to the public after all the other ferries on the river had been abandoned. It was in continuous operation for nineteen years.

James Smith needed a place for his family to live, and he also knew that travelers coming through would need food and lodging, so he built a hotel on the brow of the hill above the ferry. . . .

The lumber from which his hotel and ferry boat were constructed was hauled from the Thomas mill in the Sierra Nevada Mountains in Tulare County with Smith's ox teams. Two carpenters by the names of Ramblesberg and Haskins built the hotel and ferry boat and when completed the two projects represented an outlay of $5,600 itemized as follows: hotel—$3,000; ferry boat—$2,000; cable—$550; two brass shieves—$50.

Mr. Smith built all of his [ferry] boat out of pine wood except the knees, which were of oak. His boat was sixteen feet wide and sixty feet long, and was provided with a landing platform at each end. These landing platforms were four feet wide and extended across the entire ends of the boat, to which they were hinged. The hinges enabled the platforms to be adjusted to the varying slopes of the banks. A large strong cable extended across the stream, and the ends were attached to long, heavy timbers set upright in the river banks. This cable was suspended far enough above high water to enable driftwood to clear it at all times. The boat was attached to the cable by means of a block and tackle, connecting each end of the craft. . . . In 1860 the old rope cable was replaced with a steel one following a near accident when the rope broke. . . .

The schedule of ferry rates was as follows:
| | |
|---|---|
| One-horse rig | $ .75 |
| Two-horse rig | 1.00 |
| Four-horse rig | 1.50 |
| Six-horse rig | 2.00 |
| Eight-horse rig | 2.50 |
| Ten-horse rig | 3.00 |

Fresno County, then—until the railroad's coming in 1872—the most efficient transportation means available. The Stockton-Los Angeles road crossed the county in a northwesterly direction, featuring upper and lower detours and running through Smith's Ferry (see 4:4), Pool's Ferry slightly to the north, Scottsburg (Centerville) and Converse's Ferry. The higher elevation detour was used when the valley was flooded, and the lower when normal conditions prevailed.

The first stage on the Stockton-Los Angeles road's Fresno County portion, according to John C. McCubbin, "was a regular overland, six-horse Concord Stage Coach, and it connected Visalia with Stockton via Converse Ferry and Snelling. The name of the overseer of this line was [perhaps] a Mr. Pixley . . . A man by the name of 'Long Tom' was the driver. This overland stage was put on immediately after the starting of [Smith's Ferry in 1855. Smith] knew the stage was about to be operated when he began building his ferry boat . . . By the schedule, the southbound stage was due to arrive about 3 A.M. when all hands would take breakfast at Smith's Hotel, though no horses were changed by the drivers at the hotel. This overland stage continued to operate via Smith's Ferry until [circa 1858], when the [Butterfield Overland] road was opened from Visalia to Kingston, which was more direct."

Joining Mr. Pixley's line in late 1857 was Thomas M. Heston's "Rabbit-skin Express," carrying mail, express and passengers from Visalia to Hornitos in Mariposa County. When traversing Fresno County, the "Rabbit-skin" used the Stockton-Los Angeles road. This stage was fairly small, being drawn by two horses and seating three passengers. In June 1859 Heston sold out to an employee, Millerton resident William L. Hice. Visalia hotelkeeper Amos O. Thoms eventually became the agent for this new company.

In 1858 a new stage service began plying the Stockton-Los Angeles road. Since steamers, emigrant parties and other travelers going or coming from California could not always carry mail for the United States government, private stage contractors had to be employed to provide that service. One of them was Jacob Hall, who agreed to transport mail from Stockton to Kansas City, Missouri, for $79,999 annually. Hall's stages passed through Fresno County only six times, however; Indian attacks along other portions of his route caused an early abandonment of his enterprise.

A service competing with Hall's, far more successful and better-remembered, was the Butterfield Overland Mail. Formed by a consortium headed by John Butterfield, the company began developing its main route—from Saint Louis, across the Southwest, and up to San Francisco—after winning its $600,000 government contract on September 16, 1857. (See 4:5.) The route intersected Fresno County and a succession of stops was established: Whitmore's Ferry (Kingston), Elkhorn, Fresno City and Firebaugh's Ferry, all of which are described at length in Chapter 12.

As the most easily-reached gold deposits began

| | |
|---|---|
| Twelve-horse rig | 3.50 |
| Fourteen-horse rig | 4.00 |
| Sixteen-horse rig | 4.50 |
| Footman or one horse | .50 |
| Horse and rider | .50 |
| Pack horse | .05 |
| Sheep, in bands: per head | .03 |
| Horses or cattle, in bands: each | .12 |

Stages, about 60 per cent of transient teams.

The Smith's Ferry Hotel was a two-story frame structure containing eleven rooms, with hall above and below. It faced toward the northeast and was painted white. Mr. and Mrs. Smith did not want their children to be continually exposed to the evil influence of a saloon, so there was never a bar at Smith's Ferry Hotel.

From Smith's Hotel, stages and freight teams could be sighted far out across the dreary plains on either side of the roads. Big fourteen- or sixteen-animal freight teams, drawing a string of three heavily-loaded wagons and coming from either of the roads, would be in plain sight for a full half day before the melodious tones of the "leaders'" bells could be heard announcing their near approach.

The big barn at Smith's Ferry was usually filled with alfileria hay each year. Alfileria grew very prolifically in early days and, when ripe, could be raked up loose from the ground without cutting. When this supply of wild hay was exhausted, it was replenished with grain hay from Smith's ranch. . . .

This hotel building remained there for some years after it ceased to be used. Smith continued in charge of the hotel and ferry until the time of his death [due to pneumonia]. His widow continued with the business for a number of years until she married Clayborne Wright, who then assumed charge and conducted the business for a few years. He then moved to some other part of the state and Mrs. Wright again took charge and, with the assistance of her son, Hamilton Smith, continued the management of the property until February, 1874 when it was [sold] to J. W. Mitchell and W. E. Ross. . . .

Mr. W. E. Ross stated that when he took charge of the business in 1874, the old hotel register left by the Smiths was a massive volume and showed daily cash receipts on many occasions of over $300. . . .

Stages were now making less frequent trips, and the number of freight teams were rapidly diminishing on the old stage road. Business continued to dwindle, until finally the partnership was dissolved in [the latter part of] 1874. . . .

The old hotel that had been open to the public continuously for the previous nineteen years was then locked up and deserted. Neither the hotel nor the ferry were ever operated again.

The hotel building remained there for some years after it ceased to be used. In July, 1882, the "76 Land & Water Company" acquired title to the land where the old Smith's Ferry and Hotel were located. In 1886 they dismantled the old hotel and hauled the lumber to the ditch at Wahtoke Dam.

An enduring monument to the memory of James Smith is the oblong mountain that stands a few miles to the east of the old ferry site. This was designated as "Spring Mountain" by the men who made the original survey and subdivided the lands surrounding it some years after that. After Smith established his ferry in 1855, it was always known as "Smith Mountain," which name it has retained throughout the years.

The Honorable James Smith, whose life was marked by studious, temperate, and industrious habits, always took a deep interest in the promotion of those things which were for either public or private good.

SOURCE: McCubbin letters, Reedley Library.

*James Smith and family were the first residents in the Reedley area when he established a ferry on the river in 1855—truly a pioneer family.*

*A lone home on the prairie for about twenty years. The trees may have been planted but the prairie was treeless at that time.*

To the Corrals and Barn

To the Ferry →

Smith's Ferry Hotel —— West View

Drawn From Blueprint Floor Plans of J. C. McCubbin by K. Nickel.

(Courtesy - Oscar Noren

*The western portion of the Butterfield Overland Mail Route in 1858. Planning and staffing each station was a continuing problem. (See page 44 for Fresno County route.)*

# OVERLAND MAIL COMPANY.

## THROUGH TIME SCHEDULE

### GOING EAST.

| LEAVE. | DAYS. | Hour. | Distance, Place to Place. Miles. | Time allowed. No. Hours | Av'ge Miles per Hour |
|---|---|---|---|---|---|
| San Francisco, Cal. | Every Monday & Thursday, | 8.00 A.M | | | |
| Firebaugh's Ferry, " | " Tuesday & Friday, | 11.00 A.M | 163 | 27 | 6 |
| Visalia, " | " Wednesday & Saturday, | 5.00 A.M | 82 | 18 | 4½ |
| Ft. Tejon, (Via Los Angeles to) | " Thursday & Sunday, | 9.00 A.M | 127 | 28 | 4½ |
| San Bernardino, " | " Friday & Monday, | 5.30 P.M | 150 | 32½ | 4½ |
| Fort Yuma, " | " Sunday & Wednesday, | 1.30 P.M | 200 | 44 | 4½ |
| Gila River,* Arizona | " Monday & Thursday, | 7.30 P.M | 135 | 30 | 4½ |
| Tucson, " | " Wednesday & Saturday | 3.00 A.M | 141 | 31½ | 4½ |
| Soldier's Farewell, | " Thursday & Sunday, | 8.00 P.M | 184½ | 41 | 4½ |
| El Paso, Tex. | " Saturday & Tuesday, | 5.30 A.M | 150 | 33½ | 4½ |
| Pecos River, (Em. Crossing.) | " Monday & Thursday | 12.45 P.M | 248½ | 55¼ | 4½ |
| Fort Chadbourn, " | " Wednesday & Saturday | 1.15 A.M | 165 | 36½ | 4½ |
| Fort Belknap, " | " Thursday & Sunday, | 7.30 A.M | 136 | 30¼ | 4½ |
| Sherman, " | " Friday & Monday, | 4.00 P.M | 146½ | 32½ | 4½ |
| Fort Smith, Ark. | " Sunday & Wednesday, | 1.00 P.M | 205 | 45 | 4½ |
| Fayetteville, Mo. | " Monday, & Thursday, | 6.15 A.M | 65 | 17¼ | 3⅔ |
| Springfield, " | " Tuesday & Friday, | 8.45 A.M | 100 | 26½ | 3⅔ |
| P. R. R. Terminus, " | " Wednesday & Saturday | 10.30 P.M | 143 | 37¾ | 3⅔ |
| (Arrive) St. Louis, Mo., & Memphis, Tenn. | " Thursday & Sunday, | | 160 | 10 | 16 |

*Schedule issued September 16, 1858, shows what was a fast pace at that time. Firebaugh to Visalia took seventeen hours!*



*U.S. Mail Stage took over local routes of Butterfield in the 1860s. Ads supply details of their operation.*

*The Fresno Copper Mine, Ltd., viewed from east to west. Development was financed primarily by British investors.*

*One of five steam tractors with ore wagons used to haul ore from Copper King Mine to the railroad. Local objections caused the mines to stop using them.*

*Interior of the Copper King Mine. Reason for the photograph is not known but it appears there may have been a cave-in. The mine had four levels at 100-foot intervals.*

petering out in the mid- to late-1850s, mining's significance dwindled in Fresno County. People were turning their attention to other industries, principally stock-raising and lumbering (see Chapter 6), yet a few noteworthy gold discoveries were still being made. Late in the decade, at Clark's Bar on the San Joaquin River, Russell P. Mace and some other men built a millrace to divert the current. This method, which had worked so well at the Jenny Lind claim, paid off handsomely. Gold worth $900 was extracted the first day, and average output on succeeding days was $1,000. When this claim was exhausted, after a fairly short time, Mace mined at Temperance Flat and Mace's Flat. The latter location was below the Patterson Bend on the San Joaquin River, and both "[were scenes] of great activity and heavy workings," according to Lilbourne A. Winchell.

An article in the *San Francisco Daily Herald* for December 15, 1858, gave further details on Mace's activities, and some neighboring mining claims as well:

Mr. Sharp's claim is nearly worked out, so far as prudence dictates mining for this year. My estimate of $16 per day to each hand has been verified, including the [Chinese] employed.

Mace, [J. Scott] Ashman and Co. who have displayed so much perseverance and energy are now reaping their reward—their claim, so far as worked, turning out as well as could be desired.

Paine and Co. (purchasers into Fry claim) are progressing so busily with their work, that none of them have been visible in Millerton for some time. By last accounts, it might still be looked upon as the richest claim on the river.

The only poor diggings are on Soldier's Bar, where Agricola, and 2 or 3 others have been prosecuting their searches after the precious oro, so busily as to invite

Reference 4:5
# THE OPENING OF THE BUTTERFIELD OVERLAND MAIL ROUTE
## LILBOURNE A. WINCHELL

[After the directors of the Butterfield Overland Mail Service secured their contract,] preparations on a colossal scale were made to [inaugurate service]. Stations were selected at the most serviceable points—water being a first consideration, though there were other determining factors; shelter for the keepers and stock to be built of whatever native material was at hand—poles, rock, adobe—even, at first, rough, brush shelters in the localities free from Indian attack. Through Arizona, New Mexico and Texas strong stations and corrals were erected of high, adobe walls, for protection against the predatory tribes of those regions. Enormous supplies of hay and grain for the stage animals were hauled, in some instances, in the desert regions for long distances. Water was hauled under the most discouraging conditions, to the far out desert relay points. [In Fresno County, James Smith dug two wells on the west side for this purpose.] Hundreds of tons of requisites for man and beast were distributed and a constant supply maintained. At divisional points—main stations where drivers were relieved and passengers refreshed—horses were re-shod, harness mended, stages examined and repairs made. An army of employees were hired—drivers, guards, hostlers, mechanics, cooks, teamsters. Fifteen hundred men and over two thousand horses and mules were engaged in the work of mail carrying and supply distribution. All animals were shod, and branded O M. Most of this stock were wild—mustangs—and had to be broken in to harness practically untamed—as one early passenger said: "as wild as deer and as active as antelope."

Daring and experienced western men manned the stages. They were the greatest drivers the world ever produced—cool-headed, fearless, reliable, and upon them devolved the safety of the passengers and the sacred mail.

In the beginning light, Concord spring wagons were used, which held four passengers and five or six hundred pounds of mail. They were replaced by the big Concord coaches—"thoroughbraces"—which seated nine passengers inside and sometimes as many as ten on the outside—some on top, and two or three on the driver's seat.

The appellation "thoroughbrace" was fixed because of the leather supports, which were used in place of springs. They were fastened to the bolsters over the axletrees, and to them the body was hung. This arrangement caused the coach to rock, as a cradle, from front to rear, lessening the jolts. Thus it swayed and pitched instead of bouncing. By this motion, some passengers were affected with symptoms experienced by sea travelers.

On the level courses between near relay stations, only four to six horses were generally used, but on long stretches and in hilly or very rough localities, eight or more were necessary to make time.

When hitching up these fiery, nervous mustangs, there was a hostler holding each span by the bits—sometimes a man could control but one—while other helpers fastened the traces.

As a pair was worked into position, the lines were passed up to the driver, who was already on his seat, with his foot on the brake lever. In turn, as the wheelers, pointers, swing teams and leaders were successively fastened in, the lines were given into the grip of the man who guided them. When the hostlers cried "All set!" they jumped aside and the half-frantic mustangs lunged into the air and leaped forward on a run. No attempt was made to hold them. Keeping them in the track taxed all the driver's skill and strength. As the miles were covered, the pace steadied down, and the little, wiry natives of the plains broke into a trot, swinging along at an amazing pace. They soon learned their halting places, and when the stage rolled up to the station they were at full gallop under the cracks of the driver's long whiplash, but stopping quickly at the tightening of the lines and the pressure of the brake. Still restless, with dancing feet and tossing heads, chafing at the bits, they were unhitched and led to their stables, to rest until their turn again came around, which was in three or four days. They were then driven back to their former stopping place.

The semi-weekly trips required six or eight of the big coaches, traveling continuously night and day in both directions. Through the searing heat and dazzling sands of the deserts; in the driving winter storms of rain and snow, they were not stayed. Nothing but death or disaster stopped them. With each stage was a conductor whose duties were similar to those of a railroad train captain.

A year and a half of extraordinary accomplishment and the 2795-mile trail was ready for service. Stages left San Francisco and St. Louis, simultaneously, on the 15th of September, 1858. Upon arrival at their destinations they were given tremendous ovations. The crowds went wild with joy. Bands led the stage and the masses of exultant citizens, through the streets to the post offices. Dozens of hats were thrown into the air, trampled under foot and lost. No matter; "the Overland [had] arrived!"

SOURCE: *History of Fresno County and the San Joaquin Valley* by Lilbourne A. Winchell. Original manuscript held by Fresno City and County Historical Society.

the attention of more active miners, by whom it is supposed riches are likely to be better developed.

As the 1850s wore on, increasing numbers of Chinese miners arrived in Fresno County and worked the diggings (see 4:6). Driven from their homeland by poor living conditions, crowding and famine, many of the Chinese who came to California and its fabled gold mines were sponsored by fraternal organizations known as tongs (see Chapter 11). Forced to mine worked-over claims—money-grubbing whites never allowed the Chinese to touch virgin gold-bearing areas—they struggled to pay off their tongs and live decently. It seems likely most became content on these shores. Racial prejudice may have abounded (see Chapter 5), but food was plentiful, the cost of living was low, and wide-open spaces abounded if any had previously felt claustrophobic.

One low-yield district the Chinese worked was the Chowchilla River. Brothers Howard C. and Robert E. Gardiner, gold rush storekeepers, scouted the area in the mid-1850s to see if they should locate there. "It was reported that there were many Chinese there whose trade was very desirable, as they were generally prompt in payment," wrote Howard Gardiner later, " . . . but there was also a multiplicity of stores. Morever, the dust on the river bars was not so valuable as that on the Tuolumne, being alloyed with silver or some other metal that reduced its value to $14 an ounce. This was three dollars less than the average price. The prospect on the Chowchilla was not satisfactory, so the idea of locating there was abandoned."

Chinese miners were based at all the major gold camps. A group under Ah Hoi worked a previously-rich claim in the Red Banks area during 1856, after purchasing it from A. Myers for $100. Just above Fort Miller, Lo Ho and Company, Ah Loon, the Sue Company and others worked the San Joaquin River diggings, and thirty-seven miles above Millerton, Ah Chee and Company conducted their mining operations.

Other Chinese, like many of the whites, discovered it was easier to service a miner's needs than to mine themselves, and opened stores. Ah Lem, Ah Fook, Uz Une and Loo kept the stores that discouraged the Gardiner brothers; Hong Lee was based at Coarse Gold Gulch, and Lin Kee at Fine Gold Gulch; and the Fresno River was lined with shops conducted by Sing Hop, Mow, Ah Cone, Ah Linn and Company, Chang Kee, Ah Chuck, Lee Wah and Company and Tong Sing and Company.

By April 1857 a *San Joaquin Republican* (Stockton) correspondent had the following to say about Fresno County's gold prospects: "At present there seems to be no mining going on in the immediate vicinity of [Millerton], except by a few Chinamen, who have located along the banks of the [San Joaquin] river, where they are gardening, farming and mining alternately as they imagine their work is the most profitable. I inquired of sundry [Chinese] as to the wages they could make mining, and generally understood that they could make about a dollar a day." The reporter had some other comments to offer: "Mining in the neighborhood here seems to be in its infancy, and very few persons are

Reference 4:6

## CHINESE OF THE JOAQUIN MINES
### ERNESTINE WINCHELL

Mysteriously following [the] discovery of California gold mines appeared the Chinese at every location. As soon as the white men on the upper San Joaquin—gorgeous in black hats, scarlet shirts and white breeches—looked up from their rockers and sluices they saw little quiet brown men in faded blue and flapping garments busily digging near by. Of course the established system of staked and declared claims limited the alien operations from the first, but with the exception of a few renegades no one molested them. . . .

All sorts and any kind of habitation contented the Chinamen. Of brush and boards, of rice mats and kerosene tins, the tiny shelters were grouped on a spot hopeless for mining, and yet near to water for their perpetual ablutions. Nondescript wearing apparel was forever draped on bushes or strung on sagging cords, from mud fireplaces willow smoke intermittently arose, and horrid smells hung like an invisible unwavering mist. Lurking in a hut an old Celestial kept guard, and an unfamiliar footstep

would bring his furtive yellow face to the opening, bleared eyes blinking and pigtail dangling about his knees. It was no use to talk to him, the most persuasive accents received but the invariable emotionless response, "No savvy," in monotonous reiteration.

This creature was cook as well as guardian, and nothing human could be simpler than his duties. Three times a day he set before the gang a great bowl of steaming rice, a dish of boiled fish or pork or fowl or small game, another dish of raw or cooked vegetables and a pot of tea, everything soft, or cut into small bits. Each man helped himself and afterward washed his bowl and chopsticks, so, all in all, housekeeping duties rested lightly on the cook.

In season the caterer to the Chinese mining camp caught fish from the river. Sometimes he purchased chickens from the local housewives, his insinuating, "You got roosi-tah? How mocchee? Ess-bit? preluding the exchange of seventy-five cents for a leggy superfluous rooster from the dooryard

flock. Also, he was a dependable market for rabbits and squirrels.

Digging and ditching and washing, fresh water was all around the miners all the day, but while a thirsty white man or Indian would scoop up a drink from the stream, a Chinaman never did. Near at hand every group had a big pot of tea and at intervals one of the little Mongolians would lay down his tool, splash over to the pot, pour off a thimbleful of the tannic infusion and trickle it luxuriously down his throat.

For more than thirty years the Joaquin at Millerton staged the colorless, uneventful, plodding lives of Chinese miners. It was not the changing of the county seat or the abandonment of the pioneer settlement that finally brushed them off the scene. The time came when there was no more gold for even a Chinaman, and then the last pale little digging form disappeared from the bank of the historic river.

SOURCE: Ernestine Winchell columns.

61

at present engaged in this pursuit. The bed of the [San Joaquin] river here, in places, has proved very rich . . . [but] very little attention has been given to the development of the mines, from the fact, I presume, of it being a long way off from the conveniences of life. [A statement that must have rankled in the ears of Millertonians and mining camp residents alike.] Almost all mining operations heretofore have been confined to the bed of the river, and can only be prosecuted at a low stage of water."

The following decade proved similarly quiet where gold mining was concerned, although it did continue at all the usual places (see 4:7). No important discoveries were made, save for some rich placers located on Sycamore Creek during the 1861–62 winter. The gold was so pure that Millerton merchants gave $17.50 per ounce for it, and the area was soon jammed with miners. Lilbourne A. Winchell wrote that

Branch stores were established in the new district by the Millerton merchants; as well as drinking resorts. Steve Gaster and Jo's. [sic] B. Folsom of Millerton quickly installed these welcome institutions. [Ira] McCray started a stage line between the County seat and the new camps. Teamsters made regular trips to supply the increasing demands for supplies of all kinds. Pretentious centers of trade on the creek styled themselves Lashley City, Bannock No. 1 and Bannock No. 2. From the Doss flat to the mouth of this golden watercourse teemed with miners. Andrew Firebaugh [see Chapter 12] drove his cattle from Monterey County to a serviceable position in Watts' Valley and supplied the prodigal gold diggers with beef. Along the banks miners' tents and rough log cabins were thickly located.

Other than this strike, most mining excitement during the 1860s was focused on copper—not gold. Near Buchanan, now in Madera County, large deposits of copper were located; a mine, smelter and camp sprung up there, with Theodore Phillips as its superintendent. Charles Strivens operated a saloon there

and the Vignoli family a store. The place remained prosperous until the deposits began to play out, copper prices declined and freighting costs increased. This spelled doom for the Buchanan mine, which closed in August 1873, and eventually for others who had claims close by: Milton S. Latham's Baltimore Copper Mining Company, John M. Ault's General Grant Mine one mile northwest of Buchanan, Harry DeGroot's Green Mountain Copper Mine six miles from Buchanan, the Fresno Copper Mining Company (whose claim was discovered by John R. McCombs of Millerton and worked by Frank Dusy and others) and the Ne Plus Ultra Copper Mining Company.

The last-named enterprise, located near the Henry Clay Daulton ranch, was formed by Daulton, Dr. Lewis Leach, E. C. Winchell and John Greenup Simpson, along with other notable Fresno County residents. At one time its ore was hauled out to San Francisco, shipped from there to Swansea, Wales, and smelted, but the problems of declining prices and increasing costs brought that cycle of production to an end eventually. The May 2, 1877, *Fresno Weekly Expositor* mentioned that the mine was experimenting with a "lixivating" process: "Old iron ore is thrown [into tanks]. A continuous stream of water passes through the tanks. The decomposed ore is thrown into the water, and the copper is taken up in solution. When the water comes into contact with the iron it . . . disappears, and in its place pure copper reappears . . . The Company have on hand 5,000 or 6,000 tons of ore that can be worked to advantage by this method."

Ferry foundings were rare by now, since the mines had died down, the county's agricultural potential remained untapped and few people were gravitating toward central California. One inaugurated during this time, according to Paul A. Vandor, was "Van Valer's," five miles above Kingston on the Kings River. The owner may have been Peter Van Valer, an area stockraiser. Thomas H. Thompson's 1891 Fresno County atlas indicates a "Van Valer" property on the Kings' south side, near the location given. The ferry,

Reference 4:7

## THE GOLD DUST RATES OF 1865

NOTICE.

On and after the 1st day of March, 1865, we, the undersigned, pledge ourselves to receive and pay out GOLD DUST at the following rates only:

San Joaquin River or Bar dust, where it is not mixed with other dust, at $15.50 per ounce.

Fine Gold Gulch, Cottonwood, Long Gulch, and all taken out in small gulches between the San Joaquin and Fresno rivers, (except Coarse Gold Gulch) at $14 per ounce.

Coarse Gold Gulch dust at $16.50.

Big Dry Creek at $16.50.

Temperance Flat dust, and dust taken out at the head of Little Dry Creek, at $14.

Sycamore Creek dust, free from quicksilver and not mixed with other dust, at $17.50.

Fresno River dust, taken out below McKeown's store, at $15.50.

Fresno River dust, taken out above McKeown's store, at $— per ounce.

The above rates are as near as we can come at the value of the various kinds of dust in gold coin, and after this date we do not intend to receive or pay out anything that is not equal in value to United States gold or silver coin.

George Grierson & Co., J. R. Jones, Lewis Leach, James Urquhart, Ira McCray,

Wm. Faymonville, Wm. Fielding, S. W. Henry, Robert Abbott, C. F. Walker, T. A. Long, John White, Thomas Simpson, W. Krug, George S. Palmer, Clark Hoxie, S. J. Garrison, T. C. Stallo, W. S. Wyatt, S. Gaster, Henry Chambers, J. Lennebacker, George McCleland, J. R. Barkley, Henry Henriel, Charles A. Hart, Tong Sing, Hop Wo, Daniel Brannan, H. W. Clark, D. H. Miller, C. P. Converse, L. M. Matthews, C. G. Sayle, Ira Stroud.

Millerton, March 1st, 1865.

SOURCE: *Fresno Times*, March 8, 1865.

apparently, was on a local road and used to serve local residents, thus never gaining any great historical significance.

On the San Joaquin River, near where Highway 99 now crosses the river, another ferry was established in 1869. Charles Eldon Lewis Strivens was its operator; the enterprise lasted for only a few years, since the Central Pacific Railroad bridged this point when it arrived in 1872. There the railroad established a small community and station, Sycamore, concerning which little can be found in historical sources.

When a post office was established at Sycamore on January 14, 1887, its name was officially changed to Herndon—still applied to the general area, and the lengthy avenue that runs through it. According to Ben Randal Walker, the Herndon dubbing was to honor "a relative of a local irrigation promoter." The change was not popular locally, for some maps continued to show the town of Sycamore. It should not be confused with Sycamore Bend or Point, located nine miles downsteam and generally considered the early head of river navigation (see Chapter 12).

Though the ferries were going out of style, the stage routes in eastern Fresno County were staying active. Hice's Visalia-Hornitos stage was usually busy, and its accommodations were said to rival the Butterfield's. Amos O. Thoms quit as Hice's agent in December 1860, and Hice formed a new partnership with a Stockton stage agent, John Wilson. When the Butterfield stages stopped running in 1861—due to the Civil War's disruption of traffic and Indian attacks farther east—Hice and Wilson absorbed some additional trade and were prospering. The torrential rains of the 1862 winter, however, washed out their barn at Millerton, and the flooded valley plains cut into the number of runs. By May 1862 their company had lost its contract to carry mail and was out of business.

To take up the slack, Thoms and another Stockton stage agent, A. N. Fisher, formed new companies to ply the Visalia-Hornitos circuit. Thoms sold his company to Israel W. Davis, circa 1866. The lower detour of the Stockton-Los Angeles road came into increasing use during this time. Millerton was declining and few passengers had reason to stop at that crude, rude hamlet.

Patrick Bennett and Russell Fleming started another Visalia-Hornitos stage company, presumably replacing the Davis concern, in 1868. They managed to secure the lucrative mail contract, running eight-passenger stages three times a week, and cleared an average of $15,000 each year. By installing two relay stations and keeping twenty-two horses that could be switched at those points, travel was kept as efficient as possible. One of the stations was at Centerville, the other was a large shed east of Smith's Ferry. The ferry itself could have been used as the station but Fleming disliked its then-proprietor, Claybourne Wright.

Fleming and Charles DeLong, well-known in Millerton and, later, Fresno, usually served as drivers on this route.

Disagreements with postal authorities caused Bennett and Fleming to lose their mail contract to Lemuel H. Silman in 1870. Silman's lines ran from Tuolumne City in the north and down the San Joaquin Valley's eastern fringe to Millerton. Some time later, Silman went into partnership with one Carter and started a regular Stockton-Visalia run, "[stocking] the road with good teams and comfortable stages," according to Wallace W. Elliott. For some reason Millerton residents disliked the service, calling it "an outrageous humbug," and rejoiced when Bennett re-entered the business, serving all or part of the Visalia-Hornitos run, in late 1871. By the next year stages were running regularly from Millerton to Visalia and Merced, three times a week to each place.

After Butterfield's discontinuance of its southern route in 1861, when it shifted to using a more central road across the continent, Thoms stepped in and revived it, in part, in June 1863. He founded the Telegraph Stage Company and began running teams from Gilroy to Visalia, through Fresno County's west side and all the familiar stage stops there. The company was well-patronized and eventually extended its service as far as the Havilah mining camp in Kern County. Thoms always used the Butterfield route, unless the west side plains were muddy, flooded or otherwise impassable. Whenever these conditions existed, he took the Stockton-Los Angeles road to Smith's Ferry and cut across the central prairie in a northwesterly, drier direction to reach Firebaugh. In April 1871 Thoms sold the Telegraph Company to Henry M. Newhall and several other San Francisco investors. It continued to operate until the Central Pacific Railroad made it obsolete in 1872.

Until now, no Fresno County history has described the mining activities of the 1870-1900 period. This is unfortunate, for mining did not cease after agriculture became the county's lifeblood, and several miniature gold rushes did take place in that era. Information for these years is sketchy, but can be assembled from state mineralogist's reports, special mining publications and newspaper accounts. A comprehensive survey follows, broken down by individual mining districts. The discussion is limited to mines found within present-day Fresno County, and is not concerned with gold-producing areas of the county now in Madera County. Camps and regions that fall into that classification have been taken up before only because they were linked to the overall development of the southernmost gold mines.

Chinese continued to work the San Joaquin River, in spite of the hard work and poor pay. An 1878 summer newspaper item said: "The San Joaquin River is falling rapidly and is now fordable at many points.

63

About 300 Chinamen are scattered along both banks of the river for a distance of thirty miles, beginning about five miles below Millerton and extending up into the mountains, and are washing the sand along each bank in rockers just as fast as the waters recede. By careful inquiry among them they are found to gather from $1.50 to $2.50 a day each [not a considerable increase from 1857—see the previous section on Chinese miners], and this will continue until the water rises next winter—and each succeeding rise deposits a new supply of gold." Twenty years later, Charles A. Hart hired a Chinese crew to pick gold out of the San Joaquin sand and gravel. As the above excerpt suggests, they had moderate luck.

Temperance Flat on the San Joaquin, one of the oldest mining neighborhoods, was the scene of sporadic activity. The Martin/Sullivan mine continued producing in 1888, along with the Rattlesnake Mine two miles to its southwest and a surface claim owned by D. D. Jackson. Earning thirty-three dollars and twelve dollars per ton of ore, respectively, the Martin/ Sullivan and Rattlesnake properties were not as profitable as the nearby Bonanza Mine, opened circa 1890. Owned by H. Sherwood and A. B. Chambers, and operated by twelve to fifteen men, "all assays so far made have exceeded $55 [a ton]," said the January 1, 1891, *Fresno Daily Evening Expositor*. "Some 600 feet of tunnels have been made, and . . . the latest improved pumping and hoisting machinery has been put in place . . ." Later, in 1892, Sherwood and Chambers formed a Temperance Flat Mining and Milling Company to further develop their property, assisted with the funds of some San Francisco investors. Subsequent reports say nothing of this venture, which may have been ill-fated.

Other Temperance Flat mining properties worked during the early 1890s included the Trenton and Greenhorn mines, which took gravel from around Table Mountain and crushed it manually. "At the present writing two tunnels are being driven in the mountain 150 feet below the cap," said the May 23, 1891, *Fresno Daily Evening Expositor*, "both developing quantities sufficient to encourage the owners . . . to purchase a dry washing machine which will have a capacity of running through fifty tons of gravel per day."

The Auberry Valley, not far from Temperance Flat, boasted two excellent producers in the early 1890s. The James Harron mine, first located in the 1860s, was purchased by William Lewis, Lovely Witt and John C. Hoxie, who did little with it, and was sold in turn to Angus Marion Clark and William H. McKenzie of Fresno. The latter two partners enjoyed good fortune with the property. "In our drifting and sloping we have all along found free gold, giving from $75 to $400, and in some instances $500 a ton," said Clark in the June 25, 1890, *Fresno Daily Evening Expositor*. Before long

twenty-five men were employed at the property and a rock crusher there was operating twelve hours a day. Unfortunately, the assay range began to drop (from $95 to $45 a ton), ownership changes and suspensions resulted as output declined, and work appears to have stopped altogether after 1895.

The Cavern and Hollingshead mine was similarly profitable. Opened circa 1891 in the Auberry Valley, it was purchased by the Knob Hill Gold Mining and Development Company in June 1896. For extraction costs of $2.50 a ton, it was yielding gold-bearing ore worth between $25 and $140 a ton. Capitalized at $500,000, the Knob Hill Company issued shares of twenty-four dollars each and owned two other local mines, the Knob Hill and Live Oak.

A spate of mines, gold and copper, opened in the Big Dry Creek district after 1870. Located roughly three miles south of Auberry Valley, the first important gold producers there were a claim owned by John McDowell in the late 1870s and the Confidence and Champion mines. The Confidence, started in 1874, was first owned by James F. Dodds and a group of other investors. Tunnels were blasted at the mine site and the debris was crushed with a five-stamp, water powered mill. Yields were a consistent, if unspectacular, $8.50 to $9.00 per ton of ore. Richard Montgomery Keyes and Francesco Jensen started the Champion, which tapped a richer lode initially. In 1876, $50 in gold per ton was being extracted. By 1883 this figure was $10 per ton; there were hints the mine's operations were to be extended then, and its work force increased from seven men, yet this does not seem to have happened.

Many Big Dry Creek mines began or expanded operations in the 1880s. Fresno County mining veteran David Bice James invented a five-stamp quartz mill and installed it at the Cartwright Mine on Keyes Creek, near Big Dry, in 1880. The Cartwright produced ore that varied greatly in quality—anywhere from $15 to $860 a ton. James' mill was replaced by a ten-stamp mill owned by Doak, Anderson and Company in 1883. Quite a few gold mines were operating that year: Frank Grohs' Centennial; the Harriet Jane, an extension of the Champion lode; the Helmine; the Thorn and Peterson; and Dilly's Great Western Mine. By 1890 the Monte Cristo, owned by the Peterson brothers, and Miss S. M. Jansen's Midnight Star had been added to this roster.

The area's copper development began in 1875, when James Barkley discovered the mineral on Copper King Mountain. Unable to finance the operation, he left the site unworked until Hugh R. Knepper opened a nearby vein, circa 1890. The claim was so profitable—fifteen to twenty dollars worth of *gold* came out of each ton of copper ore—that a Los Angeles concern, the Petroleum and Smelting Company, leased Knepper's claim in 1896 and began working the mine in earnest. Much equipment was installed, a village sprung up at the site, and excitement was running high. Then, problems began. Tractors were obtained to haul the ore out; they broke down county bridges and roads and scared local horse and mule teams, which had initially been used for such transport purposes.

A spendthrift named Daley managed the mine, plundered its treasury regularly, and ultimately forced the operation to shut down after $500,000 had been expended on it. According to Lilbourne A. Winchell, Daley "upon one occasion [at San Francisco's Palace Hotel] ordered in the grille, three canvas-back ducks broiled to his taste and when the platter was set before him, he [pressed] the juices from two of the birds as sauce for the third, upon the breast alone of which he deigned to dine."

Daley's mismanagement did not end the development of the Copper King. Work continued intermittently until 1918 with over 1,200 carloads of ore shipped during the later years. Between shifts one day a rumble was heard and a plume of dust fanned out from the mine as a general cave-in occurred below the 100-foot level. Fortunately there was no loss of life, but it ended hopes for continued operation.

Another copper mine in the vicinity, located three miles east of the Pollasky railroad, was worked in 1896 by W. M. Burton, Logan Beard and John Haskell. A claim had been filed on this property in the 1860s by John R. McCombs when he discovered copper indications within ten feet of the stage road from Millerton to Big Dry Creek. He never worked it but later a group which included Frank Dusy drove a long shaft into the vein. After a considerable expenditure it was abandoned, probably because of the same problems that faced other copper mines.

This claim, five miles north of Clovis near Copper Avenue, was later worked by the Fresno Copper Mining Company. Lilbourne A. Winchell described it as an "exploitation of credulous foreign stockholders." The effort required a great financial outlay for a building and heavy mining machinery which benefited only the operators "who drained the purses of the investors. Inevitably the crash came. Exposure of the frauds left the company bankrupt, with no hope of future gain."

Winchell's charges of fraud are too general if not actually overstated. Local workers and promoters were as much victims as investors were in both mines of an unfortunate geological formation—high grade ore was near the surface but quality declined at lower levels.

An unusual use was found for the mine shaft when the hoof and mouth disease decimated the livestock of California. The bodies of the animals were buried in the shaft.

Though Pine Ridge, up Tollhouse Road from the Big Dry Creek area, is mostly considered a logging region, it had several producing mines in 1897. The General Bell mine, renamed the Providence, was being worked by seven men under Logan Beard that year, and was yielding ten dollars in gold for every ton of ore. A. Mr. Wakefield also was said to be prospering with a placer claim he had on the Ridge.

Due northeast of Pine Ridge, on Stevenson Creek, placer mining was popular during the early 1890s. A November 11, 1891, *Fresno Daily Evening Expositor* report noted that George T. Lemon, an area miner, had ground-sluiced $1,200 worth of gold dust in three months, and that "the ground is easily worked and there is an absence of boulders and cement." Later information indicates that anywhere from ten to fifteen dollars worth of gold could be panned per man, per day. The 1891 article went on to indicate that the Indians, who also were panning in the area, had not forgotten their gold-diving skills of yesteryear:

> The river and creek beds are literally specked with float and flour gold, and the Indians wade and walk along the banks until they sight an exceptionally rich spot, when they dive down with a scoop or large pan and fill it with sand and gravel. Coming to the surface, they go ashore and pan out the results, sometimes securing 5 or 15 cents worth of dust at a dive. The process is very slow and wholly original with the Indians, and they devote very few days to the search. They sell the dust to the storekeepers and obtain supplies of food in return. [As they did in 1852.]

East and southeast of Pine Ridge and Stevenson Creek, the Dinkey, Bear and Laurel creeks enjoyed a small gold rush in 1896–97. "The small mountain settlements are almost depopulated, so great has been the attraction during the past few days," said the June 12, 1896, *Fresno Daily Evening Expositor*. This mini-rush was notable for the variety of mining methods being used. On Laurel Creek, Jim Bridges was using hydraulic spraying tools to dislodge the gold; on the same creek, Logan Beard and some other men were using an arrastra to crush ore, and were obtaining sixty dollars of gold per ton; and Louis Rabidou, William Wakefield, E. F. Russell, F. R. Smith and M. T. Russell were making between seventeen and twenty dollars per day from simple placer mining.

The next year saw much activity as well, with miners pouring in from Selma, Sanger, the Auberry Valley and Big Dry Creek. Lumberman Charles S. Pierce and county supervisor Alex Smith commenced massive sluicing operations on Laurel Creek. "This is not a surface digging, as the pay gravel and dirt are very deep," said the August 17, 1897, *Fresno Daily Evening Expositor*. If Shaver and Smith were going to such lengths, the expected yield must have been considerable.

Closer to the foothills, gold deposits in Watts Valley attracted some attention in January 1898. Dr. S. L. Chapman, M. W. Parker and A. M. Highrabedian

65

staked two claims there, the Flock and '98, and felt optimistic about them. "The Watts Valley placers have been worked over several times and a great deal of gold taken out," said Chapman. ". . . We are satisfied that fine gold permeates the whole [Flock] ledge." Just what success the men had is unknown. Their hopes were probably inflated, since Watts Valley has never been renowned for its gold potential.

Sycamore Creek, as noted before, was a far more productive area. Almost due east of Watts Valley, activity there was fairly constant down to the century's turn. W. A. Clark, Asberry Wills and Frank Humphrey made a respectable discovery there in May 1880, locating a lead on Sycamore Mountain. "The ore is nearly decomposed, and can be taken out rapidly," said Clark in the May 26 *Fresno Weekly Expositor*. "It is a buried beauty unveiled . . . We have returns from six assays made in San Francisco, which give an average of $68 per ton in gold. 'How is that for high.'" The following July 21, an *Expositor* report said that the lead had been excavated to twenty-five feet and was continuing to increase in width and richness.

Also in that area was the Providence, located in 1883 and the district's sole mine in 1888. It was well-equipped; five years after its founding a ten-ton stamp mill, a sixty-horsepower engine and twenty-horsepower hoisting engine were on its property. Yields were average, in the twenty-two-dollar-per-ton range. In 1889 or thereabouts, the nearby Eliza Jane mine was worked first by V. Moore, producing anywhere from six to thirty dollars per ton of ore. After several decades of intermittent work, the mine yielded $100,000.

The Contact Mine, which lay close to Sycamore Creek, was opened in 1890 and found to be moderately rich. It was first worked with an arrastra, and its output was usually $21.25 per ton or ore, which contained some silver as well. A Hancock mine was said to be operating in this general area during 1896, equipped with a water-powered mill for crushing ore. Nothing else is known of it, though it was said to be a rich claim.

Trimmer Springs, close to the Sycamore District and today on the north side of the Pine Flat Reservoir, experienced some gold excitement in 1897-98. In the former year Dr. B. R. Clow, E. D. Jones of Tulare and J. B. Clark of Lemoore developed the Black Jack mine near there (apparently not the same Black Jack mine located eight miles north of Dunlap). Joseph Diaz began developing his Good Luck mine, also in the vicinity, at the same time. The mines were, respectively, thought to have ore that would produce $5.21 and $8.00 of gold per ton, and last for fifty years if worked with a 100-stamp mill.

By June 1898 fifty treasure seekers were prospecting around Trimmer Springs. Selmans Egbert H. Tucker, D. S. Snodgrass, J. B. Sturgess, T. J. Montgomery and others had staked claims in the area. As in many instances before, no major strikes seem to have been made there, or the standard historical references are silent about them. A. B. Smith was quoted in the June 1 *Fresno Morning Republican* as saying, "The surface indications . . . do not warrant the belief that anything more than a pocket has been discovered." Another Selman, T. R. Brewer, said he "would not give $20 for the whole gold output of the district."

The Mill Creek and Sampson Flat districts, lying approximately ten miles to the southeast of Trimmer Springs, were first worked circa 1880. A correspondent writing in the July 7 *Fresno Weekly Expositor* of that year said three mines in that area were in production— Ed Rape's Shoot-the-cat, the Monitor and the Oro Fino. The last two enterprises were equipped with arrastras, and the Monitor company wanted to build three more after a wagon road to the Kings River was completed. Another gold-bearing ledge had been discovered, and christened in the *Expositor*'s honor, and the only notes on productivity were that Rape's claim was paying six to eight dollars per ton, and "the [other] parties not wishing the result made public, I can only say they are making money." The State Mineralogist's Report for 1888 suggests that the Oro Fino, and probably the Monitor, were making similar amounts.

Sometime around 1888 the Sampson, White Cross and Davis Flat mines opened in the neighborhood. Quartz ore was mined at the Sampson, crushed in a device called a Kendall mill, and thereafter screened for gold. The Davis Flat mine used an arrastra and eventually milled 400–500 tons of ore, for a total yield worth $4,800–$6,000. In later years a five-stamp mill replaced the arrastra. Located only one mile northwest from Dunlap, the White Cross was probably the best mine in the region. According to the 1916 State Mineralogist's Report, "The former operators packed ore down by burros and sleds to the creek below (one summer about 1894) and put it through a 1-stamp mill, recovering $15,000."

Not far from the White Cross, another type of mining was taking place in 1888; there were two sizable limestone deposits and two lime kilns. The owner of this operation is unknown. In time it shut down, probably because convenient rail transportation was unavailable.

The sole mining district left for consideration is an ill-defined one—the Kings River's upper reaches. One of its canyons had a producing copper mine in 1891-93, whose ore was assayed at between 13 and 45 percent copper. The Fisk Mine, in present-day Kings Canyon National Park (see 4:8), continued operations far into the twentieth century.

Now that the moderate to fair mining successes of these later years have been chronicled, a backward look at two somewhat humorous failures will round out this chapter. Paul A. Vandor gives a good description of both:

Above Pollasky on the river bank, lay corroding, for some twenty years, a huge, iron-riveted, boiler-like, bottle-shaped structure, all that is left to recall another enterprise to take gold out of the shifting bed of the river. The boiler was the invention of a local genius, Peter Donahoo [circa 1898]. It was to be set upright in the water, sand and gravel pumped out to be worked over for the gold, [the] boiler sinking deeper to bedrock as the pumping proceeded. Ingenious, but a failure, and good money was sunk.

Then there was [in 1896 and following years] the magnificent scheme of the Ohio Mining Company. It swallowed up $200,000 of eastern money and was exploited by [Captain Frank Barrett of Selma, Truman G. Hart of Fresno and several others]. Where Fine Gold Creek, once a rich placer, joins the San Joaquin a whirlpool is formed. If the creek was once so rich, why should not be the deep hole at the confluence of the streams? Capital was interested in the showing of a diver, who had brought up from the bottom of the whirlpool a pan of gravel which showed up twelve dollars of gold. A dam was built above the whirlpool and the banks cut into to divert the creek water—a laborious and costly undertaking. The rush waters of two winter floods carried away ditch and dam. A third season and the hole was pumped dry. The first panful showed up about eighty cents worth of gold. Another fiasco was recorded.

The Ohio tried another plan later with local capitalists interested to the tune of many thousands to sluice gold out of the river bank, four miles above Cassady's [sic] bar. A costly pumping plant was erected, and when all was ready to hydraulic away the bank, discovery of a fatal error was made. The power plant had been so placed that the gravel washings worked in on the pumping apparatus and placed it out of commission. Disgusted with the outcome and doubtful of its ultimate successful operation, the Ohio marked another failure.

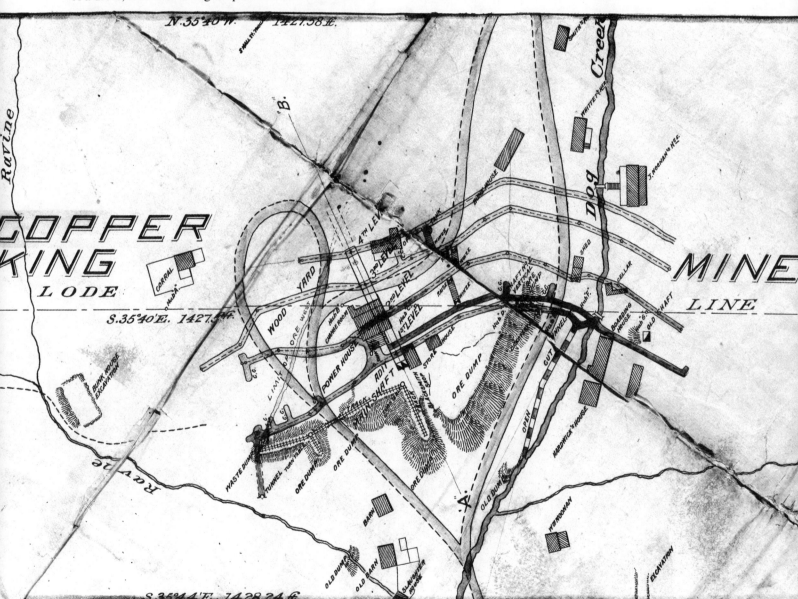

A map of October 25, 1899, reveals a Copper King Mine considerably larger than most people realize. The four levels were at 100-foot intervals and the map shows extensive tunneling at all levels. Nearby claims including Sunset, Fairview, Wabash, Amazon, Champion, Eastern Star and Dawn are shown on the complete map, which was compiled from official records and surveys of George Sandow, surveyor of the United States Department of Mines. This rare map was loaned by John B. Weldon.

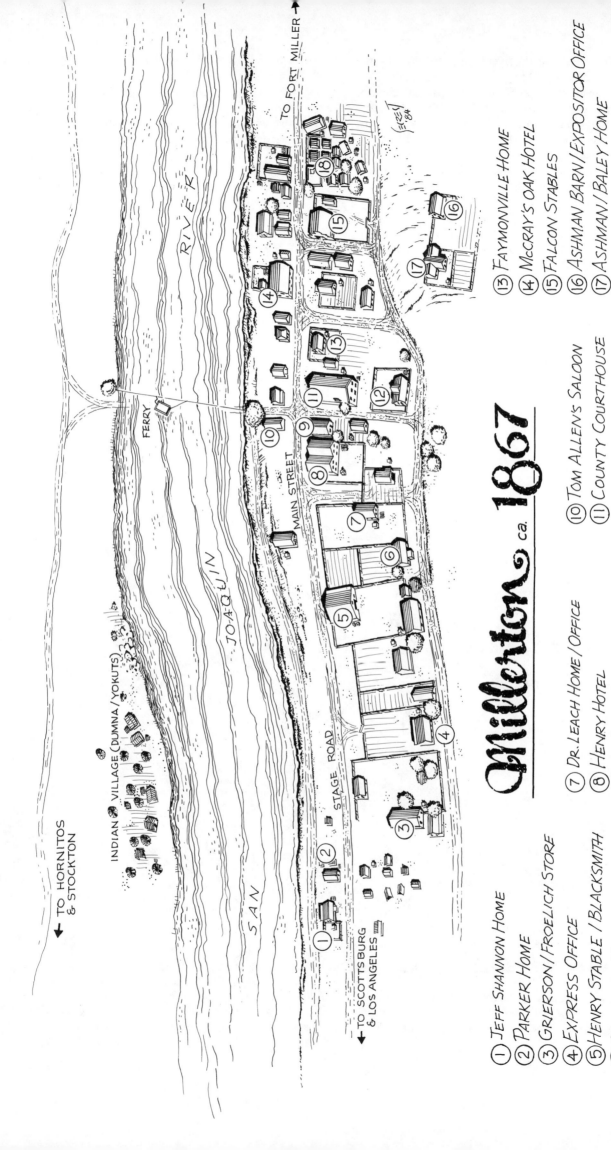

# Millerton ca. 1867

1. Jeff Shannon Home
2. Parker Home
3. Grierson / Froelich Store
4. Express Office
5. Henry Stable / Blacksmith
6. Converse Home

7. Dr. Leach Home / Office
8. Henry Hotel
9. Payne's Saloon

10. Tom Allen's Saloon
11. County Courthouse
12. County Hospital

13. Faymonville Home
14. McCray's Oak Hotel
15. Falcon Stables
16. Ashman Barn / Expositor Office
17. Ashman / Baley Home
18. Chinatown

→ TO HORNITOS & STOCKTON

SAN JOAQUIN RIVER

INDIAN VILLAGE (DUMNA / YOKUTS)

FERRY

TO FORT MILLER →

MAIN STREET

STAGE ROAD

→ TO SCOTTSBURG & LOS ANGELES

# Chapter 5
# The Fort Miller-Millerton Era

The close of the Mariposa Indian War (see Chapter 2) had brought fear to the upper San Joaquin River country. Federal Indian commissioners had concluded a peace treaty, and most of the hostile natives were being herded to the white-supervised Fresno River Indian Reservation, but no one was convinced that that ended the threat of another uprising. The local Indian population probably outnumbered the white four to one, which must have made the miners, store-keepers and ferrymen anxious. A sudden outbreak could have been equivalent to annihilation.

Major General Persifer F. Smith, head of the United States Army's Department of the Pacific at Sonoma, knew the situation could not be tolerated. On March 28, 1851, he wrote a letter to Captain Erasmus Darwin Keyes and ordered him to search for a fort site near the Fresno reservation. Keyes, then traveling with some army units accompanying the Indian commissioners, scouted the territory for a month or so.

He reported his final choice in a letter to the acting adjutant general of California on May 1, 1851: "It is situated on what is called Larione's Ferry on the San Joaquin [River] about 150 miles from Stockton, & about 8 miles above Casserdy's [sic] ferry at the crossing of the main road from Stockton to Rio Los Reyes [the Kings River]. It is easily accessible at all seasons, except when the roads in the San Joaquin Valley are ruined by the rains, and as healthy as any place in California. It is also a central position and can be reached from all points of the Reservation with a trifling out lay of labor."

Later in the month, Keyes felt encouraged to act on his selection. He penned the following letter to Indian Commissioner George W. Barbour on the 21st:

Sir: In accordance with the conversations which I have had the honor to hold with you upon the apparent necessity of having a military force situated on this [Fresno River Indian] reservation, and in the neighborhood of the San Joaquin River; and in view of the fact, also discussed with you, that we may safely pass over the country south of this river [the Kings]

with a smaller force; I have given orders to divide the escort so as to send companies B and K, 2nd Infantry, under Lt. [Tredwell] Moore, to establish a post on the site of camp Barbour, and to retain with you companies M and F, 3rd Artillery, with supplies for at least fifty days from the time of leaving this camp. To this arrangement I have already received your verbal approval, and you will oblige me with communicating it to me in writing for the information of the commanding officer of the department [of the Pacific].

As Lieutenant Moore will receive instructions to maintain the treaties with the Indians on this reservation, will you be pleased to furnish copies of those treaties for his guidance.

I am, sir, very respectfully, your most obedient servant,

E. D. KEYES,
Captain, 3d Artillery commanding Escort.

This letter represents, more or less, the birth certificate of Fort Miller—founded on May 26, 1851. Moore named the outpost, in what some said was unabashed admiration, for Major Albert S. Miller. Commander at the army station at Benicia, Solano County, and a veteran of the Black Hawk, Seminole and Mexican wars, Miller had crowded a distinguished military career into only a few years of service. He died, while still serving at Benicia, on December 7, 1852, at the comparatively young age of forty-nine.

Making Fort Miller operational was no easy task for Moore and his men. There was the matter of building the place (see 5:1), and frequent forays against local Indians were necessary (see Chapter 2). The location, contradictory to Keyes' judgment, was equally problematical and practical. Situated above the river's navigable portion, at a point where its channel was wide, the men were safe from attackers arriving by water and any flooding. For recreational or military purposes, there was easy access to the local mining camps as well. Unfortunately, grass for horses and stock animals was scarce there in dry seasons—and, since the fort was crowded close by surrounding foothills, it turned into an oven during the summer.

"[The] direct and reflected rays of the sun made it [Fort Miller] the hottest midday station on the coast," wrote William F. Edgar, the fort's first physician, in a reminiscence many years later. " . . . In June, 1852 . . . I had some curiosity to ascertain the difference in temperature between the air and the snow-melted water of the river. I took [a] thermometer from where it had been exposed a few minutes in the open air to the sun, and [when] it marked 123°, dipped its bulb into the river water, and it fell to 45°—a difference of 78°."

A small commercial community sprang up around Fort Miller shortly after its founding. The first to open a store there, according to David Bice James, was Major Lane—partner of Wiley B. Cassity in the Fort Washington enterprise downstream (see Chapter 4). Four other businessmen followed in quick succession. A character named "Big-Foot Miller" started a saloon, which shut down whenever the available whiskey flow dried up. Hugh Carlin initiated a trading post popular with whites and Indians alike; he did not use false weights to give local Indians less money for the gold they brought in, a common practice of the times (see Chapter 2). Two merchants named Moore and Boatwright had a store operating in 1851; and after freighting supplies in from Stockton, Robert ("Mike") Fagan opened another.

Fagan may have taken over the "Larione's Ferry" mentioned in Keyes' correspondence. On April 9, 1852, T. H. Wade presented the Mariposa County Board of Supervisors with a petition from Fagan, asking for a year-long ferry license. The ferry was said to be situated at Fort Miller, and the license was to run retroactively from the previous March 1. The supervisors immediately granted Fagan's request, and set rates for his ferry—and one operated downstream by Walter Harvey and Francis M. Davenport (see Chapter 4)—on June 11. A man and horse, a pack animal, and each yoke and span of livestock greater than two crossed for one dollar. Footmen were charged fifty cents, as was each wagon wheel. Other charges may have been negotiable. A few years later, the ferry near Millerton arbitrarily charged two cents to transport a sheep and set a $480 receipt record when 24,000 crossed in one day!

Dr. Lewis Leach and his partners, who operated the Fresno River's major trading post (see Chapter 4), opened a Fort Miller branch store in 1852 and placed it under the supervision of Ned Hart. Only one more store was started in the vicinity—George Grierson's, in 1856—and it folded the next year, when the fort was deactivated. Grierson's venture is puzzling, because military activity had been winding down when he opened his doors—and nearby Millerton had developed a good complement of stores, saloons and miscellaneous services for the soldiers, causing the decline in commercial activities closer to the fort.

A retrospective look at Fort Miller is always incomplete, because no rank-and-file soldier or lesser officer

Reference 5:1

## FORT MILLER—A MEMORY OF THE SAN JOAQUIN
### HELEN S. GIFFEN

The fort was situated on one of the widest reaches of the San Joaquin River, well above flood line. . . . A quadrangle was surveyed 350 feet east and west and 200 feet north and south, providing for buildings on three sides. Under Lieutenant Moore's supervision the fort began to take shape. Doors, windows, lime, shingles, kegs of powder, cannon balls, two howitzers and food supplies were hauled by wagon to a point opposite the fort on the river, and then ferried across. The block house, which has frequently been confused with a similar structure at Camp Barbour, was the first building erected. Its location was about seventy-five feet outside the compound, and it was built of logs dove-tailed together, with loopholes set at the height a man could hold a rifle. This building stood until the demolition of the fort structures to make way for Friant Dam and Lake Millerton.

The south side of the quadrangle accommodated three buildings, the one on the southeast corner being sixty-six by thirty feet with an "L" which contained the kitchen and mess hall. This also provided quarters for the officers. In the rear of this adobe was a garden which boasted the first orange trees planted in the San Joaquin Valley south of Stockton. Adjoining this building on the west was another adobe forty feet square, and next to it a small residence. To the west was a building one hundred forty feet long and twenty feet wide, built of stone and adobe. This contained six rooms and was occupied by the quartermaster, the sutler, the commissary, and two married soldiers—James McKenzie and Hugh Carroll.

To the north were the barracks, half adobe, half hewn timbers, and to the southeast the guardhouse of logs, thirty feet long and fourteen feet wide, with three rooms, two of which were cells, with heavy doors of split pine fastened by iron hinges and heavy hasps. The west line of the quadrangle was protected by a five-foot wall capped with stone. This wall ran from the southwest to the northwest corners of the quadrangle, then east to the barracks. The open line to the southeast was also protected by this enclosure, which extended to the rear of the three buildings on the south. There was a wagon gate in the west wall, and two smaller gates for pedestrians, one to the west opened on the path to Millerton, and one to the east that led to the gulch in the direction of Cassady's Bar. East of the barracks was the water gate which admitted the barrel wagon, since all water was hauled from the river.

On the rise of ground southeast of the fort enclosure was the hospital, which was completed in 1853. This had three rooms, the larger ones were used for wards, and the smaller, for the apothecary shop. A granite wall supported the terrace to the north; and a brick and stone bakery stood a short distance to the east from the infirmary, while the blacksmith shop was just below, on level ground.

The plaza, or parade ground, formed by the walled quadrangle, boasted two fine specimens of white oak, one in the center and one to the extreme west. Legend has it that one of these was used as the whipping post. It is known that flogging was not uncommon as a disciplinary measure in the army at that time, however it was usual to tie the culprit to a stack of arms rather than to a post. The flagpole occupied the center on the west wall, from which the flag fluttered in whatever breeze found its way into this small and well-protected valley. The post had the reputation of being a fine winter resort, but nothing short of an inferno in the summer.

SOURCE: *Journal of the West*, April 1963.

70

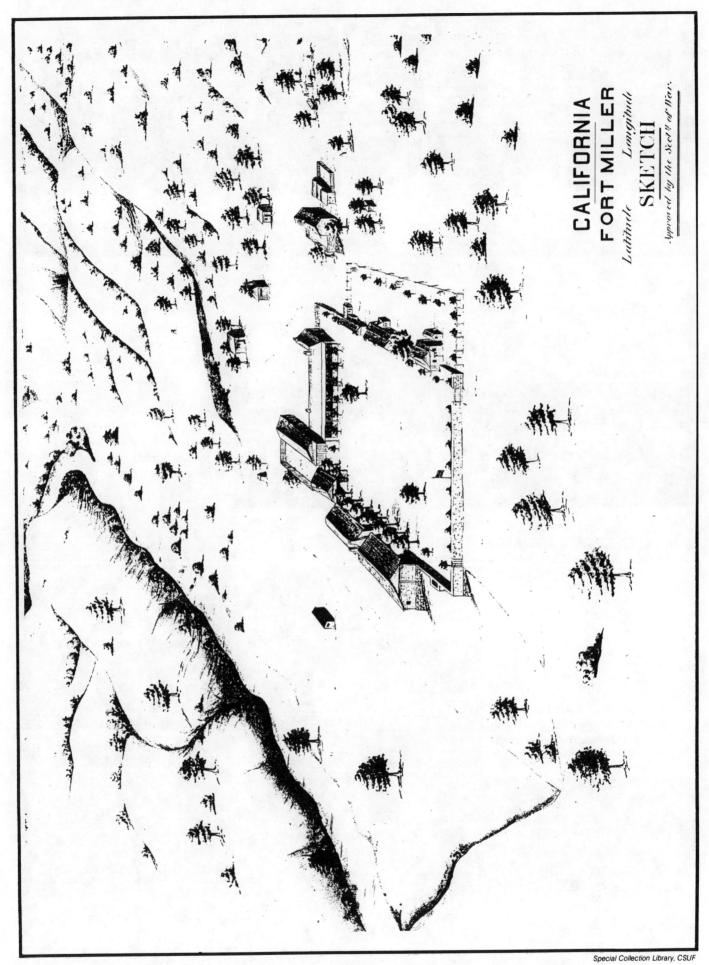

CALIFORNIA
FORT MILLER
Latitude    Longitude
SKETCH
Approved by the Sec'y of War.

*A sketch of Fort Miller done by an enlisted man in the early 1850s is believed to depict the fort dependably as well as clearly.*

*The old Block House of Fort Miller, erected without nails in 1851.*

*Fort Miller buildings looking east from parade grounds. Date of picture not known.*

*Army hospital which later housed the first public school of Fresno County.*

*Fort Miller as it appeared in an engraving in the 1882 History of Fresno. It was then part of the Judge Hart ranch.*

left reminiscences behind to describe the average man's life on the base. This is unfortunate, for several of them—Hugh A. Carroll, James McKenzie, William J. Lawrenson, Dave Brannon and Jack White—became prominent Fresno County citizens and could have been interviewed by an alert historian of yesteryear. Fortunately, descriptions of the fort by visitors and miscellaneous other sources give some insight.

"At the fort everything went on swimmingly, the men were a good lot of boys, and the officers were gentlemen," wrote William Faymonville in his 1878 *Reminiscences of Fresno County*. He obviously was not taking into account the expeditions against, and mistreatment of, Indians by soldiers; but the description was probably correct otherwise. When off-duty the men could go hunting for whatever suited their appetites—berries, salmon, deer, elk, antelope, or liquor at a nearby saloon. For those seeking other recreation, there was Theodore C. Stallo's nearby "Sebastopol" brothel.

Though there is no direct evidence, there is little doubt that those who indulged too freely, in spirits or women, were punished for their behavior. Most of the time, they were thrown into the fort's guardhouse or flogged on one of the white oak trees inside the outpost's central quadrangle. Others were condemned to a quieter type of suffering, as Assistant Fort Surgeon William J. L'Engle reported on March 9, 1857:

> ...I have to report the existence and continued prevalence of "Venereal diseases" among the enlisted men of this command to an extent likely to prove extremely prejudicial to its strength and efficiency. A reference to my daily morning reports and monthly reports of sick would discover a seeming discrepancy between those reports and this. I have to state in explanation that there exists an unwillingness on the part of the men to be placed on the sick report when they become the subjects of this disease, hence all of the cases are not reported. It has become within my knowledge that both non-commissioned officers and privates have become the subjects of primary disease the initial symptoms of which being slight and soon subsiding by self instituted local treatment [?] they have not reported themselves and secondary accidents with all their direful effects have been the result—than which no disease makes greater inroads upon the constitution or more permanently impairs the general efficiency of the man.

An enjoyable pastime, and one which helped supplement the soldiers' pay, was gold mining. The San Joaquin River's banks were always good for a few extra dollars, but the deep sands and crevices in its channel were said to contain even more of the precious metal. An officer at the fort, Captain Thomas Jordan, became aware of this and sought to exploit the situation. "He was shrewd, cunning and crafty, and always kept his weather-eye open for the main chance—in fact, he was for Jordan, first, last and all the time," wrote Faymonville.

Jordan decided to divert the river at Soldiers' Bar, a quarter-mile above the fort, convey it by canal to a quarter-mile below Millerton, and there allow the bed in-between to be worked—as with the Jenny Lind claim (see Chapter 4). He pulled together a capital stock company and soon obtained $150,000 in subscriptions for it.

Miners and military men began converging on the site, some of them working with their own equipment and hauling teams for a share of the hoped-for profits. The plan was slowly accomplished during the 1853-55 period, with a brush-and-earth dam and a twenty-foot-wide canal being constructed. When the work was finished, all anxiously awaited the first prospecting results. They were a bust. No riches had ever lain beneath that part of the San Joaquin; all the labor and invested capital had gone for nothing. Disappointment may have been widespread, but it had not been unexpected. Captain Edward Davis Townsend, an inspector from the army's Department of the Pacific, wrote the following on October 25, 1855:

> This morning I went down to see the mining operations on the San Joaquin. Captain Jordan, U.S.A., is building a dam across the River just above the Fort and expected to make a part of a fortune by selling water and washing gold. At the latter business, my experience would go to show he cannot realize much. The soldiers have their little claims on the river, and at their leisure they wash for gold using the common cradle. Some of the best miners among them make $40 to $60 a month, but that would never pay for the expensive works put up by Captain J. I rocked out eleven buckets-full of earth and made about eleven cents!

The brash captain was not discouraged by this initial failure. Though discredited and detested, Jordan managed to interest a few gullible people in a new mining venture. He believed that underneath nearby Table Mountain there was an old river channel full of clay, gravel and intermingled gold, ready for the taking. A crew of men began tunneling toward this supposed channel; then, early winter rains hit before any gold was reached. The tunnel caved in and, although apparently no lives were lost, picks, spades and wheelbarrows aplenty were swallowed by the earth. Had Jordan not retired from the mining business at this juncture, a local lynching party might well have gone after him.

The Table Mountain tunnel did not represent Jordan's final indignity. As the fort supply officer, he had to purchase hay from area farmers (see Chapter 6). One hay-raiser, John Newton, decided to pull a clever switch on the wily captain. Faymonville gives a reliable account of this incident:

Newton had foresight enough to see that a large quantity of hay and grain would be required during the coming Winter to feed all the animals kept at the fort. Jordan entered into a contract with Newton, agreeing to take all the hay Newton could furnish, at $50 per ton, Jordan to haul the hay to the fort himself. Some distance east of Jerry Brown's old place (now Hildreth's) there stands an immense rock; here Newton went to work in the Spring, cutting hay, and after having cut and cured about ten tons, he covered the rock with the hay, and, when completed, the pile presented the appearance of an immense hay-stack. Newton, Jordan and some of his men, went to inspect and measure the stack, which Jordan accepted at fifty tons. They then went back to the fort, where Newton obtained his money for fifty tons of hay, and decamped. Shortly afterwards Jordan ordered his teamsters to haul in that hay, but the first load that was taken off that pile laid bare the fraud and a portion of the rock. What Jordan said on discovering the swindle cannot be recorded here; suffice it to say that he did not pray with great devotion, but perhaps in a humiliated spirit; but there was no remedy, he had been beaten at his own game, and his bird had flown.

Fort Miller was shut down temporarily on September 10, 1856, after the Indian difficulties of that year had been successfully concluded (see Chapter 2). It was not to be fully reoccupied until 1863, for reasons that will be discussed later.

Before the fort closed, a few outsiders other than Townsend visited the area and left valuable recollec-tions of the outpost. William P. Parks, traveling with the Williamson survey expedition mentioned in Chapter 4, arrived in late July 1853 and made this intriguing statement: "During our stay at camp, Captain [Harry] Love at the head of a party of rangers arrived, bringing with him the head of the notorious robber chief, Joaquin Muerto [Murrieta; see Chapter 11]." The head was preserved at Fort Miller—by whom, and with what, is a matter of debate. William T. Henderson, one of Love's rangers, asserted that the previously-ly mentioned Dr. Edgar pickled the head in alcohol. Visalian Pasqual Bequette contradicted this account, claiming it was Dr. Lewis Leach who preserved that grisly trophy in whiskey—alcohol, for some odd reason, being unavailable. And yet another, Sam Bishop of Fort Bishop, said he ferried the rangers across the river on their way to Millerton and supplied whiskey to preserve a rapidly deteriorating head.

Two military officers arrived before Townsend to look over Fort Miller. The first, Colonel George A. McCall, visited in July 1852 and was aghast at conditions there: "[The post is]...shut out from a free circulation of air, as necessary to health in the interior vallies [sic] of California, where the heat is *extreme* during the summer months. And it possesses no advantage in a Military point of view to counter-balance this serious objection of unhealthiness, which the Medical Officer ascribes to the position of the Post." McCall said the fort should have been moved to an elevated point 600 to 800 yards away, and its key buildings

Reference 5:2

## REPORT ON FORT MILLER, JUNE 28–30, 1854

This post is at the foot of the Sierra Nevada Mountain and on the south bank of the San Joaquin River and well located for the present to overawe and restrain the Indians and protect the white settler, and should be retained some years. It is 286 miles from Los Angeles, and 160 from Benicia via Stockton on the San Joaquin River. To all these places there is a passable road for wagons except from Stockton to Benecia where there are good steamers. There is good grazing and abundance of wood and hay and some tillable land for a garden. The supplies must all come from San Francisco via Stockton except fresh beef and barley and flour. The Indians in this quarter number within 75 miles about 500 warriors who are under different local names and armed with bows and arrows, and are disposed to work for miners and others by the day, but do not wish to remove to the reservation. The American population at Millerton and this immediate vicinity may number 500, and this country is filling up with miners and the good lands being taken up. A post office should be established at Millerton where there is a ferry across the San Joaquin....

This post was established by 1t Lieutenant T. Moore, 2d Infantry, in 1851. Captain N. Lyon, 2d Infantry, assumed command 7h February, 1852. Brevet Major G. W. Patten, 2d Infantry, relieved Captain Lyon 17h July, 1852. Brevet Major H. W. Wessells, 2d Infantry, relieved Major Patten 21t May, 1853, and left the command to 2d Lieutenant T. Wright, 2d Infantry, 6h April, 1854, and 1t Lieutenant T. F. Castor, 1t Dragoons, assumed command 21t June, 1854, who with Company A, 1t Dragoons, was temporarily here expecting to move to establish a post at the Terjon [sic] Reservation.

Attached to this post is Assistant Surgeon John Campbell and Captain Thomas Jordon, assistant quartermaster.

The force consists of Company A, 1t Dragoons (Captain J. W. Gardner [Gardiner] absent sick and not at his company since promoted), 63 in the aggregate, commanded by 1t Lieutenant T. F. Castor, 2 sergeants, 2 corporals, one musician, 22 privates for duty, 6 rank and file sick, 7 rank and file on extra daily duty, one private in confinement, in all 42 present; ... 21 absent. Company G, 2d Infantry (Captain and Brevet Major H. W. Wessells on recruiting service 6h April, 1854), 35 in the aggregate, commanded by 2d Lieutenant Thomas Wright, who is also acting commissary of subsistence; 2d Lieutenant John Nugen, 4h Infantry, temporarily attached to this company; 2 sergeants, 4 corporals, 2 musicians, 11 privates for duty; 4 privates sick, 7 on extra daily duty, 2 in arrest; in all, 33 present. 1t Lieutenant G. H. Paige absent as regimental quartermaster. Thus shewing a total force of 75 in the aggregate for duty at this post.

The command as a whole was in a good state of discipline, but Company A was not instructed properly and they were mostly recruits and could not drill mounted, and had but a few horses. They marched indifferently and drilled as skirmishers and were armed with musketoon and sabre. There were but three pistols to this company. Their arms were in good and efficient order and the men in the old uniform.

The horses were old and generally worn out and but few (and here I regret I have omitted to note the exact number) and not properly shod. I condemned six California horses and one sore-backed American horse, and recommended they be turned into the Quartermaster's Department. The horse equipments such as bits, breastplates, and stirrup irons were dirty. Much allowance however should be made for the fact this company had recently marched from Bene-

replaced with adobe. Only the latter recommendation was followed, and only in part. Colonel Joseph King Fenno Mansfield, a Department of the Pacific inspector, as were McCall and Townsend, wrote a valuable report that recreates conditions at the fort (see 5:2).

Accompanying Townsend on his 1855 trip was the Right Reverend William Ingraham Kip, Episcopal bishop of California. He conducted one of the first religious services in Fresno County at Fort Miller, and wrote the following account of his visit:

> It [Fort Miller] was composed of some 20 houses most of them canvas. Two or three being shops and the majority of the rest drinking saloons and billiard rooms. The population was Mexican and the lowest class of whites and on this day they seemed to be given up entirely to dissipation.

He was also disappointed because there was no effort made to observe the Sabbath in the frontier town. When he mentioned this to military officials they quickly cleared a room and arranged for an evening service at which he officiated and baptized a child of one of the soldiers at the fort.

Fort Miller did not remain wholly unused during the 1856–63 period. Captain Edward Otho Cresap Ord commanded a reduced force there in 1858–59, taking command from Lieutenant LaRhett L. Livingston. In a letter written to his wife at Benicia, he described a somnolent military post and spoke of more recreational activities than military:

As for fare, I fare pretty well. Wyse [the fort cook] makes pretty good bread, tho' the flour is just as yellow as ever. Sometimes he gives me corn cakes and, for dinner, beefsteaks, greens and potatoes, turnips, and sometimes beans, with a cup of tea. I don't find, however, the same appetite here as in Benicia and on the Coast, either for food or for sleep. The nights are cool, though, and if I would get an early start, I think I could manage to obtain my natural rest of 11 hours[!] nightly.

I wish you were here now, darlin', for the green spring will soon be gone, the mild, quiet nights and cool, bracing mornings. The time to walk along the banks of the clear and rapid river. The trees, too, are all out and the mountain slopes, close around, are pleasant to the eye. Through an opening, only a few miles off, appears a slope of the Snowy Mountains..."

Later on, Theodore C. Stallo was placed in charge of the post, and had no objection to local families living in the deserted buildings. No record of occupants during this time was kept, and all may have lived there rent-free. Two families known to have resided at Fort Miller in 1859 were James McKenzie's (for some reason, he was not discharged and relieved from his assignment until that year) and Elisha Cotton Winchell's. The McKenzie family lived in the on-base adobe and the Winchells in the off-base hospital.

The hospital building served as the first schoolhouse for the Millerton School District, created on February 6, 1860. Winchell, a recent arrival from Missouri via

cia and had had but little time to clean up, and they were under orders for the Terjon [*sic*] Reservation. There were two laundresses to this company and the quarters were neat and comfortable altho' quite contracted.

Company G was in the old uniform with arms and equipments in good serviceable order, drilled well at infantry and as skirmishers, but the musicians were indifferent and wanted instruction. One laundress attached to this company, and the quarters were neat and comfortable although contracted.

The Medical Department was under the direction of Dr. Campbell. Hospital good, a small kitchen only wanted to complete the necessaries for the sick. The post healthy.

There is a good bakery and a magazine built of adobes, which answers a good purpose, and there are quarters sufficient for one company—all that is necessary here, and store houses of canvas, which of course are not suitable for the supplies. A good garden is had in a small valley about one-half mile off, where irrigation and suitable soil is found, and wood and grazing and hay abundant, within reasonable limits.

At this post are two 12-pounder field howitzers which require painting, but a limited supply of fixed ammunition for them, say 130 rounds, of all kinds. There is also about 18,600 ball cartridges at the post all told.

The Quartermaster's Department is under the charge of Captain Jordon, who was absent on duty. It is in good condition and the records and accounts well kept, and supplies as well stored as the buildings made of cloth would admit, but it is apparent that supplies are not safe in such buildings. There is, in the employ of the quartermaster, 17 citizens as follows: one clerk at 150 dollars per month; 2 carpenters, 150 dollars each per month and one ration; one smith at 150 dollars and one ration; one assistant forage master at 70 dollars and one ration; one acting wagon master at 100 dollars and one ration; 7 teamsters at 70 dollars and one ration; one herdsman and harness maker; two labourers at 75 dollars and one ration each; and one messenger, 20 dollars per month. Barley is had at 4 cents the pound and hay at 7 dollars the ton and hauled by the department. Other supplies [are] furnished thro' Stockton, 130 miles off over land, and it takes 12 days to make a trip with U.S. teams. The supplies are sent to Stockton by steamer and otherwise are there stored on an old U.S. vessel with a man in charge. The average quarterly expenditures in this department amount to about 9,000 dollars for the last four quarters. Captain

Jordon has at this time in his hands 7,642.46 dollars, which are deposited in the private banking house of Lucas Turner & Co. of San Francisco and not yet with the treasurer under recent regulations for reasons heretofore given in like cases.

The duty of commissary of subsistence is performed by 2d Lieutenant Thomas Wright. The supplies, generally good; the ration of coffee and sugar, too small; fresh meat, antelope and beef, the former at 12 to 15 cents and the latter 20 to 25 cents the pound, is had here: other supplies come from Benecia. No doubt a great reduction in prices will soon take place. The records and accounts are properly kept, and Lieutenant Wright has in his hands 553.46 dollars which is deposited with the assistant quartermaster for safe keeping. There is no post fund here.

The American population is so numerous within 100 miles in a northerly direction that any outbreak of Indians would be severely punished. In the mining towns there are uniform companies of militia, and every white man in this quarter is completely armed with a revolver and knife at least.

SOURCE: Robert W. Frazer, ed., *Mansfield on the Condition of the Western Forts, 1853–54*, pp. 150–53.

Sacramento, wrote the following in his diary on March 12: "After exhausting efforts to get a school house, I offered the use of my dining room and kitchen." The rooms were large, separated by what had been the surgeon's office and dispensary—"the apothecary shop"—and, by March 19, school was being held in the dining room.

Twelve students were taught at the school by Rebecca M. Baley, the seventeen-year-old daughter of Gillum and Permelia Baley. Emigrants from Missouri, the Baleys had arrived in January 1860 and were residing at the fort's commissary when their daughter got her job. Also living there was another Baley daughter, Katherine, and her husband, George Krug. Rebecca was paid fifty dollars a month for her services, with some incidental assistance given by Winchell's wife, Laura.

The first students at the Millerton District School were John C. Hoxie, Sewall F. Hoxie, Ellen Baley, Charles Baley, John Parker, Mary Parker, Jane Richards, Allen Stroud, Arza Stroud, Nevada Clark and her brother, and future county historian Lilbourne A. Winchell (the son of E. C. and Laura). When recounting the district's early history in 1927–28, the younger Winchell wrote: "From the expiration of the three months' school term in the Winchell home at Fort Miller, there was no other school [conducted] in the . . . district till the spring of 1864. This is attributable to lack of public funds, indifference of trustees, and want of available teachers competent to carry classes beyond the low primary grades. Furthermore, unattached young women were quickly snatched up by the forlorn bachelors [of Millerton] and became too busy as wives and mothers to engage otherwise."

As evidence of the last—Rebecca Baley and her sister Elizabeth shortly were wed to Jefferson Milam Shannon and J. Scott Ashman, respectively. Ernestine Winchell reported that this happy occasion went lacking in merriment. "It was the custom of the times on every possible occasion to tune up the fiddles, clear the floor, and dance all that night and into the next day. But Mr. Baley and his good wife, devoted church people, were horrified at the idea. There should positively be no dancing at a wedding of daughters of theirs, and the disappointed guests were obliged to content themselves with more decorous entertainment."

At the time of the Civil War, 1861–65, the Indian threat had subsided in the Fort Miller area, but a new one had arisen. Southern sympathizers, known as the "Knights of the Golden Circle," had organized in the Union-held states and territories, destroying property and inciting violence for the Confederate cause. A chapter had been formed in Fresno County. It met regularly at a quartz mine owned by Gillum Baley, near the Chowchilla River, and an arsenal was being built up there as well. To avoid creating suspicion,

members brought in small amounts of arms and ammunition at a time, and the stockpile grew. To complicate matters, local reports told of a man named Richard Cottrell (Deaf Dick) who paraded around Millerton yelling his support of the Confederacy and its president, Jeff Davis, at the top of his lungs. Knowledge of these incidents—along with the fact that 90 percent of the Fresno County Militia members were from the South—prompted the army to reoccupy Fort Miller.

A concerned Colonel James E. Olney, with Company A of the 2nd California Volunteers, trudged to Fort Miller in the summer of 1863, arriving on August 3. After the men crossed the Chowchilla River, near the dreaded Knights hideout, Olney ordered them to load their muskets because they were in enemy territory. "When he arrived at Millerton, with 'all the pomp and circumstance of glorious war,' he found that he had about as much use for soldiers there as he would have had in Kansas, or in Iowa," noted Faymonville.

The feared Deaf Dick was found to be a harmless town drunk. To be safe, the soldiers detained him and asked him to swear loyalty to the Union. Cottrell shouted even louder support for Jeff Davis. Hoping to break his will, the soldiers filled a sack with sand and made him carry it on his shoulders, up and down a nearby hill, one or two dozen times. Cottrell continued hollering about Jeff Davis, and another hour of punitive labor had no effect on his sympathies. The frustrated soldiers decided to release the diehard secessionist, and he appears to have caused them no further trouble.

Olney was soon joined by companies B, G and K from the infantry. No trouble erupted in Fresno County because the Knights and the Union League, the latter a boisterous group itching to make trouble, were kept apart by the army's watchful eye. Only one other instance of punished disloyalty during this period has been documented: "William Fielding, an Englishman, thought it would be a smart thing to resist Provost Marshal Van Valer, and refused to answer questions," wrote Faymonville. "He tried the experiment and was arrested and sent to the fort, and from thence to [military prison] Fort Alcatraz, where he was kept for several months to ruminate on his folly. He was finally released, came back to Millerton, and shortly afterwards went back to England, if not a wiser and a better, at any rate a madder man."

With their worries so minimal, Fort Miller's men had few serious duties. Tensions eased enough for Company G to be sent to Camp Babbitt at Visalia, another Union island in a sea of Confederate sympathy. When they were not engaged in cursory drilling, target practice or hauling wood, hay and water in from the outside, the soldiers built a new adobe officers' quarters and a granite-and-rock guardhouse, the latter never finished.

Discipline at Fort Miller became increasingly lax. "The Millerton groggeries [saloons] drew the idle soldiers as infallibly as a magnet draws iron," wrote Lilbourne A. Winchell, "and there was no day that, at some hour, a reeling 'blue coat' might not have been seen in the streets of the town, or on the homeward road, or, if overburdened by an excessive load of 'tarantula juice,' lying sprawled dead drunk along the trail, under the shadow of a tree or shrub." The usual penalty for this behavior was a short term in the guardhouse, along with a bread-and-water diet and exercises like the one given Deaf Dick.

Olney was compelled, eventually, to stop Millerton merchants from selling liquor to the soldiers. (At which time a new "groggery" opened outside the unofficial town limits, above the Point of Rocks.) In a way, he was being hypocritical. The officers kept their own collection of fine liquors on the base and imbibed them just as freely as did the enlisted men in town. Olney was not immune from this, as an August 1864 incident proved.

The colonel's wife was away to escape the valley heat, which allowed Olney to spend more time devoted to after-hours carousing. After one exhilarating night Olney stepped out of bed, ate breakfast and dressed, struggling to maintain his composure. He then stepped outside and, as erectly and solemnly as possible, began walking toward his troops—all arranged in the main quadrangle, for it was review and inspection day. Olney probably wondered why the soldiers had such strange, twisted expressions on their faces while he performed his duties. The reason was obvious to anyone of sober mind. Fort Miller's commander was performing his inspection with every part of his uniform intact, in perfect order—with the exception of his pants.

As the Civil War waned, the infantry companies began to leave Fort Miller, the last one on October 1, 1864. The post was then re-manned by Company A, 2nd California Cavalry, under Captain Loring and Lieutenant Hepburn, who commanded until the final abandonment on December 1, 1864.

Clark Hoxie was appointed Fort Miller's caretaker after the evacuation, and as before, the outpost did not stay vacant. Families, among them Andrew Firebaugh's (see below and Chapter 12), lived there briefly when traveling, settling new homesteads, or after being ejected from their residences because of calamities or improvements.

Olney returned in 1866 and auctioned off many of the fort's buildings. The property itself, with a few of the structures intact, became Judge Charles A. Hart's Fort Miller Ranch. William H. McKenzie later bought the ranch—and his heirs tried to save it when Friant

Reference 5:3

## ODYSSEY OF THE AKERS FAMILY

*Although the Akers family did not leave a large amount of written information of their pioneer experiences, we are indebted to Donna M. Hull and associates for a very detailed genealogy including detailed information about the experiences of the family. Space does not permit even a brief review of the family's activities but the following excerpts give a limited idea of the hardships of Delilah and Henry Akers and two of their twelve children. The same hardships were, of course, experienced by many other pioneers.*

Delilah Miller, born on April 17, 1802, in Kentucky, was rather tall and slender with blue eyes like her mother's. A person of strength and resourcefulness, she was capable of carrying on through any emergency which struck her family. In Estill County, Kentucky, in 1820, at 18 years of age, Delilah married Henry Akers. Henry was a large, well-built man of courage and adventure, and at 19 years of age he was much younger than the average man who married in those times. His ancestors had migrated from England to Holland, then to Virginia. He was a woodsman, an outdoorsman, and a frontiersman—always moving toward the new frontiers. He was also interested in farming and ranching. Delilah and Henry were bilingual, speaking another language unknown to their children.

Texas was offering 640 acres of land to the head of any family who agreed to settle there. Henry Akers always preferred to live near a stream with trees and rich soil. This, along with the offer of land, must have been his reason for choosing this area as their next home.

In 1847, Jim "Doc" Lewis and Smith and Harvey Akers [the latter two sons of Henry and Delilah] came to California to scout the area and to decide where to bring the family. They had decided to bring the family to California, and they were looking for a place to settle.

After the trip in 1847 to explore the possibilities in California, it is difficult to say why the family waited so long to decide to migrate to California. Possibly the idea of gold was the ultimate motivation beckoning them westward. By the first of 1852, a large caravan of people were making plans for their journey to California.

Although considerable opposition was expressed by some members of the family, one day early in March 1852, 200 covered wagons moved out of the Austin vicinity. It must have been a sight—impressive and emotional. These covered wagons were oxen-drawn, the wheels had wooden axles.

The second part of the trip crossed about 500 miles of vast dry plains and problems began: problems of no water or brackish water, problems of little feed for the stock, problems of children fretful with the heat or illness, problems of no game or fish. On other trains many people had died of thirst on the long, dry, hot stretches of plains even though scouts were sent ahead to try to locate water for the oncomers.

The Indians were active and treacherous everywhere, but none as cunningly treacherous and vindictive as the Apache Indians of the southern states. One very unusual thing about the Akers train was that they were not bothered by the Indians, except once when they attempted to stampede the stock.

It was somewhere during the Arizona crossing that the only recorded fatality of the trip took place. Illness attacked Viney [Malvina Akers] and Doc Lewis' 2½ year old daughter Amanda and she died May 22. The grieving mother, again pregnant with their son Harvey, left her little girl by the trail. They wrapped the body in a quilt and buried it in the middle of the road, then ran all the wagons over it.

By now the train was in more distress. There were great barren stretches of land and the weather was more than summery. It was just plain HOT! Food was scarce. Water holes were few and far between. Also this was rattlesnake country, and adults watched the children carefully.

Dam was proposed in the 1930s. But the government eventually obtained title to it, and now Millerton Lake covers Fort Miller's site. The blockhouse was dismantled, moved to Fresno's Roeding Park, and opened as a museum on November 14, 1954. It can still be seen there.

Millerton, Fresno County's first seat and the nearby fort's namesake, did not begin its brief life with that name. The *San Francisco Alta California* of September 26, 1851, reported that a new mining camp, Rootville, had been established in the San Joaquin River foothills two months earlier. Rootville became Millerton in time; the exact date of the name change is unknown. "It was all a 'rag town'—canvas tents for saloons, boarding-houses and stores," wrote David Bice James. Until lumber mills could be started, no durable building materials were available—and freighting timber in was prohibitively expensive.

The name "Rootville" offers conjectural evidence that Sonoran miners from Mexico (see Chapter 4) stopped to pan for gold there. The Mexicans, like South and Central American miners, worked streams with *bateas*—bowls made from tree roots. In California, according to Lilbourne A. Winchell, *bateas* were hewed "from the massive, plate-like roots of the buckeye, which were devoid of straight grain, being of twisted and interlocked growth, which obviated splitting of the bowl when wet in the process of washing gravel, or 'panning' as it is called by the Americans. The bowl was very light and perfectly adapted to the use made of it." It also was said that one *batea* could hold as much as ten American miners' pans. Thus, it seems reasonable to speculate that Rootville was named when someone spotted Mexican miners using roots to pan for gold.

Rootville/Millerton's earliest residents appear to have been Jesse Morrow, William Bowers and David Bice James, all involved in local mining ventures. By 1852 two new families named Richards and Williams had arrived, and Fort Miller storekeepers Hugh Carlin and "Mike" Fagan had established new businesses in town. (Carlin occupied a brick building, the first of its kind there. In 1866 the Millerton Courthouse was erected next to it, and after the town's demise the two structures were all that was left to mark it. The Carlin building was destroyed in 1927.) L. D. Hughes also started a store about this time, backed by James G. Clarke and a Mr. Cummings (the W. B. Cummings of Fresno City?—see Chapter 12). In time a Wells, Fargo agency was located there, and it eventually fell into the hands of a later storekeeper, George Grierson, and his successors. There were undoubtedly other arrivals and

Tucson was a flat-roofed, unprepossessing desert town, but at least supplies were available there. From there it was a long dry scorching trip to the Gila River, and the Pima Indian villages.

The Akers train remained in the Pima village for quite a time, recuperating from the first part of their journey and gathering supplies for the second. The Indians became so fond of them that they did not want them to leave and warned their friends of the Apache Indians across the mountain who would most likely massacre the train. Ten wagons decided to leave for California despite all the warnings. Of the ten only four arrived safely in Millerton, California. Some wagons broke down beyond repair and some people dropped off the train to settle along the way.

Once the border of California was reached the immigrants tended to be jubilant and have a feeling that they had arrived. The Akers clan was a long way from Fort Miller where the last covered wagon would stop. Near them was the deadly Colorado (Mojave) desert with its 95 miles of shifting sands. Ahead were mountains to climb and rivers to cross and winter floods to endure. But the thrill was evident—they were in California! [They proceeded to the San Joaquin Valley.]

Although the end of the journey was near, the families were now entering a lonely part of the long trail. "By April 20, 1852 there were only three houses in the vast territory bounded by the Coast Range on the west and Utah Territory on the east. One was on Tejon Pass, another was the ill-fated Woods cabin in the Four Creeks area and last was the house on Kings River of Campbell who ran the ferry." There were no towns for supply, no homes for hospitality and those who came were on their own.

[Their early problems in Fresno County are related in the text. In the spring of 1853 they settled on the Upper Kings River.]

The Akers built their family home under an old oak tree that still stands several miles northeast of present-day Centerville. It was a two-story house, boarded on the outside with split shakes.

### Malvina and Jim Lewis

Born in the Kentucky country known as the "dark and bloody ground," Malvina was the first child of Henry and Delilah Akers. They called the baby "Viney." Like the next brothers and sisters of the family, Viney had no opportunity for education, and could not read or write.

She married in 1836 at the age of 13. An adolescent bride, she was expected to mature during marriage as was the frontier custom in the 1800s. Within a few months, however, she was back with her parents as a widow. Her young husband had been knifed to death by a bandit on the front step of their wilderness honeymoon cabin.

Now, neither a child nor a wife, Malvina walked with the wagon train to Fort Smith, Arkansas, and finally on to the Austin District of Texas. Here, in 1839, the family would attempt to establish the good life. And here, on January 2, 1841, Malvina married for a second time, to a man named James Henry Lewis, a carpenter. He proved to Malvina that he was a good one.

Malvina could be proud of her husband. He helped the Akers boys—all highly skilled hunters—bring in the meat which kept the wagon train healthy during the months on the westward trail [when the family decided to move on to California]. His trade as a carpenter was useful in repairing the wagons. But most helpful of all was his ability as a "yarb" (herb) doctor, which earned him the permanent nickname of "Doc." With him he carried a handwritten book of herbal remedies. Administered with good sense to patients who had confidence in him, Doc's prescriptions were good medicine.

The Akers wagons finally reached Four Creeks, California in November 1852. Viney and Doc waited for the flooded, boggy land to dry so that their wagon could roll north to Millerton. The next few miles of the journey accomplished, Viney gave birth to her seventh child while the wagon train paused at Kings River. The baby, named Harvey, was born January 28, 1853.

In a few days, the Akers were on the final journey to the San Joaquin River. Their destination was the tent mining town of Millerton.

Soon, the family decided that the brawling, lawless town was not a fitting place to

departures during this earliest period; the lack of personal reminiscences and newspaper accounts for this period, however, makes it impossible to gain details.

An influx of citizens who would become important to the area began in 1852–53. Colonel Henry Burrough of Burrough Valley and the Coalinga Mineral Springs (see below and Chapter 12) became one of the town's pioneers. Saloonkeepers Thomas J. Allen and Theodore C. Stallo took up residence, and ferry owners Charles Porter Converse, Joe B. Royal and Stephen A. Gaster appear to have been intermittent citizens—their respective businesses were located some distance from Millerton. Jesse Morrow took over "Mike" Fagan's ferry, or was backed by Fagan in a different ferrying venture. Hugh A. Carroll, the Fort Miller soldier, became Morrow's partner in the next year. Other newcomers included attorneys Claudius Golon Sayle and Charles A. Hart, physician H. Du Gay, sheepherder William Rousseau and John McLeod. McLeod was born in Oregon, of Indian and white parentage, to a brother of famed Hudson's Bay Company fur trapper John McLeod. Another noteworthy development of this year was increased emigrant arrivals, especially that of the Akers party, which endured many hardships on its way to California (see 5:3).

By now there was enough commercial activity to warrant the creation of a Millerton post office, on October 11, 1853. After two periods of discontinuance (November 17, 1854 to June 30, 1855, and October 7, 1863 to October 6, 1864) it merged with the Fort Miller post office on December 23, 1874. Reasons for the transfer are unclear. Millerton had lost a lot of its population by that time, but was not dead, and the Fort Miller post office—presided over by Charles A. Hart until its discontinuance on April 5, 1876—was certainly near no commercial center.

The first postmaster at Millerton was Edward P. ("Ned") Hart; following him, by dates of appointment, were Hugh A. Carroll (June 30, 1855); Clark Hoxie (December 16, 1858); L. D. Hughes (August 18, 1860);

raise children. Influenced by Malvina, who was a full marriage partner during the major decisions, Doc Lewis moved his brood to a permanent resting place at Fine Gold Gulch. Doc purchased a combination tent boarding house, saloon and store from Malcolm and Shepherd.

The other Akers brothers and sisters took their children back to Kings River where they settled to stay.

Malvina is reported by several historical sources to have been the first "white" woman permanent resident in a large region between Mariposa and the San Joaquin and remained the only one until 1855. Then a pioneer named John Gilmore brought his wife and son from Indiana and established a home nearby on Willow Creek, near O'Neals in present-day Madera County.

Not that Viney had time to be lonely! In addition to caring for the immediate family of nine and helping Doc with the store, saloon and boarding house, she put her fingers to work making well-tailored shirts. These were sold in the store to miners who gladly paid $5 each for them.

Even the little girls Sarah Jane and Mary did their part to earn money. They learned to present a dancing act on top of the bar. [?] Lonely miners tossed miniature bags of gold dust to the dancing children in gratitude for the opportunity to reminisce of little ones left behind.

The home on Willow Creek was sold and a new ranch was purchased north of the Kings River in the foothills. The ranching years were meager ones. Although there was little money, there were more marriages and more grandchildren to brighten the declining years of Doc and Viney.

Doc died first, on January 24, 1892. Malvina died on January 21, 1901.

### Harvey and Jane Akers

Harvey Akers was a frontier-pushing pioneer born on November 29, 1826 in Kentucky. He made three early trips to California: in 1847, in 1852, and in 1861.

For the twelve years the Akers family lived in Williamson County, Texas, Harvey had managed to acquire some cattle of his own and brought them to California in 1852. He was an efficient cattleman and farmer. Soon he and his four brothers formed a partnership and began acquiring land and stock in the Centerville District, or what was then called the Upper Kings River area. In the fall of 1853 he rode horseback to Mission San Gabriel and returned to Kings River with a bundle of mission grape cuttings tied to his saddle. In 1854, with the help of his brother Bud, he planted about two acres of vineyard just below Kings River cemetery, north of Centerville and east of the cemetery below the bluff. This resulted in the first vineyard in the community. Harvey also planted about two acres of peach trees about this same time.

Harvey lost most of his cattle in the 1859–60 drought, and he needed to replenish his herd. He returned to Texas in 1860, and since the price was cheap at the time, bought a lot of cattle. He left the cattle with his brother Smith, who was living with his young family in Spicewood, Texas. The Civil War broke out and all his cattle were lost, except ten head which were later brought to California.

When Harvey arrived in Burnet County, Texas in 1860, he was "foot-loose and fancy-free" until he saw a young woman, Martha "Jane" McHaley, 17, laboring in the cotton fields. He told her, "That is no work for a woman to be doing. Come to California with me!" They got their marriage license in Burnet County, Texas on April 10, 1861, and were married the same day in the arch in the rear of a covered wagon shortly before leaving for California.

She persuaded her people to come to California with them. Harvey led this 50-wagon train, leaving Texas in early April 1861 and arriving in Kings River in October of the same year. They had many terrible hardships on this train. There was a young married couple, and during the journey, the wife had her baby. She had a terrible time, and both she and the baby died during childbirth. The husband was so upset he nearly lost his mind. This train took seven months to make the journey, an average of thirteen miles a day. There were seven deaths on the journey; six were buried on the plains, the last one buried at Los Angeles.

Harvey and Jane first settled in the Kings River area. Harvey was very industrious, never letting the loss of most of his herd get him down.

Just two months before his death, Harvey and Jane celebrated their golden wedding anniversary. This was very quietly done because he was not well. Harvey died on June 17, 1911 at his Hughes Creek home. He left his widow well provided for. Harvey was a thrifty man and had acquired many assets. When he died his estate was appraised at $55,097.94.

After Harvey's death, Jane continued to run the ranch with hired hands [and] to hold big Christmas parties at the ranch. One account in the December 28, 1913, issue of the *Sanger Herald* related the following:

"Aunt Jane Akers gave a three days' Christmas party to her relatives and friends at her new bungalow on Hughes Creek."

She died December 20, 1922.

SOURCE: *And Then There Were Three Thousand*, Donna M. Hull, 1975.

George Grierson (April 27, 1863); Francesco Jensen (January 2, 1868); Otto Froelich (October 25, 1869); Charles A. Heaton (April 4, 1872); and Charles J. Garland (June 20, 1872).

The year 1853 also was important to Millerton because it gained a sister city of sorts. Dr. William F. Edgar, then residing at Fort Miller, told what happened in his reminiscences: "About this time certain parties conceived the idea of laying out a town down the river—a short distance above where the Southern Pacific Railroad now crosses it—to be called Joaquina. They cut a sort of landing on the bank, and induced a steamboat to come up during high water and load at the place; but I believe it was the first as well as the last steamboat that landed there, and Joaquina remains as it was—a town of the imagination." Unless Edgar confused Joaquin with the nearby ferry enterprises of Charles Porter Converse, Walter Harvey or Francis M. Davenport (see Chapter 4), no clue exists as to who its developers were.

The first true hotels in Millerton—as David Bice James noted, there were canvas "boarding-houses" in the earliest days—were built in 1854. Colonel Henry Burrough's was the best, featuring a large double (M-shaped) roof, and can be spotted in Frank Dusy's 1870 photograph of the town. Canadian Ira McCray, a transplanted sawmill man from Tuolumne County, and Virginian George Rivercomb opened the other establishment. It seems to have been a ramshackle or nondescript structure, nothing like the substantial Oak Hotel McCray built several years afterward.

It is intriguing to note that McCray brought with him a black man and woman—"Tom" and Jane Dermon—who were probably the first of their race to settle in Millerton, and in Fresno County for that matter. (Blacks accompanying the Jedediah Smith and John C. Fremont parties did cross through the county's boundaries; see Chapter 3.) Jane, said to be a freed slave by some and a runaway by others, was from North Carolina. She appears to have served as a domestic for McCray upon her arrival at Millerton, later going into business for herself—a remarkable achievement for a black woman then. "Tom" was the trusted cook and manager for McCray's hotels. He handled both jobs well, although, as Lilbourne A. Winchell noted, "Tom" was a complete eccentric when it came to dress styles:

> His shirt and collar [were] of snowy white linen; [and he also wore] a rigidly correct black tie, a blue or black velvet vest, [and] his jacket and trousers were of find cloth. In excess of these he wore a series of short dresses reaching to the knees, from petticoat out. The under garments [were] of linen and silk, and on gala days his overshirt was of velvet or satin. Seen for the first time Tom was a figure to hold the astonished attention of the beholder . . .

Slightly less remarkable than "Tom" was the coming of religious services to town. David Latimer, a traveling Methodist who rode on horseback between Millerton and Scottsburg (Centerville), is thought to have been the first minister in both hamlets. The next year, Bishop Kip made his aforementioned visit to Fort Miller.

The mid-1850s marked Millerton's golden era. Now that Alexander Ball's Sierra sawmill was functioning (see Chapter 6), lumber could be had and the canvas tents of earlier years were fast disappearing. Saloons and gambling dens were flourishing, frequented by rough miners who staked their hard-earned gold dust on whatever monte, faro or poker games they could find. Dashing gamblers and cardsharps, clad in white silk shirts, velvet vests and black broadcloth coats and pants, did their best to outwit the less experienced players. Stages ran constantly (see Chapter 4) and their arrivals, signalled by a distant horn-blow, were major events—for they brought news, mail, money or loved ones, the most precious commodities in that crude mining camp. And a host of characters plied the town streets—Mexicans and Spaniards in leggings, open jackets and sombreros, and their women, "the painted, short-skirted, jewel-decked [senoritas]," according to Lilbourne A. Winchell, "[and] the buxom, barefooted squaw in red calico and plaited hair . . . " There were as yet few white women in the neighborhood, other than the wives of Hugh Carroll and William H. McKenzie, Fort Miller soldiers.

Being "first" sometimes has its disadvantages, as Eliza Carroll and Ann McKenzie found out one day when they took a walk to a nearby Indian rancheria. Never having seen a white woman, some Indian women rubbed and pinched their white skin to see if the white would come off. Mrs. McKenzie escaped but Mrs. Carroll was stripped naked. Mrs. Carroll in 1852 gave birth to a daughter, Mary S., the first white child born in the county.

Business developments of this period were considerable. George Grierson and Francesco Jensen, two Danish immigrants, and Gomer Evans started a store in 1855. It was located at the western edge of town, with Grierson's home at the rear of the business. Jensen branched out from this enterprise early, erecting a trading post on Willow Creek (near present-day O'Neals, in Madera County), but returned to Millerton once more and lived there three years before moving to Big Dry Creek. San Franciscan Evans was not in the partnership long, returning north to become a bank cashier. Like all the other stores of this period, the Grierson-Jensen-Evans venture had to carry an incredible array of foodstuffs, utensils, medicines, liquors, wearing apparel and other items (see 5:4).

Ira McCray purchased George Rivercombe's interest in their hotel somtime in the mid-1850s and began working toward a more elaborate venture. On June 9,

1855, McCray purchased Jesse Morrow's crude San Joaquin River ferry—a boat hitched to a cable running overhead, with the cable tethered to a large oak tree on the Millerton side. McCray also purchased the property on which the oak tree stood (that and the ferry cost $200), and forty acres belonging to Morrow, on the river's north side (and opposite the town?) for $2,500.

The latter location became the site for McCray's $15,000 Oak Hotel, said at one time to be the finest establishment of its type between Stockton and Los Angeles. It consisted of separate units, one-story and two-story, with the previously-mentioned oak tree in a courtyard between them. The dining room, forty-eight feet long and sixteen feet wide, was presided over by McCray's servant, "Tom." Though netting covered the doors and any dishes or containers, flies were a constant menace. To keep them away from the patrons, servants had to pull, back and forth, a light framework suspended from the ceiling and festooned with paper fringes. A barroom was located in the part of the hotel just off the street—equipped with mirrors, pool tables, paintings of nude women and two private rooms for card playing. In those precincts miners were known to lose all their worldly fortunes, and stock raisers the tax money they had brought into the county seat for payment.

McCray continued to expand his Millerton holdings. By investing in an adobe warehouse to the east of the Oak Hotel, owned by Stephen A. Gaster and Joe B. Royal, he was able to gain a little more space and construct a large livery stable. Over its double doors was a painting showing horses, a falcon and women hunting, with a sign proclaiming "McCray's Falcon Stables." The same name (Falcon) also was used to denote McCray's ranch near the Kings River (see Chapter 6). James W. Rankin eventually joined McCray as a partner in the hotel, ferry and stables, but sold out (as Rivercombe had before) for $5,000 in December 1858.

Next to the Oak Hotel was Jane Dermon's house. She was probably still working for McCray at this time, but had successfully branched out into several businesses of her own. She sold Southern-style meals, cakes, breads and pastries, and took in washing from many of Millerton's residents. Through these contacts she got to know many people well, and was quick to drop everything to nurse them back to health whenever they got sick. When she died in 1865, her friends—predominantly, if not entirely, white—gave her a proper funeral and burial in Millerton's unofficial cemetery, across the river from the town.

The outstanding event of 1856, at least for Millertonians, was the creation of Fresno County and the designation of their town as the county seat. This was the culmination of a process that had begun, essentially, when California gained statehood on September 9,

Reference 5:4

# A TYPICAL PIONEER STORE

Stores in those days provided, usually in one room, everything known to be used by the regional inhabitants. For the miner, picks, drills, shovels, gold pans, six- or eight-tined sluice forks, perforated sheet iron for his rocker, quicksilver for amalgamating in sluice or arrastre, black powder and fuse; nails, as cut from sheet iron—square sided, tapering and broad headed. To adorn his person, all manner of raiment—from felt hat to heavy, nail-studded boots. Clothing, in variety, was kept for general use.

Staple provisions were in full supply; but the coffee in original 150-pound sacks, was unparched; tea came in large, foil-lined boxes direct from the Orient; small, tough, dark-colored dried apples from Oregon, cut in quarters—skin, core and all—were threaded, like beads, on cotton strings, dried and packed in small barrels. They were purchased by the consumer, in festoons, to the desired quantity.

White sugar, in broken lumps, was a rare and expensive luxury; the brown came in woven 50-pound grass mats from Hawaii, and in barrels from remote refineries. In summer time the dark sugar solidified in the barrels to the consistency of rock and was, perforce, mined out in chunks with a crowbar. Real, thick, black, New Orleans molasses was to be had in kegs. Flour, in sacks, red

and bayo beans, bacon, rice were perennial fare.

Soda, cream of tartar, and Preston and Merril's "yeast powders," in small cans, provided leavening. No fresh fruits were obtainable, except at Christmas time a small supply of red Oregon apples, and small Tahiti oranges sold for fabulous prices. Other than Italian sardines and Baltimore oysters, canned food stuffs were rare; ordinary condiments were stocked—pepper, mustard, and common spices.

Red calico in great quantity lured the savage eye—dark blue, a close competitor. All housewives' needs were in evidence—clothing materials, some fine fabrics, dishes, pots and pans, steel-bladed table knives and three-pronged forks—the latter used, by most individuals, solely for spearing lumpy viands; the knife was the dependable instrument for food conveyance. Saddles, bridles, hair cinchas and ropes, spurs, pack saddles and panniers, cording in selected sizes; guns, pistols, powder, percussion caps, lead and bullet molds, buckshot and smaller pellets. No fixed ammunition nor breech loading firearms were in use. Nostrums in variety—pills, powders and plasters, calomel and castor oil; "Mustang Liniment"—good for man or beast; toilet luxuries were chiefly represented by highly-scented bear grease, in

small bottles, colored red or yellow. Dandies anointed their hair and mustachios on gala occasions with this delectable perfumery. The exacting used, also, bay rum and "Florida Water," prodigally sprinkled over handkerchiefs and coats. Powerfully pervasive were the expensive grains of pure India musk indulged by the especially discriminating belles and beaux.

(Whew! How the ball room reeked with the complex odors. Ne' mind! Everybody was happy!)

There was not regular retail competition with the saloons; but barrelled "licker" supplied the store patrons' wants by the bottleful. An ornate glass container, with artistic, steel-plate label, bearing an animated scene of "St. George and the Dragon," was in popular use—"Hostetter's Bitters" was a panacea for ennui and all other human ills. Thousands of bottles of this 95 percent alcohol elixir were handed out by all merchants and saloons. Not a trail, of the many radiating from Millerton and the Kings river settlement, that was not blazed by these regretfully emptied, square sided, corrugated, whisky bottles!

SOURCE: L. A. Winchell, "History of Fresno County," unpublished manuscript.

81

# HOW
# *Fresno County*
## EVOLVED

FRESNO

|  |  |
|---|---|
| | CUT OUT IN 1861 |
| | CUT OUT IN 1870-72 |
| | ADDED IN 1874 CUT OFF IN 1876 |
| | CUT OUT IN 1874 RETURNED IN 1876 |
| | CUT OUT IN 1874 |
| | CUT OUT IN 1887 |
| | CUT OUT IN 1893 |
| | CUT OUT IN 1909 |

MARIPOSA

MERCED

MONTEREY

SAN LUIS OBISPO

TULARE

FRESNO COUNTY
ESTABLISHED - 1856

1849. Twenty-seven "original" counties were formed at this time, the largest of which was Mariposa. It embraced a huge chunk of territory, ranging from the Stanislaus River on the north, to the Utah Territory (now Nevada) line on the east, the northern part of Los Angeles County to the south, and the crest of the Coast Range mountains to the west. In all, Mariposa County took in nearly 20 percent of the state's land surface—most of it uninhabited, and containing all of present-day Fresno County.

As people began filtering into Mariposa County, subdivision became necessary. Its southern edge was conveyed to Los Angeles County in 1851; Tulare County was carved out of its southern regions in 1852, and Merced out of its northwestern corner in 1855. The latter two county formations embraced areas that eventually became part of Fresno County. At its inception Tulare County's northern boundary line extended a few miles above the Kings River and roughly paralleling it, after which it went down the ridge separating the San Joaquin and Kings rivers' tributaries. Merced County, during this brief 1855–56

## Reference 5:5

# FROM WHENCE CAME THE NAME OF FRESNO

**Fresno, frez'-no: River, Flats, Dome, Grove of Big Trees** [Madera]; **Fresno: County**, city. Fresno is the Spanish name for 'ash' and was doubtless applied because the Oregon ash, *Fraxinus oregona*, was native there. Goddard's map shows Ash Slough north of the [Fresno] river [near Chowchilla]. Rio Fresno is mentioned in the San Francisco *Alta California* of April 2, 1851, and the name appears as Fresno River on Tassin's map of the same year. The stream is shown as Fresno Creek on Gibbes' map of 1852 and is mentioned as Frezno River in the Indian Report. This phonetic spelling was also used when the county was created and named, April 19, 1856 (*Statutes*, p. 183). Before 1860 an attempt was made to establish a Fresno City at the site of the present station of Tranquility (Goddard's and Hoffmann's maps). When the Central Pacific reached the site of the present city, May 28, 1872, the name was applied to the station. In 1874, Millerton, county seat and all, moved to the new station.

[In addition to the Oregon ash, the broad-leaf or water ash was also reported to have grown here but all are scarce now. Neither are the same as the Eastern ash which pioneers had known and used for fine woodwork. Ash trees here were used extensively for barrels and wagon wheels.]

SOURCE: *California Place Names*, Erwin G. Gudde, 1949.

# FIRST ARRIVALS

The first influx consisted of Mexicans of the province of Sonora, Chilians and a few Chinese. These, principally, took possession of the southern mines, or those on the San Joaquin and its tributaries.

SOURCE: *Frost's History of California—1854.*

## Reference 5:6

# THE FORMATION OF A COUNTY
### From California State Register, 1857

FREZNO COUNTY
(County Seat—Millerton)

Frezno County, organized 1856. Boundaries: North by Merced and Mariposa, east by Utah Territory, south by Tulare, and west by Monterey.

TOPOGRAPHY—This county was formed from portions of Mariposa, Merced and Tulare, and contains that section of the mining region known as the extreme Southern Mines. The agricultural land in the county is situated in the vicinity of King's River, and is represented to be well adapted for grazing purposes. Number of acres in cultivation, including the Reservation, 2,000.

LEGAL DISTANCES—Not yet established by law (from Millerton to Stockton about 140 miles).

### OFFICERS

| Office | Name | Residence | Salary |
|---|---|---|---|
| County Judge | Chas. A. Hart | Millerton | $2,500 |
| District Attorney | J. C. Craddock | Millerton | 1,000 |
| County Clerk and Recorder | J. S. Sayles Jr. | Millerton | 1,000 |
| Sheriff and Tax Collector | W. C. Bradley | Millerton | 1,000 |
| Treasurer | Geo. Rivercombe | Millerton | 1,000 |
| Assessor | John G. Simpson | Millerton | 1,000 |
| Surveyor | C. M. Brown | Millerton | 1,000 |
| Coroner | Dr. Du Gay | Millerton | Fees |
| Public Administrator | James Smith | Kings River | Fees |
| Supervisor | John R. Hughes | Millerton | Per diem |
| Supervisor | John A. Patterson | Kings River | Per diem |
| Supervisor | John L. Hunt | Huntsville | Per diem |

(The terms of all of these expired in October, 1858.)

THIRTEENTH JUDICIAL DISTRICT—Hon. Edward Burke, of Mariposa, judge district court; sessions, second Monday, March, July and November.

SIXTH SENATORIAL DISTRICT—Senator: Hon. Samuel A. Merritt of Mariposa; term expires January, 1859.

MEMBER OF ASSEMBLY—Hon. Orson K. Smith of Woodville.

AGRICULTURAL RESOURCES—Wheat, 1,000 acres; barley, 500 acres, and vegetables, 500 acres.

FRUIT TREES—But little attention has as yet been devoted to the culture of fruit. There are two vineyards in a forward state, and a few fruit trees, which appear to thrive remarkably well.

LIVE STOCK—Horses, 1,400; mules, 200; asses, 150; cattle, 18,650; calves, 2,650; sheep, 1,000; swine, 4,000; goats, 50; total 28,100. Assessed value, $360,000.

MINERAL RESOURCES—There are several important mining streams, principally worked by Chinamen. Amount of foreign miner's tax collected $1,000 per month.

WATER DITCHES, ETC.—There are two extensive water ditches in the course of completion; one steam saw mill and two quartz veins, represented to be remarkably rich.

MILITARY POST AND INDIAN RESERVATIONS—Fort Miller, Frezno Farm and King's River Farm Reservations are located in this county.

FINANCES—Receipts from date of organization July 1 to December 1, 1856, $6,281.15; expenditures, $4,268. Amount of taxable property, principally stock, $400,000, tax collected, $6,912; foreign miner's tax collected $1,200 per month.

POPULATION—Votes cast, 319; Indians, 1,300.

ATTORNEYS—Millerton: O. M. Brown, H. Clark and James T. Cruickshank.

PHYSICIANS—Fort Miller: Wm. J. L. Engle; Frezno River: D. J. Johnson, Lewis Leach; Millerton: W. A. N. Dulgnay (Du Gay).

The first meeting of the supervisors-elect was held on June 23 of Hughes and Patterson, J. M. Roan having failed to qualify wherefore Hunt was chosen at a special election ordered at this initial session, besides which the county was declared formally organized. Patterson was succeeded by J. E. Williams in February, 1857. Clark Hoxie elected in May to succeed Hunt and S. W. Rankin in August to supersede Hughes.

SOURCE: California State Register, 1857.

period, had all of Fresno County north of this boundary and west of Converse's Ferry on the San Joaquin. Central California residents who petitioned the state legislature asked that "Frezno County" (a phonetic spelling used in early records and soon abandoned) be created out of Mariposa, Tulare and Merced counties.

The reasons for the county's formation were simple. Millertonians and others living in the area hated to take the dusty, winding and often impassable roads to the different county seats to conduct official business. Local mining and lumber industries were growing in significance, and it was believed that the other counties were neglecting the greater Millerton area. The name "Fresno," applied to the prospective county, was taken from the Fresno River that ran through the proposed boundaries; the origin of the name is explored in 5:5. After considering these arguments, the California Legislature passed an enabling act to form the county on April 19, 1856, and a creative enactment was passed the following May 26. Ira McCray, James Cruikshank (a new Millerton attorney), Hugh Carroll, Charles A. Hart, O. M. Brown, H. M. Lewis and J. W. Gilmore were appointed as commissioners to form the county.

Meeting at McCray's Millerton hotel, the commissioners established ten voting precincts and scheduled county elections for June 9, 1856. The precincts were located at familiar landmarks, all mentioned previously save for one—C. A. Yancey's ranch on the Chowchilla River. The others were Dr. Lewis Leach's store on the Fresno River, John Lavert Hunt's store on the same river, J. Scott Ashman's store on Fine Gold Gulch, Upper Camp and Gaster's on the San Joaquin River, Gaster and Royal's trading post (Mono City) on the San Joaquin, Millerton, Firebaugh's Ferry, and the Kings River ferry near Scottsburg. (The results of the elections are described in 5:6, along with other miscellaneous details concerning the early county.)

When the Fresno County Board of Supervisors first met at Millerton on June 23, 1856, the county was declared formally organized. Its boundaries, in a rough sense, could be delineated as follows. The northern borderline was the Chowchilla River; at the place where it meets the San Joaquin River, the boundary was drawn straight southwest to the crest of the Coast Range. To the west, the line followed the Coast Range crest. The southern line can be visualized by imagining a line drawn straight southwest from Reedley's site to the Coast Range crest; in the other direction, a jagged easterly line was followed for sixty miles. After that point it turned abruptly, and straight, northeast until it hit the California state line. The eastern boundary was the state line itself.

Present county boundaries are nothing like those described above. Everything east of the Sierra Nevada crest was ceded to Mono County in 1861. During the 1870s, Mariposa County got a small northeastern segment of land back and the Tulare County boundary was redefined, with a net loss of territory to Fresno County. Much of the extreme west, all of it mountainous, went to San Benito County in 1887. The greatest loss occurred in 1893, when politicians and businessmen north of the San Joaquin River successfully agitated to form Madera County. (Because of this, many events that occurred within the present-day Madera County boundaries have been omitted from this volume. A few, which have relevance to Fresno County's history as a whole, have been recounted.) The transfer of some land in southwestern Fresno County to Kings County in 1909 gave the county the contour it retains today.

As the county's largest settlement, though unincorporated, it was only logical that Millerton was chosen as the first county seat. It was there that the famed, and still-extant, Millerton Courthouse was built—but after the county had existed for ten years, and needed the extra space to manage its affairs. At first, a modest brick building owned by Judge Charles A. Hart and rented for fifty dollars a month, was adequate for governmental needs. At this point there was a greater need for a good jail; prisoners could no longer be incarcerated at Mariposa. County Clerk James Sayles, Jr. placed advertisements in the *Mariposa Gazette* and *Mariposa Democrat* for a suitable contractor.

The supervisors decided to let Colonel Henry Burrough build the county jail for $6,000. Ironically, he had underbid two men, Alexander Wallace and one Mitchell, for the job—then hired Wallace as a subcontractor to do the actual construction. Wallace appears to have accepted the job, at an obviously reduced rate, because he counted on cutting corners with his work. Though the jail was made of a pine framework, with brick walls and a heavy shake roof, it was insubstantial. Wallace told the board, in February 1857, that his work had been proper in every way . . . but he was lying through his teeth. This led to a novel situation, laughable now and highly embarrassing to main contractor Burrough, reported by William Faymonville:

When finished, a day was appointed for [the jail's] acceptance by the Board of Supervisors. A German (B. G. P. Van Dempster, who had been caught stealing potatoes] was confined in the new jail when the Board of Supervisors, accompanied by the Colonel, went to inspect the structure and ascertain if it was done according to plans, &c. The prisoner informed the Colonel that he would scratch out of that institution in less than twenty mintues; in fact he had removed two or three of the bricks, just to show the Colonel how easy the thing could be done. The Colonel became alarmed, and begged the fellow for God Almighty's sake not to scratch out until it was accepted by the Board of Supervisors, otherwise he would be a ruined man. Whether the Colonel offered other or more substantial inducements, can only be conjectured; at any rate the fellow remained in jail until it was formally accepted by the Board of Supervisors, and then, with the aid of a tenpenny nail scratched out and made his escape.

In 1858 the county grand jury admitted the obvious: the jail had not been built to specifications and was useless for holding prisoners. (People confined there would often break out to gambol in the nearby hills, returning only for meals—which were excellent, since they were prepared at local hotels.) The jail became a bigger and bigger joke until the supervisors decided to tear it down in March 1863. William L. Harshfield and William H. Crowe were paid $200 to do the job. Bricks were to be saved from the demolition and resold at not less than five dollars per thousand; the bricks were never sold and the county lost an important revenue source (its expenses yearly were only a few thousand dollars in this period). Until the Courthouse was built in 1866–67, prisoners were taken to Mariposa and housed there under contract with the sheriff. When that was unfeasible, the town hotels were used for "incarceration"—which must have hardly seemed like punishment.

Meanwhile, the county government was experiencing growing pains and needed to move. After rejecting an offer to buy Hart's brick building for $1,200, the officials moved into a building owned by Ira McCray and leased for forty dollars monthly. Its upper floor had three offices and its lower floor was a makeshift courtroom; the latter must have been fairly large, since thirty-eight chairs could fit into it.

The late 1850s and early 1860s was a time of modest expansion in Millerton. Stroud's butcher shop was added during this period, as were Dr. Leach's practice and residence (marooned in Millerton during an 1860 storm, he decided to stay), and permanent residences for Theodore C. Stallo, Charles Porter Converse, William H. Parker, Stephen A. Gaster, Joe B. Royal and a new saloonkeeper, George McClelland. Canadian Simon W. Henry built a new two-story hotel, with accompanying saloon and blacksmith shop, that became a popular resort (see 5:7). County records indicate that Henry had to answer for many assault charges—he did not tolerate foolishness, malicious mischief or outright violence on his property.

A few people associated with the town began building homes outside its unofficial limits. S. H. Hill and Clark Hoxie lived at Hill's Flat, a piece of land made semicircular by the river's bend, near Fort Miller and opposite from it. Judge E. C. Winchell and family, initially Fort Miller residents (see above), relocated near the mouth of Winchell's Gulch, a stream one mile east of Millerton that fed into the San Joaquin River.

Another "suburb" of Millerton developed after 1856, when Chinese and their businesses were ejected from the town. Mining activities had brought many of them

Reference 5:7

## THE BALL AT THE HENRY HOUSE

The opening of the "Henry House," on the evening of the 22d inst., was a gay, festive and brilliant affair. Your absence was regretted, but understood to be unavoidable. Nevertheless, you will be proud to know that the tripod was faithfully represented; that ——— covered himself and the Times office with laurels, by his gallant bearing, courtly demeanor and artistic execution of numerous difficult passages in the art terpischorean. You will grieve to hear the profound sighs that doubtless, ever-since, struggle out of the depths of his bosom, indicative of an arrow, lodged in the recess of the heart. Who the fair maid, whose melting orbs of ebon or azure hue, launched the resistless shaft, may never be known; but *she* should be primarily answerable for any shortcomings in his department, this week, at least.

The new landlord, most ably seconded by the ladies of his household, did "the hospitable," in the most approved style. The valuable services of the ubiquitous and ever-ready "Tom," of the Oak Hotel, were also brought into requisition, in the culinary bureau. As a necessary consequence, the supper was all that heart could wish. The tables groaned under a load of roast turkeys, ducks, and plump, juvenile porkers, flanked by pyramids of cakes and a profusion of all the delicacies, usual to festive occasions—

and the appreciative guests, upon the signal being given, did ample justice to the "layout" before them.

But the centre of attraction was the neat and exceedingly pleasant ball-room, where were gathered a large and gay assemblage of "the beauty and chivalry" of the county. Never before, since Fresno became a free and independent republic, has there been, within its limits, so large a collection of the fair sex, with the exception, perhaps, of one or two occasions. And the native graces of the ladies were greatly heightened by the excellent taste manifested in their attire. Many of the dresses were rich and elaborate, and all were exceedingly appropriate and attractive. The gentlemen—to their honor be it said—were on their best behavior, and, like knights of the olden time, were gallant, courteous and attentive. No discords marred the harmony of the party—thanks to the absence of all intoxicating influences, save the fascinating smiles and bewitching glances of the lovely creatures who ruled the hour. So mote it ever be!

The music was excellent, the calling good, and added much to the pleasure of the occasion. Hour after hour, the giddy dancers revelled in the delightful mazes of the waltz, the polka, the schottische or the cotilion— each one bent on enjoying himself to his

utmost, and ministering equally to the enjoyment of the rest. Under such circumstances, no one could fail to be pleased with the entertainment; and the shrill clarion of chanticleer assailed the frosty morning air long before the joyous assemblage reluctantly pronounced their mutual adieus, and withdrew from the festive hall.

Much has been written and said of the evils of dancing; but the veriest cynic, witnessing the cordiality of such reunions as these, would surely acknowledge them more productive of social good than a twelve-month of philippies; and methinks, could he be once drawn into the magic circle of the cotilion, surrounded by sylph-like forms and beaming glances, twinkling feet and murmuring voices, his flinty heart would quickly melt—his emancipated soul cast off her slavish fetters; and with the first squeak of the fiddle, he would thrill with an *inexpressible-all-over-ness*, and frantically shout—

"On with the dance! let joy be unconfined;
No sleep till morn where youth and pleasure meet,
To chase the glowing hours with flying feet."

SOURCE: *The Fresno Times*, March 1, 1865, p. 3.

85

Millerton in 1870 from the north bank of the San Joaquin River. This famous picture
is one of the few existing photographs by Frank Dusy and the only one of Millerton
by anyone. Note remnants of an Indian village in right foreground.

Fresno County's first Courthouse in
1868. To the left of it is the Wm. Faymonville residence. The Court House
Exchange on the right was better
known as Payne's Saloon.

First county offices were in the twin
gabled Henry's Hotel, half of which
is shown in this picture from the side.
It was to the right of Payne's Saloon
in the upper picture.

# Millerton-Fresno Pioneer Leaders

**AH KITT**
*Operated a blacksmith shop at Millerton and Fresno in partnership with Jefferson Shannon.*

**J. SCOTT ASHMAN**
*Served as Fresno County sheriff from 1859 to 1867, and again from 1871 to 1873. While in office he formed a posse to pursue Vasquez and his gang.*

**GILLUM BALEY**
*Pioneer at Millerton, was elected county judge in 1867 and served for twelve years. When the county seat moved to Fresno in 1874, he was elected county treasurer and served two years.*

**WM. FAYMONVILLE**
*Wrote first history of Fresno County. A popular leader, he held dual posts of county clerk and auditor, 1863-68, and was in real estate sales and development.*

**J. W. FERGUSON**
*Founder and publisher of Fresno Weekly Expositor and Fresno Daily Evening Expositor. Active in many community activities and assemblyman from the area.*

**DR. LEWIS LEACH**
*This Millerton pioneer was a partner of Major James Savage, a prominent physician, merchant and land developer, and founder and president of two early Fresno banks.*

**SAM WING GEE**
*Chinese pioneer. Photograph taken by R. W. Riggs of settlers who moved from Millerton to Fresno.*

**JEFF SHANNON**
*Butcher, deputy sheriff, blacksmith, land agent for real estate division of Southern Pacific and first station agent in Fresno, in 1872.*

**JAMES H. WALKER**
*Farmer, sheep raiser, member of legislature, 1862-63 and 1871-73, and sheriff, 1867-71.*

**E. C. WINCHELL**
*Served as first superintendent of Fresno County Schools in 1860. He and his family lived in the adobe building at Millerton known as the "Hospital."*

**OTTO FROELICH**
*Shown with his wife and daughter Maren. A Danish immigrant to Millerton in the early 1860s, Froelich established one of Fresno City's first pioneer stores in 1872.*

87

to the upper San Joaquin River area (see Chapter 4), and a fair number had settled at Millerton, including storekeepers Tong Sing and Hop Wo and (later) blacksmith Ah Kit. For a time their presence was tolerated in the village, and the merchants were allowed to conduct their businesses—which, by law, they could have been forbidden to own. They even sold miners' and other supplies to the white population at good prices. After the county's formation, though, the Chinese were banished to some level land adjacent to the San Joaquin River, between Millerton and Fort Miller. Local whites suddenly decided that their odd language, eating with bowls and sticks, refusal to drink river water and—most loathsome of all—bathing nude where unsuspecting people might glimpse them, were unacceptable to the community at large.

The Millertonians had no excuse for treating the Chinese as cruelly as they did. Morality among the white citizens was horrendously lax in those days, and contemporary standards would likely adjudge the Chinese more virtuous. "[Everything] was conducted in a loose, devil-may-care style," wrote William Faymonville. "County Court was adjourned one day, in order to give the jury an opportunity to attend a horse-race, and the Board of Supervisors would adjourn twenty times a day in order to go and take a drink."

If a person came into town looking for an official to sign a deed, certify a mining claim or record a document, that official would almost always be found in a saloon. There, according to Lilbourne A. Winchell, inquiries made of the bartender could produce responses like "No, he's not been here, [he's] over at Stroud's, playing poker . . . Been at [George McClelland's saloon] all morning—him and the district attorney and the clerk and the coroner is settin' in a big game . . . No use for you to see him, he's drunk now. Gi' me the paper; I'll give it to him tomorrer when he sobers up."

This type of indulgence could lead to aberrant behavior, as a now-famous story—also related by Winchell—demonstrates:

Late one night after a long session of poker and whiskey in McCray's bar room, a district attorney, a county clerk, a justice, a lawyer and another companion—all well under the control of many drinks—agreed that they were hungry. At that waning hour of the night, the hotel cooks and all other servitors were sound asleep. In their drunken disregard for anything, they filched some bread from the kitchen pantry; but wanted something more. Across the street from the hotel lived [Jane Dermon]; she had some chickens, and the boozey officials robbed her hen-roost, and proceeded to fix up a chicken supper. On a fire built in the street they roasted, or burnt, the half-picked, half-dressed fowls. With these and the stolen bread and more whiskey they held a bestial feast—tearing and devouring the raw flesh like savage beings. The car-

ousal did not cease till near daylight, when some were dead drunk, sprawled in the dust of the road, and the others barely able to stagger sottishly away from the scene of their debauch. Incredible? It will be hard for those who [read] this tale, at this far day, to believe that utter degradation of those officers of the law; but unimpeachable testimony has long supported the truth of the story!

Even Winchell's father, Judge E. C., became caught up in Millerton's free-wheeling spirit. An article in the July 18, 1891, *Fresno Daily Evening Expositor* testifies to this:

The people at Millerton were great people for social entertainments. That was the headquarters for all the surrounding country, and people came from Kings River [Centerville], Fresno Flats [Oakhurst], Fine Gold and other places, to attend the dances at Millerton, which was the county seat and the principal town in the county. A dancing teacher was hired, and everybody began to learn to dance—old miners, old stockmen, old gamblers, old preachers, and of course all the young people in the whole country.

A memorable dance is recorded, which took place in early days. It took place one night in the courthouse. Judge Winchell was county judge then, and had given his permission for the dance to be held in the courtroom. When court adjourned that evening the Judge mounted his old gray horse and rode home, leaving the dancers to enjoy themselves.

The next morning about 9 o'clock he reached the top of the hill above town, and heard the dance still in progress. It was time to call court, but he thought he would let them finish that set before disturbing them. So, he stood in the door and watched them. The music filled him with desires to join in and take a whirl; and soon he found himself swinging round the airy circles as lively as any of them, and probably more lively, for they had been dancing all night, and he was rested. When that set was done he concluded he would join in another. So he did, and another and another till he forgot all about the court; and they danced until high noon, when the meeting adjourned to meet that evening at Judge Hart's to renew the dance.

When Millerton marked its first decade, it was still a rude, ramshackle town with many more cheap frame buildings and tents than more substantial structures. Floods, in the 1861–62 winter, wiped out a large proportion of the town. A number of buildings subsided, and the lower floor of the Oak Hotel was filled with sand and silt. The town citizens should have learned from this disaster—rebuilding with stone and brick buildings at a greater distance from the river—but that never happened. Millertonians liked to have easy access to water and since there was only one well in town, it was a lot simpler to throw together more shacks and tents than to bother with planning and sound building practices. Convenience was the overriding factor to the carefree Millertonians in those days.

Progress was being made on some fronts. About the time of the flood, the Reverend Daniel Dade, a Catholic priest, moved into town. Assigned to the Visalia parish in May 1861, he contracted malaria there and was sent to Millerton, where the climate was said to be more healthful. While there he stayed active in religious doings, holding regular services (probably at the Burrough hotel). His genial presence and Irish wit soon endeared him to the locals, and even to those who frequented the saloons and gambling dens. Eventually Dade returned to Visalia, but he often visited friends at Millerton and conducted weddings there.

In the spring of 1864 Laura A. Winchell (Mrs. E. C.) opened a new school at her Winchell Gulch home. (The area had been without a school for four years.) It served young scholars from a wide geographical area, from as far north as the Chowchilla River to as far south as the Kings, and several points in-between (Fresno River and Big Dry Creek). A large room was eventually built to house the school, which was actually a private academy. Pupils ranged in age from six to nineteen years, and instruction went from the ABC's up to the McGuffey's Fourth Reader and Physical Geography grade.

Another important development of this, the Civil War era, was the founding of Fresno County's first newspaper, the *Fresno Times*. It was the brainchild of Ira McCray, who felt that the county needed a means to publicize itself. To this end he enlisted the help of Samuel J. Garrison, former co-publisher of a Visalia secessionist sheet called the *Equal Rights Expositor*. Rioters had destroyed his printing plant and offices in March 1863, so Garrison, who seems to have been between jobs, was happy to move to Millerton. He set up shop in a ramshackle building close to the Oak Hotel, where local citizens and soldiers from Fort Miller would help him work issues off the press. Unfortunately, problems besieged this enterprise, ranging from marauding hogs (see 5:8) to low circulation, so the *Fresno Times* expired after ten issues. Publication began on January 28, 1865, and ended the following April 28. The curious of today can review a complete file at the Fresno City and County Historical Society or the Fresno County Free Library, although historically valuable material is lacking. Garrison, mindful of his previous experiences, saw fit to make the *Times* duller and less controversial than the *Equal Rights Expositor*.

The last major improvement made in Millerton was the erection of a county Courthouse. This was a four-year undertaking that began when the board of supervisors purchased a sixty-six- by three-hundred-foot lot, centrally located in Millerton, from William Rousseau on May 11, 1863. On the following June 9, an adjacent lot of similar dimensions was sold to the county by Stephen A. Gaster and Joe B. Royal; the combined lots, which cost $650, were thereafter known as "the courthouse lot." The store, stable and fencing that had been on the Gaster-Royal lot were sold at auction, R. B. Thomas was paid $100 to develop plans and specifications for the Courthouse, and advertisements were placed in the *Mariposa Free Press, San Francisco Weekly Bulletin, Weekly Sonora Union Democrat, California Weekly Republican News* (Sacramento) and *Tulare Times*. Bids were slow to come in, Thomas' plans were somehow rejected or never delivered, and the project languished.

Eventually plans by Charles S. Peck of Mariposa

Reference 5:8

## EDITOR GARRISON VERSUS WILD HOGS

Millerton did not stand in need of scavengers any more than many another town, but it had more than its share. It is doubtful if there ever was a town of that size that was bepestered as Millerton was with hogs. They came in from the hills in all directions, and the only way to get rid of them was to kill them. Dogs could make no impression on their tough hides. Besides, they could kill a dog quicker than a dog could kill them. They were of that old, long-snouted, lop eared breed, with heads like alligators and backs like a saw. They were always on the verge of starvation, and there was nothing on earth that they would not eat.

They rummaged over the hills and devoured the grain on the ranches, until it came to be a problem what could be done with them. They went in herds, and would come into the town at night and break open the cellar doors, and push into kitchens, and upset cupboards, and play havoc generally.

But the boys met their match at last, and many a long snouted old veteran of twenty summers slept the sleep that knows not breaking. In the course of time a man went to Millerton and started a newspaper. No sooner had the hogs heard of it than they set out to visit the place one night to see what could be found in the line of eatables. They never had seen a printing office, and they did not know but that it might contain a great many good things to eat.

So, one night they paid a visit under the leadership of an old-timer who had crossed the plains with Fremont in 1848, and had roamed the hills about Millerton eating acorns ever since. They pushed the cellar-door of the printing office open and went in. They were perhaps somewhat disappointed by not finding all they looked for, but they made a tolerable mess on the rollers used to ink the type. After that they upset everything in the cellar and took their departure.

The next morning when the editor of the paper saw what had been done he made up his mind to destroy the whole herd. He went out and hired a man to lie in ambuscade the next night with two revolvers, to shoot the hogs when they came back to visit the cellar again.

A man named Seymour agreed to do the shooting. He was a large hograiser himself and wanted to get the wild hogs killed off so tame hogs would have a chance. Accordingly, it was a pleasure as well as a duty to shoot the hogs.

The next night the herd came, pushed the cellar door open and went in. Seymour hid outside with his two revolvers, while the editor took a pole and drove the hogs out of the cellar. Seymour shot 12 times as they passed him and killed 12. He was greatly pleased until he found that they were not wild hogs at all but were his own that he had killed.

SOURCE: *Fresno Daily Evening Expositor*, July 18, 1891, p. 2, c. 1-3.

County were approved, and three bids were received and considered on June 11, 1866. George Chittenden wanted $20,000 for the job, Peck and William Hillenhagen $18,500, and Charles Porter Converse $17,008.25. The supervisors were reluctant to let the irascible, shifty Converse (see Chapter 11) have the job, and appointed Claudius Golon Sayle, Fresno County district attorney, as the project supervisor. For further safety, County Clerk William Faymonville and Sheriff J. Scott Ashman were appointed to referee disputes between Converse and Sayle.

Construction work on the Courthouse stretched from mid-1866 to mid-1867. Bricks for the building were burned in a kiln behind Grierson's Millerton store. Granite for its foundations, window sills, entrance and entrance steps and jail portion was quarried from a location a quarter-mile below town, on the San Joaquin River.

The building slowly took the following form: On the ground floor, a large entrance—the only one to the building—confronted a main central hallway leading to the clerk's, sheriff's, treasurer's and surveyor's offices on either side. The walls were wainscoted, and the windows had solid iron sheets for shutters. At the end of this floor were two jail cells with heavy granite walls and floors, with one window each, secured by six bars apiece.

The second floor was reached by mounting an inside staircase, just to the right of the entrance. On that level there was a small jury room, a large courtroom and a thick pine plank floor throughout. Exterior dimensions of the building were thirty-six by fifty-four feet; the outer walls were of brick (save for the jail's bare granite construction, which gave the whole an unfinished look) and the roof was made of shaped shingles. A final touch was the addition of a marble plaque, reading "Erected 1866," in the building's pediment.

Until the county seat's transfer, the Courthouse worked well and was the setting for some interesting incidents (see Chapter 11). Once Millerton began its decline, Joseph Bell Folsom, an early area resident (see Chapter 4) lived there. The building also was used as a schoolhouse in 1878 and as a social gathering place. In the years afterward, bats, pigeons and other animals used the place as a refuge, and vandals took their toll. A report in the May 10, 1892, *Fresno Daily Evening Expositor* said: "The glass is nearly all broken out of the windows, the wooden doors are gone, and the floors are somewhat bulged on account of the rain beating in at the windows; the plastered walls are all scratched up by lead pencil marks . . ." This destructive process continued well into the twentieth century; in 1927, marauding high school students from Fresno shot the marble plaque apart.

When construction on Friant Dam threatened to inundate the Courthouse, in the early 1940s, the Native Sons and Daughters of the Golden West had it carefully taken apart, with every piece numbered for relocation. The remains were taken to a storage site near the base of the dam. More than two decades later, in 1964-65, the California Division of Parks and Recreation was given funds to rebuild the Courthouse on Mariners Point, overlooking Friant Dam and Millerton Lake. After five years of work and $154,000, the Courthouse was restored to its original splendor and has been open to the public ever since.

The Courthouse's completion marked the apex of Millerton's development. Approximately six months afterward—on December 24, 1867—a massive flood destroyed much of the town, broke its spirit, and sent it into a decline from which it never recovered. Early snowfalls in the neighboring mountains, followed by warm rains, had washed acres of foliage and trees into the San Joaquin River and its tributaries. The waters began rising, but Millerton was spared for a time: a large mass of debris had collected north of town, creating a dam that held back much of the torrent that was building. The pressure became too much, however, the dam crumbled, and a huge wall of water ripped through Millerton on Christmas Eve. Logs were caught up in the floodwaters and acted as battering rams, pulverizing everything in sight. The famous

Reference 5:9

## CHINESE EXCLUSION IN MILLERTON

At a called meeting of the Citizens of Millerton held on the 30th day of December, 1867 for the purpose of taking into consideration the locating of the Chinese population heretofore occupying the Town of Millerton . . . J. Scott Ashman was duly appointed Chairman and Wm. Faymonville, Secretary.

It was resolved that a Committee of five be chosen for the purposes above indicated, to wit: to ascertain and define the limits of this town within which no Chinese inhabitants shall be allowed to reside . . . On motion C. A. Hart, Ira Stroud, Lewis Leach, J. M. Shannon and Otto Froelich were unanimously chosen as such committee and in-

structed to report to this meeting tomorrow, at 7 o'clock P.M. to which time the meeting adjourned. Meeting at 7 o'clock, P.M. Tuesday, December 31, 1867, the Committee Resolved, That all persons wishing to erect Buildings for the occupation of Chinese, be requested to build on the West side of the first creek below Shannon's house . . . On motion, the aforesaid resolutions were unanimously adopted.

On Motion, the following Resolution was also read and adopted, to wit: Resolved, That it is the express wish and desire of this meeting that all Chinese female inhabitants be requested to remove from the limits of the

Town of Millerton, to the ground designated in Resolution No. One so soon as the same can be effected without serious detriment to themselves, or to those whose property they are at present occupying.

On Motion, the meeting adjourned,

Wm. Faymonville, Secretary

[The last motion undoubtedly referred to prostitutes and they obviously did not want to inconvenience the owners of the houses in which they were working.]

SOURCE: Minutes of the meetings.

oak tree at Ira McCray's hotel was torn out by its roots, and the buildings and ferry there were dashed to pieces and washed away. All of the wooden buildings at lower elevations were smashed like kindling, and water lapped ominously at the base of the Courthouse. After the worst had hit Millerton, the flood continued to hurtle down the river with tremendous force. Logs were deposited at the California Ranch and Banderita Flat where impromptu sawmills were set up, though not always at a profit (see Chapter 6). Some of the wreckage was said to have reached San Francisco Bay!

Christmas Day, 1867, dawned on a ruined Millerton. While there had been no casualties—waters had been mounting for several days, and everyone had moved to higher ground—the destruction of property, businesses and hope had been appalling. John Linnebacher, who had opened a store there in 1865, had most of his building washed away and lost much stock; he went insane, and had to have his affairs managed by a guardian. James E. Denny, who had moved to Millerton a year after Linnebacher and had built another store—out of brick and timber scraps from the Courthouse construction—also was wiped out. Unlike Linnebacher, he began anew in Visalia. Even George Grierson, a longtime merchant (given Millerton's brief history) became discouraged after the walls of his adobe store were soaked and slid away, leaving only the rock foundation, supporting timbers and a roof atop it. He and his family left for Denmark on May 1, 1868, and Francesco Jensen took over the business. Within a year Jensen was succeeded by Otto Froelich, who in turn became a prosperous Fresno merchant.

Ira McCray suffered the worst fate of all. His finances had become shaky after 1862-63, when he failed to collect on debts owed him and his business began to languish. The flood completed his ruination, and he left Millerton destitute. He attempted to build a new fortune in the Arizona gold mines, met with no success there, and drifted back to the new town of Fresno. There, he lived off of friends and any convenient almsmen. In the late 1870s he contracted cancer of the hand and began failing. He died a pauper at the county hospital on October 5, 1877, most likely cared for in his last days by ex-Millertonian and generous spirit Dr. Lewis Leach.

The Christmas Eve flood was not the last disaster to hit Millerton. In a fit of rage, townsfolk banished the Chinese—who seem to have crept into their midst again—a mere six days after the flood (see 5:9). The act seems strange; townsfolk should have been more concerned with rebuilding than airing prejudices.

The Chinese were picked on whenever a convenient opportunity arose, as this item from the July 10, 1872, *Fresno Weekly Expositor* shows:

OUGHT TO BE ATTENDED TO.—We direct attention to the horribly filthy condition of that portion of our village, known as Chinatown. [The Chinese had apparently moved back again!] It is a perfect pestilence-breeding cesspool. At this time, in particular, when the terrible small pox is running rife throughout the State, this "sink of iniquity" should be looked after, as should a case of that dreadful disease occur in our midst, this infamous locality alluded to would do more to spread it, by aid of its miasmatic and offensive atmosphere, than any exposure could possibly do. The citizens should organize themselves into a committee and compel the filthy slaves to be more cleanly [*sic*]. It is better to take precautionary measures than to have half our citizens stricken down by loathsome disease.

The writer was probably mistaking cramped and disorderly living conditions for uncleanliness. As noted before, the Chinese were just as hygenic as the whites who lived then, if not more so.

Two and a half years after the flood, calamity struck just before another holiday. Blacksmith D. B. McCarthy had been storing Fourth of July fireworks, obtained at Stockton, in his Millerton shop. When he and a party of revelers—possibly drunk—decided to test a Roman candle on the night of July 3, 1870, flames from the candle found their way into the shop, and to the remainder of the fireworks. A brilliant, raucous blaze erupted; Simon W. Henry's nearby hotel was soon caught up in it, as was S. Levy's Farmer's Exchange Saloon. Of Henry's loss, which was $8,000 or so, the July 6 *Fresno Weekly Expositor* said: "He has had a terrible stroke of luck; has been flooded out once, had his blacksmith shop burned down once previously, and blown down once."

The aforementioned *Expositor* was one of the few bright spots amid this murky decline. A successor to the ill-fated *Fresno Times*, it commenced publication on April 27, 1870. Its first owners were J. H. Peters and John W. Ferguson; Peters left the business in November 1871 and was replaced by Charles A. Heaton. Ferguson bought out Heaton's interest in October 1873, since Heaton wanted to enter the Millerton real estate business, and was the sole owner for many years afterward. Chicard and Company freighted in a Washington hand press and other printing supplies from Stockton. Costs were so high that the *Expositor* had to forsake a building it had planned to use, and printing was conducted in a stable for eight months. For some time after that, the shop of an accommodating carpenter was used. Unlike the *Times*, circulation grew steadily after an initial press run of 200 copies.

In the year of the *Expositor*'s founding, Millerton seemed vital enough. There were four stores (three of them Chinese), Otto Froelich's express and post office, three saloons, Michael Donahoo's and Simon W. Henry's livery stables, James Thornton's butcher shop, McCarthy's blacksmith shop, and single shoemaker's, tailor's, drug, barber, saddlery and furniture shops.

Yet everyone seemed demoralized and fatalistic about the town, as the *Expositor* lamented in July 1870: "Everything is dead or on the rapid decline. No buildings of any value, no churches [nor were there ever any in Millerton], no society and no permanency about anything. Such should not be the case . . . and such would not be the case were the town located almost anywhere else in the county. As it is, it is unhandy for all sections. It is off the line of travel [the mining excitement having died down] and has no inducements for people to settle in it, even though there was room to build suitable houses to live in, which there is not." Indeed, houses were renting from six to twelve dollars a month, and even old Fort Miller remained fully occupied by area residents; but no one wanted to live in the dirty river town that had never been rebuilt completely after the 1867 flood. There was a crude, unsettling feeling about the place that made all Millertonians uncomfortable.

Despite the sentiments of townsfolk, the 1870s—the last days of Millerton's pre-eminence in Fresno County—saw a few improvements. In October 1870 a Good Templars lodge was founded—Fresno County's first secret society—and the Fresno Lodge, No. 186 of the Independent Order of Odd Fellows was created on February 23, 1871. In June 1873 the latter group opened a town cemetery around a hill and just behind Millerton; only half a dozen or so burials were ever made there.

After the destruction of McCray's ferry in the 1867 flood, "Walker" (probably James Null) and William Faymonville opened a replacement service, and in 1872 Faymonville, James Walker and Dr. Lewis Leach opened another ferry at Wester's Flat, site of an old Pitkatchi Yokuts village about a mile below Millerton. Stage service was available to several different points (see Chapter 4), and after the town of Fresno was founded in 1872 Charles W. DeLong and Russell Fleming ran a line from Millerton to that prairie town.

Fresno's proximity to the newly-established Central Pacific Railroad, and to agricultural enterprises as well, assured that it would eclipse Millerton in a commercial sense. Almost as soon as it was founded, and began to show promise, people began to suggest the county seat be moved there. A March 23, 1874, election made the transfer a reality (see Chapter 7) and Millerton was doomed. With mining gone, and its location now off the beaten track, it had no reason to live. Practically everyone began moving out, some dismantling their homes and businesses and hauling them to Fresno. Wallace W. Elliott's *History of Fresno County* describes the Millerton exodus thus, and wrote a succinct obituary of the town:

Expositor of September, 1874, says: "The glories of Millerton have departed, and in a few more days it will live only in name. One by one the buildings are being torn down and moved to Fresno. Last week Faymonville's and Dr. Leach's offices were torn down, and Judge Sayle's residence and office is following suit. Dixon's residence will soon go the way of the rest. Over two years ago Otto Froelich led the van by tearing down his store, and last spring the *Expositor* office followed suit, and during the last month the great exodus commenced. Farewell, poor Millerton."

At a later date it says: "Joseph Sayer, the Millerton shoemaker, stayed there until the last, and finally moved to Fresno. He says he 'don't could have stood it any longer; Millerton is shoost like a ranch; you don't can see nobody all day long; Sharley [Charles] Garland don't got but one goostomer, and that's Bill [Faymonville], and he's goming Fresno.'"

One attraction near Millerton apparently did not come into its own until after the town had all but disappeared. A mere three-quarters of a mile below Millerton on the opposite side of the river—and known to the locals since the 1850s, although a January 14, 1874, *Fresno Weekly Expositor* report called it a "newly discovered Bethesda"—was the Millerton Sulphur Springs. The waters there issued from five separate springs named Indian Geyser, Diana's Bower, Fresno Bubbler, Invalid's Delight and Cupid's Boudoir. There also was a spring issuing from the granite bedrock near the river's edge.

Sometime during the 1870s or 1880s, a hotel or bathhouses seem to have been built there. It is certain that, in 1890, William R. Hampton's hotel on the San Joaquin River (see Chapter 13) was dismantled and moved to the sulphur springs.

The springs received no further notice in the newspapers but they obviously were popular with those who liked to bathe in warm (seventy-one degree) sulphur water. The state mineralogist later reported (mineral water, you know) that at one time the spa had "eighteen tent cottages and a twenty room hotel." The springs issued 17,000 gallons in twenty-four hours. They served visitors and remained there until 1942, when Millerton Lake's rising waters necessitated their destruction.

Dreams of another sulphur spring resort led to the founding of Thermal in the late 1880s, just five miles southwest of the Millerton springs. Applicants for a post office said it would service a resort near some hot sulphur springs (hence the name) but the project never came into being. In any event, the post office was established March 5, 1889, on the James Ferguson ranch, at the southeast corner of Millerton and Auberry roads.

A store and bar were opened at about the same time; and on March 5, 1895, a Thermal School District was founded with L. J. Henrici, Frank Martinez and James Ferguson as its trustees. None of these enterprises lasted for long. The post office was transferred to Auberry on January 15, 1900, the store and bar are

*The Thermal postoffice and store established to serve a sulphur springs resort that never materialized.*

HENRY AKERS

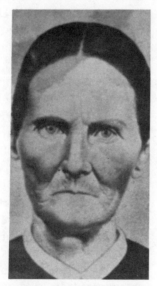

DELILAH
MILLER AKERS

JAMES D. COLLINS
*One of Fresno County's first teachers, he established the "Academy" school at Big Dry Creek in 1870. He farmed and was elected sheriff in 1898 and served for eight years.*

FRANCESCO JENSEN
*Millerton merchant, first postmaster and general store owner at Big Dry Creek in 1870.*

long gone, and the school district lapsed for lack of students in 1907, having had only six in its previous term. Wells in the area still bring in sulphur water most often but there are no plans for a resort.

One may broadly propose that mining and get-rich-quick visions led most early settlers to Fresno County, but in a specific sense that is just not true. The early settlements south and east of Millerton had a largely agrarian and stock-raising base from their earliest days, and, unlike the rambunctious residents of Millerton and other mining camps, the people were oriented toward education, church and the family. Auberry and Big Sandy valleys, Big Dry Creek area and Watts Valley were bellwethers of the many towns in the county that developed with the rise of agriculture, the influx of more genteel farmers, and the advance of a relatively stable civilization in the county circa 1875.

John Greenup Simpson, William Harshfield and William Lewis Lovely Witt were the earliest settlers at Big Dry Creek, arriving in 1852. Of these men, Simpson eventually assumed the greatest importance to Fresno County. When latter-day homesteaders in the area got discouraged with their crop returns and left, Simpson unhesitatingly bought them out—his holdings increased to 7,000 acres. He became a prominent stock raiser, served as the first county tax collector, and later as a superintendent of county schools.

Harshfield and Witt have long been recognized as being among the earliest hay and grain farmers in the county (see Chapter 6). They sold their holdings to Charles Porter Converse of Converse's ferry circa 1854; three years after that, Converse sold his Big Dry Creek holdings to Millerton hotelkeeper Ira McCray. By dismantling his old hotel and stables there, and replacing them with the more elaborate Oak Hotel, McCray was able to build a new, similar operation at the point where Big Dry Creek crossed the Stockton-Los Angeles stage road. Beyond this point, it is said, no other buildings existed on the prairie during the 1850s, save for William Helm's small cabin six miles to the west. McCray's enterprise seems to have endured until his financial reverses of the 1860s; it is unknown if anyone took it over after that time.

As the 1850s progressed, a wide variety of people began moving into the Big Dry Creek area. Among them were "Little Dog Johnson," so called because of a small terrier that followed him constantly; William Adshead, a brick and stone mason; Louis Henrici, John Shaid and Lewis Stemder, who began ranching in 1855; and stock raiser Major Wyatt, who settled on Wyatt Mountain (six and a half miles south of Millerton) circa 1859.

"An episode [typical of the era] on the Wyatt ranch was the 'barn raising' about 1867, when the men of the neighboring hills came to lift into place the hand-hewn, wooden-pegged frame, and further aid in the building of the major's new barn," wrote Ernestine Winchell.

"The women and children came, too, on horseback or in the farm wagons, bringing quantities of food, which was supplemented by all the resources of the Wyatt larder. This was a festive occasion long remembered." In the early 1870s, Wyatt died after being thrown from his horse out in the middle of the plains on a hot summer day. By the time he was found, barely alive, heat prostration and sunstroke had placed him beyond hope. His sons took over the ranch for a time, but moved on after a few years.

One notable arrival of 1868 was Francesco Jensen, who moved down from Millerton and opened a small store. When Big Dry Creek gained a post office on March 25, 1870, it was established at this store, with Jensen as postmaster. This post office was the first in the county not situated on a major river. A September 4, 1872, *Fresno Weekly Expositor* notice said that "Mr. J. has recently received a large assortment of groceries, dry goods, clothing and drugs. He also keeps a superior quality of liquors, particularly brandy, for medicinal purposes."

Most arrivals of the 1860s were involved in stock raising. A few came from Solano County with their flocks of sheep: Major Thomas P. Nelson, David Cowan Sample and William Walter Shipp in 1868, and Thomas J. Hall and Thomas Jaynes the next year. Nelson, Sample and Shipp formed what became known as the Mississippi Settlement, in an area to the south and west of Big Dry Creek. John W. Potter and Richard Freeman also were sheepmen in the area; numbered among the farmers were Arnold Bonnifield, James Berry Jack and two men named Heiskell and Wainscot. There also was a farmer and windmill manufacturer, John Doak.

Others who came to Big Dry Creek in the late 1860s were Lewis P. Clark and Jesse Blasingame, the latter an Auberry Valley hay farmer who raised horses, cattle and sheep on an extensive flatland spread.

A Mississippi School District was formed on May 4, 1869—which attempted to swallow the Millerton School District two years later. Instead, the Millerton district absorbed the Mississippi—perhaps because of attendance fluctuations, as was often the case in those days. It was not until June 4, 1879, that the district was reorganized. In 1877, while still part of Millerton, the school was conducted by William Long, who taught forty-two students and had an average attendance of thirty in his classroom.

In the early 1860s a circuit rider, Henry Neal, met regularly with members of the Methodist Episcopal Church South in the Big Dry Creek area. About 1865 the Reverend Joel Hedgpeth became the regular minister. In 1869 the congregation built what is believed to be the first church in Fresno County. John G. Simpson donated the land for the church, and other costs were covered by popular subscription. A square one-room building with a steeple and bell, it still stands today, on

Madison Avenue just a quarter mile north of Highway 168 in Academy. The church building was attacked a few years ago by woodpeckers which drilled holes all over it—the holes making excellent nests for bothersome bees. Stucco on the outside walls and corrugated iron sheeting on the roof ensure that the church should be around for many more years. Services still are held there at least four times a year, the attendees being mostly descendants of Big Dry Creek pioneers. The church operates in cooperation with the Clovis United Methodist Church.

"The Reverend Joel Hedgpeth was greatly loved by all his people," said one of his descendants. "Once he was offered the opportunity of becoming a bishop in the area, but he refused, maintaining that he was a small man, a little man and a plain man—and he belonged to the people here who were also plain people, and there in this small church he wanted to remain with them. And he did. Later he was at one time 'churched' [upbraided] for refusing to preach fire and brimstone; he believed that love alone was the power. In spite of this rebuke by his church, he continued as the preacher of the little church; his followers just would not do without him." He is buried in the cemetery not far from the church.

The outstanding event in Big Dry Creek's history was the construction of its academy in 1872 (see 5:10). The connection of the community with this institution has been so pervasive that, in modern times, the Big Dry Creek name for the area has been supplanted by "Academy." The shift began on May 8, 1876, when an Academy post office was established, only to be discontinued on July 6, 1877. It was revived on April 22, 1892, merged with Big Dry Creek's post office on August 10, 1893, and save for one lapse the Academy post office lasted well into the twentieth century.

As for the academy itself, it came into being when there was a public clamor for a school. Leaders in the district—Alfred Beard, W. T. Cole, L. P. Clark, Jesse Blasingame, Jesse Musick, Andrew D. Firebaugh, A. C. Thompson, Cladius Golon Sayle, W. L. Greenup, Ira Stroud, Francesco Jensen and John A. Stroud—formed a private corporation, capitalized at $50,000, to construct the school. The cost was only $3,170, which paid for a rather impressive building. "The size of the building is 36 x 54 feet, veranda on two sides, and on the front, [the veranda is] eight feet in width," said the November 20, 1872, *Fresno Weekly Expositor*. "The school-room is 33 x 35 feet with ante-rooms on each side of the building. The recitation room is 19 x 20, a very light and comfortable room. The ceilings clear 12 feet. The building is ceiled throughout with alternate redwood and pine."

As its name suggests, and the appended description confirms, the academy set its sights higher than all other Fresno County schools of the period. Its more diligent graduates could qualify to teach school in their own right, or proceed to college entrance—an impossibility in any other county school. Because of the overall shortage of teachers, the academy's establishment was a windfall for the developing county school system.

James Darwin Collins and his wife, Ann, taught at the academy for its first two years; they were said to be outstanding teachers. Later on, Professor William A. Sanders was hired to teach there for eight dollars a day—an astronomical salary in that era, and indicative of the academy's high standards. When he completed

Reference 5:10

## THE BIG DRY CREEK ACADEMY

The Academy is situated in a beautiful oak grove on a dry knoll, a short distance from Dry Creek, a small mountain stream which makes its way down from the mountains through a long line of oak, willow and cottonwood trees; and winds its way over the plains toward the San Joaquin, but is lost in the sands before it reaches its destination. . . . The school is well supplied with maps, charts, cards, etc. Among other objects of interest, is a well selected library of fifty-six volumes, (enclosed in a black walnut book case), including Webster's Unabridged Dictionary, eight volumes of the American Cyclopaedia [sic], "Rollin's Ancient" History, and works of Science, History and Biography; a fine set of blackboard, 3x80 feet, and a flower stand with eighteen varieties of common plants.

The school at present numbers fifty pupils in regular attendance, and is for a country school, well graded in all branches from the First Reader to algebra, geometry and physiology. Drawing is taught to the primary scholars only; but all sing daily. Indeed, there are a number of excellent singers, and while a score of voices raise on the soprano, the other parts are well carried; and as good singing is quite a rarity in schools, the people of Dry Creek are quite proud of the accomplishment.

The Dry Creek Literary Society keeps pace with the school in point of progress, and although its young, promising orators may not quite excel the modern public speaker in "lip service," yet in modesty, common sense and manliness, they take the lead.

The Academy was designed for a high school, and was built by private parties at a cost of about $3000. The first school was taught by J. D. Collins in '72-3; since then the school has been large and prosperous. And at present thorough sympathy exists between parent and teacher, indicating that the people are awake to the best interests of the common schools. The design of a high school has not been given up, and there are many things in favor of such a movement: First, the extreme healthiness of the neighborhood: Second, a good house: Third, a thoroughly moral neighborhood—something to be highly recommended to the youth of the present generation. . . .

The present teacher, Mr. F. W. Blackmar, cannot be too highly eulogized for that nameless "knack" of conducting the school exercises, the just result of fine scholastic attainments, thorough professional training, and the natural tact and courtesy so charming to all with whom he comes in contact. Surely the people of Dry Creek are to be congratulated upon such an acquisition, for in no better hands is it possible to confide the educational, moral and social advancement of their children. Under such guidance as his, the Academy school is certain to prosper in the near future, becoming as it deservedly should "The School" of Fresno County.

SOURCE: *Fresno Weekly Expositor*, January 24, 1877, p. 3, c. 3.

the school year in May 1876, it was reported that he had seventy-five students enrolled, with an average attendance of fifty. By 1877 Sanders had been succeeded by Frank W. Blackmar, and—sadly—the higher-level curriculum had been dropped, making the academy a mere elementary school. The building was later moved, was reduced in size, and never regained its former importance.

A backward glance at Big Dry Creek would be incomplete without mention of social activities there—which seem to have been considerable. From the *Fresno Weekly Expositor* of February 16, 1876:

The young people of this neighborhood seem to partake of the general good feeling, and signalize their sentiments by having frequent parties. I attended one at Mr. [John] Doak's on the 5th inst. Quite a number of persons were present, and everybody enjoyed themselves hugely—especially when supper was announced. It was the best meal I ever partook of. Turkeys were served by wholesale, and pies, cakes and other nick-nacks were equally abundant. After supper the young folks acted several charades in a creditable manner. Amid the enjoyments of the evening the ladies did not forget the privileges conferred upon them by reason of it being Leap Year. It is my opinion that several conquests were made on that evening. One lady went so far as to propose and was accepted. Fearing that the young gentleman would back out she insisted on having the ceremony performed immediately. After some hesitation the gentleman assented, and the ceremony was performed by Rev. John Doak. As the lady immediately abandoned her new-made husband, he made complaint before judge [W. T.] Cole and a decree of divorce was granted. The party broke up at a late hour.

From the *Fresno Weekly Expositor* of January 3, 1877:

I had the pleasure last night of being one of the many persons who enjoyed themselves at the Big Dry Creek Festival. There were about two hundred persons assembled, or the school house which is about thirty-six by fifty, was so densely crowded that it was difficult for one to have elbow room; and he had to keep his pegs straight under him if he wanted his corn crib safe. But assembling there was not all; the Dry Creek students had promised to entertain the people on this occasion, and they never went back on their word; for we had not more than got ourselves snugly tucked in some ten year old boy's seat, with a desk about six inches lower, we supposed, than a mechanic could get . . . [before] we heard the sweet strains of music start, and turning our eyes in the direction of the stage, we saw a huge instrument, which looked like it was or might be the father of all music pans, and behind it was seated a pretty little girl of about fourteen years, with rosy cheeks, curly hair, a dimple chin, and pretty blue eyes; and she seemed to be a princess of music, for

when she began to play, everything quieted into silence—even the babies, dogs and Arkansaw whittlers were mute. Prof. Blackman [*sic*] then gave the Christmas tree's inaugural address; next followed a long train of declamations, singing, etc. Finally this part of the performance drew to a close, and they unveiled the Christmas tree, which had looked all along like a piece of Montgomery [Queen's Circus] tent cloth; but now the change had come; they lit up the tree with an innumerable quantity of [items], and we could plainly see doll heads, jumping jacks and quilts and blankets about a foot square. I heard afterward that the receivers of the quilts and blankets did not go home that night; but two or three of them got together and spliced, to try the durability of their presents . . .

About five miles north of Academy, in Morgan Canyon, another community had been "founded" a year earlier. It was 1876, the year of the United States centennial, and canyon residents wanted to form a school district. They patriotically selected the name Centennial, and the county schools department accepted the name and petition for formation. The only problem was that, somewhere in the paper-shuffling, the name was changed to Sentinel. Nobody seemed to be concerned; it took only a few weeks for the residents to pitch in and build the twenty-four- by twenty-eight-foot schoolhouse, supplying it with wall maps, a globe, a dictionary and furniture, and employing B. A. Hawkins as its first teacher. Soon the school had an enrollment of thirty-six and an average attendance of thirty.

Amid all the excitement, no one thought to change Sentinel back to Centennial, and it retained the former name throughout its existence. The settlement was soon served by two traveling ministers (B. Birkhead and W. Howard) and, although lacking a church congregation, boasted an enthusiastic Sunday school. On April 7, 1880, another milestone was passed when the Sentinel post office was created.

As to the economy of the area, "the country in this vicinity is now almost entirely utilized as a stock range for cattle and hogs," said the January 17, 1877, *Fresno Weekly Expositor* of the Sentinel neighborhood. " . . . The soil is of excellent quality, producing large crops of grain and hay wherever cultivated, which cannot as yet be rendered profitable owing to the difficulty of getting the proper machinery into this [foot-hill] portion of our county. Fruit trees of all kinds grow luxuriously and produce bountiful crops and the largest and most luscious fruit, while the many farms under cultivation are abundantly supplied with living springs of the purest water." William Corlew was said to be the area's leading farmer, and the pre-eminent stockmen were Louis Studer and a partnership composed of Daniel Hedrick and one Nichols.

Sentinel's post office and store were three miles southeast of the school, at the intersection of the Millerton and Toll House roads. A roadhouse was

The Academy schoolhouse, with a class of students collected on the porch, probably sometime in the 1880s.

Post office at Academy soon after it was established in 1876.

Plaque recognizing role of Academy in the county's history, erected by Jim Savage Chapter, E Clampus Vitus.

ACADEMY

ONE QUARTER MILE NW OF HERE IN A GROVE OF OAK TREES ON THE SOUTH BANK OF DOG CREEK WAS ESTABLISHED THE ACADEMY IN 1872. IT WAS THE FIRST SECONDARY SCHOOL IN FRESNO COUNTY. L.O COLLINS, LATER SHERIFF, WAS THE FIRST TEACHER. JUST EASTERLY OF THE ACADEMY STOOD THE SMALL M.E. SOUTH CHURCH BUILT IN 1869 AND STILL IN USE.

THE STAGE ROUTE FROM VISALIA TO MILLERTON PASSED NEARBY AND SOON A SMALL VILLAGE SPRANG UP-INCLUDING A HOTEL, STORE, STABLES, AND POST OFFICE, TO WHICH THE NAME "ACADEMY" ATTACHED. LATER IT WAS A STOPPING PLACE FOR THE TOLLHOUSE TEAMSTERS.

MANY OF THE COUNTY'S EARLIEST FAMILIES SETTLED HEREABOUT ENGAGING FIRST IN THE SHEEP AND LATER IN THE CATTLE BUSINESS. MANY OF THEM AND THEIR DESCENDANTS NOW REST IN THE NEARBY PIONEER CEMETERY.

DEDICATED NOVEMBER 19, 1967
JIM SAVAGE CHAPTER
E CLAMPUS VITUS

*First church in the county—the Methodist Episcopal Church at Academy—is still in use. Picture is after it was given a protective coating against woodpeckers.*

*A stationary thresher on the Smith ranch in the Big Dry Creek area, circa 1880. Note steam power unit on left—modern for that day.*

## FORGOTTEN TOWN

The earliest recorded townsite in the county is that of June 14, 1865, by George Rivercombe of Georgetown, of thirteen lots on Jones' Flat west of Big Dry Creek. Discovery was made in the record book of mining claims. Lots one to seven, each fifty by 100, ran back to the hills, and eight to thirteen to the creek, lots located on both sides of a central street. The ink sketched townsite notes the existence of a "China house" on lot eleven, and south of townsite and at right angles with it marks out a 400-foot wide mill lot. The lot owning locators were: J. D. Woodworth, Henry Burroughs [*sic*], Ira McCray, Dr. Lewis Leach, William Faymonville, and Rivercombe. It was probably a mining camp, but the oldest Dry Creek pioneer has no recollection of it and the record might not have come to light but for an accidental discovery.

(From Paul A. Vandor's *History of Fresno County*.)

*Ad in January 1865* Fresno Times.

built nearby on the creek by a man named Taggart. Liquor, clothing, tobacco and food could be bought there, and horses and teams could be rested at a watering trough. "At this place an improvident or belated traveler could buy crackers and sardines for a lunch," wrote Ernestine Winchell, "or even obtain a hot meal of bacon and beans, hot biscuits or flapjacks, coffee or green tea. Though he lived alone, the proprietor was himself able to prepare the simple viands generally expected."

The Sentinel school lasted until January 14, 1932, but the post office had a somewhat more tumultuous history. It was deactivated on July 31, 1883, reinstated from February 3, 1888, to March 30, 1897, and revived again in the early twentieth century. What happened to the neighborhood store is unknown.

A more enduring community, Auberry, was located seven miles north of Sentinel. Its name and location have confused beginnings. When miners Albert and Absolom Yarborough arrived in Fresno County from Tennessee, circa 1860, they located in a valley near Temperance Flat. Through casual pronunciation the valley, named after the Yarboroughs, was unofficially christened Auberoy, Aubery, and finally Auberry. Here a settlement of stock raisers and sheepmen evolved, among them John Sutherland, T. F. Blair, F. C. B. Duff and the Corlew family.

On June 12, 1884, an Auberry post office was established in the southern end of the valley, near what is generally identified as Marshall Station. In 1888 it moved a mile and a half south, near the edge of Table Mountain. In 1906 it was moved again, this time eight miles north to New Auberry. The upper end of Auberry Valley had a post office from 1888 to 1899 near the junction of Auberry and Big Sandy roads. It was officially named Lodge but locally called Big Sandy post office and often confused with the Auberry office. In 1902 it was re-established, in 1903 moved three miles north to Old Auberry, and discontinued in 1904.

Various newspaper stories recorded the emergence of a more closely-knit community in the valley. The October 8, 1884, *Fresno Weekly Expositor* reported that a Christian camp meeting had been held there during the previous September 19–October 1:

> The grounds were nicely fitted up by Brothers Hall. Aubury [sic], Corlew and others with an arbor 60 x 100 feet long, covered with shakes and partly sided up. Board tents were also made and everything comfortable and convenient at an expense of about $300. Brothers Dewitt, Logan and Shelton presented the simple story of the Cross in a forcible and impressive manner, ably assisted by Mrs. Tuttle, who had charge of the singing. The attendance at first was small, but as the news spread the people came in and the interest increased until the results were rarely ever equaled in so sparsely settled a community. There were 36 confessions and baptisms, and many took fellowship.

> Strange as it may seem for these times, politics were not thought of, at least not mentioned. At the close of the meeting much interest was manifested; $150 raised for missionary purposes, and $100 for the expense of the meeting . . .

The April 29, 1885, issue of the same newspaper demonstrated that recreational activities were most popular in the young settlement:

> BASE-BALL.—A correspondent writes us from Auberry valley that an interesting match game of baseball was played there on the 18th instant, between the Toll House and Auberry clubs. The latter won the game, the score standing 21 to 27. The Auberries feel rather jubilant over the affair, as this is the second time they have beaten the Toll House club. They are now searching for other clubs to conquer. In the evening after the match the young gentlemen composing the clubs, accompanied by a number of young ladies, repaired to the premises of J. W. Cavin and took possession of his barn, cleaned the floor and had a social dance. . . . Abe Yancey says the Toll House boys, after their defeat, went home and practiced all day Sunday, and now feel confident that they can scoop the Auberry's in another contest.

As the nineteenth century progressed Auberry remained little more than a wide spot in the road. The 1894 Fresno County directory notes only one business operation in town, T. L. Rose's general merchandise store—which also housed the post office. Mining activities helped keep the area lively (see Chapter 4), and other enterprises were being developed on a modest scale. The April 17, 1894, *Fresno Daily Evening Expositor* noted that "the new settlers are crowding on the deeded [government] land, both east and west, north and south—they don't bother—I suppose it is because the needle points that way." Their motivation was, apparently, to engage in agricultural and stock-raising pursuits. The *Fresno Morning Republican* of May 1, 1898, talked of how "crops are light, but no complete failures . . . Parties are bringing stock from all over the county to our chapparal hills. Lots of feed here as long as it lasts."

The area was devoted primarily to raising cattle and the settlers did their best to keep it that way. A correspondent for the *Fresno Daily Evening Expositor* wrote on April 17, 1894, "Sheep have been kept out of this valley for nearly twenty years, but they are here now. . . . Going to start sheep shearing tomorrow. . . . The Palisades look grand with their mantle of green, but the motley sheep turn them reddish color which is disagreeable to the cattle."

As in most of the foothill communities, ranchers in the off seasons drove teams for nearby lumber mills or cut and sold oak firewood in the valley towns. There also was considerable mining, especially along the San Joaquin River, and some participated as owners or workers. There were many optimistic reports on the mines, such as a letter dated February 27, 1889, from L. Ben to the *Expositor*:

Fortune surely must be smiling on this locality, as all the miners seem to have "struck it rich" at once. There seems to have been unusual activity in the mines lately. The Chamber & Sherwood, Solivan, Temperance, Cal Bono, James Herron, the Crystal and the Farley are all showing up fine. Each seems to rival the other in size and richness, and their owners in developing them, while the Jackson & Clark, at present the "El Capitan" of them all, is running fullhanded and with vigor, with preparations for putting in hoisting works and more men. This mill, under the able management of Harry Ayers, is running at full capacity....

In all their optimistic reports they failed to include any dollars-and-cents reports, but since their efforts extended for over twenty years, some mines must have been profitable enough to encourage others.

The Auberry region played host to a number of school districts during the nineteenth century. Oldest among them was the Big Sandy, formed on May 3, 1875, with G. A. Hough, F. C. B. Duff, and T. F. Blair as its first trustees. It was conducted by A. H. Day in 1877, and the January 3 *Fresno Weekly Expositor* of that year said that "the building is quite comfortable, having easy and commodious desks capable of seating some forty-odd pupils whose daily exercise in the various branches taught, is a delight to listen to." The district took its name from the Big Sandy Creek and Valley, approximately five miles northeast of Auberry Valley. As for the school itself, it was on Auberry Road, near the Big Sandy Creek.

An Auberry Valley school district was organized not long after the Big Sandy, on August 8, 1875. S. H. Bond was its first teacher, and Thomas Luke, Joel Holbert, and W. L. Corlew its first trustees.

Where Big Dry Creek flows from Pine Ridge onto the foothills lay Toll House, a settlement born in the wake of the toll road established there in 1866–67 (see Chapter 6). It was started in 1868, just after the road was opened to traffic. James F. Morgan of Morgan Canyon and Henry ("Doc") Glass started blacksmithing businesses that year to service the teams and wagons that were constantly passing by. Charles Abraham Yancey opened a hotel there the same year. "Yancey is a very accommodating fellow," said the April 28, 1872, *Fresno Weekly Expositor*. "[As] an instance: The 'big hill,' up which runs the toll road, is difficult of ascension, and teams frequently get stalled. Abe has a "pulling team" which he lends to teamsters in distress. Cy Dean got stalled the other day, and Abe's famous team, a black horse and a mule, was sent to the relief. It was hitched to the wagon, and commanded to 'get up,' which it didn't proceed to do; the combined strength of seven men succeeded in pushing the wagon against the horses, and they started."

Logging and teaming activities inevitably populated the area, which made it necessary to form a school district—the Pleasant Vale—on May 6, 1872. Sallie Foster was the first teacher, succeeded by Reuben H. Bramlet. The school was a mile below the Toll House settlement to better serve the residents, whose homes were clustered in that area. Dorothy Poling has given an interesting description of it:

... It consisted of one room with an "anteroom" on either side of the front entrance, one for the boys and one for the girls. These were used to hang wraps, store lunches, and, frequently, to administer a strap or limb from a tree to an erring student. The second Pleasant Vale school was located [on the same property] as the first, and was built on practically the same plan. Although the first school had one teacher, who taught nine grades, the second reduced the grades to eight. A one room school has its advantages. While another, more advanced grade is "up front" on the "recitation bench," one with a wandering mind can learn what is in store for future grades ...

Toll House prospered along with its namesake road in the latter nineteenth century. Michael J. Donahoo opened another blacksmith shop, Henry Rea a general store in 1874, Adams and Malcom an additional store about the same time, and G. Pierce Baley, Abner W. Petrea, and one Barker hotels to compete with Yancey's. A succession of saloons opened for business as well; their proprietors' names seem to have been forgotten. Henry Rea became the town's first postmaster on May 8, 1876; except for a lapse between November 13, 1884, and February 2, 1885, it has operated ever since.

In the July 1, 1891, *Fresno Daily Evening Expositor* a correspondent said this about Toll House: "The village is a very small one, but is nice and secluded. On three sides it is surrounded by very steep mountains. Half the town belongs to A. B. Yancy [*sic*], and the other half to Mrs. Barker [widow of the aforementioned hotelkeeper?]. It is said that all the houses here are owned by one or the other of these persons. There are not more than thirty houses in the town, and only two of them are painted. The most of them seem to have been built about the close of the Revolutionary War."

The description may have been unflattering, but the town was alive and kicking. There was a town baseball club known as the Mountain Boys, a Good Templars lodge founded circa 1893, and even a Toll House Literary Society. It met with a similar group from Burrough Valley on February 8, 1890, and discussed an apt question for pioneering Fresno County residents: "Has the extermination of the American Indians been justifiable?"

*Toll House in 1881. (From engraving of W. W. Elliott)*

*Pleasant Vale school at Toll House after consolidation. This is not the building
constructed in 1872 when the huge district was established
but is on the same site.*

101

*Sarvers's Peak at Toll House photographed by R. W. Riggs in 1882. Yancey's Saloon is at right. Note the original Toll House Road along the base of Sarver's Peak, which was constructed in 1866–67.*

F.C.C.H.S. Archives

*Mountain post offices. On the left the Burrough Valley office and store, long closed but still standing (1983). On the right the Sentinel post office on Toll House road, founded in 1880 but date of picture is unknown.*

Sierra Union School

*Mountain schoolhouses. The one on the left they wanted to name Centennial in observance of the 1876 centennial, but somebody didn't understand and it became Sentinel. On the right is the Mechanicsburg school after it was moved to the hamlet of the same name.*

The town's most notable feature was the road running through it, originally private but sold to the county in 1878. Full of steep grades and tight curves, it was hard to negotiate in later years with an automobile—much less a span of a dozen mules or oxen pulling three or more wagons! It was an equally awful, precarious ride going down or up. "The lumber teams . . . went down like chunks of visible thunder," wrote Ernestine Winchell. "Towering blocks of chain-bound yellow boards loomed through banks of gray or tawny dust, crashing, rumbling, thudding—reverberant. Brakes shrieked and howled like attendant imps. Yet one man, a strap in one hand, a rope in another, a horse between his knees, courage in his heart and demoniac craft in his head, controlled the prodigious phenomenon." These difficulties were ameliorated to some degree in 1892, when Angus Marion Clark, George L. Hoxie and others incorporated the Fresno and Pine Ridge Toll Road Company and constructed an easier route, roughly paralleling the old road. In December 1896 this company sold out to the county for $7,500.

Moses Mock, who was skillful mechanically as well as in the lumber trade, drove the first motorized vehicle on the old road during the 1880s. Fascinated by the steam engines that ran sawmills, he wanted to apply the same principles to power a wagon. He built several small prototypes—one that worked, and some that did not—and wanted a full-scale model, but lacked the funds to have one made. For some spare money, he ended up selling his plans to an Eastern manufacturer—who applied them successfully, and made a fortune selling steam wagons.

In 1886 Mock, who had still not lost sight of his dream, purchased a steam wagon someone else had developed. It cost $555.75, and freighting costs from the East equaled that amount. Used for hauling lumber on the Toll House grade, and for quartz crushing near Sentinel, the wagon was inefficient and did not live up to expectations. Mock eventually sold it to grain farmer Clovis Cole, who found it was useless as a harvester as well.

The man who knew the Toll House road best was Abner W. Petrea, owner and driver of the Toll House and Fresno stage line. For years he took passengers up the grade from the town, to the Grapevine Spring, past turns called Cape Horn, Cape Cod and the Cape of Good Hope, and—after reaching the summit—along a level portion named the East grade after one who conducted a saloon alongside it.

Everyone attested to Petrea's competency, speed and good humor as a driver. "When we engaged passage on the stage we were not promised a serenade on the last twelve miles of the road, but Allen [sic] Petrea entertained us with songs as he drove and we felt as though we had Sousa's band on a Pullman car," wrote John Shirley Porter in the July 5, 1898, Fresno Morning Republican. It was said in 1892 that Petrea

had driven 50,000 miles—equal to a journey around the world, twice—in Fresno County during his career. Seven years later, after many more miles, he sold out to Joseph House.

The Pleasant Vale School District deserves special mention as the largest school district in the county. When organized in 1872 it covered all the county east of a line extending irregularly from Temperance Flat to Trimmer Springs—about 2,200 square miles.

Two nearby schools, organized from Pleasant Vale territory, were the Mechanicville and Manzanita. Although the small hamlet named Mechanicville was only three miles south of Toll House, the school was six miles south on the Pittman Hill road. It was organized August 4, 1875, with Andrew Firebaugh and C. M. Bennett as trustees. Two young men who had just come from Virginia, Alfred Hoffman and Samuel Harris, did their part to get the school afloat: Hoffman built it, and Harris served as its first teacher. The school was later moved near the hamlet.

The Manzanita district organized March 16, 1898, with John Lewis as teacher. It was about three miles west of Toll House at the junction of Lodge and Black Mountain roads. These two districts and Pleasant Vale later joined to form the present Sierra Union District, which serves some 900 square miles.

The earliest settlers in Burrough Valley, two miles southeast of Toll House, were Colonel Henry Burrough and George Rivercombe, former Millerton residents who arrived in 1853. (See chapters 4 and 12.) They both appear to have continued residence in the almost-circular, 4,000-acre valley during the 1860s, with a brief lapse for Rivercombe; he went east to join the Confederate army. (Legend has it that he named all his farm animals—a mule, horse, dog, rooster, sow and oxen—Jeff Davis, in honor of the secessionist cause.)

In subsequent years the valley became a minor agricultural center. Stock raising took place there, and a January 29, 1887, Fresno Daily Evening Expositor report said "[the] hay crop is always sure. People do not raise grain for market, but they cut everything for hay, which finds ready sale at from $10 to $15 per ton . . . There are numerous springs of pure water in the valley, and many of the families are thus supplied with water. The valley is especially adapted to fruit-growing. A good portion will produce fruit without irrigation after the first or second year." Later, William Dunlap became noted for his apple orchard there, Chester Burnett for his apricots and Charles Williams for his blackberries.

For recreation, the aforementioned article said that valley residents turned to music, baseball, literary discussions, debating and spelling bees, "all of which are largely attended and appreciated." A probable location for some of these activities was the Chester Burnett ranch, where a store was located in the late 1880s and a post office was established on October 2,

1889. In August 1890 Burnett announced plans to erect a three-story building—store and post office on the first floor, church facilities on the second and a public hall on the third. Whether it was ever constructed is unknown.

Burnett's ranch was located at the junction of the Burrough Valley and Auberry roads, as was a similar spread occupied by Andrew ("Dewey") Spence in 1888. Just west of Spence's home he built a store in 1899 (an eventual home of the Burrough post office), and earlier he had donated land on the northeastern corner of his property for a Seventh-day Adventist church. It was an important institution for many years—even having an academy, headed by C. H. Maxwell—but, after the valley's population declined in the early twentieth century, the church was moved to Orosi. Additions have changed its appearance, but the church is still in use.

Early Burrough Valley was home to two school districts, both organized on May 4, 1882. The Mountain View, a quarter-mile east of the site of the Spence store, had J. H. Anthony as its first teacher and George Hutchings as its first board clerk. Three and a half miles southeast of this school was its Sycamore counterpart. Miss M. Matlock was its first teacher and J. W. Rice its first school board clerk.

Watts Valley, two miles southeast of Burrough Valley, was originally called Pope's Valley after its earliest settler. Hezekiah S. Pope. "Pope settled in the late '50s, but arrest for deadly assault induced him to jump bail and flee the country," wrote Lilbourne A. Winchell. Little else is known of him, other than the fact that he was a miner and owned a bar called "Popesville" on the San Joaquin River. After his departure the valley was rechristened after another resident, C. B. Watts.

"Our Valley has the largest supply of good white-ash wood of any portion of Fresno County," wrote a correspondent in the February 28, 1887, *Fresno Daily Evening Expositor*. "Our main dependence, aside from stock, is on wood. Wood is legal tender among us, and is good as gold. The price is hardly sufficient to make a good return for our labor." The writer lamented that there was no rail transportation out of the valley, which would allow for high-volume export and increased sales of the wood "and all would be enhanced."

As to entertainment, he/she further commented that "a large audience gathered to listen to a debate and other literary exercises. This was the first literary entertainment this valley has ever had . . . Our usual mode of enjoyment is dancing, which is well enough, but here it is the sole amusement."

More "modes of enjoyment" were added by 1892, as the April 15 *Fresno Daily Evening Expositor* of that year indicated:

> The mettle of our baseball club was tried to its utmost last Sunday in a lively tussle with the Burrough Valley boys, but we held our own with a score of 21 to 20. The Burroughs have been the champions of the mountains for the last two years. The game was an exciting one from start to finish. The Burroughs were in the lead in the fore part of the game, but the superior batting of the Watts Valley boys saved the day. The features of the day were the catching of Mel Duncan, the fielding of Selby and the batting of Telliver, Kuhn and Hale . . .
>
> Surprise parties are getting quite popular in our valley. A party of young folks gathered together a week ago last Friday night and adjourned to the residence of Mrs. Bettie Mitchell and tendered to her a most agreeable surprise. Dancing was the main feature of the evening, and was indulged in by quite a number of the lads and lassies, who, it is needless to say, enjoyed themselves in a most pleasant manner . . .

The first school district to function in this area was the Watts Valley, organized on May 8, 1878, with trustees G. W. Dill and E. S. Musick. Later, on February 12, 1890, it was joined by the Hawkins school district, named after county schools superintendent B. A. Hawkins. Jessie Whitney was its first teacher and H. F. Bonnifield, E. P. Barrett and Isaac Hale made up its first school board. The schoolhouse was roughly two miles west of the aforementioned Sycamore School.

Back on the Toll House road, due west of Burrough and Watts valleys, lay two enterprises that figure significantly in the history of that thoroughfare—Humphreys' Station and Scotty's (see Chapter 10).

Six miles southwest of Humphreys' Station and just two miles from Academy, a new post office opened on July 8, 1886. It was named Letcher for F. F. Letcher, a Fresno County supervisor and area farmer, and after a time J. C. Brigham established a store there that incorporated the post office. On May 7, 1887, a Letcher school district was formed to further augment this embryo town, with Mrs. I. H. Chapman as its first teacher and H. H. Budge its first board clerk. Little else happened here down to the time the post office closed, on January 15, 1915. There was some copper mining in the area (see Chapter 4), and it is possible that Letcher—who was a partner in several local mining ventures—may have wanted to make his namesake village into a copper-smelting center or some such. If this was so, his dream was never realized.

# Chapter 6

# Livestock, Loggers and Sandlappers

The rise of Fresno County's first major business can be traced to some hungry miners' stomachs. When fortune seekers crowded in during the 1850s, foodstuffs were almost impossible to find. Local agriculture had not been developed—people preferred seeking gold to game. Horses, stages and small boats were the main modes of transportation, making it impractical to convey large food shipments to the San Joaquin Valley. Then a few entrepreneurs realized that building a local cattle industry offered an ideal solution to the problem.

Before 1849 California's Spanish and Mexican settlers raised large herds of cattle in relatively populous areas of the state, principally for their hide and tallow value. With the state's small population, there was little need to slaughter cattle for meat. The gold rush changed this situation. After years of being valued at four dollars a head, demand for beef in the mining areas pushed prices to thirty-five dollars a head.

It did not take long for the cattlemen to make the most of these boom times. From the coastal and southern ranches, cattle drives to the hungry miners in the Sierra foothills became a regular occurrence. Wild cattle, descended from strays that had roamed the San Joaquin Valley for years, were rounded up systematically. Early Fresno County settlers began small-scale ranching; notable among them were Peter Crawford

Appling, Tom Overton, Abe Yancey and S. H. T. Frakes.

The Fresno County cattle market grew in line with the population. Small operations gave way to large, causing the rise of several local cattle barons. Settling near Scottsburg on the Kings River in 1853, William Hazelton and John A. Patterson became the first "barons" of that area, building large herds from stock purchased in southern California and Mexico. The story of how they got their start in the business is worth repeating.

After mining in the Mariposa diggings for a while, Hazelton and Patterson became monte dealers and came out $20,000 to the good after one night's work. The next morning Hazelton told Patterson, "John, we made a 'big killing' last night . . . Let's quit! I want you to promise me, and I will promise you, never to play cards again for money. We've got enough!" To this Patterson agreed, the bargain endured, and both men soon made respectable fortunes.

In 1857, three men arrived in Fresno County who followed Hazelton and Patterson's lead: David Burris, Jefferson James (see 6:1), and John Sutherland. Burris and Sutherland, the latter an English immigrant and ex-miner, based their herds on the lower Kings. Three years later Cuthbert Burrel of Sonoma County arrived in the same area with 1,300 head of cattle and settled on

Reference 6:1

## JEFFERSON JAMES, EARLY PIONEER OF THE WEST SIDE

*In January 1959 the Fresno County Historical Society published the first issue of its quarterly, "Fresno Past and Present." Biographical sketches of early pioneers was announced as a regular feature, and the first one was of Jefferson Gilbert James (most often J. G. or Jeff), one of the earliest and most successful settlers on the West Side. It was based on a paper read at the preceding quarterly meeting of the society by Mrs. Fred M. Garrison, then of San Joaquin, now of Fresno. We have edited slightly to conform with her later writings, condensed some of the twentieth century information, and* *added a few notes from other sources as indicated.*

In Spanish times the area of the James Ranch was part of what was called "The Tulares," and was inhabited only by Yokuts Indians. It was traversed by several Spanish exploring expeditions, and was mentioned in Fremont's diary when he passed through the area in 1844 and again in 1845.

Jefferson G. James came to California, accompanied by a brother and a cousin, in 1850. They were moderately successful as gold seekers and they returned to Missouri when they had "made their pile." With his share of the money Jefferson James bought some cattle, drove them to California, and made a handsome profit. In 1857 he and a partner, James Douglas, purchased some cattle in Los Angeles, drove them north to the Central Valley, first stopping at Kingston, and finally moving them to the head of the Fresno Slough where he decided to settle.

He purchased as much land in the area as he could and by 1860 he had built a home near the original Fresno City. He brought his bride [Jennie L. Rector] to this home in 1860.

the Elkhorn Ranch (see Chapter 12). His presence is memorialized in the place names of Burrel and Elkhorn. The last of the old-time barons to establish themselves in the county, and the most important, were Henry Miller and Charles Lux (see 6:2).

Drought plagued the San Joaquin Valley in 1851, 1856 and 1863–64. The cattle business was not hurt by the first two, since it was in its infancy, but the last was disastrous. In later years Henry Miller reminisced that "we lost two-thirds of [our] cattle. We could not drive them off because everybody's cattle were out there, and in moving my cattle I would have to move all the others."

Many less visionary cattlemen were discouraged by this experience. They rushed to sell, causing prices to fall to $1.50 a head. Miller took a whole different view of the situation, confident that conditions would improve. After buying more land and cattle when prices were low, he outdistanced all his competitors once the drought was over. The Fresno County cattle business was no place for pessimists.

During the 1860s, when more than a million head of cattle roamed the mid-San Joaquin Valley ranges, it became necessary for ranchers to hire cowboys. These men were responsible for grazing and watering the animals, periodically rounding them up, and driving them to marketplaces. It was a job that could scarcely be matched for sheer tedium.

Working from dawn to dusk, a cowboy traveled miles over the valley plains in a typical day, with only a hat for shade and a revolver for protection. He would sit on his horse for hours, leading cattle about, watching for strays and staying alert lest a rustler show up. His home was the open range, his bed any place where he could throw down a few blankets and catch some sleep. For doing all these chores, he was paid only once a year. Any clothing, food or supplies he needed were furnished by his employer, who dutifully deducted their cost from the lump-sum payment.

Cattle roundups and drives were usually scheduled by groups of ranchers who lived close to each other. During roundups, the cowboys met at a chosen spot

Bancroft (H. H. Bancroft, *Chronicle of the Builders of the West*) says, "... In 1860 he [James] bought out Douglas, five years later he took in as partner George F. Smith who brought the Fish Slough farm into the firm, and in 1873 he bought out Moses Selig who had previously purchased Smith's interests. The property comprises 57,000 acres ... in Fresno County extending from two to three miles in width, and about fifteen miles in length, on either hand of the great slough which receives the water of the San Joaquin [and Kings] River[s]."

In 1867 he moved to the present headquarters of the James Ranch and built his permanent home there. By this time he owned about 72,000 acres and he controlled even more. He was able to do this because he could buy up the rights of other land owners who had not been able to survive the dry years. He also purchased land that was under water during the rainy seasons—inundated by the various sloughs and channels of the San Joaquin River during flood stages—and built a systematic system of drainage for this swamp land. By 1890 he had 150,000 [elsewhere reported as 161,000] acres under fence, with 36 separate ranches.

Mr. James employed a great many people on his ranches, and many pioneer families got their start as employees or as tenants of the James Ranch. Sam Williams was a well-remembered pioneer who started out as a tenderfoot rider on the ranch. One of the many James Ranch projects was the building of a large canal to carry water from the San Joaquin River, from a point several miles east of Mendota, southwesterly towards his ranch. However, he was unable to put the canal into operation because of litigation which ensued with Miller and Lux over riparian water rights.

In 1908 James decided to sell part of the Fish Slough Ranch to colonists, and appointed his son-in-law, Walker Coleman Graves, Sr., general manager of the J. G. James Land Company. Mr. Graves named the new colony Tranquillity, in honor of his birthplace, the Graves ancestral home near Lexington, Kentucky. He sold the first farming land in Tranquillity to Wade Williams, Judge S. V. Brown, Frank Johnson, Carroll Covington, Earl Slater, Hans Hansen, Chris Thompson Hansen, Eugene Tully, J. E. Epperson, Pete Jorgenson and many others.

Referring to James' local activities, Paul E. Vandor, in his 1919 *History of Fresno County*, wrote:

"Mr. James spent life's closing years in San Francisco conducting a great wholesale cattle business. He was prominent for the legal battles that he waged in the courts of the state for eleven years. These were begun in 1889 and involved not only Miller & Lux, the greatest cattle and irrigation holding firm in the state, but also the California Pastoral and Agricultural Company, a British corporation, and the San Joaquin and Kings River Canal and Irrigation Company, another Miller & Lux enterprise. In all, Henry Miller instituted six suits against James, while the latter had one against him. These were waged with bitter determination by the cattle kings yet never became personal in nature.

"The point whether James could take water from the San Joaquin and the Kings was involved in all. James' lands did not abut directly on the river but were on the slough and watered by the overflow. He contended that this entitled him to take water from the river above him. The contention was resisted. The decision by the supreme court after long litigation was for James. ...

"James was prominent locally also through his connection with the Fresno Loan and Savings Bank, capitalized at $300,000 and organized in 1886 and with him as president two years later. In the panic of 1893 it closed its doors and there was a scandal that it should have received a large deposit of public funds only a few hours before the closing of the doors. Its affairs were liquidated and settled by the late Emil F. Bernhard after long years. The bank erected the Land Company building at Mariposa and J, which passing through several hands at price record deals is the present property."

Bancroft wrote of James' San Francisco activities, "In 1866 he removed his residence to Stockton, and afterward to San Francisco, where he has since continuously resided, looking after the business here, and making monthly visits of supervision to the rancho. ... Mr. James was elected a member of the board of supervisors in San Francisco in 1882. ... The popular confidence in Mr. James was reasserted in his appointment to the board of education, to fill the unexpired term of Charles Kohler, deceased, and he was duly elected for the ensuing term, which began January 1, 1889. [Later he was the Democratic candidate for mayor but was defeated by the late Adolph Sutro who carried the day with his promise that if elected he would give San Franciscans a single five cents street car fare to the ocean beach for popular recreation.] ...

"Mr. and Mrs. James [had] but one child [Maud Strother James], the wife of Walker Coleman Graves, a Kentuckian of excellent family, liberal education, and a high order of talent, who is assistant district attorney of San Francisco, and actively engaged in the profession of law. ... The grandparents take great pride and comfort in their bright and handsome grandchildren, Jefferson James, Walker Coleman, Jr., and Rector Graves ..."

John A. Patterson, with William Hazelton, brought the first cattle to the Kings River area.

Fresno sheep and grain pioneer William Helm, Sr. in 1865. Helm acquired 16,000 acres of land and owned 22,000 sheep.

Jefferson G. James was a rugged pioneer on the West Side from 1857. This picture is after he had moved to San Francisco, possibly when he was a candidate for mayor of that city. He maintained his interests in Fresno County including operation of more than 150,000 acres of farm land.

Headquarters of the Jefferson James ranch was located at the head of Fresno Slough near what is now Tranquillity.

*In 1862 William Hazelton and his wife, Mary Akers, moved their house near the Kings River to higher ground on Trimmer Springs Road after the flood of that year.*

*As the Hazelton family grew they enlarged their home by adding a second story. The two dark trees in the front yard are the orange trees planted by Mary in 1866.*

*One tree, now nearly 120 years old, has been cut back severely but is still bearing. The other died about fifteen years ago. The family still has a large orange grove on the early homestead.*

where thousands of head of cattle were roped, branded and sold. Purchases were certified by tying the cattle, branding the previous owner's mark on the animal's shoulder, and applying the new owner's mark to the side.

With ample opportunities for socializing and endless work to be done, roundups always had an exhilarating air about them; drives were far different. Making sure a herd made it safely to San Francisco or Stockton could be a deadly dull task, as Ernestine Winchell noted:

> A wagon carried the supplies ahead, camping for the night where wood and water were found together within a day's travel of the steers. Through the time of darkness part of the vaqueros at a time, in relays, rode quietly round and round the ruminating band; before it was light the men breakfasted by the campfire, for at dawn the cattle rose to feed, and then were slowly moved on their way, every precaution being taken to keep them from losing weight. During all the hot hours they were permitted to rest, placidly chewing somnolent cuds while the cowboys, again in turns, dozed under their sombreros or rode monotonous guard.

The Fresno County cattle that did not end up in distant markets, of course, were slaughtered and consumed at home. When word went out that a butcher had obtained some fat steers, people were quick to track him down and ask for some good cuts. The butcher sold any leftovers by hitching up his wagon, traveling to the mining and logging settlements, and selling his wares to a less finicky crowd. In this endeavor they were sometimes joined by enterprising cattlemen who herded their animals into the camps, set up tents, commenced slaughtering and peddled fresh beef. Dairymen, who were slowly establishing themselves (see 6:3), also found these areas to be a good market.

Many of the aforementioned cattle ranchers also became involved in hog and sheep raising. Early on, Millerton-area settlers Jefferson Milam Shannon and S. B. Coffee realized the importance of the hog business. Chinese miners hungry for pork were scattered throughout the neighborhood, so Shannon and Coffee started swine farming in 1854. They provided pork at the then-excessive price of twenty-five cents a pound, and the Chinese were happy to pay any price for it. Historians have suggested snickeringly that the men squeezed more than a fair profit out of this business. They insisted on weighing all pork they sold, and all gold they took in exchange, on their own scales.

The late 1850s and 1860s saw swine farming spread to other areas of Fresno County. Charles A. Hart, J. Scott Ashman, Newton and Perry Murphy, F. C. B.

Reference 6:2

# HENRY MILLER
## WALLACE SMITH

The greatest cattleman in the San Joaquin Valley measured in terms of acreage and astuteness was Heinrich Alfred Kreiser. When he was a little peasant lad in Germany he herded the pigs and the calves. One day he lay in the grass watching his charges and like Little Boy Blue he fell fast asleep. His mind went on a journey and he saw countless herds of cattle with a Double H (H.H.) mark on their left hips. Such marks and such long horned cattle had never been seen in all Germany. Suddenly a huge, long-horned bull prodded him and he awakened to find a little calf playfully disturbing his slumber. The telling of his dream aroused the jeers of those who heard it, excepting only his mother. But the vision persisted. Might not one "H" represent Heinrich; what about the other? He was puzzled. No Joseph appeared to interpret his vision.

This boy eventually went to New York, worked in a meat market, met an American-born German shoe salesman named Henry Miller, and when the latter was unable to utilize his ticket to California, Heinrich Kreiser bought it at a reduced price and went by boat via Panama to San Francisco. The ticket carried the name Henry Miller and was non-transferable. So Kreiser became Miller and Miller became the guiding genius of Miller & Lux, and Miller & Lux became the cattle kings of the San Joaquin Valley.

The accidental change in name seemingly brought also a change in good fortune.

The new Henry Miller arrived in San Francisco with $6.00; secured a job in a butcher shop; made and peddled sausages; and finally decided in order to improve the quality of beef that he must become a producer as well as a retailer and wholesaler. So he went to the San Joaquin Valley. He rode his horse through the red-pillared groves of coast redwoods, crossed the Coast Range, and on the interior slope he paused and beheld his future kingdom. And suddenly he rubbed his eyes. Over the plain, spread out in the distance like a golden sea, were many cattle and the brands on their left hips were the Double H! Was he a little boy back in Germany fast asleep?

Miller must have reached the *Sanjon de Santa Rita* ranch somewhat agitated. But he did not show it. He calmly discussed with Henry Hildreth, a fourth owner of the ranch, the local conditions of the cattle industry. Hildreth was dissatisfied; he wanted to go back to the gold mines. He offered to sell his 8,835 acres for $1.15 an acre and his 7,500 cattle for $5.00 each. With his cattle would go the Double H (Henry Hildreth) brand. Miller accepted—after awhile. He could not be hurried, even to make dreams come true. . . .

On his return to San Francisco Miller visited a cattleman, a tall Alsatian named Charles Lux, whose ranch lay along Baden Creek. At that time they were competitors in the markets of San Francisco. Soon they were to pool their interests, increase their holdings, and make the firm of Miller & Lux famous. They agreed on a policy of buying and never selling land. Each man possessed what the other lacked and the combination proved irresistible. The first land purchased by Miller in the San Joaquin was Hildreth's interest in the *Sanjon de Santa Rita* which had originally been granted to Francisco Soberanes about sixteen years before Miller made his purchase. . . .

Miller remained an active figure in California until the Panama-Pacific Exposition held at San Francisco in 1915. The next year he passed away. The little boy from the Black Forest of Germany left to his heirs two large banks and their branches, many reservoirs and irrigation systems, a million cattle, and deeds to a million acres which carried with them control of many times that amount of land. The dream of his boyhood had been abundantly realized.

SOURCE: *Garden of the Sun* (Los Angeles: Lymanhouse, 1939), extracts from pp. 193–96.

Duff and Jesse Blasingame all took it up in the Big Sandy and Yarborough (Auberry) areas, as did Harvey Akers near Scottsburg. When compared to cattle ranching it had a fair share of advantages. Hogs ate almost anything, reproduced rapidly and could be secured with simple brush-and-log fences.

The earliest sheep-raisers in Fresno County were ranchers Henry Clay Daulton and Jonathan Rea, who began maintaining flocks in-between the Fresno and Chowchilla rivers circa 1853. To the south, the Big Dry Creek area eventually boasted several prominent sheepmen, among them William Helm, Thomas J. Hall, Thomas Jaynes, J. W. Potter, Richard Freeman and L. P. Clark. (To stay close to his flocks Helm, in 1865, built the first house on the Fresno County plains.) Moses J. Church and John A. Patterson were among the first to have flocks near Centerville. Fresno County's most famous entrepreneur, Frank Dusy, grazed his flocks on what later became the Fresno townsite. (For a portrait of the early Fresno County sheep industry, see 6:4.)

Initially sheep, like cattle, were used as a source of meat. When it was realized that Fresno County plains and mountain meadows could be used for large-scale sheep raising, this situation changed. In 1867 Patterson began importing French and Spanish Merinos noted for their wool rather than their mutton. Others followed his lead, which was an expensive proposition; five years later, Dusy and a partner paid $3,000 for twenty pure Merinos. Nonetheless, wool-growing became an important enterprise within a short time. An October 23, 1872, *Fresno Weekly Expositor* report said that "the immense amount of wool now being sent to the [Fresno] railroad station . . . is astonishing to visitors. The oldest resident of our county, having but little idea of its immense and valuable resources . . . [exclaimed] in pleasurable surprise . . . 'Is it possible that all this is the product of Fresno County?'"

The multiplying of cattle herds and farms on the valley floor during the 1870s made competition for grasslands stiff. More and more sheep were taken into the Sierra for grazing, but unfortunately, the situation was desperate in the highlands as well. A quarter million or more sheep could roam in that area at one time, causing disputes over grazing lands to erupt. When Pine Ridge sheepman W. B. Harris' property was invaded by a Mr. Saulter's flocks in 1871, he reciprocated by herding his animals onto Saulter's land. A Saulter employee named Brooks, while riding on horseback around the property, saw what was happening and told Harris to stop. Harris, also mounted, ignored the request. Brooks then shot at Harris and missed. Harris began galloping toward him and took a bullet in the mouth. Leaving Harris for dead, Brooks fled the scene. No known reports tell of his being captured.

Fresno County's eastern mountain regions were not valuable to the itinerant sheepmen alone. The vast forests there were an ideal source of building materials, firewood, fence posts and other necessities, enabling a lumber industry to develop rapidly after 1852. John Harms and James Hulse (Hultz) are credited with starting the county's first sawmills in that year, at Redwood Creek and Corlew Meadow respectively. After two years Harms' mill was sold to Charles Porter Converse and Bill Chidester, who moved it to Crane Valley. About the same time Alexander Ball bought the Hulse mill, moved it to the north end of Corlew Meadow, and lost it to fire in 1859. According to Paul A. Vandor, Ball was "a rough and ready and good-

Reference 6:3

# A PIONEER DAIRY
## ERNESTINE WINCHELL

In the early summer of 1874 John Nelson, then twenty years of age, and Joe Carter, his cousin a couple of years younger, thought it about time to go into business for themselves, so they hired a bunch of about forty cows with young calves from Nigger Gabe Moore of Centerville and in June opened a dairy over the ridge northeast of Musick Meadow. This was a beautiful grassy stretch bordered by towering pines and drained by a small tributary of Stevenson Creek.

There was then no wagon road beyond Humphreys' sawmill at what was afterward called Littlefield's, but the boys had their packhorse loaded with beds and supplies and, independent of roads, drove the cattle through the timber to their destination. A two-room log house was there, with a fireplace for heating and cooking, a log milk house built over a welling spring and floored with rough flakes of granite, and all the necessary implements, corrals and pens.

The milking corral was built of logs laid one above another, and held in place by stakes set on each side and crossed at the top, carrying still another log in the crotch. Through the gate John and Joe drove the bunch, big and little, to rest for the night.

In the morning the calves had their first lesson in gentling. One by one they were roped and then dragged and driven through the small gate from the corral to the calf pen, the pasture gate was opened, and they were free to come and go as they wished for grass and water. The cows were driven out on the range to graze, the musical tinkle of their many bells sounding far through the quiet woods. Late in the afternoon, guided by the bells, the boys on horseback gathered them back to the corral.

From convenient pegs large tin buckets were hung well out of reach of hoofs and horns. The calf pen gate was opened, half a dozen of the hungry little chaps were allowed to pass through, and like catapults they made for their mooing mothers and began supper. Then, in a few minutes, they had another lesson.

Separated from their banquet by force, steered by a stick tapping on one side of his head and propelled by painful twisting of his tail, each little fellow was hustled through the gate to the range, and after the six had been in that way expelled each young dairyman seized a quart cup and hastened to fill it from a dripping udder. Once filled, he poured the milk into the nearest bucket and hurried back for what might remain. This was repeated until all the calves had taken about half the milk each from their mother, had been turned out to graze for the night on the open range, and the cows had all been stripped dry. Two or three quarts night and morning after feeding the calf was considered a pretty fair yield, as indeed it was under the conditions that prevailed.

SOURCE: Ernestine Winchell columns.

natured man, a hard worker by day and ardent poker player by night," and the latter vice contributed to his declaring bankruptcy after the mill was destroyed.

The early sawmill operators and their employees worked under rough conditions. Living in tents or shacks (and sometimes outdoors, when weather permitted), a lack of roads and fast transportation isolated them from the pioneer settlements only a few miles distant. In the solitude of the great pine forests, their entertainments were few: perhaps some card games, sing-alongs and campfire socials. Their existence was an endless cycle of chopping, cutting and hauling wood. It was a dreary regimen, hampered by difficulties Lilbourne A. Winchell has described well:

> The crude mills were of small daily output—5,000 to 6,000 feet being their individual capacity. The machinery was of the most primitive design: A log carriage was fixed into position; the long-bladed upright saw hung from a framework over the carriage, and when in action the teeth made a downward stroke through the log, cutting only when in that direction. Against all modern methods the saw was advanced with each stroke till it came to the end of the stationary log, but was stopped when within three or four inches of cutting out. Drawn back to its original position, the sawing continued ripping the log into the desired lumber dimension. Having finished the divisions the log was now given a half-turn on the carriage, and the saw again cut the slices into proper widths. For ex-

ample: Having first divided the log into four-inch sections, it was turned and sawed into two-inch strips— thus producing 4-inch by 2-inch scantling. There remained a cluster of huge matches, all attached to each other at the butt. It only remained for the attendant to pull them apart, which was easily done. In this manner all kinds of lumber was produced. The motive power was delivered from a big water wheel, driven by a race from the dam.

Transporting lumber was not easy, either. Again, let Winchell tell of the difficulties faced by James Fisher, who built the first road leading out of the Ball Mill in 1855:

> Out of that precipitous, granite-covered and brush-grown slope he gouged out occasional boulders, hewed away a fallen log here and there, cut through some impenetrable thickets of scrub oak, mountain mahogany and buckthorn, and by following down the bottoms of narrow, steep and rock-studded gulches improved the primitive track over which thousands of feet of lumber had been already conveyed by ox teams, under conditions incredible to any except the pioneers. ...On some of these terrific plunges wheels were rough-locked with heavy chains, and in other places the pitching loads were held back by heavy logs chained to the rear axles. [If] safety further demanded the onrush was checked or eased by snubbing the wagon to trees.

Reference 6:4

# LOW WAGES AND POOR FARE: EARLY-DAY SHEEP RAISING

It has not been a great while since Fresno County's principal industries were confined almost exclusively to sheep and cattle raising, and the former largely predominated.

The sheep industry was then conducted upon a large scale, and many who engaged in that industry owned flocks containing from 10,000 to 40,000 head.

Sheriff [John M.] Hensley and a number of old-time sheep men were discussing the situation yesterday.

"There are few men," said Mr. Hensley, "now engaged in sheep raising who followed that business when it was the principal industry of the county.

"The old-timers have long since abandoned it to engage in other more profitable pursuits which the country now affords.

"I shall never forget some of my experiences in the early days, long before the county was organized.

"I had a job under an old fellow named [John A.] Patterson. He taught me the business. His camp was located in the foothills on the upper San Joaquin [River]. I held that job just two years and I swore every night that I would throw up the situation the next day. Hard work? Well, I should rise to remark. We had no dogs in those days to assist in herding. I did that myself, with the help of a horse.

"I remember one day the feed was getting pretty short, and old Patterson came to me and wanted that I should go in search of greener fields. 'Do you think you can manage the flock,' said I. 'Why shouldn't I,' said he. 'Don't you think I know my own business[?] You go, but don't be gone more than three days.'

"I went as directed, but I knew the old fellow would have trouble. There were about 11,000 in the band, and I was well acquainted with them. Patterson didn't know these sheep a little bit.

"After an absence of three days I returned to the camp. Before reaching it, however, I looked for Patterson and the sheep where I had left them. His wife told me that she had not seen him since I left. I went out and climbed the hurricane deck of one of the tallest neighboring hills, and what do you think I saw? The whole country, for a space of ten miles in circumference, was dotted here and there with sheep. I saw the horse but couldn't see Patterson. After a ride of a few hours I came upon the horse and Patterson, completely winded, [lay] panting in the shadow of the animal.

"'I give it up, John,' said he. 'So do I,' said I, and you can bet your life I did. Why, it would take six years to get those sheep together again.

"While I was with Patterson I never did any shearing. That was one of the unpleasant duties of which I was relieved.

"I packed my blankets and started down the San Joaquin. When I struck the place where Herndon now stands I found another camp. It was owned by an old man named Eaton. His flock numbered about 20,000. This was the shearing season. The sheep were bunched off in small parcels and run into brush corrals, where they were relieved of their wool by about fifty men of all nationalities.

"It was a hard matter to get shearers, and I was given employment at once. You talk about life in the far West, but that was the toughest place I ever struck.

"I will never forget my first day's experience as a shearer. The men employed were more like wild beasts than human beings. Nearly all of them spoke different languages, and their wants were made known by signs.

"I struck the camp in the evening and was provided with a pair of shears and told to go to work the next morning.

"I was awakened long before daylight and called to breakfast, but before I could get my clothes on everything had been devoured. All that remained was a few bones and some bunches of dirty wool that had been scraped into the middle of the table. Mrs. Eaton told

Foothill and valley towns continued growing after the 1850s, so the lumber industry expanded to meet the demand. George McCullough and Thomas Winkleman set up another mill in Crane Valley in 1859, a year before the Converse-Chidester operations closed. Before the McCullough-Winkleman sawmill shut down in turn (1872), George Sharpton moved his mill from the mouth of Mill Creek to Crane Valley, thus assuring continuous logging activity there.

Southeast of Crane Valley, others were being attracted to the lumbering potential of the Pine Ridge. Deciding there was a local need for sugar pine shingles, brothers J. H. and J. N. Woods arrived in the area during the summer of 1866 and began manufacturing them. After accumulating a large supply of shingles the Woodses faced a problem: getting them to market, since there was no road leading out of the ridge. True do-it-yourselfers, they cut out a crude trail from their camp to Sarvers' Peak for freighting purposes. Since wagons could not handle the 1,000-foot drop from the peak to Dry Creek (and thence to the valley), the Woodses had a wagon carried up to the mountain piecemeal and reassembled for use on the trail. This rough road was the first Tollhouse grade built. Until its later extension, the shingles had to be hand-carried in bundles down from Sarvers' Peak.

Near this time Mariposa lumberman John W. Humphreys visited the Pine Ridge area and was impressed by its lumbering potential. Urged on by his Fresno County friends, Andrew Jackson Thorn and Spyars Singleton Hyde, Humphreys dismantled his sawmill in late 1866 and deposited its pieces at the foot of Sarvers' Peak. With the labor of Humphreys' men, some local settlers and a Chinese gang from Millerton, a road was carved up to the divide separating Big Dry and Sycamore creeks. This still did not reach the Woodses' road. In order to transport the sawmill to Pine Ridge, it was necessary to carry it to the new grade's end, send the wagons hurtling down a slope (soft ground and strong brakes kept them from going out of control), and guide them up another trail before reaching the Pine Ridge. Under the supervision of Moses Mock, Humphreys' sawyer, the machinery was set up at a predetermined location. Its first output furnished the flooring and roofing material for the new mill.

While this work went on, a team of workmen completed the Tollhouse grade from Sarvers' Peak to the Woodses' road. Heavy rains in late 1867 washed away a large portion of the grade. The bad weather was a hazard to travel but a boon to lowland lumberman Jim ("Black") Phillips, at least for a time. Near Sycamore Point on the San Joaquin River 100 acres or more had been covered with trees washed down from the mountains. Obtaining the engine and boiler of a threshing machine, Phillips set up a sawmill on the point and commenced a simplified logging operation; half the work was already done. There was only one hitch, and it spelled the scheme's doom. The trees' rough journey from the mountain slopes had imbedded rocks underneath their bark; if a saw hit one it was dulled or broken. Before long Phillips was spending more on saws than he was taking in for lumber, and he wisely quit the business.

From the late 1860s to early 1870s logging flourished in Fresno County, with the greatest activity centered in the Pine Ridge area. Teamsters, driving five or six yoke of oxen, hauled lumber out easily via the improved Tollhouse grade. Humphreys and Mock expanded their operations, selling their first mill to M. J. and Michael Donahoo in 1869–70 and opening new operations in Bransford and Hoxey meadows. These were known as the Clipper No. 1 and No. 2 mills.

At all times the mills and freighters were busy. "It is said that the saw mills do not turn out lumber fast enough to supply the demand," said a report in the August 20, 1870, *Fresno Weekly Expositor*.

Although lumber could be purchased cheaply at the mills, it was expensive to haul it any farther. Freighters charged forty dollars to carry a thousand board feet to the valley floor. This situation attracted the attention of Caleb Dickerson Davis, M. M. Jack and "Black" Phillips, who contemplated building a flume from the

---

me that if I wanted breakfast I would have to get up a little earlier, which I was cautious to do afterward. I had a good appetite in those days, but I went to work that morning without breakfast.

"When I struck the corral I found four men fighting over a sheep. Wherever an easy-shearing sheep was found, there was always a row about who should shear it. The men were using their shears as weapons and one poor fellow had his throat badly cut, but survived his injuries and continued his labors. I asked one of the men engaged in the rumpus how often they took these spells, but the fellow couldn't understand me and made no reply.

"I thought noon would never come that day. I was never so hungry in my life. At last I heard the bell, but before I could let the sheep I was shearing up two men ran over me and threw me into an unconscious state. The bell caused a regular stampede, and four or five others beside myself were knocked silly by the shearers in their haste to get to the dinner table. We had mutton for dinner, but precious little did I get. If we found any part of the internal mutton which was not suitable for the digestive organs to take hold, we were told to lay it on one side of our plates.

"Talk about cruelty to animals; you ought to see those fellows shear sheep. When the poor dumb brutes did not lay perfectly quiet the shearer would stick his shears into it, clip his lips and perform other acts of cruelty. I was never more disgusted in my life. The corral looked like a slaughter pen, and the shearers were bloody from head to foot.

"That wasn't what made me quit after working there all day," concluded Mr. Hensley. "I stood everything until that evening [when] I saw the boss settle with one of his men, and then I threw up the sponge. The man with whom he settled had been at work three months. He had charged him with three pairs of shears and brought the hired man out in debt to him about twenty-five cents. I saw there was no money in the business and quit."

SOURCE: Fresno County Scrapbook 1870-1899, pp. 1713-14, taken from *Fresno Daily Evening Expositor*, July 10, 1890, p. 8, c. 1.

*Moses J. Church, best remembered for his early and consistent leadership in irrigation. A blacksmith by early training, he became one of the first to raise sheep in Fresno County, and encouraged farming and the colony system.*

*Artist's concept of one of several confrontations over the diversion of water for irrigation.*

Centennial Selma

*Workers and work camp of Fresno Canal and Irrigation Company, the early and large combination of the ditches of Easterby and Church.*

F.C.C.H.S. Archives

113

Beast killer was an early title given the Toll House grade. Artist's route line makes it look easy, but to it must be added hundreds of curves as the road followed every little gully and avoided all the big rocks and most of the narrow ledges. Sarver's Peak is on the left.

Early type mountain cabin—apparently one of the better ones.

"Fresno County for the poor man. The mild climate admits of cheap buildings to begin with." So said an appeal to prospective settlers in the 1890s.

mouth of Bear Creek down to the valley flatlands. After rounding up some investors in 1873, the men constructed a mill on Pine Ridge, with a flume to come later. The mill was built out of parts Phillips had salvaged from his Sycamore Point venture. Plagued by incessant breakdowns and technical problems, this operation, called the "Flintlock," failed to prosper. It closed in 1876, and the flume idea was never realized.

To round out this portrait on Fresno County's earliest industries it is now necessary to discuss the most important—agriculture. Farming has been undertaken in the county for more than 130 years and its beginnings can be traced to the gold rush era.

The first farmer of any significance was Major James D. Savage (see chapters 2 and 4). In the wake of the Mariposa Indian War, one of his jobs as a Fresno River Reservation official was to teach local Indians the rudiments of agriculture. "J. R. W.," a correspondent for the *San Joaquin Republican* of Stockton, reported the following on March 3, 1852:

> During my sojourn, the Major took much pains to explain his "modus operandi" with the Indians. He is quite extensively engaged in agriculture, is sowing about 350 acres with small grains, 140 acres with corn, beans, peas, potatoes, squashes, pumpkins, tomatoes, beets, onions, carrots, parsnips, cabbages, radishes, &c., for the Indian rations for 1852 and 1853, and for the purpose of supplying the neighboring miners with such articles fresh, and at lower rates than they can be imported from below. Each Indian, or family, has a patch of its own, within his enclosure, of similar variety, except the small grain, the Major furnishing them with seeds, teams, farming utensils, &c. at his expense . . .

In 1852, Samuel A. Bishop harvested a wheat crop on the Fresno River Reservation, and William Lewis Lovely Witt and William Harshfield began cutting wild hay on the Dry Creek bottomlands. At the same time Bud Akers brought some grape cuttings to the Scottsburg (Centerville) area, planting them on the banks of the Kings River.

Other farmers, encouraged by these experiments, began establishing larger-scale operations in 1853. Akers' brother Harvey traveled to Los Angeles, obtained a number of mission grape cuttings, and planted them near the present-day intersection of Belmont Avenue and Trimmer Springs Road. Up north, at Temperance Flat on the San Joaquin River, Billy Martin established himself as Fresno County's first diversified orchardist. Arriving in 1851, he worked first as a miner, but began dabbling in agriculture shortly afterward. He sent for apple seeds and peach pits from his Vermont home and began raising those two fruits. On a trip to San Jose he obtained grape and fig cuttings and set those out as well. By the mid-1850s Martin was regularly supplying the residents of Miller-

ton and nearby settlements with fresh fruit. Children always looked forward to his visits because he gave them peaches—a delectable, hard-to-find treat in those days.

The early successes of the Akers brothers and Billy Martin were emulated by other pioneers. On his Falcon Ranch (located in the Kings River bottomlands), Ira McCray set out 7,000 scions of grapes in 1859 and established a good-sized vineyard. Some three years later orange trees were growing on property owned by William Hazelton, Harvey Akers, Caleb Dickserson Davis and Charles A. Hart. Below Tollhouse Captain J. N. Appleton, a retired English navigator, planted a vineyard and an orange grove in 1864 that kept producing for more than a half-century.

Because the Civil War had interrupted the flow of cotton from the South, local interest in cultivating the crop began to heighten. E. W. Burchfield of Santa Clara and James Kincaid were the first county residents to enter this business; Kincaid planted 100 acres near the Kings River in 1865 and Burchfield 200 (presumably in the same area), according to the *Fresno Times* of January 28 and March 15, 1865. Conditions for developing these crops were crude. Planting was done by hand, rows were laid out erratically with stakes and strings, and ginning and baling were likewise products of manual labor. Most of the cotton was shipped outside Fresno County, but several pioneer women made heirloom quilts of it—thus preserving a part of these historic crops.

By modern standards it seems incredible that Fresno County's earliest farmers grew anything. All planting and harvesting was done by hand, sometimes with the assistance of local Indians or Chinese. The use of fertilizers was virtually unknown. During most of the 1850s there was no irrigation; rainfall and periodic flooding were the only ways to water crops. This type of dependence could be disastrous, as the 1854 drought and floods in 1862 and 1867 proved. (Those two events wiped out most of the Kings River crops, including the vineyards of Harvey Akers and Ira McCray.) It must also be remembered that no pesticides were available, making every crop vulnerable to an insect attack. Yet the farmers persevered, even when every imaginable calamity befell their meager existences. The problems experienced in developing the Easterby Ranch (or Banner Farm), the county's first significant enterprise, attest to this.

On July 29, 1868, A. Y. Easterby of Napa County purchased more than 5,000 Fresno County acres from the San Francisco "German Syndicate." The syndicate was so named because most of its members, including Friedlander, were of German descent. Easterby, a world traveler who had seen irrigation work in many countries, was convinced he could make the Fresno plains blossom forth in a similar fashion. To this end he retained the services of a Napa sheepman, Moses J.

Church, whose flock was starving and in desperate need of pasturage. He suggested that Church relocate to Fresno County, where he could feed his sheep and explore the agricultural possibilities. Church consented to this plan, scarcely realizing what adventures awaited him.

The first challenge Easterby and Church faced was getting an experimental crop going. They claimed a farm site near Millerton, drilled a well and put in some wheat in late 1869. Virtually everyone believed this venture would fail. According to one story, County Recorder Harry Dixon was loath to record Easterby's title to the claim; he felt that only a fool would try farming the dry, sun-baked plains.

Initially Dixon was proved correct. Light rains in the spring of 1870, along with the trampling and grazing of cattle, ruined the first crop. Easterby remained unshaken. Looking to the southwest of his first farm, he saw greater promise where he had purchased other lands, near Fancher Creek and the Kings River. It was here that the Easterby Ranch was laid out.

There were problems aplenty in starting the ranch.

For regulated farming to commence, water had to be obtained from the nearby Kings. There was no way to convey it. All the irrigation projects of earlier years that stemmed from the river's banks were unsuitable for Easterby's purposes.

The earliest existing canals had been built by the Yokuts Indians—probably the Wimilchi, Apyachi or Nutunutu tribelets—and were in the wrong place to do Easterby any good. "In the development of irrigation at the Laguna de Tache [see Chapter 3] in 1900 to 1902, I found that numerous small ditches had been dug from the river for irrigation," wrote Ingvart Tielman in *The Historical Story of Irrigation in Fresno and Kings Counties in Central California.* "... I am sure the Indians ... learned the principles while living at the Mission[s]." Considering the plentitude of food sources in central California (see Chapter 2), it seems surprising the Indians would rely on such methods. Perhaps they had acquired tastes for fruits and vegetables brought to California by the padres, and were trying to cultivate them in their ancestral lands.

John Pool's ditch, dug in 1854 near his ferry (see

Reference 6:5

## THE TRIALS AND TRIBULATIONS OF MOSES J. CHURCH

[In 1868] a cattle man named Yank [William] Hazelton claimed not only possession but the ownership of all the plains from the foothills of the Sierras westward, and he had his vaqueros well instructed. When he ascertained Mr. Church's object [to dig irrigation ditches] he began to plan mischief, and there is no question but that the intention was to drive him away or make away with him in some way.

The first demonstration that was made on the plains gave Mr. Church some idea of the spirit that the cattle king possessed ... After he had commenced [digging] ditches a few of Hazelton's vaqueros, with some others, came to Mr. Church on the plains. They were on horseback while he was on foot. They ... handed him a bottle and asked him to take a drink.

"Thank you," observed Mr. Church. "I never drink."

"Boys," said the leader of the gang, "let us all take a drink to convince this old man that we are not going to poison him."

At this time Alburtus Akers, who was the spokesman, remarked: "We'll convince him that we'll drag out his existence over the plains if he don't obey our orders," at the same time dangling a rope which he held in his hand.

"What are your orders?" asked Mr. Church.

"That you leave this county at once," was the reply.

"By what authority do you give me such orders as this?" asked Mr. Church.

"I am Yank Hazelton's vaquero and I am representing him," replied Akers, adding: "He owns this county, and therefore you must leave."

... Without molesting him further they galloped away ... A few days afterwards a company, some of those who had visited him formerly, and among them Yank Hazelton, came and surrounded Mr. Church. He did not know Hazelton but it was he who said:

"You had been ordered to leave here several days ago, and you have had ample time to get out of the county, and if you don't obey orders and go we will have to do what we came here to do—to drag your existence out over the plains with that rope ... "

The determined eye of Mr. Church was upon him, and in that sarcastic manner for which he is noted he replied:

"From the demonstrations you have been making I am satisfied that you own the land, and now what are your orders?"

"Well," said he, "you see that band of sheep over yonder? We found your boy with them and we ordered him to get behind them and not stop until he was out of the county, and he is obeying like a little man. You must get in behind them and get out ... I am Yank Hazelton."

"Your request, Mr. Hazelton, is unreasonable and unjust. I can't leave my house, my horses and grain; besides, it is nearly night," replied Mr. Church.

Hazelton turned to the crowd and said: "Well, boys, this is pretty plain talk. What will we do with him?"

Paul Stover, a German carpenter, said: "If he no go his cattles is all dead. If he stay I bees the carpenter, and I makes his little house for him [meaning his coffin]."

"Well," said Mr. Church, "your request is unreasonable, even if you own the land ... If you have any demonstration to make you may as well do it now. There is only one man

to witness it;" and as he said this he pointed to a friend who knew what was going on. They hesitated. "But," continued Mr. Church, "if you'll give me reasonable time to gather up my things, I'll go ... "

The next morning, when Mr. Church went to arrange for a change in location, he found his house and barn torn down and his feed burned up or destroyed. They did not visit him, as they promised. It was not his intention to leave the county nor abandon the work he had engaged in ...

After [Church] constructed the ditch some distance a man named [Alburtus?] Akers, who belonged to the Hazelton gang, met him and after pledging him to secrecy as to his informant, told him that there was a plot to have him assassinated, and that he was in the plot. The other men who were to do the job were Caldwell, Glenn and Hutchison. He did not believe the story, thinking it a plan to frighten him to leave. But a few days after another one of the gang came and informed him in like manner, telling him how they proposed to proceed. They were to catch him at Centerville when getting his mail, spit tobacco in his eyes to insult him, and as he would undertake to resent it they would shoot him down. Glenn was to spit in his eyes, and when Church went to the post-office one day for his mail Glenn was there; but he passed out a rear door, and the trap did not work.

The next move to assassinate him was to find him at his home. This was to be done by Glenn and Caldwell. Again Akers and Hutchison notified him and he was on his guard. He was called upon as he was warned, and he sent his wife and daughters out to tell them that he was there and would be out in a

116

Chapter 4), could not be used by Easterby either. It was on the wrong side of the Kings and probably in disrepair. A canal near present-day Piedra, built by Jesse Morrow, William Hazelton and Harvey Akers in 1860, lay too far north for feasible expansion as well.

There were, however, two other canals that looked promising. One had been built by Anderson Akers and Spyars Singleton Hyde in 1866 and purchased by the Centerville Canal and Irrigation Company two years later. The other, built by J. B. Sweem in 1869, was located a half-mile below the Centerville company's ditch. Both extended from the west bank of the Kings, watering small farms in the direction of Easterby's ranch, although stopping short of it. An 1870 survey by Robert Edmiston, made at Easterby's behest, showed that this system could be extended to the bed of Fancher Creek—always dry save for periodic flooding and spring runoffs. Since the creek ran through Easterby's property it would thus be possible to irrigate it.

After learning these facts Easterby purchased the Sweem ditch for $1,800, Church posted an appropriation for 3,000 feet of water in July 1870, and expansion work began. A hitch developed when the expanded Sweem ditch threatened to intersect the Centerville canal; its owners refused to grant a right-of-way. Easterby responded by buying them out. On May 16, 1871, his now-extensive irrigation holdings, were consolidated as the Fresno Canal and Irrigation Company.

While Church and Easterby worked out their irrigation difficulties, another problem arose. Hazelton and other Kings River cattlemen did not want farmers taking up their grazing lands, and this led to some ugly confrontations (see 6:5). The would-be agriculturalists were not intimidated. Late 1871 found Easterby's irrigation system partially functioning, wheat growing on his ranch and settlers moving into the Fancher Creek area. In his capacity as a federal land agent, Church had personally encouraged many of the settlers to make Fresno County their home.

Other quarters of the county also were bustling with agricultural activity. Along the San Joaquin River, Millerton gambler and racehorse fancier Billy Christy

moment. At the same time he told his wife and daughters to remain and hear what was said and see what was done. They went, and soon Mr. Church appeared. Caldwell first accused him of trying to steal one of his horses, calling him vile names, hoping to have some pretext to kill him . . . The women stood by and gave the men no opportunity to kill him and they drove away.

Another plot was to kill him and Easterby, and they came very nearly doing it. The plan was to catch them at Jacobs & Silverman's store [at Centerville], in which the postoffice was kept, when after their mails. There was no warning of this plot and they went into the store, and while there a crowd of cowboys came in, when Caldwell charged Easterby with some crime. When he denied it Caldwell struck him on the cheek with his open hand. Easterby opened a rear door and passed into a small room, and Church was left alone. Then Caldwell struck Church a heavy blow with his fist on the jaw, and as he dropped his hand he quickly raised it again with a pistol someone had placed in his hand from behind. Church then dodged behind the counter and ran towards the door when Tom Bates, a powerful man, called for him to stop, and he did, thinking Bates was his friend. But Bates grasped him by the shoulder and gave him a violent jerk, tearing the arms from his coat and shirt, leaving his arm completely naked. He finally got out of the store and a friend took him into a wagon. They then began hunting for Easterby and found him one of the maddest men in the county. The cowboys had gone and Easterby immediately sent for Lawyer Brown of Visalia and Judge [C. G.] Sayle of Millerton. They both came, but nothing was done. Nothing could be done at that time with safety . . .

On another occasion, while Mr. Church was at Centerville for his mail, as he was passing to the door from the postoffice, which was in the rear, a man named Smith [stood] by the counter, leaving a narrow passageway. As Mr. Church was passing by him he threw a handful of sand into his eyes, hoping to blind him, and followed it up with a blow in the face. Mr. Church struck back, and kept backing him towards the door. In passing that way a man named Paul Stover, who was sitting on the counter, kicked [Church] in the jaw with a violence that almost broke it but it did not stagger him. He continued his fight to get out by striking at and backing Smith towards the door. He was almost at the door when Bill Glenn, who was standing on a pile of sacks on the other side from the counter, kicked towards his head. Mr. Church dodged the blow and threw up his arm, which caught Glenn's leg and threw him headlong to the floor, when he lit on his head and shoulders. By this time Church had fought his way to liberty, and he was literally covered with blood from the nose, where Smith had struck him. Once outside he turned about and saw a crowd of twenty or more of the gang, and he said:

"If you want to kill me, why don't you do it? If you only want to whip me, why don't you come one at a time? Now is your opportunity, and I'll give you the best I've got."

At that Tom Bates and Alburtus Akers started out of the store and went directly towards Mr. Church, each with a revolver in his hand. Just as they got to him they parted and passed across the street to what was then known as Lem Farrar's saloon. "They took a drink and bought a bottle of whiskey, and I knew what that meant," says Mr. Church. He then got in his buggy and [drove off] . . .

On the way he stopped at DeWolf's, and Mr. DeWolf was perfectly shocked at his appearance . . . He was so angry that he ran to the back room, got a pistol, and handing it to Mr. Church, whom he knew never carried a pistol, saying: "Here, take this, and do not disgrace it, nor allow yourself to be disgraced while carrying it."

Mr. Church took the pistol and as he started away he saw five or six men not one-half mile away, coming at full speed. He jumped into his buggy, determined to reach the [Fresno Canal & Irrigation Co.] headgate before they caught up with him. It was only a quarter of a mile and he arrived there in time to inform his foreman, Mr. [William C.] Powell, of what had happened, and who saw the men coming. He sent Mr. Church down into the excavation before the crowd arrived, who were by this time inflamed with whisky. The Chinese also saw them and knew what it meant, and they fled quickly to their tents; and in a few minutes they went back quietly to work, each one armed with a pistol.

The first inquiry was for Mr. Church, and Mr. Powell told them that he was not far away. They were not satisfied, and saw that they must use a little diplomacy. They offered Powell a drink, which he took, and then they said they wanted to treat Mr. Church.

"Well," said Powell, "Mr. Church don't drink. I would advise you to go away peaceably, for if you attempt any injury to him or his property you will be riddled with bullets . . ."

Cussing the Chinamen, they took the advice of Mr. Powell and galloped away and for some reason, this was the last serious attempt to assassinate Mr. Church . . .

SOURCE: Fresno County Scrapbook 1870-1899, pp. 254–55, taken from *Fresno Daily Evening Expositor*, December 25, 1895, p. 1, c. 4–6.

had established an orchard-vineyard operation to rival Billy Martin's. Dry Creek farmers were prospering; a year before, in 1870, the first thresher to be operated in Fresno County made its debut on the ranch of a Mr. Hewlet. In the mountains and foothills, Abe Yancey and Colonel Henry Burrough were successfully raising wheat, rye and barley, though they were still relegated to dry farming. William Taylor, a Flint Rock Valley corn farmer, was getting a yield of sixty bushels per acre.

Despite these encouraging signs, it was uncertain if Easterby's vast schemes would work. The year 1872, however, fulfilled everyone's highest expectations. Under Church's supervision, the Fresno Canal system was completed, drainage ditches were dug on the ranch, and an eight-mile fence was constructed to keep out cattle. The result: a bumper crop producing four million pounds of wheat.

Easterby's ranch had hit an early peak (see 6:6) and other farmers were also enjoying great successes. Fancher Creek's agriculturalists harvested a respectable 200,000 bushels of grain in 1872. Kingston farmer-stockmen Justin and Jonathan Esrey realized an average fifty-five bushel an acre yield on their wheat crops.

Nearer to the Easterby Ranch, Caleb Davis, W. Kipp and J. Hutchison were faring well with Kings River cotton crops. Milton McWhorter and John Altman also were cultivating the white gold. "We are said to be the first people to raise commercial crops of cotton in California," said McWhorter years later—an exaggeration. "The crop Altman and I raised was a bumper. We harvested more than two bales of cotton per acre. Altman and I went to Louisville, Kentucky and bought a cotton gin and press and shipped them to California. We . . . operated it by means of a water wheel set in an irrigation ditch. We sold the cotton to the Oakland Woolen Mills for twenty-two and one half cents per pound. I cleared $5,000 on my share of the crop. The girl who later became my wife helped me pick it." This commodity found ready markets in San Francisco and elsewhere, since the arrival of the Central Pacific Railroad in April (see Chapter 7) had lowered the price of mass transportation. Indeed, the 1872 boom happened largely because farmers knew the railroad was coming and planned accordingly.

Landowners in the northern part of Fresno County launched several impressive agricultural and irrigation ventures in the early 1870s. The most ambitious of these was the San Joaquin and Kings River Canal Company, incorporated in February 1871. Backed by the Miller and Lux enterprise, Isaac Friedlander, William S. Chapman, San Francisco banker William Ralston and J. Mora Morse, the company's objective was to build a canal from Kern Lake in Kern County to Antioch in Contra Costa County. This scheme, which would have allowed boats to travel the San Joaquin Valley's length, was probably too ambitious for its time. Given the railroad's advent, it was perhaps unnecessary.

After running into financial troubles early on, the San Joaquin Canal Company was taken over by Miller and Lux and its plans changed. Instead of a valley-long canal, the company built a ditch roughly parallel to the San Joaquin River, tapping that source just below where it met the Fresno Slough. For diversionary purposes a large brush-and-framework dam was erected in front of the canal. Its thirty-foot height allowed boats to pass over it during high-water conditions. Later, the dam was rebuilt with pilings and equipped with a collapsible weir to one side, allowing the passage of boats at any time. From this point the canal was extended more than 100 miles, to Orestimba Creek in Stanislaus County. Through lateral trenches extending from its main trunk, the canal watered experimental orchards, alfalfa and cereal crops on Miller and Lux land. The total cost of the venture: $1.3 million.

On the Kings River two important irrigation schemes developed in the wake of Easterby's venture. Judge B. S. Booker incorporated the Kings River & Fresno Canal Company in 1871, and Daniel Spangler constructed a ditch leading from the Kings to Lone Tree (in the present-day Kingsburg area) in 1872. The modest Spangler venture soon became viable while Booker's plans were slowly realized.

Booker's original intention was to build a canal going in the same direction as Easterby's, from the Kings River to Fancher Creek. This project languished until 1873, when local nurseryman L. A. Gould and others purchased Booker's interests. Work commenced immediately to expand the ditch to Gould's

Reference 6:6

## "ONE GRAND FIELD OF GRAIN"

Within four and a half miles of Fresno is the immense farm of Mr. A. Y. Easterby, planted and conducted by Mr. Chas. S. Lohse. Mr. Russell Fleming hitched up a fast team at Fresno and drove us up to this big enterprise. We were shown over the place by Mr. Lohse, and if anything in the world will overcome the incredulous minds of those who are determined upon swearing that our plains is but an immense sand desert, this certainly would. Here stretching away in every direction as far as the eye can reach is one grand field of grain. Three headers, and a steam thresher and upwards of fifty hands have been at work for several weeks in harvesting the crop, and there is still some three weeks' work left on hand. Forty tons of wheat per day is being shipped to San Francisco by rail from Fresno—the product of this farm, and 1000 tons are to be shipped between now and the 1st of August. On the ranch is about twelve acres of corn which stands fully ten feet in height, while melon and pumpkin vines loaded with their products are to be seen in abundance. . . . A branch of the Fresno Irrigation company's ditch extends through the farm, and if turned loose would flow into the town of Fresno in about two hours' time. One hundred and fifty acres of corn will be planted by Mr. Lohse, so soon as the wheat crop is harvested . . .

SOURCE: *Fresno Weekly Expositor*, July 10, 1872.

farm; it reached there by August. Unfortunately, difficulties arose that required him to tap temporarily into the Easterby system. Aside from that problem, Gould did quite well during the 1873 and 1874 seasons. Fruit trees, vines, alfalfa and grain all flourished on his property (today bounded by McKinley, First, Belmont and Blackstone avenues in Fresno).

Closer to the Easterby Ranch, newer farms threatened to overtake the lead of that pioneering experiment. H. Voorman, B. C. Libby and George Eggers were each farming some 1,000 acres of wheat; combined acreages for the crop in Fresno County amounted to a staggering 100,000. In the same neighborhood August Weihe was undertaking a diversified agricultural enterprise like Gould's while Francis T. Eisen, later Fresno County's pre-eminent vineyardist, was getting his start in that business (see 6:7). Along the Kings and elsewhere cotton cultivation reached its peak. Fruit and grain crops later became less expensive to harvest and ship, but before this happened Albert Henry Statham, William Helm, Caleb Dickerson Davis and others prospered with their small cotton acreages.

Completing this picture of prosperity were the small farmers, whose numbers were fast multiplying in Fresno County. Plots lining the rivers and irrigation canals were quickly snapped up, and if this proved too difficult or expensive, other options were available. A windmill-well combination could be used to water the dry plains practically anywhere. An August 20, 1873, report in the *Fresno Weekly Expositor* mentioned that this method irrigated two or three acres adequately. If all else failed, there was still the possibility of dry farming. Andrew Reed of Elkhorn said in 1873 that farmers there were clinging to that method. Land was cheap, thanks to the absence of irrigation canals, and

that was incentive enough for some individuals to settle in the area.

At this point, only one factor militated against the full-scale development of Fresno County agriculture. Cattlemen had backed off from their vicious opposition to farmers but their herds still roamed the plains, eating and trampling crops at random. While larger farmers like Easterby and Gould could fence in their holdings, at great expense, small farmers could not afford that protective measure. Consequently, their crops were left at the mercy of the cattle. "Sandlappers"—farmers who settled on public lands, usually on small plots—could have a whole season's work wiped out in a few hours. Every unfenced farm was exposed to risk, and the situation worsened steadily.

Unlike the earlier farmer-stockman conflict, the "no fence" issue (as it came to be known) ended with one side the clear loser. The number of farmers was increasing in Fresno County; their interests were allied with the Central Pacific and other railroads who wanted to transport their crops; and together these groups wielded increasing pressure on the state legislature to protect their interests. Against this tide of opposition, coupled with overstocked ranges and a drop in livestock prices, the cattlemen fought hard. State Senator Thomas Fowler, a cattle owner representing Fresno County, successfully defeated many proposals to restrain the animals. Once he was voted out of office in 1873, though, support for his cause in Sacramento evaporated. Pro farmer-railroad legislators were growing in number; a change in their political fortunes was inevitable.

On February 4, 1874, the "no fence" law was enacted by the California Legislature. It did not obligate cattlemen to fence in their herds, although its provisions made such action necessary in most instances. As long

Reference 6:7

## FRESNO COUNTY'S EARLIEST FARMS: TWO REPRESENTATIVE DESCRIPTIONS

From the *Fresno Weekly Expositor*, March 12, 1873:

On last Saturday we visited the place of Messrs. C. G. Frash and F. T. Eisen, which is about four miles from the new town of Fresno... Mr. Frash informed us that he had traveled considerably about the state looking for a location but had seen none, taking all things into consideration, that suited him as well as his present location, in this county. These gentlemen have 1,280 acres of land and are now engaged in plowing and planting. They have three gang plows running, besides several single ones preparing the already plowed ground for setting out grape cuttings. In all there are some twenty men employed on the place. They have 200,000 grape cuttings, and all of foreign varieties, [and] will plant 10 acres of cotton and corn and grain, enough for their own consumption. Mr. Henry Reemer is engaged in building a house and barn and

other necessary buildings...

From the *Fresno Weekly Expositor*, July 9, 1873:

It was our pleasure on last Saturday, in company with W. W. Hill, Esq., to visit... the place of Mr. Aug. Weihe... Fortunately Mr. Weihe himself was at home, and we enjoyed a very pleasant visit. Mr. [John D.] Forthcamp is Superintendent of the farm... Mr. Weihe has about forty acres of cotton which looks exceedingly well. In fact we do not remember to have seen a more promising field. The stalks are now about ten inches in height, and very thrifty. Mr. Weihe, last winter, imported banana trees from Panama which he planted on his place. The voyage from the Isthmus, coupled with the disastrous weather of last spring, militated greatly against the trees and it was thought they had died, but about two weeks ago two of them came up from the roots and are grow-

ing vigorously in the open air. They have leaves on them about eighteen inches long ... This is the first attempt to grow this valuable, but delicate, tropical plant in this valley and in our torrid atmosphere they promise to be successful... Water for irrigation here is obtained from the Fresno Canal and Irrigation Company. When Mr. Weihe dug the well on his ranch he had to sink some sixty feet for water, but since he commenced irrigating his land water flows into his well from the top of the "hard pan," only about twenty feet from the surface. The nearest point of any of the branches of the canal to the well is 150 feet. Mr. W. has a number of very large cottonwoods, which he obtained near this place, which are growing thriftily, and in a very few years he will have an inviting and valuable farm... During the past spring Mr. Forthcamp informs us that he has planted out 12,000 almond trees and 300 lemon trees, all of which are doing well.

as a farmer placed "visible and well-defined monuments" marking boundary lines on his property, he was entitled to confiscate any cattle that wandered onto it. Livestock owners needed to be notified only if they lived six miles from where their animals trespassed, and if they (the cattle) could be identified. And cattle could be reclaimed only after farmers were reimbursed for keeping them, at twenty-five cents per day.

Cattle owners quickly took all the hints suggested by the law, which took effect on February 20. Workmen began scrambling over the ranges, fencing in the holdings of Miller and Lux, Jefferson James, John Sutherland and many lesser barons. Wealthy Miller was about the only cattleman who did not complain about the expense. In truth, he did not mind the law since it solved a constant problem—his herds getting mixed up with others.

Fresno County's remaining barons must have winced at fencing costs. To enclose Sutherland's holdings south of the Kings it was necessary to haul in 15,510 redwood posts and 413,000 feet of Oregon pine boards to the Kingsburg depot in eighty railroad cars. This material was then assembled into a fence twenty-three and a half miles long. In 1874 dollars the total cost was well over $25,000. To fence in a mere 160 acres averaged $2,240.

The passage of the "no fence" law signaled the end of Fresno County's cattle era. Barons, herds and ranches remained after 1874 (and remain still) but the business, stymied by droughts and price fluctuations, never regained its onetime prominence. Agriculture, which had survived many initial tribulations, now began emerging as the county's premier enterprise. An editorialist in the September 15, 1875, *Fresno Weekly Expositor* was moved to remark:

It is evident that the era of doubtful wheat crops on large areas ... of sparse population, poor living conditions, hideous shanties, and, generally, of a condition of things which seemed to be specially inaugurated for the purpose of rendering this beautiful county as repulsive as possible ... is now passing away. Each acre within twenty miles of Fresno will yield its two hundred and fifty dollar harvest of raisins, prunes, figs, citron, oranges, lemons and other products with which the markets of the world have not yet been supplied, and with which they can never be glutted.

This prediction probably seemed ludicrous to many, extravagant to others, and rather modest to a few when it first appeared. We know now that the optimists were right, but even they must have been dumbfounded as they witnessed Fresno County agriculture's wild success in the following years.

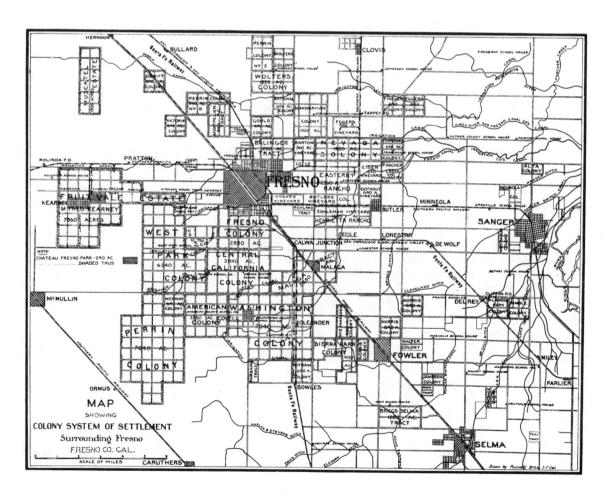

MAP
SHOWING
COLONY SYSTEM OF SETTLEMENT
Surrounding Fresno
FRESNO CO. CAL.

# Chapter 7
# The New Town on the Plains, 1872-1885

The city of Fresno owes its existence to a grain field, a railroad, and a foresighted man. When the Central Pacific Railroad started building a line down the San Joaquin Valley on December 31, 1869, its directors wanted to locate a new town near the middle of the route, but were not certain where to place it. In late November 1871—several months before the tracks reached Fresno County—Central Pacific director Leland Stanford, railroad official Alban N. Towne, and one Colonel Grey visited the A. Y. Easterby ranch. It was a thriving wheat field in the middle of a bleak prairie, and impressive to the touring officials. Stanford was moved to declare: "Wonderful! Here must we build the town!"

Immediately following Stanford's visit the Contract and Finance Company (a real estate subsidiary of the Central Pacific) bought 4,480 acres, most of them west of the Easterby property and near the proposed railroad route. The new townsite was approximately ten miles southeast of Sycamore, in a desolate area where Dry Creek drained into the plains. Seemingly a bad location, it had one advantage: closeness to Easterby's ranch and the center of other anticipated agricultural ventures.

Events began crowding in fast. On March 23, 1872, the Central Pacific's southbound rail construction crews completed a temporary bridge over the San Joaquin River. The site of Fresno was reached in late April, with sidetracks, turning tables and a depot erected there shortly afterward. In May Edward H. Mix surveyed the town into 320- by 400-foot blocks, with 25- by 150-foot lots and twenty-foot alleys. The railroad held a land sale for these parcels on June 26, 1872, prices ranging from $60 to $250, depending on location.

Because of its central placement, a few county entrepreneurs reasoned that Fresno would become an important shipping and commercial center. To cash in on this imagined prosperity, a few began setting up businesses in the new town. James E. Faber was the first storekeeper, setting up his establishment in a tent. His first provisions, purchased at Stockton, could not be regularly delivered to Fresno because of an obscure

Central Pacific regulation. Thanks to an understanding conductor the goods were surreptitiously thrown out along the tracks north of town, where Faber retrieved them later.

Following Faber was Millerton storekeeper Otto Froelich, who set up a rival store across the tracks. About the same time R. Daily built a small restaurant and rooming house (with one guest bedroom). Frank Dusy and his partner, William M. Coolidge, set up pens and corrals near the tracks for their sheep-raising activities. Loading chutes were built for the use of local cattlemen, principally Jefferson James.

Other pioneering businesses were Anton Joseph Maassen's restaurant and saloon, where water (obtainable only from wells, of which there were few) sold for twenty-five cents for two bucketfuls; M. A. Schultz's hotel and saloon; B. S. Booker's variety store; John Wyatt's livery stable; John W. Williams' blacksmith shop; Pete and Jim Larquier's restaurant and hotel; and George McCullough's lumberyard. Froelich became the town's first Wells, Fargo agent on May 22, 1872, and stage driver Russell Fleming its first postmaster the following August 28 (see 7:1). By November 1872 Fresno had four hotels and restaurants, three saloons, three livery stables, two stores and one or two houses, with many railroad workers living in tents.

The year 1873 found a thriving town on the "sinks of Dry Creek." During a two-month period eighty cars of wheat, thirty of cattle, and seventy-five of sheep left the depot, while 100 cars of merchandise were received. Regular passenger service between Fresno and other towns was established. Trains left for Merced, Lathrop, San Francisco, Stockton, Sacramento and the East at 2:10 a.m. daily, and 4:50 a.m. Sundays. Southbound, trains left for Goshen, Tulare and Tipton at the same daily time, but at 9:45 a.m. on Sundays. Few new businesses were opening up, but no one disputed the town's prosperity. Some began suggesting that the county seat be moved to this bustling prairie locale.

In the *Fresno Weekly Expositor* of March 18, 1874, "A Disgusted Millertonian" voiced the sentiments of more and more county residents. "The progress of

121

[this] town has been like a cow's tail—downward," he wrote. "It is a disgrace to the wealthy and prosperous county of Fresno that its County Seat should be located at so poor and mean a village as Millerton, a place without a store or decent building . . . "

An election had already been scheduled for March 23 to decide if the county seat should stay in Millerton or be moved to one of several suggested locations. Fresno received 417 votes, Centerville 123, Lisbon (a proposed site located on Big Dry Creek north-north-west of latter-day Clovis) 124, and Millerton, only 93. Historian Paul E. Vandor wrote that "tradition has it that whiskey was carried in basket[s] and ladled out in tin cup[s] by railroad bosses to their workers at the polls," since their votes were decisive and the railroad had an obvious interest in the relocation.

Millerton residents now began following the lead of carpenter Thomas Whitlock, who in mid-1872 had been the first to desert that bleak hamlet for Fresno. In early Septmber 1874 William Faymonville's and Lewis Leach's offices, Judge Claudius Golon Sayle's residence and office, Harry Dixon's residence, Simon Henry's blacksmith shop and stable, and other Millerton buildings were dismantled and hauled down to Fresno. The *Expositor* had preceded most of these individuals and businesses, having produced its last Millerton edition on April 15 and its first Fresno edition exactly one week later. The last major moving activity was the transfer of the county hospital patients to the plains on October 3, via Russell Fleming's stage. Dr. Leach supervised the removal.

If anything established Fresno for good, it was this protracted move from Millerton and the increased population and activity it brought. A July 1874 informal census counted four general stores, two fruit stores, one drugstore, three hotels, two restaurants, two livery stables, six saloons, two law offices, two physicians, one tinsmith, one saddle shop, two butcher shops, three blacksmiths, one tailor, the *Expositor*, and twenty-five private residences.

Reference 7:1

# FIRST FAMILIES OF FRESNO

### ERNESTINE WINCHELL

Immediately [when] the tracks of the Central Pacific railroad . . . reached the sinks of Big Dry creek nine miles from the San Joaquin river activities other than those of groundsquirrels and road runners began to stir that part of the great valley.

At this time, April 1872, the prospect far and near was entrancing to any eye that saw. Poppies in sheets of flame; cream-cups and white forget-me-nots and four-o'clocks like splashes from the milky way; pools of (can't read)-eyes reflecting the azure of the sky. Purple and crimson and gold, rose and lilac and pearl of all the wild blossoms so well known to every child of today, besides many that 55 years of cultivation have totally destroyed.

Horned toads and rattlesnakes loafed on the warm crests of hogwalllows; ground-squirrels were yelping, and under tufts of lupine palpitant jackrabbits sniffed the air. Baby owls blinked nestled in abandoned holes, and blackbirds whirled through the sunshine. Over the colorful perfumed plain swept bands of antelope, their white flags like foam of the sea; elk and mustangs grazed at the edge of the plain.

But for none of these had the children of the railroad eyes or ears. Dropped on the trampled right of way with lumber or tool or goods, they gave their whole attention to their various businesses of life. The adoptions rolled up with wagons and teams, and each contributed a share to the settlement that was called Fresno station. Busy as ants they came and went—to and from Millerton and Coarse Gold and Stockton; Scottsburg and Kingston and Visalia; New Idria mines and Salinas and all the coastward towns.

The first family man to get that grip on the new land that is represented by a home was Russell H. Fleming. By the time the flowers had faded and the owlets had feathered he brought his wife and children from Millerton to a small house he had erected on what the map said was Mariposa street, between H and I.

On the remainder of that half block Mr. Fleming built stables and corrals for the vehicles and teams he used in his passenger stage business and the U.S. mail contract between the county seat on the river and the station by the railroad. These structures also accommodated the animals and wagons of the freighters who headed there from all points of industry in the hills and along the banks of the San Joaquin and Kings river.

In June Mrs. Fleming began to make the first home in Fresno—children about the doorstep and a cloth spread on the table. But there was not a tree to shade her thin walls and roof from the pelting sun; not a blade of grass in her yard. An iron stove to cook the food and a pile of wood for fuel. A hand pump to supply the water—and a path of Hades to woodpile and well-curb, back and forth a score of times a day, in sun of summer and wind of winter.

Not Mrs. Fleming alone, but also the women who followed her to Fresno in their turn to make homes for their optimistic and adventurous men. The aristocracy of that day were they, rising to the heights of heroism without ostentation, enduring martyrdom without complaint. Proud and brave, they met unflinchingly the conditions that were the fault of no human will.

Every stitch of clothing for themselves, their men, their children and their houses they washed with their own hands, dragging water for the purpose from the depths of the arid ground. From flaming stove to blanketed table they carried heavy flatirons, turning out marvelous heaps of starched and ruffled gleaming garments that gratified even their housewifely pride in work well done.

To those homes established in Fresno that summer of 1872 winter brought only another set of trials. Uninterrupted, the winds tore across the gray plain, shook the frail dwellings and filled them with icy breath. Rain thrashed the thin roofs and trickled under any crooked shake. Fog let down a clammy veil that drifted in rags through every crack.

By the end of the decade the isolation at least was over, for there were then many homes in the Fresno that in 1874 had become the county seat, though household conditions were bettered little beyond added rooms. Trees were growing, but too small to afford real shade. Wood from the hills was still the fuel for cook stove and heaters. There were a few windmills, but the homes with piped water were rare.

To those intrepid women who had braved the hardest of the trying early days, life grew easier from year to year until they were taken one by one to their reward. The heaviest of the burdens were lifted from their gallant shoulders, wind and rain and fog were shut from their comfortable dwellings, and flowers grew in their yards.

In the great city of today their names are all but forgotten but their homekeeping, duplicated in scores of other pine board shanties, is the rock upon which the metropolis of the Valley is reared.

SOURCE: Ernestine Winchell columns.

When Fresno's townsite was laid out by the Central Pacific, it offered four city blocks on high ground, intersected by Fresno and O streets, for county use. The blocks, labeled A, B, C and D on the town plat maps, were a gift horse the city fathers chose to look in the mouth. Lilbourne A. Winchell later had this to say about the selection: "How would the people ever be able to walk that long distance over the red-hot plains [the town's commercial center then being located along the railroad tracks and H Street], through tangles of sticky mint, tarweed and tumble weeds; and thread through the thickets of sage brush and lupine that covered the site,—without shade, and no liquid wayside refreshment? Unthinkable!"

Accordingly, the railroad donated a new set of four blocks—these intersected by Mariposa and L streets—for the eventual site of county buildings. By September 25, 1874 a temporary building for county offices had been built on the latter location. There was room enough in it for the county clerk, recorder, surveyor, treasurer, tax collector and sheriff. The district attorney, however, was relegated to using an anteroom of Len Farrar's Magnolia Saloon for offices, and court was held above the Shannon and Hughes store and saloon. Rude as these accommodations were, they were tolerated because a new Courthouse was in the making.

On March 27, 1874, Fresno County was empowered to sell $60,000 worth of bonds to finance construction of a Courthouse. The California Bridge and Building Company of Oakland won the building contract on May 14 for $56,370, began to burn bricks, and laid the foundation less than five months later. The cornerstone of the building was laid on October 8 in a Masonic ceremony. Contained in that box were newspaper accounts of the Courthouse construction, a Bible, gold and silver pieces, historical notes "of the first twenty years of the San Joaquin Valley," Dixon and Faymonville's map of Fresno Couty, and miscellaneous other items.

In accordance with the design of Sacramento architect A. A. Bennett, the Courthouse slowly began to take form. It was a box ninety-five feet long, sixty feet wide and fifty-seven feet high, topped with a dome that brought its height to 112 feet. Some 800,000 bricks were used in its construction.

The building was formally accepted by the county on August 19, 1875, a move that did not please the Grand Jury empaneled at the time. Its members inspected the building and claimed to find evidence of inferior ironwork, vaults that were not fireproof, and use of poor building materials. A subsequent tour of the building by two architects and two contractors found these claims to be without merit. "But it does seem strange that a building so utterly bad should be constructed under the eyes of our citizens, many of whom were mechanics [laborers], and more or less of whom daily visited the work, without the defects of some of them being discovered," commented the November 17, 1875, *Fresno Weekly Expositor.*

To dress up the buildings's appearance improvements were made in later years: an ornamental fence around the property in 1876, trees, palms and shrubbery planted by Gus Witthouse in 1878, and a replacement redwood fence in 1883. The building also was supplied with its own windmill and water tank, a luxurious feature (for that time) that cost $1,350.

Housing was scarce during Fresno's early years. The April 29, 1874, *Fresno Weekly Expositor* remarked that no building in town was vacant and "the most ordinary shanty brings from eight to twelve dollars a month rent." As late as September 12, 1883, the same paper commented that "our streets are paraded every day by home-seekers who find it impossible to get any kind of a house to inhabit; and when they find an empty shanty the exorbitant price charged for it is enough to scare any reasonable person."

Homes built during the 1870s were little more than simple frame cottages, some bigger than others and a few with second stories. Construction became more elaborate in the next decade. William Betteridge built himself the town's first brick house in 1882, with five rooms and a big bay window. A six-room house built by Rollin R. Roberts in the same year featured a stained-glass front window and carpets throughout. Both residences had high ceilings, a feature that became almost standard in later years as a method of dissipating summer heat.

At first Fresno's business establishments were housed in tents, then in flimsy frame buildings, and later in brick buildings and "business blocks." Substantial brick buildings were constructed by E. C. Winchell and John W. Shanklin in 1881, Frank H. and Kate Ball in 1882, and Angus Marion Clark and William H. McKenzie about the same time. The "blocks" were generally more imposing and important. When commercial lots became expensive after 1874 (in that year, some went for $600), investors hit upon the idea of erecting large commercial buildings with rental spaces for businessmen and professionals. This idea soon caught favor.

One of the first "blocks" was built by W. H. Donahoo in the early 1880s. On its bottom floor were plenty of glass windows for merchants to display their wares, and the upper floor was reserved for office space. In the single year of 1883, when business activity was building up to a peak, there was a tremendous rash of "block" building: E. Gilmour, Luke Shelly, Walker Drane Grady, J. M. Burleigh, Albert H. Statham, G. R. G. Glenn and Charles G. Hutchinson all got into the act, with most of the structures named for their builders. The two-story Hutchinson Block, located at the later site of the Security Pacific Bank Building, was handsomest of all.

Fresno's few hotels were so crowded by 1874 that reservations had to be made a day in advance. Not surprisingly, there were many entrants in this business. Early hotels included Maassen's International, Jerry Ryan's Star Hotel, and William Lawrenson's California Hotel (the old Larquier House), all of which opened in 1874. The Henry House, which opened on May 10, 1875, was Fresno's first high-quality hotel. Built for $15,000 by blacksmith Simon W. Henry, it contained thirty-eight rooms, all beautifully appointed and carpeted. It was taken over by Jesse Morrow in 1877 and renamed after him.

Worthy competitors to the Henry/Morrow House emerged in 1882, when the two-story, sixty-nine room Ogle House and the United States Hotel of Jerry Ryan were built. This was Ryan's third entry in the local hotel field (he had built the Washington in 1876). In 1883 he erected yet another—the California, and in the same year John W. Williams built the elaborate Grand Central Hotel. The latter property was purchased by financier Fulton G. Berry in 1884.

Among the young town's saloonkeepers and saloons were James Faber's "Senate," Len Farrar's previously-mentioned "Magnolia," Harry Mendies and William Lawrenson's "Courthouse," Fred Kramer, O. James Meade, and Harry Z. Austin. They were eventually joined by M. A. Blade, Austin and A. G. Bell's "Mist," and a quaint resort known as "Miller's Beer Depot."

It took little time for Fresno's puritanical elements to notice these developments. An effort to form a temperance league was made as early as 1873; a Good Templars lodge (which was prohibition-oriented) was formed on January 25, 1875; and a Temperance Alliance was operating by 1883, the same year that a Mrs. Holyoke, representing the Woman's Christian Temperance Union, lectured in Fresno.

No busy frontier town could long do without general merchandise stores. As with the other essential businesses, a healthy complement of them developed quickly. L. Davis of Snelling opened a clothing, variety and grocery store in August 1873, and Levy and Brother a general store in January 1874. Elias Jacob of Visalia and George Bernhard of Mariposa opened similar establishments the following June and October. Jacob had purchased Otto Froelich's store and was bought out in turn by his clerk, H. D. Silverman, and Louis Einstein in early 1875. Silverman died two years later and was replaced in the partnership by Louis Gundelfinger, with the business bearing only Einstein's name after that time. Its closest competitor was a general store operated by Adolph Kutner and Samuel Goldstein; the two sets of businessmen continually competed against each other by enlarging their stores, building warehouses, opening branches in other towns and offering better merchandise (see 7:2).

Also rising to early prominence in the merchandising field were J. Brownstone, Charles DeLong and William Vellguth. The latter's highly diversified business sold drugs, dresses, millinery and "fancy" items, and housed a barbershop and bath house as well. Somewhat later entries were the Saxe and Davis store and Solomon Wollner's I X L Store, founded in 1881.

Robert Simpson opened a butcher shop in 1873, with others following soon afterward: George Sutherland and W. E. Williams in the same year, and the Fresno Meat Market, E. P. Nelson and George Bernhard, the next. John W. Coffman joined Bernhard by 1881, and business was good enough that year for them to slaughter 630 hogs and put up 12,000 pounds of lard, 19,200 of ham and 102,000 of bacon. Unfortunately for patrons, prices for meat in Fresno stores were raised in 1882: porterhouse steak went up to twenty cents a pound, loin steak was eighteen cents and round steak fifteen. John C. Nourse, Gillum Baley, W. T. Mattingly, W. T. Riggs and others ran regular grocery stores during this period, while George Bates and B. S. Booker limited themselves exclusively to the fruit trade.

Early rough-and-tumble Fresno even had room for shops that catered to feminine needs. Mrs. William Vellguth was the first to enter the millinery trade—in a corner of her husband's store. Miss Mattie Card and Miss A. McDonald started a competing business in 1875, and the field was broadened to include a Mrs.

Reference 7:2

## THE WONDROUS WARES OF KUTNER-GOLDSTEIN

An Expositor reporter while meandering down Mariposa street yesterday evening in search of an item, got caught in the immense throng that was pressing down the street, and before he knew what he was doing, or thought what he was about, he found himself jammed into the dry-goods department of Messrs. Kutner & Goldstein. The quick eye of the manager of the department, Mr. Myerstein, caught the sparkle of the $1000 diamond that sparkled in the items-man's immaculate shirt-front, and the immense golden fob-chain that dangled from his watch-fob, and at once concluded that it was one of our rich vinters, who having disposed of his season's crop, was looking around for something elegant to present his wife. The clever salesman seized his arm and in a twinkle had him up before a counter and was unfolding to his astonished gaze, the most beautiful things in the line of lady's goods, and at the same time kept up a continuous talk, describing and praising up the goods and detailing the prices. There were doll-maus and circulars in silk plushes, satin rhadames, grosgrain silk, silk mattassey, and the lord only knows what other kind of materials; they were fur lined, fur trimmed, cut pompadour, and spangled and bangled and what-knot. Next he opened on him with a volley of silks of all shades, colors and styles; following with shodah, damask, and dress goods of every description, and the latest fashion, and there was—but alas! the poor reporter's brain was in a whirl, and he made a rush for the open air muttering "$50," "silk plush," "$5 a yard," "$75," "wife," "$150 pattern," etc. He is now in bed, with a nurse sitting by laving his head with ice water. But his mind seems hopelessly ruined.

SOURCE: *Fresno Weekly Expositor*, October 11, 1882, p. 5 c. 3, in Fresno Scraps, p. 497.

In 1874, Otto Froelich's pioneer store, at H and Mariposa in Fresno, was purchased by Elias Jacob, H. D. Silverman and Louis Einstein. The following year Silverman and Einstein purchased Jacob and Company, and subsequently it became Louis Einstein and Company.

Louis Einstein (above) and his Pioneer Store (left), southeast corner of Mariposa and H streets, Fresno.

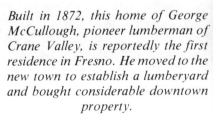

Built in 1872, this home of George McCullough, pioneer lumberman of Crane Valley, is reportedly the first residence in Fresno. He moved to the new town to establish a lumberyard and bought considerable downtown property.

125

*The county's first Courthouse in Fresno, built in 1876 for $56,000.*

*Mariposa Street and the new Courthouse in 1877—
population 500.*

*The same street twenty-five years later—population 20,000.*

*Fresno in 1876 from front of the Courthouse.*

*Morrow House at Tulare and K streets about 1880. Jesse Morrow was the proprietor after 1877.*

*Blacksmith and wagon shop, necessary in every city, was operated by W. Robertson in the early 1880s.*

*By 1881 the city boasted a Fresno Water Works, with L. Anderson as superintendent.*

*Madary Planing Mill and Box Factory, founded in 1879, sold much of the lumber needed to build the new town.*

Black and Miss Williams in December 1876. Mrs. M. J. Hughes and Mrs. Anna Vandergaw opened additional shops by 1881, and in 1883 Mrs. E. Gilmour started selling trimmed hats, bonnets, baby things, and fine embroideries and lace. A canny businesswoman, Mrs. Gilmour always made a point of wearing her latest and best fashions to church in order to inspire prospective purchasers. As if the activity in this trade wasn't sufficient, a Mr. and Mrs. Lamb opened a new millinery store in 1884 that specialized in bonnets and hats imported from France.

Blacksmith, livery, harness, saddle and related businesses were staples in young Fresno. Despite the iron horse's availability, the more conventional type still had its uses—especially for short distance travel. Simon W. Henry built his blacksmith shop and stables in 1874, with Alexander Tombs, John W. Williams, Albert H. Statham, Joaquin Lamonthe, and Elijah Wimmer following his lead in the next several years. In the early 1880s the Simpson brothers, Thomas R. Brown, Charles Hogdon, M. F. Lockhart, J. R. Sullinger, George Harron, James Harrison, Charles Johnson, George Keller and Martin McNally had joined their ranks, along with harness makers F. N. Bedford and C. A. Kramer, and wheelwright H. J. Schwap.

Among Fresno's livery stables of this era the Hughes, built in 1882, stood out. It could hold fifty vehicles, always had twelve span of horses on hand, and took care to wash customers' buggies in the shade so that the paint on them would not blister. An associated business also operating in this era was W. Robertson's Manufactory, which built wagons, agricultural implements, carriages and buggies. "All of his work is made upon honor, and he takes pride in warranting all that leaves his shop . . . The place presents the appearance of an immense hive, as indeed, it is," said the August 30, 1882, *Fresno Weekly Expositor.*

In the growing Fresno of this era lumber was always much in demand, although few entered the business. D. E. Bundy, Frank K. Prescott and Charles S. Pierce were the only lumber dealers of note, with Whitlock and Young, J. Banta, and M. R. Madary operating planing mills to finish the raw products. Madary's mill, built in 1881, also had an adjacent box factory and wood yard. All of these finishing enterprises burned in 1882 but were soon rebuilt.

The town's first flour mill was operated on Mariposa Street by Calvin Jones, an emigrant from the Kings River country. Powered by a small boiler and engine, his operation had a limited capacity. He quit the business in 1878, when Moses J. Church built a larger mill on Fresno and N streets. By running a branch canal from his Fresno Canal system (see Chapter 8) into town on a fifteen-foot drop, Church was able to power his mill, later dubbed the Champion, by water. It was enlarged in 1880 and made into a four-story building with a 120-barrel-a-day grinding capacity. O. P. Wil-

son, manager of the Champion, sold flour to retail and commercial customers at the same price. To his mind it remained the same commodity, no matter who bought it, and he saw no logic in a sliding price schedule.

Five banks serviced Fresno in its earliest days. The first was named, unsurprisingly, "The Fresno Bank" and was incorporated by Otto Froelich and Captain Charles H. Barth in the fall of 1874. Permanent quarters were set up in March 1875, but a year later the bank collapsed. The business climate in town was not strong enough to support a bank, Barth had overextended himself and could not pay a sizable debt to the government, and the Bank of Nevada had to take over his share of the business.

In August 1876 Thomas Fowler and Lewis Leach teamed with Froelich to inaugurate "The Bank of Fresno." It opened the following December 2 and survived until July 1877, when "the present stagnation in business, and the excessive taxations and restrictions imposed . . . rendered it . . . impossible to continue at a profit," according to the July 9 *Fresno Weekly Expositor.* The bank, capitalized at $250,000, had sold stock amounting to $47,600. Its directors ordered a dividend of seven dollars paid to all remaining shareholders.

There were no new entries in Fresno County banking until October 26, 1881, when the Fresno County Bank was formed and Lewis Leach selected as its first president. It had capital stock of $100,000, paid up by March 16, 1885—the day the bank reorganized under a national charter and was renamed the First National Bank. In the meantime Leach had moved over to the presidency of the Farmers Bank of Fresno, which had been organized on March 8, 1882 with $100,000 in capital stock.

Before Fresno's incorporation in 1885 yet another bank joined the local financial ranks: the Fresno Loan and Savings Bank, organized in 1884 and eventually basing itself in an opulent, three-story brick headquarters that cost $65,000. Like its immediate predecessors, it was capitalized at $100,000. W. T. Oden was the bank's first president, and later was succeeded by cattleman Jefferson James.

Journalistic development in Fresno was quite lively in the town's formative years. After resettling in a Tulare Street frame building, the *Fresno Weekly Expositor* continued to prosper and moved into a new, two-story brick headquarters in the spring of 1881. It assumed daily status on April 3, 1882, increased its size from a five- to a six-column format on April 2, 1883, and to a seven-column format on April 3, 1884. Beginning in May 1875, the *Expositor* was joined by the *Fresno Weekly Review* of Charles A. Heaton, a former employee; the new newspaper ceased publication seven months later. Said the *Expositor* of its demise: "One paper can live in Fresno County while two are sure to starve."

On September 23, 1876, a new entry, the *Fresno*

*Republican*, was published in a first edition of 750 copies by Dr. Chester Rowell. He was associated with a local group of Republicans known as "The One Hundred," which formed a support base for his newspaper but probably did not number that many. Nevertheless, Fresno's growth brought more Republicans to the county (previously a Democratic stronghold), and the newspaper did well. It was sold to S. A. Miller on April 26, 1879, with the stipulation that "its policy, politics or name should never be changed" and that it could never combine with the *Expositor*, a Democratic organ. John W. Short became Miller's editorial partner in 1881 and they published the paper jointly for several years.

Other newspapers operating at this time were a satirical review edited by Ledyard F. Winchell and the *Fresno Weekly Democrat*. The *Democrat* was the brainchild of W. S. Moore, formerly of Franklin, Kentucky. Like most newspapermen of his day (and all who worked in Fresno), Moore ran a sideline printing business to keep his newspaper afloat.

Fresno's first doctor was H. C. Coley, who opened offices next to Schultz's Hotel in 1874. He carried on a grocery, general merchandise, drug and medicine business to supplement his income. Following him in August of that year was Anna Cramer, the town's first nurse and midwife. A month later Fresno had only one health care facility, a ramshackle hospital presided over by Dr. Lewis Leach and later deemed unfit for use by the county grand jury in September 1876. In November of 1876 the county purchased a lot from Charles Crocker, bounded by R, S, Tulare and Mariposa streets, to build a $3,527 replacement hospital that could accommodate twenty patients.

The next important development in this area was the creation of a county medical association on December 22, 1883. Its first president was Dr. Chester Rowell, publisher of the *Republican* newspaper, who had resided in town for nearly a decade.

A. C. Bradford was the first lawyer to locate in Fresno, in March 1874. He soon found a partner in Judge E. C. Winchell, who moved down from Millerton three months later. By 1876 Walter D. Tupper and W. H. Creed, along with Walter Drane Grady and R. H. Daly, had created other partnerships. They were all based in the county Courthouse. Later, in 1885, Winchell initiated a new partnership with Daly. By that time many new attorneys had settled in town: W. Barry, J. B. Campbell, E. D. Edwards, Henry C. Tupper, John Goss, E. J. Griffith, Milus King Harris, E. D. Larkins, Aurelius ("Reel") Terry and Harry Dixon. Most of these men eventually served as judges, district attorneys, or both.

In spite of the town's development otherwise, there was no school for the forty-six boys and thirty-four girls living in and around Fresno in 1872. A school district was formed on February 6, 1873, with trustees

J. W. Williams, B. S. Booker and R. Daily. The railroad donated a block of land off Tulare and M streets for a school, but an election to approve a $3,000 construction bond for it failed. As a temporary measure, private funds were solicited for Mary J. McKenzie to teach a class in the second floor of Booker's store.

A new election on August 29, 1874, reorganized the district. A $4,000 schoolhouse bond issue was approved 48 to 2, and Otto Froelich, B. S. Booker and J. W. Ferguson were installed as trustees. With Reuben H. Bramlet as the teacher, and Georgia Ellis as his assistant, the Booker building was again used as a schoolhouse for forty students until a school could be built. Finished later that year by Joseph L. Smith, at a below-budget cost of $2,699, it opened on January 4, 1875, on Tulare near M Street. At first it served fifty students, but a few had to be turned away until Mattie Patten could be hired to fill out the teaching staff. The school, nicknamed the "Pink" for its color, was operated in the serious and conscientious manner of those days. Beginning in 1877 monthly report cards were issued showing the number of days tardy and absent, along with class standing for all students. Examinations were also no-nonsense (see 7:3).

Bramlet, his wife, Euphemia, and John Dooner continued as teachers in 1878. Fresno's growth had made it necessary to build a larger school. The California Legislature authorized the district to issue $15,000 worth of bonds, and not long afterward contractors Frank and C. S. Peck began building the new school. Formally known as the Central School, informally as the "White" or (later) the "Hawthorne," it cost $10,500 and could accommodate 400 students. It opened in September 1879 on the eventual site of the Memorial Auditorium, and was up to full capacity by 1885. In that year D. S. Snodgrass was principal, and teachers were restricted to teaching their particular specialties— mathematics, reading, language, geography, penmanship, drawing, music and physiology.

Fresno's first library was founded by the short-lived Fresno Social and Literary Club in 1876. When that organization disbanded, books were returned to the members who had donated them. Another library, privately funded but intended for public use, was begun in 1883. It occupied rooms in the Donahoo Block and was open from 4 to 10 p.m. on weekdays and 10 a.m. to 4 p.m. on Sundays. Lumberman W. J. Foster made an initial donation of 125 books and Moses J. Church donated 110 more, so the library got off to a substantial start. The first president of the library association was W. R. Doty, and the first librarian was E. L. McCapes. Support came from 110 charter members who each donated five dollars annually.

The Fresno post office functioned in a variety of locations after its founding in 1872. Charles DeLong, then a salesman for Otto Froelich, succeeded Russell Fleming as postmaster on November 14, 1873. The office remained at Froelich's after the store was purchased by Jacob and later Silverman and Einstein. Eventually fifty call and fifty lock boxes were installed there. Later, the post office was moved briefly to the Fanning Brothers variety store, then relocated in February 1876 to a new store owned by DeLong alone. Froelich became postmaster on May 29, 1880. He moved the office to the John Donahoo building and gave it its own room for the first time. It remained there when Nathan W. Moodey succeeded Froelich on July 6, 1882, but was removed to the new Hutchinson Block two years later.

Although it has long been a municipal service, the delivery of water to Fresno's citizens began as a private business. In the beginning, the only way to get water was to dig a well (as Anton Joseph Maassen did), or set up a well-windmill combination (William Vellguth was the first to do this, to supply his barber shop and baths). But there were problems: windmills were expensive, hand-pumping was laborious and time-consuming, and some businesses were too close together to make wells practicable.

To resolve these difficulties at a hoped-for profit, Lyman Andrews and George McCullough set up the Fresno Water Works in July 1876. A 100-foot well with a seven-inch casing was drilled to supply the city, a 23,000-gallon storage tank was erected, and mains were laid under the city streets at a cost of $3,000. According to Todd A. Shallat, monthly rates were nominal: "$1.50 for a family of five, 10¢ for each additional person, $1.50 for a garden, and 50¢ for the family cow." Fresno's citizenry was so appreciative that a commemorative banquet was held for Andrews and McCullough on October 14, 1876.

In May 1877 the company was sold to the Fresno Water Company, in which Andrews and McCullough retained a financial interest. An additional 12,000-gallon tank was added to the system in 1878, another well and a steam pump were in service by 1881, and by the next year 17,000 additional feet of pipe had been laid. These extensions to the system, however, made maintaining pressure difficult. Dissatisfied customers began tapping into Church's Mill Ditch for water, and some went without. To overcome this difficulty Holly duplex pumps were installed in 1884, designed to pump 34,000 gallons of water per hour directly into the mains. As a result, "water [could] be thrown over the highest building in town," according to one contemporary report.

Another municipal convenience, the Fresno Gas Company, was created on March 31, 1881. Capitalized with $50,000, James R. Smedberg was its first president, Dr. Lewis Leach was its first trustee and was empowered to sell stock, and the company was to serve a projected 200 customers. Apparently problems developed after this initial organization, for the first meeting of the "Fresno Gaslight Company" was held on December 16, 1882, with Leach elected as president and William Faymonville vice-president.

Hardware dealers Donahoo, Fanning and Company set up the works. A gasometer that could produce 25,000 cubic feet of gas per day was installed, along with mains and other necessary equipment. Although Fresno's population was barely over 1,000, the works were built to serve a town of 12,000 to 15,000 population. Company directors had noted that small gas works in Modesto and Merced had been outmoded by rapid growth, and did not want to make the same mistake in Fresno.

After Alexander Graham Bell invented the telephone, Fresno people "began to try what they could do with boxes and wet batteries and tin-can receivers," according to Ernestine Winchell, but in July 1882, S. A. Miller set up a twenty-line switchboard in his *Republican* office. Some fifteen subscribers signed up initially, and no directory was required; Mrs. Miller, the operator, could connect anyone by name. The cost of monthly service was four dollars—comparable to today's rates in raw dollars, and probably higher counting inflation. A substantial clientele was soon built up (see 7:4).

A grim, albeit necessary, service for Fresno was inaugurated when its first cemetery was opened in 1873. It was located on ground owned by William H. McKenzie on the east side of town, and was soon joined by another cemetery at the corner of Calaveras and M streets. Due to frequent flooding the McKenzie cemetery was abandoned in 1876, with the bodies removed to the block bounded by Kern, Inyo, C and D streets. The owners of this new graveyard were H. C. Warner and W. J. Bennett, town undertakers. On August 18 of the next year fire visited this new location, and by the time three more years had passed it had become too crowded. A second relocation was made—this time to a tract near the corner of Fresno Street and Church Avenue.

The condition of this new graveyard, out on the bleak prairie, soon became a minor scandal. It inspired the following ditty:

> I would not claim it as a home,
> Nor e'en a place to die.
> For out on yon sand hills bare,
> Your dear and dead ones lie.

To correct this situation, Thomas E. Hughes sank a well in 1883 to provide water for foliage. Moses J. Church later built a canal out to the cemetery for an additional supply.

The planting of evergreen shrubs and trees later proliferated, and at last Fresno had a decent graveyard. But, once again, the town's needs began to outstrip the available space. In April 1885 Church decided to donate eighty acres, out on what later became Belmont Avenue, so a number of organizations could bury their dead. The gift's one stipulation was that the organizations had to move out of their spaces in the old cemetery. This was agreed to and the Mountain View Cemetery was created, with subdivisions for varied groups: Episcopal, Seventh-day Adventist, Catholic and Christian cemeteries and Liberty Cemetery for veterans, along with Masonic, Odd Fellows, United Workmen, Forester and Knights of Pythias graveyards. The bulk of these still exist in the same location.

The sole service that did not keep pace with Fresno's growth, or modernization in general, was street maintenance. Town thoroughfares were unpaved and unlit, were often choked with refuse, and were not graded. Water collected in them during winter seasons and made travel difficult. Occasional efforts were made to improve the situation. An public appeal was made to clean up the streets in 1874. Russell Fleming and William Lawrenson installed street lamps in front of their businesses in the same year, and a few streets were graded in 1875 and 1876. Yet there were still problems.

The September 2, 1874, *Fresno Weekly Expositor* said that streets and alleys "are in a disgustingly filthy condition . . . [and] are covered with old bones, hats, boots, dead dogs, decaying vegetable matter, old clothes, tin cans and the like, and the consequence is a most disgusting and pestilence-breeding effluvia constantly pervading the atmosphere." Part of the problem was that dogs roamed free. One wag suggested that

Fresno be rechristened Dogtown, since there were three of them for every human.

By the 1880s the situation was hardly improved. Despite grading, Mariposa Street "[seemed] to be converted into a giant duck pond," said the October 11, 1882, *Fresno Weekly Expositor*. The same paper said on September 12, 1883, that "the filth and garbage of the house are thrown out indiscriminately to fester and fill the air with the most deadly fumes. No attention is had to drainage or cleanliness."

Lack of church facilities prompted another problem. Ministers came to the young town infrequently, and never regularly; one of the first religious services in town was conducted by the Reverends L. Dooley and Alexander Odum in May 1875. The *Fresno Weekly Expositor* of the following August 4 mentioned that "it is a disgrace that a town as large as Fresno should be without a church edifice . . . a town without a church looks a little uncivilized." This situation soon changed (see 7:5).

The Reverend Odum helped organize the town's first congregation, the Methodist Episcopal Church South, in early 1875. The original numbers were but seven: Judge Gillum Baley, his wife and three daughters, and two other women. The Reverend H. B. Avery was the first pastor, and the first church building was built at Fresno and L streets in 1876 for approximately $3,500. Avery preached the first services in the church during

Reference 7:3

## SCHOOL EXAMINATIONS

R. H. Bramlet, Principal of the public schools in this village furnishes us the following synopsis of the examination of the B, C and D classes in his school, and the standing of the pupils:

B CLASS:

1st.—Reduce 648-720 to its lowest terms.

2d.—Tell what kind of a fraction 728-21 is. Reduce the same to a whole or mixed number.

3d.—Reduce 13⅝ to an improper fraction.

4th.—What kind of a fraction is 7-8 of 12-15 of 9-14? Reduce it to a simple fraction.

5th—.What is the sum of $3/4 and $2/3?

6th.—What is the sum of $½, $¼ and $2-5?

7th.—A boy earned $⅞ and spent $½; how much had he left?

8th.—What cost ¾ bushels of corn at $4-5 per bushel?

10th.—If one hat cost $3½, how many can be bought for $21?

Percentage:—Clara Shanklin, 55; S. J. Ashman, 100; H. G. Ashman, 60; Alice Williams, 38; Alice Daly, 80; Idria Shannon, 75; Alexandria Schultz, 83; Wm. E. Henry, 20; Willie Guard, 100.

SOURCE: *Fresno Weekly Expositor*, October 13, 1875, p. 3 c. 2, in Fresno Scraps, p. 1111.

Reference 7:4

## THE 1883 FRESNO TELEPHONE DIRECTORY

Fresno Telephone Directory—office in Republican building. Office hours from 7 a.m. to 12 m. and from 1 to 6 p.m. All bills collected monthly in advance. List of subscribers—1. court house (clerk's office); 2. Harris & Burleigh; 3. Dr. Rowell's office; 4. Dr. Rowell's residence; 5. Donahoo, Beesley & Oden store; 6. Expositor office; 7. Porteous' blacksmith and wagon shop; 8. Eggers' vineyard; 9. Dexter stables; 10. William Faymonville's office; 11. Ducan Brothers' stables; 12. Burk's drug store; 13. depot; 14. Robertson's machine shops; 15. sheriff's office; 16. Louis Einstein & Co. store; 17. Dr. Leach's office; 18. Donahoo, Beesley & Oden warehouse; 19. George Bernhard's wholesale liquor house; 20. Morrow house. Note:—Subscribers are cautioned against allowing the use of their telephones by non-subscribers. In case such unauthorized use is permitted, the manager is instructed to remove the instrument.—S. A. Miller, manager.

SOURCE: 1883 clipping, Fresno's Yesteryear's File, Fresno City and County Historical Society.

*Fresno Bee Photo*

*Mrs. S. A. Miller, first telephone operator in Fresno, in 1883.*

*Fresno Volunteer Fire Department, July 1877. Top row: Charles Wainwright, John Elam, Lephonso Burks, Harry Rea, Charles DeLong, Louis Einstein, Charles Over-holzer, N. D. Gilbert. Lower row: Fred Kramer, George Strine, Frank Tadlock, Steve Spano, John Dwyer, William Lawrenson, Lee Gundelfinger (chief), Will Silvers, John Welsh, William H. McKenzie, Andrew Basso, John Boyle.*

*Second flouring mill, established in 1878 at Fresno and N streets by M. J. Church. This is after its enlargement in 1880.*

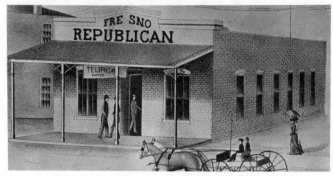

*Fresno's two newspapers in 1881.*

132

*Main business section of Fresno, north side of Mariposa Street, 1882.* F.C.C.H.S. Archives

*Fresno's first jail building (1883–1959), Courthouse Park. Inmates included Sontag and Evans, and Dr. F. O. Vincent (convicted for the murder of his wife in the 1890s and the only Fresno County prisoner ever hanged.)*

FCCHS Archives

FCCHS Archives

*Wife of Millerton pioneer Ah Kit, with her son, J. S. Kit (on right), daughter-in-law and grandchildren.*

133

*The flood of 1884 isolated these businesses on the east side of H Street. Two men poling a boat supplied help for some—when not posing for a picture. This also gives us the only known picture of the Ogle House.*

*The flood of 1884 showed the danger of being on the sinks of three creeks, but the town was little better prepared when another wet year flooded it again.*

*Fresno in 1885, looking north from the Courthouse. Intersection at bottom (left) is Fresno and M streets, with the Champion Flour Mill ditch running down the center of Fresno Street. Prominent buildings: Saint John's Church (center, site of present City Hall built in 1941), Saint James Episcopal Church (right center), White School (upper right), and Champion Flour Mill (right).*

Thanksgiving of that year, lecturing on "The Goodness of God." Baley served as church steward, class leader, trustee, Sabbath school superintendent, janitor and local preacher, probably filling more lay offices than any other member of a Fresno church. Avery was followed in the church ministry by I. L. Hopkins, T. L. Duke, and A. L. Hunsaker in that institution's earliest years.

Saint James' Episcopal Cathedral was organized in late 1879 as a mission by the Reverend D. O. Kelley. Its precursor was the Trinity Mission, organized in January 1874 by the Reverend William Ingraham Kip. It apparently did not survive. Services for Kelley's mission were first held at Walter D. Tupper's law offices, then at the Magnolia Saloon, and then at the town schoolhouse. After a while a $1,300 subscription was filled to build a permanent church, and Kelley obtained an additional $1,000 from friends in the east. The cathedral was opened on April 3, 1881, at Fresno and N streets, and consecrated on December 7, 1884. The total cost was $4,000 which included a parsonage, and overall construction took four years.

In 1879 local Catholics were said to be "nearly as poor as the desert they lived in," but eighty or so of them took up a collection to build a church. On May 6, 1880, C. S. Peck agreed to build one for them at Fresno and M streets for $9,195. A few weeks later, on June 26, Father Valentine Aguilera founded Saint John's Catholic Church. The church building was completed the following October. Father Aguilera, who had previously served in Visalia, was the congregation's first pastor.

The Methodist Episcopal Church was organized in December 1881 by the Reverend Adam Bland. Its first resident minister was Martin Miller, who was succeded by F. M. Pickles, J. R. Gregory, S. J. Kaeler and

G. W. Woodall in the early years. A house of worship, located at K and Merced streets, was built two years after the church's founding.

On March 18, 1882, the First Baptist Church was formally organized, although cottage prayer-meetings had been held before by local Baptists. There were seven charter members, and one of their first acts as a congregation was to pledge $600 per year to pay a permanent minister. T. T. Potter came to Fresno six months later to take the position, and he and his wife proved to be unusually faithful exemplars of the gospel. At her own expense, Mrs. Potter built a chapel for Fresno's Chinese and invited them to her home to hear lectures about Christianity. During the tenure of a later minister, J. C. Jordan, a $6,000 church was built at Merced and N streets and dedicated on June 28, 1885.

The Reverend S. V. Blakeslee founded the First Congregational Church in May 1882 with eight members. The church was suspended when the minister's health failed but was revived on January 19, 1883, by the Reverend George E. Freeman. At first, Freeman's congregation met in an old shack and, later, at Donahoo's Hall. In the latter location Freeman not only preached, but played the organ, led singing activities and the Sunday school, acted as janitor, paid the church's monthly rental fee of twenty dollars out of his own pocket and built the membership to fifty. Fred Banta was given a contract to build a church for the group in February 1884. It cost $5,000, was occupied the following June, and dedicatd in September of that year. Church membership fell when a contingent of Armenian immigrants began attending services in 1884–85. They were viewed with suspicion and prejudice, as were most ethnic groups of that era. This issue tore the congregation apart several years later. (See Chapter 14).

Reference 7:5

## "A FAIR ATTENDANCE AT THE USUAL SERVICES," 1883

Yesterday opened up with a cold, raw wind, but this did not hinder a fair attendance at the usual services. At the Methodist Episcopal Church, the pastor, Rev. F. M. Pickles, was found at his desk, and addressed a good audience from Romans xii, 17.... The Episcopal Church was well-attended, and the usual service held. Rev. D. O. Kelley, the rector, preached a good discourse... Rev. T. T. Potter, of the Baptist Church, occupied his pulpit, and at the close of the services administered the ordinance of baptism, according to the formula of that body, immersing the convert in the canal, above the school-house.... Rev. G. E. Freeman, the latest of our city pastors to arrive, preached to the Congregational society in the hall occupied by Prof. Tiffany, of the High School.... The Methodist Church South was occupied all day by Rev. Mr. Jones and his coadjutors, who are founding Evangelical Temperance Alliances in this part of California. The pulpit in the morning was occupied by Rev. W. N. Cunningham, of Visalia, who spoke of "Our Indebtedness to Christ." The afternoon was occupied in a social service, addressed by Samuel Fowler of Tulare. Mr. Fowler stands 6 feet 8 inches, and is a recent convert to temperance and religion. He is better educated to contend with Indians and wild beasts than with moral evil. He impresses his audience with the conviction that he is a near relative of the celebrated Sampson, and could knock the bottom out of a rum barrel, and knock in the skull of an ordinary man in one stroke. He is full of good nature, and raised an audible smile more than once. He is a terror to rumsellers, tricky politicians and preachers that lack nerve. Hon. J. W. Bones gave one of his eloquent and characteristic addresses, followed by Revs. Messrs. Pickles, Potter and Freeman, of Fresno. The evening service was largely attended, with excellent music led by Mrs. Tuttle, of Central Colony, who also sang alone once or twice during the service. Rev. F. H. Wales, of Tulare, gave an address on the subject of the [Temperance] Alliance and its fundamental principles, declaring that the Alliance was organized to strengthen the bonds of fraternity, battle infidelity, raise the standard of piety, and stay the tide of intemperance. He was followed by Rev. Barder of Selma. After some questioning raised by Rev. Mr. Pickles, touching upon secret societies, had been answered, the Fresno County alliance was formed with about 60 members, and J. W. Hinds elected president. A meeting under the auspices of this society will be held on Saturday night at the same place.

SOURCE: *Fresno Weekly Expositor*, February 7, 1883, p. 9 c. 3. In Fresno Scraps, p. 574.

Reference 7:6

# A MASQUERADE BALL, A CONCERT, A CELEBRATION AND STREET SCENES: FRESNO SOCIAL LIFE IN THE 1880s

The masquerade ball, in new City Hall, last night, given under the auspices of the Odd Fellows, brought together, as it usually does, a large concourse of people, some as maskers, bent on having a jolly good time, and others as spectators, who assemble to see the fun. The hall had been tastily decorated for the occasion by W. A. Richardson, thus greatly improving its appearance. Excellent music was furnished by Boyle's string band. To say that the ball was a complete success does not more than do the subject justice, and to E. J. King, the veteran Odd Fellow, and the indefatigable Charley Wainwright, is due the greater share of the praise for this result. The prize for the best sustained lady's character was awarded to Mrs. J. O. Litten, who as "Topsy" puzzled all to fix her identity. The character was well sustained. J. O. Litten, as the Irish wood sawyer, was awarded the gentleman's prize. There were some other very excellent characters, among which we noticed Mrs. J. G. Moodey as the peanut vender; Walter A. Linforth as a Chinaman, who ran a washhouse. It was a fine representation of the wily "celestial," and, in our opinion, the best sustained character in the room. W. J. Bennett, as a deaf, dumb and blind organ-grinder, followed by his faithful dog, was tip-top. He was made up well, but it was at the frightful sacrifice of his goatee. Mr. Schenck, as a photographer, also is worthy of notice; he took some excellent pictures, and had lots of fun. But to enumerate the especially good characters would require too much space; suffice it to say that all the maskers looked well, or horrid, according to the characters assumed. The following are some of the principal characters assumed by the maskers: J. L. Iovovitch, Admiral Porter, K. B. C., the finest costume worn during the evening; Miss Emma Donahoo, Scotch Lassie; Maggie Mathews, Italian Peasant; Miss Ella Holton, Cinderella; Miss Maggie Davidson, Italian Flower Girl; Miss Minnie Packard and Mrs. Sanderson, Fresno Cannery Girls; F. Fiester, Monkey; Ed McCardle, Cavalier; J. R. Austin, Schoolboy; Mrs. C. E. Brimson, Spanish Princess; M. Duwald, Clown; H. Roemer, Domino; W. W. Phillips, Happy Hottentot; F. Davidson, Schoolboy; Miss M. Shundler, Domino; Mrs. Starr, Domino; W. D. Grady, Domino; B. K. Badger, Jester; Capt. Crooks, Domino; Frank Dusy, Louis XIV; L. F. Winchell, Fireman; S. Ashman, Romeo; J. F. Bedford, Vaquero; L. A. Blasingame, Bull-fighter; M. K. Harris, Uncle Sam; Wm Donahoo, Bocaccio; Miss L. Crow, Fortunio; L. A. Winchell, Don Juanatio; W. S. Badger, Middy; Miss Ella Bedford, Folly; Miss Sadie Burleigh, Spanish Princess; Miss Ida Studer, Cinderella; Mr. Higgins, as a '49er; Mrs. M. J. Hughes, Farnieta; H. E. Burleigh, English Swell; E. B. Davis, Sailor; Miss Nellie Smith, Hunt-

ress; Charles Packard, Harlequin; J. H. Glass, Devil; John Stevens, Clown; M. J. Madary, English Officer; Mrs. Mattie Rea, Italian Brigand; J. J. White, French Pero; W. F. Burks, Harlequin; A. M. Swanson, Louis XIV; A. Boshardt, Turk; A. Babcock, Desperado; Frank M. Schenck, Photographer; Samuel Woldenberg, Romeo. A fine supper was served at midnight in Zeis & Seeburg's Restaurant, connected with the hall.

The second concert given by the Blair sisters last evening drew out a fair-sized audience of our music-loving citizens. It is a lamentable fact that the concerts given by these talented ladies were not as well patronized as they deserved, which was due in a measure to the lack of proper advertising. Artistically the concerts given by the trio are very satisfactory. Miss Susie is wonderfully gifted as a violin soloist, playing with an artistic finish rarely accorded to one so young. Miss Josephine possesses fine execution on the cornet and when she has acquired the muscular power of lip necessary to produce a firm cornet tone will be withoug doubt one of the leading soloists in California. Miss Sallie has a rare gift of accompanying, and aside from her musical accomplishment is an artiste of no mean ability, having painted very nicely her own concert dresses, and in many ways bringing her artistic ideas into play for the benefit of the trio. The stage presence of the sisters is very pleasing, their dressing very tasteful and manners very winning. The ladies will repeat their visit in the course of a few months and it is to be hoped our citizens will assist them in their musical education by giving them a large audience. They are hard students, very nice ladies aside from their music, and striving very hard to perfect themselves in the branch of art they have chosen.

* * *

New Year's was celebrated in due form by the denizens of Fresno. About all the business houses were closed, and the general effort of all seemed to be directed to one point, viz.: "To be happy." The young gen-

tlemen who had made preparations to receive their lady friends, were rewarded by numerous visits, and right well did they entertain their callers. They had prepared elegant lunches for the occasion. Many men who had not made preparations to "receive," went about paying calls to the various saloons, and the result can be well imagined. They got very "happy," and at the same time got in a condition to make them feel like swearing off. All in all the day passed off exceedingly pleasant.

* * *

Anyone to see Fresno on Saturday evening could not help being impressed with the idea that our town is a business place. In fact, it partakes very much of the character of a city. Last Saturday evening as a reporter passed along the streets he had his attention arrested by the busy scenes transpiring about him. An auction sale of second hand furniture, etc., was in progress in Popovich's auction rooms on Front street, a crowd of people were present buying; the saloons adjoining were crowded, and the stores all along Mariposa street presented an attractive and beautiful appearance under the brilliant glare of the gaslight; hundreds of ladies and children were tripping to and fro making purchases, and scores of nimble clerks were busily engaged in supplying their wants. The strum of a banjo and the hum of voices at the corner of Mariposa and I streets, where a large throng was congregated, told of an auction sale in process at the IXL auction house. The ceaseless tramping up I street of hundreds was heard. They were attracted in that direction by the strains of music from the Adelphi. The church bells tolled for Saturday evening meetings, and devotees were rapidly hurrying to the houses of worship. The mingling of hundreds of voices, the clatter of horses' hoofs and the rattle of wagons, concomitants of a busy city, were all here. And this was Saturday night in Fresno.

SOURCES. in order of presentation: *Fresno Weekly Expositor*, January 10, 1883, October 31, 1883, January 9, 1884, and July 1, 1885.

The African Methodist Episcopal Church was organized in 1882 by the Reverend Aaron S. Walton, the First Presbyterian Church on January 20, 1884 by the Reverend H. Budge, and the Christian Church on June 16, 1884. Meeting places for these congregations varied widely: a blacksmith shop at one time for the A.M.E. church, Nichols' Hall for the Presbyterians, and Donahoo's Hall for the Christian Church. The latter congregation, however, did not waste time before building a permanent church for itself at Mariposa and N streets. The cost of the structure, dedicated in October 1885, was $3,300. James Logan, W. T. Shelton and J. B. Johnson were the earliest ministers there.

In the fall of 1874 Fresno's first social club began holding regular meetings—the Independent Order of Odd Fellows, which had transferred its lodge down from Millerton. Meeting in temporary quarters at first, the organization later erected a lodge at Mariposa and I streets. The November after the I.O.O.F. transfer a social club was organized to hold dances, and a temperance organization, strangely named the Dashaway Literary Society, was formed. It initially had twenty members and E. C. Winchell served as president.

Added to these clubs the following year were the Good Templars, which soon attracted forty members, and the Masons, who organized at Magnolia Hall on May 9, 1875. Groups founded in 1876 were of a more intellectual nature. A Fresno Social and Literary Club was founded with E. C. Winchell as president, and a Democratic (Tilden) Club was formed in August, with 153 members, to support that year's presidential ticket.

For a four-year stretch no new organizations were formed, until a United Workmen lodge was founded on April 21, 1880 with twenty-three members. The organization of the Knights of Pythias Vineland Lodge followed on December 14, 1881, with forty members, and the Pomona Council of the Legion of Honor in the same year. The Native Sons of the Golden West, whose members had to have been California residents since 1855, formed Fresno Chapter No. 25 in December 1883. Thomas E. Hughes was elected president. In 1885, a ladies' auxiliary to the United Workmen Lodge (Martha Lodge No. 39, Degree of Honor) was formed with sixty members, along with Atlanta Post No. 92 of the Grand Army of the Republic (a Union Civil War veterans' association) and a Sunday afternoon literary society that attracted nearly three hundred members!

Young Fresno was also rich in other types of recreational organizations. The March 10, 1875, *Fresno Weekly Expositor* reported that two local clubs, designated "Fresno" and "Magnolia," had played a baseball game the previous Sunday. This was the first recorded instance of the sport being played in town. These early clubs gave way to a Fresno Base Ball Club by 1876, a Central Base Ball Club by 1879, and the most important early team—the Fresno Stars—in the spring of 1883. Milus King Harris was the first presi-

dent of the Stars club, which soon developed a respectable record. A June 2, 1883, *Fresno Weekly Republican* report said that the team "played a match game on their grounds in the north end of town . . . with a 'picked' nine. Judging from the score, which stood 40 to 0, the nine was picked a little too soon." The Stars beat another local team later, then lost to Lemoore's club, but "fully redeemed whatever their reputation might have suffered" by defeating the Visalia Eclipse on May 27, 1883.

Another recreational group of this early period was the Fresno Brass Band, formed in 1876. When it folded in 1883 the *Fresno Weekly Republican* commented: "Fresno can't possibly get along without a brass band. It is essential to patriotism, tone and good morals of the town. The Fourth of July is approaching, and every one knows that a Fourth of July celebration without a brass band would be a dismal failure."

For a small prairie town, Fresno boasted a wide variety of entertainments in its early days (see 7:6). Dancing was so popular that a New Year's Eve event at B. S. Booker's hall had to be followed by a New Year's Day dance, and a Washington's Birthday ball was announced at the same time. Mollie Livingstone's Blue Wing was another popular dance hall, and most of the town's hotels and saloons held similar events. Dances were held wherever large, flat spaces were available. When the Fresno Fruit Packing Company opened its cavernous insides to the public on May 26, 1882, Professor Smith's Quadrille Band played and the six hundred or so people attending danced until half past three.

Traveling circuses were another popular entertainment. Conklin's Great United States Circus was the first to exhibit in Fresno, on August 14, 1873, tenting on the north side of the railroad reservation. Following Conklin's troupe was the San Francisco Circus and Collection of Performing Animals in August 1874, Montgomery Queen's Gigantic Menagerie, Circus and World's Fair in October 1874, and Adam Forepaugh's Great Circus and Menagerie on April 8, 1878.

Forepaugh's show was one of the major circuses of commented that " . . . the whole country has been on que vive to see it, therefore, to say that everybody attended, will be within the limit of truth." The circus portion of the entertainment "was good, there being good riders, fine horses, nimble tumblers, and daring and dexterous [*sic*] trapeze performers . . . The herd of performing elephants . . . was alone worth the price of admission. The elephants . . . moved like clockwork . . . The great pyramid of elephants was performed as truthfully as pictured in the bills."

The 1880s brought new forms of entertainment. Fresno now had a regular skating rink owned by Charles Newell, and in 1883 the Fresno Fair Grounds Association built a racetrack and buildings on the same site occupied by today's Fresno District Fairgrounds. The association appears to have been formed in March 1875 and to have purchased land from William Helm at the same time, but financial troubles or a lack of interest kept the association virtually moribund for almost a decade. The one-mile track eventually built was said to be excellent. Fresno was placed on a regular racing circuit and track events attracted people from all over the San Joaquin Valley.

More culturally inclined citizens were treated to the opening of Walter Drane Grady's Opera House, located on I Street, in March 1884. Among its first attractions was the Katie Putnam Theatrical Company. As Lena the Madcap, Miss Putnam "gained the good graces of the audience at once," according to the March 19, 1884, *Fresno Weekly Expositor*. "They laughed at her girlish pranks and hoydenish ways and sympathized with her in her afflictions and applauded her triumphs." The Mastodon Minstrels followed on May 6, 1884, singing tunes such as "How Much Does the Baby Weigh" and "Yes, My Love, I'll Meet You."

Boxing also became popular at this time; matches were held all over town. A June 17, 1884, series of bouts between local and visiting pugilists featured "a jig dance [that] was heavily encored" by John Devine.

Holidays were usually celebrated with much fanfare. Fresno's New Year's celebration was held by M. A. Schultz, at his hotel, in 1873. Heavy rains postponed the event for one week, but the delayed festivities were lively and no one was disappointed. July Fourth was always an exciting event, as Paul E. Vandor's account of the 1873 activities attests:

The celebration was "a grand success." George Zeis was marshal of the parade which disbanded at the railroad freight depot for the literary program. The Glee Club of Messrs. Williams and Son, W. T. Rumble, and George Zeis, Miss Mary J. McKenzie, Mrs. Whiteside and the Misses Melissa and L. Gilkey sang a "patriotic ballad." Rev. T. O. Ellis Sr. made the invocation. The choir sang again and J. W. Ferguson read the Declaration of Independence. More singing and the poet of the day read "An Invocation to Liberty," Miss Lizzie Gilkey impersonating the Goddess of Liberty. More singing and J. D. Collins, the teacher of the Academy school, delivered the oration of the day, introduced by B. S. Booker as President of the Day. Then followed a song of patriotic nature and the benediction. Then the festival in aid of the school with "grab bags, ice cream stands, fruit stands, ring cakes and 'sich like'" and "the whole affair passed off without a single thing to mar it." Ball in the evening was "a grand affair." About fifty couples attended and "the supper was strictly first class as was indeed the whole affair," with general good feeling prevailing.

It took until 1874 for a proper Christmas celebration to be held in Fresno—at Farrar's Magnolia Saloon. To make sure the affair went off properly, some Fresno boys journeyed to the Millerton area, cut down an imposing digger pine, and brought it back to serve as the first town Christmas tree.

These formative years witnessed the development of a divided Fresno. The whites reserved the east site of the railroad tracks to themselves. Anyone who fit a different description, including whites of a disreputable

Reference 7:7

## ACROSS THE TRACKS

### ERNESTINE WINCHELL

Although the Fresno of early days was quite democratic in some respects, lines of color and caste were automatically drawn. Those citizens whose training and experience had been in observance of class distinctions brought a measure of social bias with them, influencing their actions inevitably.

The shop of Ah Kit, the Chinese blacksmith from Millerton, was located at Fresno street and I, but was soon removed to a place across the railroad where others of his people had already settled. There Hop Wo and Tong Sing, also of the San Joaquin, established their respective houses of the mercantile business.

The boundaries of Chinatown were definite from the first, and as other classes and colors made their appearance in appreciable numbers they formed their own communities upon adjacent blocks.

The first formal burying ground was laid out on the west of where Elm avenue came into town, but as soon as the Chinese found they could not inter their dead just where they pleased they bought land for the purpose on McKinley avenue.

For ten years or so few had any idea that Fresno station would grow or change, and of them none could predict in what direction or in what manner. There were but a score or two of buildings strung along the steel rails that ran diagonally across the unlimited stretch of barren hogwallows....

Tulare street was the main thoroughfare of the alien quarter. By way of this street and the railroad reservation a turbid tide of evil humanity flowed into Mariposa street from across the tracks. To the unsophisticated eyes of Fresno womanhood and Fresno youths there was nothing, however, to differentiate a man drunken from a west side saloon or one from the east.

Occasional groups of Chinese women, sometimes leading quaint little children, and all in gorgeous silken and embroidered attire, were of great interest and wonder. Strange things were whispered of these slim creatures with shining bare heads and impassive, painted, ivory faces.

Any day might be met by a bevy of young white women who also drifted up Mariposa street from the mysterious districts. Bare-headed, they, too, had elaborately dressed hair, and features creamed and rouged. Over long dark skirts they wore half-fitted smocks, buttoned in the back and reaching about to the knee. Though there was not a trace of garishness or immodesty in this costume, even young girls came to understand the meaning.

In and out of stores and hotel lobbies these women tripped, chatting and laughing among themselves, shopping, seeing and being seen. They made no disturbance, but no one can now say what seeds of sorrow and distress were sown.

Eventually municipal regulations put a stop to this parade, and Fresno maids and matrons were protected from the chance of meeting a group of women from across the tracks. But for long years after that they might at any time be forced to step aside for reeling men who were as likely to have reached that sordid state on one side of the railroad as the other.

SOURCE: Ernestine Winchell columns.

138

or criminal character, was obligated to settle on the west side of the railroad tracks (see 7:7). The Chinese, who made up the largest part of the west side's population, had first tried to settle around Schultz's Hotel but were later banished across the tracks. They held occasional ethnic festivities, the significance of which escaped the town's whites.

Of an 1883 Chinese New Year celebration the *Fresno Weekly Republican* said "the wild, weird melody of the Chinese violin, of the tam tam and yangtees-huldabaloo float in the evening air until about 4 o'clock in the morning, when the last musician falls under the table in a state of helpless intoxication." The November 19, 1884 *Fresno Weekly Expositor* commented as follows on a Chinese fair held in Fresno: "The show consists of a large number of gaudy pictures . . there is a statue [which] is supposed to be able to strike terror into the hearts of all who have strayed from the path of honesty, but our idea was that [the man depicted by the statue] had sat down on a tack or made a supper of green apples."

Transients, who thronged Fresno's streets from its inception, also were disliked and misunderstood. One farmer, visiting town in 1879, was so besieged by tramps that he decked the ninth one who asked him for money and almost got beaten up himself. Three years later, when tramps were said to be "[shadowing] kitchen doors to the discomfort of the housewives," the March 1, 1882, *Fresno Weekly Expositor* noted that one man had taken to buying bakery tickets for bread loaves and handing them out when panhandled. Thus "his dollars [purchased] twenty loaves of good bread, instead of eight drinks of whiskey, as before."

The problem was bad enough the next year for the *Expositor* to remark, on November 5: "A better way . . . would be to have a law by which they could be arrested and sold . . . Great burly men, dirty, but fat, and otherwise well conditioned, well able to work and earn an honest livelihood, comprise the great majority of the grand army of tramps."

Fresno, in its infancy, suffered through an astounding succession of natural disasters. The first to strike was a series of earthquakes on February 4, March 20 and 26 and October 18, 1872. The worst activity occurred on March 26. These were the Owens Valley earthquakes, centered on the east side of the Sierra and said to be the worst in California's history. The largest shock lasted for about nine minutes in Fresno, followed by a two-hour quivering motion and hundreds of aftershocks.

A series of uncommonly hot days followed in the summer of that year, and in the summers of 1874 and 1876 as well. Of the 1874 heat wave, the July 15 *Fresno Weekly Expositor* said: "We have no fears of cremation now. It would be impossible to incinerate us. We are a salamander . . . By the free use of ice water, lemonade, ice cream, whiskey, and other creature comforts of a cooling nature, we are enabled to pass through this fiery ordeal with a rare degree of patience and fortitude."

The 1880s brought other unusual occurrences—a small snowfall on February 7, 1883 (the first of significance in Fresno); on April 16, 1884, a tornado that tore up two barns, one warehouse and a house; and—most significant of all—the great flood of February 1884. Heavy rains caused Red Banks, Dog and Dry creeks to swell and dump torrents of water on Fresno. No dams or drainage systems existed, which meant that the "sinks of Dry Creek" would fill naturally. The basement and billiard room of the Grand Central Hotel was flooded to the ceiling, as were other similar establishments, with furniture floating at the top. J. W. Ferguson's house, located in a depression, was in a similar plight and his wife and children had to be rescued. Trains continued to run, but passengers had to be transported to town on flatboats. Most townspeople were inexperienced in their use, and when one capsized a battle broke out between its "captain" and one of the passengers. Among town businesses Madary's Planing Mill, the Hughes Stables, Rasmussen's beer hall, the Star Hotel and the Stanislaus Brewery were said to be hardest hit.

Fires hit almost all Fresno County towns in the nineteenth century, and Fresno itself was not spared from this destructive force. For its first few years the town was lucky; the first recorded fire was one that burned up a mailbag in July 1872. No serious fires happened for some time after that date.

All the city had to protect itself at first was a Babcock extinguisher in the Jacob and Company store, which was rendered ineffective by an unknown tinkerer around July 1874. It was used to fight an open fire that month—with absolutely no effect. When a lamp exploded at the Magnolia Saloon the next month it had to be snuffed with blankets, and in October a fire at Schultz's Hotel was controlled only because William Lawrenson had dug a well nearby and had installed a force pump and hose.

The citizenry was aroused enough to discuss fire prevention in January 1875. A $200 subscription was raised, and a benefit ball for volunteer firemen held on March 17, yet nothing constructive was accomplished. Another meeting was held on May 28. Again, nothing was agreed upon except a proposal to form a stock company and lay pipes and cisterns. The *Fresno Weekly Expositor* suggested no further action would be taken "at least not until after the town burns down," and it seemed this observation would come true. Only Lawrenson's rig kept a February 19, 1875, blaze from spreading farther than Joaquin Lamonthe's stables. A bucket brigade had to quell a May 1 fire on the California Hotel's roof (with some assistance from a force pump owned by the International Hotel).

A series of 1876 fires galvanized townsfolk into

action. On January 11, 1876, Lawrenson's saloon, the Bishop and Company drugstore and Russell Fleming's office building all burned—a loss of $13,700. Three weeks later the Law and Foster carpentry shop was lost, and on July 12 the Blue Wing dance hall and two others went up in smoke. In the first of these blazes desperate firefighters had to scoop water out of puddles standing in the street.

On February 24, 1877, justifiably concerned citizens organized the Fresno Hook and Ladder Company at Magnolia Hall, with Leopold Gundelfinger as its chief. A hook and ladder truck was obtained for the group but, curiously, it was not used during a September 28, 1879, fire that destroyed Luke Shelly's restaurant, J. Schell's jewelry store and the Fresno and Morning Star hotels. Some claimed that, for unknown reasons, its wheels were usually fastened to the floor. This was the case when the truck was destroyed in a July 23, 1882, fire. That conflagration swept away the Hughes stables, William Vellguth's store, Ryan's hotel, Magnolia Hall, the French Saloon, the Ogle House, the Metropolitan Hall, George Bernhard's house, Edward Faure's barbershop and twenty-six other buildings, for a loss of $250,000.

Firefighting was made easier after the board of supervisors established a board of fire commissioners on May 14, 1881. It was not effective at first, and a proposal to form a fire district at the same time was unsuccessful. The commission eventually did manage to get two cisterns installed, purchase a fire engine in July 1884, and establish an I Street stationhouse. The fires continued, however.

An arsonist started a fire in George Bernhard's liquor store on February 21, 1883, that firefighting efforts kept from becoming a major disaster. A blaze the following June 27 did $40,000 worth of damage. The Winchell and Griffith building, John W. Williams Building, Tombs' saddlery shop, the old Odd Fellows hall, and buildings owned by Walter Drane Grady and David S. Terry all went up in smoke.

Fresno had enjoyed nearly a two-year respite from serious fires until twelve buildings in Chinatown went up on February 21, 1885: a restaurant, two or three brothels, two laundries and a gambling house were claimed in that blaze (see 7:8). Then two other fires, even more destructive, hit on February 27 and March 2 of the same year. The first wiped out Baker and Johnson's and Yeargin and Morgan's grocery stores, J. C. Herrington's saddlery shop and four other buildings for a loss of more than $42,000. The second struck Woldenburg and Foster's furniture store, the Combs and Hogan saloon, Nick Petkovich's fruit store, Car-

Reference 7:8

## "SAVING THEIR TEMPLE"

The saving of the gorgeous Chinese Temple was a splendid piece of work. Isolated from the rest of the burning block, it seemed, at first, in no great danger, though showers of live sparks and dead ashes swept over it on the morning breeze. All its devotees had fled. Only the high priest of the great and mighty Joss faithful remained. He took position about fifty feet in front of the edifice, and calmly facing the approaching fire, began with indignant gestures and low and broken ejaculations to warn the fire-fiend not to come any nearer. His thin, swarthy features, upturned to the red light, his lank form, uncovered head, swaying queue, with his long arms tossed high above his head and now singly, now together waving off the destroying demon, would ordinarily have sufficed to scare off any half dozen of common tophet-imps. The first effects of his incantations were seen in the swarm of half-scorched and wholly frantic cats that darted out of the blazing houses and dashed along the borders of the flames to places of fancied security. Thus far, the high priest had made his fight against the fire, unaided and alone—his being the solitary figure in the midst of the sandy street, the outer edge of which was lined with a crowd of listless spectators, and tumbled masses of Mongolian goods and chattels—around and among which, ubiquitous street Arabs were peering and prospecting to find their clean Sunday shirts and collars. So they said. Suddenly, the undaunted servant of Joss was vigorous-

ly reinforced by an agitated son of Confucius, who gallantly charged on a low wicket fence some fifty yards to leeward of the Temple and at first dash, tore off three or four laths. Then rushing thirty or forty yards to the westward, and still further away from the fire, he made a similar onset on a similar fence and achieved another brilliant victory. But even all these herculean efforts failed to check the fire on the windward (northward) side of the Temple, so that it now seized upon the last house in the row, only 150 feet distant from the solemn Cathedral de la Joss. Very soon its sugar-pine roof and adjacent shed covered with shakes, began to emit faint blue vapors of smoke—fatal precursors of outbursting flame. But the high priest never budged. He set his face like a flint toward the fire, defiantly advanced a step or two toward it, flung his lank arms higher and more wildly in the heated air and rattled off his anathemas in still louder tones. He gave no heed to the gathering crowd about him and gave no commands to his countrymen. His frenzied eyes rolled from the fire to the Temple—from the Temple to the fire, while his lips kept up their exorcisms—his arms their imperative gesticulations. Thus he held the red foe at bay, as Wellington, the French at Waterloo, or Leonidas, the Persian at Thermopylae, though all witnesses said the Temple was doomed, for its smoking sides seemed just flashing into flame. Just then a bareheaded Chinaman tumbled out of a hut in the rear of

the Temple with a wooden wash-bowl containing a quart of water. Rushing to a corner of the shed, he heaved a mighty heave, and threw almost a pint of the fluid on its roof. Thrilled by this daring act another followed suit and got a few drops on the wall. The struggle between the priest and the devil was now at its most sublime height, and among the lookers on, the odds were in favor of the latter personage about two to one. Higher and higher rolled the hot billows, higher and more madly waved the sacerdotal arms, higher and higher ran the bets of the sympathising crowd, though no coin was put up to speak of. The scene grew intensely interesting. All the paling stars in the six o'clock sky peeped down and held their breath, and the sun himself tugged and scrambled to get his eye over the ragged edge of the dark blue wall of the East, before the contest ended. But such deadly combat between mind and matter could not very long continue. The fiery plumes of the burning house began to droop and lower. The roof fell in—the walls crashed over, the heat subsided and the temple was safe. Golden-winged victory perched on the twisted top-knot of the priest. And yet there are worldly-minded cynics who say they don't know.

SOURCE: Fresno County Scrapbook 1870-1899, p. 510, taken from *Fresno Weekly Expositor*, Feb. 21, 1885, p. 9, c. 3.

140

gile and Madsen's butcher shop, and other buildings for a loss of perhaps $35,000.

Added to this roster of 1885 fires was a September 7 blaze that struck south of the Grady Opera House and nearly claimed that structure. Bucket brigades had to be called in for this fire because suction on the fire department's engine had shrunk too much, a hose to be used with a fireplug turned out to be too short, and a replacement hose had to be obtained from the railroad depot. By the time these difficulties had been overcome, many buildings had burned down.

Despite these and other travails, Fresno continued to grow. Its population climbed to 1,112 in 1880 and 3,464 in 1885, yet the town remained a collection of buildings on the prairie rather than a full-fledged city. There was no police force, sewer system or truly efficient fire department, and cattle were still roaming the dusty streets that became winter lakes. These deficiencies needed to be addressed, and the only way to solve them was formal incorporation as a city.

Foresighted citizens had held meetings to discuss incorporation as early as June 5, 1874, June 13, 1876, and in March 1878, yet there was never enough interest demonstrated in the issue. Later on, the board of supervisors scheduled an incorporation election for December 1, 1883, that failed, as did a similar proposal on May 3, 1884. There were many who agreed with the *Fresno Republican* when it said, the year before, that "... our experience in the incorporation of towns of this size has not been favorable. There is always somebody with an axe to grind, and jobbery and cornering usually result in getting the town hopelessly in debt." Incorporation foes even went so far as to get a black man to parade the streets during one election, advertising his campaign for city marshal, as a way of scaring white voters.

Incorporation finally won, 277 to 185, in a September 29, 1885, election. Saloon men were against it because of license fees, and property owners feared an increase in taxes, but enough were convinced of the potential benefits to make the issue pass. William Faymonville, W. L. Graves, Thomas E. Hughes, J. M. Braly and Arthur Tombs were elected trustees, W. B. Dennett city clerk and assessor, C. T. Swain town marshal, W. H. McKenzie, treasurer, and S. H. Hill, recorder. The first meeting of these officials took place the following October 27, and on November 28 a municipal code of 510 sections was voted into effect.

A mere thirteen years after its birth, Fresno had now passed into sudden maturity. It was no longer a tentative town on the prairie. Local industries and institutions had been founded and were thriving. Social events and organizations were now an accepted part of life. Most significant, a small legion of people had found the town to their liking—for business, its people, its camaraderie or whatever—and were determined to stay. A cycle of continued progress, with only incidental misfortunes, had begun that has not yet found its end.

*Engine No. 1 with hook and ladder of Fresno City Fire Department in front of the City Hall, circa 1890.*

141

*Vintage Fresno*

*Many promises and easy terms are used in posters to sell Central California Colony land.*

*How it all started—ad made great promises for what became known as Johnson grass.*

*An early ad for the famous Fresno Scraper.*

# Chapter 8

# Watering the Parched Land: Agriculture, 1870-1887

Bernhard Marks was desperate. A former school principal and mining investor, his burning desire was to be a farmer—and he was floundering in that new occupation. After he bought and planted a 1,400-acre grain ranch near Stockton in 1874, faulty levees broke and inundated his property. Steamboats ran over his crops, and his simultaneous effort at dairy farming failed. Frustrated and unsure of himself, he did not know where to turn. Then, he went to a Stockton grange convention in 1875 and heard a speech that changed his life.

The speaker was W. A. Sanders, schoolteacher and sometime agriculturalist in Fresno County. He told the farmers about the area's tremendous agricultural potential, which had been confirmed by the experiments of Easterby and others (see Chapter 6). Marks was impressed by the talk, and a notion entered his mind. Land and irrigation rights could be had for little money in Fresno County. An investor could purchase both on a large scale and offer smaller, watered lots at a price that would ensure a good profit.

Intrigued by this idea, Marks tried to talk one of Fresno County's largest landowners, William S. Chapman, into it. A colonization scheme of this sort had never been attempted, and Chapman did not think the county's desert lands offered any inducement to potential settlers. Yet Marks persisted in his arguments and Chapman eventually was convinced of their merits. Plans were made to fulfill Marks' new dream only a few weeks after the Sanders speech.

By August 1875, Marks, Chapman and William H. Martin, another San Francisco financier, were offering 192 twenty-acre lots in the Central California Colony. It consisted of six sections of land lying to the southwest of present-day Fresno. Purchase terms were tempting, even for that day: $150 down and $12.50 per month until a $1,000 debt was retired, *at no interest*. The buyer of the first lot, J. H. Sewell, was even given a cow, seed and grain. Soon, settlers from diverse backgrounds and locales were buying lots. If not brisk, sales were steady. Some thirty-six adults and eighteen chil-

dren had settled in the development by December 1875.

The following year was full of trials for Marks' fledgling scheme. Moses J. Church's Fresno Canal and Irrigation Company, which had contracted to deliver water to the colony, met many problems in fulfilling its obligations. A specially-constructed extension of the company's main ditch kept caving in, and it took until March 1876 to get water to some of the colony. Other settlers had to wait until branch canals could be built to their property, or take the risk of dry-farming.

Whole experimental vineyards that Marks had set out the previous year dried up. Martin pulled out his investment. Chapman thought of doing so, as did some of the settlers. It was only Marks who remained firm. "So confident was I of success that I made no calculation of failing," he said in the March 30, 1892, *Fresno Daily Evening Expositor*. "I went into it to win..."

In time the doubters were proven wrong. By 1877 beets, potatoes, corn and melons were flourishing in the Central California Colony. Vineyards and orchards also were being planted, as were strawberry and blackberry patches. Some 200 people had settled on the lands and had formed a self-sufficient, if tiny, community. There was a lumber yard, blacksmith and wagon shop, doctor's office, grange organization, a school with twenty-three students, and even a dramatic club in this frontier environment. Transportation around the colony property was easy, since Marks had had a grid of streets laid out. These roads were given names that have survived unto today, and were beautified accordingly: Cherry Avenue was lined with nine varieties of cherry trees, Elm Avenue with cork elms, Fruit Avenue with different fruit trees, and Fig Avenue with White Ischia fig trees. Marks made these plantings in the hope they "...would lend comfort and cheerfulness to the scene, and make the people feel contented...[The] most important thing in founding a colony is to have the people contented."

Since Central California colonists were said to have cleared the purchase price of their lots in one year's worth of farming, and the soil was undeniably fertile (tree branches were said to break under their loads of fruit), others tried to imitate Marks' success. In the year that the Central California Colony became viable (1877), two new colonization ventures began: Moses Church's Temperance Colony and S. A. Miller's Nevada Colony.

Like Marks, Church offered twenty-acre lots adjoined by branch canals for easy irrigation. There was a catch: all land purchasers had to "bind themselves to use every effort to preserve the sanitary condition of the colony by preserving the purity of the air [i.e., refrain from smoking]. They are not to make or sell any intoxicating liquors and are not to belong to any secret organization or encourage such institutions." Church, a devout Seventh-day Adventist, insisted that his colonists be of a high moral character. He apparently lost nothing by this gambit; the colony was sold out by March 1878.

Miller was less selective about his Nevada Colony settlers. For $750, or $100 down and $20 per month, any taker could obtain a twenty-acre lot in that development. It was located due north of the Easterby Ranch. Only twenty-four of these lots were sold; Miller concentrated his efforts on selling 80- and 160-acre parcels that ultimately housed some of the county's great agricultural estates. The colony derived its name from the fact that Miller had once been a Nevada miner, and he induced some of his acquaintances from that sojourn to buy into his venture.

One of Fresno County's more important colonization ventures got under way in 1878, when Wendell Easton and J. P. Whitney purchased eleven sections of land to the south and southwest of the Central California Colony. Various-sized lots in this tract—the Washington Irrigated Colony—were offered for sale at reasonable terms. A mere $700 bought a twenty-acre lot and a fifty by seventy-five foot lot in the townsite of Covell, named after the colony's agent and superintendent, A. T. Covell.

For reasons that are unclear, this scheme encountered early sales troubles. Easton journeyed to Germany, Australia and Sweden to persuade potential settlers to emigrate to the San Joaquin Valley. He spent $25,000 on advertising—with no immediate effect. He chartered a train to take people from San Francisco to the colony; again, no luck. In desperation he chartered a second train. This time, 500 people came and 385 lots, or five of the eleven sections, were sold! Additionally, Easton's entreaties to the Swedes seem to have worked. Henry Larsen, C. A. Erickson and M. J. Lindrose were among the colony's earliest settlers.

This colony bore many resemblances to the Central California. It obtained its water from the Fresno Canal system; fruit-growing—mainly peaches, pears, apricots and grapes—was its mainstay; and the farmers

brought the Covell (later Easton) community to an early sophistication. A school, a literary and agricultural society, a dramatic club and a Swedish Methodist Episcopal Church were all functioning there by 1881.

The 1,920-acre Scandinavian Colony, located to the Nevada Colony's immediate northwest, enjoyed a far easier success than did the Washington. It was established in 1878 when some San Francisco Scandinavians purchased land from pioneer Fresno County agriculturalist Henry Voorman. The colony's early settlers were mostly of Nordic descent (although anyone could buy lots there), and a square mile's worth of property was sold the week after lots were placed on the market. Considering the price, this was not surprising. A twenty-acre lot initially sold for $450, and land prices remained so low that the colony was sold out by April 1882. By that date 700 acres had been planted in orchards, vineyards and alfalfa, and unimproved lots sold for double their 1878 price.

With the advent of several other important developments, colony settlements in Fresno County reached a sort of peak in 1880. To the immediate west of the Washington Irrigated Colony Charles Henry opened the 3,200-acre American Colony for settlement. Originally intended for "old-line" American colonists (hence its name), the colony began playing host to people of all nationalities soon afterward. At an early date it had 200 settlers and a gross annual product of $300,000.

While the American Colony was being started Henry and Julius Wolters laid out a 1,020-acre colony to the north of the old Gould Ranch, and to Fresno's immediate south Thomas E. Hughes was offering lots for sale in his 2,880-acre Fresno Colony. Word of Fresno County's agricultural prosperity was beginning to circulate by this time; after scheduling some train excursions á la Easton, Hughes had no trouble selling half his colony's land in three months. The quick sales must have been gratifying to him, since he had worked as a shepherd and fledgling real estate agent two years before. Hughes had been so strapped for funds to buy the colony's irrigation rights that he had to sign five sections of his land over to Church, by now sole Fresno Canal and Irrigation Company owner. Despite these struggles, Hughes turned an immense profit on what land was left. Purchased for $6.50 an acre, the sale price of Fresno Colony lands averaged $40 to $50 an acre.

As the foregoing has shown, a variety of crops were grown in Fresno County during the early colonization days. This was a transitional period. The raisin and wine industries had not yet risen to pre-eminence in the county; farmers in 1880 had 73,000 acres in wheat compared to 1,000 in vines. Wheat-growing had assumed temporary importance for several reasons. The warm, dry valley summers made the grain hard and good, and a low British tariff—combined with crop failures in that country—allowed American wheat to find a ready market there.

During this period Robert Brownlee, lessee of the Easterby Ranch, had all 2,500 acres of that property in wheat; Jeff Donahoo and Peter Hansen of the Centerville area had approximately 3,000 acres of wheat combined; Abner J. Doble had 1,000 acres near the Kings River bottomlands, and about 16,000 acres were planted to wheat in the Kingsburg area. Rains in 1878 and destructive winds in 1880 took their toll on the crop, but the large acreages being farmed offset the losses—and profit margins ranged from 15 to nearly 100 percent.

County statistics for 1879, the year in which vineyard popularity increased dramatically, show that there were 26,809 peach trees, 7,427 apple trees, 5,683 pear trees and 5,579 fig trees. Pear and peach orchards were concentrated on the colony lands and places like the Eisen, Gould and Eggers farms; apple orchards were found mostly in the foothill areas and fig trees in various valley locations. The December 8, 1880, *Fresno Weekly Expositor* remarked that there was a great demand for fruit and farmers were putting in more orchards for the next season.

Citrus fruits, by contrast, had not become established; there were but 97 lemon and 960 orange trees in the county, according to the 1879 statistics. Uneven valley temperatures killed off a Nevada Colony lemon grove that year, and two years before H. Madsen of the Central California Colony had lost his oranges to frost. Only Joseph Burns of Centerville was having good luck with his orange groves, luckily situated in the then-unknown foothill "thermal belt." It was later discovered that the belt had even, year-round temperatures, which are necessary for consistent citrus production. The Eisen farm on the valley plains reportedly had thirty producing orange trees at this time. Proper tending, luck or both must have been responsible for that result.

The increase in colony lands, and of farming in general, prompted the expansion of some irrigation systems and the creation of others. Between 1875 and 1876 the Fresno Canal system went through a frenzied period of growth. Its main canal and headgate were enlarged to carry 1,100 cubic feet of water per second, the main canal was excavated to the Central California Colony and was then taken to a point twelve miles beyond. In addition, the Fresno Canal company took over the Kings River and Fresno Canal system, constructed to service the Scandinavian and Wolters colonies. This left the company with the responsibility of watering all the colony lands described previously. Farmers in the Kingsburg, Liberty (Riverdale), and later-day Selma and Fowler areas were located too far south to tap into these systems and were forced to build their own. A number of cooperatively built, managed and owned irrigation canals came into being to meet this need.

The Emigrant Ditch Company was created in 1875 when a group of Wildflower men decided to give up dry farming and incorporate with $20,000 in capital stock. The company secured water rights from the Fresno Canal company, which had been given legal title to much of the Kings River water flow, by agreeing to expand the Fresno company's main canal, as described above. After completing that work the Emigrant Ditch Company built its own canal, tapping Cole Slough on the Kings and extending west for twelve miles. Work began on June 14, 1875, was finished on August 15 of the same year, and by 1882 the main canal and its distributing ditches were watering 6,000 acres.

A more ambitious undertaking, the Centerville and Kingsburg Irrigation Ditch Company, was incorporated on March 12, 1876. A. B. Cole, T. C. Bratton, W. J. and J. C. Berry, and I. N. Parlier were among the notable pioneers associated with this venture. Its goal was to water the plains around Kingsburg and the Selma townsite by tapping the Kings two miles above Centerville and stretching the main canal westward.

The Centerville and Kingsburg irrigation system was built in an unusual manner. Local farmers who had incorporated the company "bought" shares of it by agreeing to excavate a given chunk of the main canal with their own labor. In addition, any shareholding farmer who wanted a branch ditch running to his property had to build it himself. Remarkably, most of the canal was completed by October 1, 1877, after only six months of actual construction. This happened in spite of technical problems (see 8:1), and the need to increase the company's capital stock from $12,500 to $35,000. Expansion and improvement work continued in the 1880s, when the system's overall cost rose to $75,000 or more. It eventually embraced forty-four miles of main and branch canals and watered 15,000 acres.

With the Selma-Kingsburg area now irrigated, farmers in adjacent districts were encouraged to begin three new irrigation systems in the early 1880s. Most important of these was the Fowler Switch Canal Company, formed in late 1883 by Caleb Dickerson Davis, C. L. Walter, Abijah McCall and Frank Dusy. The Centerville and Kingsburg labor-stock swap method was used to finance much of this canal's construction—$110,000 initially. Work commenced in 1883.

The Fowler Switch main canal began 300 feet below the Fresno Canal company headgate and went westward for twenty-seven miles, with important branch ditches tapping it along the way. The Cleveland Ditch delivered water to the area between Malaga and Fowler; the Western Canal went through the area due south of the Washington Irrigated Colony; and the Elkhorn Canal serviced the western fringes of the Wildflower area.

145

Of lesser importance were the six-mile, $15,000 Liberty Canal, completed in 1881 by farmers in the Liberty (Riverdale) area, and the Kirby Ditch, built a few months before by C. K. Kirby and H. A. Peterson to water lands west of Fowler. Both canals used the Kings, directly or indirectly, as a water source.

A multitude of small irrigation canals were built around the lower Kings before 1881. Among the earliest were the Riverdale and Turner ditches, built in 1875; the Vanderbilt Cut, connecting Cole and Murphy sloughs so as to increase the latter waterway's flow (and irrigation of adjacent lands) in the same year; and the Last Chance and Lower King's River ditches, which snaked through portions of Fresno and Tulare counties and were partially built *circa* 1876.

Water flows were erratic through this region, necessitating constant repair work on these canals. In 1881 the Lower King's River Ditch put its fourth headgate into use, the previous three having been destroyed by flooding. Rancher John Sutherland and Poly, Heilbron and Company (owner of the Laguna de Tache grant) were also using canals, in this same region, and at the same time. Nothing certain is known about their construction, extent, or purpose.

The San Joaquin River, an obvious irrigation source, was mostly left untouched during this period. Only one scheme, that of the Upper San Joaquin Irrigation Company, attempted to supplement existing Miller and Lux canals and it was a miserable failure. It was started in the late 1870s by Dr. E. B. Perrin and his brother, Robert, who wanted to bring water to a quarter-million acre area north and northwest of Fresno. They had purchased much land in this vicinity at $2.50 an acre and reasoned that watering the property would shoot land values up to $40 an acre. With the aid of some San Francisco financiers and Barker and Fillibrown as contractors, they began building a diversion dam, headgate and sixteen-mile main canal in 1878. The canal's intake was situated somewhere around Cobb's Ford. Unfortunately for its developers, the light volcanic soil of the area tended to dissipate when excavated and watered. Constant cave-ins and work stoppages caused the Perrins and their investors to drop the project in 1882

A short time afterward J. L. N. Shepard and Egbert Judson of San Francisco took over the Upper San Joaquin canal project. The new investors tried blasting a channel parallel to the river and alongside its bluffs, which was a slow, expensive process. At least $120,000 was spent on explosives in a single year. The Upper San Joaquin canal idea was abandoned in 1887, after a considerable sum of money had been expended on it. Estimates of the entire cost range from $300,000 to $3 million.

During the 1880s the raisin and wine industries began capturing more interest than any other Fresno County agricultural enterprise. The hot, dry summer days and cool, moisture-free nights produced a sweet

Reference 8:1

## DISAPPOINTMENTS AND DELAYS: BUILDING THE C & K CANAL
### GEORGE B. OTIS

The year 1877 was a very dry year and the vegetation on the plains dried and died, without rain and blew away till the surface was as bare as a swept roadway. All through the fall and into the next year to the 25th of January the heavens were as brass and the prospect was not encouraging. During the long dry months and under the blazing days the "digging the canal" went on. Some "chunks" were finished and presented such an unexpected feature that demanded some explanation. The portion just east of the railroad and including a 100 feet to the end of the Centerville and Kingsburg Irrigation District Canal, excited much interest among the railroad men and as the teams were busily finishing the scraping close to the track, a freight train stopped and the crew gathered and inquired all about where the canal started ...

The general need crystalized into a concentrated effort and with steady energy, without a halt the plan was consummated. But even in canal building, experience will develop unexpected trouble. The general fall of the land surface is over five feet to the mile to the southwest and as water will move quite briskly at a few inches to a mile fall, it was soon discovered that the water was having a roaring good time tearing along the newly excavated waterway. Rushing to one side it would dig into a bank and tear out the sandy soil and bear it away on to some quiet spot and build up bars of sand that could divert the current and multiply the damage till it was plain that "something had to be done," and that right quickly ...

"Well, it has to be controlled by putting in drops, the current is gone mad and the fall of the land is far too much for the sandy soil to keep the water in the canal and without it is held down to a slower pace the work will be absolutely ruined." So said the [canal] engineer and all could see it was correct, but oh, what a disappointment and delay. But these were not the men that ever despair ... and the work began of grading the canal to stretches of levels that could be controlled, holding up the flow and dropping it over falls of wood onto floors that restrained the power of the weight against the crumbly sides of the canal and then on to another "drop" the waters [sped] for another convulsion and general tear around.

Carloads of lumber ordered from afar—patiently hauled in through the sand from railroad to where it was to be used and dozens of men, scores of teams—a veritable village of constructionists.

It was a costly remedy, but it was a perfect success and the gates were slowly opened and the "drops settled" and little by little the flow was increased and soon another "dee-fic-al-ty," as one of our neighbors from up in the pines of "Far-away," called it—arose and could be very plainly seen. It was a Something that was unique to this sandy, silty soil and "not laid down in the books," it was the total collapse of the soil when saturated, just as the effect of water poured into the sugar bowl would lower the surface ... As the banks and the bottom of the canal became soaked, saturated there [*sic*] collapse appeared in frightful holes, cracks, chasms, down which often the whole force of the stream would go for varying periods. The effect often was for a levee to utterly vanish and the gap let out the entire flood to race away over the distance, going through the same performance as when confined to the banks of the canal. No time was lost to send a fleet rider away to the head gate to shut off the water and after awaiting till the place had dried, for the common expression was "It would bog a blanket, or drown a shadow." It was a fearful spectacle to behold and think what if a man should be caught in one of those swirls of water that would disappear into the bowels of the earth with an ominous growl that would have been certain

grape that ripened early. New vineyards were sometimes brought into bearing within two years, rather than the usual three. Dealers and wholesalers, reluctant to buy domestic products rather than Spanish raisins or French wines, changed their attitudes by the mid-1880s. Prices were lower and quality equal to foreign samples, if not better. Add to this the fact that vineyard profits per acre averaged $100 to $300—when it took *fifty* acres of wheat to clear a similar amount—and it is obvious why the vine established its supremacy among Fresno County's different crops.

Fresno County's raisin industry began on a fluke. When the hot summer of 1875 dried some of Francis T. Eisen's experimental grapes on the vine, he decided to pick, stem and pack them, sending them to San Francisco as a "Peruvian importation." These raisins caused an immediate sensation. Their reception may have been why Bernard Marks laid out his unsuccessful two-acre vineyards at the Central California Colony that year. Whatever the reason, two other important vineyards were set out the following year.

The first was known as the Hedge-Row, owned and operated by four San Francisco women schoolteachers—Minne F. Austin, Lucy H. Hatch, E. A. Cleveland and Julia B. Short. It consisted of 100 acres in the Central California Colony and was producing by August 1878. In that year thirty twenty-pound raisin boxes were packed, followed by 300 boxes the following year and 7,500 in 1886. Profits grew in proportion with the increased production. Minnie Austin was able to retire after ten years in the business, as were several of her co-investors.

Truman Charles White came to Fresno in 1876 with $325 and a strong desire to enter the raisin industry. With the help of his sister-in-law, Mrs. Julia A. Fink-Smith, and some Muscatel grape cuttings obtained from R. B. Blowers of Yolo County, he started his Raisina Vineyard that year. Situated on eighty acres next to Cherry Avenue, this enterprise produced raisins that consistently won top honors at state fairs and exhibitions. In 1886 he obtained the princely sum of $480 per acre for his crop while Minnie Austin received but $179.

In the Central California Colony neighborhood other settlers were quick to follow the lead of these pioneers. Captain E. A. Rowe and Mrs. J. A. F. Smith were producing raisins in 1879, according to the October 20 *Fresno Weekly Expositor* of that year. This vineyard's crop was said to be " . . . of excellent quality . . . clean, large, plump and juicy."

Elsewhere in Fresno County, huge vineyards were gearing up for production. The Robert B. Butler and Joseph Goodman (see 8:2) vineyards were planted in 1879. Butler's 640-acre vineyard was fully planted by 1885, making it the largest in the state. Annual yields of $200,000 to $250,000 gross profit and two million pounds of raisins were common in subsequent years.

Throughout the early and middle 1880s vineyard mania hit Fresno County. "Everyone wanted a raisin vineyard," said farmer G. N. Vanwormer of Fowler. "The banker and the butcher, the clerk and the bookkeeper, all went mad in the rush for raisin property . . . " Prime improved agricultural lands were selling for $1,000 per acre. If they already had vines they were

death to any one caught in the current. Holes left after some of the breaks were as large as the railroad depot at Selma.

The "holes" filled with water would be blue with the great depth. Remember that the canal was built over a soil without moisture for a depth of 40 to 50 feet down to a "water level." The bed of the canal after one of those runs to when it has to be turned out to repair looked like a case of "total wreck," causing delay and long hours of scraping soil into the holes and building levees.

Then there was no restraining grass roots and willows to bind the loose soil as there exists today, no Bermuda forming a sod so strong that its manifold roots defy the wash of the channel.

In the first years of irrigation the canal was inoperative from the necessity of repairs a majority of the seasons . . .

The passing of the canal current under the railroad was a feature of irrigation, new here and the proper making of the passageway was not laid down in the books of engineering.

The result of consultation with the railroad officials determined a box-like structure of plank and the advent of the water to the box or culvert was anxiously awaited and watched. Night came and the entire flow was

going down a hole . . . Mr. McCall, for whom the McCall avenue was named afterward, and myself, were instructed to watch the culvert all night. "If the water comes before the midnight passenger train, put a danger light of red on the track and have the conductor and engineer examine the prospect."

The advance of the water was changed into a retreat and back the current went as another sink hole was developed, perhaps a hundred feet from the roadway. In the darkness of the night and amid the roaring of the water and the breaking of the earth and its tumbling into the sink hole, made any near inspection extremely dangerous, and so the only thing to do was to stand on the bridge and watch and wait, with covered lantern, looking down the road for the southbound train. The water arrived and gurgled and hissed and sank and reappeared, advanced a little, retreated and enclosed the culvert, and as it sank into the earth, released or drove out the air and made a sound much like a boiling pot as it disappeared into the ground.

The train came in sight and the red light was placed in the center of the rails and a hundred feet away the train stopped . . .

The engineer, conductor, roadmaster and superintendent of this division carefully con-

sidered the risk of crossing, or of having the water turned out and the ground allowed to dry and settle.

The sounding rods, sticks, all showed that the surrounding ground was as soft as mush. Lanterns held in anxious hands, dozens of silent observers, the clear starlight night, all made a striking picture of the uncertainty of the venture to cross. All opinions were finally centered on the engineer's dictum, and when he said he would venture it, we all stood back away from the train and as the huge locomotive reached the wooden box-culvert it seemed as if it would sink into the water as the weight came on to the culvert, but the engineer hesitated not a second, but opened the throttle and in a second or two the weight was on the other end and that settled, but the first end arose, and so it rocked up and down as every passing car crossed, and for several trains it looked very risky, but at last settled solid and as firm as today.

SOURCE: George B. Otis, *Reminiscences of Early Days, The Pioneer Days of Selma and Surrounding Country.* Press of the Selma Irrigator, July 1911. Selections here from pp. 16-19, 30-31.

maintained, and if not they were plowed up and replanted in vines.

Despite the high prices, large-scale vineyards were still being set up. William Forsyth began his 160-acre operation, near Red Banks Creek and Olive Avenue, around 1880. A. B. Butler started his vineyard, which grew to 480 acres, in March 1881. C. A. Kirby and H. A. Peterson, of Kirby Ditch fame, put in a vineyard with dimensions similar to Butler's in January 1882. Other notable raisin vineyardists of this era were J. W. Pew, J. P. Thomas, N. W. Trezevant and J. W. Gould.

The explosive growth of the county's raisin industry can best be seen in production figures. In 1882, 80,000 pounds were produced; in 1884, 800,000, a 1,000 percent increase; and 7 million in 1887, nearly nine times the 1884 figure. Increased production bestowed both prosperity and problems. When Fresno County's raisins began making their way back to Eastern markets in Chicago and New York City, commission agents who bought from growers sought to cut prices. The agents seemed to be anticipating a raisin glut and wanted to protect themselves. "It is, we think, a well-established fact that the ordinary commission merchant is cold-blooded, and cares but little for anybody but himself, and, therefore, he is always ready to sell,' moaned a reporter in the December 8, 1886, *Fresno Daily Evening Expositor*. Luckily for growers, there was no glut at this time. The increased supply seemed to have triggered an increased demand. However, they had barely tasted the difficulties commission agents would give them in succeeding years (see Chapter 15).

Closely related to the raisin industry, wine making in Fresno County followed a similar pattern of development. Wines established themselves a little more easily than raisins because the *phylloxera*, a vine-ravaging insect, had wrecked many vineyards in France and northern and southern California. Fortunately, it never touched the central part of the state.

As with raisins, Francis T. Eisen was the father of Fresno County's wine making industry, producing 200 gallons in 1875. In the following year he built a 40,000-gallon capacity wine cellar on his property and began buying grapes from other sources at thirty dollars a ton. He did not have enough producing vines to keep his operation busy. By 1881 his yearly vintage had grown to about 80,000 gallons and he was producing Zinfandel Claret, Zinfandel Port, Dry Sherry, Sweet Malaga, Riesling and other varieties. With a 250,000-gallon annual production in 1885, he remained one of the county's top wine makers.

Following Eisen's lead in 1879 were Robert Barton and George H. Malter. Both were German immigrants who had come to America, been successful in miscellaneous business ventures, and hoped to become richer yet in Fresno County agricultural ventures. In all likelihood, they exceeded their expectations.

The Barton estate, purchased for $8,000 in 1879 and improved for $350,000, was sold for $1 million eight years later. Bounded by present-day Cedar, Chestnut, Belmont and McKinley avenues, in 1883 it embraced 530 acres of vineyard, a twenty-acre fruit orchard, a wine cellar with a 200,000-gallon capacity and a grape brandy distillery that could produce 40,000 gallons a year. The premises featured a mansion surrounded by fountains, Kentucky bluegrass, Lombardy poplars and Italian cypress.

In its time Barton's estate was the agricultural showplace of Fresno County, and an exceedingly productive one. Its vintage, as more vines came into bearing, went from 75,000 gallons in 1883 to 360,000 in 1886, more than a third of the county's wine production for that year. Barton's cellar was especially noted for its white wines and Sauternes. (For a description of Malter's enterprise, see 8:3.)

Incorporated and planted a year after Barton's estate was started, the Fresno Vineyard was a similarly profitable venture of some San Francisco financiers. The group included Martin Theodore Kearney—William S. Chapman's private secretary and, during the 1880s, an investor in several Fresno County agricul-

Reference 8:2

## THE GOODMAN VINEYARD

The Goodman vineyard, adjoining Barton's on the east, is one of the most carefully and neatly cultivated of Fresno vineyards. This vineyard is the home of the well known author and journalist, Joseph T. Goodman, who is at present abiding under his own vine and fig tree. Thirty acres of this vineyard were planted four years ago, before its purchase by Mr. Goodman. Only about one-half of those vines grew, and the vacant places have since been filled out by replanting. The entire vineyard, which consists of this 30 acres of bearing vines and 60 acres of one-year-old vines, is planted to raisin grapes, making a vineyard of 90 acres.

There are 130 acres in the tract, the remaining 40 being devoted to grain, pasturage, a family orchard and grounds surrounding the residence. The latter is situated near the east line, an avenue planted with poplars leading to it from the west side.

The residence, the surrounding grounds, raisin packing house, stables, etc. are all arranged with an eye to taste, convenience and comfort. There is one building here the like of which can probably not be seen elsewhere. Its dimensions are about 20 feet square. The exterior is quite ornamental, but the interior is as plain and devoid of ornamentation as a Quaker meeting house. Mr. Goodman has dubbed this isolated room the "Scriptorium," after the name given the rooms in which the monks of the middle ages retired to do their writing, the penalty for intrusion into which by any female or other unprivileged person was death. It is in this room that Mr. Goodman, when wearied with the toll of vineyard and farm, retires to pursue his literary labors. We believe, however, that he has somewhat modified the rules which governed the monkish "scriptoriums."

During Mr. Goodman's absence of several months the past winter and spring, Mrs. Goodman has had full charge of the vineyard and has managed the work in progress very successfully.

The first raisins on this vineyard were made last season, the product of 15 acres of bearing vines being 400 boxes. The yield this year will be considerably larger.

SOURCE: *The Fresno Weekly Republican*, June 28, 1884.

148

tural ventures. The vineyard was situated in 400 acres of the old Easterby Ranch, which—after being owned by Nevada silver baron William S. O'Brien and the Bank of California—was subdivided into the A. B. Butler, Malter, Margherita and Herman Granz vineyards.

It took only two years for some of the Fresno Vineyard's vines to reach maturity, at which time 55,000 gallons of wine were produced. Three years later, the yield was 325,000 gallons. There were also brandy-producing facilities and an orchard of sorts. Fruit trees were planted along the irrigation ditch banks, rather than shade trees, to form a windbreak against the frequent prairie gusts. This vineyard produced Zinfandel, Burger, Riesling, Muscatel, Blaue Elba, Malaga, Angelica and a host of other wines. Its production facilities were destroyed by fire in 1887 but were rebuilt soon afterward.

The 160-acre Eggers Vineyard of George and Herman Eggers, although established in 1873, did not begin producing wines until 1882. Much of the brothers' 5,760 acres were planted in wheat and barley in the early years, until production shifted over to wine grapes in the early eighties. Figures for the first vintage are unavailable, but production was 65,000 gallons in 1884 and 125,000 in 1886. This vineyard produced all the typical wines—Claret, Angelicas, Ports, and white. Due to start-up costs, it took until 1885 to turn a profit.

Other notable wine vineyards of this period were operated by Herman Granz, the Fruit Vale Winery Company, A. P. Adams, the Kirby Vineyard, D. Duquesne, the Henrietta Vineyard and a host of smaller operations. Around 1880 an independent winery and distillery was operated in Fresno by Dr. Lewis Leach and Otto Froelich. It handled approximately 30,000 gallons annually and, with the other enterprises, pushed

Reference 8:3
## THE MALTER VINEYARD

The Malter vineyard is situated about four miles from the city of Fresno, and occupies a portion of sections 5 and 17 of township 14 south, range 21 east. It is conveniently situated between two of the best roads in the county and the soil is a fine quality of red loam. It was originally a part of the Easterby and Henrietta ranchos and for many years was used for grain and cattle raising. [In the Sunnyside area.]

In 1879 G[eorge] H. Malter purchased 480 acres, a portion of which he has since sold. The land at that time was a grain field, but the success of the Eisen vineyard, which adjoins it, suggested its fitness for grape raising and Major Martin Denicke was employed as an expert to investigate the matter. Acting on his advice Mr. Malter at once undertook to plant 320 acres, giving the enterprise entirely in charge of Mr. Denicke . . .

After some years of work, when it was demonstrated that the vineyard was a paying investment, Mr. Malter commenced to improve and beautify the land with the profits of the crops. Before that time his grapes were taken to the Margherita Winery to be treated and made into wine.

The first building constructed was, of necessity, the cottage, then the winery and distillery, and lastly the magnificent residence which is just about completed . . .

The winery now consists of two large buildings—the fermenting house and storage house.

The fermenting house is two stories in height and is built of adobe. It contains seventy-two fermenting tanks, each having a capacity of ten tons of grapes. They are arranged in six tiers, one above the other, so as to economise [sic] space and facilitate the operation of handling. There are two elevators which take the grapes from a large platform, upon which they are dumped from the wagons. By this means there is no delay to the teamsters, as three wagons can unload at the same time. There are two crushers to which the grapes can be taken, and from which they can be dropped into any one of the seventy-two tanks in a moment. This gives a daily capacity of 100 tons. All the various kinds of wine are produced, and the quality is of the best.

All of the wines from the Malter vineyard are disposed of in large lots, most of which are made to order in lots of from 50,000 to 100,000 gallons. No wine is sold at retail. One ton will make from sixty-five to eighty-five gallons of sweet wine, and about twice the quantity of dry wine. Sweet wines are worth from thirty-five to forty cents a gallon.

Over 3,300 tons of grapes were worked in this winery last year.

The storage house is two stories in height, 40 x 120 feet, and has a capacity of 250,000 gallons. It is also built of adobe. Nothing which can in any way add to the facilities for the keeping or storing of wines is wanting in this building.

The distillery was built in 1888, at the same time as the winery. From time to time improvements have been added until today it is one of the most complete distilleries in the State of California. It is so constructed as to be capable of distilling pumice or fermented grape juice to a very high proof brandy, and accomplished the process of rectification and distillation in the same operation.

The pumice still consists of two 1,000 gallon stills which are separated alternately. The alcoholic vapors pass through fourteen rectifying chambers to the coolers and produce pure and high proof brandy at once. The fusil oil, which is worth a great deal more than the brandy, is caught separately during the operation. Most of this fusil oil is purchased by Eastern manufacturers who very likely use it for adulterating purposes.

Grape syrup is made from pure must. For this purpose Mr. Malter has constructed a building and provided it with all the acknowledged improvements for the manufacture of this valuable article of commerce.

The juice for making syrup is first clarified in two pans eight feet in diameter; from this it passes into a pan five feet wide by twenty feet long. This pan is divided into three compartments. It is charged in the first and the pure syrup is taken from the third. The process goes on continuously. The apparatus is capable of making 500 gallons of pure syrup in 24 hours. Syrup containing 60 per cent of sugar is worth 50 cents a gallon.

The muscat vines, for the purpose of making raisins, were planted but two years ago and have scarcely yet come into bearing. They produced $1,000 worth of raisins last year.

The grounds of the Malter vineyard are as beautiful and well laid out as any in the county. The trees and flowers are young as yet, but they are grown sufficiently to show the promise of their future beauty.

A fine avenue leads from the entrance to the center of the grounds, where the residence and other buildings are situated. The avenue is lined on both sides with eucalyptus and cedars. A row of fan palms divides the road into two drives.

The grounds about the residence and cottage are beautifully laid out and contain a large variety of flowers. In a few years it will be hard to find a handsomer place than the Malter vineyard . . .

SOURCE: *Fresno Daily Evening Expositor*, February 3, 1891, p. 2 c. 1–3, in Fresno Scraps pp. 43–44.

Fresno County's wine production to over 1 million gallons annually by 1886.

With the steady increase of fruit and raisin production in the county—especially raisins—facilities for processing these crops were needed. The first of these was a fruit drying and small canning establishment built in 1879 by the California Fruit Drying Company in Fresno. This operation apparently did not last long. The 1881 Fresno County directory states that no cannery was operating in the county.

To fill this void William Faymonville, M. J. Donahoo, Thomas E. Hughes and others incorporated the Fresno Fruit Packing Company on March 6, 1882. The need for this Fresno-based business must have been crucial, for it was operating three months later. The factory produced canned goods in an efficient, assembly-line manner. After being sorted and peeled, green fruits would be packed in cans, syruped, sealed and sent to steam baths where they were cooked "in such a manner as to preserve . . . all natural juices and flavor," according to an August 23, 1882, *Fresno Weekly Expositor* report. Once this phase was completed, the cans were stacked in pyramids, left to cool and labeled.

Following a period of management by the Cutting Packing Company of San Francisco, the Fresno Fruit Packing Company was purchased by the George W. Meade and Company packing firm, also of San Francisco, in December 1886. Renamed the Fresno Fruit and Raisin Packing Company, Meade enlarged its new facility the next year at a cost of $600,000. Large new receiving, sweating and packing rooms were set up. The boiler and engine room was reconstructed to run economically: fruit pits were used as fuel. This expansion program, however, proved too costly and the facility went bankrupt on December 29, 1887.

In the meantime, another packing house had opened in Fresno to service fruit growers. The Pacific Fruit Company inaugurated its new facility on July 29, 1887, with Fresno nurseryman W. M. Williams as manager. It was originally intended to compete with the Meade house, only to find itself alone by year's end.

Early fruit-packing ventures in Fresno County were not restricted to the county seat. When the Hedge-Row

Reference 8:4

# RAISIN MAKING
## M. F. AUSTIN

The sun-laved shores of the Mediterranean offer to the vine no finer soil and climate than the warm plains of Fresno Co. The abundant water supply from the snow-filled canyons of the mighty Sierras gives health to the vine and size to the berries, while the long summer heat fills the grape with all lusciousness. When the early September days pour a torrid heat upon the plains, the rich clusters put on a golden tint, the royal amber of full ripeness.

Sun and water and warmth can do no more; the vintage time has come. To make sweet raisins, filled with jelly and of a fine brown color, it is important that the grapes shall show this yellow color. Picking early, so as to be first in the market, does not mean good raisins. The grapes, when thus ripened are carefully cut from the vine and laid upon small platforms, made of smooth sugar pine and raised from the ground by inch cleats. These platforms are three feet long, and two feet wide and are capable of holding from twenty to twenty-five pounds of green grapes.

They are then placed on the open spaces between the rows of vines and left for the action of the sun and air.

In picking the grapes, care should be taken not to handle the bunches so as to rub off the delicate bloom. In nine days after picking, the raisins are sufficiently dry on the upper side to admit of turning over. This is done by placing an empty platform upon a filled one and reversing quickly. If skillfully done, no fruit will be thrown off.

In five or six days after turning, the raisins are sufficiently cured to be removed from the platforms. This is the only really delicate part of the whole business, requiring much judgment. The more care the better raisins. If the raisins have part of their juices, still liquid, unconverted into jelly, so that a drop can be squeezed out by pressing the raisin between the thumb and finger, it is unfit to be put into the "sweat-box," as it will eventually mould or sour after packing; and if too much dried, the consumer will never know the deliciousness of properly cured raisins; therefore a careful inspection of each tray must be made and imperfectly dried raisins be removed; after which all dust and dirt must be vigorously fanned from the tray.

They are now carefully slipped from the tray into large boxes called sweat boxes, which are three feet long, two feet wide and one foot deep. After a layer (consisting of the contents of three or four platforms) has been placed in the box, a large sheet of Manilla paper is laid upon them, then another layer of raisins and paper alternately until the box is filled. The boxes are now taken from the vineyard to some cool building and allowed to stand from two weeks to a month. The moisture passes into the stems, making them pliable and an equilibrium is established through all the raisins in the box.

At the end of the proper curing time, the raisins pass into the hands of the packers. These pack from the layers on the Manilla paper into galvanized iron trays, fitting comfortably into the boxes which go to market. These trays have false wooden bottoms and are all balanced on the scales before packing. All imperfect raisins and superabundant stems are cut out from the bunches, which are then neatly placed in the trays until they contain five pounds of fruit.

They are then pressed in a lever press; the fancy paper wrapper is now placed upon the iron tray, a steel plate over that, and all reversed over the box in which they are to be packed—the slide is removed when the compact five pound layer, with its paper wrapper falls into place in the box; the paper is folded over and the box is ready for its successive layers. The standard California box holds four layers, or twenty pounds. When all the layers are in the box, a fancy label is placed upon the top—cover nailed on and the box stenciled with the owner's name. This constitutes a box of table raisins.

It is understood that the quarter and half boxes contain the finest bunches and largest berries—while the whole boxes may have smaller and less perfect bunches and some loose raisins. All small, loose raisins are packed as "cooking raisins," according to the option of the packer.

There seems to be no good reason why California and Fresno county especially shall not produce raisins equal to old Spain, when we have learned that the best results follow the greatest care in details. We must not forget that Spain has had centuries of experience which has been transmitted from generation to generation while we are novices in the business, with all things to learn.

M. F. Austin

SOURCE: *Fresno Republican 1881 Directory.*

and Raisina vineyards began harvesting their first crops (usually with Chinese labor—whites regarded grape-picking as a menial task), there was no alternative except to pack raisins at the vineyard (see 8:4). Other large-scale raisin growers, such as Armenian immigrant Hadgi Agha Peters and A. B. Butler, opened packing houses in 1885. Butler's packing house was comparable in size to the Fresno Fruit Packing Company and could employ 250 men.

The early agricultural development of Fresno County was not accomplished easily. At different times, three sources of difficulty—irrigation disputes, the Southern Pacific Railroad and farm pests—threatened to end, or simply upset, the laborious process of making the desert bloom. The story of these malevolent forces has never been told within a single, comprehensive narrative. What follows is an attempt to fill this gap in Fresno County history.

First, the irrigation disputes. They began with the Fresno Canal system which, on August 10, 1875, was granted a right to use the waters of the Kings River. (The Kings River and Fresno Canal system was simultaneously denied a right to appropriate water, which is why it joined the Fresno Canal system fifteen days later.) Soon afterward ditch companies on the lower Kings, and later the owners of the Laguna de Tache, began contesting this ruling in court.

The Fresno Canal company's main canal, it was claimed, would take too much water and leave appropriators downstream with nothing a times of low water. Besides—and this was the point advanced by the Laguna de Tache's owners—water appropriations violated the doctrine of riparian rights. This concept, originated in England, stated that landowners with property next to a river were entitled to have such water flow past their lands undiminished in quantity or quality. On these grounds, more than 200 suits were eventually filed against the Fresno Canal company. Its legal defense costs eventually exceeded the construction costs of its distribution system.

Other difficulties arose when the Fresno Canal company fell apart financially in 1875. It had originally been owned by a consortium—William S. Chapman, Frederick C. Roeding, A. Y. Easterby and Moses J. Church—but fell into the Bank of Nevada's hands in the wake of its financial difficulties, and was sold back to Church in 1876 for $28,000. By 1877 Chapman and the Central California colonists had reversed their allegiances. Church, they said, had built a faulty branch canal system through their property that allowed water to run off as waste or collect in ponds. Church contended that he had not been paid for irrigation rights, which had to be renegotiated with each change in Fresno Canal company ownership. The courts believed Church and a new agreement was drawn up after much wrangling. At one point, according to the December 20, 1879, *Fresno Weekly Republi-*

can, "Chapman enjoined the colonists from interfering with the water, and the canal company from turning it off. So the water [continued] to run until the Lord, the Devil, or W. S. Chapman [saw] fit to interfere."

A year later, the riparian controversy began building. In late 1882 Sinon C. Lillis, a one-fiftieth owner of the Laguna de Tache, had a crew of his ranch hands tear out Fresno Canal company diversion dams on the Kings and rebuild them at other points. (Constructed perpendicular to the headgates, these dams brought a more consistent water flow into the canals.) The idea was to conduct water to the east side of the Kings, where it would reach the small Laguna de Tache irrigation works—at the time, alfalfa was being grown there. The Fresno Canal company crews retaliated by rebuilding their old dams. After several more rounds of removals and rebuildings the Laguna de Tache owners, along with Kings River cattleman John Heinlen, filed riparian injunctions against the Fresno Canal, Centerville and Kingsburg, and Fowler Switch companies in early 1883.

Church, ordered to shut off the Fresno Canal headgate in March, refused at first. Water was, after all, essential to agriculture—now the brick and mortar of Fresno County's economy. Then, fearing the penalties, he relented and the *Fresno Weekly Republican* of March 31, 1883, remarked that "... the people of [Fresno] were aroused as if a bombshell had fallen in the streets ... Messengers were sent through the various colonies, carrying to each owner of orchard or vineyard the news that the ruin of his peaceful home and the means of subsistence for himself and family were threatened."

Immediately a citizen's committee, calling itself the Fresno County Water Company, was formed by Bernhard Marks, A. B. Butler, J. W. North, Martin Denicke, M. T. Sickal and Robert Barton. The men posted a new appropriation, claiming that the water had been used by farmers for eight years and neither Church nor the riparianists could take it away. When Church tried to shut down the headgate after the water company's formation, an angry mob stopped him. Tensions between the farmers, irrigationists and riparianists continued throughout the year (see 8:5).

Irrigation troubles subsided in 1884 because the Kings River ran high and there was plenty of water for everyone. The Laguna de Tache owners looked the other way if a headgate, closed by prior injunction, was mysteriously opened. The next year, they did not tolerate this behavior. In a succession of 1885 rulings Poly, Heilbron and Company got the courts to order the permanent closings of the Fowler Switch, Centerville and Kingsburg, and Kings River and Fresno Canal portion of the Fresno Canal system. Yet the headgates remained open in many instances. "This is a plain and forcible indication," said the *Modesto Her-*

# "THIS IS WAR AND WAR IS NOT PLEASANT"
## ERNEST J. NIELSEN

The year 1883 was an extremely dry year. The wheat crop had been a failure. A small amount of water was running in the river, but in the middle of July the Centerville and Kingsburg canals abruptly went dry.

William H. Shafer, at that time the Superintendent of the C[enterville] and K[ingsburg] System, was ordered to go to the headgates and determine the cause. He returned and reported to the directors that the Fresno system (of which Moses Church was the guiding figure) had built up the diversion dam at Centerville and was diverting all of the water from the systems into the Fresno system.

A committee from the C and K System, one of which was Shafer, called upon Church and called his attention to the fact that all of the water was being diverted into his system. They also called his attention to the fact that he was restrained by court action from diverting any water from the river, just as they were. They also stated that they had no desire to call his violation to the attention of the courts and asked for a share of the water.

Mr. Church told the C and K committee that he was powerless to act, since the people had taken the operation of the canals from his hands.

The C and K committee returned to Kingsburg and decided to determine if the statements of Church were true. They accordingly instructed Shafer to go to the headgates and turn all of the water out of the Fresno system and back into the river and then remain at the point and see who came to turn the water back into the Fresno system.

It was not long before Shafer was to have this question answered. It was J. M. Loveland, Church's own superintendent, who came to turn the water back into the Fresno system. Loveland remarked, "Who had the nerve to turn the water out of our canals?" To which Shafer replied, "I did and I think you have your nerve to take all the water from the river." Loveland replied, "Well, I'm turning it back into our system." Shafer replied, "I don't intend to stop you, but I'm going to watch you do it."

Shafer then returned and reported his findings to the directors. They again went to Moses Church, informed him of their findings, and asked him, as friends and neighbors, to permit some of the water to go down the C & K system. To this Church agreed, but with the stipulation that the water be taken from his waste gate. The directors immediately saw his point, since if this was done, they would have acknowledged his right to dam the river and take all the water. The C & K directors refused these terms and Church declined to let them have any water in any other manner.

The C & K directors returned to Kingsburg for a meeting with their attorney and their Superintendent Shafer. The attorney informed them the legal advice was difficult to give. Any legal action might take years to decide. But he stated, "If it is the advice of your attorney that you seek, I cannot give you any. However, not as a lawyer, but as a man, if my family depended on the water in the ditches which you have built yourselves, if my crops were dependent on water from the river, I would blow up that dam that is keeping water from reaching my ranch, which I thought I was rightfully entitled to."

After meeting with the attorney, the directors met outside his office and Shafer remarked to Mr. T. C. Bratton, "Here is our solution." I. N. Parlier, the president of the C & K system, remarked, "How can we blow the dam with powder, since powder will not function in water?"

Shafer replied, "We can blow the dam with dynamite."

Parlier added, "But who will get the dynamite and who will blow the dam?"

Shafer answered, "I will get the dynamite and I'll blow the dam."

While the group was still discussing the intentions to blow up the dam, the telephone operator at Kingsburg came into the group. He was asked what he wanted. To this he replied, "A telegram is just as personal as the U.S. Mail, but in this case I feel I must tell you that a telegram has just been sent to the Fresno Irrigation Company, informing them of your intention to dynamite the dam."

With this information, it was decided to wait at least a week, since it was certain that the directors of the Fresno Company would station guards to prevent any action at the dam.

At the expiration of the week, Shafer asked A. A. Smith, then postmaster at Kingsburg, and Samuel Moffett to go to the Sol Sweet store at Visalia and purchase the dynamite. The only other place where it might be purchased was at the Kutner Goldstein Company in Fresno. Purchase in Fresno was to be avoided, since it was certain that, if this course was taken, the Fresno group would soon receive word.

Moffett and Smith made the purchase and were instructed to meet Shafer and Capt. T. C. Bratton (of Selma and a Civil War veteran) at Ray's Ford. Ray's Ford is a point where Lincoln Avenue now ends at the Kings River and is also a point where the Kings River makes a 45 degree turn. This crossing was at a point where the river had a hard cobble bottom. The group met on August 2, 1883. Moffett, when met, displayed his 25 pound box of dynamite, which had been wrapped in cotton and which he described as "eggs." Someone in the group laughed at the cotton wrapping around the box and Moffett replied, "I was cautioned against subjecting it to any hard jar, so I bought the cotton. The women at home can always make use of cotton, so it will not be wasted."

On the morning of August 3, 1883, the group prepared to dynamite the dam, after having gone from Ray's Ford to the diversion dam on the east side of the river, so that they would not be detected. When they arrived at the dam site, Shafer carried Captain Bratton across the river on his shoulders. Bratton had been wounded in the Civil War, and the hip injury that he had suffered in the war caused him to be careful not to aggravate the condition by getting into cold water.

Moffett insisted on being permitted to assist Shafer in placing the dynamite. To this and other requests by his companions, he refused. Shafer contended that any injury that might be suffered by Moffett would become widely known as well as the incidents relating to such injury.

While Shafer was engaged in placing the dynamite, the superintendent of the Fresno system appeared. Again it was J. M. Loveland. When he shouted across the river, "What are you doing?" Shafer replied, "We are going to dynamite your dam."

Still shouting, Loveland replied, "Don't you know that you will get into a pack of trouble for what you are doing?"

With this, Shafer replied, "Of course we know that, but this is war, and war is not pleasant. We are determined to get the water that we are entitled to, trouble or no trouble."

Shafer lit the fuse and ran. The dam was blown and boulders were blown 50 feet in the air. Water rushed into the C & K canal system and remained there for a period of two weeks. Shafer had his men remain at the site and they were told to engage in "target practice" during this time, to discourage any attempt to repair the dam. Two attempts were made during this time, when Church sent a crew of Chinese to the scene. They were frightened away.

After these two attempts, J. M. McCardle, the constable of Fresno, was sent with a warrant for the arrest of Shafer. Shafer and McCardle were friends and Shafer readily submitted to arrest.

On the way to Fresno, McCardle questioned Shafer and he was told the entire story. McCardle had no great affection for the actions of Church and told Shafer so in a few well chosen words.

McCardle told Shafer that he could not be brought into court until the following day and that he had no desire to place him in jail. He said that his own family was in the mountains, or he would take him to his home. He then asked Shafer, "Have you any money?" Shafer replied that he did.

McCardle then replied, "I don't think you will run away. I'll put you up at the Grand Central Hotel for the night."

On the following morning Shafer appeared in the court of Justice of the Peace S. M. Hill. The lawyer for the Fresno system was George E. Church, later to become district attorney. Shafer was charged with

*Bernhard Marks, developer of the county's first agricultural colony.*

*Francis T. Eisen, father of Fresno County's raisin and wine industries.*

*James Porteous, inventor and owner of Fresno Agricultural Works.*

*James Porteous' first blacksmith shop, erected on the bare Fresno County plains in 1874.*

FCCHS Archives

FCCHS Archives

*The Fresno Scraper picking dirt and debris on the left and dumping it out on the right.* FCCHS Archives

*Minnewawa, the estate of Dr. I. S. Eshleman and daughter, Minnie, founder of Minnewawa Creamery Corporation. She is sitting on the upper porch and he is walking the dog.*

*T. C. White's label features his beautiful home and a medal awarded his raisins in 1885 by Mechanics Institute in San Francisco. Above is his home, the packing shed to the left and Mr. and Mrs. White in the garden.*

*Most of the early colonists lived in simple houses such as this one in the Scandinavian Home Colony belonging to Anton and Louisa Henningsen. The Henningsens were representative of many. They left this sabbath picture and their daughter-in-law, Mrs. Helene Henningsen, preserved their life's story in a book,* Anton and Louisa.

*ald*, "that the people are higher than the law when the law is in conflict with their interests."

The farmers' plight looked grim during 1886. The California Supreme Court ruled, in the *Lux v. Haggin* case, that riparian law took precedence over anyone's appropriations. A smug Sinon Lillis made an appearance before the Centerville and Kingsburg company's board of directors. He offered to drop further litigation in exchange for a sizable chunk of the canal company's stock and asked for comments. The canal company's president responded: "You want us to give you half of our canal. I will see you in hell first."

Again, an injunction was approved to turn the Centerville and Kingsburg canal's headgate off. Later it was turned back on by persons unknown. Separate attempts by the canal's superintendent and board of directors to turn off the headgate ended when they were confronted by a crowd of men disguised with pillowcases on their heads and armed with rifles.

The situation was irremediable. The Centerville and Kingsburg company could do little other than to pay court-imposed fines for illegal water use. Similar incidents took place at the Fowler Switch headgates.

With thousands of California acres in farmland, it was apparent that *Lux v. Haggin* would have to be modified. This happened on March 7, 1887, when the Wright Act of Assemblyman C. C. Wright of Modesto was passed by the California Legislature. Under its conditions, landholders who could obtain irrigation in a given area, from an existing source, could petition a county board of supervisors to form a public irrigation district. Once two-thirds of the affected area's voters approved, bonds for formation could be issued and the district organized.

Riparianists fought the Wright Act, only to have it affirmed by the U.S. Supreme Court. In later years, as will be seen, it provided a meeting-ground for diverse irrigation interests in Fresno County.

Unlike the riparianists, the Southern Pacific Railroad provided farmers with problems that could not be legislated away. Although the railroad had brought a practical form of transportation to the valley, thus opening up valley products to wider markets, it proved to be the farmer's foe on two counts: land titles and

freight rates. The background of the former subject is well known.

When the Southern Pacific proposed building a line through a certain region, the federal government would give it lands adjacent to the intended route. Sensing a good financial opportunity, the Southern Pacific induced settlers to move on these lands while the railroad gained formal title to them. Once full government approval was obtained—a process that took years—the settlers were allowed to purchase their property.

Many settlers moved onto land in the Mussel Slough country lying in Fresno and Tulare counties. The people there spent $400,000 building irrigation works and intended to stay—only to find, when their lands were offered for sale, that prices ranged from $24 to $35 an acre. The farmers, who believed prices would be around $2.50 an acre, were upset. Some were priced out of their homesteads, stayed on the Southern Pacific lands anyway, and were forcibly ejected.

On May 11, 1880, U.S. Marshal Alonzo W. Poole tried to carry out a Southern Pacific eviction on the Henry J. Brewer farm. It was situated just inside the Fresno County line and in the Mussel Slough country. When Poole and a party of men arrived, they were met by an armed group of settlers. Displeased with negotiations they had held with the Southern Pacific, a few of the settlers had formed a militia. When the two sides faced each other, angry words were exchanged and shots rang out.

To this day no reliable account concerning this battle, or who started it, exists. The participants all told different stories. Nor is it necessary to reconstruct what happened; the reader is referred to J. L. Brown's *The Mussel Slough Tragedy* or Wallace Smith's *Garden of the Sun* for that data, too lengthy to recapitulate here. What mattered was that seven men, on both sides of the issue, died in the fray and the Southern Pacific's reputation never looked blacker.

Seven settlers were tried later in the year for their part in the Mussel Slough fight. They were found guilty of resisting an officer, paid $300 fines, served eight-month jail terms and were regarded as folk heroes throughout California. (Railroads, like today's

"malicious mischief." Years later Shafer often remarked "malicious, yes; mischief, no."

Church proved his case against Shafer without question; but, all during the hearing, Shafer's attorney made no objections and offered no evidence to the contrary. Shafer became alarmed and whispered to his counsel, "When do you start defending me?" The reply was, "Relax, don't worry."

At the conclusion of the presentation of the case by Church, Shafer's attorney rose and addressed the court with these remarks, "Your honor, the case has been proved without queston, but certainly you must be aware of the fact that the scene of the alleged

crime was very close to the county line. The prosecuting attorney has failed, in presenting his case, to prove the jurisdiction of this court. He has failed to show whether the crime was committed in Fresno or Tulare County. In the absence of such information, I move that this case be dismissed."

Justice of the Peace Hill was smart enough to see that he had a hot potato in his lap. Had he decided against the defendant in this case, as the evidence indicated, he would have acknowledged also the violation of the Fresno Canal Company against the injunction to take water from the river. Their own violation of the injunction would have been a

matter of court record by the mere act of finding the defendant guilty. He welcomed the opportunity to dismiss the case. He did so, much to the relief of all parties concerned, once they realized the importance of the case.

This single act by Shafer ended all further attempts on the part of any company to take all the water from the river and was the actual beginning of peaceful ways and means to partition the water to all intereted parties, in accordance with their legal rights.

SOURCE: *Garden of the Sun*.

Big Business and Government, were never held in high esteem by the people they served.) Meanwhile, the Southern Pacific offered a 12½ percent reduction on some of its land prices and used gentler tactics in evicting settlers.

The Southern Pacific's freight rates caused continual grumbling among Fresno County's farmers. In 1883, a fifty-four-dollar surcharge was tacked on freight carloads going to San Francisco—simply because Fresno had not been classified as a "terminal shipping point"—and it went up to seventy dollars in 1886.

Raisin growers became increasingly concerned and met at Fresno's Grand Central Hotel on August 14, 1886 to discuss the problem. The growers complained that wine makers got a break from the Southern Pacific because their cooperage was sent out at a standard rate, but shipped back at a lower rate. (Wine makers complained that raisin growers got their trays back at no cost.) A delegation from the meeting was sent to meet with Southern Pacific officials in San Francisco where, apparently, nothing happened. This was one of the few formal challenges Fresno County farmers gave the Southern Pacific. It seems likely that ever-rising crop prices during this period quieted many voices that otherwise would have been raised in protest.

Farm pests and pestilences in early Fresno County were many. The first agricultural enterprise to encounter problems with insects was the Eisen Vineyard, which combatted grasshoppers in 1874, red spiders in 1875, and grape moths in 1876–77. The first two pests attacked grape foliage—bad because leaves shelter grapes from the sun and heat—and the fruit itself. The moth attack required a crew of twenty men to work for six weeks, hand-picking larvae off vines. In later years the Eisens had trouble with army worms, thrips and a grape "cancer." They killed the worms by whacking vines with a stick, causing the worms to fall onto sheets of paper spread below, and pouring them into pans of coal oil.

Scales and wine-slugs were prevalent in 1883, taking their toll on the Raisina and Barton vineyards and orchards. T. C. White killed the scales by spraying his prune trees with a double dose of lye. The slugs, which had abounded at the Fresno Vineyard the year before and had been eaten by a flock of hawks, were killed off in a more ingenious way: turkeys were herded into the vineyard to feast on them! Fresno banker and rancher John Hyde Braly used this method most successfully in 1885 (see 8:6). This same method was used against grasshoppers that year, when they caused extensive fruit damage in the Selma area. Arsenic pastes made by nurseryman George C. West and Francis T. Eisen also were effective. There was only one problem with this treatment—it fueled rumors that Fresno County produce was poisoned.

Johnson grass, a longtime nuisance in Fresno County, was introduced under circumstances that have mostly been forgotten. Professor W. A. Sanders began selling it, in the early 1880s or before, as something to plant in alfalfa patches. It was said to keep gas from building up in farm animals—a serious problem, since alfalfa tended to bloat and sometimes kill the poor creatures. When farmers began putting in "evergreen millet," as Sanders called it, new difficulties arose. It crowded out alfalfa completely, spread indiscriminately, and was ignored by the animals as food. Farmers quit planting the "millet," now known as Johnson grass, by the mid-1880s—but it remains today.

Whatever the problems faced by Fresno County's farmers, people grew increasingly eager to join their ranks. Chartered train excursions from San Francisco, San Jose, Colusa County, Stanislaus County and other California locations streamed into the state's center constantly during the 1880s. They were always welcomed in a courteous, and sometimes extravagant, fashion. When a trainload of 254 people arrived in Fresno on August 17, 1881, they were serenaded by the Fresno Brass Band, officially welcomed by Judges John W. North and E. C. Winchell, and conducted through special grape displays in the town's major hotels. A board of trade was established in 1885 to better coordinate promotional ventures such as these and to advertise the county to the outside world.

Fresno County home-seekers came from places other than California as well. M. Theodore Kearney spent much of 1885 traveling through England and Germany, encouraging people to settle on the colony developments he was opening up. Moses J. Church, ever the Fresno County promoter, journeyed to Indiana in 1887 and brought many prospective settlers back with him. The county also welcomed large numbers of settlers from DeWitt County, Illinois, that year, along with a sizable contingent of Volga Germans (Germans who had established ethnic colonies in Russia).

A significant immigration wave to Fresno County began in 1881, when Hagop and Garabed Seropian purchased some orchard land. They were from Armenia, a small Middle Eastern country and the oldest Christian state in the world. Long preyed upon by the neighboring Turks, who resented their dominance in business, agriculture and banking in that part of the world, Armenians began coming to America in large numbers by 1874. (In that year an Armenian named Yanakian—or, in translation, Normart—visited Fresno, but did not stay.)

The Seropians were impressed with Fresno County. Through correspondence, they induced their brothers Simon, Kevork and Hovannes, along with Stepan Shahamirian and Bedros Bedrosian, to come in 1882. Hadgi Agha Peters and Krekor Arakelian, later prominent melon growers, came in 1883. The latter arrived with a group of approximately forty men, women and

# OF WORMS AND TURKEYS

## JOHN HYDE BRALY

From my infancy I had heard and later read about the grass-hopper and army-worm invasions—from old Bible times to the pioneer days of bleeding Kansas, where the army-worm destroyed every green thing that met its onward march; where the "grass-hoppers became a burden," obscuring the sun like a cloud as they flew through the air; where, alighting, they devoured everything green or dry; were so thick at times on the railroad tracks as to stop the trains; where they ate the paint off the cabin doors; where they even gobbled the iron shoes off the mules as the latter tried to kick away the hoppers—for which final whopper, by the way, I do not vouch.

The Fresno grasshopper and worm invasion of which I am about to tell was not as bad as that, but it was bad enough.

The worms that came upon [my vineyard] were produced from the eggs of very large moths, each moth laying thousands. They chose as the repository for their millions of eggs the underside of the leaves of wild sunflower, hogweed and grape. The eggs being smaller than the smallest mustard seed one moth could and did stick dozens of those mites on the underside of one leaf. These hatched out in a few weeks into tiny worms which began at once to eat the leaf and, growing very rapidly into maturity, they would be as long and thick as a man's finger. They then turned into the chrysalis stage, from which would again come forth other moths to repeat the process.

We had heard that worms were appearing in places in the colonies, and had seen the big moths flying about, but we had not yet awakened to the slightest apprehension.

One day at noon Cochran, our foreman, came to the bank and reported an invasion of army-worms. He told me it was serious. He said they were entering our vineyard on a line nearly a half mile long, devouring every vine in their march.

I was, of course, much excited. I told Cochran to go over to the hardware store and buy two dozen spades and shovels, hurry home with them, take a plowing team, and with all the men he had, white and Chinamen, immediately plow and cut a ditch on the west side where the worms were entering—and then get water running through it as soon as possible.

Meanwhile, I went over to Chinatown and hired a dozen or more Chinamen and scurried them off to the fight. I next went to the stores and bought all the little scissors they had, at twenty-five cents apiece.

I hurried to the schools and offered ten cents an hour to children over twelve years old to snip worms, and then I rushed off to "Martha's Vineyard" [an adjoining, infested vineyard].

When I saw that army of worms, with its frontage of nearly half a mile, slowly but determinedly moving into the vineyard; and when, on careful inspection, I found our entire vineyard infested with a myriad of eggs and worms just hatching, my excitement knew no bounds.

By dark the ditch was finished and water was flowing through it. That slightly checked the invasion from without, but all night I kept men with lanterns and shovels, instead of "billies," working against the invading worms—for, instead of turning back from the running water, they tumbled into the ditch in such numbers as to stop it up with drowned worms, making a bridge over which other worms would crawl. The men's duty was to keep the ditch clear and the water running, which, accomplished, completely checked the invasion.

But the millions of worms already hatched in the vineyard could in four weeks' time destroy it completely.

Mamma was waiting outside the house for me and for the whole story. As we talked the intensity of our feelings increased and our courage rose. Suddenly I jumped up, cracked my heels together twice, and said: "Mamma, by the Eternal, the worms shall *not* eat up our vineyard."

We had discussed every possible plan and had hit upon the Turkey—good old Thanksgiving Gobbler!—as our only hope. Yes, we would get turkeys—buy every turkey in the country.

Cochran was called and told to have Daisy and Nellie—the horses that had brought the family through the flood—in the best possible trim and harnessed to the buggy at sunrise the next morning. He was also told to prepare turkey-yards, perches and feeding troughs for the coming swarms of turkeys.

Mamma and I were off the next morning just as the sun, red-eyed, was peeping over the distant peaks of the Sierras, with only two thoughts in our minds—millions of worms, and turkeys to eat them!

We first invaded Fresno colony; drove, early as it was, to the peaceful homes and at once asked if there were any turkeys for sale, and at what price. We found that all would sell, some at one price and some at another. We took all we could get at any price—the bargains always closed with the fewest possible words and in the quickest time—and sped on to the next place....

We reached home at dark, having driven about ninety miles and bought nearly a thousand turkeys. Feeling sure we had saved "Martha's Vineyard," we laid us down and slept.

The next morning wagon-load after wagon-load of turkeys began to arrive, Cochran having everything ready for their reception.

It was truly a sight worth seeing. By night we had nearly a thousand turkeys on the place, making things pretty lively with their clacking noises.

Early the next morning the man in charge of them turned them loose in the vineyard, and the war on the worms began. It was most interesting to hear and see the mother turkeys leading their little "turks" to the charge.

In a few hours their crops were filled with worms, and they were then driven into the shade of the orchard trees, where they would spread themselves out, wings and legs, for all the world as though they were dead, remaining that way until about three o'clock in the afternoon, when their keeper would arouse them and again turn them into the vineyard.

In three hours they would again fill up on worms and be brought home, where long troughs of hot bran-mash and red-pepper would be awaiting them. They were crazy for that red-pepper mash.

Often wondering how many worms the flock would consume in a day, something happened which set us computing them. One evening a turkey the size of a chicken broiler met its death by accident, just as it was coming in with its afternoon catch. Our son Arthur opened its crop and counted out fifty-three worms (many of them yet alive), three grasshoppers, and two little grapes swallowed by accident. Seeing that this was not an average-sized turkey we calculated that the birds would each eat not less than one hundred and fifty worms a day—thus making one hundred and fifty thousand worms destroyed per day, or four millions in thirty days.

So the days passed on for a week, and the birds had been once over the vines, and this before the worms were large enough to do much harm. The next week they swept the vineyard again. In two more weeks the vines were clean and every bush was trying to outdo its neighbor in growing and maturing fine clusters of grapes.

Our flock of turkeys was now greatly in demand, so we hired them out for twenty dollars a day until our second crop of worms was ready for picking, when we brought them home for the purpose.

From that time until Thanksgiving Day, with the worms all gone, we fed the turkeys on Egyptian corn, until they were large fat birds, and, I think, the finest bunch of turkeys ever massed together in California. We sold them to a firm in San Francisco at twenty cents a pound net. And so, besides saving our vineyard, they netted us about fifteen hundred dollars clear profit.

Our family and friends who ate turkeys from that flock say, even yet, that there never were such fat, juicy turkeys as those raised on Fresno worms—which, *ab initio*, were raised on grape juice.

SOURCE: *Memory Pictures, An Autobiography* by John Hyde Braly.

children from a town called Marsovan. They made up the first large contingent of Armenians to settle in the county.

After 1882 colonization and irrigation schemes continued to proliferate in Fresno County. Perhaps the most notable was the 76 Land and Water Company, formed on June 7, 1882, by P. Y. Baker, H. P. Merritt, Charles Traver, I. H. Jacobs, C. F. J. Kitchener, Francis Bullard and Thomas Fowler. The name was derived from a cattle brand previously used in the area where the company was located. Baker got the idea to form the enterprise after droughts had forced many landholders in the upper Kings River area into bankruptcy and large acreages there became available. A $400,000 irrigation system was built by the investors to water 310,000 acres they purchased for less than ten dollars an acre. By 1884 the 76's main canal was operating and settlers were buying land at five dollars to thirty-five dollars an acre, with a five-dollar-per-acre water right.

Notable irrigation developments of this period included the Millrace Canals, built in 1882 to connect two branches of Murphy Slough on the Kings River and extend another ditch twelve miles north of the slough into agricultural land. The Ashbrook Ditch near Liberty, which tapped Cole Slough, was expanded in the following year. Nearer to the Millrace Canals, the Reed Ditch was built about this time. It was four miles long and capable of irrigating 1,500 acres.

The year 1885 saw the construction of several important irrigation works. Jefferson James built the James East Side Canal, fifteen miles long and able to service 5,000 acres. It tapped the east side of Murphy Slough for water and was later expanded to carry seventy-five cubic feet of water per second.

The Cameron Ditch, with its headgates at Patterson Slough (also on the Kings River), was built about this time, along with the larger Crescent Canal. Local settlers built the latter ditch (cost: $33,120) by organizing a $75,000 capital stock company of 150 shares, 29.5 of which were sold. A $500 share entitled the owner to irrigate 320 acres. The canal's headgate was on the Kings River and went into use during 1887. In that year Fresno County had $2 million worth of canals that could irrigate 610,000 acres of land and carry 3,500 cubic feet of water per second—a far cry from the situation of twelve years before, when the Fresno Canal system's main unit was the only important irrigation system in the county.

In the area surrounding Fresno five important colony ventures opened in the early- to mid-1880s. The 960-acre Union Colony of William Archibald Fisher began offering five-acre lots for $1,000 to $1,250 in 1883—a clear example of the increase in land values. Moses J. Church, Bernhard Marks and E. A. Braly opened a new tract for settlement in the same year. Called the Church, Marks and Braly Tract, it adjoined the Central California and Washington Irrigated colonies, was said to have good, level soil, and took up nearly ten sections of land. As with the Central California Colony, distributing ditches were built to every lot in the tract.

A one-time Bank of California tract was christened the West Park Colony and offered lots for purchase in 1884. It was situated due west of the Fresno and Central California colonies. In August 1885, M. Theodore Kearney began selling off his Fruit Vale Estate, purchased in 1883 and lying in and around today's Kearney Park. Finally, E. B. Perrin of Upper San Joaquin Canal fame began offering his Perrin Colony lands for sale in 1887. These were located mostly to the north, northeast and northwest of Fresno.

The lands immediately around Fresno were being developed rapidly. Because of this crowding, it was apparent that colonies would have to be founded elsewhere in the county. This began in 1882, when Dr. J. L. Cogswell started his Coulson Colony near Centerville. Little is known about his venture other than that it had a perpetual, unassumable water right from the Centerville and Kingsburg Canal Company. The Fowler area, circa 1884, witnessed the beginning of four significant colonies: that of Charles Lewis Walter (320 acres) and Charles H. Norris (1,920 acres), and the Sierra Park Colony of C. K. Kirby (2,560 acres) and Nye-Marden Colony (800 acres), organized by Mrs. E. M. Nye and W. H. Marden. In the Kingsburg area, two colonies were established in 1886: the Kingsburg and Kingsburg-Riverside, the latter actually closer to Reedley (see 8:7). The Malaga Colony of G. G. Briggs, near the settlement of that name, began functioning about 1882, and by 1887 the Selma vicinity had six colonies—Nebraska, Sanders, Clifton, Wildflower, Liberty and Briggs' Selma Tract.

As agriculture in Fresno County entered its adolescence, industries related to it started springing up. The development and manufacture of farm implements had reached an early stage of sophistication. Nurseries were now needed to provide the trees, shrubs and vines that were constantly in demand. W. M. Williams opened such a business in 1882, three miles east of Fresno. He offered pear, peach, apricot, nectarine, prune, apple and walnut trees, different varieties of cypress, and Chinese shade trees—to mention just a portion of his stock. Two years later Frederick Roeding, son of George Christian Roeding, opened a similar enterprise—the Fancher Creek Nursery, adjacent to the Eisen Vineyard. In 1885 Frank D. Rosendahl started another nursery near Kingsburg.

Shortly after the formation of the Washington Colony, local farmers banded together with some Central California Colony settlers to form a dairy. It was the first large-scale supplier of butter, cheese and milk in Fresno County, and was productive enough to send periodic surpluses to San Francisco for sale.

Riggs and Son, an egg distributor, carried on a similar trade, shipping 144,000 eggs to San Francisco and Oakland in a seven-month period during 1885.

Some time later, Minnie Eshleman started the Minnewawa Creamery Company on her father's Minnewawa Ranch, which had been cut out of the old Henrietta Ranch and was watered by Fancher Creek. Gifted with a keen business sense, she managed the ranch and was the first to produce high-quality butter in the county. Her methods were publicized through lectures and articles, and gained wide acceptance throughout the state. A herd of prize Holstein cows was built up at the ranch, which became one of Fresno County's true agricultural showplaces. In addition to a wide variety of conventional crops, Miss Eshleman grew olives, almonds and watermelons at her ranch when they were uncommon in the rest of the county.

Despite the advent of vineyards, interest in—and production of—other crops remained relatively stable. Wheat-growing had yet to decline. The Kingsburg, Selma and Fowler areas remained heavily planted in the crop during 1886, when the value of the county's production was placed at $2.5 million. The 76 country was described as "one continuous wheatfield," with almost all its acreage planted in grain. Hot, dry northern winds in 1886-88 damaged the crop, but Fresno County hung on to its position as the state's third-highest wheat producer. Alfalfa was another popular crop, always planted for stock feed. No farm was considered complete without a patch.

Orchard activities in the early- to mid-1880s moved away from citrus fruits to other varieties. The Burns and Hazelton orange groves continued to prosper, and Alfred Baird was doing well with oranges and Sicily lemons near Big Dry Creek. Unfortunately, the failures of previous years had diminished interest in these crops. Far more popular were apricots, then being grown in the Fresno Colony by A. O. Anderson and J. H. Harding, and Albert Covell in the Washington Irrigated Colony; peaches, which were thriving on the Gould and Barton ranches; French and German prunes, being cultivated at the Eggers, Butler and Fresno vineyards; and Bartlett pears, which the Minnewawa Ranch and Butler Vineyard were growing in appreciable quantities. (Most of the major vineyards had good-sized orchards.)

While generally not so profitable as vineyards, orchards could still provide a reasonable return for farmers. The *Fresno Morning Republican* of August 12, 1887, reported that A. C. Bryan of the Washington Irrigated Colony had received $135 for the 10,800 pounds of fruit his fifty-four Early Crawford peach trees provided. The trees were situated on a mere half-acre, which made his return comparable to what raisin growers were getting. One year before, a Mr. Robertson of the same colony had gotten a $300 per acre yield for pears—also respectable.

Another fruit that was generating some curiosity, though it did not become a major crop until later, was the fig. Stephen Mitrovich, a Yugoslavian immigrant, and Melcon Markarian began growing White Adriatic figs near Fresno in about 1884. Three years later I. N. Parlier planted a fig tree on his ranch. The tree later became the largest of its kind in the

Reference 8:7

# THE RIVERSIDE COLONY

## C. J. ANDERSON

The first Swedes came to the Riverside Colony in the latter part of the 1880's. In the decade and a half following, many more came. They had been a part of the great immigration from Sweden which took place in the latter part of the nineteenth century. Most of them had settled in the midwestern states where they took up agriculture and other occupations. Many of them came to California and to this area, while others came directly from Sweden.

They loved the sun-kissed land of this valley; a sharp contrast to their native northland of Sweden, and they were quick to realize the possibilities of the rich soil and the abundance of water from the snow-capped Sierra Nevada Mountains for irrigation. And their first problem was to construct ditches to carry the life-giving water to the arid land. And here they resolved to raise their families to love God and their country.

On 10 and 20 acres of land they worked from dawn to dusk raising different varieties of fruit trees and vines, so the families could do as much harvesting as possible themselves. There was always an acre or two of alfalfa to raise feed for the team of horses and the family cow. A flock of chickens and a pig or two were a "must." Not to be the owner of these accessories would be impractical indeed.

With the coming of the first cold weather in the Fall, the pig had to be slaughtered. The men would cut up the meat into the desired cuts, some of it to be salted down. The women industriously rendered the lard and ground the proper portion for meat balls and potato sausages. Some of the other tasty dishes were pickled pigs' feet and head cheese, which were reminders of the saying that the only portion of the hog that can not be used is the squeal. These meat delicacies were a "must" at the Christmas season's festive board, together with the traditional "lutfisk."

On Sunday, old Dobbin furnished the motive power of bringing the whole family to church. The various conveyances consisted of carts, spring-wagons, buggies, and surries. Some rode bicycles. On Sunday nights some of the young people preferred walking in groups to church, for their own reasons. . . .

On the weekly trip to town, the surplus eggs and butter were traded for groceries. As the lower bridge was built as late as 1908, we had to cross Manning Bridge, a mile further north, to get to Reedley. It was interesting to see how the purchases would come out. Those were the days of dusty, unimproved roads, button shoes, black family parasols, outside plumbing, celluloid collars, staved garments for ladies, open vehicles, eggs packed in bran or oats in a bucket, bonnets for girls, and good straw hats for boys.

The heart of many a boy was thrilled when he could accompany his dad to Reedley on a lumber wagon to deliver fruit to the market or packing-house, and to accompany him when he brought the horses to the blacksmith to have their hoofs trimmed and shod.

The working days for both men and women were both long and hard, and yet it seems that they had more time to visit with their friends and neighbors than we have today. Those days are unforgettable.

## Phantom Shelbyville: One of the Greatest Swindles That Accompanied the Boom Era

Along in 1889 a briliant idea occurred to a man who was running a theatrical show around the big Central States like Indiana and Illinois, Ohio and Nebraska. It was the boom era in Fresno County, when, as a cold matter of fact, $100 was paid in gold coin for what would bring at most $10 today.

This man, who chanced to drift through Fresno, conceived a notion to tempt people to his show with a gift lottery proposition, in which Fresno County, then springing into prominence as an agricultural country, flowing with milk and honey, was to figure. Every person who attended this show was given the opportunity of becoming the owner of a lot in Shelbyville, Fresno, Cal., which to this day [1901] is beautifully and regularly laid out on the county map as a striving city. Go out to the land and it is the most desert waste that mortal man ever laid eyes on.

The gullible Easterners argued that if they could obtain a town lot for nothing in fertile and sunny California they could either sell it outright for a good sum of money or go over and take possession of a cheap inheritance. The women took the same view and they patronized the show in every town it visited. They also acquired title to Shelbyville lots.

The theatrical philanthropist who was giving away lots thus had a good title, and he made more money out of the scheme than has any owner of a lot in the phantom town on the alkali plains. The highest assessed value that ever was placed during the boom times on a Shelbyville lot was $4, and the philanthropist collected almost that much from every lot owner for his deed, notarial affidavit and seal.

There are hundreds of such deeds at the County Recorder's office, and on many of them not even the fee of recording has been paid. The greater portion of the town site of Shelbyville is owned by the State, having reverted to it for delinquent taxes. The lots are not worth the taxes assessed against them and how little that is can be readily computed on an assessed valuation of $4, the highest value ever placed on them, with a rate of $1.25 to $1.40 on the $100. If all the taxes on Shelbyville deeded lots were paid, it would not be sufficient, and has not been to pay for the services of the deputy assessor handling or the assessment book covering Shelbyville property.

There is a town in Indiana called Shelbyville, and it may be that this gave title or name to the scheme. The printed deeds, which even to this day float into the Recorder's with inquiries concerning the value of the lots, are indorsed "Dan'l of Shelby," probably some theatrical name which may have given the name to the colossal swindle. It was a little gold mine for the speculator, who had bought the land in this county for a song and turned the title deeds on a subdivision principle loose among the confiding suckers of the East, who wanted to see his show anyhow.

So far as can be established or gathered the name of this enterprising trader and showman was Guy Webber, who described himself as of Jersey City, Hudson County, N.Y.

So far as the title to the Shelbyville land was concerned, Mr. Webber could read that title clear. He bought and paid for it, and had the deed recorded, but as to the value of the land, except for alkali and hard pan, and as a hiding place for the coyote, no man knoweth unto this day. The town of Shelbyville is in plain view from the Jameson depot of the Southern Pacific railroad, being half a mile northeast of it, and between the depot and the San Joaquin River. The site of Shelbyville covers four sections, or 2,600 acres, less half a section immediately contiguous to the depot.

The rest approaches the river and consists of the purest alkali land, on which not even a mortgage or salt grass can be raised. It is like unto the country around the Dead Sea in Palestine, where even the birds fly high in passing over it. West and south of Jameson station there is plenty of good land, within half a mile of the depot, but Shelbyville is "per se." It looms up in solitary grandeur. At one time it had a value as grazing land, but with the bringing of water for irrigation the alkali in the subsoil was forced to the surface, and today not a blade of grass is on the land.

The leanest and hungriest but self-respecting coyote or jack rabbit that wishes to cross the plain to the wheat ranches beyond will make the widest detour rather than cross the inhospitable and alkali desert, Shelbyville.

The County Recorder has at various times been deluged with inquiries as to the cash value of Shelbyville lots, some holders of title being willing to sacrifice them without ever having seen them, and of course to the advantage of the purchaser, for anything from $50 to $5,000 a lot. The number and variety of these letters is wonderful, and it is a pity they have not all been preserved and framed. Most of the inquiries came in from 1892 to 1894, but they still come in fitfully. At the same time it is to be recorded that on the site of Shelbyville, which shows up on the county maps large and square, there is not a building for which a tramp would exchange his coat, and not a foot of ground in cultivation.

It was one of the greatest and most astute swindles that marked the boom era, but the promoters have naturally justified themselves by saying that no one really suffered very much. The people who went to the show in the Central West had their fun for their money, and some of them drew two lots in Shelbyville, so that they were only out $2, with about as much again for a deed for a piece of land which was surely worth that much. It is like the old fox hunter's justification of fox hunting. "The huntsmen like it, the hounds like it, and it has never been quite proved that the fox did not like it."

—From the *Fresno Evening Democrat*, November 23, 1901.

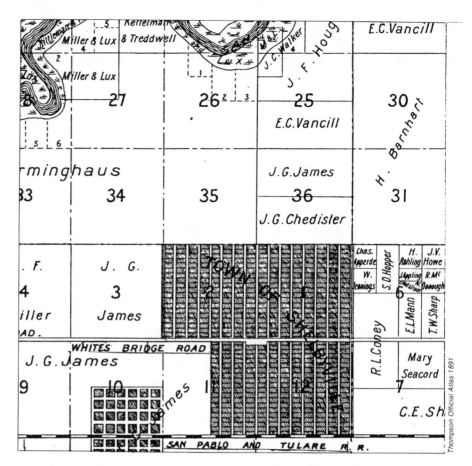

160

world. Eventually it had to be supported with a framework, and finally became so heavy that it collapsed of its own weight in 1945.

With the *San Francisco Call, Harper's New Monthly Magazine, Pacific Rural Press* and other publications extolling Fresno County's prosperity during the 1880s, along with the Board of Trade promotional efforts, a boom in real estate was inevitable (see 8:8). It happened in 1887 and was properly described by Lilbourne A. Winchell as a year of "frenzied finance." Excursion trains from San Francisco and Los Angeles arrived in Fresno daily, bringing with them a multitude of people interested in farm land. The *Fresno Morning Republican* remarked later that "real estate men just stepped out on the sidewalk to expectorate a mouthful of tobacco and sold a couple of forty-acre tracts before they could escape to their offices . . . "

The number of transactions made required the county recorder's office to add two copyists to its staff, and the magnitude of the deals themselves were often staggering. Fresno financier Fulton G. Berry sold $186,000 worth of property in five days; $1,000,000 worth of land changed hands in April alone; and unimproved tracts that had sold for $50 to $200 an acre a few years before were now going for $250 to $1,000.

Cutthroat tactics among real estate agents were common. The June 4, 1887, *Fresno Daily Evening Expositor* complained that when some agents heard that another was ready to clinch a sale, the eavesdropping agent would tell the prospective buyer that he or she was about to purchase worthless land. To make the sale firm, these interlopers were often bought off with a percentage of the transaction—and, presumably, made to promise future silence. The *Expositor* called for an end to "this guerrilla business . . . that amount[s] to little less than blackmail." One imagines that it persisted until the boom's end in 1888.

From the founding of the Central California Colony to the time of "frenzied finance," Fresno County had experienced unparalleled expansion of its agricultural industries. The bleak valley prairie was now dotted with thousands of farms, orchards and vineyards. Across the flatlands an imposing network of canals and access ditches was in place, all of which had made the miraculous agricultural growth possible. Best of all, the majority of farmers were living comfortably—some extravagantly. They had been forced to weather big problems, ranging from the Southern Pacific to tree scales, but their overall prosperity was not daunted. To say there had been a "boom year" was erroneous. It had been a boom era, and whatever frustrations and misfortunes surfaced within it seemed merely insignificant.

Reference 8:8
## BOOM FEVER

From the *Fresno Expositor*, August 17, 1887.

There is a more bouyant feeling in real estate at present than has ever been known here. Buyers are coming in from every quarter, and all bargains find ready purchasers. Many a man who has picked up a quarter or half section of land for Government prices a few years ago, and who settled down thinking to make a living for himself and family raising grain, has been confronted with an offer to purchase his property at prices so far above what he ever dreamed of its being worth that he seems dazed at the thought that he should so suddenly spring into opulence. But there is a reason for this rapid increase in values.

Fresno County's true worth is being understood. It is the one part of California where the grape grows to perfection, and the one section that can rival Spain in the production of raisins. Our people have not heretofore understood the true value of its lands. If land about Stockton is worth $200 per acre to grow wheat on, how much better is Fresno County land worth $500 per acre to grow the more valuable raisin grape. Our lands are too cheap. They are better worth a thousand dollars per acre than lands in less favoured localities are worth $300. Never will land in Fresno County be cheaper than it is now. It is now at the bottom of the ladder, so to speak. Its ascent will be marked and rapid.

From the *Fresno Republican*, April 22, 1887.

Real estate transfers are still on the increase both in number and amount of money involved. Fresno County, with a population of about 25,000, records more transfers than the city and county of San Francisco, with a population of over 300,000.

—

The daily hotel arrivals in Fresno are only exceeded by those of two other points in the State—San Francisco and Los Angeles. If this is not a very large straw, indicating the direction of the coming breeze we are badly mistaken.

From the *Fresno Republican*, April 22, 1887.

Some five years ago D. J. Vaughan, who had been a moderately successful miner at Iowa Hill, in Placer County, accepting the order of the Courts that the hydraulic mines must be shut down, gathered together so much of his worldly effects as he could convert into coin and struck out for greener fields and pastures new. Having heard of Fresno County he made his way hither, and after looking about for a time, invested in an 160-acre farm near the race track at $50 per acre [$8,000]. He paid part cash, relying on some notes and mortgages that he held in Placer County being paid in time to make future payments, but in this he was disappointed at the time, and made an application for a loan of the amount needed, and was not looked on with favor by capitalists. However, his own money came in soon, and the land was cleared of debt. This much preliminary. Mr. Vaughan has held the place for five years, made some improvements on it and also made considerable money out of the soil, and a few days ago he refused the offer of $250 per acre for his investment, or $40,000. This is more than D. J. cleared in twenty years' mining.

From the *Fresno Expositor*, August 24, 1887.

Last Saturday was an exceedingly lively day at the Recorder's office. On that day there were sixty-four instruments filed for record, viz.: One assignment, 49 deeds, two bonds for deeds, five mortgages, five releases, one declaration of homestead, and one *lis pendens*. To a man up a tree it looks as if things were lively, even if the boom has not struck Fresno. We doubt if anywhere in California, outside of the southern counties, there is greater activity in the sales of real estate.

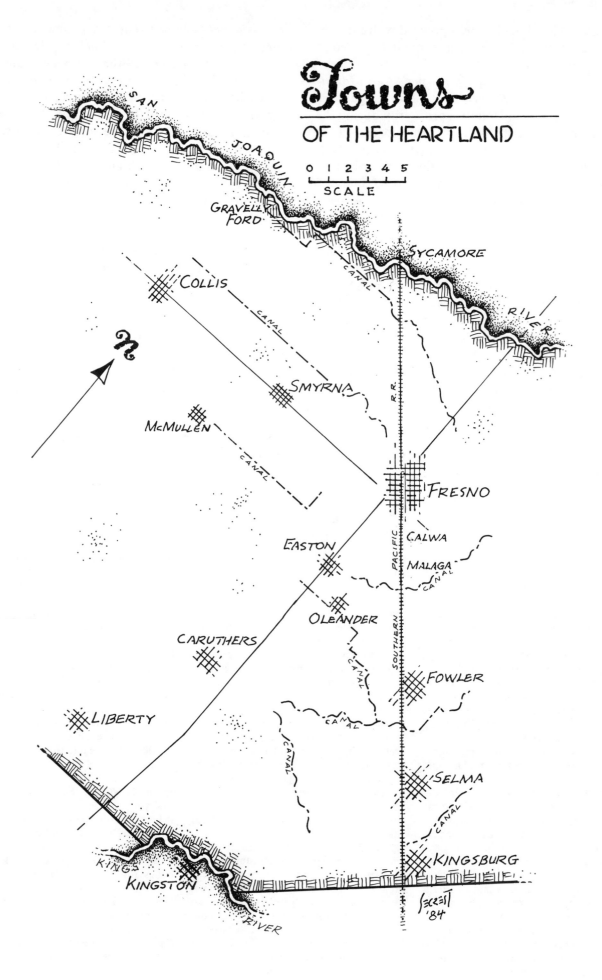

# Towns
## OF THE HEARTLAND

SCALE
0 1 2 3 4 5

SAN JOAQUIN

GRAVELLY FORD

SYCAMORE

CANAL

COLLIS

CANAL

RIVER

R.R.

SMYRNA

CANAL

McMULLEN

CANAL

FRESNO

PACIFIC

CALWA

MALAGA

CANAL

EASTON

OLEANDER

CANAL

SOUTHERN

CARUTHERS

CANAL

FOWLER

LIBERTY

CANAL

SELMA

CANAL

KINGS

KINGSBURG

KINGSTON

RIVER

SECREST '84

# Chapter 9
# The Heartland

As the introduction to this book notes, the saga of Fresno County's towns has been mostly ignored in previous historical treatises. This chapter, along with three others that follow it, represents an effort to compensate for this deficiency. In the nineteenth century alone, the county boasted many settlements with appreciable (if not sizable) populations, all of which have stories that deserve to be noted—for the sake of present-day residents, completeness of the historical record, and anyone who might be curious.

To this end, the present chapter considers "Towns of the Heartland"—meaning the central county, where wagon trails, stage routes, railroads and agriculture built up a host of prosperous communities. Later chapters will consider settlements in the county's west side, east side and Sierra Nevada regions.

Perhaps the earliest "heartland" town was the Liberty or Riverdale settlement, roughly twenty miles south of Fresno. It took its name from the earlier Spanish-Mexican hamlet known as La Libertad (see Chapter 3). This was in Manuel Castro's *Laguna de Tache* land grant but no settlement ever evolved from that. The beginnings of Anglo residency, and predominance, in the neighborhood are equally difficult to chart, but seem to have commenced in the early 1870s. On October 4, 1874, a Liberty School District was formed with its schoolhouse two miles north and one mile east of the future site of Riverdale.

Stories conflict, but the Riverdale name must have arisen from the fact that the Kings River and its many sloughs were nearby. It was attached to the area's post office, which was established by James Powell on July 1, 1875, a mile or more northeast of the present town.

By 1876 a Riverdale school had been created with H. L. Benson as its teacher. It appears to have been private, for a county Riverdale School District was established on May 7, 1878. The earlier school either ceased operating before that time, or was swallowed by the new public district.

In late 1876 a grange organization was formed by the local farmers, amid much holiday merriment. After electing its officers at Squire Thompson's house "the

members and their invited guests fell to dibbling in the yellow legged chickens and roast turkeys, followed immediately by a general hoeing down of those great piles of cake, pie and other sweetmeats so generously provided by . . . the mothers and daughters of our land," said "Sarah Jane" in the January 3, 1877, *Fresno Weekly Expositor*. The season also had featured an exhibition at the Liberty schoolhouse and a dance at George Smith's house with a Mr. Snedding providing music on his fiddle. A contemporary report referred to it as "waxing the horse-hair."

The Liberty Canal Company was incorporated in 1879 (see Chapter 8). Its works, along with those of the nearby Millrace Ditch, gave the surrounding plains a good water supply—when irrigation rights disputes did not interfere. The district began attracting many farmers, among them Abner Doble, Ben Hill, Andrew Reed, W. H. Farmer, A. Ashbrook and B. H. Barrett. Most of them prospered, and the *Fresno Daily Evening Expositor* of February 1, 1887, said that "grain grows remarkably well . . . The higher land is of the quality known as white ash land . . . and admitted to be the very best of fruit land . . . poplar trees set out from cuttings on Cottle and Luce's place two years ago are now from eighteen to twenty feet high."

Stock-raising was still the mainstay of a few people in the vicinity, notably Cuthbert Burrell (see Chapter 6), but raising hay, alfalfa and miscellaneous fruits had become popular as well.

Though everyone around was busy tilling the soil, cultural concerns did not go neglected during these times. "Rev. Mr. [T. H.] Bauder will preach here next Sunday . . . Rev. Mr. Reams will lecture on temperance on the 3d of May . . . We have a Band of Hope with 47 members; a good Templar[s] lodge with 21 members [both being temperance groups]; also Sunday-school every Sunday, and preaching every other Sunday," said an April 23, 1884, *Fresno Daily Evening Expositor* story.

After 1882 a local dairy business started in earnest. A January 25 report of that year, in the *Fresno Weekly Expositor*, said "[it] will do well here. As dry as everything is at present, those that are making butter cannot complain, and the butter is of good quality." The same newspaper noted on April 25, 1883, that "butter making has commenced in earnest." A Mr. Hill had recently sold several of his milk cows, for which he realized good prices. In 1890 a full-scale creamery opened (see Chapter 15), and by 1894 Job Malsbary and J. Turner were operating regular dairy businesses.

For the grand sum of $600, the Liberty school was expanded in 1882. A Mr. Tiffany taught there in 1883, and Alice Shepard in 1899. In the latter year, the Riverdale school had Alice Applegarth as its teacher. Each school had an average attendance of twenty students during this period. Joining these older districts were the nearby Crescent, formed on May 7, 1886 (presumably named after the area's canal system), and the Summit Lake on May 5, 1887, with A. W. Eddy as its first teacher. The Summit Lake district was absorbed by the Crescent on April 5, 1889, but was reorganized on March 2, 1897, with Amelia A. Meyer as its "new" first teacher. It was again annexed to the Crescent district in 1900, after the district apparently ceased operating.

As did Firebaugh, the town of Kingston formed its nucleus around a ferry—L. A. Whitmore's. He established it circa 1854 on the town's later site, apparently with no official sanction; his first ferry license was issued on April 2, 1855, by the Tulare County Board of Supervisors. The minutes describe his ferry as being "two miles downstream from Crumbly Ranch," an obscure and unremembered landmark. (The site of Kingston lies opposite the Kings River from the town of Laton.)

On November 7, 1855, the supervisors authorized Whitmore to map a county road from "where the Slough leading from Tulare Lake joins the San Joaquin," to Whitmore's ferry and along the east side of the Tulare Lake to Fort Tejon Pass. All of these locations were in Tulare County at the time. On the same day, the supervisors gave permission for I. S. George and T. D. Maltby to lay out a road from Elkhorn Creek to Visalia, on the most direct route practical. The road was never built, but George became Whitmore's partner in the ferry enterprise.

When the supervisors convened again, on February 3, 1857, they issued a license for Whitmore and George to operate a ferry together from December 12, 1856. No indication was given for this retroactive arrangement, but it was obvious that the ferry was the one at Kingston. The license location was given as "at this Ferry on the Kings River"; no others seem to have been operating at this time. At the same February 3 meeting, the supervisors agreed to build a road from Visalia to the Whitmore-George ferry, because of popular demand. It is uncertain how long the partnership endured, for George's name is not found in records after this date.

Whitmore's wife was a Yokuts Indian, and it was because of her that he lost his life in early 1859. Kings River settlers had been rounding up local Indians and placing them on reservation lands (see Chapter 2), and Whitmore's wife and children were to be included. Apparently he was out of the ferry business by this time, for the Sacramento Union of February 10, 1859, noted: "L. A. Whitmore, formerly owner of Whitmore's Ferry on Kings River was recently shot in his own house by Dr. Workman, one of the leaders of the lower Kings River anti-Indian men, backed by ten or fifteen of his party for no other cause as yet known than to gratify the evil passion of a mob . . . "

Following Whitmore's death, the ferry property was sold at auction in July 1859—perhaps to James E. Denny, who is known to have owned the ferry sometime around 1859-60. In turn, Denny sold the ferry to Oliver H. Bliss; the exact transfer date is, again, unknown. Bliss appears on the 1860 U.S. Census as a Kingston resident and "ferryman," but he may have been leasing the property from Denny.

February 6, 1860, the Kingston School District was formed. According to educational historian John Dow, Kingston "was the first public school in Fresno County to receive state apportionment [$1.73 in 1862-63!], to operate continuously under state terms, and to employ a qualified and credentialed teacher."

The original district comprised much of the county's southeastern quarter. Among its first teachers were two county schools superintendents, E. S. Kincaid and H. M. Quigley. The Fresno Weekly Expositor of January 31, 1877, had this to say about the school: "Mr. [G. W.] Keran [its teacher] has charge of some twenty-five or thirty little ones in a school building which might be made much more attractive by the judicious expenditure of a little money, for better furniture than that now in use, and a couple of coats of paint for the outside . . . " Despite two reductions in size, the district existed in 1899 with Uriah Bock as its sole teacher. It had managed to outlive the settlement that had spawned it.

Other school districts of the area were the Lake (formed on August 9, 1865) and Lillis (February 4, 1896). Early teachers of the districts were Ann W. Morton and May McCardle, respectively.

Although Kingston obtained a post office on November 17, 1859, it grew little in the following decade. Until 1866 there was little other than the ferry and stage station. Bliss, the owner, seems to have had big plans for the town. He leased 800 nearby acres from Jeremiah Clarke in 1865 (purchasing them in 1871), and had the town surveyed and platted in late 1870. In 1869 he built a simple bridge, made of lashed-together planks, across the Kings. It was the first of several, since the unruly river was prone to washing any poorly constructed bridge away. By 1872 Bliss had built a pontoon-type bridge "by means of two boats and additional planking," said the September 4 *Fresno Weekly Expositor*. It thus afforded "travelers an opportunity to cross the river without delay, in low stages of water as well as high."

In addition to Bliss, who eventually opened a livery stable, the town's earliest businesses were Moses Fleishman's store, managed by Launcelot Gilroy; another store operated by Levi S. Sweet and Company; William G. Sanderson's and L. Reichert's hotels; and John Abbott Davidson's medical practice. Later on, in 1873, Gilroy and Charley Coe clerked at a store that had been opened by Centerville merchant Elias Jacob. Louis Einstein, later of Fresno mercantile fame, was another clerk there. The store was eventually linked by telegraph to its Centerville counterpart, a remarkable innovation for those days. By 1876, there were a few new local entrepreneurs: H. F. Sloane had a store, with Ed Erlanger serving as his clerk, and a Mr. Hanks and Mrs. G. N. Furnish were operating hotels.

Despite its partial isolation, Kingston was not lacking in social activity. The Methodist Episcopal Church South held large revival meetings near the town in September 1870 and again a year later, attracting crowds of several hundred each time. A small tent city was set up each time for the gatherings, and a restaurant was maintained for the ardent faith-seekers.

Also popular was a racetrack built by William Sanderson in early 1872. Foot and horse races were conducted at the mile-long track, which became a fixture of some importance. A Kingston Jockey Club was eventually formed, and the purses for some events were considerable. The May 15, 1872, *Fresno Weekly Expositor* reported that Harry Weaver and Addison Henning had engaged in a foot race for sixty dollars, and the March 12, 1873, issue mentioned that a $500 horse race was to be held on April 23. The local horses expected to be entered included Henning's "Bullet Neck," N. W. Randall's "Stonewall Jackson," J. T. Kennedy's "Mare" and Buck Randall's "Scissors."

Outlaw Tiburcio Vasquez's bold raid on Kingston brought statewide notoriety to the town in December 1873 (see Chapter 11), but it languished afterward. Bliss sold his properties on April 1, 1874, to nearby rancher John Sutherland for the then-considerable sum of $30,000. Others began leaving the community; it shrunk to such insignificance that its post office wsa transferred to the Sans Tache station on June 30, 1890. Wallace W. Elliott's 1882 Fresno County history explained the town's demise succinctly: "[Since] the railroad has been completed through the valley [Kingston's economy being based on stage and horse-and-buggy traffic], its glory has measurably departed."

Seven miles northeast of Kingston, a more enduring town came into being during 1873. A few months earlier, the Central Pacific railroad had laid its tracks outward from Fresno and through this point (see Chapter 7). Officials decided that a switch at this location would be useful, so they called it King's River in honor of the nearby waterway. Substitute names for this "official" designation, Draper(s)ville and Farleyville, were used locally—honoring two early area settlers, Josiah Draper and Andrew Farley.

A post office was established on June 24, 1874, with the name of Wheatville, but changed to Kingsbury in November of that year—probably to honor Sanford Kingsbury, a Pacific Improvement Company clerk. In February 1876 the post office was changed to Kingsburgh—perhaps to honor the nearby river again, perhaps because it was a little easier to say—with the "h" being dropped in January 1894.

Draper, Farley and Thomas Cowan, Sr. were the first settlers in the area that became the town, arriving in late 1873. Grain was already being shipped from the switch; forty-eight cars of wheat from the Grangeville area were moved out that year. Plans had been made to locate a large railroad roundhouse and yards there until—so one story goes—Leland Stanford saw the impressive Easterby Ranch and decided to build at Fresno instead. Nevertheless, King's River Switch could boast of a twelve-by-fourteen-foot, one-door, one-window private school in 1873; a hotel run by Farley, with Simon Aaron's store in its basement; and a saloon with a competing store owned by Simon Harris (see 9:1).

The following year saw the establishment of Charles Endicott's blacksmith shop; another hotel run by Draper and his wife, "Aunt Lida"; a Wells, Fargo office with Harris as agent; a post office run by Farley, who received twelve dollars yearly for his services; and a wooden, twelve-by-sixteen-foot railroad station, with I. A. Marshall as its first depot and express agent.

Throughout the late 1870s Kingsburg grew little; the 1880 census recorded a population of eighty-eight. With agricultural activity focused mainly around Fresno, the March 8, 1876, *Fresno Weekly Expositor* noted that there was still much vacant land around Kingsburg. The important events of this period were the formation of a public school district on May 3, 1875; the town's first major fire on July 14, 1877, which consumed Aaron's store and Hugh Dolch's saloon; and the arrival of entrepreneur Solomon H. Loomis, who served as the town's barber, painter, paperhanger, gravedigger, undertaker and cabinetmaker at different times.

When a black barber moved into town one day and began providing competition, Loomis began advertising free haircuts. This rough example of discrimination, all too common at the time, succeeded: the new barber soon had to move out of town. Yet the sign stayed up and people kept asking for free haircuts. To them Loomis responded, "What? Do you think I'll give you a shave and a haircut for nothing?"

As farming ventures began to fan out from Fresno in the 1880s Kingsburg grew, more than tripling its population by the decade's end. Railroad lands were snapped up eagerly in 1881 and the boom year of 1887 saw the Wristen, Erickson and North Kingsburg tracts added to the town. Lots in them were priced from $30 to $150. The *Kingsburg Herald*, cranked out by R. Wheeler on an old Washington hand press, began publication in 1888 and lasted for two years. Draper Street, the town's main thoroughfare, was made as wide as Market Street in San Francisco in anticipation of people and increased traffic that never arrived.

A sizable migration to the Kingsburg area took place in 1886, when Andrew Erickson and approximately fifty Swedish families arrived from Ishpeming, Michigan. The Swedes wanted to settle in a prosperous farming community. Erickson, acting as advance agent for the group, had been much impressed with the Washington Irrigated Colony and the farm of Frank D. Rosendahl, another Swedish immigrant, nearer to Kingsburg. According to the *Fresno Weekly Expositor* of December 8, 1886, most of the families came with $5,000 each, and the newspaper commented that "their enterprise will do wonders toward developing the great fruit growing industry in this section of the valley."

The grain-shipping business increased enough for three warehouses to be built in Kingsburg during the early 1880s. One was owned by the railroad and two were in private hands, with a total capacity of approximately 10,000 tons. Even with that holding capability,

farmers were often unable to store their crops; the town was the busiest wheat-shipping point in Fresno County. This kept Kingsburg's economy strong throughout the decade.

During the eighties Einstein, Gundelfinger and company of Fresno, S. Davis and Company and R. B. Clark conducted general merchandise businesses; George Bunch and Jolly and Johnson had butcher shops; Dr. J. F. Burns, A. C. Mayfield and Mrs. W. W. Scott, at different times, conducted drug and variety stores; and W. T. Garner had a fruit and vegetable store. Kinchloe and Shafer and G. W. Harris ran saloons—the town had a complement of three during this period. The Axtell, Welch and Ward hotels opened up to compete with the Draper, or Temperance, establishment. In 1887 the Kingsburg Improvement Company, a town mercantile association formed to erect commercial buildings, built a $10,000 brick hotel (the Kingsburg or "Brick") that overshadowed the other operations.

The blacksmith trade, vital to any frontier town, was served by A. Bariau, the Borchers brothers, and C. J. Clark; A. T. Butler and Levi Garrett had livery stables; C. H. Davis a wagon- and carriage-making shop; and Deane and Garner a saddlery shop. There was at least one doctor in town (R. M. Osborn) and a law and real estate office also was in operation. The Valley Lumber Company had a yard, Wehmeyer Brothers operated a planing mill and furniture store, and an agricultural

Reference 9:1

## WHAT WAS KINGSBURG LIKE BACK IN THE GOOD OLD DAYS?

What was life like in Kingsburg in 1875?

It was frontier country in those days and life was rugged. A picture of Kings River Switch, the little crossroads later to become Kingsburg, is given by Jake Harris, who with his father operated the Harris general merchandise store, in stories in early editions of the Recorder.

In those days grapes and peaches were unknown and one day when a Chinaman from Visalia who had been to Fresno with a load of fruit passed through here on his return he still had a bucket or two of peaches in his wagon. With alacrity Jake made a dive for the peaches and made away with a handful before the Oriental had an opportunity to voice his disapproval. In those well nigh fruitless days they were like apples of gold on platters of silver to Jake's palate, said the Recorder.

The population had little to amuse itself with and the arrival and departure of trains (two a day, both at night) was an event which always "brought out the usual bunch of fellows." Woe be to the luckless traveler who chanced to stop off for he was sure to be hailed by the crowd with shouts of "free bus to Draper's Hotel." What made it so funny was the fact that the little log structure that went by the name of hotel was just across the

corner and less than half a block away.

In those days there were no wells and water was hauled from Kings River with the roads so rough that much of it slopped out of the barrels before reaching its destination. Lem Harp was engaged by the elder Harris to dig a well at the location of the Ideal Grocery at $1.25 per foot. An abundance of water was hit at 17 feet and that was the first water well in Kingsburg.

Meat was a luxury and a rarity. One day Harris asked a trainman to bring him a piece of meat from Stockton and he would pay him for it. The trainman did as requested. But there was no ice and when the meat arrived the Harris family buried it rather than ate it. "However, once in a while Andy Farley would kill a sheep and divide it up with his neighbors and everybody would have fresh meat for a while."

Harris said that one might suppose that operating a store would not be profitable. But it was. Every little railroad station was like an oasis in the desert to the sheep and cattle ranchers and grain growers scattered from the foothills of the Sierras to the foothills of the Coast Range. It was not unusual for these people when shipping their stock or grain from the Kingsburg depot to stop in at the Harris store and lay in a supply

of nearly everything they needed for a period of three to six months, their bills running up into the hundreds of dollars at a time. Invariably the purchases were in cash; credit was unknown and unexpected. There were no towns off the railroad and customers would come from a radius of 50 miles.

The depot was actually just a rude platform where freight and express were unloaded to which the owners might come and help themselves.

The valley was barren country. There was no irrigation in the Kingsburg district and no trees. There were no tall buildings to obstruct the view and John Forney, who came to Kingsburg in 1883, said that on a clear day from atop a building in Kingsburg one could see the buildings in Fresno. In the dry summer months the powdered ground of the hit or miss roads winding across the plains here and there caused horses or vehicles to throw up clouds of dust which could be seen for miles. In this way people always knew when some one was approaching the village.

SOURCE: *Kingsburg Recorder*, November 18, 1954, p. C8.

166

works was run at different times by E. M. Morgan and Lemuel Harp.

Kingsburg's growth was reflected in the formation of the nearby Clay and Eschol school districts on June 9, 1880, and the steady growth of its own school. Professor Landrum Smith and his wife conducted the Kingsburg school, housed in a three-room building, in 1887; they were successors to Professor W. A. Sanders, J. W. Traber and Mrs. D. H. Smith.

With the possible exception of Fresno, no Fresno County community had a more intense development of religious institutions than did Kingsburg in the 1880s. Methodist Episcopal and Methodist Episcopal South churches were established in 1884; the latter burned down in 1887 and was soon rebuilt. Holiness and Baptist congregations also were founded about this time, only to move away by 1887. A Mission Covenant Church was started in 1886, conducted at first by the Reverends Carl Anderson, Jacob Danielson and J. F. Gilberg. It organized a Sunday school in 1891 and changed its name to the Swedish Mission Christian Church in 1896, when the Reverend A. Hollner was pastor.

On September 6, 1887, the Swedish colonists from Michigan organized the Concordia Lutheran Church —the first Lutheran church in the San Joaquin Valley—with the Reverend A. Anderson as its first pastor, succeeded by A. M. L. Herenius (1889-1893), and Dr. P. A. Mattson (1893-1900). The Swedish Methodist Episcopal Church began in 1888, when the Reverend J. H. Andrews of San Francisco organized a religious class of six Kingsburg married couples. The Reverend E. G. Rosendahl was the first formal pastor of this congregation in 1888-89.

Community organizations thrived in Kingsburg during these times. There were active Knights of Pythias and Good Templars lodges in the early 1880s, the latter of which had 100 members in 1887. There was also a literary society which, according to a January 12, 1881, *Fresno Weekly Expositor* report, had recently discussed "the momentous metaphysical question of the relative powers of the male and female brain . . . we have philosophers in our midst who do not hesitate to grapple with questions which Locke, Cousin Hamilton, and other famous mental giants failed to decide." There was also an orchestra that gave regular concerts and a town hall (the Harp and Ball) where club meetings, dances and other social functions were held.

For the less sophisticated there was horse racing, and the May 31, 1882, *Fresno Weekly Expositor* said this about a recent track event: "One young man present, after betting all his money, bet his hat and boots, and walked hatless and bootless over the ground offering to bet his breeches against six bits that his favorite would win the race. The race was won by Confidence and Elmer saved his wardrobe, besides winning a pocketful of money."

The 1890s were a time of prosperity, misfortune and assorted small happenings in Kingsburg (see 9:2). On the favorable side of the balance sheet, a bank (the Bank of Kingsburg) was established on November 7, 1891. Sinon C. Lillis was its president and W. S. Hopkins its cashier. A raisin-packing house was in operation by 1893, under Lemuel Harp's supervision. The Kingsburg Cooperative Packing Association, formed on September 10, 1896, opened a packing house that succeeded that operation and was later part of the California Raisin Growers' Association cooperative.

Some new businesses had been established by this decade. A Mrs. Flewelling ran a millinery and dressmaking shop (later sold to two women named Larson and Davidson), D. T. Ward was the town jeweler, news agent and telegrapher, and John Forney was the local agent for Victor bicycles—a relatively new invention selling well in 1896. Phone service between Kingsburg and the Laguna de Tache land grant was established by 1895, and the Sunset Telephone Company offered service to other points in 1898. A footnote of interest: the town had a postmistress, Lucille Morgan, from 1894 to 1898.

Nationwide depression and a series of fires tempered Kingsburg's progress just before the century's turn.

Reference 9:2

## KINGSBURG COMMOTIONS

Some weeks since W. S. Hopkins, our bank cashier, in trying to catch a chicken with a 32-calibre Remington succeeded in perforating three inches of picket and scanting, the slug passing on plowed a little trench in the street and veering to the right broke a window pane, split the air just above Mr. Farley as he lay on his bed, penetrated the partition and reached the home base in the next room. As soon as Mr. H. found that no one was hurt he hastened to return the borrowed gun and is of the opinion that boys ought not to be allowed to discharge fire arms in the village . . .

On Tuesday last our butcher Ed. Poulson, attempted to kill a beef with a very dirty gun. The bulls went wild and so did the cow. Rushing upon her assailants, she unhorsed Poulson's man, George, goring the horse in the breast and nearly killing the animal. Meanwhile Ed. could not assist his man, as his own horse was bogged in the Kingsburg-Centerville canal, in which he had taken refuge and from which he was rescued with difficulty. Finally the men got away, came to town, cleaned the gun and renewed the battle, bringing down the "critter" at the eighth shot on a 200-yard range.

On Thursday a strange dog that had been stopping upon his own invitation with A. C. Bryan for a few days, became rather too familiar with that gentleman by pressing his teeth into the flesh of his leg. The compliment was returned with the old shotgun and a few jolts across the head from the heavy end of a singletree [an iron crossbar used with harnesses] for emphasis. Familiarity not only begets contempt, but often something more substantial. The treatment given the dog they say, broke him entirely of his bad habit . . .

SOURCE: As above, on p. 1445, taken from *Fresno Daily Evening Expositor*, June 26, 1893.

Farmers and merchants were dispossessed of their property, and the Bank of Kingsburg moved to San Francisco in October 1895 for want of business. As for the conflagrations, a later *Kingsburg Recorder* account mentioned that "a person leaving Kingsburg in 1890 and returning in 1895 would hardly have recognized the town . . . whole blocks were swept away in a single night." All four of the town's hotels were destroyed—the Temperance in a December 18, 1896, fire and the opulent Kingsburg on July 22, 1898. The latter blaze also did away with the lumberyard, Salvation Army barracks and a few private residences, at a loss of $20,000.

Kingsburg's school, in early 1890, employed three teachers and served 120 students. It regularly closed the school year with a program put on by the students and a grand picnic, but one wonders how pleasant a place it really was. When a circus came to Fresno County and schoolchildren talked about cutting class to see it, an unsympathetic teacher threatened to give zeroes to anyone absent that day. Later on, in 1898, a Miss Maxwell resigned her teaching position at the school "owing partly to indisposition [sickness] and partially to the unwarrantable treatment received from the principal," according to a January 30, 1898, article in the *Fresno Morning Republican*. Joining the Kingsburg School District in 1892 was another—the Harrison Joint Elementary District, which was formed on March 9.

Churches and church-related activities assumed great importance in this phase of Kingsburg's history. The Swedish Methodist Episcopal Church, Kingsburg's fifth church, was formally incorporated on December 1, 1891, and wasted little time in erecting a church building. The Methodist Episcopal Church South had ladies' and youth societies that gave "entertainments" frequently. The women served election day dinners at the Kingsburg Hotel, held sewing and social bees, and conducted what was called a "hard times soshul" for the church parsonage's benefit in April 1895. Charles Flewelling and Myrtle Roberts took first prize for best costumes at the event: sackcloth and ashes. At the church itself, an activity took place on January 27, 1897, that most houses of worship would forbid today: "The occult mysteries of astrology are being most opaquely expanded by an ancient sage at the M.E. church south. The reading or horoscopes is quite marvelous," according to a *Fresno Daily Evening Expositor* report.

For those with less pious inclinations, Kingsburg offered many other fraternal and recreational pursuits in the 1890s. There were regular dances and balls held at the Kingsburg Hotel and another town hall, Maxwell's. Some parties were held at private homes. The *Fresno Morning Republican* of January 30, 1898, said that "a shadow social was given at the home of Mrs. Lena Draper Saturday evening last. The young men

bid on the shadows of the fair damsels, and each man who secured a shadow was entitled to escort that 'shadow' to supper."

The town literary society, which had lapsed into oblivion, was revived about 1898 and tacked "debating society" onto its name. A Kingsburg Rifle Club and an Epworth League had been organized by 1893, and an Independent Order of Foresters lodge was added in early 1897.

Athletically-oriented citizens built a bicycle-racing track in 1896–97; "A. B. Loomis is the champion on furlong heats, while J. F. Forney acknowledges no peer at one-fourth mile or more," said the January 27, 1897, *Fresno Daily Evening Expositor*. A baseball team was organized about this same time. When the new century arrived it was apparent that Kingsburg, commercially and socially, was a place destined to remain on the map.

The agricultural development that allowed Kingsburg to progress so well figured heavily in the development of two hamlets to its west—Wildflower and Caruthers.

Wildflower, eight miles west of Kingsburg, had a short and uneventful history. It was founded circa 1876 and was nicknamed the "Duke Settlement" for reasons now unknown; its proper name probably came from someone's observation of the native flora. The earliest residents were mostly grain farmers, although a February 12, 1879, *Fresno Weekly Expositor* report mentioned that 2,000 apple, peach, apricot and pear trees had been set out recently. Instead of relying on dry farming, the nearby Emigrant Ditch was available later for irrigation purposes.

Until the boom era of 1887, land was cheap because of Wildflower's relative isolation. An 1883 report mentioned that parcels reachable by irrigation still were available for ten dollars an acre: "The land is level and of such composition that water running around a 40-acre lot, by means means of percolation and a capillary attraction will make the tract as prolific producer independent of rain."

The Duke School District was organized on January 3, 1877, to serve the Wildflower area. Its first trustees were Clark Joplin, John Yeargin and A. B. Atwell; Ella Guard and Edith Carpenter were among its earliest teachers. According to one student, Maggie McNamee Leavelle, the school was at Clovis and Clarkson avenues and burned down in 1885, at a $500 loss. Classes were then shifted to a church, where one schoolteacher—for seventy-five dollars a month—taught sixty-five students spread over nine grades.

A Wildflower post office was inaugurated on June 21, 1878, possibly by the area's premier merchant—P. D. Jones. By 1879 his store had $12,000 worth of merchandise and a large adjoining warehouse, and had been joined by a hotel operated by James Flood. Few other entrepreneurs came to join Jones; the 1894

The ranch and residence of Elisha Harlan, Riverdale, circa 1880. The post office was housed here before it was moved into town. As dairying developed in the area the town promoted the title of "Cream City."

J. B. Welsh's hotel in Kingsburg circa 1881 when only ninety people lived in the town.

The first business in Caruthers was John J. Truman's store, on the right, which also became the post office in 1892. On the left is John Lot's saloon.

Fresno Almanac

Fresno County directory lists the town's businesses as his store (where the post office was located), William McElroy's blacksmith shop and dairies operated by William Dickinson and Joseph Minghetti.

Diptheria struck ten or more Wildflowerians in 1879, but the epidemic did not daunt the town's spirit for long. The Duke Literary Society was formed about that time for the purpose of debating scholarly and political issues. On March 8, 1879, the members discussed whether "might, not right, rules the world," according to the March 19 *Fresno Weekly Expositor*. "The affirmative gained the question . . . The society also publishes a paper, devoted to mirth, comical advertisements, and side-splitting puns." Unfortunately, one reason for the group's formation was the discussion of the new California constitution—and when that issue lapsed, so did the society. A Good Templars lodge, sixty members strong, was founded in 1881 and a baseball club functioned during the 1890s, but apparently not even these social amenities could prevent the community from sliding into obscurity. On June 21, 1898—exactly twenty years after the post office's founding—it was transferred to the nearby Conejo branch, and Wildflower officially ceased to be.

As Wildflower declined, a newer settlement—Caruthers—was on the rise, helped by the fact that it lay on the Southern Pacific's Los Banos-Armona route. After the tracks angled southeasterly at Collis (where a small station was put into service eventually, in 1892), they came through a region near the home of sheepman/grain farmer William "Billy" Caruthers—roughly ten miles northwest of Wildflower. Although the ranch was connected to the outside by a twice-a-week stage that ran to Kingsburg, Caruthers recognized that the railroad would be a bigger boon to his bailiwick. Grain farmers in the area—Caleb Dickerson Davis, Ben Barritt, George Forsyth, George Prather and Caruthers—were in need of a shipping outlet. Caruthers, in 1888, decided to go after it by offering the Southern Pacific a half-section of land. He proposed that the railroad establish a station named Caruthers on the site, offer town lots for sale there, and give him half the proceeds. The plan was accepted and John Mills was dispatched as the first agent.

The local grain interests were so anxious to have warehousing facilities that two were built before a switch and siding could be installed. By hauling lumber in from Fresno, Costigan, Cohen and Company and the Grangers Bank of San Francisco got their storage quarters up promptly. Jess Walden and Denny Donovan, in that order, were the first managers of the facilities. According to Caruthers historian Laura Wickham Sinclair, "Teamsters from [Kingsburg] drove their ten-horse teams daily into Caruthers during the harvest season, sometimes coming as late as ten or eleven at night. The warehouse had to be opened so the wagons could be unloaded and started again on the homeward trip . . . When the wagons arrived in the daytime, the local children would beg for rides, thinking it great fun to ride on the swaying high seats of the grain wagons."

The warehouse construction encouraged Fresno's Valley Lumber Company to open a branch alongside the tracks, with H. A. Adams as its manager. There was no hotel or boarding house for Walden, Donavan and Adams to stay in when they first arrived—they had to stay with the accommodating Caruthers family. The situation was remedied when Mr. and Mrs. Apoleon Kanawyer opened the town's first hotel, a two-story edifice, in 1892. It was sold to George Sutherland in 1893 and, assuming it was the same structure known as the Pioneer Hotel, was sold to Joseph Gibson in 1897 and was refurbished extensively.

Caruthers obtained a post office on August 25, 1892. Joe J. Truman, the town's first storekeeper and resident, also served as the first postmaster. H. A. Adams bought out Truman several years later and inherited the postmaster's job as well. A man named Marks is said also to have operated a store—unsuccessfully—in town. Other businesses included Jim Williamson's blacksmith shop, D. E. Lawton's Star Saloon and Joseph Gibson's saloon and restaurant opposite the depot.

The town school district was launched before the post office—on February 29, 1892. Either Edith Clark or Ella Vanderburgh was the first teacher. School was first held in a small structure used as a community hall. The Methodist Episcopal Church South also used the building until it could build its own church. Funds were collected for that purpose by two traveling ministers from Tennessee; one ran off with the money, and fund-raising had to resume amid much sheepishness on the part of the church leaders. A church was built eventually, and monthly services were conducted. Local adherents of the Baptist faith worshiped at Chicago Hall, meeting-place of the grange organization, at Elm and Conejo avenues.

Caruthers residents enjoyed a number of recreational pursuits in the 1890s. Weekly dances attracted people from as far west as Elkhorn, and as far east as Kingsburg. Blue-rock shooting tournaments, using mechanical birds, were the rage in 1896, and the April 12, 1897, *Fresno Daily Evening Expositor* noted that a "sciopticon-phonographic exhibition" (equivalent to a narrated recording paired with a slide or filmstrip show) was to be held in the village. Nor was the comical lacking in the town's early years, as the March 20, 1896, issue of the same newspaper noted:

Mrs. Bert Beall of Riverdale challenges the world as lady pedestrian. She is teaching music at Caruthers and started on her bicycle for Caruthers a few days ago. Mrs. Beall is not a small woman by any means and as the wheel was a safety only in name it broke right in two in the middle when Mrs. Beall was eight miles from home and she had to return home afoot. Mrs. B. will give the horse his place hereafter when she wishes to make long journeys in teaching.

East of Caruthers and northwest of Kingsburg, settlements on the main Southern Pacific tracks—Selma, Fowler and Malaga—were growing and prospering. Selma, which ultimately became the most important of the three, was founded in 1880. Early in that year, four area farmers—Jacob E. Whitson, E. H. Tucker, Monroe Snyder and George B. Otis—began pleading with the Central Pacific to establish a non-agency station and siding. The first pair wanted the station on lands Whitson claimed and Tucker had been given an interest in, near the intersection of the Centerville and Kingsburg canal and the railroad tracks. Snyder and Otis favored a site they had claimed southeast of the Whitson-Tucker property.

It was finally decided that the Whitson-Tucker plot was better. Snyder and Otis obtained an interest in it, the railroad was given a strip of land inside this parcel, and the Selma townsite was born. It was surveyed by Caleb Dickerson Davis in June 1880, with the first auction of lots held by the town's fathers on the twenty-sixth of that month (see 9:3).

Commercial and educational developments already established in the area necessitated Selma's founding. There was a railroad section house and workmen's quarters nearby, built in 1872. The Frey brothers, immigrants from Switzerland, had built a mill powered by the Centerville and Kingsburg canal in early 1880. At the town's birth, it was served by three nearby schools—the Valley View, Canal and Franklin—all established on May 7, 1878. The first-named school was eventually moved from Selma's outskirts into town, on a lot donated by the Frey brothers. The Central Pacific opposed the move, and timbers it owned were necessary to transport the schoolhouse

across the Centerville and Kingsburg canal. To accomplish the task, citizens had to "borrow" the necessary materials while the section boss was visiting in Kingsburg on railroad business. Along with these enterprises and schools, two religious congregations were functioning in the neighborhood—Presbyterians and United Brethren, who began holding services in 1878 and 1879, respectively.

Continued controversy has surrounded the naming of Selma. The first name proposed by the town's fathers was Whitson, for obvious reasons. It was scrapped because the railroad already had a Whitney station and the names sounded too much alike. Irwin, after Governor William Irwin of California, was then proposed, but was dropped when the railroad said it had an Erwin station. At this point it gave the founders their choice of four names: Dalton, Weymouth, Sandwich and Selma, the last chosen because the Frey brothers said it was the name for a "beautiful, amiable, sweet-tempered maiden" in their native country. But how did the railroad get the name in the first place?

In later years a woman named Selma Gruenberg Lewis said that her father, an adviser to Central Pacific founder Leland Stanford, had shown her baby picture to Stanford. He was suitably impressed, so the story went, and had the name put on the list of possibilities. A more credible tale, remembered by separate witnesses (Mrs. Lewis was the sole source for her story), was that the name was suggested to honor Selma Michaelsen Kingsbury—wife of the Sanford Kingsbury mentioned previously. Unfortunately, research has not proven this story or discredited the other.

During what was left of 1880, Selma barely grew. At the year's end it could boast of only a grain warehouse on the railroad reservation, I. Brownstone's general store (built on a lot donated to him by the town founders, who badly wanted a store in their midst), a hotel run by W. D. Read, and Rhoades Hall—actually a saloon—operated by Andrew J. Rhoades. A post

Reference 9:3

## AN "EXCURSION"

### GEORGE B. OTIS

The plans of Mr. Tucker were to have an excursion and a public sale of lots. As the trains were to stop at the new station when the switch was laid and the little box of a depot with no agent was erected, Mr. Tucker thought the sale would be a good introduction to the world.

The date was set forth on the posters and the train neared the stopping place, the hopeful quartet of town daddies, clad in their best, were on hand to show where the future solid blocks of buildings were to rise. The one deputized to hawk off the lots at a good price, was ready to mount a wagon and with lusty voice proclaim to the further limit of the great crowd that would sure come on the train—that the "First choice of lots" was

now offered at auction—"make your bids gentlemen."

The train stopped—the expectant crowd must have been slow in alighting, in fact it did not get off—it was not there to get off.

The engineer rung the bell and with one tiny little toot, to the wee city on the plains the four hopeful ones were left to still own their lots.

A. Barieau, farming one mile east had been a harness maker and he took a lot and put up a box 8x10 and a skin of leather was left by the train on the depot platform.

Mrs. W. S. Staley has a photograph of the postmaster, J. E. Whitson, standing in the door of his store and postoffice. He at first carried the entire mail in his pocket and

the photo gives a vivid comparison with the necessities of the surroundings.

Frank B. Burton opened a modest little hotel where the present planing mill is and Barieau bought a car load of lumber and sold it out for cash while he stitched the hide into harness.

W. D. Reed was building the flour mill for the Frey Brothers and he built the house recently torn down and removed from the Vincent block, as his residence and it was followed by the first smith shop, after Reed had finished framing the mill. The shop was across the street from where Isaac Townsend has his iron shop now.

office was established on August 12, with Whitson as postmaster and sole mail deliverer; he kept all his office equipment in a cracker box. There were intermittent social activities, too; the Frey brothers held a ball at their flour mill on July 20, and a town literary society was organized on November 27.

Selma's development in earnest began in 1881. That year saw the erection of another hotel (Nat Johnson's Commercial), two blacksmith shops, three saloons, a livery stable owned by Tucker, a wagon maker, a harness shop, a shoemaker, a baker, a saddler, a milliner, and seven more stores. The Fresno County directory for 1881 reported that there were more than 100 buildings in town, and the population was approximately 200. Other indications of growth could be seen in the establishment of Knights Templar, United Workmen and United Woodmen lodges; the founding of two new school districts nearby, the Walnut on May 3 and Prairie on May 4; and the addition of Methodist Episcopal and Christian congregations to the community.

A Congregational church group was added during the following year, as was the Terry school district on May 4. Selma also gained its first newspaper—the *Weekly Free-Lance*, which operated in September and October before expiring—and lost its Valley View Hotel, express office, tinsmith's shop and post office to a December 9 fire. The loss was a then-considerable $15,000, and it left the town's main commercial avenue, West Front Street, devastated.

As the town progressed through the 1880s and early 1890s it began to develop a fair share of amenities. A good-sized railroad depot was completed in January 1884; by 1887 it was among the five busiest shipping points in the southern San Joaquin Valley. The station burned in 1887 but was quickly replaced. More than 2 million pounds of raisins left it in 1892 alone.

When a crude switchboard was set up in T. R. Brewer's drugstore in the fall of 1885, Selma obtained its first telephone service. The exchange connected only five local businesses at first. Service to Fresno was made possible in 1889, and to San Francisco and Los Angeles the following year. A reading room association, which operated a small library, was formed on February 25, 1888, the same year a board of trade to promote town interests was started.

Competing waterworks, owned by D. A. Dunbar and a Mr. Buckland, began serving Selma in mid-1887 and were consolidated on July 1, 1889. The operation was later known as the Selma Water Company. M. G. Elmore organized the Selma Gas and Electric Works in June, 1889—it offered only gas service at first, provided by a coal-fired plant—and Charles M. Blackman began providing electricity on a regular basis on February 20, 1893.

Property in the young town was becoming increasingly desirable. When local developer J. G. S. Arrants platted a twenty-acre subdivision to Selma in 1886, he expected to realize $600 from sales and got $6,700 instead. More town lots were laid out in the next year; depending on location, prices ranged from $150 to $500. Settling in Selma was a risky business, though.

Reference 9:4

## SELMA'S HOUSES OF REFINEMENT

### J. RANDALL McFARLAND

Boom towns of the West possessed curious characteristics. Literally thrown together on frequently unlikely sites, their populations had not had time to establish deep community roots. Ways of life, most generously called crude, were routinely endured. At the same time, the pioneers who threw aside their pasts for futures on usually unproven ground were often of intellect. Newspapers, books and magazines were avidly read. Entertainment was what the settlers could concoct, or that which was on the live stage. In Selma were two institutions which insured that the finer things in life were not passed by.

These were the Unger Opera House and the Whitson Hotel. Located diagonally opposite each other at Second and Whitson streets, they allowed Selma to assume proportions of cultural pretentiousness many times its size, creating moments and memories of magic.

Of the two, the opera house came first and endured the longest, but for a few fleeting years the two were in concert. Between them,

an insatiable thirst for the nation's finest drama and actors and an appreciation for excellence in hotel accommodations were awakened in Selma.

The Whitson Hotel was among the West Coast's finest hotels. It was conceived in the summer of 1887 when Selma's boom was at its peak. In September, J. E. Whitson bought out his partners and commissioned the hotel's construction, at a cost of $52,000. All 100 rooms in its three stories on the northwest corner of the intersection were finished with redwood and hardwood floors. All had electric call bells, and running water was piped to the upper floors. Guests entered on the corner through elegant plate glass doors. Nothing in southern Fresno County was so plush as the hotel's parlor, reading room, billiard room and elegant bar. The dining room was large and grand enough to double as a ballroom. The ground floor was shared with other stores and offices.

At the front desk was the Whitson's register in which all guests, including those enjoying a meal, were asked to sign. The big black

book quickly became the town's social register, elaborately listing all theatrical companies and private parties....

There were grand nights in the ballroom, with the register telling of dinners and dances large and small. The Christmas season of 1889 was a particularly busy one with social dances before the holidays and a masquerade ball at the Unger on Christmas Eve, with dinner, at the customary stroke of midnight, in the Whitson. Such occasions were the equals of the finest hostelries anywhere, and it was only the morning's light over the still-demanding land which could break the spell.

Dawn of the 1890s, however, came up troubled and grey. J. E. Whitson may have seen it coming for he managed, at least on paper, to more than recover his massive investment with sale in February 1891 of the hotel and 350 of his remaining lots. After the big fires, the heart of downtown Selma had migrated across the tracks and there, in mid-1890, the $27,500 Hauptli building at Mill and Second streets was opened. It also had a hotel, which began serving guests in Sep-

Fires from 1885 to 1889 wiped out sizable portions of the city, and the lack of a regular fire department put every building in town at risk.

The first fire of real importance struck on September 20, 1885, when the pioneering Brownstone store and several vacant buildings burned at a loss of $20,000. Blazes on May 28 and June 18, 1887, hit businesses along West Front Street—the Louis Cohen store (both times), the Gem and Missouri saloons, E. E. Shepard's law offices, the local justice court and a variety store. Mrs. H. L. Bailey's ice-cream parlor burned on September 15–16, 1888, along with the Diederich blacksmith shop and the post office—the third time the post office had been hit by fire.

A February 25, 1889, conflagration destroyed the Renfro House, St. George stables and other businesses. Additional fires on August 6 and 16 wiped out the *Selma Irrigator* newspaper, the Cohen, Rosenheim and Barieau buildings, the Cohen block and many other businesses. (After setting up shop at the nearby *Selma Enterprise* offices, a reportorial wag from the *Irrigator* remarked: "Today's issue may be somewhat scorched, but others will be better.")

The organization of a fire department was imperative, and was accomplished on August 29, 1889. It was financed through a fifty-cent tax on each $100 of assessed valuation. August Young was the first fire chief, replaced one week later by H. P. Gay, and there were fifty-six charter department members. On their first call, only a bucket of water was needed to quench the flames they found at a private residence. They provided more intensive service when fire hit the German Hotel on December 16, 1889, and the *Enterprise* office on June 16, 1890.

To serve Selma's growing population—which shot from 1,000 to 1,837 between 1887 and 1890—many new businesses were formed. J. H. Say opened his two-story Renfro House on May 22, 1884, with a formal ball. The German Hotel was opened in February 1887, the opulent Whitson Hotel (see 9:4) in mid-1888, and the Hauptli building and hotel in late 1889. The number of saloons went from four in 1884 to six in 1889, with all of them doing a brisk trade. When Nick Tischer's Star Saloon burned in 1889, he reopened hurriedly—in his basement!

In the boom year of 1887, the Bank of Selma opened for business with John A. Stroud as its president and D. S. Snodgrass its cashier. It was set up with $100,000 in capital stock, 60 percent of it held locally, and in 1891 moved into a substantial $7,500 brick building. On May 19, 1892, the *Fresno Daily Evening Expositor* remarked that Selma now had seven general stores, two "family grocery stores," two clothing stores, two large lumberyards, a planing mill, a raisin packing house (established in 1889), five blacksmith shops, two butcher shops, seven hotels and five livery stables. The flour mill was still in operation, having been purchased by Christian Bachtold in 1886 and greatly expanded. Some $50,000 had been spent to erect brick buildings. No longer a tentative settlement on the plains, Selma was building itself to last.

Two newspapers were established in Selma during the 1880s. The first, the *Selma Irrigator*, commenced publication on April 3, 1886, and was prosperous enough to start publishing daily on March 15, 1888. Democratic in politics, it was owned by Walter T. Lyon, nephew of the *Fresno Daily Evening Expositor*'s J. W. Ferguson.

To give the *Irrigator* some in-town, Republican competition, Jacob Whitson, S. J. Mathews and C. J.

tember 1891 as a boarding house and two years later as a first class hotel. Smaller, it had less overhead, and for its guests was more convenient.

Under a succession of owners the Whitson reeled. J. E. Whitson apparently still held enough paper that the depression, followed by the hotel's closure in 1894, proved to be a personal financial disaster.

It was suggested in 1896 that the hotel be made into a business college. The hotel housed Selma High School's classes in 1896 before the high school building was completed.

More lasting was the enjoyment created by the two opera houses which bore the name of Charles Frederick Unger, a native of San Francisco who first came to Selma in 1881. He was a rancher, drayman, building mover and bookstore operator; but for 35 years, his was the name Selma connected with entertainment.

Most boom towns could claim an opera house, to play to the tamer side of those whose lives were frequently tough and always rough. Unger, in the fall of 1888, took possession of the popular local assembly facility known as City Hall and moved it from the site it had occupied since built in 1881 at Second and Tucker streets. Its new location was on the east side of Whitson Street just below Second Street.

It was an opera house in name only. The building was simple and of frame construction. An addition was built for an expanded stage, to be 20 feet deep with a 20-foot arch. Six standard sets of scenery were prepared.

On Nov. 28, 1888, final arrangements were made and that evening at 9 o'clock the Riggs Theatre Orchestra opened a ball with a grand march, ushering in a new era in Selma's social life. Supper was served at the Whitson Hotel, not yet open for business.

Unger's first playbill was that of Dec. 19, 1888, when the play, "The World," was presented. In the years which followed, the opera house's unpretentious boards were trodden upon by the best of Broadway. First of these, on April 12, 1889, were Tyrone Power and his wife, Ida Burroughs. Frank Mayo, later a New York star, played the Unger on December 3, 1889, in "Hamlet" and again January 27, 1890, as "MacBeth." A few days later another future Broadway star appeared with the Stanley Burlesque Company. Henry Chanfru was already known as a fine actor when he played in "The Arkansas Traveler" Oct. 17, 1889. Greatest of them all was the Shakespearean actor Edwin Booth who played on the Unger stage May 25, 1889, he of a family of classical actors and brother of President Lincoln's assassin. There were other great shows, such as "Uncle Tom's Cabin" in 1890 and 1892; and an old-fashioned medicine show by Texas Tom's Concert Company on Feb. 19, 1889.

They were drawn to Selma not by the crude facilities, but because the road shows could try out in Selma for a night seeking favorable reviews in Fresno papers, with the cast comfortably accommodated in the Whitson. . . .

SOURCE: *Centennial Selma.*

173

Walker started the *Selma Enterprise* on June 23, 1888. It was published as a weekly save for a brief spell in 1888 (during an election season) and in 1889-90, when it appeared daily. The newspaper ran into trouble in 1890, when it was discovered that political candidates were buying its "silence" for prices ranging from twenty-five to seventy-five dollars.

After this embarrassment, the *Enterprise* was sold to Victor I. Willis, who served as its business manager and chief executive. His wife, Loretta Melissa Willis, directed "editorial policy" and was the newspaper's sole reporter. She helped further the cause of many civic and community organizations during the 1890s and ranks as the most important woman in early Fresno County journalism.

Education continued to hold an important place in Selma's development. It was necessary to erect a new two-story, three-room Valley View schoolhouse in mid-1884, and in 1888 a bond issue had to be passed to enlarge that structure. The Fruitvale and Atlanta school districts were formed near the town on May 5, 1885, and May 9, 1888, respectively. A private high school offering college preparatory courses was founded in Selma in 1885—an important step, since the only other county town with a high school was Fresno. The school folded in 1886 when Principal Samuel N. Burch ran off with Lillie Buckley, one of its teachers.

Selmans were left without a high school until August 29, 1892, when the Selma Union High School opened. Charles J. Walker, principal of the Valley View school, was appointed head of this new institution and kept his old job as well. The high school had been voted into existence the previous February 27, and was supported by a tax of sixteen cents for each $100 of assessed valuation in the school's district. Its enrollment doubled in three months, and the school offered no fewer than twenty-two distinct courses to its students.

Religious bodies continued to proliferate in Selma down to the turn of the century. The town's Congregational group established its own church in 1883, only to disband about four years later. Other early congregations began building houses of worship: the United Brethren in 1884, the Methodist Episcopal group in 1886, and the Cumberland Presbyterian Church in 1888. New congregations were being established as well, among them the First Baptist Church (1885), the Seventh-day Adventists (1886), Saint Joseph's Catholic Church (1888, served by visiting priests until 1913), the Evangelical Colony Covenant Church (1890) and Harmony Christian Church (1896). (The Harmony Christian Church's structure, still in use, can be seen today at Selma's Pioneer Village.)

As something of a testament to Selma's growth, two churches moved into the town from neighboring communities: a Methodist Episcopal Church South from Wildflower in 1886, and Saint Luke's Episcopal Church from Clifton (Del Rey) in 1888. By 1892 Selma could count ten churches in its midst, with a combined membership of approximately 500.

Like most other Fresno County towns, Selma had a healthy complement of special and fraternal organizations. Perhaps the most important were the Masons, who formally organized on October 24, 1884, and moved into an imposing temple in 1890. Additional organizations founded before Selma's incorporation were the Independent Order of Odd Fellows (September 27, 1883), Grand Army of the Republic chapter (an organization of Union Civil War veterans—March 1886), United Ancient Order of Druids (August 1887), Native Sons of the Golden West (June 1887), Knights of Pythias (1888), Woman's Christian Temperance Union (1889), and Independent Order of Foresters (1890).

Selmans could choose from many entertainments in these days. Dr. Hiram S. Shelton formed the Selma Brass Band in April 1885, which gave many well-attended concerts. A baseball team was formed in the same year; it played its first game against Kingsburg on June 1 and lost 40 to 8. An interdenominational young people's group was formed in 1889, and in the same year the Selma Fair Grounds and Race Track Association opened a horse racing track that proved popular for four years. Prize fighting, held in an arena behind George Owens' saloon, was popular in 1891 until a police raid (and fines given to the spectators) put a damper on such activities. Another place that provided recreational refuge was Stroud's Pond, a 160-acre lake created when the county water table rose. John A. Stroud equipped it with boats, picnic tables and a bath house.

As the year 1893 began there was agitation to incorporate Selma. Some saw this as a maneuver by Prohibition elements in the town, so that municipal anti-saloon ordinances could be enacted. Others saw it as a way to clean up the streets, which were always filthy, and keep them from becoming lakes in the winter. Eventually a petition was sent to the county board of supervisors, which put the proposal to a March 4 election vote. On that date Selma became a city by 124-54, with Christian Bachtold, C. M. Kilbourne, T. R. Brewer, William P. Graham and J. E. Whitson as its first board of trustees. The corrugated iron shed that housed the fire department doubled as city hall. Under these austere circumstances, the city's first-year revenues were $4,165.94 and expenditures, $2,824.46.

True to the expectations of some, the new government began the next year installing rain gutters and filling in low elevations to correct drainage problems. A few still thought such actions were negligible and incorporation was an unnecessary frill. One Selma resident, P. W. Corbley, went so far as to get a "disincorporate Selma" bill passed in the California Legislature. Under the measure, which gained approval, only one-quarter of the city's voters were

*Selma's main business district in 1887 was on West Front Street and included a saloon, a confectionery and a couple of unmarked buildings. Several people were willing to get in the picture on a winter day.*

*Iron Irrigator Windmills were an early Selma product, an outgrowth of Charles M. Blackman's Selma Foundry and Machine Works. He also made dynamos after using one in 1892 to launch the first electric light service in Selma—the second in the county.*

*Office of the* Selma Daily Irrigator, *with J. J. Vanderburgh (in front of door), his wife and the newspaper staff, in 1896 just after he bought the paper but before it reverted to a weekly. Walter T. Lyon founded the newspaper in 1886.*

*In 1897 the $5,000 plant of the Selma Creamery Association was completed with a cold storage plant and equipment to make butter and cheese. C. H. Schmit, the manager, was from Denmark.*

*Frank Dusy and wife, Catherine. He was a pioneer sheepman whose sheep once grazed where Fresno now stands, the first photographer of Fresno County, noted Sierra explorer and early day civic leader. Photo taken in November 1873.*

*The Dusy home near Selma, considered the most beautiful home in the county when built.*

*This mill was built four months after the original mill burned in 1896.*

SELMA FLOURING MILL.

*The old Saint Ansgar Lutheran Church which was located at Manning and Bethel avenues. It is now part of Selma's Pioneer Village.*

*Wagonloads of wheat await unloading at Selma railroad station at corner of East Front and Second streets.*

*Valley View School, first built in 1884 with addition of 1888. The number of students indicates the rapid growth of the city and the emphasis on education.*

*In 1889 Selma's newly organized fire department proudly display their new equipment. Note most volunteers have acquired uniforms.*

*Header cutting grain between Kingsburg and Selma in 1882. Kingsburg was then the major shipping point of wheat in the area. The young lady brought lunch out for the crew—or just wanted to have her picture taken.*

needed to approve a petition for a disincorporation election. Corbley apparently got the required number of signatures and placed them before the board of trustees on May 3, 1895. When the envelope supposedly containing the petition was opened, it contained only two blank pieces of paper. Corbley cried sabotage—which his opponents must have committed—and demanded an election anyway. The trustees demurred. No actual petition had been presented to them.

Few civic improvements were made in the 1890s. Pacific Bell announced plans to compete with the established Sunset Telephone Company in 1895, and secured permission from the trustees to open another exchange, yet nothing came of the plan. Blackman's electrical works, plagued by storm damage in September 1896 and a dynamo burnout the following November, was shut down in September 1897 for lack of customers. Frank L. Keller started a new system in November 1898 that was later taken over by John T. Chick of Sanger, who ran a similar enterprise there. A few months later T. B. Matthews and J. G. S. Arrants revived Selma's gas works, which had been shut down for some time.

Selma in the 1890s was a conflict-ridden town. Different groups asserted their rights from time to time and got a large share of the townspeople upset. In 1893 and 1894, Salvation Army members created a few ripples when they played their musical instruments on the street. They were defying a municipal ordinance—aimed at them, and intended to stop horse runaways and the like—forbidding them to do so. A trial was held for one of the law's violators in February 1894. His defense was that he was following the will of God, which automatically superseded the laws of men. The jury's will superseded the Lord's and returned a conviction. The ordinance stayed on the books for many years.

Another municipal problem erupted later in the year, when an "industrial army" of 180 men—protesting increased mechanization in that year of depression and unemployment—visited Selma. The men were permitted to camp on the city's south side and were well-treated, but city officials were worried that they might incite a riot. By beefing up the city's police force and forbidding public speeches, nothing got out of control. The "army" departed peacefully.

Prohibitionists caused a stir in April 1895 when they induced city trustees to approve a measure forbidding the consumption and sale of alcoholic beverages in Selma. The measure, unique in California at the time, did not stick. Prospective and established saloon owners soon challenged its authority, and the city sheepishly granted a few liquor licenses in late August. The Woman's Christian Temperance Union remained a powerful force in Selma, however. It was joined by a Prohibition Club on June 28, 1898, and an Anti-Saloon League in November 1899.

One problem that refused to leave Selma alone was fire. An April 22, 1893, blaze on East Front Street ruined the Jarrett building, Commercial Hotel and some stores; the Cumberland Presbyterian Church burned on April 7, 1894; and the Frey-Bachtold flour mill, so prominent in Selma's history, was destroyed by fire on December 19, 1896.

The business climate in Selma remained good during the economically turbulent 1890s. A dairy association, cyclery, broom factory and confectionery, all established in 1895, helped bolster the town's economy —as did the Coalinga oil boom of the same time (see Chapter 12). Beginning with the Producers and Consumers Oil Company in 1895, many west side oil companies made Selma their headquarters. It was a commercial center, a source of well-drilling and other equipment, and had better transportation facilities than the bleak oil country. By 1899 the Home/Blue Goose, Selma, Hawkeye, Alaska, California and Colorado, Elwood, Anglo-American, Farmers, Elkhorn, Landon and Tidal Wave oil companies were operating in Selma, and had helped the local bank's deposits exceed $1 million.

The town's two newspapers were also fairly prosperous at this time, although the *Irrigator* had to return to weekly status in late 1896. They were both sold during the 1890s, the *Irrigator* to John Jay Vanderburgh in 1896 and the *Enterprise* to John W. Aiken and F. G. Gill in 1899.

With the addition of a new school district (Central, southwest of town, on March 5, 1894), P. F. Adelsbach's night school for adults in 1897, and a kindergarten in 1899, Selma had rather comprehensive educational facilities for a town its size. Yet they remained inadequate to some extent. The steady increase of students at Selma Union High School and the Valley View School prompted the latter to evict the former from the building both used in December 1895. The high school conducted classes in the vacant Whitson Hotel until a new McCall Avenue campus was completed in 1897 for $3,990. It featured a lecture hall/auditorium, library, laboratory and several classrooms—all in one building—and was opened in time for the fall term's start on September 13.

Athletic and other recreational activities continued strong in Selma throughout the 1890s. The high school football team trounced its Fresno counterpart on December 25, 1894, and also in a January 1, 1895, rematch that 2,000 people attended. Interest in the sport was so intense that R. T. Staley organized a Selma Football Club in September 1896, when the high school decided not to field a team for the season.

Baseball also was popular, with one town team being organized in October 1897 and another, with semi-professional status (the Selma Dudes), set up in 1899 by T. R. Brewer. Activities of a more cultural nature were not always available at this time. The town's Woman's Christian Temperance Union reading room was closed for want of patrons in November 1895, although there was enough support to found a Wednesday Literary Club in 1898.

The Selma Brass Band lost its financial backing in 1894 and was replaced by two others: the Selma Juvenile Band in March 1898 and the Selma Cornet Band of E. S. Reichard in September 1899. In *Centennial Selma*, J. Randall McFarland relates the following anecdote about the former band:

> The boys became fairly accomplished musicians, and had some lessons in business. Some concerts they played in Fresno brought $25, but in Selma the rate was usually $5, and the boys had once found themselves rewarded with sodas instead of promised money.
>
> It was because of this that the band got involved in a heated political feud in September 1898. A concert was scheduled on the little bandstand on the southwest corner of East Front and Second streets. The Republicans, at the same hour, planned a large rally two blocks to the west at the Whitson Hotel. When no one showed up for the rally . . . V. I. Willis investigated and found a thousand people listening to the band. He offered the band $5 to play for the GOP rally, which he moved to the bandstand. Then, the boys learned Willis planned to pull the old soda payment switch. The band pulled up stakes and moved to Second and High streets, followed by the entire crowd. Willis fumed and wrote scathing criticism of the band, which had so successfully played on.

The town of Fowler owes its name and existence to State Senator Thomas Fowler (see Chapter 6). A cattle raiser in the area, he decided to obtain shipping facilities for himself and his neighbors sometime around 1872. The Central Pacific, Fowler's constant ally, was happy to oblige him soon after its Fresno County tracks were built. By 1874, and probably before then, there were cattle pens, loading chutes, sheep-shearing corrals and a siding at Fowler. Sheepman Frank Dusy (see 9:5) and cattle rancher Jefferson James, along with the senator, were among the first to take advantage of the railroad's largesse.

Reference 9:5

## FRANK DUSY

### J. RANDALL McFARLAND

Frank Dusy—miner, agriculturalist, photographer, soldier, patriot, oil promoter, quarry developer, sheepman, social activist, horse trader, lawman, mountaineer, explorer, sportsman, irrigationist, inventor, businessman, brickmaker, adventurer, fraternal brother and family man.

Frank Dusy from his youngest years thrived upon rebounding from personal misfortune with the promise and adventure of a new life. He developed a boundless energy which, even when his parents died at an outbreak of cholera when he was but eight years old, sustained Dusy. His parents were French-Canadians and Dusy had been born in Melbourne, Ontario, in 1836. Says the 1882 History of Fresno County, "In early life he was bound out under English law for seven years to learn the shoemaker's trade, but disagreed with his master before the term expired and ran away to New Hampshire at the age of 11 years and worked as a farmer's boy." Dusy also learned the quarrying business while in New England—after having told a judge he would merely run away if returned to the shoemaker's work.

How Dusy came to California is a subject of some historical disagreement. Nearly all sources, including the 1882 history of the county and the late, eminent historian of Selma, Ernest J. Nielsen, say Dusy came to San Francisco by steamers and isthmus crossing in Panama from Boston, arriving in San Francisco on Oct. 4, 1858.

In any case, Dusy quickly migrated to the Mother Lode and met with above-average success in mining, according to some sources. Others say his experiences in Tuolumne, Stanislaus and Mariposa counties cost him

"$200. and nine months hard work." Dusy did not stay long in the mines as a prospector but turned to supply for a short time, engaging in the produce business.

Always a man of progress, Dusy next became one of the state's true pioneers in the new art called photography. It was an untried industry, but Dusy put it to work, lugging a huge camera on a pair of pack mules with a portable darkroom where—according to an intimate friend, the late William H. Shafer of Selma—Dusy sensitized his plates and developed them on the spot. Many historians feel Dusy's greatest work was his photography, first in Fresno, Mariposa and Merced counties. Certainly, his picture of Millerton in about 1870 must rank among the most historical, no other photos of the old Fresno County seat having survived.

Either on a war patrol chasing two rebel guerrillas or engaged in an antelope hunt in the same area—leading historians disagree—Dusy observed oil seepages in the sandy hills of Vallecitos Canyon, 10 miles south of present-day Coalinga. Dusy is often credited with having discovered the oil-laden land, but the historian Latta states others were engaged in some work in the same area as early as 1861. It was, however, Dusy along with John Clark, Charles Strivens and W. A. Porter who filed possessory claims on 160 acres of black gold land on Dec. 16, 1864. The oil, when taken to Millerton, caused quite a stir in the usually quiet, original county seat of Fresno. But without experience, tools, refineries or markets, Dusy and his partners quickly sold their interests to the San Joaquin Petroleum Company. . . .

It was in the latest years of the 1860s that Frank Dusy came to the plains above where Selma would later thrive. Only in those days there were no towns, no trees, no canals, railroad or settlement. Grasslands with winter feed on the open range only suitable for sheep grazing existed and it was into that business that Dusy next turned. At first he worked as camp tender for William Helm, visiting camps and furnishing supplies to the herders. It gave Dusy the opportunity to learn the sheep business.

When the opportunity arose to secure a squatter's camp of a cabin, well and small corrals from a sheepherder moving to a site near Parlier, Dusy bought the crude facilities. It was government land and the sale merely involved possession. Unfortunately for Dusy, the site (in the section southwest of the present McCall and South avenues, three miles north of Selma) was an odd-numbered section and included in the Central Pacific Railroad land grant. Years of litigation later were to result. Dusy's sheep business quickly grew and he began the annual practice of summer migration with his flocks which later resulted in vast exploration and discoveries in the Sierra, as the sheep ranged in the mountains.

When rails of the Central Pacific Railroad reached what was optimistically designated Fresno City in May 1872, Dusy immediately took advantage of the improved transportation and loaded the first freight ever to be shipped from the new station, wool, onto the cars directly from his wagons. The "city" he found consisted only of the railroad construction crew's tents.

Dusy's sheep business did not eliminate

179

Between 1878 and 1881, Fowler's sole resident was a turkey rancher named John S. Gentry. According to Ernestine Winchell he sold "bottled and plug goods" to the sheep and cattle drivers who came by, and watered their horses for twenty-five cents per drink. (The price seemed exorbitant, but the water had to be pumped by hand.) Gentry's store and cabin consisted of two crude, whitewashed buildings described as having "no floor, no roof worth mentioning, and the walls would not compare favorably with the average hen coop . . . "

Things began improving in 1882. Agricultural activities were beginning to dominate in the surrounding countryside, so A. B. Armstrong built a grain warehouse that was joined by two others soon afterward. The railroad, noticing that there was no major shipping point between Fresno and Selma, built a handsome depot that summer. Fowler's townsite also was platted at this time, and an auction of railroad lots was held in August. These developments induced Gentry to add a second story to his glorified chicken coop and call it Gentry's Hotel. Earlier, in May, he had begun operating a post office with rural free delivery. The lack of settlers in the area, however, put the post office in jeopardy. Gentry urged his townsfolk (all ten to twenty of them) and more distant neighbors to write as many letters as they could, lest the government discontinue the office.

When the Pacific Improvement Company ran an excursion train from San Francisco to Fowler in 1883, it sold $11,000 worth of property in a one-day land auction. The town quadrupled its size (to about 100 residents) and even got a private day school going, with Eva Beckwith as its teacher. A public school district, the Princeton, was established nearby on May 4, 1883, and a year and two days later the Fowler School District was organized. Its first classes were conducted by Rose Beckwith in the depot until a $1,500, one-room schoolhouse could be built. Cecelia Williams was hired as the first permanent teacher; the staff expanded to three by 1899.

An October 8, 1884, *Fresno Daily Evening Expositor* report said that Fowler had two stores (one operated by a man named Spofford), a saloon and a livery stable in addition to the aforementioned businesses. Its first

---

other pursuits. In the 1870s, he made several trips into Nevada and returned to the valley with bands of 300 or 400 horses to be sold. For a time, in one of his least-chronicled experiences related by his son to Latta, Frank Dusy was a deputy sheriff of Merced County. Wearing the badge, the account goes, Dusy had one of his near-fatal experiences.

In 1872, Deputy Sheriff Dusy was trailing the legendary bandit, Tiburcio Vasquez, who was in the midst of his reign of terror across the generally lawless San Joaquin. Tracking the Vasquez gang to a small two-room shack on Cottonwood Creek southeast of present Madera, Latta says, Dusy approached on foot, apparently unarmed and was captured by two of the Vasquez gang who took him to the cabin. The bandit, pleased at a lawman so easily delivered to him, invited Dusy to dine with him. After dinner, in the other room of the shack Vasquez determined to rid himself of Dusy and drew a long knife, rushed at Dusy who pulled a revolver hidden in his boot and struck Vasquez over the head. Dusy threw himself against the side of the cabin, breaking through the boards. While fleeing toward the nearby creek, bullets fired by Vasquez's men found the mark. One, said Latta's account, struck him and lodged where it rested for 15 years. He ran to his horse despite the wound and made a clean escape.

Dusy's sheep operation continued to grow. By 1877 he was able to report 73,643 sheep had been sheared at his headquarters, by then removed to Fowler's Swith, in the just-concluded season, an average of 1,800 a day by his Chinese labor.

In the summer months, Dusy retired to the cool upper elevations of the Sierra Nevada where his sheep had the freedom of feeding on lush vegetation. The region along the drainage divide between the San Joaquin and Kings River was the Sierra domain. Dozens of mountain features were discovered and named by Frank Dusy as he searched for new grazing lands. He is believed to have been the first white man to view and explore the untamed regions of the upper Kings River area, particularly on the north fork. Headquarters was at Dinkey Flat on Dinkey Creek, so named by Dusy when his pet dog, Dinkey, was killed by a grizzly bear at the stream.

Greatest of his discoveries and explorations was Tehipite Valley, in 1869. Dusy was exploring pastures along Crown Creek. He shot a bear and the wounded animal ambled rapidly along a small trail. Dusy gave chase and saw the hulk of the bear disappear on a roll. Approaching, no bear could be seen. Instead was the majesty of the Tehipite Valley. Dusy, upon exploration, became stranded overnight on a narrow crevice and a major, day-long struggle up nearly vertical cliffs was required for what seemed to be an impossible escape. Dusy's report was the first to be made to the public regarding the inspiring canyon which is still so inaccessible. The 1882 county history says an entrance to the valley other than an Indian trail was discovered in 1878 and, quoting Dusy, claims "the trail must have been made at least 20 years before by white men, as trees had been felled by axes and other evidences of white men's work were noticeable. In the valley were found remains of a campfire and a grave on which stood a pair of boots, mouldering and crumbling with age." In 1879, Dusy first photographed the canyon. . . .

For all of his adventuresome spirit, Dusy became domesticated in 1873 with his marriage to Catherine Ross. He built for her a log cabin at Dinkey, their summer home, and bought more land, this for a home in Section 6, Township 15 S, Range 22 E, just southwest from the old Prairie School and cemetery at what are now McCall and American avenues near present-day Del Rey.

Dusy was becoming more of an agriculturalist. In the valley, he had seen the railroad slowly start to bring change to the land, putting in the past the day when his shack just north of modern Selma was the only building between Fresno City and Kings River. Said the Fowler Courier on May 26, 1894, Dusy "naturally looked with disfavor upon the coming in of settlers upon his sheep range, but when he saw they were going to come anyway, (he) quietly and wisely disposed of his sheep and settled down to a new order of things, and began taking a very active part in all enterprises for the advancement of the country." Actually, Dusy was still running sheep in the Sierra each summer, but on his lands upon the plains he had planted wheat, which he soon supplemented with alfalfa, corn and tree fruit. . . .

The plains were being made to come alive with water. The Fresno canals were long established and, after 1878, the Centerville and Kingsburg branches were beginning to spark intense cultivation in the southern parts of the county. Most of Dusy's holdings were in between, generally along the highest portion of the sandy plain. Irrigation was the answer and Dusy jumped to the lead to help create a new artificial stream.

In 1882 Dusy filed a claim for 1,000 second feet of Kings River water to be run in a canal along the top of the "ridge." C. L. Walter, a Fowler pioneer, recalled in 1908 that "there was quite a discussion as to what the name should be, the Dusy Ditch and the

banker was Frank Donaho, its first doctor was named Jarrett, its first justice of the peace was Tom Dean, and its first constable Charles Glazier. Dean resigned after Glazier arrested a vagrant whom the justice felt compelled to release; he said he did not care to work with a too-vigilant peace officer.

Several years later, in 1886, other businesses had opened up in town: the Grand Hotel (built in 1885 and the first true hotel), a Kutner-Goldstein store, Samuel L. Hogue's real estate and insurance office, a lumber-yard, a Wells, Fargo office, and a blacksmith and wagon maker. Added to this list, in 1889, was the Fowler Fruit and Raisin Packing Company, with local farmer Captain Charles H. Norris as the company's president. It was sold three years later to Chaddock and Company, another packing concern.

In 1890 Fowler had a population of 335 and had become a significant shipping center. Some 688 carloads of grain, 153 of raisins and fifteen of green and dried fruit left the depot in that year. The town's three warehouses, which could hold 7,000 tons of grain, were usually bursting at the seams. E. W. Burton and P. W. Hastie's real estate office was doing much business, and a January 1, 1891, *Fresno Daily Evening Expositor* feature about the town mentioned that "every available structure [was] in demand" and no buildings were vacant. Pratt and Manley's general store, a drugstore, a meat market and another blacksmith shop had all joined the town's business roster by this time.

Prosperity continued well into the 1890s as the town added another packing house (the Phoenix, in 1895) and a newspaper, the *Fowler Courier*, one year before that. It began publication under C. P. Ruffner on May 19, continued under his proprietorship for five months,

Selma Canal being suggested. I maintained that the Fowler Switch Canal was the proper name, to which Mr. Dusy agreed." So it was the Fowler Switch Canal which was constructed starting in 1883. It was considered to be the finest irrigation canal in California. . . .

Drawing great public attention, work on the Fowler Switch Canal proceeded until March 1883 when water was first turned into the new ditch. Almost immediately, the spring flood washed out the headgate. Another was constructed and the canal was opened for use. Then, the Fowler Switch Canal Company was slapped with Tulare County Superior Court injunctions forbidding diversion of water from the river to protect downstream holders of riparian (natural) water rights. The Fowler Switch Company was in the same situation faced by other canal companies but years of litigation resulted. The headgates were closed—officially, at least. Water flowed nearly every season with, on many occasions, armed farmers, wearing barley sacks with their clothing turned inside out as a mask, guarding the headgate to insure their crops would receive vital water.

To Frank Dusy, who had invested heavily in the Fowler Switch Canal, it was a severe financial blow. . . .

It did not take Dusy long to recover. Taking advantage of a granite quarry claim he had filed nearly 15 years before he opened another new career. He received the contract for granite in the new Fresno County Courthouse additions and in several San Francisco structures. The state's monopolizing granite suppliers quickly bought Dusy out.

The sale's receipts were used by Dusy to construct what was probably the San Joaquin Valley's grandest house of the 19th century on the east side of McCall Avenue between South and Parlier avenues. It was three stories high with a cupola on top, from which, it was said, Dusy could watch his ranch employees in a 160-acre orchard.

It cost $15,000 and was of the most advanced design to combat the valley's intense heat. There were heating ducts and running water. Even a second floor toilet was included. It was said Dusy planned to make the third floor into a grand ballroom, but it was never finished. Bricks for the house came from Dusy's own brickyard, which he had developed between Hanford and Kingsburg. The soil created cherry brick evident in some Selma buildings standing in 1975 which Dusy supplied with brick. He used part of the money from his brickyard profits to pay off the canal debt.

But more crises loomed for Frank Dusy. In the early 1890s with his house under construction, the years of litigation between the Southern Pacific and Dusy came to an end regarding the possessory title which a much younger Dusy had innocently acquired from the squatter herdsman for Section 15 of Township 15 S Range 22 E, the railroad's alternate section. Not only did he lose the land but, in the end, the court ordered Dusy to pay a substantial sum to Southern Pacific for use of the property. Said the Fresno County Enterprise upon his death in 1898, "Some of the best land in this vicinity he held at one time, and might have owned at his death but he stubbornly resisted what he considered the extortion of the railroad company, and in the fight over possession lost; but he would not yield the principle to save the land." The school lien application he filed to start the litigation upon learning the railroad held title to what he thought was his land failed to persuade the court that Dusy had any right to purchase the property. . . .

Another blow came on June 3, 1894, when Mrs. Dusy died. Most historians say she was stricken while in the Sierra on a trip with Dusy, ill from the hardships of the trip. A popular story was that she had fallen down the lovely staircase in the foyer of the dream house her husband had constructed for her. In any case, she was dead at the age of 43.

That year was one of depression on top of the other financial setbacks. His cattle business went broke at the same time after a series of poor feed years. Little furniture remained in the huge house. Dusy, with what doubtlessly was a huge grocery bill (then paid only annually), apparently could not make the payment and Kutner-Goldstein of Selma foreclosed on the property.

After this incredible string of reversals, Dusy again changed courses, and careers. It was the Klondike era and Dusy set off for Alaska to resume his old life in the mines. At Cook's Inlet with a company of 10, he found encouraging prospects in a placer mine and founded what he called the Fresno Mining Company. The next year, in 1896, he chartered a small steamer, and with many problems and difficulties, hauled 100 Fresno County men to Alaska. He made another trip with other difficulties in 1897 and suffered a slight stroke. Still another trip north occurred in 1898. His son, Chester Dusy, told Historian Latta that the elder Dusy, despite what difficulties he experienced, found financial success in his mining and pack train operations at Six-Mile Creek and Cook's Inlet, making more money in the last two years than in the previous decade.

Late in October 1898 Dusy returned to Selma feeling fine. On Nov. 9, after greeting friends on the street and following election returns, he went home and, late in the evening, fell ill. Death came within a matter of minutes. . . .

Very few of his many careers and interests did he live to see brought to full potential, but he started or influenced them all. He dreamed dreams which never quite came true, but in the true spirit of the California pioneer he was, Frank Dusy left this valley a better place for the civilization he knew would follow.

SOURCE: *The Selma Enterprise*, October 23, 1975, pp. 1–2.

and was then purchased by Howard Harris and Charles Looney. The two men brought out the first issue of the *Fowler Ensign* on October 20, 1894, and it has continued publication ever since. Another indication of Fowler's economic health was indicated by C. T. Cearley's 1898 Fresno County directory, which listed five "contractors and builders" in town: A. T. Baker, A. Davidson and Son, Frank Lyman, S. W. Pierson and W. H. Runciman.

The First Presbyterian Church was the first to organize in Fowler, under the direction of the Reverend I. N. Hurd and J. S. McDonald, on December 5, 1886. It used the town schoolhouse for services until occupying its own structure on May 4, 1887. Nearly four years passed before another church, the Christian, was organized on May 11, 1890. The congregation met in Fowler's Good Templars Hall for the first few years of its existence and ran into a snag when it tried to occupy its own permanent building in June 1893. A schoolhouse thirty feet wide had been purchased to move onto the church's twenty-six-foot wide lot. P. W. Hastie, owner of the adjacent property, refused to allow the move—and posted a guard on his property—until the building was narrowed. The reason for Hastie's reaction is not known, but the building was modified as he wished.

After the Christian Church's establishment, a United Presbyterian Church was formed on May 31, 1890, with the Reverend William Brown as its first minister, followed by the founding of Saint Michael's Episcopal Church in 1891. Like its fellow Presbyterian church, the newer congregation was quick to build its own house of worship and dedicated it on April 10, 1891.

After the founding of its own school district, Fowler was soon surrounded by others to serve the nearby population. The Monroe School District was established on May 4, 1885; the Iowa School District on May 5, 1887; the Magnolia School District on May 9, 1888; and the Horace Mann School District on March 16, 1896. The first teachers in the districts were Mrs. R. J. Morrow, Miss E. J. Boyer, Fannie Stone, and Rose Homan, respectively.

In Fowler itself, the old school was replaced in 1889 with a $10,000, two-story structure that accommodated 100 students. On August 26, 1898, voters approved formation of the Fowler Union High School. It opened the following October 10 in the town grammar school, drawing its twenty-six students from the aforementioned districts. Hamilton Wallace of Stockton was the first principal, and Eleanor Bennett the first teacher.

For a small town, Fowler developed an impressive array of clubs and organizations in its early years. First was the Good Templars Lodge, organized in 1885. It soon occupied a two-story hall eventually taken over by the Independent Order of Odd Fellows, which had been established in 1890. During the ensuing decade, other groups appeared on the scene: the Farmers' Alliance, Woman's Christian Temperance Union, Pickwick Club (for debates), the Bachelors' and Elite clubs (for socializing) and the Knights of Pythias (fraternal).

Reference 9:6

## FOWLER'S SOCIAL SCENE, 1891–1893

*Fresno Daily Evening Expositor*, April 27, 1891:

The Young People's Endeavor Society of the Christian church gave a very pleasant social at the hall on Friday last. The house was called to order by President M. R. Harlan, who announced that a short program would be presented, after which every one could remain and have a good time. The following are the names of those who took part in the exercises:

Quartette... Lulu Harlan, F. Lyman, Belle Patton, Milt Harlan, Carrie Barnett, assisted by Lum Landrum.

Select Reading... By the President.

Piano solo... Miss Lilah Stewart.

Cornet and piano selection, "Gavotte"... F. Lyman and Lulu Harlan.

Recitation... Miss Mollie Davis.

Cornet solo, "Long Ago"... Prof. John G. Willis and Miss Landrum.

Essay, "Mother"... Lena Pool.

Trio... Lulu Landrum, Belle Patton, Lulu Harlan.

Recitation... Fred Nelson.

Cornet solo... J. G. Willis and Lulu Landrum.

The programme was very interesting and was well received. Afterwards all remained and conversed in a very satisfactory manner and enjoyed the refreshments which was [*sic*] served by those genial young ladies. The late hours having arrived reminded the people that it was time to disperse, which they did and were well pleased with the evening's exercises. It is hoped that the young people will try and repeat one of a similar nature at no distant date. Many people from Oleander, Lone Star, Malaga, Iowa, Fresno and Walnut were present to enjoy themselves at the social.

*Fresno Daily Evening Expositor*, February 16, 1892:

Rev. J. C. Lynn's house was the scene of a happy lot of young and old people Friday evening, who gave them a good old fashioned house-warming, having just moved into their new house in town. The carriages commenced to arrive early in the evening and continued for some time. The company consisted of 84 persons. Various games were indulged in and a new feature for this section of the country in the way of a topic conversation. The ladies were given a slip of paper with a topic, also the gentlemen. The ladies hunted up their partners for the subject. Fun? Well, I rather think so—music, songs, etc. At a convenient hour a sumptuous repast was served which fitted nicely in a vacant space. The young people of the United Presbyterian church gave as a slight token of remembrance of esteem for the pastor, an elegant china tea set. The presentation speech was made by Miss Fennell, and was responded to by Rev. Mr. Lynn... A royal good time was had and the small hours were growing large ere they journeyed homeward.

*Fresno Daily Evening Expositor*, November 15, 1893:

The Episcopal fair was a very nice affair. The ladies decorated the hall with chrysanthemums, palms, etc., in a very pleasing way. The novelty booth was arrayed with many fine works from the needle to tempt buyers. The supper was a great success. About 5 p.m. a programme was rendered as follows: Double quartet, "Mary Had a Little Lamb;" flute solo, Mr. James; vocal solo, Miss Conlan; musical coffee pot, Mr. Baell; piano solo, "Polish Dance," Miss Eva Turner; vocal duet, "Happy Swallow," Mrs. Captain Norris, Miss Lavity; double quartet, "Speed Away."

SOURCES: As above, all found in Fresno Scraps.

*Fowler's Seventh Street looking west at the turn of the century. The dirt street is lined on the left with the Phoenix Packing Company, Kutner-Goldstein grain warehouse, Valley Lumber and Frank Lynum Packing Company, and on the right by Kutner-Goldstein's, M. Brady general merchandise, Hamilton's cafe and Platzek's Harness Shop.*

*Thomas Fowler, Kings River cattle baron and owner of the famous 76 brand. The town of Fowler is named for him.*

*Captain Charles Henry Norris, Fresno pioneer who settled on three sections of land where present-day Fowler is located.*

*Every town had a horse shoeing shop, and Fowler had E. T. York. At one time C. E. Smith had the Fowler Shoeing Shop.*

*Fowler's Grand Hotel at Seventh and Main streets.*

183

There also were youth organizations attached to the First Presbyterian and Christian churches, a Ladies' Aid Society of the latter church, and a philharmonic orchestra. Scarcely a week passed without one of these groups hosting a function (see 9:6). One of the more popular community events was a Washington's Birthday celebration, held in 1895 and 1896. Approximately 3,000 people attended these festivities, which featured balloon flights, foot races and football games.

In this era no club in Fowler was more important than the Fowler Improvement Association. It had its genesis sometime in 1889, when Mrs. Amos Harris (see 9:7) and a dozen or so women formed the "King's Daughters." This group provided clothing, food and moral support for Fowler's poor and a family of motherless children. After some months passed, the women reorganized as the Fowler Improvement Association on August 19, 1890. By holding teas and dinners, the association raised money to have Fowler's dirt streets sprinkled and, in 1898, began planting the town's streets with eucalyptus trees to provide shade. No water system had been built in the town, so the women paid a man named Jordan Young to water the trees—which eventually numbered 700—by hand.

In addition to these activities, the FIA opened a town reading room soon after its founding and backed the local prohibition groups. Little money was spent for the club's own needs (it met in a converted chicken coop) and its members devised ingenious ways to attract people to its fund-raising socials. The February 23, 1892, *Fresno Daily Evening Expositor* remarked that the FIA was about to give a "Russian Tea" social, where patrons would be served by women in Russian peasant costumes and could choose from "a Russian bill of fare; pay for what you get, 5¢ each article."

The last town established on the Central Pacific tracks, Malaga, has a past that cannot be charted with much precision. Pre-1900 newspapers paid little attention to the hamlet, and later historians have ignored it almost entirely. It took its name from the G. G. Briggs agricultural colony (see Chapter 7) in which it was established, and is said to have been partially platted in 1883. A school was founded on May 4, 1885, with George W. Cartwright as its first teacher. Presided over by Sadie Tyler and Sallie Porter in 1889, the school had to expand (to a four-room structure) several years later.

In 1885 John D. Cartwright started manufacturing light-weight pruning shears in the village. This item became popular and later allowed him to accumulate a sizable fortune. About this time the Southern Pacific built a depot at Malaga. Because of increasing fruit shipments from the area, it had to be enlarged in 1890 and 1893.

Reference 9:7

# IN OCTOBER

### ERNESTINE WINCHELL

An epochal month was October in the experience of Antoinette Pelham Harris. On the 22nd. of October, 1837 she was born; October 26th. 1861 she became the mother of a son and a daughter; on the 25th. of the month in 1916 she passed from life. There were other significant October dates, but the one that first concerned Fresno county was October 2nd., 1881 when she came to Fowler with her family from the former home in Stanislaus county.

Sadly to the dismay of Mrs. Harris the new house awaiting her stood stark and alone in an uninhabited land. Though the situation of the building was on one of the sand ridges washed up by overflow from storm-born creeks of the hills, not more than two or three dwellings could be seen in any direction—spectral and far-away. No plantings of any kind; the roads were wandering wheel tracks through the sparse dead weeds. Twice a day a passenger train, and occasionally a rattling string of freight cars, rolling and shrieking, to and fro from the busy places in the world were all that visibly tied her to the life she had known.

Educated in Olivet college, a Michigan institution of particularly high ideals, trained in the normal department of Ann Arbor university, and having taught school for a number of years, Mrs. Harris had exceptional qualifications. Before Fowler had any

schools she taught her son, Howard, and finally prepared him to take a business course in the Stockton college. Also in her home she coached Estelle Miller for the county examination for teachers which the young girl passed at the minimum age and with excellent percentages.

Mrs. Amos Harris gave much attention and encouragement to the Fowler District school. Miss Agnes Henry opened the first term with 26 pupils, and she found a pleasant home with the C. L. Walters, but later on, when her own little house was sufficiently stretched, Mrs. Harris boarded successive teachers for several seasons. Fully to comprehend all that meant one must have taught a country school in the horse-and-buggy days. To Mrs. Harris herself it was merely one more way to aid her community—so to nourish and counsel and encourage the young woman that each day she was able to bring to the class room a new fund of vigor and inspiration for the work.

Never physically strong, it was wonderful that she accomplished so much, but, driving her fat roan mare to her low-hung phaeton Mrs. Harris could be depended upon to do more than her share of the work in every meeting and entertainment. In 1887 she organized the first Sunday school in Fowler, and as time ripened she built up a Band of Hope and a chapter of King's Daughters.

With Mrs. D. W. Parkhurst she created the Fowler Improvement Association. She was active in the Woman's Christian Temperance Union, and one of her last initiatives resulted in the private kindergarten during the year of 1896. In the meantime, after her fiftieth birthday in 1887, she had completed two full courses of Chautauqua reading, and in those two diplomas had a very sweet and modest pride.

Mrs. Harris talked of a public reading room when to everyone else it seemed visionary, but she was a women of visions that she spared no effort to make real. When, continually encouraged by herself, the Fowler Public Library became a fact her interest never failed, and she indefatigably read and studied to extend its usefulness to the limit. Through the *Fowler Ensign*, published by her son, Howard A. Harris, she helped her townspeople still more, backing the editor in every uplifting and progressive move.

To the man who leads the way, who lays up the wall, who carves the rock, who directs the stream—all honor. To the woman who, in the life of her community does all this—not only honor, but loving memory.

SOURCE: Ernestine Winchell columns.

As the 1890s progressed, Malaga did not become a truly significant town (see 9:8), but bustle compensated for its lesser status. The large El Modelo raisin packing plant of A. D. Barling, founded in 1889, was nearby, as was the Olivet Packing Company—opened at about the same time. These operations were joined by the Fresno Raisin Company packing house in 1892, and a year later the Olivet company expanded its facilities greatly. Many of the goods produced by these enterprises moved out of the Malaga depot, and the surrounding vineyards were always abuzz with activity.

"There is a variety of grape pickers at Malaga on the large vineyards," said a September 20, 1892, *Fresno Daily Evening Expositor* report. "We have almost all nationalities here. There are Americans, Indians, Japanese and Chinamen. It is quite a problem with the ranchers to know which class of help they prefer . . . It all depends on how close you watch them."

Two settlements with an intertwined background—Oleander and Covell (Easton)—got their start about the time of Malaga's founding. As with Malaga, colony development (this time, of the Washington Irrigated Colony—see Chapter 8) was the motivating factor in their creation.

Located on land around the corner of Cedar and Adams avenues, Oleander was the first to gain a post office—on January 10, 1881. The first postmaster, Judge J. W. North, wanted to name the office Washington Colony but federal authorities declined his request, saying there were too many similar post office names. North then took the advice of his daughter, May, and adopted Oleander because of the many oleander bushes surrounding the colony.

Along with North, some of the earliest settlers were Captain Daniel C. McLaughlin, W. H. Baldwin, Mrs. F. A. Estes, the Squire brothers and C. H. A. Davis. With land prices as low as twenty and thirty dollars an acre, and irrigation water readily available, the lots around Oleander were snapped up quickly and planted in grain, peaches, apricots, alfalfa and nectarines. "There are every now and again sales made of the few vacant lots that were unimproved and it will be but a short time till you will see every lot around here fully improved," said a correspondent in the September 10, 1889, *Fresno Daily Evening Expositor*.

In the late 1880s, when raisin growing had become the rage in Fresno County, Oleander was home to several packing concerns: the Curtis Fruit Packing and Fresno Raisin companies, and smaller operations run by H. E. Cook and Napoleon Viau in their own vineyards. A Griffin and Skelley house was running by 1894, and growers and packers alike were said to be producing superior raisins. "We have no alkali land to speak of, and no other drawbacks against which to contend," said A. C. Bryan, Fresno Raisin Company vice-president, in 1891. "Another product in which we can't be beat is the Oleander girls. They are the prettiest in the county, and we have half a mind to use the photographs of half a dozen of them for [our] label . . ."

The first buildings in the settlement were Judge North's house and post office, and a small shanty belonging to W. H. Baldwin. The post office moved from residence to residence thereafter, first going to Mrs. Estes' home and then to J. D. Galloway's. By 1884 there were thirty houses in the neighborhood. Five years later there was a telegraph station and talk of lining the streets with lights, and paving them with vitrified bricks. The last two civic improvements appear not to have materialized; after all, Oleander never became an incorporated entity.

Tom Elliott operated a town store in 1889, but the major mercantile business throughout the nineteenth century was Robert J. and E. W. Wilson's store. Robert J. eventually went into partnership with a man named Harding. Oleander also played host to an iron windmill factory, the Zephyr Wind Engine Company, which drilled "water, gas, oil or any other kind of wells" for the locals.

Only three fires of any consequence disturbed Oleander in its infancy. One struck an all-purpose building on April 10, 1893, that had previously housed the Cosmopolitan Hotel, a grocery store, the post office and the area school. George Ruggles had been using the place as a harness shop before the fire; it burned to the ground, and the loss topped $2,000. A September 1, 1899, blaze, helped by the explosion of a powder canister, destroyed the Wilson and Harding store—the second time it had burned in seven years. (The first incident's date has gone unrecorded.) No cause was discovered for any of the fires.

Located off the main Southern Pacific line, Oleander was served by daily and weekly freight teams until the Valley Railroad (see Chapter 14) was placed through it in 1897. On April 4, at 9 a.m., workers came into town and started laying tracks alongside the post office. A crowd began gathering to watch the workers, which must have cheered, and otherwise inspired, the laboring men. By 6 p.m., the track had been completed to a half-mile south of the post office.

An Oleander school district was formed on May 12, 1883, with Miss M. D. Fletcher as its first teacher. It was initially conducted in a house loaned by a Mr. Langdon, and attendance grew rapidly—there were eighty-seven students in 1889. Hattie Bolitho and Miss M. Purcell were subsequent teachers at the school, which had a woman principal—Jennie Beardsley—in 1899. A dancing school also was. opened in town during 1890, managed by a Mr. La France. "There is at present 18 pupils with the number increasing at a rapid rate," said the January 22, 1890, *Fresno Daily Evening Expositor*.

The Oleander Congregational Church was organized in 1892, according to one source, but it may have been operating as early as 1889. The Reverends G. J.

Binder and J. Overton were among its earliest ministers. Services were held at a var ety of locations until a permanent church was built in 1895. Soon allied with the congregation were a Church Endeavor Society, Young People's Church Endeavor Society and a Ladies' Aid Society. The only other religious organizations in town during the 1890s were a Danish Missionary Society, formed in 1892, and the Salvation Army. The latter group held "large and enthusiastic meetings every Thursday evening in Wilson's hall [above the town store]," said the March 30, 1896, *Fresno Daily Evening Expositor.*

Other clubs and organizations of note were a Good Templars Lodge organized in 1889, a Social Club formed in 1890, a Hoot Owl club devoted to fishing and hunting, an Oleander Dramatic Society (that was working on a drama called "Comrades" in 1894) and even an Old Maids' Club. Of it the *Expositor*'s correspondent, "Dixie," said this on March 30, 1896:

Very few people here are aware that an old maids' club exists in this vicinity, and it was not till the other day that we knew of the existence of such an organization, and it was only by promising that no names would be mentioned that we were given some information about its mysteries. The membership of the society is small and limited and contains names of ladies who are so sweet and pretty that we never dreamed that they had reached that period of life when the chances of marriage are rather slim. But the members of this club are not of the marrying kind. Without doubt they have been courted and perhaps have had offers of marriage, but they don't believe in it. Think there is lots of unhappiness and no independence in that state, and prefer living lives of virgin purity. We do not care to have our hair pulled by making public any of their written principles, but can truthfully say that they do not accept these words of the poet:
I am ashamed that women are so simple
To offer war where they should kneel for peace;
Or seek for rule, supremacy and sway,
When they are bound to love, serve and obey.

Oleander's social scene was exceedingly active for a settlement its size. The town social club and Ladies' Aid Society were constantly hosting ice cream socials,

picnics, sheet-and-pillowcase balls, rug-making bees and dances. When a May 24, 1889, dance was held on a floor that was cleaned and waxed too thoroughly, "people not knowing . . . would have thought every dancer under the influence of something stronger than water. You never saw such [grand] and lofty tumbling. It was in singles and pairs, and sometimes it looked as if an entire quadrille was trying to stand to heads." A more typical social event, held in 1895, was described thus:

One of the most pleasant parties of the season was given by E. W. Wilson at his home on Cedar avenue, New Years' night. A fine turkey dinner was enjoyed very much by the family and a few friends about 6:30. We must, besides the splendid dinner, make special mention of the salad, Mrs. Wilson surely excells [*sic*] in making it. Invitations were out for a hop later in the evening, and about 8:30 all were tripping the light fantastic to the excellent playing of W. J. Godley. In another room cards, chess and social converse held their sway. During the evening the guests were favored, first 'The Old Bridge,' sung by Mrs. E. W. Wilson and Mrs. Frank Galloway; J. Brandon came next with 'Forgive, Forget'; 'Sweet Marie,' by unknown. All retired late in the evening to their homes, deciding that Mr. and Mrs. E. W. Wilson as host and hostess could not be outdone.

For the more athletically-oriented there were football and baseball teams in town by 1894, presided over by an Oleander Athletic Association which also seems to have held sway over a Cricket Club. "It is said they will go down to Hanford next month to wipe the Hanford Cricket Club off the face of the earth," said the October 17, 1894, *Fresno Daily Evening Expositor.* "Go slow, boys." On December 1 the newspaper reported: "The Hanfords won by quite a large score." The football team had better luck later in the month, whipping Selma's team on the gridiron. Football was so popular that a Juvenile Football Club was formed around 1894, and a regular athletic club was instituted by J. M. Sinclair and Wallie Barr in late 1896.

The beginnings of Easton have been discussed, along with those of the Washington Irrigated Colony,

Reference 9:8

## GREAT IS MALAGA

*Fresno Daily Evening Expositor*, January 17, 1893:
Here in Malaga, though to a passerby we may appear unimportant, yet "appearance are often deceitful," and we really do occupy an important position in Fresno County. I am afraid to call Malaga a town for fear some one would take me up on it, for when one begins to sum up the business buildings it does not take long to count them, as I can sit here, and looking out the door and window I can count one two-story school

house and general merchandise store, two packing houses, one hotel, one blacksmith shop and the railroad depot, and I can see it all, but when one looks at it from a business point of view, from a knowledge of what it really is, it puts on a different aspect. For example, we have this past season shipped more produce from here than any other shipping point on the railroad between Fresno and Tulare city. What other one item will, forge a place to the front faster? The railroad company have [*sic*] recognized that fact

and in a short time will construct a new depot, and I believe the time is not far distant when we will see new residences springing up in our midst. We are so near our county seat that it is a most acceptable place for those who do not care to live in the largest town in the county. Thirty minutes' drive or eight minutes by rail . . .

SOURCE: As above, on pp. 1500-1501 Fresno Scraps.

in Chapter 8. Its post office was created on February 2, 1881, briefly discontinued from August 3 to October 22, 1883, after which it operated until a merger with Oleander in 1902. Early accounts of the town are scarce; what is known suggests that it was nicely maintained. In 1888 numerous wells were drilled along unpaved Elm Avenue to keep it free from dust. Eight-to ten-horse teams, towing a wagon with a pump and tanks, would fill up at the wells and drive down the road, sprinkling water as they went along. The same year saw a committee organized to purchase cemetery property, though this was not accomplished until 1893 when the Washington Colony Cemetery was opened.

Until the 1887 boom times little seems to have happened in the town, but a July 24, 1891, *Fresno Daily Evening Expositor* correspondent said: "Easton proper consists of two merchandise stores, one owned by [George B.] Rowell and [George L.] Johnson, the other by W. S. Marks. The first store is also a post-office; the other includes a drugstore. We also have two blacksmith shops [probably operated by Samuel J. Hender and Eugene Bradford at that time], a dress-maker, two physicians [one named Laird, the other J. F. Summers] and a barroom all situated on Elm avenue, our main thoroughfare, and five and one-half miles south of Fresno."

Other businesses that opened in town before the century's turn were the Five-Mile House, a hotel operated by a Mr. Kiser; the Easton Packing House, managed by Milo Rowell in 1893; Dougal McCaig's blacksmith shop; W. S. McMillin's painting business, and the Baird brothers' meat market. By 1898 the town had four churches—Swedish, Methodist Episcopal, United Presbyterian and Lutheran. Their ministers in that year were L. Dahlgren, G. E. Foster, W. W. Gordon and P. Rasmussen, respectively. Dahlgren and Goddon had, by that time, served their congregations for four years or more.

During its formative years, many school districts sprang up around Easton. The town became an educational hub after May 12, 1892, when the Washington Union High School District was formed to serve seven students. Among its first teachers were H. Barker, C. S. Taylor, Jr. and A. Sorensen.

A number of local school districts were ultimately joined with the high school district. The oldest of these was the Orange Center, organized on October 3, 1876. It operated in temporary quarters before moving into a permanent schoolhouse, on Central Avenue between Fig and Elm avenues, around 1877. In 1899 its teacher was Rose Homan and its principal Anna Lehman. Closer to Easton, the Washington Colony School was organized on May 15, 1897. It was first housed in a building twenty feet square, with one teacher and seven pupils. By 1880 so many new families and children had arrived that the local households paid twenty dollars each toward a building fund, and a new schoolhouse was built. Even that structure was inadequate after a few years and had to be replaced, with the old school being moved across the street and becoming Easton's town hall.

In the 1880s, when the population continued to increase, more school districts were created: the Fresno Colony (on May 6, 1884), West Park (May 4, 1885), Braly (May 7, 1886) and Pomona and American Colony (both organized on February 26, 1889). Some early teachers were Ida Waggoner, Mary Crofoot and Alice Kimball of the Fresno Colony, Alice M. Root of the American Colony, and Minnie Roff and Frances Conn of the Pomona. The colony school districts were in the agricultural tracts of the same names; the Braly's location was probably at Jensen and Braly avenues, and the Pomona's at Fruit and Central avenues. The 1890s saw the creation of three more local school districts: the Gill (on February 16, 1891—Lucy Dorman and Mary Hines among its earlier teachers); Perrin Colony (May 9, 1893—Helen Tuohy and Hattie Taylor); and Manning (February 27, 1899).

Although it was a larger settlement than Oleander, Easton seems to have cultivated a less active social scene. There were only two social clubs (the Ideal and Hedge Row) that hosted the usual festivities of the times. Of a Hedge Row leap year party given in 1892 it was said that "if you don't go, it is because you are afraid the ladies will make a wall-flower out of you."

For those of a more scholarly, or perhaps pugilistic, bent, there was the Washington Colony Literary Society. Of the group the April 17, 1894, *Fresno Daily Evening Expositor* had this to say: "Saturday evening of last week the . . . society accepted a challenge from a similar society in Gill school district to discuss the evils and merits of the American jury system. The Gill contingent set forth the viciousness of the California juries in a manner so offensive to the native sons that were present that the former lost the decision and were obliged to soothe the savage breast with 'music by the band' to obviate a fight."

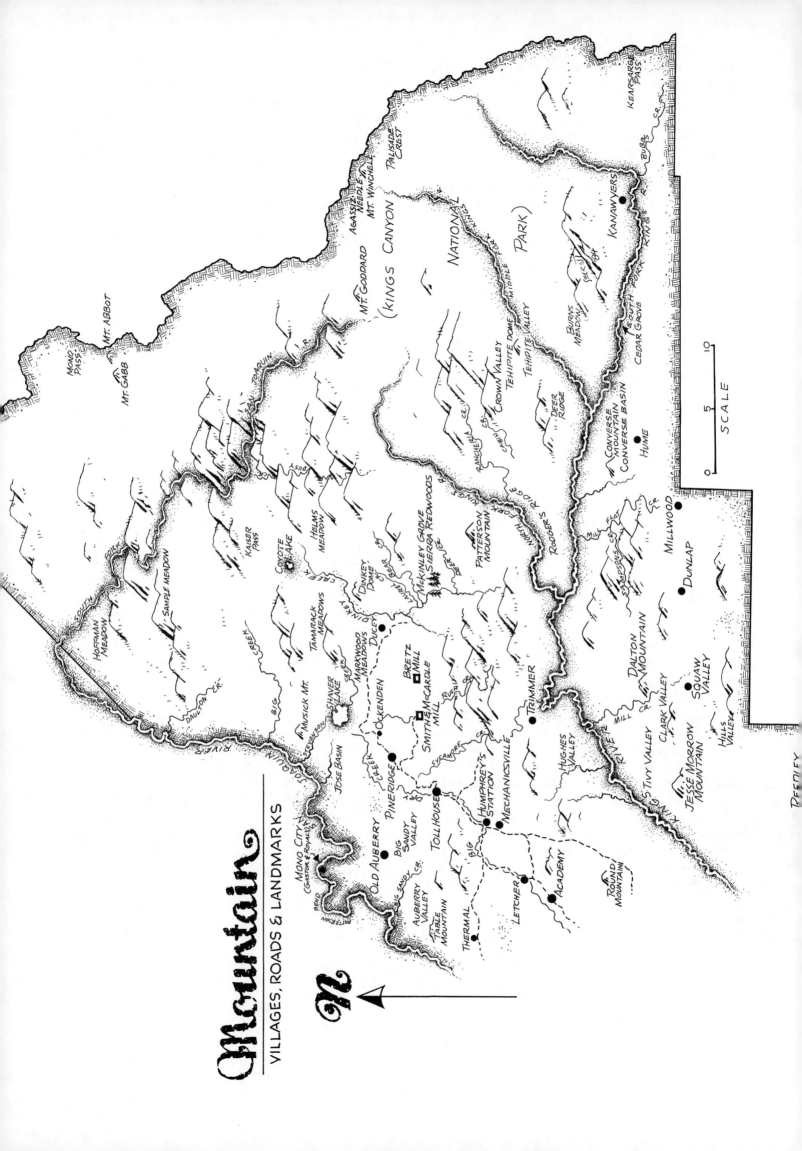

# Chapter 10
# High and Low Sierra

The early explorations into Fresno County's extreme eastern edge—the foothills and the Sierra Nevada—did not end with the visits of Joseph Reddeford Walker, John C. Fremont, William Robert Garner and the Mariposa Indian War battalions (see chapters 2, 3 and 4). In the 1860s, new travels and discoveries began in the area, partially out of economic necessity. Sheepmen from the lower elevations had to feed their flocks in the mountain meadows, since plains pasturage was often scarce (see Chapter 6).

By bringing their flocks into the San Joaquin River watershed north and east of the main river, Henry Clay Daulton, Jonathan Rea, A. S. Raynor, Colonel J. P. Lane, Joseph Barrett, B. S. Birkhead, Samuel Cassidy, John M. Hensley and the Qualls brothers became familiar with that region and the Kaiser Creek Basin. William Helm staked out grazing lands in the "short-hair" country, the San Joaquin River-Kings River divide, and Frank Dusy, William Carpenter and Henry Coolidge ran their flocks on the north fork of the Kings River and Rancheria Creek areas. Other early Sierra sheepmen included Thomas P. Nelson and W. W. Shipp, who operated along Laurel and Bear creeks, and William Markwood and one Hall, whose territory included the Big Creek area. It is tragic that none of these men left a record—save for Hensley—of their activities, and of the waterways, peaks, forests and meadows they must have discovered.

It is easier to chart the explorations of a group contemporary with the old-time sheepmen—the official California geological survey, led by geologist Josiah Dwight Whitney. Created in 1860, as the gold rush activity was waning, the survey's mission was to find new mineral resources ready for exploitation. Survey members visited a wide range of locales, finally arriving in the Fresno County Sierra in late July 1864; earlier they had twice traversed the San Joaquin Valley plains. Moving up from Visalia, and guided by some Owens Valley prospectors familiar with the territory, the party inched up the Kings River's south fork.

"It was a horrible trail," wrote expedition diarist William Henry Brewer. "Once, while we were working along the steep, rocky side of a hill, where it was very steep and rough, old Nell, our pack-mule, fell and rolled over and over down the bank *upward of a hundred and fifty feet* [italics Brewer's]. Of course, we thought her killed ... Strangely, she was not seriously hurt."

After following paths their animals could barely handle, the party found its way into the upper Kings River Canyon, today part of Kings Canyon National Park. Brewer's description of it was rapturous:

We left there the next morning and worked up the valley about ten miles. Next to Yosemite this is the grandest canyon I have ever seen. It much resembles Yosemite and almost rivals it. A pretty valley or flat half a mile wide lies along the river, in places rough and strewn with bowlders [sic], and in others level and covered with trees. On both sides rise tremendous granite precipices, of every shape, often nearly perpendicular, rising from 2,500 feet to above 4,000 feet. They did not form a continuous wall, but rose in high points, with canyons coming down here and there, and with fissures, gashes, and gorges. The whole scene was sublime—the valley below, the swift river roaring by, the stupendous cliffs standing against a sky of intensest [sic] blue, the forests through which we rode. We would look up through the branches and see the clear sky and grand rocks, or occasionally, as we crossed an open space, we would get more comprehensive views.

On July 20 the men did further exploring. Members Charles Hoffmann and Richard Gardiner found it impossible to scale some of the canyon's walls—which went up 2,000 feet or more. Brewer noted that he "climbed over bowlders [sic] and through brush, got up above two very fine waterfalls, one of which is the finest that I have ever seen in this state outside of Yosemite." They continued to trudge on, climbing more than 4,000 feet in altitude while traveling an actual distance of only five miles. A rattlesnake was encountered and killed—surprising, they thought, because of the 10,000-foot altitude—and a mountain grouse was killed and cooked, making for "splendid eating."

The Whitney party continued eastward, up Bubbs and Charlotte creeks, continuing to brave the hazards about them. "In places the mules could scarcely get a foothold where a canyon yawned hundreds of feet below; in places it was so steep that we had to pull the pack animals up by main strength," said Brewer.

Eventually they crossed the Sierra summit and entered Owens Valley from the west. Proceeding northward there, the men later ventured westward and recrossed the summit at the Rock Creek-Mono Creek pass on August 2. They soon found themselves on the San Joaquin's middle fork, where Brewer said the party spied "a grand view, but as it is so similar to those already described I will give no description. . . . Rides over almost impossible ways, cold nights, clear skies, rock, high summits, grand views, laborious days, and finally, short provisions—the same old story."

After naming two peaks Abbot and Gabb—for Henry Abbot, a member of the Williamson expedition (see Chapter 4) and Whitney expedition paleontologist William Gabb—the men went down Kaiser Ridge and eastward through a break in it. Their objective was to scale Mount Goddard, previously noticed on their Kings River traverse, and named after engineer-geographer George Goddard.

"We camped at about two thousand feet," wrote Brewer,

> and the next day four of us started for it—Hoffmann, Dick, Spratt (a soldier), and I. We anticipated a very heavy day's work, so we started at dawn. We crossed six high granite ridges, all rough, sharp, and rocky, and rising to over eleven thousand feet. We surmounted the seventh, a ridge very sharp and about twelve thousand feet, only to find the mountain still at least six miles farther, and two more deep canyons to cross. We had walked and climbed hard for nine hours incessantly, and had come perhaps twelve or fourteen miles. It was two o'clock in the afternoon. Hoffmann and I resigned the intention of reaching it, for it was too far and we were too tired.

Lilbourne A. Winchell theorized that the route taken was through Helm's Big Meadow, and then Dusy's, Clark's and Fleming's canyons.

From this point the party wandered into the extreme northeast of Fresno County, until the party reteamed with some soldiers attached to it. The soldiers had gone to Fort Miller and gotten supplies—Brewer and the others were living off dehydrated bread and tough jerky. Reunited, they began inching up the San Joaquin's north fork. Before leaving, Brewer wrote a vivid impression of life in the unspoiled mountains:

> Around us, in the immediate vicinity, were rough bowlders [sic] and naked rock, with here and there a stunted bushy pine. A few rods below us lay two clear, placid lakes, reflecting the stars. The intensely clear sky, dark blue, very dark at this height; the light stars that lose part of their twinkle at this height; the deep stillness that reigned; the barren granite cliffs that rose sharp against the night sky, far above us, rugged, ill-defined; the brilliant shooting stars, of which we saw many; the solitude of the scene—all joined to produce a deep impression on the mind, which rose above the discomforts.

The next expedition of note was led by Judge E. C. Winchell and Captain John N. Appleton in late September 1868. Traveling along the Kings River-Kaweah River divide, the men made their way to the upper Kings, crossing Glacier Creek and traveling to Crescent Lawn, "a spacious meadow encircled on the southeast by a grand arc of granite mountains thinly clad with pines," wrote Winchell in the September 11, 1872, *San Francisco Call.* From there the men proceeded north and northeast, gaining 12,000 feet in altitude and seeking the magnificent canyon spotted by the Whitney party.

After coming down one slope, the men noticed a series of jagged granite mountains. Though the others were setting up camp and making a fire, Winchell could not wait to see if the fabled canyon might be visible from the peaks. The scene he beheld was well-described by Appleton in the October 16, 1872, *Fresno Weekly Expositor:*

> Below was a huge chasm through which trugged [sic] one of the river's tributaries, now pitching itself over a precipice, then fretting and forming among the massive boulders, again dashing into cascades—the spray playing and sparkling in the sun, which yet found the way into the canyon. Further on were the foothills undulating in picturesque beauty; beyond was the Joaquin plains, looking like an ocean, save where you could trace by the timber on their banks the two rivers, gracefully winding their way. Through them the atmosphere was so pure, so clear that the vision was only bounded by the Coast Range of mountains, far in the distance; to the Northward and Eastward the mighty Sierras [sic], their lofty peaks topped with eternal snows glistening in the sun was one of those grand panoramic views seldom seen, but once seen, is never after forgotten . . .

The vista peak was named Winchell, after E. C.'s cousin, Alexander, a geology professor at the University of Michigan. (Later it was given the appellation Lookout Peak, and the Mount Winchell name was transferred to a peak on the northern edge of Kings Canyon National Park.) After pouring some liquor on the mount and giving it a christening, the men descended into the canyon. Appleton said they found "a beauty and symmetry looking like some gentleman's park, and rising some little distance from the river was a most remarkable rock. It had at a distance, all the appearance of a huge cathedral, its walls were from sixty to one hundred feet in height, perfectly perpendicular. On examining it we found the walls covered with hieroglyphs, among which the figure of a cross was very prominent."

Making their way farther up the canyon, the men hunted for mountain grouse and fished for trout, with their amazement over the scenery steadily mounting. The canyon kept narrowing, with its massive walls thrusting farther and farther upward, dwarfing the travelers. Winchell described what was seen, and the names given to the geographical features, in the September 12, 1872, *San Francisco Call*:

... Opposite Kettle Brook are the "Pillars of Hercules," towering at the portals of the stony realm beyond; and next, on the same side, is "Appleton's Peak"—a sheer, blank wall, near whose top the great pines that plume it seem but a span long. "Leach's Peak," on the south side, fills the angle made by the Brook. The *cañon* here is but one-fourth of a mile wide, but rapidly widens again and contracts in elliptic form, making a rude oval, half a mile wide, and thrice as long, named "The Coliseum." Its lofty, fringing cliffs are yet nameless. At the eastern end a furious torrent darts out of a steep gully on the north side, with deafening roar, and gave us trouble in crossing, for which we repaid it with the title, "Thunder Creek." Further [*sic*] on is a second, irregular ellipse, a mile long, its northern wall a broad, angular peak, the "Pyramid of Cheops." On the south "Three Sisters" correspond in form to the "Three Brothers" of Yosemite. Another stream emerges from a glen east of the Pyramid, to which, because of its proximity to the copper mine alluded to in the early part of this sketch, we applied the name "Malachite Creek." The deposit of ore crops out 400 feet above the valley on the east side of this rivulet, and appears to be of rich quality. A third swell in the *cañon* seemed so nearly circular, being only three-quarters of a mile long and of almost equal width, that we called it "The Rotunda." Its enclosing heights are yet unchristened. Finally, beyond, is the noblest apartment of the series. The great *cañon* of Kings River is here abruptly terminated by a magnificent granite tablet which stands across the valley and faces the west. Two similar tablets uplift from the green floor, at right angles with the former, on opposite sides of the river, thus constituting the three inner walls of a vast Titanic temple, open to the setting sun. But through the enclosed, inner corners leap into this enchanted, and enchanting, arena, two bold and glassy torrents from the north and the south—new-born of the snows—which, rushing together, instantaneously coalesce, forming the jubilant South Fork [of the Kings] and sweep in matchless beauty and wedded gladness down through the embowered and rock-walled valley.

The party reversed course and was back in the Millerton area, where Winchell and Appleton lived, by early October.

An August 1872 visit to Dusy and Carpenter's sheep camp on Dinkey Creek, and areas beyond, was chronicled by William Faymonville in the August 28, September 4, 11 and 18, 1872, issues of the *Fresno Weekly Expositor*. Traveling up the Toll House road from Millerton on horseback, Faymonville visited Pine Ridge and the Markwood settlement north of it (see below), then crossed eight miles over the mountains to the sheep camp. From there Faymonville, Dusy and E. P. Kester went to a grove of sequoias located six miles away. Now known as the McKinley Grove of Big Trees, the area had been discovered two years earlier by George Statham, son of sheepman Albert Henry Statham, and it had some incredible specimens. "The largest tree, the Gen. Washington, measures twenty feet six inches in diameter," wrote Faymonville.

Several other trees were measured—none of which was less than fifty-seven feet in circumference—and it was noted that many of the trees had been vandalized by bears. "In one place we measured out of curiosity, the highth [*sic*] to which one of these beasts had reached with his claws, and it marked nine feet six inches from the ground ... In another place, while measuring the highth [*sic*] of one of the smaller of the fallen trees ... my attention was drawn to a number of fresh bear tracks, all about the log. I remarked to Mr. Frank Dusy, that I thought we had 'better be gettin' away from there.'"

After these minor adventures the men feasted on broiled mutton, bread, tea and doughnuts. "The latter article was concocted by Mr. Dusy, before we left Dinkey, and I can vouch for their being 'nifty,'" said Faymonville.

Taking an easterly course, the men went through large forest ranges, with moist soil and fresh green underbrush. "About five o'clock in the afternoon we passed the sheep camp of Mr. Thomas Hall, and finding a fine bunch of venison hanging convenient, and there being no one at home, we concluded to help ourselves with a portion of it ... The ride of the afternoon, the mountain air, or something else had aroused our appetite[s] to a lively pitch, and it was but a short time before each of us had a 'right smart chunk of venison' impaled on a forked stick, and broiling it over a bed of coals."

Heading for another Dusy sheep camp on Oso Creek, the men met with some incidental dangers. While riding along one trail, Faymonville heard a rattlesnake. "I have frequently heard it said that 'snake oil' was good for rheumatism, but not being afflicted with that painful malady, I had no use for the oil of this particular snake, so hurried my horse on." Kester dismounted and shot the snake, which had eight rattles and a button.

Upon reaching camp the men found many signs of bears, which was bad since the animals preyed constantly on the mountain sheep flocks. The tracks of a particularly vicious bear—"Old Stub," named because of an odd indentation found in his tracks—were spotted, and around midnight one of the men tried to bag a bear he heard. His revolver sounded and the beast let out a ferocious yell, but neither blood nor wounded or dead animals could be found later.

From Oso Creek a trip was made into the Tehipite Valley Dusy was so familiar with (see 10:1), and while looking down from the heights, the men engaged in some scenic vandalism. "We rolled off a few rocks from the cliff, and we could see and hear them for minutes plunging and crashing beneath us," wrote Faymonville. "Sometimes they would go hundreds of feet without touching, then they would strike a projecting cliff, but would bound off again, and with increased vigor, go rustling down, finally lodging in a ravine three thousand feet below us."

Wishing to explore the lower reaches, the men started downward, but not without a mishap. "The mountain side was very much steeper than I had supposed, and to make matters worse, was covered with loose broken rock, rendering it almost impossible to get a foothold, frequently sliding thirty and forty feet. . . . .Occasionally we were compelled to crawl on hands and knees through the thick bushes. . . . An hour and a half of this kind of traveling rather took the 'vinegar'

out of me, and the more so, when I discovered that we had made but little over a third of the way down."

Faymonville nevertheless continued the descent, suffering considerable bruises and blisters and a badly sprained knee. "It seemed as if every time I fell, it was on a cactus plant. Certain portions of my person were pierced and repierced by the sharp leaves. There is one virtue these 'sword leaves' have. . . . A person may stick one of them into his flesh as far as possible, and it will pull out as easily again as it went in without breaking off." Upon reaching the valley floor he was too tired to do anything except spread out on the Kings River's sands.

Camp was made in a natural structure, consisting of two large boulders roofed by a large sheet of granite. There was a floor of white sand, since the river had flowed through this rock shanty at one time. Faymonville spotted a three-stage waterfall in the valley and named it "Nonpareil," but someone else later changed the name to Silver Spray.

The men looked around for two days, then exited up another precipitous trail until they reached a previous camp on Clarendon Creek. Continuing in an eastward direction, Faymonville noted that "vegetation entirely ceases, except an occasional juniper or tamarack, which is battered and torn from frequent war with the

Reference 10:1

## A TRIP TO TEHIPITE VALLEY

On the 11th of July, 1879, our party of five, thoroughly equipped, armed and provisioned, left the hospitable mountain home of Mr. and Mrs. Frank Dusy, on Dinkey Creek, en route for the grand canyon of the middle fork of Kings River . . . with hopeful hearts, and amid the laughter of our friends, who bade us adieu, we entered upon the arduous undertaking of climbing thirty-five or forty miles nearer the summit of the Sierra Nevadas; over a rocky and precipitous country, clad with chapparal and pine forests. . . .

After six long hours of obstinacy on the part of the donkeys, and of toil and vexation on the part of the riders, we reached the North Fork meadows, sixteen miles from Dinkey, and our camping-place for the first night. This is a delightful and romantic spot in the valley of the north fork of Kings River, one of the many cases of verdure in this wilderness of rude and ragged mountains . . . Here we gladly halted, and sought rest and refreshment after our weary initial day . . .

The next morning, after a refreshing sleep and a hearty breakfast, we packed our provisions, blankets, etc., on the two donkeys and a mule, and leading them, made the rest of the trip on foot. As the rugged way now made it impossible to ride further, we here left our horses, staking one and hobbling a second, expecting they would await our return. But the sequel showed that our confidence had been misplaced. Slowly toiling

eastward about six miles, over a broken and rock-strewn country, we stopped for lunch and to take a rest before entering the stupendous canyon of the Middle Fork, which our guide, Mr. Dusy, informed us was only a mile distant.

Reanimated by this assurance the space was quickly passed over, and at 4 o'clock P.M. of Sunday, July 13th, we stood on the brink of the cliff and gazed with wonder and awe upon one of the grandest views to be found in the Sierra. A grassy slope reaches to the very edge of the chasm, the bottom of which is more than a vertical mile below, and as one looks shudderingly down the giddy abyss he sees the majestic stream of the Middle Fork, appearing no larger than a brook, as it glistened in the sun. To the east we beheld mountains of solid rock, capped with snow, and increasing in grandeur and height as they near the summit, which was dimly outlined against the sky, in the far distance. Lingering with enraptured visions we were loth to withdraw our eyes from a scene at once sublime and awe-inspiring, at the warning by the lengthened shadows, that our time was limited, so with reluctance we left the spot and pursued our way down the steep and difficult route that led to the bottom of the valley.

No route has ever been found by which animals could be taken into the canyon of the Middle Fork till about a month ago, when some prospectors discovered a trail

that evidently was made many years ago. It is said that about 1860 a party of Mexicans discovered gold in the canyon, and while engaged in mining there a party of white marauders encroached upon them, but were driven out. In return they caused the Mexicans to be murdered by the Indians, that they might become possessors of the gold. So much for rumor, now for fact. The path by which we descended winds round a ledge of rocks for a distance, and is very narrow. At one abrupt turn the ledge is broken off, requiring an artificial substitute. Here a tree has been felled across the break, then brush and rocks piled in to make a safe passage way. Doubtless this work was done many years ago, as the stump and log are old and decayed, and the "blazes" on the trees marking the trail have grown over till they are scarcely visible. In the valley we found an ancient grave, an old camp-ground, a venerable pair of boots, and remains of branches of trees used to make a corral, with other indications of an early habitation.

As we plunged down the dangerous and flinty way, we came to a place where we were compelled to unpack our mule, in order to get around a narrow point on the ledge. But we determined to try the little donkeys without unpacking. So one of the party took a donkey by the head, while another seized his tail with a death-like grip, and in that manner, steadying the burro's nerves, made the passage in safety. The descent of two and a

elements ... The mountains are more like rocky crags—sharp and precipitous, and black and barren—the patches of pure, white snow alone relieving the eye from the monotonous black." After reaching what they believed to be the Sierra summit range, the men proceeded westward. Within three days Faymonville was back at his Millerton home.

In the next few years the Fresno County Sierra had some illustrious visitors: famed naturalist/conservationist John Muir (see 10:2), and artist Albert Bierstadt, who arrived in 1874. Bierstadt was enthralled with the upper Kings River Canyon, and transferred the panorama he saw there to canvas. The resulting work was received enthusiastically. It is said that the painting was exhibited in San Francisco and was later sold to an Englishman for $50,000, whereupon it was taken back to his home country. Contemporary research has not disclosed who now owns the painting, if it still exists. Another notable visitor, in 1875, was Sierra enthusiast James Mason Hutchings. Botanist Albert Kellogg and photographer W. E. James accompanied Hutchings on this trip; all called at the Kings River Canyon and, like everyone else, marveled at its grandeur.

Frank Dusy led other expeditions to Dinkey Creek, where he maintained his summer home, and beyond during the late 1870s. Accompanied by one of his partners, P. F. Peck, Dusy ventured from his sheep camp on Simpson's Meadow and explored the Palisade Basin during the 1877 summer. "They were out two nights [on foot] and carried only one Henry rifle and some camp bread and bacon," wrote Lilbourne A. Winchell. "They worked northeasterly as far as the creek now called Palisade and found near the palisade wall a glacier. Dusy told the author of the wonders of that region, which account resulted in a prolonged exploration of that region in 1879."

Embarking again from Simpson's Meadow the following year, Dusy and Professor Gustav Eisen (see Chapter 8) visited Tehipite Valley and roamed the area, crossing the Kings River sixteen times over a two-and-a-half-day span. An ardent Sierra devotee, Eisen visited the southern Palisade range that same year. Four years earlier he had explored the McKinley

half miles is very tiresome, owing to a loose soil and shifting rocks, down which the trail winds its tortuous way. But we arrived safely in the valley before sundown, tired enough to eat our suppers in haste and go to sleep.

As Mr. Dusy's chief object in visiting the valley on this occasion was to take photographic views of the principal points of interest, we, early next morning, loaded ourselves with the camera, acids, glass, and other articles required to take pictures, and, guided by him, started off up the river about a mile, to where a vast amount of drift-wood has collected, forming a bridge across the stream, which here is divided into many branches. Crossing them without accident, and climbing up the chaos of rocks that for ages have been falling from the cliffs, on the south side of the canyon, we reached a suitable point, overlooking the valley, about five hundred feet above the river. Mr. Dusy was soon in readiness, and proceeded to take a copy of the Dome and the north side of the valley, but, owing to the hazy condition of the atmosphere, he did not succeed in getting a presentable picture. So we clambered down again to the river by a shorter route, wading nearly waist deep in the icy waters, across to our camp. The mountain air produced a singular drowsiness, and it was sometimes with difficulty that we could keep our eyes open, particularly after dinner. We arose next morning, with old Sol looking down upon us, reproachfully, as if chiding us for scorning the splendors of a mountain dawn. Hurrying through breakfast, we again waded the river, and once more climbed the rocky debris to our former point of observation. This time the artist obtained admirable representations of the Dome, the Valley, and the Falls under the Dome. Pleased with our success we returned to camp, re-crossing the river at a place where it was necessary for us to partially disrobe, and to carry our boots and unmentionables together with our photographic materials, in our hands....

A general view of the valley, which is three miles long by one in width, is magnificent and sublime. Great white mountains of rock on either side, cleft by deep canyons, down which icy torrents tumble and roar; beautiful green meadows, dotted with copses of willow and oak; the bright colored flowers; the several branches of the river, with their transparent waters, bordered on one side with a bar of white sand, that glistened like snow in the sun, all combined to make one of the fairest pictures in Nature's gallery. The grandest feature of all is the superb and majestic Dome, which rises 5,330 feet above the level of the river, on the north side of the gorge. The Indians call it "Tehipite," signifying high rock, and that name we decided by formal vote it should wear forever, and that the same name should also be applied to the valley. We recorded our resolve on a written notice, conspicuously posted, and also inscribed it on the blazed trunk of an oak tree. Be it known, therefore, to all the earth that the lordliest mass of granite in the Nevada range, is the Tehipite Dome, in the Tehipite valley, on the middle fork of Kings River.

On the opposite side the rocks rise 6,000 feet high, though not vertically. The falls, under the dome, come from the waters of Crown Mountain Meadows, and pour over the cliff in a series of cascades, and in three distinct falls. The lowest one is perhaps 300 feet high, and breaks into spray before reaching the bottom. Because of its great beauty we named it the "Silver Spray Cascade."

Our work being completed, we prepared to ascend again to the outer world, when at the last moment we found that our pack mule had eloped. After vainly trying to make our patient donkeys carry his load with theirs, two scouts volunteered to pursue the recreant. Wearily climbing out of the canyon, they followed his muleship six miles, and found him hied homeward. The scouts brought the truant mule into the canyon the next morning, and we at once prepared to depart. At 1 o'clock p.m. of the 17th we began to struggle up the precipitous side of the gorge, and at 6 o'clock reached the summit without accident. We had to unpack the mule and steady the donkeys by ears and tail, as before, at a narrow pass. Here one of the donkeys lost his footing, and for a moment was suspended by his extremities over a yawning gulf, 1,000 feet deep. Had either of those appendages failed him, or the grip of his drivers been less firm, sad would have been his fate, to say nothing of the precious treasure he bore in his panniers. He was fully conscious of his danger, and trembled all over when the crisis was past. At the summit we met and encamped for the night with Messrs. Doak, Tadlock, Sample, and Collins brothers, who were on a prospecting tour towards Mt. Goddard and the higher Sierras [sic].

Our next day's trip was on foot, sixteen miles to the North Fork, where we found our truant horses grazing on the meadows. Once more, on the morrow, we were all gaily mounted, and driving our faithful donkeys before us, rode joyfully out of the chaotic world of mountains, canyons, forest and chapparal which we had been exploring, into the more attractive region which borders Dinkey Creek, our point of departure.

Montero

SOURCE: *Fresno Weekly Expositor*, July 30, 1879, p. 2, c. 3–5.

Grove of Big Trees. The affection he developed for the sequoias proved important in later years, when he was attached to the California Academy of Sciences in San Francisco and asked to testify before a congressional committee about redwood conservation. There was talk of throwing all the big tree ranges from Yosemite to Tulare County open to lumbering, but Eisen's subdued, persuasive testimony prompted the legislators to act otherwise.

Dusy's last major explorations took place in 1879, when he became the first to compile a comprehensive photographic record of the Sierra (see 10:2). He was followed in this undertaking by Lilbourne A. Winchell, who made some views of Tehipite Valley and the surrounding country in 1887 with a "modern dry plate camera." (Only crude wet photographic plates were available to Dusy.) Winchell's efforts were later exhibited at the Chicago Columbian Exposition of 1892–93, and at the San Francisco Panama-Pacific Exposition of 1915.

Reference 10:2
## JOHN MUIR ON BIRDS, SOUNDS, SMOKE AND SEQUOIAS

[John Muir made three forays into the Fresno County Sierra. The first was in August 1893, when he set out from Yosemite's Mariposa Grove with botanist Albert Kellogg, Billy Sims and Galen Clark. They toured the upper San Joaquin River canyons and Sequoia belt, where Muir admired the climbing skills of mountain sheep and decried the logging operations that were in their infancy. The party also ventured into the upper Kings River canyon, which Muir greatly admired and returned to visit in the summer of 1875. From there he and a new party, composed of Charles E. Washburn, George B. Bayley and "Buckskin Bill," a mule skinner, went up Kearsarge Pass and into the Owens Valley. Muir returned to the Sierra alone that September, save for a "little brownie mule," to learn about "the peculiar distribution of the Sequoia and its history in general." Once again, he explored the upper Kings River canyon and Dinkey Creek. While visiting these places, he jotted down the following observations in his journal.]

Upper San Joaquin River, September 1 [1875].

*Birds.* Now a wide-winged hawk heaves in sight—sailor of the air, fish of the upper sea, with pectoral fins ten times as big as his body—so high you scarce hear his fearless scream.

Now comes a cloud of cranes with loud uproar—"coor-r-r, coo-r-r"—breaking the crisp air into greater waves with their voices than with their broad brown wings, their necks outstretched as if eager to see farther and go faster, their legs folded and projecting back like the handle of an umbrella....

A little dusky crested bird dwells among the willows, keeping the twigs in tremor, though seldom seen. Now a linnet flits across the open and lights on willow sprays, making shimmer of shining leaves like the beautiful disturbance made by ducks plashing down from the sky into a sunny mirror-lake.

Jays with guttural notes hop from limb to limb, leaving stiff dead twigs in fine vibration like the fibers of a violin.

Woodpecker is drumming on hollow logs, tapping dead spars. Then comes the way-cup with golden wings colored like October leaves, clad in perpetual autumn, the dearest of the woodpeckers, elegant in form notwithstanding his short barbed tail....

Now we hear the loud cackle and chuckle of the logcock, prince of Sierra woodpeckers, larger than a pigeon, with ivory [lead-gray] bill, crimson head and jet wings, making the woods ring, loving the deepest dells where the sugar pine and sequoia grow tallest and cast dim shadows. Astonishing how far they are heard in calm weather drumming on dead sequoia tops.

Now a hummingbird as big as a bee alights wing-weary on a twig, and begins to smooth his feathers....

The squirrels send down showers of burr scales and purple seed-wings and bark that flicker and alight like snowflakes.... The Douglas squirrel gives forth more appreciable life than all the birds, bears, and humming insects taken together. His movements are perfect jets and flashes of energy, as if surcharged with the refined fire and spice of the woods in which he feeds. He cuts off his food cones with one or two snips of his keen chisel teeth, and without waiting to see what becomes of them, cuts off another and another, keeping up a dripping, bumping shower for hours together. Then, after three or four bushels are thus harvested, he comes down to gather them, carrying them away patiently one by one in his mouth, with jaws grotesquely stretched, storing them in hollows beneath logs or under the roots of standing trees, in many different places, so that when his many granaries are full, his bread is indeed sure. Some demand has sprung up for sequoia seeds in foreign and American markets, and several thousand dollars' worth is annually collected, most of which is stolen from the squirrels.

Middle Fork Kings River, September 10

Huckleberries are ripe here at nine thousand feet.

Nature makes beautiful use of smoke. During September and October the Indians fire dead logs in hunting the deer, and shepherds do the same in making ways for their sheep. Great smoke springs are thus started, which, oozing and curling forth into the still Indian-summer air, make whole skies of smoke. The sun, especially in the morning, fires this new sky and burns it white, producing a truly glorious effect....

From the Middle and North Forks' divide glorious views are obtained of all the Kings River Kingdom—the wideness of the valleys grassed with pines, the grandeur of their architecture on canyon-edges and all along their fountains, and the sweet, gentle beauty of their meads and gardens.

I have yet to see the man who has caught the rhythm of the big, slow pulse-beats of Nature.

Last eve I heard a night bird I would gladly lie awake a week to know. Its note was very musical, flutelike, very soft and sweet, yet brave, cheerful, and clear—'Ka-wu'kuk, ka-wu'kuk.'

Camp near South Fork, Kings River. Undated.

*Sequoias.* While camped recently in a fir grove near the head of a tributary of the Merced, I caught sight of a commanding granite dome looming above the trees, called Wah-Mello by the Indians, and, though now studying trees, I could not resist running to its summit. Here I obtained glorious views of the forests filling the Fresno Basin, vast expanses of yellow pine stretching many a mile, forests of sugar pine with outstretched feathery arms, and, towards the southwest, the kingly sequoias rising high in massive, imposing congregations. There is something wonderfully impressive in sequoias at a distance. Producing foliage in dense masses, they can easily be recognized miles away. One is seen crowning a ridge, rising head and shoulders above companion pines, with inexpressible majesty on his massive crown, or they are beheld in dense, close-together companies, their fine outline curves exceedingly distinctive....

A supremely noble kind of tree. Redwood was once more widely distributed, but not the *Sequoia gigantea.* The sequoias are the most venerable-looking of all the Sierra giants, standing erect and true, in poise so perfect they seem to make no effort—their strength so perfect it is invisible....

Sequoia is a serious-looking tree, but not so serious as the juniper. Instead of standing silent and immovable with only its light outer sprays like the tentacles of barnacles, sensitive and full of motion, the sequoia waves and sings gloriously in the great winds and leads all the forest choirs.

SOURCE: *John of the Mountains,* Journals of John Muir, Linnie Marsh Wolfe, ed., pp. 224–28.

*Tehipite Dome as photographed by Frank Dusy, with L. A. Winchell, in July 1879.*

*E. C. Winchell completes ceremony naming Winchell Peak for his cousin. The name was later transferred to a peak north of North Palisade where it has remained.*

*Tehipite Valley, as photographed by L. A. Winchell in 1893. (Two prints spliced together.)*

*An engraving of a painting, "Scene in Paradise Valley," by the famous painter A. Bierstadt, probably about 1875. Efforts to locate another Bierstadt of the Kings River area have been unsuccessful. This one reportedly sold for $50,000 in 1885.*

In 1879, before his photographic activities started, Winchell followed his father's lead and made some pioneering forays into the Fresno County Sierra. Rather than paraphrase his account, it is presented in full here:

In the summer of 1879 the author visited the Palisade basin and prospected the region in its larger aspects. *Cañons* were followed, ridges climbed and the glaciers examined. It was a treasure house of riches far greater than any hidden beneath the surface. Cutting the sky the most colossal of all Sierra crests reared its adamantine spires, walling a world of *cañons*, peaks, dashing ice torrents, unassailable heights, green parks bordered and starred with exquisite alpine flowers, which fringed even the snow banks. A giant realm— awful, austere, beautiful in its scarred and chaotic majesty. A world to behold; no pen nor brush may picture it. The transcendent glory of the mighty Sierra Nevada.

Snuggled at the feet of the great wall may be seen ice—solid ice—glaciers—vestiges of primordial ice fields. The largest of these lies at the northeastern base of the reigning peak of the Palisades,—now called North Palisade.

During this adventure the author named three spires of the crest: Dusy's Peak (renamed by later visitors, and now known as North Palisade); Agassiz-Needle and Mount Winchell retain their original titles. [Agassiz was named to honor naturalist Louis Agassiz, Winchell for the aforementioned Alexander.]

Palisade Creek, Dusy Creek, Glacier Creek, Grouse Valley, and two frowning guardians of a wild portal, Erebus and Nox, were additional names bestowed at that time. The regions were impassable for any domestic animals except the burros of the Basque sheep men [see below] and they entered by one pass only...

In the fall of 1879, the author and a companion climbed Mount Goddard; scaling the wall at the northwestern front, to the eaves of a long slope of broken and jagged rock, which ended at the western of the twin apexes marking the mountain's summit. Two or three hours were spent in comprehension of the superb panorama by which they were surrounded. A monument about three feet high was built of the slabs of slate-like fragments strewn about. A record, dated September 23, 1879, was signed by the author and L. W. Davis, and deposited in an empty baking powder can, which was buried in the center of the monument. So far as is known, and endorsed by prominent mountain men, this was the first completed ascent of Mount Goddard. Descent was accomplished by following a snow and ice-filled gash, or crevice, which cuts the cliff from top to bottom, near its western angle, and in which Davis nearly lost his life, when he slipped on the ice, and flat on his back began to slide down the two-thousand feet [*sic*] trough, at an angle of about 30° or 35°. A large, protuberant rock-point against which one foot caught was all that saved him from becoming a shapeless form of bone and flesh at the bottom.

From Mount Goddard exploration was made of a high and rough territory, at headwaters of North Fork of Kings River and through the network of ridges and *cañons* extending to the head of Crown Valley and along the almost impossible divide reaching from Goddard to the Middle Fork of the Kings.

The autumn was exceptionally warm and free from storms; and the months of October and November contributed to a prolonged and intimate exploration of the high country.

The only other noteworthy exploration—if it can be called that—of this period was the first occupation of the upper Kings River Canyon. On November 14, 1877, W. A. Clark, William Hicks, William Hilton and L. M. Grover left Visalia and headed for Copper Creek in the canyon, where they built a large log cabin. Abandoning their pack animals (for it was a drought year, and stock herded to the mountains had eaten all available pasturage), they noticed sheep, horses and cows passing through their camp. All the animals had been turned loose by desperate owners, and died of starvation or were eaten by the local bears and panthers. The men turned the tables on the bears and ate them, and feasted on squirrels, quail, pigeons and grouse besides. It was a mild winter, and the living was relatively easy.

Later Copper Creek residents were Apoleon Kanawyer and his wife, Viola, who opened a two-story hotel, pack station and grocery store called Kanawyer's Camp in 1881. Down the Kings River somewhat, at Cedar Grove, John Fox and Hugh Robinson built another hotel in 1896. It was a rough-hewn product made out of local resources—"log walls, a shake roof, a puncheon floor and openings for windows," according to one account. These were the first settlements of their type in what later became Kings Canyon National Park.

Not all the early venturers into the Sierra had an easy time of it. Sometime in the 1880s, Joseph Medley and Newt Murphy decided to herd some hogs into Jose Basin, just north-northwest of Pine Ridge. The early winter was at hand, but conditions were accommodating enough; the men were able to live in a lean-to bark shelter, and burned a log or two when they needed warmth. Then light snows began to fall, and while the hogs did not mind (it acted as an insulator when they slept), Murphy began to panic and feared that he and Medley would become trapped in the basin.

Medley had his fiddle with him and tried to keep up spirits by playing "The Girl I Left Behind Me" and "Oh Susannah," but it was no use—Murphy remained a nervous wreck. Finally, as the snows began to mount appreciably, Medley's brother, Marion, donned skis to check on the men. Indeed, they were nearly trapped and an evacuation was planned. Sadly, the hogs could not be herded out. There was too much snow on the ground, and they became mired when they tried to move any distance. "There were pitiful white bones in plenty scattered along the creek when springtime next came to Jose Basin," wrote Ernestine Winchell, "but the hardy skeletons of Joe Medley and Newt Murphy were still encased in their own tough skins." Their loss was a reputed $4,000.

Though sheepmen were beset with similar problems, their numbers expanded during the early 1870s and afterward. William Helm joined the Coolidge and Dusy enterprise after Carpenter bowed out, and Dusy's Canyon, Helm's Big Meadow and the Crown Valley were used by the men as pasturage. Helm left in turn during 1874; Dusy and Coolidge thereafter used Crown Valley, Blue Canyon and some ridges to the canyon's southeast known as the "Alpine Camps." William Markwood reached out and put his sheep on Cutts Meadow, Pittman and Tamarack creeks, and Dinkey Lake. His partner Hall took up lands in Hill's Meadow, between Deer Creek and the Kings River's north fork, for his flocks.

Other sheepmen and their ranges included John A. and Elisha Patterson, whose animals inhabited the large Patterson mountain range; L. P. Clark, who corralled his sheep in a basin called Clark Canyon;

Henry Ross, on Ross Mountain and Woodchuck Creek; Albert Henry Statham, between Deer and Dinkey creeks, and on Rancheria Creek; the Collins brothers, in the Crown Valley area; D. C. Sample, between Deer Creek and the Kings River's north fork, and in lower Crown Valley; W. T. Cole, between Bear Creek and the Kings; Potter and Freeman, in Blayney Meadow, and on upper Kaiser Creek; Henry Glass, I. A. Melvin and W. F. Blayney, on the San Joaquin River's south fork at different times; the Boze Ely and Blasingame families, on the Bear Creek divide; Pete Ramband and Pete Giraud in the Palisade Basin; Robert M. Wood, on Woods Creek and the adjacent Kings River's south fork; the Dougherty brothers, in the Granite Basin—along with Frank and Jeff Lewis; and brothers Chester and George Rowell on the Kings River-Kaweah River divide, usually at a place known as Rowell Meadow.

The 1890s saw an increasing number of Basque sheepherders, from the Pyrenees region of northern Spain and southern France, enter the Fresno County trade. Many came to California because it was easy to make a living here and return to their homelands with a nice profit. Of them the December 15, 1896, *Fresno Daily Evening Expositor* said:

> They have usually a wagon and two or three dogs... In about ten years they return to their native land with a competence. It is figured this way. A wagon and a pair of horses can be picked up for less than a hundred dollars. The dogs are mostly a gift... In the summer, [the Basques'] pastoral home is in the high Sierra, where the pasture is; in the autumn, he moves down to the foothills; in the winter, he is on the plains where the grass is growing green under the early rain. He moves along as Jacob did with his flocks and herds. He reaches Huron or Panoche Creek, where the grass is good until the springtime, and slowly moves across again to the Sierra to avoid the summer heat on the plains. In this way these Basque herdsmen, who can live on 25 cents a day, are worth $3000 or $4000 at the end of ten years...[The sum is not considerable today, but was a small fortune for those times.]

Although it had to weather an occasional drought year, or fluctuation in wool or mutton prices, the Fresno County sheep industry fared well until the early 1890s. Concern then began to mount about the effects of long-term pasturing in the mountains, and some began to wonder if the sheep belonged there. Wild grass and weeds were becoming rare, and erosion had gotten serious. The sheep ate all plants to the ground and consumed their seeds as well, which kept the soil in a denuded state. Winter snows would thus melt more quickly, creating floods and high-water conditions in the lakes, streams and rivers. Sheep also had a tendency to pick up Johnson grass seeds in their wool, while pastured in the valley, and were introducing that menace into the Sierra. Even their travel patterns had a deleterious effect on the land: "It is a habit of sheep in their wanderings through a hilly country to travel along the sides of hills, rather than up and down," wrote Hu Maxwell in the October 3, 1892, *Fresno Daily Evening Expositor*. "By so doing they trample paths, one above another, running in horizontal and parallel terraces. The appearance of a hillside thus trampled is a series of benches . . ." When rains came, water poured down the "benches" and washed the earth away, creating miniature gullies.

Senator John F. Miller of California had recognized this situation as early as 1881, and was concerned about the increased logging operations in the Sierra as well (see below). In that year, he introduced a bill in Congress to convert some of eastern Fresno County into a national park. The area proposed was too extensive, and the sheep and logging problems were not serious enough, so Miller's bill went nowhere. Nine years later, however, there was sufficient concern in Congress to create Sequoia National Park (on September 25, 1890). Its specific goal was to protect Tulare County's Sierra regions. On February 14, 1893, a more ambitious undertaking—the Sierra Forest Reserve—was created to promote selective and carefully managed lumbering, reforestation and recreational activities in the area between Yosemite and Sequoia national parks. (Yosemite National Park had been created on October 1, 1890). Apoleon Kanawyer was the first ranger selected to serve in the 4 million-acre forest reserve, renamed the Sierra National Forest on July 25, 1905. It retains that title today.

The Sierra National Forest was created, in part, to impose a near-ban on sheep-raising activities within its precincts. In 1899 rangers were stationed at Jose Basin and on Big Creek, commonly-used entrances to high mountain trails, to keep the men and their flocks out. This helped preserve the forest, but enforcement was always problematical. An 1898 drought in the valley forced sheepmen to look askance at the rules if they wanted to save their herds. Consequently, Special Agent J. W. Zevely of the Department of the Interior ejected more than 170,000 sheep by mid-summer. The sheepmen resorted to artifice in outwitting the rangers. One who fell victim to their tricks was Dave Fowler, stationed at Ockenden. An August 29, 1899, report in the *Fresno Morning Republican* told how Boze Ely pulled a switch on him:

Ely started up to the mountains with two large bands of sheep, both belonging to [Lee] Blasingame. When he reached Pine Ridge he was met by Fowler who warned him not to enter the reservation under penalty of arrest. The sheepman declared that he had no intention of violating the law but Fowler's suspicions were aroused and he determined to watch Ely and his sheep. The latter got wind of the fact that he was being watched and determined to outwit the reservation guardian just for fun.

Ely had two large bands of sheep. So he quietly watched until one very dark night and then gave the herders command to drive one of the bands on into the reservation. All the bells were taken from the sheep and the least possible noise was made. The herders actually passed within a few feet of Fowler's house as they drove the sheep.

The remaining band was divided into two smaller flocks. When the guardian of the reservation woke up the next morning one of his first acts was naturally to ride around and see if Boze Ely's sheep were still outside his domain. He saw the two bands and concluded Ely was obeying the law. In the meantime, half of the sheep were well on their way into the heart of the reservation and they remained there for two months without detection . . .

Sheepherding, along with mining and early lumbering activities, brought permanent settlers into the high and low Sierra regions. The communities they built were among Fresno County's smallest—and remain so to this day—but they have full, varied and intriguing histories. The remainder of this chapter will discuss all the important Sierra settlements; segments on the towns of Pine Ridge and Millwood will include discourses on lumbering after 1875. Chapter 6 covers the period before that year.

Pine Ridge, approximately eight miles east of Auberry, was more a loosely-defined area than a true community. Its center was near where John W. Humphreys and Moses Mock set up their sawmill in 1866-67 (see Chapter 6). Humphreys took some lumber from one of the early production runs and built a home for his family on a nearby mountain slope. They lived there until the mill was relocated in 1874 and Prussian immigrant August Beringhoff, one of Humphreys' employees, purchased the home. He added a barn, a general store (the first of its kind in the neighborhood), and became known to all—as an effort toward Americanization—as Gus Bering.

The Bering enterprise lasted for less than a decade, for he died in 1882. Adolph Lane and L. B. Frazier subsequently purchased the store, with Frazier's wife selling twenty-five-cent meals at the Humphreys' home (now a restaurant) to teamsters and passers-by. Three years later Bering's widow, Rose, took over the restaurant and store, hiring John Barker as a clerk. She sold out circa 1890. Previously known as "Bering's Store," the name changed to "Kenyon's" in honor of new proprietor Silas W. Kenyon.

Following this change of ownership at the store, a number of improvements took place at Pine Ridge. A post office was established on April 19, 1892, and on April 3, 1894, a school district was formed. Its first teacher was Mrs. N. E. Whitten, and the first trustees were Kenyon, Samuel Jennings (Kenyon's brother-in-law and business partner), and R. H. Patton. The continued increase in local lumbering activities had brought more families to the area, necessitating the formation of the school district. By 1899 another had to be started. On April 4 of that year the Meadow District was organized with Katie Coates as its teacher and C. C. Corlew, W. H. Van Ness and W. D. Barnes its trustees.

On the Pine Ridge business scene, Kenyon's store was joined by William Stephenson's butcher shop, a blacksmith shop, and a dairy operated by Thomas E. Bacon. Of the latter the June 29, 1892, *Fresno Daily Evening Expositor* had this to say: "By the way, the butter made at this altitude, where [the cows] roll in such luxuriant grass, and [are] supplied with pure cold water, is not equaled anywhere, not even excepting the famous dairies along the coast. There seem to be conditions peculiarly adapted to the manufacture of gilt-edged butter not found anywhere else."

The economic mainstay of Pine Ridge, as indicated above and in Chapter 6, was obviously the lumber industry. Only the significant developments in that trade can be noted here. Paul A. Vandor believed there were eighty-four sawmills that operated on the ridge, "according to the tell-tale sawdust dump piles," and there may have been more. Some of the logging businesses functioned for many years, but sawmills and headquarters buildings were frequently moved—which has caused much historical confusion. Others operated so briefly that all remembrance of them has disappeared.

John W. Humphreys and Moses Mock, the dominant forces in Pine Ridge lumber during the early seventies, continued their leadership in the latter part of the decade. Their Clipper No. 1 mill at Bransford Meadow produced until the fall of 1878, processing six million board feet and logging approximately 300 acres. Afterward, the mill was moved to Kentuck (later Kenyon) Flat, about a mile northwest of Pine Ridge. Over a two-year span two and a half million board feet were cut and 160 acres logged there. At the same time Mock was prospering with a sawmill of his own, situated on Taylor Creek and a mile southeast of Pine Ridge.

In 1880 Michael J. Donahoo bought the Kentuck Flat mill, now exclusively Humphreys', and moved it to Taylor Creek. It produced the same amount of lumber as in its previous location, again over a two-year period. Three miles west of the ridge, storekeeper Gus Bering got his start in lumbering that year. Taking in Fresno lumber dealer William Foster as his partner, he set up a double circular, steam-powered mill whose two-year output amounted to three million board feet. Bering and Foster used horse teams and wagons to haul out the lumber, a Pine Ridge first; previously, everyone had used oxen teams. After Bering's death the mill was sold, as was his other business, to Lane and Frazier, who moved it to the site of Humphreys'

first mill (see Chapter 6). In the 1883–85 period, six million board feet were cut at the relocated mill and 450 acres logged around it.

A less productive, but enduring, sawmill operation was founded in 1880 by Joseph Bretz. It was located just outside of what was later Okenden on what is now known as the Bretz Mill road. Here some two million board feet were cut, and shakes and shingles were produced; the June 18, 1892, *Fresno Daily Evening Expositor* remarked that "J. E. Bretz is clearing the fallen trees out of his mill yard, getting ready to fire up his old perpendicular locomotive and begin the manufacture of shingles. He is making arrangements for a big run this summer." A few miles to the south-southeast, also in 1880, Cy Ruth of Big Sandy built his Paiute Mill. Situated at the base of Mount Baldy, the operation was later purchased by C. M. Bennett and moved to various locations, finally ceasing production in 1905.

Mock, tired of his Taylor Creek mill for some reason, relocated to Rush Creek in 1881 and set up a double circular, steam-driven plant. The surrounding timber was excellent and plentiful, but there was no good road leading out of the site. Tons of lumber were backed up at a time for want of expedient transportation. A frustrated Mock sold out in 1885 to John Smyth and James McCardle, who built an adequate— if treacherous and winding—road out to Widow Waite's station on the Toll House road. Thereafter the mill was exceedingly profitable. By the time it stopped producing in 1912, sixty million board feet had been processed.

John W. Humphreys re-entered the lumber business in 1882, after an absence of several years. He set up a sawmill at Ockenden's site with Michael J. Donahoo as his partner. They found the going somewhat more difficult than in previous years; timber lands had to be purchased at $2.50 an acre. After superficially logging the area, taking out seven and a half million board feet, Donahoo and Humphreys sold their shares of the mill to a young Englishman named William Ockenden. Ockenden purchased Donahoo's share of the mill in 1886 and bought out Humphreys the following year. He moved the operation some two miles west and produced four million board feet in 1888–89. As a result the nearby forests were considerably, though not entirely, ravaged, a fact pointed out by the July 1, 1891, *Fresno Daily Evening Expositor*: "The surrounding woods have been robbed of all the forest trees, and present a desolate appearance, but the young trees that are growing up furnish fine shade and a delightful place to wile away the hours."

Two other sawmills started in 1882 were built by sets of partners, Cy Ruth and William Kipp, and Adolph Lane and one Bolling. The latter mill, located close to the Lane-Frazier mill, cut 10,000 board feet daily and had a total output of three million board feet. C. M. Bennett started a double circular, steam-driven saw-

Angelo Reckas

*Ockenden, one of the largest mills and later a resort on Highway 168 about two miles before Shaver Lake. There are no visible remains of the operation.*

FCCHS Archives

F.C.C.H.S. Archives

*Pioneer August Bering, who established a store at Pine Ridge in 1875 at the site of J. W. Humphreys' first sawmill. At left, his store in 1882.*

*Four- and six-horse stages served the mountain area. The riders appear well protected from the dust.*

F.C.C.H.S. Archives

Alice Carleton

*The tray mill at Ockenden with a typical team of oxen used for many years in most mills.*

*A donkey engine used to pull logs by cables out of the woods or over a hill, or to let them down a slide.*

Alice Carleton

201

mill in 1883, a mile and a half upstream from Mock's 1881 enterprise. "There were several accidents at this mill and three men were killed in one season," wrote Bert Hurt in his *Sawmill History of the Sierra National Forest*. "One man fell into the saws at the mill, another was killed in the woods, and Bennett's brother was killed when a boiler blew up at the mill. About 9,000,000 feet were cut and 450 acres logged over. Logging was done with ox and horse teams over two-pole chutes. The mill closed down the summer of 1886."

Alonzo Littlefield set up a simple up-and-down sawmill, powered by an overshot water wheel, in 1887. This operation was on the Pine Ridge grade, a mile and a half north of Bering's Store. "There he fixed up a shop where he made brake blocks for the lumber wagons and helped the teamsters with other emergency repairs," wrote Ernestine Winchell. " . . . This land had been cut over by Humphreys' sawmill in 1874, but here and there remained a pine tree that could be made into shakes, to add to the small income his needs required. About 1894 he sold his land to Ernest Van Vleet for a cattle range." Littlefield had to range over a 160-acre spread to obtain his lumber, and cut a total of three million board feet.

Humphreys and Mock reteamed in 1888 to build a new sawmill at Swanson Meadow. Situated near Ely Mountain, a dozen miles northeast of Pine Ridge, this was a fabulously rich timber area—twenty-six million board feet were taken out of 110 acres before the plant shut down in 1892. "At this mill, the logging was done by heavy teams of mules and horses, which was an innovation in woods methods," said Lilbourne A. Winchell. "Heretofore oxen were universally used to haul the big trucks, the only exception[s] having been at [Bering's and] Lane and Frazier's mill . . . "

C. M. Bennett moved his operation from Rush Creek to Stevenson Meadow in 1888, employing John Sage as his millwright, and horse and oxen teams for hauling. At this location, logged until 1900, 300 acres and seven million board feet were cut. At the same time Bennett was moving, Jesse Musick and his sons installed a double circular, steam-driven mill near present-day Shaver Lake Heights. Its eventual output was sixteen million board feet, taken from 600 acres of almost-untouched forest. Ox and horse teams, together with heavy wagons, were used for transport. This mill operated well into the 1890s, and a box factory was later added to it. Accounts suggest it burned sometime before the turn of the century.

The last important sawmill to open near Pine Ridge was Charles Cummings'. "Charley Cummings took the Ockenden mill over and moved it about a half mile farther into the timber, setting it up . . . the fall and winter of 1889," said Bert Hurt. "It operated four seasons, closing down the fall of 1893. Cummings was a redwood operator in Santa Cruz County before

going to Pine Ridge, and when he started the Pine Ridge operation he used the coast methods of logging. Ox teams and cross-skid roads [were employed] and when the hills were too steep for cattle to get off the skid road, the logs were skidded to the road with men and jack screws . . . About 17,000,000 feet were cut and 600 acres were logged over."

Fewer mills opened on Pine Ridge during the 1890s because so much of the surrounding, easily accessible territory had been ravaged by previous operations. "At many places on Pine Ridge may be seen the effects of having the forest removed," said the August 10, 1892, *Fresno Daily Evening Expositor*. "The mills have cut out the marketable timber, and fires have killed all the undergrowth, until now, in many places, the mountains are desolate and low, where a few years ago they were covered with dense forests." Still, there was a need for construction materials throughout central California, so the exploitation of the timber continued.

William Stephenson and C. M. Bennett built a double circular, steam-powered mill at Stevenson Meadow during 1890. The enterprise lasted for two years, logging 150 acres and cutting three million board feet. It was purchased later by the greatest logging enterprise ever to operate at Pine Ridge—the Fresno Flume and Irrigation Company. Incorporated on October 29, 1890, it was capitalized at $500,000, offering 5,000 shares at $100 apiece. Fresno businessmen J. M. Haskell, R. B. Johnston, L. J. Miller and H. L. Musick formed the company and acted as its first board of directors, together with Frank Bullard of Yolo County.

The directors purchased 12,000 acres of timberland in the Stephenson Basin area, hoping to build a large sawmill and a flume that would run down to the valley floor, but problems intervened. Fights broke out among the directors regarding assets, liabilities and rights-of-way for the proposed flume. The enterprise languished for the first part of 1891; then, a man associated with the company was quoted in the May 30, 1891, *Fresno Daily Evening Expositor* as saying that " . . . litigation is at an end and there will be nothing of that sort to hinder or embarrass the proceedings in the future. The work is free to go ahead now—that is, it is free so far as the dismissal of these law suits can make it free . . . Everything was compromised, and it was satisfactory to all concerned."

Difficulties apparently continued, for it was not until July 1892 that flume construction began. Vast quantities of lumber were needed for that project, and were provided mostly by Caleb Dickerson Davis' Bonanza Mills. Sensing a good business opportunity, Davis contracted to supply four million board feet, log 300 acres and cut as much as 40,000 board feet a day to satisfy the terms. At one time this operation was said to be the most productive on Pine Ridge, and a box and tray factory was added to it. Fire destroyed everything at the operation on December 9, 1893. The loss was $40,000, wholly covered by insurance. Reconstruction began immediately because the flume was still under construction and the need for lumber remained acute. The sawmills of Charles Cummings, C. M. Bennett and others were enlisted to help take up the slack.

The Bonanza Mills fire was one of many difficulties encountered in the flume construction. Marking its route along Stephenson Mountain was an onerous task: "As it happens the grade of the flume runs along down the face of a high cliff of rock, and the engineers have to be let down by ropes to the proper place to put the hieroglyphics on the solid granite front instead of driving stakes in the ground, and they dangle about in mid air," said the June 29, 1892, *Fresno Daily Evening Expositor*. If conditions were right, a mile of flume could be built in ten days, but never easily, as the August 2, 1892, issue of the same newspaper noted:

> The construction for the last week has been retarded on account of natural barriers. Stephenson creek had to be bridged, and that took several days. And the precipitous granite walls . . . [have] been another drawback.
>
> It is out of the realms of the laughable for men to be lowered in rope baskets, fastened to a tree a hundred feet above, and hang there against the face of a smooth granite wall, hundreds of feet above Stephenson creek, and a hundred feet from the top of the cliff, and drill and blast a foothold on which to commence the flume. Then when there is a foothold made on which the men can stand, they hold with one hand to ropes fastened above and work with the other. To make a flume of such huge dimensions as this one, over such difficulties is slow indeed.
>
> An enterprising photographer comes upon the scene to get some negatives of the picturesque scenery surrounding the flume. But the abyssmal[*sic*] depths of the yawning chasm, the rugged walls of the beetling cliffs, the dash and roar, the turbulent waters, and the men dangling in mid-air unnerved the poor, uniniti- ated picture man. And when a tremendous blast, a thousand feet away, threw a fragment that tore a hole through the flume a few yards from him, he picked his way as carefully and hurriedly as possible back up the canyon. He has not been heard of since.

To provide water for the flume, a $16,000 dam was built across Stephenson Creek in late 1892. Thirty- seven feet high and two hundred feet long, it covered nearly 12,000 acres—until warm rains and a flash flood washed much of it away on December 24, 1892. "The noise was beyond description, causing the ground to tremble," said one report. "The rolling of boulders that weighed hundreds of tons added to the roar of the water. Trees were snapped like straws. It was well that nobody lived below the dam, for nothing could have been saved. The reservoir was so large that a long time was required to empty it."

This and the previous difficulties caused more shake- ups among the company's directors. Once the prob- lems began to mount, Michigan lumbermen Charles B. Shaver and Lewis P. Swift took control of the com- pany, bringing with them considerable expertise and a spate of new investment money. (In time the dam and reservoir behind it were made whole again. Both were named after Shaver, and though the Fresno Flume and Irrigation Company is long gone, the designations remain today.) Though the flume was completed to Dry Creek after a reasonable interval, and could be ridden by errant thrill-seekers (see 10:3), the year 1894 dawned before appreciable quantities of lumber began flowing to the company's Clovis headquarters and processing plant (see Chapter 13). Before one penny of return was realized, $300,000 had been poured into the sawmill, dam, flume and valley plant.

The company's mill, built at the northwestern edge of present-day Shaver Lake, was an impressive enter- prise. "[Eight] miles of steel cable threaded the forests; equal miles of log chutes carried the train of logs drawn by powerful donkey engines stationed at commanding points," wrote Lilbourne A. Winchell. "A logging rail- road with geared locomotive received the loads at various wood stations, and delivered the logs to the lake, from which they were floated or towed in rafts by a little steamer, to the mill." There, a work force of 300 men had a 500-horsepower saw to work with, and could produce 155,000 board feet in twenty-four hours. The *Fresno Morning Republican* of August 26, 1898, described typical goings-on there in this manner:

> Those who wish it may ride on the lumber carriage, but hereafter I will just walk, for during the sawing of a 50-inch log we rode, or rather were jerked, backward and forward a few dozen times. Then, when the log needed turning, and the steam log turner, or "nigger," as it is commonly called, would jump up from the regions under the floor and whirl the huge log over, it seemed like some evil genius that would grasp us with his teeth if we ventured too near.
>
> The saws are 68-inch for lower and 54-inch for upper, and no logs have been taken to the mill that needed blasting before being run through the saws. Saws are changed about every three hours, and it is rather dangerous to examine them too closely when they are in motion.
>
> At night the mill is lighted by electricity, there being a dynamo and separate engine for it in the mill; and lights are placed on the lake also where a man is busy piloting logs to the little cart that runs on a wire cable and goes down under the water to receive the log. The little cart, like a king fisher, dives down for its prey, grasps it firmly in its talons on its back, then comes creeping over the dam, dripping with water.

This operation was so streamlined that it frequently flumed too much lumber to Clovis; work shifts were briefly laid off until the flatland crews could catch up

203

Angelo Reckas

*Fresno Flume and Irrigation Mill on Shaver Lake, to right, where lumber was cut to go down the flume to Clovis. The road was on the old dam.*

Cliff Fields

*Mill yard at Shaver Lake. Note three branches of flume which bring lumber from different sections with all ending up in Clovis.*

*Wagon team hauling the always essential firewood out of the Sierra foothills to Fresno, 1895.*

FCCHS Archives

204

Cliff Fields

Armstrong's store and hotel at Pine Ridge. The store was originally Bering's.

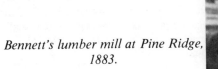
Bennett's lumber mill at Pine Ridge, 1883.

F.C.C.H.S. Archives

with the backlog. When the mill closed in the fall of 1914, it had cut *450 million* board feet of lumber and logged *15,000* acres, staggering quantities that set a Pine Ridge lumber production record.

Although the Fresno Flume and Irrigation Company dwarfed its competitors, others were still encouraged to start logging operations in the vicinity. Timberlands remained, for some previously-logged stands were coming back, and there was always the possibility of going deeper into the virgin woods. John Sage's double circular, steam-powered mill, established in 1893, had enough trees to choose from so that it could cut 15,000 board feet a day. Its timberlands ranged over 100 acres; six-horse teams and wagons were used for hauling, and before this sawmill shut down in 1898 three million board feet had emerged from it.

A year later, Jerome Bancroft and Winn Litchfield set up a sawmill whose exact location near Pine Ridge is uncertain. It was described at length in the August 3, 1898, *Fresno Morning Republican*:

The next place visited [by a party of flatland vacationers] was Bancroft's settlement at which place Mr. Bancroft has had his mill situated four years [Litchfield apparently had left the partnership]. The number of men engaged at the mill ranges from thirty to thirty-five, and the mill continues at work every day and Sunday nights. Lumber, cleats, boxes and trays are manufactured daily. The daily capacity for lumber is from 30,000 to 35,000 feet; for cleats, 15,000 to 20,000; for trays, 2,000 to 3,000; and about 1,000 boxes. Mr. Bancroft and sons own about 400 acres of timber land and have an apple orchard with 2,000 trees planted, besides a garden and a competent gardener who has charge of the vegetable department and supplies the boarding house with every kind of vegetable common to the valley. The mill has been running since May and will continue until snow falls. Mrs. Bancroft hospitably entertained us and served us fresh fruit from the valley, which was greatly appreciated by us and it was with reluctance we departed from her pleasant home. There is a dance hall at that place and Saturday night dances afford entertainment for those who trip the light fantastic.

This mill was destroyed by fire in July 1899.

Reference 10:3
## EXCITING FLUME RIDE

Editor Expositor:—No person who has not had the strange, new and exciting experience can form any just conception of a ride from Stephenson creek, beyond Pine Ridge, to Dry creek, in the flume which now reaches a point on Dry creek eight miles below the Toll House. Perhaps at no other place in the world can one have that thrilling experience, that romantic excitement; for, while there are many flumes, both in this State and elsewhere, yet this one, in some respects at least, is the most wonderful of them all. It sweeps in graceful curves through forests of giant pines, magnificent cedars and towering firs, skirts the walls of granite mountains, passes along the brinks of cliffs, precipices and bluffs, which fall sheer down hundreds of feet and in places almost thousands of feet . . .

There were six of us in the party, consisting of Mr. Shaver, superintendent of the Pine Ridge flume, Mr. and Mrs. L. P. Swift, Mrs. H. L. Musick, Miss Ida Musick and Miss Lena Backer. The start was made from the head of the flume, at the dam on Stephenson creek, at 8 o'clock in the morning, a beautiful August morning in the mountains.

But first, just before starting on the journey, a word or two in description of the boat is proper, for when once under headway there will be little time to describe it, for there will be other things to look after and attend to. The flume is in the shape of the letter V, and has sides about four feet high. Down this the water flows and the flume boat is made also in the shape of a V, to fit the flume.

The end of the boat pointed down the flume is left open, in order that the water may enter and hold the boat steady. Slats are nailed across the boat from side to side, and lengthwise with the boat on these slats a plank is laid, on which the passengers sit, balancing themselves, and by that means balancing the boat, which they soon learn to do very nicely . . .

All things being ready at 8 o'clock in the morning, we balanced ourselves carefully in the boats, and with a quick start the boats were under way, gliding smoothly and gracefully round curve after curve down the canyon of Stephenson creek, not very rapidly at first, and it was a good thing for us, as it gave us an opportunity to grow accustomed to the novelty before we came to the swift and reckless places in the journey.

Before the first mile is passed the Bonanza mill is reached, and then immediately the flume runs out along a bare rock, forming the side of a mountain. Far beneath is the rugged canyon of Stephenson creek, filled with huge boulders. In building the flume along this place the workmen had to be let down from above with ropes, and they swung by ropes while they drilled holes in the wall of solid rock in which to fasten the timbers which support the flume. We flew rapidly across this giddy place and sat quietly in the flume boats and let them go. We could not have stopped had we so desired; for when you once set out upon that journey, there are only a few places where a halt can be made.

In places the flume from this point has a descent of two and two-thirds feet to the rod, and when all was ready the flume boat with its six passengers shot forward, down the flume at terrific speed, while we all shouted with rapture, for we took no thought of what would happen if a trestle should give way, or if some accident should wreck the boat and send us all over a cliff, perhaps hundreds of feet into the canyon . . . After the head of Dry creek was passed the descent became more rapid . . .

At length the Toll House, with its dusty sheds and old barns appeared in sight a couple of miles away and more than a thousand feet below us. We sailed round the brink of the cliff of solid granite on the west side of Dry creek, so high that the buzzards were soaring beneath us in the canyon.

We had now passed all the dangerous and exciting places on the journey and the mountains were left behind, and the flume entered the foothill, where the descent, while considerable, is much less than where it pitches down the face of the mountain and sweeps hurriedly round the bluffs.

When we came to the end of the flume we took conveyances and proceeded to Fresno.

Of course the boats are never taken back. The only way to take them would be to haul them with teams, and that is not necessary. Each boat makes one trip and that is all. It reaches that bourne from which no flume boat ever returns.

One of the Party.
Fresno, Aug. 31, 1893.

SOURCE: Fresno County Scrapbook 1870-1899, pp. 1257-58, taken from *Fresno Daily Evening Expositor*, September 1, 1893.

Another mill, three miles northeast of the Pine Ridge settlement, was operated by brothers Frank, George and James Landale during this same era. A modest operation that employed twenty-five men, cut 30,000 board feet daily and had a box factory, it burned on July 17, 1896. It was said that 500,000 feet of lumber were destroyed in the blaze, the loggers' cabins were destroyed, the men had to be put up at Kenyon's, and the loss was $10,000.

The year 1898 saw a flurry of sawmill openings on the ridge. Abner W. Petrea set one up just south of the Bretz mill, where 700 acres were logged over seven years and twenty-one million board feet cut. Like the better mills of its day, it had a double circular, steam-powered saw and could handle 30,000 board feet daily. William Kipp opened a mill with similar capabilities in the spring, a mile south of Kenyon's. Cattle and log wagons did the hauling; 100 acres were logged and a million feet cut before the mill closed in the fall of 1899. Much of the vicinity had been logged before, and the young, available timber was not of prime quality.

A short distance southwest of Kipp's mill, Bert Moore operated another in 1898–99 that was much more productive, with 2.8 million feet of lumber cut, and 160 acres logged, with horse and mule teams doing the hauling. The only other significant mill to open that year was owned by W. W. Wilson and Elmer Damon. Sam Eversole was the superintendent there and Damon became the sole owner shortly after the mill was started. "Twenty men are employed and about 160 pounds of beef are required each week for them, as they have mountain appetites," said the August 3, 1898, *Fresno Morning Republican*. "Lumber is the only thing manufactured, and 14,000 feet per day is sawed."

In addition to the sawmills—and, usually, in conjunction with them—box, shingle, shake, tray and cleat factories operated at Pine Ridge during the eighties and nineties. "The first box mill was built by [W.] Millard Ewing and [W. S.] Bouton the season of 1885 . . . and it operated until the summer of 1889, when it was lost by fire," wrote Bert Hurt. "About 2,000,000 feet were cut, and about 100 acres were logged over. Only the best trees were felled and the timber was bolted in the woods. It was hauled to the mill in wagons with horse teams. Power was secured by the use of steam."

In subsequent years, similar enterprises opened. The June 18, 1892, *Fresno Daily Evening Expositor* remarked that "[there] seems to be no limit to box factories this year in this part of [Pine Ridge]. In addition to the large one at the foot of the mountain, at the Toll House, there are no less than seven at Pine Ridge." Their names have gone unrecorded.

Pine Ridge's reputation was not based solely on lumber. In the 1880s and 1890s, the place was a popular resort for flatland residents who wanted to escape valley heat and enjoy the cool mountain air and verdant scenery. "I have just arrived at this place in a heavy rainstorm," wrote a correspondent in the June 21, 1882, *Fresno Weekly Expositor*. "On the road I saw quite a large delegation of the residents of Fresno, among them was our genial friend Reese, H. Ross, W. M. Williams, --- Burch, and Frank Dusy. They had their families with them, who were going to the mountains to rusticate for the Summer. Most of them were not very favorably impressed with the beauties of the mountain climate. But it is usual to have a storm about the beginning of June."

While there, vacationers could camp in the open (see 10:4), or retire to any number of resorts. Kenyon's hotel was a favorite, in winter and summer both. During the former season, a nearby meadow would freeze and create a huge, natural ice rink. Many visitors skated there, as well as Indians who used bear jawbones in lieu of skates! Two other popular resorts were described in the August 26, 1898, *Fresno Morning Republican*:

Shaver is a very nice camping place, as there are many neat shanties scattered about, while a store and postoffice make the campers imagine they have every luxury of the valley. The boarding house was the most welcome sight about noon, and the meal we secured was both plentiful and substantial. We did not see a saloon in the little town, but there were two about a mile away, standing close together, and an undertaker's sign on a tree between them.

Armstrong's Grove, about three miles from Ockenden, on the Shaver road, was very inviting with its signs, "Free Camping Ground Here," and the place presents a clean and lively appearance. Cottages were numerous, while a dance hall and a photograph gallery were prominent buildings, hidden among the trees.

Extended quotations from the *Fresno Daily Evening Expositor* of August 18, 1894, and August 17, 1896, respectively, will serve to re-create the recreations of ridge vacationers:

Last Wednesday night a jolly party of seventy-five persons assembled at a campfire of the Baird brothers of this city, held at their camp at Burrough meadows. They were entertained by violin and vocal music, and dancing. Henry Eversole was "floor" manager and Sam Eversole danced a fling—"The Fusileers." Miss Lucy Baker and the Misses Owens sang, and according to the decision of the EXPOSITOR'S informant, "they were the head of the class."

. . .

Last Saturday evening a pleasant hop was given at the Damon dancing hall, midway between Ockenden and the Dam. Thirty-five couples were in the grand march. Good music was rendered by the Fresno Troubadour Club, and the evening seemed to be well spent.

The Fresno Troubadours arrived at the dam a few days ago. Truman Lippincott, a member of the club, will arrive in a few days. The boys have pitched their tent along the side of a large rock, just above the F.F.I. Co.'s cook-house. They are a jolly lot, and expect to stay here about a month, and will aid much in making the mountaineers cheerful.

Ockenden, just up the road from Pine Ridge, was the site of another resort. "It has been a place of encampment for people from the plains for the past twenty-five years," said the July 1, 1891, *Fresno Daily Evening Expositor*. "The water is fine and cold as ice. The woods are cool and the sunshine is just warm enough to make the shade sought after. The place is now owned by Thomas J. Okenden [brother of William], a young Englishman, who has a store and hotel here."

The place became so popular that Ockenden expanded it in 1892, and built a large hall for dances,

balls and other social functions. A year later, on July 24, 1893, a post office was added to these facilities. By 1898 there were enough permanent settlers in the area to justify founding a school district, the Butler, on May 16. Lewis P. Swift, Charles Griffin and A. N. Cressman were its first trustees, and Hattie Adams was its teacher in 1899.

Activities available at Ockenden during this period included picnics, parties at the local lumber mills, watching the loggers at work, or visiting Sunset Rock, a quarter-mile away from the settlement. The latter place, as the name suggested, was a good spot from which to watch sunsets. "The reservoir at the power house can be seen in the distance, a beautiful lake of silvery whiteness," said one onlooker. "As the sun descends behind the mountains it seems like a gigantic ball of fire resting on the mountain tops in the distance, and across the hills and valleys appear rays of purple and red light, a sight beautiful and inspiring,

Reference 10:4

## CAMP LIBERTY ON PINE RIDGE

Editor Expositor: On leaving Fresno some 12 days ago, I believe, I promised to drop you a line on my reaching the mountains. This promise, given in a moment of absent mindedness, I will now endeavor to fulfill, though writing for the newspapers, to the unpracticed pen, is an undertaking of no small magnitude. . . .

The road to Italy is over the Alps, so the way to Pine Ridge is, as most of your readers know, over the Toll House road; but most of your readers are totally ignorant of what that term, the "Toll House road," fully implies.

To say that that part of it from Letcher's to the Toll house is a disgrace to Fresno county, is drawing the matter in as mild terms as now occur to my mind. In all Fresno county this is the only present outlet that we have for our vast wealth of pine forests, and this road is traveled as much, perhaps, as any other three roads in the county, and yet it is filled with boulders, roots of trees, gullies, washouts and every other conceivable obstruction, to that extent that traveling over it in a light vehicle is attended with constantly recurring cuffs, humps and wrenches to the body and limbs of the rider and ever present peril to the stability of the vehicle. A little later in the season the road up the mountain is still worse, and really dangerous . . .

Arriving on the mountains in the cool, refreshing shades of the pines, the steep grade, the dust, the rocks, the heat and all other petty annoyances are speedily forgotten in the improved and reinvigorating condition of mind and body caused by the high altitude and clear atmosphere.

GORGEOUS SUMMER PALACE

Instead of camping near one of the numerous saw-mills in this region, as most people usually do, who come up here, we moved

a few miles closer to the summit and erected a gorgeous summer palace on the side of a gentle shady slope, near a green meadow intersected by a beautiful brook and in striking distance of Tom Bacon's dairy and Bill Stephenson's butcher shop.

After making our house and preparing it with a long airy veranda, where we sit and smoke and talk and rest our eyes upon the manifold beauties which nature has so lavishly scattered around, we raised upon the very apex of our structure, the comb of the roof, as it were, the American flag, the stars and stripes, and christened our new abode "Camp Liberty," which, being interpreted, means that everyone is at liberty to do as he pleases.

Notwithstanding the difficulties of the approach to this region, you must not conclude that we are wholly wanting in social events. A day's ride among the secluded dells and shady groves hereabouts will reveal the fact that a large number of young ladies, worn out by the winter's gaieties in the cities and towns, and tired of the heat and dust of the plains, have hied themselves away to greener and fresher bowers, and like the acacia, they are

"Beautiful none the less,

For blooming in a wilderness."

Of course when young people are in the same neighborhood social gatherings and good times generally are brought about. Last week it was given out that there would be a dance at Stephenson's mill on Saturday night, and a little after nightfall of that day, when the stars had come out and were shining down from their placid heights with a sparkling brilliancy, only seen in high altitudes, numerous couples, some afoot, some horseback and some in vehicles, could have been seen winding their way to the scene of mirth and festivities. On arriving at

the place a huge bonfire blazed and crackled in front of the hall door. Some dozen old fellows, like the writer, smoked their pipes of peace around the fire and viewed the gaieties from this safe distance through the open door. Within, two fiddlers, on a high perch at the end of the room, twanged away, while on the floor eager hearts "chased the glowing hours with flying feet." There were no dresses of flimsy white stuff, or swallow-tail coats, low-cut vests, or pump slippers, but, like Tom O'Shanter, the fun was glorious. Such grace of movement, lightness of step and genuine, old-fashioned dancing I have not seen for many a long day.

MOLASSES AND MUSCLE

Last night the doors of Camp Liberty were thrown open to the neighboring ladies and gentry for a big candy pulling, known in some of the northwestern states, I am informed, by the more elegant and classic expression, "taffy jerking." The candy was duly pulled until it had the appearance of raw silk. After the candy the company gathered around the bonfire, which had furnished light for the occasion, and sang songs, religious and otherwise. "From Greenland's Icy Mountains," the sweet strains of "Annie Laurie," "Bonnie," "Sweet Bessie," etc., etc., filled the "rocks and braes around" until the hooting of the owl, the barking of the fox on the distant mountain side, warned the light-hearted singers that soon the "eye of morn" would open in the East. Next week we go deer hunting up in Tamarack, and if we have good luck I will send you word.            H.

Camp Liberty, Pine Ridge, July 20, 1890.

SOURCE: Fresno County Scrapbook 1870-1899, pp. 1218-20, taken from *Fresno Daily Evening Expositor*, July 9, 1890, p. 8, c. 1, 2.

but to discribe [sic] it in all its beauty and grandeur is impossible."

Beyond Ockenden lay another vacation and recreation spot, Markwood Meadows. The area was first settled by sheepman William Markwood, mentioned earlier in this chapter. He was killed on August 15, 1876, when his horse shied and threw him off a cliff. Before then, the meadows had been developing as a resort of sorts; William Faymonville talked of staying there, with Aquilla Loveall and his wife, during his 1872 excursion into the Sierra. Elliott's 1882 Fresno County history referred to the place as being "a favorite summer resort for a number of families, who have built comfortable homes for their use. . . . It is a beautiful plateau, level as a floor, and at the proper seasons is covered with a luxuriant carpet of green grass." This held as true fourteen years later, when the August 17, 1896, *Fresno Daily Evening Expositor* said, "Markwood seems to be the favorite camping spot this season. Parties are given there, and good social times are had."

Early property owners at the Markwood Meadows included Thomas Ockenden, his brother William, Mark H. Collins and Phineas Loucks. An odd story is attached to Loucks, who arrived at the nearby Laurel Creek area in 1887. A peripatetic county resident, he left his wife and children in their cabin on the creek while he tended to some beekeeping at Centerville. Local residents were concerned when heavy snows fell in the area and there were no signs of the Loucks family, but Phineas remained blasé about the situation. The cabin had been built to withstand any disaster, he said, and plenty of food had been placed there earlier.

When the spring of 1888 arrived, Mrs. Loucks and her children emerged from the cabin—just barely alive. Pregnant at the time of her isolation, she died in childbirth aggravated by weakness the following July. After burying her in a nearby meadow, Loucks moved to Selma with his children for a time. He seems to have left them with friends and/or family; in any event, he disposed of them so he could return to the cabin alone. Apparently aggrieved by his wife's death, he became a morose hermit. Neighbors spotted him only once in a great while; in April 1892 he was seen at Kenyon's, and no one saw him for weeks afterward. The August 10, 1892, *Fresno Daily Evening Expositor* tells the remainder of this sad tale:

> A couple of months afterwards some men passing by his cabin, found it deserted. In the woods near by they found his tools where he had been at work making shakes. From all appearances the tools had been lying there many weeks. No trace of Louks [sic] could be found, and he has not been heard of since. It is the belief that he became insane and wandered off into the mountains and died.

South of Pine Ridge were other timbered areas and the Kings River—with several communities between them. Sixteen miles southwest of Pine Ridge was another loosely-knit community, based around Round Mountain and Fancher Creek and generally known by the former name. Thomas Flippen and Joseph Elliott were the first to start farming and stock raising there, in 1869. They were followed by Joseph Imrie the next year, and N. E. Qualls, S. E. Qualls and A. H. Barringer in 1872. "It was not many years before every bit of the land was taken up in homesteads, pre-emptions, timber-culture claims, or purchased from the state, with actual homeseekers with families and ambition," wrote Ernestine Winchell. Soon fig, orange and cereal crops were being cultivated on the red clay soil about the mountain's base.

In 1873, Round Mountain school district was formed by Flippen, Elliott and S. B. Qualls; the men also served as its first trustees. Classes were conducted at Flippen's home by a Miss Greenleaf until a schoolhouse could be built the following year. A February 21, 1877, *Fresno Weekly Expositor* article mentioned that the school had fifteen students (five boys and ten girls), could easily accommodate thirty-five to forty—though it was small—"and the furniture, homemade, is sufficient and comfortable." W. S. Sorrell was listed as the teacher, and the article expressed amazement that his usual attendance was twelve students out of the fifteen. "Very few, if any, of our county schools can show like this, which may be generally understood as a significant though silent indorsement [sic] of Mr. Sorrell's excellent methods of conducting school exercises and making them interesting . . . "

Two obscure settlement areas were located a half-dozen miles southeast of Round Mountain. Lilbourne A. Winchell's *History of Fresno County* relates virtually all that is known about them: "Tivy Valley's first settler was one of the Commissioners who organized Tulare County. He was a surveyor, and laid out many of the valley townships. Joseph A. Tivy's old chimney . . . may yet be seen [1927–28] near the road leading up the south side of Kings River. C. F. Cherry was a pioneer in Clark's Valley." The latter location is distinguished by the fact that it housed two school districts: Clark's Valley, organized on August 4, 1873, and the Camden, founded on May 7, 1886. The latter district's attendance seems to have been minimal, for it was annexed by the Clark's Valley school on May 5, 1887.

Five miles due north of Tivy and Clark's valleys lay the Hughes Valley, first settled by John Hughes—one of the first Fresno County supervisors. He presumably arrived there in the fifties or sixties; there is little known about him, save for the fact he had two left thumbs.

A better-remembered settlement was five miles to the northwest of Hughes Valley—Trimmer Springs.

As the name suggests, springs with medicinal qualities began to lure vacationers and others there, circa 1884. At that time, or shortly thereafter, a hotel was built. It was probably owned by Morris Trimmer at first, for the place was called Trimmer in 1887 although men named Luce and C. L. Harrigan were the proprietors. Shortly thereafter, a post office (called simply Trimmer) was established, on July 27, 1889. It continued for several decades, save for an October 24, 1890, to May 6, 1892, lapse.

By 1891 Trimmer seems to have again obtained ownership of the springs and adjacent property. The hotel there was never elaborate, being nothing more than a large, plain, barnlike structure. An eighth of a mile behind it were the springs and numerous cottages surrounding them. The waters were piped into a tank and distributed to bathhouses and the main hotel. "Although strongly impregnated with various minerals, the smell and taste of the water of one spring is not unpleasant," said a July 3, 1890, *Fresno Daily Evening Expositor* report. "But the other is so strongly charged with sulphur that the suggestive odor of rotten eggs arising therefrom renders it rather unpalatable." Plans were made to pipe the water direct to Fresno and ship it out in barrels, for profit and publicity, but the scheme never materialized.

At first Trimmer Springs could be reached only by a road that went through Watts Valley and down Sycamore Creek. This kept it from becoming too popular, but the situation was remedied when a road leading out to Centerville opened in the early 1890s. Thereafter many persons from Fresno, Malaga, Selma and Dinuba began patronizing the place, with whole families coming for weeks of simple, pleasurable recreation. Fishing in the nearby Kings River was always good; speckled and lake trout were plentiful (and some samples weighed up to three pounds), and at low water stages angling for catfish was easy. Other diversions were described in the August 17, 1891, *Fresno Daily Evening Expositor*:

The campers amuse themselves by romping the hills when strength and disposition concur, hunting, boating, fishing, cards and croquet; but, alas! no lawn tennis . . . But one other diversion—the greatest and best of all—must not be overlooked, namely, "riding on the flume." The Kings river flume [see below] is near by and affords opportunity for that grandest of mountain sports. The novelty, with just enough danger to make it attractive, of boarding and debarking makes it the ambition of everybody. Occasionally a bold navigator makes a mistake and is half-drowned, but up to date no one has met his fate. Two young gentlemen from Fresno quit the raft on one occasion and swam a mile with little damage further than the wetting of their clothes and the ruin of their watches.

According to Mrs. Ivan Drake, Squaw Valley—a dozen miles south of Trimmer Springs, on Mill Creek—was named in 1851, when two white hunters visited the area during the time of Indian hostilities (see Chapter 2). Only women and children were found there, since the men were fighting in distant locales—hence the name. Two years later the first incidental white settler arrived—Enoch Smith, who grazed his cattle in the mountain meadows. Circa 1860, he and several other families became regular residents.

Stock raising and farming remained the economic mainstays for some years afterward. Though the former was a profitable business, it had its problems, as a Squaw Valley correspondent in the May 6, 1885, *Fresno Daily Evening Expositor* attested:

The men who have a habit of picking up a rope and not having the least idea that there is a horse at the end of it—if you were to question them—and of driving off neighbor's cattle and selling them just for fun; and borrowing provisions when the owners are absent, are beginning to be too common thereabouts; they are so numerous that when an officer comes to take them away at the expense of the county [the thieves] are kept informed of his whereabouts and can keep dark. I am credibly informed that Sands Baker, Mr. Lisman, Mr. Caldwell and others have lost cattle this Winter at their hands. An officer and Traver butcher, I am told, were in Stokes' valley after two of them for some theft, and stopping at a house—one of the thieves being in the house at the time—was informed that the suspected party was not there and had not been. I would not vouch for these reports, but I believe they are substantially correct. It has come pretty near to the pitch that if the officers cannot bring these thieves to justice the people must. We cannot, and will not, stand such insecurity to property. We claim to be law-abiding citizens, and will only resort to such measures but for self-preservation. Rumor has it that a certain gentleman is packing provisions to some of these fellows now, but as to the truth of it I am unable to say.

Another trouble we have to contend with is this: Ever since the settlement of the valley it has been the custom—and an agreement was drawn up and signed by most of the settlers, in substance as follows—that all should erect reasonable fences, and keep the same in repair, and if anyone has a breachy animal it should be taken care of. With this exception stock of all kinds should run at large and have the benefit of the outside land. Lately one of our neighbors, ignoring the agreement and taking advantage of the "No Fence" and other laws [see Chapter 6], has sown his grain, with no fence at all, and we have the choice of the fun of keeping in the saddle or turning our stock into grain fields. According to my understanding of the "No Fence" law he has us at a disadvantage; but as the case stands, submission means deprivation of means of support, from the fact that the main dependence of farmers here is stock-raising, and they cannot without the aid of vacant land raise their stock. They cannot during the time their crops are growing give support to their stock and, consequently, submitting to this invasion of justice is not to be thought of. A meeting to this end will be held to-morrow. [The resolution of this and the other problem, if any, are unknown.]

Farming was a modest enterprise in the earliest days. An 1885 report said that while 1,000 acres in the valley could be profitably farmed, only 300 to 400 were being cultivated. By 1897 these same 1,000 acres *were* planted in hay, wheat and barley—the major crops in the decades before—and the area's prominent farmers included John Price, J. C. Silver, A. B. Hartman and two men named Burk and Rich. Raspberries, strawberries and pea vines also were being grown at that time, as were radishes, turnips, onions, cabbages and tomatoes.

With the farmers and stock raisers came wives and children, and to serve the latter several school districts were formed. The Squaw Valley was formed first, on August 8, 1871, and Mrs. Ivan Drake sketched its early years (see 10:5). Following it were two neighborhood school organizations, the Hills Valley district (on April 5, 1875; it was reorganized on April 4, 1895) and the Cherry, organized on May 4, 1882.

The passage of time added more progressive touches to Squaw Valley. A post office was created on November 7, 1879, with Joe Downing as postmaster and thrice-weekly mail from Centerville, and later Sanger. When the Kings River, which the deliverymen had to cross, and other waterways ran too high, there was no mail service at all. A Sunday school was functioning by 1897, but no church seems to have been established before 1900. One of the visiting preachers at the Sunday school, a Reverend Mr. Parkhurst, was described this way by a local in 1897: "His words were

hardly suited to the place; he was enthusiastic, a little too much so in fact; but I believe he will improve, as he is but a boy." The only fraternal organization in town during these early days seems to have been a Good Templars lodge, founded in 1885, with a membership of twenty-four that year.

Holiday celebrations, dances and other socials were common occurrences at Squaw Valley. The end of the school term always brought special festivities celebrated with alacrity. The May 3, 1882, *Fresno Weekly Expositor* described one such occasion:

. . . Yesterday the school term for this district closed. The patrons of the school gave the teacher and children a dinner on a grand scale, and extended a general invitation to visitors. Friends of the little folks and patrons came from ten to twenty miles to partake of the festivities. About 2 p.m. the table was spread with meats, cakes, pies, fruits and candies, and a general display of good things that would have been a credit to any confectioner's store outside of the large cities. The children dined first, then the visitors, and lastly, the patrons. Three large tables in all, making in round numbers 200 persons. In the evening an exhibition was given by the children, all performing their various parts exceedingly well. The careful training of their esteemed teacher, Mr. Mayo B. Carrington, was plainly noticeable throughout the entertainment. The spectators were more than pleased. Mrs. Rodgers, an old resident of the place, remarked, at the close of the exhibition, that she had resided there for nearly thirteen years and had never seen anything approaching the talent displayed that day by the children. I believe the teacher goes from here to Fine Gold Gulch to teach. Evidently he carries with him the hearty good wishes of his late scholars and the thoughful people of

Reference 10:5

## LIFE AND SCHOOL IN SQUAW VALLEY
### MRS. IVAN DRAKE

The first Squaw Valley School stood across the road from the present one, on what is now our ranch. It was built in 1871. Who the earliest teachers were, we do not know, but in 1875 a Mr. Flourney of Virginia was the teacher. Being a southerner, he called door "doe," flour "flo," store "sto," etc. It made teaching difficult to first graders. Gertrude Burk, later Mrs. Traweek, and John and Charles Drake attended his school. Miss Laura Chandler taught for two years. In 1878, Owen Holmes, whose father was a Superior Court Judge in Fresno, taught the school. He was followed by Ruffin Borden of Madera. Miss Nettie Meyers, who was the next teacher, got fired because she played cards nights with the family where she boarded. Mayo Carrington taught in 1882, and he had a big school. The money to pay the teacher's salary was raised in the district. The people who donated money were called school "patrons."

One spring morning when Harry and Oliver Burk were walking across the Kelly field (now a part of our ranch), Mr. Kelly hurried out of his house saying, "Last night I thought the moon was arising, but it was the schoolhouse a-burning down." As it was near vacation time, there was no more school until Fall.

In 1888, Mr. Boren . . . deeded land for a new schoolhouse and also for a cemetery. The schoolhouse was built as was customary then with the windows on two sides. This building burned while I was teaching there. In its place a modern cement block schoolhouse with every convenience was built. I enjoyed teaching several years in it.

When Ivan Drake was a little boy attending the Squaw Valley School and playing at recess, Sontag and Evans drove up in an old cart and talked to the school children. They had camped all night near a spring in Red Gulch, what we now call Red Hill, located at

the foot of Bear Mountain. They had eaten their breakfast at Eli Downings who lived near the Drake place. From the schoolhouse they went up to Young's Cabin, near what is now called Sontag Point, because it was a lookout. The next day, they had a fight with officers.

Every Sunday we had Sunday School at the schoolhouse with a large attendance. We also had hay rides, quilting bees, spelling bees, basket suppers, all night dances, Indian Pow-wows, a literary society, where we put on 4-act plays, the participants coming on horseback or buggies for miles to practice, and ball games. Some ball games were played with neighboring teams like Dunlap. Bill True, Ivan Drake, and Everett Drake were the star players.

SOURCE: *Beginnings in the Reedley Area* by Katherine Nickel, pp. 57-58.

*Hundreds of huge trees (California Sequoia Gigantea) were taken from Converse Basin. This one had a twenty-six-foot diameter and everyone turned out to get in the picture.*

*Hotels such as the Red House Hotel were essential in Millwood—a remote place in the logging era.*

*Millwood post office at the turn of the century. Mr. and Mrs. W. C. Barnett are enjoying the sabbath.*

Irma Grosse

212

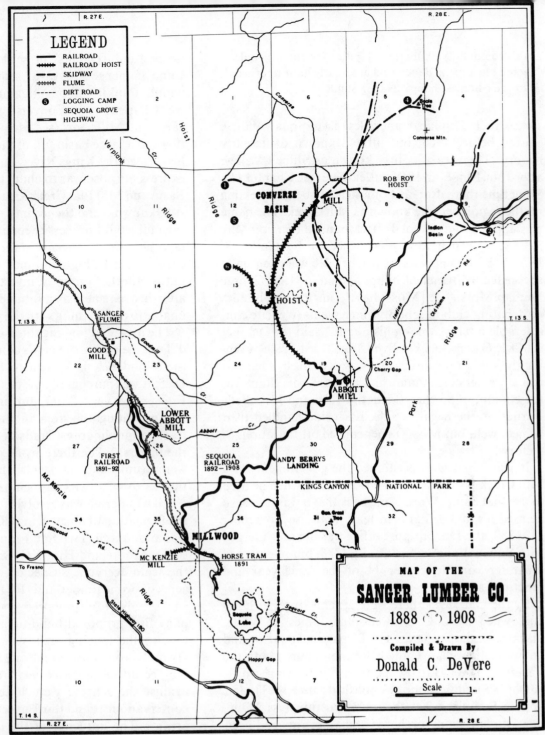

They Felled the Redwoods

*The flume, constructed of twelve- and fourteen-inch boards over an inch thick, carried thousands of board feet of lumber to Sanger every day.*

213

this community. After the exhibition the young people joined in a social dance, and at an early hour returned to their homes, happy as "big sunflowers."

Assuredly Dunlap, eight miles east of Squaw Valley, existed before 1900, but little is known of its early history. The area was first known as Shipe's Valley, after John Shipe, an 1868 settler there (see Chapter 11). Sometime thereafter, as homesteaders began trickling in, the region became known as Mill Creek. The name was applied to a school district founded there on May 3, 1875. When it formally opened on September 8, 1876, J. B. Sargent was the teacher. He was eventually succeeded by Blanche Phillips and, in 1881, by George Dunlap Moss. "He [Moss] has . . . instituted a lyceum or debating club in school, which seems to excite considerable interest among his pupils," said the October 6, 1881, *Fresno Weekly Expositor*. "Last Friday evening the subject for discussion was: Resolved, That war was a greater curse than whisky. Miss Lydia Blunt was the champion on the affirmative side, and Miss Belle Turner on the negative side. Each side handled their subject well, but Miss Turner carried off the laurels of victory . . . "

It was Moss who petitioned the government for a Mill Creek post office, and was rebuffed when he tried to use that name. Word came back that it was taken, so he used his middle name instead. Thus, on November 13, 1882, the Dunlap post office was born. It merged with Squaw Valley's on July 17, 1885, but re-emerged separately on November 11 of the same year and functions still.

By the mid-1890s there were general stores at Dunlap owned by C. C. Traweek and James T. White, blacksmith shops operated by Benjamin Anderson and John W. Howell, a United Brethren church with the Reverend J. W. Harrow as its pastor (having grown out of a Sunday school established circa 1881), and Sophia E. Wilson was the town "postmistress." Outside Dunlap, many orchards and vineyards had been set out during this era. The Foster family gained fame for its apples in Fresno and other valley communities. Mountain spring water was fortunately available for irrigation, since the valley canals and ditches obviously could not extend to Dunlap's high altitudes.

After the Mill Creek school's formation, two other neighborhood educational institutions emerged: the Harmony Valley, established on June 9, 1880, and the Hopewell, founded on May 6, 1884, with A. A. Judson as its first teacher. A lack of population caused the Harmony Valley district to close in 1885. It was re-established a few years later, again was unable to sustain itself, and was annexed to the Hopewell on May 5, 1889.

Eight miles east and northeast of Dunlap, no one would have attempted farming and stock raising, as the land was too mountainous and remote. It possessed

no real inducements for settlement—but it did have some immense groves of sequoias, which got some people thinking about logging possibilities. The first was Charles Porter Converse, who, after his checkered career at Millerton (see chapters 4 and 11), moved there to a large basin full of the trees. In January 1876 he formed the Kings River Lumber Company, whose express purpose was to chute logs out of the Converse Basin and Mill Flat Creek areas—as they were, and are still, known—and thence into the Kings River, where a sawmill would process them at a lower elevation. The fact there were no roads in the area, and that start-up costs would be high, doomed the idea. Converse sold out to another group of investors only a week or two after his scheme was announced. They were likewise unable to do anything with the proposed logging plans.

The dream of logging this isolated part of the Sierra did not die with Converse's company. A sawmill called the Woodcock is known to have operated there in 1885; it was purchased by Pine Ridge lumberman L. B. Frazier that year. Later, during 1886 and 1887, people began visiting the area in droves, purchasing huge tracts of public forest lands at $2.50 an acre. Some of the buyers, taken there by anxious real estate agents, were drunks and transients; there was much speculation as to what was happening.

All wondering was resolved on April 24, 1888, when the formation of a new Kings River Lumber Company was announced. Two San Francisco lumbermen, Austin D. Moore and Hiram C. Smith, had been running the scam everyone suspected, and had gotten 30,000 acres of prime timberlands for their trouble. To log the vast stands of fir, pine, cedar and redwoods, the company first proposed building a railroad from Centerville to the logging area, where there would be two sawmills—one above and one below the snowline, so they could be operated year-round. Formal protests against the scheme were lodged at Washington by conservationists and those upset by Moore and Smith's artifice. The influence of the lumbermen proved too pervasive. A federal agent was dispatched to the scene, and his report was wholly favorable to the purchasing methods and anticipated logging activities!

The first part of Moore and Smith's plan proved impractical, so it was scrapped in favor of constructing a flume, with a dam and reservoir to provide it with water. As with the Fresno Flume and Irrigation Company, initiated a few months later, a lumber processing plant was needed at the flume's end as well. At first, it was expected that the facility would be placed at Fresno, but the town fathers of Sanger came up with a better deal for the lumber company—sixty-five free acres just outside the town—and it was accepted on August 29, 1889 (see Chapter 13).

Teams and wagons labored over rough mountain trails to haul in materials for the two sawmills. After much hard work during the first half of 1889, the upper

(Sequoia) and lower (Abbott) mills were opened on July 6 and August 26, 1889, respectively. The flume began to go up on July 29, with lumber supplied by the Sequoia mill, and a crew of Chinese workers started building a dam on Mill Flat Meadow that August. As the dam's height rose to fifty feet a lake, named Sequoia, was created, covering 125 surface acres. Simultaneously the flume increased in length until its fifty-four miles were complete. It followed the course of Mill Flat Creek up to its junction with the Kings River, where it crossed to the other side via a 450-foot suspension bridge. From there, it roughly paralleled the river until it ended in Sanger. To help correct jamming and washout problems, a telephone line was strung along the length of the flume, connecting eleven observation stations with the main headquarters.

The *Fresno Daily Evening Expositor* of July 3, 1890, gave a good description of the flume-building:

Just above the [Kings River] bridge men are stationed who catch out planks as they float down the flume, and nail them together into boxes, with a triangular piece of inch board at one end. On board these boxes the heavy braces of 4 x 6 lumber are placed, and they are put in the flume, down which they are carried by the rapid flowing water. When a box reaches the end of the flume already built, the end piece is knocked off, the box is fitted into its place and nailed securely and the next one is floated down. [The boxes were prefabricated flume units.] About eighty of these boxes are put in place in a day, when circumstances favor, and as each is 16 feet long this means a progress of nearly a mile in four or five days.

The boxes, as they are floated down the flume, consist only of the first two planks of the "V," [which is what the flume looked like in cross-section], so there remain two more planks to be nailed on each side, and the cracks to be battened over. To do this work a large force of men are [*sic*] employed.

Ahead of the crew laying the boxes is another raising the scaffolding on which the flume lies. As the flume has passed over precipices so steep that the surveyor could not take the levels of the different stations, and through country so rough that the timbers had to be carried on men's backs to where the scaffolding was to be raised, it can readily be seen that the position of these men is no sinecure. The scaffolding is raised in length 16 feet high, each length being called a bent. Thus there were seven bents required in one part of the flume. This means that a scaffolding has to be built seven times sixteen feet or 112 feet off the ground and so built that the flume would have a general descent.

Over eighty men are employed at the flume. Their salaries range generally from $60 to $90 per month. Out of this they have to provide sleeping accommodations for themselves, and pay $18 per month for board, which, though good and plentiful, is sometimes, through the exigencies of the position, rather scant as to variety. Most of the men live in tents,

although many without discomfort, unroll their blankets on the ground and have the sky for their only canopy . . .

The flume has been pushed along as rapidly as possible, under the management of C. B. Eads, a young but veteran flume builder. The work has often been retarded by jams caused by the rushing of lumber down the flume and the breaking of several boxes, and wreckage of bents following the enormous strain put upon them by the piling up in one place of thousands of feet of lumber, and the backing up of an immense volume of water. But the worst is over now. There are no more precipices or 125 feet deep chasms to be crossed, and Mr. Eads looks forward confidently to having the flume at Sanger in three to four months . . .

Eads' prediction was correct, for the flume reached Sanger on September 3, 1890. It was capable of handling an immense volume of lumber—250,000 board feet daily—and in its first five months of operation nearly twelve million board feet were chuted down to Sanger. The mills cut the lumber at a rapid rate as well. A "race" between them on October 3, 1889, resulted in the Sequoia's winning—76,000 to 72,000 board feet. Several years later, if run day and night, they were able to produce 155,000 board feet in twenty-four hours.

"A huge band saw has displaced the previous double circulars," said a report in the June 26, 1893, *Fresno Daily Evening Expositor*. "A few minutes is sufficient to convert a large log into broad planks. On leaving the band saw this broad board is seized by two men who stick it on to rollers and from here it passes into the edger. Here two other men carry the different pieces to two cut-off saws, where they are cut in proper lengths, placed on cars, run into the yard and piled. But little is wasted at this mill. The slabs are cut into lengths of about four feet and piled, as also are the edgings, and ultimately shipped in the flume to Sanger, where they are sold for wood . . . "

At first the timber could be reached with ease from the mills, but increased deforestation—as early as 1891, when the company took out twenty million board feet—obligated the building of narrow-gauge rail lines farther into the Sierra. Chutes were positioned to connect with the lines at different points, which made loading easier. The lines snaked through the mountains on treacherous curves and trestles, and on steep grades; on one, a locomotive could propel itself by gravity while heading down. Building these facilities was a hazardous business, as Hank Johnston noted in *They Felled The Redwoods*:

In April, 1892, the Visalia Weekly *Delta* reported that 50 Chinamen [*sic*] and 20 white men were building a "seven-mile railroad" running northeast from the upper mill. During the grading, an unfortunate accident occurred. One of the Chinese workmen placed three charges of black powder in an obstructing rock. Only two charges exploded. After a short wait, the Chinaman indiscreetly approached the third charge to investigate the problem. As he reached the area, the last charge suddenly went off "blowing the heathen to bits." It was intended at first to raft the remains down the flume to Sanger but for some reason they were transported by wagon to Visalia instead.

During the early 1890s, a town sprang up around the Sequoia mill and was christened, rather expectably, Millwood. A post office was founded there on June 22, 1894, and businesses in the town by then included a general store, a butcher shop, a livery stable, saloons and two hotels—one named the "Red House," the other the "Sequoia" or "White House." For those needing their services, a shoemaker, photographer, barber, blacksmith, doctor and undertaker were available. Recreational activities (see 10:6) included croquet, boat rides on Sequoia Lake, baseball and visits to a red light district about a mile south of town.

In the earlier years, Millwood's population was mostly made up of loggers, living either in dormitories or in shacks with their families. The composition changed after 1894, when a good county road from Sanger was extended to the town and flatlanders began to use the place as a vacation resort. By February 8, 1898, the village had grown enough so that a Millwood school district was founded. Lizzie Dobie was its first teacher, followed by Ida Moore.

When the 1893 panic hit and construction starts fell off in the United States, the Kings River Lumber Company was placed in a perilous position. It attempted to pay its workers with sixty-day time drafts in July 1893, and a strike was hastily organized. "I quit this morning, and I shall not strike another lick nor bore another hole nor drive another pin until I have a guarantee that my money is ready," said employee Clarke Jennings at a workers' gathering. Moore somehow managed to patch over this difficulty, but a year later the mills were closed by court order while the company struggled with its creditors.

To save the lumber company Moore and Smith undertook considerable refinancing and reincorporated as the Sanger Lumber Company on October 15, 1894, capitalized at $600,000. In the ensuing months, it proved impossible for them to turn the company around. Moore was broken financially after that, although Smith continued as manager while the creditors took possession and decided what to do with the property.

Only twenty-five million board feet were cut in 1896, and greater production was necessary if the company was to break even. Smith deemed it necessary, at this juncture, to take an existing railroad line past Hoist Ridge, where it ended, and directly into the virgin timber stands of Converse Basin. There a two-band, steam-powered mill was set up and 400 men employed. New methods were devised to accomplish logging there (see 10:7), and everything seemed to proceed smoothly, but the operation proved a disaster. Only sixteen million board feet were cut in 1897, the creditors were furious at Smith, and he was ruined—declaring bankruptcy in a Fresno court, where he claimed $798,138.13 in liabilities and no assets.

The previous reorganization brought new creditors into the Sanger Lumber Company, with the San Francisco branch of the Canadian Bank of Commerce heading the list. Its manager, George H. Collins, became the lumber company's de facto head. While the bank shopped around for a buyer, it appointed Frank Boole as the new lumber company manager. By 1899,

Reference 10:6

## A FINE AMATEUR ENTERTAINMENT

About two weeks ago Jim Berry's camp [Sequoia Mills] was treated to a fine amateur entertainment.

Clark Jennings was master of ceremonies and performed his part in a highly efficient manner.

The first on the programme was a recitation by Miss Bertha Neer. She received the plaudits of the audience for her splendid speaking.

The next was a song by Miss Retta Hurt, who executed her part with credit to herself.

Andy Wells then favored the audience with a comedy, accompanying the acting with a banjo. He was dressed as a colored gentleman and his inimitable acting brought down the house.

The next in order was a sermon on "Spirits" by G. W. Freece. Mr. Freece represented the old "hardshelled" Baptist minister, long tailed coat and a bottle of spirits in his pocket. His acting was splendid and he received prolonged applause.

A violin and banjo duet was then given by Andy Wells and Nat Bradshaw, which was good, and it was duly appreciated by the audience.

Mr. Wells then favored those present with a song, representing a darkey [sic] sorrowing over departed friends, and his sobs in connection with the banjo and the song were ludicrous in the extreme, bringing down the house.

Frank Shirrell then delivered a declamation, showing himself a speaker of no mean order.

Fred Wright, an amateur gymnast, gave an exhibition of his skill. He appeared dressed in tights, and performed some very difficult feats with apparent ease.

Following the tumbling was the "Missouri Drill" by Nat Bradshaw and J. Eldridge, which was done in a very creditable manner, the house being convulsed with laughter at their grotesque actions.

Clark Jennings next exhibited the workings of his telephone with improvised apparatus. He passed a string around through the crowd, requesting each one to take hold of the string. A large number took hold of it. When all was ready he remarked: "I have fished in many streams in my life, but I never had so many suckers on one string before in my life." The audience saw they were sold, but took it in good part.

W. Kitzmiller, the genial roustabout, favored the house with "Next is Something Else." He is a fine amateur actor and a general favorite with the boys, and his acting was received with great favor by all.

This concluded the performance for the evening, and all went home . . .

SOURCE: *Fresno Daily Evening Expositor*, September 20, 1893, p. 1, c. 2.

216

prosperity seemed to be returning under his steward-ship, if a May 13 *Fresno Morning Republican* article was any indication:

> Millwood is livening up for the season. Men are slowly coming in, teams line the road loaded with both freight and passengers. The yards are being repaired for receipt of lumber and a new hydraulic apparatus for unloading the cars is being put in. Gangs of men are repairing the hoist and mill, loggers are felling timbers, and about a mile of new skid road is under construc-tion. It is expected the mill will start about the 20th instant. Men are in demand, both at Millwood and Converse basin, as owing to the prospect of plenty of work in the valley this season, not so many are going in as has been the case for the last two seasons.
>
> It would be hard to find a more beautiful or inter-esting camping place than Converse Basin, with its pure water, bracing air and wonderful forests, and the remarkable and extensive operations of the lumber company in handling the giant timber there found.

Reference 10:7

## IN THE REDWOOD FORESTS OF THE SIERRA

Far up in the heart of the Sierra Nevada mountains, fifty-two miles from the town of Sanger, stands the plant of a great lumber company. With lands comprising 12,000 acres, this company has within its boundar-ies thousands of the largest trees in the world.

Here is the home of the Sequoia Gigantia [*sic*], California's most massive product. For thousands of years these wonderful trees grew and thrived, exercising upon the valley below their peculiar climatic influence, until man with his greed for gold appeared upon the scene, not many years ago. Then the work of destruction began, and now bids fair to shortly exterminate the greatest growth of the vegetable world.

The "Sequoia Gigantia," [*sic*] commonly called redwood, is not to be confounded with the ordinary redwood which is so abundant along the Coast Range mountains. While the redwood proper often attains a great height, it is considered small in comparison with the Sequoia. The quality of the lumber obtained is also different. Sequoia lumber is extremely brittle but capable of taking on an extremely high polish, which makes it highly desirable for ornamental purposes, while redwood is of coarser fiber and more ten-acious, consequently forming better build-ing material.

### LOGGING SCENE

Probably there is no business nor occupa-tion less familiar to the general public than the logging of the forest giants. Imagine woods so dense that the sun seldom if ever penetrates, and instead of the familiar oak, pine, spruce and fir, trees whose height aver-ages 300 feet, and whose diameter often exceeds twenty-five feet, and such is a forest now being converted into marketable lum-ber.

First, into the woods come the chute builders, who hew down tall, straight, slen-der trees of not more than one foot in diameter, which are stripped of bark and branches and laid so as to form a cradle or skid. They act to the logs as rails to a horse car. Chute building is done under the direc-tion of an experienced woodsman. He lays out the path to be followed, and with his axe hews the "box" in the ends of the pole, making the connections fit perfectly and leaving no projections to obstruct the run-ning of the logs. Along the line of the chute a tow-path is constructed, wide enough to accommodate a team of ten horses, two abreast. This done, the actual logging be-gins.

The "fallers" or "markers," as they are sometimes designated, select the tree to be felled, and after looking carefully over the adjacent ground to decide which is the most level spot available, cut a deep notch in the side of the tree in the direction of the fall. This is so accurately done that, when felled, a tree twenty feet in diameter will not vary a foot from the marker's estimate as it lies upon the ground.

Now two brawny woodsmen armed with a 16-foot cross-cut saw and axes begin opera-tions. First two deep notches are cut in the side of the doomed leviathan, opposite to each other, into which spring-boards are placed so as to form a foot rest. Often the men work fifteen feet above the ground, when the base of the tree is gnarled or ex-ceedingly wide. The sawing is begun directly back of the marker's notch and a little higher up. Hour after hour, frequently for two days, these two men swing steadily to and fro, manipulating their saw, and showing not the slightest sign of fatigue, although the work is hard, tremendously hard, even to a woodsman. Suddenly a slight cracking sound is heard. Instantly the sawyers shout a warning cry of "Look out below," at which signal everyone within hearing skurries [*sic*] to a place of shelter. "Zip, zip, zip, zip," goes the relentless saw. The crackling becomes louder and more frequent. Then the mighty tree leans forward a trifle, rights itself, leans a little more, then finally with a terrific snap it topples, slowly and gracefully, but gather-ing headway each second until with a crash and roar like a peal of thunder it strikes the earth which quivers under the impact of the blow as if shaken by an earthquake.

And so is the growth of thirty centuries undone in a day.

The next act in the work of destruction comes with the advent of the cross-cutters, who saw the tree into logs of twelve, sixteen and twenty foot lengths. This done, each log is hauled by a long steel cable, operated by a powerful donkey engine, to the chute where, by skillful maneuvering on the part of a crew of men "swampers," it finds a resting place in the chute; and there the most interesting and also the most dangerous part of the work begins.

### SHOOTING THE LOGS

The chute is carefully greased where the ground is level and still more carefully sand-ed on the down grades. A team, generally of ten powerful horses or oxen, is hitched to the log by a chain connected with a hook termed a "grab," shaped like the ordinary fish hook but without the familiar barb and so con-structed that should the log run faster than the team the hook drops from the chain, freeing the log . . . a gradual incline leading to the level finally brings the log to a landing, where it is loaded upon flat cars preparatory to its trip to the mill.

But when the down grade is reached it begins to slide by its own momentum. The chain unloosens from the hook, and a stream of fire and smoke trails from back of the log. Faster and faster it runs, making a peculiar ringing sound, known to every woodsman, and gathering headway each instant. . . .

To the cars is attached a mammoth cable of more than a mile in length and of great strength. This cable winds around the great drum of an extremely powerful hoisting engine, which hauls the cars on a track up a steep mountain, and by the same means lowers them on the opposite side to the railroad.

At the mill the log is unloaded, placed upon a platform which travels backward and forward on a short track. With each forward trip the log is brought into contact with a great band saw, revolving many hun-dred times a minute. As each board is sliced off it is conducted by rollers to the "edger," a series of wicked-looking buzz saws set in an iron frame. By these the plank is cut into marketable widths, loaded on handcars, rolled to the yards and piled with others for seasoning. Six months later, the lumber being sufficiently seasoned, is shipped by flume fifty-two miles distant to the com-pany's factories at Sanger for manufacture and distribution. A considerable part of the stock goes to Germany, for use in the manu-facture of lead pencils, and so part of the majestic towering giant comes back to us in its new form, an insignificant lead pencil.

J. P. Cullen

SOURCE: *Fresno Daily Evening Exposi-tor*, August 21, 1897, p. 2, c. 1, 2.

# Two Tales of the Low Sierra

## The Corlews of Auberry

### Muriel Wardlaw

Mr. Joseph Prather and his wife Lorraine have given us this story of their mountain home and the pioneers who homesteaded the land. I have used almost in its entirety a narrative written by Beryl Corlew Byrd, the mother of Lorraine Prather.—Muriel E. Wardlaw.

John H. Corlew, a descendant of French Huguenots whose surname was originally spelled *Corlieu*, was born in 1827 in Missouri. He joined the enthusiastic forty-niners in California to mine for gold along the banks of the San Joaquin River. Not meeting with immense success, he returned to Missouri, and there was married to Miss Eliza Sexton.

Two sons were born during the first years of the Civil War, Charles Clifford, in 1861, and William Cloudsley, in 1862. John Corlew, a staunch southerner, joined the Confederate army, leaving at home his small sons, and his wife expecting a third child. The end of the war brought him only tragedy with the death of his baby daughter at ten months, and soon afterwards, the death of his wife....

John Corlew returned to the far west again in 1874, taking with him his thirteen year old son, Clifford. They rode on the second through-train from the east, finally arriving at Modesto. Corlew concluded that the San Joaquin Valley "will never be anything but a dry desert with no chance of irrigation water," so they rode on farther south and into the foothills of Fresno County, knowing there would be water from springs there.

The two stayed for a time in Old Auberry Valley, raising a few cattle and sheep. From that place he wrote [to his family to come west and] bring his younger son, Cloudsley, with them, which they did.

This place at the foot of the canyon was a well traveled thoroughfare in those days, and was also an ox cart road to the first lumber mill in the vicinity, Ball Mill, established in the early 1850s and located atop the high ridge adjoining the ranch on the east.

Cliff became a teacher as soon as his age would permit his obtaining a certificate.... Dora McDonald became engaged to Cliff. She took up a timber claim of 160 acres not far from the old Ball Mill site.... To Clifford and Dora's union came five girls, named Beryl, Gladys, Eunice, Dorothy and Anel. Eventually he obtained land in connection with the claim, to the amount of 1,380 acres of beautiful yellow pine timber. Later this was known as Corlew Meadows, now known as Meadow Lake. A single cabin was built as the beginning of the outpost, which was a stopping place for teams and people on their way from the valley to the mountains. The accommodations became an eating house, a store and post office, camp grounds along the meadows and a feed yard for horses and wagons. A man by the name of Bennett built a mill on the place and all the timber was cut except eighty acres, reserved for cabin sites.

...Cattle and hog rustlers were a plague to these early settlers. After knowing for some time that they were losing both cattle and hogs, they determined to track down some of the aggressors. Leaving the ranch about day break one morning, they rode into some very rough country north of the San Joaquin River. About noon they came upon

their quarry where some beef steak was broiling and sputtering over a camp fire. They were cordially invited to partake, which they did. When they finished they ordered their host to dig up the beef hide, which was plainly branded with Cliff's 30 branding iron. The thieves were commanded to saddle their horses and lead out. These men were cautiously herded for two days and nights until they reached the Fresno jail, where the ring leader received two years in prison for his role....

During the years many changes came about. Clifford went to Sugar Pine to visit his daughter, Dorothy Peterson, who lived there with her husband, and was fascinated with the work at the big mill and all surrounding activities. He heard of the mineral warm springs down Lewis creek about one and a half miles. He went down and found mineral in the land as well as in the water, so he took up mining claims and built a rustic cabin on the hill overlooking the falls. Into the log "pot-hole" he piped the ninety-eight degree water from the spring. Corlew's granddaughters, whom he wrote of as his "four little pearls," were on hand to swim in the pool from morning to night whenever possible.

It was in this area, among the surroundings he loved, that Cliff Corlew, "the cliff man," as he called himself, wrote his volumes of poetry about the glories of nature, and his love for God and for his fellow man. The book "Sierra Sanctum" was written here. And here he is buried, in the place where, by his own direction, his grave was to be.

—From *Ash Tree Echo*, Vol. 3, No. 2, pp. 57–60.

## Scotty's, A Mountain Groggery

### Ernestine Winchell

[At Humphreys Station] Dry Creek ripples down toward the Valley at the left, and in front comes in at an angle the less traveled track from Centerville by way of Pittman hill.

A few yards further on the level space along the roadway is littered with the remnants of the old buildings of [John W.] Humphreys' station where in the busy freighting days of the eighties and nineties the lumber teams stopped over night, where meals were served to the teamsters and other travelers, and where the horses were watered through the wagon-stage era...

Over the waste and wreckage of earlier times, over the simple affairs of this, [Scotty's] weather-worn old saloon building keeps uncanny watch. Sardonic, sinister, furtive, it leers at the passer-by, hinting of evil secrets, suggesting a sly pride in sordid history, insolently defiant of report. A very hobo of a house, slipshod, dirty, ragged, not old enough in years for dignified infirmity, but decrepit with the premature decay of the dis-

sipated and abandoned.

Late in the seventies it came into its ignoble existence, and during the eighties was noisily alive, glittering with the gaudy containers of cheap wares to eat and to drink, throbbing inside with vile impulses and vicious acts, sanctimoniously pretending to be no worse than others of its kind.

For twenty years the thing flourished like the green growth in slimy pools. One manager succeeded another, each taking his turn of pouring liquor, or dispensing cards, or sitting—shirt-sleeved and impressive—on the front porch, but the character of the place never changed. Stories of drunkenness and robbery and cheating were told outside its walls, whispered a degree higher up in the moral scale, and impatiently hushed at the next advance as too mean for attention.

Never was there a clean brave tragedy, nor an honest red-blooded crime to dignify it. There was the pitiful poisoning by accident of a child who followed his father within the grimy doors. Indians became dangerously drunk, or even expired in agony at a discreet and uncriminating distance, but no man died on the spot with his boots on, of

hot lead or cold steel.

That many visitors departed from its portals more or less capably on their own feet, but shorn of honor and self respect, of health and cash and hope, was the one clear charge that could be brought—a charge never pushed by any abject victim, for there would be no proof that he came out in any way different from the way he went in. Crafty, indeed, were the wayside saloonkeepers, and of this place the craftiest of all. Even now when questions are asked there are hesitant, fragmentary answers, vague, opposing—and long, uneasy silences. The wary evasiveness is intriguing, and sharply it whets the curiosity. A story there must be, for mystery loads the air...

Scotty—who he was, whence he came, whither he went, there appears to be none to say. Such public knowledge of him as there once was has died away. His identity now seems to be one of the dark secrets hidden by the blank, inscrutable, sneering visage of the staggering, disreputable structure that still bears his name—a name that winter rains or summer fire may some day wash clean of his association.

# Chapter 11
# Outlaws, Lawmen and Assorted Rascals

The foregoing pages have given, in truth, an idealized portrait of early life in Fresno County. While some misfortunes and hard times have been mentioned, Horatio Algeresque stories of people making their fortunes in farming, mining, logging and other businesses have predominated. As an undeniable part of the historical record, those stories must be related—but to stop with them would make this volume incomplete. For the young county sheltered many who sought illegitimate fortunes, or violently demonstrated their frustrations when the good life eluded them. By means ranging from thievery and murder to vice and bunco, they sought to shift the economic balance away from the honest, upstanding citizenry. As in any relatively civilized society, the criminal element did not succeed—but its attempts to prevail always provide fascinating tales.

No one can dispute that early Fresno County was a wild, rough-and-tumble place. "We have seen men go stalking into religious meetings with revolvers and knives strapped to their persons ... and it is a sure thing to see men at dancing parties swing the fair ladies around in the mazy dance with a battery or two of firearms about them," commented the February 1, 1871, *Fresno Weekly Expositor*. While such behavior seems extreme even in these crime-conscious times, it was a raw age when men had to be prepared to defend their rights. William Aldridge, said to be the "Lone Republican" of Fresno County, had to cast his 1856 presidential election ballot under armed guard. Two secessionist-minded hoodlums named Davis and Hill had threatened him with violence if he committed that simple act.

Street fighting and fisticuffs were common during Fresno's infancy. "From 1874 to 1880 it did not take much of an argument to start a fist fight," said early resident George Bernhard. "[All] you had to say was 'You are another' and fists would fly until one or the other would holler, 'Take him off.' Then, after a few days, all would be forgotten and they would be better friends than ever. Of course there was some shooting, sometimes a man before breakfast and another before

dinner, but not often. However, Fresno became known as a fighting town. They used to say when the train arrived at Sycamore (now Herndon), the conductor would announce that Fresno was the next town and that you had better get your guns ready ... "

At least there were good reasons for the brawling. A gun battle broke out at Fresno's Larquier House in October 1872 after an attempt to disarm one of its Mexican patrons; he had become boisterous because a young woman had refused to dance with him. Nearly two years later one William McCracken was run out of town for being a "sport" of no "particular advantage to the town." He was pummeled in public by seven men dressed in Ku Klux Klan outfits after he refused to flee Fresno. Two of his tormentors were caught eventually. In a town where such occurrences were too common, one was fined thirty-five dollars and the other freed for lack of evidence.

Significant crime and violence also ran rampant (see 11:1). During the early mining period, the aforementioned Davis and Hill preyed on sluices regularly. Claim-jumping was another popular pastime. In the Dennis area, thieves helped themselves to mining equipment and scattered pay dirt tailings whenever the claim owners were away. At least one criminal adopted a more forceful means of dispossession. John Donaldson and William Russell, who worked the valuable Red Banks area seven miles above Millerton, were murdered brutally in 1855. Donaldson was shot, Russell dragged to death, and a sizable gold horde kept in their cabin was missing. Russell's body was pierced with arrows to suggest an Indian raid. A more likely culprit was Jim Hewitt, who delighted in frequenting local saloons, stealing gaming pots while there and coercing miners into buying drinks for him. Hewitt disappeared soon after the Red Banks incident and, some said, was spotted later in Idaho.

Throughout the early decades murders were committed for reasons varying from serious to downright trivial. The first man to die violently at Millerton, according to David Bice James, was a Texas badman named "Screwdriver" Smith. When Smith asked a San

# THE CARNIVAL OF BLOOD AND OTHER TROUBLES AT TRABUCCO'S TAVERN

Among the hills in the northern part of Fresno county, at the old ford of Fresno river, may be seen a few fragments of what once was a rude house, never a building of much size, and now almost entirely gone. Four boulders, that were the cornerstones of the building, still lie where they were placed in 1851, when the house was built. A few fragments of wood lie here and there, scattered about the hillside near the old road and a heap of rusted cans and broken bottles a few steps to one side are all that the traveler who passes this way will now see to mark the spot on which once stood the frontier tavern in which were enacted some of the bloodiest tragedies in the early history of California. [It was here] where Lemas Trabucco's tavern stood, and where he ultimately lost his life...

The story of Trabucco's tavern has never been told. The whole history never can be told, for some of those who might have told it are beneath the leaning seynite slabs on the hillside. But there is much of it that may be collected from those who still remember a part and have heard the rest from others.

John M. Hensley, now sheriff of Fresno county, was a resident of that vicinity during much of its history. . . . An Expositor reporter has gleaned from his recital the story of Trabucco's tavern, and the tragedies that were enacted there.

The tavern was built of rough, oak logs, set in the ground side by side like pickets, with one door, two windows without glass, and a roof made of pine shingles, split from logs, and in their rough state. Within the tavern there were no arrangements made for sleeping, except to wrap in blankets, which the traveler must furnish for himself, and sleep on the floor, which was of hewed logs laid upon sills.

The chief source of revenue to Trabucco was his saloon, a few yards from his house. . . . The whole outfit consisted of two barrels, with a board laid from one to the other for a bar, and a few black bottles of whiskey, and some glasses. A roof of brush and grass kept out the sunshine and the rain. There were no walls, unless the walls also were of brush leaned against the poles that supported that supported the roof.

A crowd of idle ruffians were always loafing around Trabucco's saloon, either drinking or gambling, or most probably both. They were men who had little fear of law and little respect for justice.

One of the first incidents in the history of the place, which Sheriff Hensley can remember, occurred when he was a very small boy. He was playing near the saloon one hot summer afternnon, when a stranger came riding down the road on horseback. He had his blankets tied behind his saddle, also a camping outfit, such as a tin pan, a little sack of flour, a cup, and a few other articles like a traveler in those days usually carried with him. A revolver was strapped to the horn of his saddle, as was then the custom.

The traveler rode leisurely by, spoke to no one, and passed on. The men in front of the saloon stopped their drinking and gambling, and looked after the stranger.

"He thinks he is too good to drink with us," said one.

"Too stingy to treat," spoke another.

"Too selfish and stuck up to stop and be sociable," chimed in the third.

"Let us take a shot at him for luck," some one suggested.

"Agreed!" replied the others in one breath and they instantly drew their six shooters and fired at the man who was now some distance down the road, and unsuspecting his danger.

At the report of their pistols, the traveler reined in his horse, turned in his saddle and returned the fire. He shot only once, but he aimed better than the half dozen who had shot at him; for one of the men fell dead.

The traveler without saying a word, hung his pistol again on the horn of the saddle and rode away as though nothing had happened. There was no pursuit. The graveyard on the hill had another occupant that evening. It was not the first, however, as a number of graves were already there.

Things were rather quiet after that for some time. But in about a year another man was shot. It was never understood who did it, but it was a very general belief that it was done for meanness, and with no purpose to kill any particular person. A man who was known in that country as Captain McEwin stopped in company with some others one night at Trabucco's tavern, and was lying on the floor asleep, when about midnight some one fired through the open door and broke McEwin's leg. The rude visitor escaped without being seen.

The incident so preyed on the mind of J. B. Coffey, a resident of that county, who was also asleep on the floor when the shooting occurred, that he became a raving maniac and ran off to the mountains, and from that day to this has not been heard of.

The next event in the story was the murder of Captain Brown, a cattle man who had a range in the hills above Buchannan, and who frequently was at Trabucco's. That day he had stopped at the saloon, and had remained long enough to become drunk and boisterous. In the quarrel and fight which followed, Captain Brown was shot through the lungs and died in a few minutes. It was unknown who fired the fatal shot, as there was promiscuous shooting on both sides, but Brown died believing that Trabucco had shot him on an old grudge, and his last words to those standing around were, that they should not let Trabucco's gray hairs go down in peace to the grave. Trabucco was then an old man, having spent his whole life in scenes like that. The dying curse of Captain Brown was soon to fall upon him. Brown was buried the next morning in the fatal graveyard on the hillside, in the silent company of others who had died of violence.

The dying request of Capt. Brown, that Trabucco should not be allowed to die a peaceful death, was granted sooner than any one had expected. When the men came back from Brown's burial, they commenced drinking, and soon the events of that day and the day before were mentioned.

A large number of Mexicans were present, having been attracted to the place by the excitement. When they all were in their cups the Americans began to charge Trabucco with having killed Brown. This he denied, and the Mexicans took sides with him, and the quarrel became violent and general. Only a spark was needed to ignite the conflagration, and the spark was soon cast. An Indian named Antone shot a man named Cameron, and instantly "One Arm Frank," as he was called, a white man, shot the Indian Antone. The ball struck him in the eye, but did not kill him.

This was the signal for a general fight, and the scene that followed is known in the history of the frontier as "The Carnival of Blood."

When Antone fell, his brother, named Jack, began shooting, and immediately a man named Burton fell dead, shot through the neck. Trabucco sprang over the bar of his saloon, and joined in the melee. "One Arm Frank" was struck in the forehead and fell dead beside Burton. A Mexican who was lying at one corner of the house, so drunk that he knew nothing of what was going on, was struck by one of the random bullets and never knew what hurt him.

In the meantime the friends of Brown had singled out Trabucco and were firing at him from all sides. No less than half a dozen times he was struck, but none of the balls proved immediately fatal. Finding himself outnumbered, and also weak from loss of blood, Trabucco left the saloon and fled to the tavern. He tried to barricade the door, but had not strength enough to do so, and lay down upon the floor in the back part of the room, with his pistol in position to shoot anyone who should attempt to enter the house. The men did not care to run the risk, and kept their distance. But a Mexican who had been lying asleep at some distance, and under the influence of whisky, awoke, and staggered up to the door, without knowing what was going on. Trabucco did not ask any questions or wait for any explanations, but as soon as the Mexican's form darkened the doorway, the report of a pistol from within was heard and the Mexican fell lifeless to the ground.

Trabucco was never seen alive again. The men would not enter the door for some time. But at length, when all had become quiet, and when repeated calls had failed to bring an answer from within, the men went to the tavern and found the old man, Trabucco, dead on the floor. The wounds he had received had proved fatal, and Captain

Francisco gambler, Dan Woods, for a ten-dollar loan during a card game and was refused, Smith threatened to kill Woods. The next day, an armed Woods returned to the scene and waited for Smith. James tried to warn Smith, whom he characterized as "not a bad sort." He did not reach him in time and the ambush was successful. A sympathetic jury later cleared Woods.

During the first county elections George Bingham became drunk at the Roan's Store (see Chapter 4) precinct, started swinging an axe-handle around, and was shot and killed when he began annoying Frank Kerwin. Kerwin was tried in Mariposa for the crime, found innocent and, ironically, met his death at Roan's Store after an altercation with a Chinese.

In 1856 one Frenchman shot and killed another at Thibault's, near Roan's Store, when the other man began tearing down his house. History has forgotten the deceased man's intentions, and the grand jury was unconcerned enough to refrain from an indictment. At Peyton's grocery store near Scottsburg (later Centerville), in 1865, a man named Satterfield met a similar fate. The August 30 *Visalia Weekly Delta* reported that

> Satterfield, who was a dissipated man, had been beaten badly by John Shipe, and was, while again drunk, threatening Shipe in the presence of [one Tom] Jeffers; Jeffers cautioned him not to meddle with Shipe, as if he hurt him he would have others to deal with, &c. Jeffers finally became very much excited, and drawing his pistol, told Satterfield he would shoot him then, and he believed he would shoot that button, indicating one on Satterfield's coat. Satterfield replied that he certainly wouldn't shoot a man in that way,

when Jeffers raised his pistol and fired, touching the button and shooting Satterfield through the breast. Satterfield did not fall at once, but upon Jeffers saying, 'I've got you, you are my man,' said he thought he was, Jeffers then swore if he was not he would make him so, and just as Satterfield was staggering to fall, shot him again through the head. Jeffers than went to [William C.] Caldwell's [Falcon Hotel], reported the murder and then escaped and has not since been seen.

Another fatal altercation of this period was Jim Harron's stabbing of Frank Stiddam at Temperance Flat. Harron served twenty-five years at San Quentin state prison for his crime, which centered on the ownership of an Indian woman.

At times circumstantial evidence or the mere suspicion of murder was enough to initiate a lynching. This tended to happen when the suspects were members of a racial minority group—always the Indians or Chinese—or when the predominating white citizenry saw no use in a trial. In 1864, one accused murderer came close to justice, and missed because of the vigilante noose. He was a local Indian working with a sheepherder, with whom he had argued, and was accused of killing him. An Indian woman identified the suspect and a trial began at Millerton. During lunch recess one day six men grabbed the suspect, carted him off to Winchell's Gulch and hanged him from a nearby oak tree.

Note of interest: The lynchers came to the site minus rope and, it appears, untied the calf of future Fresno County historian Lilbourne A. Winchell to obtain some. He recalled the incident with a strange wistful-

Brown's dying request had been granted more speedily than anyone at the time had thought it possible.

The next day the graveyard on the hill received accessions in goodly numbers. The two Indians, Antone and Jack, were the only two who were arrested for participating in "the carnival of blood." They were, perhaps, as little deserving of punishment as any, but they fell into the clutches of the law and were sent to the penitentiary one year each. Antone took advantage of the privileges afforded at the prison and learned to read. Afterward he learned to write, and now lives in this county, and reads and writes both Spanish and English.

Trabucco's tavern, and the saloon, passed into new hands, but it does not seem that it was a change much for the better. Though some of the worst characters had been killed, there were still plenty left.

About this time there were many camps of Chinamen all up and down the gulches, mining for gold. Every few days reports would come in that a China camp had been robbed. . . .

One day a report came in of a robbery of some camps in the country above, and the men at Trabucco's all looked surprised.

Evidently they had not done it. They became enraged to think that outsiders were coming into the country to rob. Evidently they considered that to themselves alone belonged the monopoly of robbing the China camps. They started up the country to search for the intruders, as they called them. They captured a young man, who was a stranger in that country, and who could give no correct account of his whereabouts the night before. Under threats of death he confessed that he had been one of eleven—all the others being Mexicans—who had done the robbing. With this they took him out and hung him. They did not bury him in the graveyard on the hill—he being a stranger—but made his grave in the middle of the road. Soon afterwards the road was changed, and a board was placed at the head of the grave.

Some time afterwards it was heard that the same gang of ten Mexicans were again in the country, and would probably rob the Chinese camps. It was the custom of the robbers to shoot through the tents, and the Chinese would then run off and leave all they had to the robbers. Considerable quantities of gold dust were often found in the tents.

But the white men of that country were opposed to having outsiders come in and

rob. So, when they heard that the Mexicans were in the vicinity, three men who lived near hid themselves in a China tent, where it was supposed the robbers would pay a visit. They were not mistaken. That night the Mexicans came and discharged their pistols into the tent. The Chinese ran as usual, but the white men remained. The Mexicans sprang off their horses and ran into the camp to secure their booty.

Just as they lit a candle, the white men fired, and three robbers fell lifeless, and several others were wounded before they could escape. They were followed, and all of them were either killed or captured before they could get out of the country. This took place at Baley Flat a few miles from Trabucco's tavern.

The change of ownership in the Trabucco tavern did not bring a change for the better. It continued to be a rendezvous for all the rough characters in the country.

SOURCE: Fresno County Scrapbook 1870–1899, pp. 1150–53, taken from *Fresno Daily Evening Expositor*, June 27, 1891, p. 2, c. 1–3.

ness: "The amazed and indignant boy [L.A.W.] ran to the house and called his mother, who . . . [was] helpless to interfere . . . The lynchers were not apprehended and the case was closed, even for the youngster who next day curiously sought out the gallows tree and viewed the ghostly figure slowly swaying at the end of his stolen tether."

Indians often felt the brunt of swift justice in later years. In 1873 two Indians were hanged for killing a Chinese sheepherder near Jones' Store, and another was hanged for assaulting a white girl. The latter crime apparently happened near Millerton; the suspect fled to Centerville, was apprehended and lynched a half-mile below the county seat. About this time two more Indians were hanged at Academy for robbing a Tollhouse store. They fled into the mountains, were found at a San Joaquin River sweathouse and returned to Tollhouse where they were nearly lynched. After being cleared or let out on bail by a Fresno court, they were intercepted on their way back to the mountains and strung up.

The most remarkable killing of this period happened on September 16, 1867, an election day. Two candidates for sheriff, J. Scott Ashman and James N. Walker, had been engaged in a bitter contest. When a Walker partisan, Charles Porter Converse, started to leave Theodore Payne's Millerton saloon he was nearly brained when Ashman man John Dwyer threw a rock at him. Converse fell to the floor, stunned. Dwyer's partner in the assault, W. H. Crowe, administered another blow. Unfazed, Converse arose, shot and killed Crowe and fired at Dwyer, who was running away from the melee by that time. Eventually tried and acquitted, Converse still had to spend some time in the Courthouse jail—the first occupant of the structure he had built the year before!

The reasons for several other early homicides have been lost. It is unknown why one Johnson killed Wharton at Texas Flat; why one Keener shot and killed his father at Fresno Flats (Oakhurst); why Gus Gray murdered Tom Overton at the Fresno Crossing on July 5, 1852; why Henry Sagehorn shot and killed Ralph Moore at Texas Flat in 1857; and why a Mexican axe-murdered Aaron Arnold on the upper San Joaquin River in 1870.

Centerville-area rancher Benjamin Andrews was slain in 1870 for a reason appreciably less important than politics—hog pasturing. Jerry Ridgeway and Joseph Burns, who were raising the animals in the neighborhood, received a curt note from Andrews that read, "If you don't keep your hogs out of my meadows, I'll shoot every one of them." When Ridgeway subsequently sought Andrews to discuss this matter, an argument erupted. Andrews ran for a gun, Ridgeway picked up a rock and readied his defense, but thought better of it and retreated.

Ridgeway had several other encounters with Andrews and, as he said in the *San Francisco Daily Evening Bulletin* of October 9, 1871, "was often compelled to go far out of my way to avoid meeting him." On July 31, while starting on a hunting trip with some friends, Ridgeway ran into Andrews again. "I rode along toward him: when within about sixty yards he exclaimed, 'I've got you, you ------,' at the same time firing his shot-gun at me, but missing me," said Ridgeway. " . . . I shot at him with my revolver, and struck him in the left shoulder, his load striking me in the left side, filling my arm, side and neck with shot, he then turned to club me with his gun, when I fired a second shot, striking him in the breast, and I fired a third after his fall . . . he said to me, 'Don't kill me,' and I replied it was too late, and fired again."

Reference 11:2

## DISPENSING JUSTICE TO THE JUST AND UNJUST

A good story is told of the manner and the machinery by which justice was obtained and the laws administered on Fine Gold river in early days. The system suggests the primitive institutions among men in the early ages of the infant world, before the statute and common laws had taken different names, and before municipal law was heard of. It was a revival of the faultless practice in vogue in the days of Abraham, Isaac and Jacob, when the whole legislative, judicial and executive departments of the government were in the hands of one old patriarch, from whose word there was no appeal, and against the wisdom of whose decision none ever dared to raise a voice.

Sheriff [John M.] Hensley was the originator of this effective government on the Fine Gold. . . . [He] had large bands of sheep in that region at that time, and spent his time there. He superintended the business and had a dozen or more Mexicans to do the

herding. . . . By mutual consent and by a sort of spontaneous intuition, they made up their minds to place him as a ruler, a sort of justice of the peace over them.

There was no regularly elected officer whose authority was recognized on the Fine Gold then; and there was no one likely to contest Mr. Hensley's title to office, or to molest him or make him afraid.

From near and far the people over all that region of country brought their disputes and their misunderstandings to Mr. Hensley to have them adjudicated and passed upon. Such a thing as an appeal from his decision was never dreamed of. . . .

The great secret of Mr. Hensley's success in rendering satisfaction was that he always decided according to the evidence and common sense, and there is an aptness to see this, even among herders and miners. They can appreciate a righteous decision as well as the most learned clients that ever confronted the

great high priests of the Sanhedrim of the Pharisees.

Often about the frontier store, where the people were gathered together, they would draw knives, or unlimber a battery of six shooters in each other's faces, and threaten death and destruction to all before them; but all Mr. Hensley had to do was to command peace, and every knife and pistol disappeared.

In course of time they came to regard him as able to interpret and execute law, and also to manufacture it; and if a disputed point came up for decision, he simply made law to suit it, and met every emergency as it arose. . . .

A fugitive for more than a year after this incident, Ridgeway was later apprehended in San Francisco and brought back to Millerton in 1871. He quickly escaped jail, was discovered in an Arizona mining camp and returned to justice. Most of the prosecution witnesses had left Fresno County by then and he was acquitted. Ridgeway went to Cerbat, Arizona, where a cautious man killed him in 1873 after Ridgeway had made a drunken death threat to him.

Quarrels of an undetermined nature were responsible for other killings. A Mr. Nicholas, storekeeper for A. Vignola at Dennis in 1862, was murdered while trying to quell a riot. Two groups of miners, one American and one Mexican, entered the store and began arguing. When a fight broke out and Nicholas unsuccessfully tried to stop it, he dashed into a back room and came out with a pistol. Before he could fire, one Major Brown wrestled him to the floor. While Nicholas was prostrate and Brown was grappling for the gun, a mob member smashed Nicholas' head in with a plank.

Tollhouse storekeeper and ex-saloonkeeper Theodore Payne was killed after some kind of dispute in 1873. He was arguing with his partner, George Tripp, when a black teamster named John Williams fired into the store and fatally wounded Payne in the leg. As Williams fled the scene, John Morrow and Riley Anderson shot his horse out from under him. He served a two-year sentence for the killing. "It was always believed that there was conspiracy between Tripp and the Negro to get Payne out of the way," said Lilbourne A. Winchell.

Little is known of early Fresno County justice. The existing anecdotes on the subject, however, are illuminating (see 11:2). One of the earliest stories concerns Mike Tubbs, an *alcalde* (something of a combination judge, mayor and miscellaneous political functionary) when Fresno County was still part of Mariposa County. He was noted for prescribing whipping as a punishment for crimes, and if this was the case the "prescription" was never less than two dozen lashes. When an Indian came before him for trial after stabbing another Indian, Tubbs passed an unusually severe sentence: seventy-five lashes, ears to be cropped, and hair shaved off. The Indian endured the first two ordeals with barely a whimper, but the shaving of his head was more than he could take! He jerked and thrashed around while the operation took place, and once it was over he broke from his captors, running madly out of camp and wailing at the top of his lungs.

Decorum was absent from the early courts. There was one instance in which Lewis Leach sued a Frenchman for $350 and won. Just before the time to appeal had run out the Frenchman's lawyer, James Cruikshank of Millerton, headed for Roan's Store—meetingplace of the appropriate tribunal—to seek a new remedy for his client. A few local boys knew he was coming, greeted him with carousing and some good "tarantula juice," and within a few hours of arrival the barrister was out cold. When he awoke the next day, Cruikshank realized he had been taken . . . and the appeal time had expired!

Another time, defense attorney E. C. Winchell paused in the middle of a trial to review a statute. The judge and district attorney, not wanting to wait, silently departed for a saloon and liquid refreshments. When Winchell looked up from his books, he saw a courtroom minus two-thirds of its necessary officers.

Despite their importance, early crimes were not dominated by the random acts catalogued above. Gang violence, if not more important, is better known, well-documented and was almost as extensive. Some of California's most noted criminals used Fresno County as a hideout (especially at the California Ranch, Arroyo de Cantua, and Las Juntas on the west side), a robbery target, or both. Of the gangs to make their way into the county or its later borders, the earliest and most significant were led by Joaquin Murrieta.

Born in his ancestral home of Pueblo de Murrieta, Sonora, Mexico, Murrieta came to California with the 1849 gold rush. He first tried honest work as a miner in Calaveras County at Murphy's New Diggings. While there, some rowdy Americans found a pretext to jump his claim, beat him and rape his wife, Rosa Feliz Murrieta. After these incidents the Murrietas moved near Angels Camp, where Murrieta dealt monte in a blue tent known as the Carpa Azul. An ugly incident occurred there that turned him against the law for good. Murrieta's brother, Jesus, who also had made the California trek, was accused of stealing a mule he had legitimately sold to miner Bill Lang. Jesus was lynched, and for assumed complicity Joaquin was horsewhipped. The surviving Murrieta, in frustration and revenge, began cutting a bloody trail across California.

His first item of business was to track down the miners who had wronged him. After scouring the countryside he found perhaps fifteen of them at different times, roped them, and dragged them to death behind his horse. Knowing that peace officers, vigilantes, or both would soon be trailing him, Murrieta spirited his wife to a hideout in Niles Canyon, Alameda County, and began plotting more sinister moves. For purposes of criminal activity—mostly horse thievery— he formed a number of gangs commanded by himself and assorted relatives of his living in California: Joaquin Valenzuela (a cousin), Joaquin Manuel Carrillo Murrieta (his half-brother), Joaquin Juan Murrieta and Manuel Duarte, the last better known as "Three-fingered Jack" due to his lack of two digits. (Hereafter "Murrieta" will denote the gang overlord alone.)

The gangs were headquartered at the Arroyo de

Cantua, near present-day Coalinga, at an adobe house with a barn and brush-and-pole corral. It was an ideal hideout location, featuring a series of gullies, caves and lookout vistas. To this day a trio of small mountains, affording a good view of the area, are known as the Joaquin (or Three) Rocks. At the Cantua brands were changed on stolen horses by a sub-gang under Pedro Gonzales, after which a group under Teodoro Valenzuela ran the animals to a southern dispersal point— the Rancho de Berruga in Sonora, Mexico.

The gangs began operations no later than mid-1852. At that time a posse of uncertain origin tracked some of them to the San Luis Gonzaga ranch (now covered by the San Luis Reservoir in Merced County). A surprised Murrieta and a few lieutenants fled south. An Indian band living near Tejon Pass in Kern County, led by Chief Zapatero, captured the retreating bandits and divested them of some booty. Legend has it that they were stripped before being released, adding a humorous touch to the incident. In any event the July 3, 1852, *Weekly Alta California* verified the incident: "Jose Zapatero, another chief, has since taken a number of horses from some Soneranians [*sic*], which were pursued to the Tejon, and delivered them over to the authorities." "Them" is probably a reference to the horses and not the gang members.

Murrieta gang activity seems to have quieted, for a time. But on November 21, 1852, they were heard from again after the shooting death of General Joshua Bean, of the California Militia, near San Gabriel. Bean— brother of Judge Roy Bean, "Law West of the Pecos"— may have been wise to gang activities and planning retaliatory measures. Murrieta's involvement seems certain. His brother-in-law, Reyes Feliz, was quickly apprehended for the murder, and referred to gang activity at his trail. A conviction followed, after which he and two others connected to the crime were hanged.

After the Bean murder, the Murrieta gangs moved north and embarked on an unprecedented series of robberies and murders. In late 1852 and early 1853, Chinese miners were being robbed and killed constantly in western Calaveras County. The white miners remained somewhat complacent until two of their own were killed at the Phoenix Quartz Mills, also in that vicinity, in January. Two county posses then went after the gangs. One of them caught up with a bandit group on January 30, but the mounted robbers shot their way past the lawmen and escaped.

Reference 11:3

## BATTLE AT THE CANTUA

### William T. Henderson's Account, as
### Interpreted by Frank F. Latta

"Joaquin's rendezvous was supposed to be in the Coast Range, in the vicinity of the Cantua [not until *after* Love and his Rangers arrested Jesús Féliz], and Captain Love's command *finally* went in search of him. For months, signal fires had been kept burning on the higher peaks, [principally on Las Tres Piedras, Piedra Azul and on Black Mountain near Las Tres Piedras] in the vicinity of the Cantua, presumably to guide Joaquin, El Famoso, and his command to shelter in case at night they should be on the San Joaquin Plains."

Actually these signal fires were used to send messages of any kind to Las Tres Piedras whenever Murrieta or Valenzuela was there, or to other places at any time. It was in order to receive and answer these messages that these two Gang captains stayed at Las Tres Piedras instead of down at the Oak Tree Camp or at the Adobe Headquarters, both on the lower Arroyo Cantua. . . .

"When Capt. Love's company arrived on the Arroyo Cantua they found a large camp of Mexicans, there being eighty-three men and three women. ["One hundred," said Jesús Féliz. "Twenty-five, no more," said Avelino Martinez: Both of these men were eyewitnesses.] When questioned as to what they were doing there they said that they were engaged in catching mustang horses, large numbers of which were then running at large on the plains. [Capt. Love pretended to be registering mustang runners for the purpose of collecting a State Tax.] A few days after they arrived in the vicinity of the Mexican Camp [within eight hours] the latter all scattered out and disappeared, having evidently become alarmed and gone to warn Joaquin."

Joaquin and several of his band were at Las Tres Piedras, while the remainder of the Gangs was branding the band of 300 Joaquin Juan Murrieta-Tres Dedos Circle M horses and mules to be taken to Rancho La Berruga in Sonora, Mexico.

"Capt. Love started with his company to follow them, and on the morning of the 25th of July, 1853, at about daybreak, came upon a Mexican camp on the Cantua, right where the creek debouches on the plains." This would be about correct for the south side of the creek. On the north side the plains extend about a mile farther upstream and several small gulches come in from the north. These afforded cover for several of the Gangs when the battle was going on.

"There were two Mexicans on guard, they were taken prisoners, and four more were found asleep in the bed of the creek."

The prisoners were Antone López and José María Ochovo. They must have been at some distance, or behind a bend in the creek bank, or this would have alarmed everyone.

"As the command rode up, one of the sleepers sprang up, and put on his heavy Mexican hat. [This is the hat Frank Sálazar claimed to have in his museum in the old stone jail in Hornitos.] He ran toward his horse, which was tethered on the opposite side [north side] of the camp."

Other accounts have this man washing the sore back of a "bay," meaning *bayo* or dun; a buckskin horse. This was El Tigre, the pet saddle animal of Joaquin Murrieta. El Tigre had a sore back and also had gone lame on the trail.

"Mr. Henderson, having seen Joaquin before, concluded that this was the man, although his face was so covered that he [Henderson] could not get a fair sight at him. [Other authorities have stated that the only member of the Rangers who knew Joaquin by sight was Wm. Byrnes (another California Ranger). Unquestionably, this was thrown in by the *Expositor* reporter to strengthen Henderson's story.] He spurred his horse and made up to the Mexican and commanded him to stop, the Mexican by that time having reached his horse."

Now both were on the north side of the creek. Also other authorities have placed Byrnes and several other Rangers on this side (the north) of the creek, "so the camp could be covered from both sides."

"Meantime Capt. Love began interrogating the Mexicans as to their business. They uniformly replied that they were catching mustangs. In the meantime, Joaquin, for so the Mexican proved to be, [If one considers all authorities, he is convinced at this

In early February the Murrieta casualty toll began climbing. Chinese miners remained a special prey of the outlaws. Six were killed on the Cosumnes River at the beginning of the month, numerous bands of them were robbed and driven away from their diggings, and a February 20 raid of one Chinese camp made the gangs $30,000 richer. Unsatisfied with that take, the outlaws robbed more Chinese at Rich Gulch a few days later and took approximately $10,000. Other racial and ethnic groups were not neglected in this sweep. An American named Joseph Lake was killed on Jackson Creek and a German teamster was robbed of $600.

Once again a posse was formed, this time under Deputy Sheriff C. A. Clark of Amador County. Once again it encountered gang members, this time while another Chinese camp was being raided. Once again the posse was unable to catch up with the bandits, who had spied its approach early on. To compound the posse's frustration, it had arrived too late. The men discovered that several Chinese were dead and $3,000 had been taken.

Those living in California's mining country were either paralyzed with fear or running away from the Murrieta menace. "Our citizens are either returning home or seeking foreign shores in hope of finding that protection that cannot be afforded here," said the *Calaveras Chronicle*. The state offered $1,000 for Murrieta's capture, and countless posses were combing the eastern foothills and Sierra for him.

One man, Ira McCray of Sawmill Flat, Tuolumne County, was itching to do something and had let many others know his desire. A gang henchman poisoned his well as a result. Fortunately, the poison was so potent that it was discovered before anyone was harmed. McCray then visited the mining town of Columbia and obtained a howitzer to protect his store, firing it on his return trip to dissuade any potential robbers. Tired of the scenery or the need for self-protection, McCray soon moved to Millerton and became one of its important citizens (see Chapter 5).

Spring found Murrieta and some of his men in northeastern Mariposa County, where they raided Prescott's ranch and stole horses on March 4, and probably killed five Frenchmen on Bear Creek soon afterward. Now more drastic action than a reward offer was necessary. Mariposa County citizens peti-

particular point, Byrnes being some distance away, no one present had any idea who this man was. He was simply a Mexican they didn't want to get away.] had made several attempts to go to the place where he had slept, to secure his saddle and pistols, but the persuasive influence of a double-barreled shot-gun in the hands of Mr. Henderson had kept him back.

"A considerable amount of parleying was done, most of the answers being made by Joaquin. At last Capt. Byrnes, who was some distance behind, came up."

Byrnes, having been sent by Love to cover the camp from the north side of the creek, must have gone farther down stream to cross. Such a detour could have been done in order to avoid being seen at close range and so arousing the suspicion of the men in the camp. This route would have placed him "some distance behind."

"He knew Joaquin very well, and as soon as the latter caught sight of the Captain [Byrnes was Acting First Lieutenant] he jumped on his horse to fire at him, but his horse shied and the shot missed.

"Henderson followed in close pursuit, and Joaquin, as an only hope, jumped his horse off the bluff some twelve feet high, into the bed of the creek. [Evidently Henderson and Byrnes were between the bareback rider and the crossing of El Camino Viejo, the Old West Side Road.]

"Being barebacked, he slipped from his horse and fell on his back on the ground. Col. Henderson [Here *Private* Henderson of the Rangers suddenly has been elevated to full Colonel, outranking by three grades even his Commanding Officer, Captain Harry Love.] followed him, and as he sprang over the cliff, he for the first time convinced himself that he was pursuing Joaquin. The fall had knocked his hat off, which had been fastened on his head by a broad black ribbon, and his face was left uncovered, and the broad scar on his cheek was plainly visible.

"Almost as quick as a flash Joaquin sprang to his feet and again mounted his horse. Henderson dropped his shot-gun and pulled out his revolver, and, not desiring to kill Joaquin, shot at his horse, with a view of breaking one of his thighs, but the ball missed the bone. They were both riding at breakneck speed down the bed of the creek." Note that they were traveling *downstream*, away from the hills which offered the only protection within reach. The horse had been staked north of the creek and about opposite Murrieta Spring.

"Coming to a low place in the bank of the creek, Joaquin turned his horse to ride out, as he did so Henderson fired again at the horse, striking him in the same leg and very nearly the same place. The blood streamed from the wound, the ball evidently having cut an artery.

"Col. Henderson now was convinced that his only chance to capture Joaquin was to shoot him, as the Mexicans in the rear were already shooting at him, so he fired at the fleeing desperado and hit him in the small of the back, the ball passing through him, still he clung to his horse and urged the animal forward. At this time John White, of the command, rode up, and he also fired at Joaquin, who was leaning forward on his horse, and the ball struck him just above the one fired by Henderson, and ranged upward. [This is a minor detail, but, under the circumstances, with all three men on running horses, certainly several yards apart and much excited, who could determine who shot who where?]

"This caused him to fall from his horse, but, mortally wounded as he was, he still tried to escape, running at the best speed possible toward the hills. [Here someone has reversed the direction of flight.] Henderson then fired at him, and shot him through the heart, and even then he had the vitality enough to call out in Spanish to his pursuers to cease shooting, as he had enough." [This last activity would have been entirely impossible if he had been shot directly through the heart. And to determine this the man must have been cut open, something that never has been claimed.]

"Three-fingered Jack, taking alarm when his chieftain fled, also started off afoot at the height of his speed, trying to reach the hills and brush. He was shot nine times before he fell, the last shot being put through his head by Captain Byrnes. This gentleman than cut off the hand of Three-fingered Jack and the head of Joaquin, and brought them to Fort Miller, where they were preserved in spirits by Dr. Edgar, the surgeon at the military post." Note this last, as later Wm. Howard [another California Ranger, in 1890] is quoted as saying, "Jim Norton took a bowie knife and hacked off the head of the bandit chief, which was placed in a sack with Jack's hand."

tioned the state to raise a company of rangers to run down the Murrieta gangs. After some weeks of deliberation the legislature agreed to this demand on May 17, and a company of twenty men was enlisted at Quartzburg, Mariposa County, eleven days later. Its captain was Harry Love, a gruff bear of a man and a seasoned veteran of the Texas border wars. The California Rangers, as they were known, were commissioned for three months and were to be paid $150 a month, each man furnishing his own supplies.

The Rangers began moving fast; during June robberies were a daily occurrence in Mariposa County. They soon recovered thirty-one stolen horses and captured three gang members. Two of these bandits were sent to Quartzburg for trial—unfortunately, "Judge Lynch" interfered before they could be brought to a proper tribunal.

By early July the Rangers' presence had made it too hot for the gangs. Murrieta and his men left Mariposa County for the safety of the San Joaquin Valley's west side. Love and his men traveled from San Juan to San Luis Obispo looking for the gangs, then scoured the Tejon Pass area. Guided there by Reyes Feliz's previously-captured brother, Jesus, several scores of gang members were found in the latter location on July 18. Many horses were there as well—a trek to Sonora was in progress. The Rangers could do nothing except take down the names of the bandits, since they were outmanned and outgunned at this juncture. This encounter was a stand-off, each side presumably unsure about what the other would do.

The Tejon Pass incident made everyone in the Murrieta gang nervous. They split up and went in separate directions, some to Santa Barbara County, some to Sonora, and Valenzuela, Duarte and Murrieta back to the Cantua. There, on July 25, a gunbattle happened that spelled the end for the Murrieta gangs (see 11:3). Although only six men reportedly were killed or captured, the assault broke the bandits' collective spirit. Only a handful of members continued criminal careers, notably Pio Linares, with many of them going straight.

What happened to Murrieta after the Cantua is an issue that may never be settled. Historian Frank F. Latta asserts that he was not killed at the battle, being camped a short distance away when it occurred; that he helped bury the dead afterward; that he left for Niles Canyon and Rosa afterward, but was wounded by officers looking for outlaws while on his way, died from the injury and was secretly buried at his homestead. Latta maintains that the head taken by the Rangers from one of the Cantua bodies was not Murrieta's, since it was said to have a dark complexion and black hair. This description, and testimony of ex-gang members, led Latta to believe the head was that of Chappo, an Indian who ran with the gangs. By contrast Murrieta is said to have had blue eyes, a light complexion and light brown hair. Yet published descriptions of the head, appearing in August 1853 issues of the *Stockton Herald* and *San Francisco Herald*, say that the head had blue eyes, light complexion and light brown hair! This, coupled with the fact that Love obtained numerous affidavits certifying the head as Murrieta's, suggests that Latta's theory cannot be accepted as definitive until better evidence surfaces.

The Murrieta onslaught remains unparalleled in California history. It was five years before anything like it arose in Fresno County—the gang of Jack

Reference 11:4

## THE MASON-HENRY GANG: A DOCUMENTARY HISTORY

[The items given here, from the *Visalia Weekly Delta* of November 16, 1864, detail Mason and Henry's first strikes in Fresno County. For clarification's sake it should be mentioned that they killed Hawthorne at Hawthorne's Station, rode south to Elkhorn Station and killed stationkeeper Robinson there, and then headed north where "Dutch Charley" was murdered. Evidently the *Delta* was confused about Mason and Henry's political sympathies, calling them "peace Democrats"—supporters of presidential candidate General George McClellan, Abraham Lincoln's opponent—when they were actually Confederate sympathizers.]

The Murder of Mr. Hawthorne.—The circumstances in the case of the killing of Mr. Hawthorne, another victim of the McClellan raiders upon "Lincolnites," are, in substance, as follows: It seems that at about 12 o'clock at night of the 8th, two horsemen rode up to the barn belonging to Mr. Hawthorne's premises, who keeps another Stage Station on the road to Gilroy, and called out to two men sleeping therein, "hello boys, let us in, we are cold." Recognizing the voices they opened the door, and when entered, their arms were demanded under a threat of death if refused, and when their pistols were delivered up, they said they did not intend to harm a hair belonging to them, but that they were going to kill the "old man," that he was a d—d black Republican and he must die, and that they were going to give hell to other Lincolnites. They then charged them to remain perfectly quiet while they were doing their work in the house, and no harm should come to them. They then went to the door of the house where Hawthorne was sleeping, and called to him; he also recognizing the voices, opened the door without hesitation, when they shot him through the head, killing him instantly. They remained sometime inside, rummaging about and drinking liquor at the bar. When they came out they fired off the pistols belonging to the two men in the barn, and gave them back to them, telling them that they had killed the old man; said he died harder than any one they ever saw die. One of them said, you'll be questioned about this, tell them that I killed him. I, Jim Mason; and tell them what I did it for. These men say they tried to remonstrate with them before the killing; asked if it did not seem hard to kill that poor old man; asked what he had ever done to them. They answered nothing, that he had been a good friend to him (Mason), that he had eaten at his table, drank with him and slept with him, but he was a d—d black Republican, had voted for Lincoln and must die.

After finishing their hellish work, they told the "boys" that they were going to take a fine pair of stage horses, and persisted in taking them in spite of their remonstrances, but they finally became fractious and got away, and made their escape. They then departed, and in the morning we find them at their work, at the next station.

The McClellanite Raiders.—We have met Mrs. Robinson, the widow of one of the men murdered on the 8th and 9th, and from her

226

Cowan and one Hart, in 1858. Like Murrieta, the men made a specialty of robbing miners, Chinese and American, until a chance event ended their careers. While hunting cattle between the Fresno and Chowchilla rivers one day, George Greer and James Bradley spied the two bandits and opened fire. A bullet smashed into Cowan's head, killing him. Dr. Lewis Leach kept the resulting skull as a souvenir of the encounter. Hart, wounded in the fray, was captured, tried at Millerton and sentenced to a term at San Quentin.

In 1863 a new gang took to the Cowan-Hart robbery pattern. Its members were Jim Raines, brothers Al and John Dixon, Jim Hall, Tom McCauley (known as Jackson), and men named McDowell, McIntyre and Hosler. They made regular raids on the Coarse Gold and Fine Gold country, most notably sacking the Coarse Gold Chinese store. By 1864 the local citizens formed a posse and chased after the marauders. Al Dixon was promptly caught and hanged; he has the distinction of being the first to suffer that fate in Fresno County. His brother John's life was saved, thanks to the intervention of an unknown man from Fresno Flats (Oakhurst).

Other gang members soon got wind of the plot against them and scattered. Raines did not depart from the area. A married man, he had no desire to leave his home. By lying low he was safe for a time; then, he made the mistake of insulting the Fort Miller provost. A contingent of soldiers was dispatched to Raines' home where he appeared with a revolver and threatened to shoot anyone who tried to capture him. A gunbattle ensued that ended with Raines' capture.

Interned at the Fort Alcatraz prison for several years, Raines was back in Fresno County by 1868, settled in the mountains east of Centerville. He started a new cattle-rustling and hog-stealing business which resulted in a new posse's being formed, led by John Shipe. One night Shipe knocked on Raines' door, posing as a tired hunter. The wary Raines stalled for two hours before letting him in. When he did, Shipe's gun rang out fast, and Raines' career—and life—were over.

The dispersion of the Raines-Dixon gang did not dissuade Tom McCauley from a life of crime. He sojourned at Los Angeles, then returned to Fresno County and hid out in the mountains above the Kings River. Here he met a sheepherder and fellow Confederate sympathizer (these being Civil War days) named John Mason. McCauley adopted a new alias, Jim Henry, and the men decided to launch a new crime wave in Fresno County as the Mason-Henry gang (see 11:4).

After being tracked outside the county boundaries, the outlaws stole horses in Merced County, robbed a store there, and pulled down telegraph wires near Firebaugh's Ferry for good measure. They then headed for the Tejon Pass-Kern River country, where they robbed another store, killed a sheepherder named John Johnson, robbed some traveling families and got involved in at least one gunbattle. A contingent of

we gather the main facts connected with the killing of her husband. She says that on the morning of the 9th, at about 8 o'clock, being alone with her little children, and still engaged in doing up her morning work, she noticed two men on horseback, coming up the road at a slow pace, and off approaching the house she saw they were strangers to her; and after the meeting salutations were passed one of the two enquired did they "have any barley," to which she answered in the affirmative, but that her husband, Mr. Robinson, was away, having gone the day before to King's River to the election, and that she was momentarily expecting his return. Then they led their horses to the water trough and asked for a vessel to drink with themselves, which she procured; and after satisfying their thirst they very leisurely mounted and bade her good morning and rode away as they approached, quite slowly, which fact she was led more particularly to notice from the circumstance that a little pet dog, belonging to the children, and of which they were fond, persisted in following them after her earnest attempts to call it back. But her duties hard pressing upon her, she had returned to them, and, tho she was outside the door and was looking for her husband's return, she had not noticed the approach of the wagon in which he was riding, until she heard the report of a gun not more than a quarter of a mile from the house, and instantly heard and recognized the cries of her husband, and when the smoke lifted saw him start to run, when two rapid pistol shots were heard. After their victim was dead the villains enquired of Mr. McCollough, the owner of the team, how he had voted? and on being answered that he did not vote at all, told him to go and take care of the woman and children. That they were after Lincolnites; that they had given some of them hell and would give others the same. After the lapse of some time, the man—McCollough —started to the house with his team, when he and Mrs. Robinson retreated to the inside of the house and made vigorous preparations to defend themselves against the murderers, who were loitering about near the premises; but finally, somewhere between ten and eleven o'clock, after making several feints as if to charge upon the house, they wheeled their horses and rode off rapidly; and, owing to a cloud of smoke which had arisen, she could not see clearly the direction taken. The statement which McCollough gives, who witnessed the killing, is in substance as follows: He says they had passed the two men some distance, when Mr. Robinson, noticing their dog following, alighted, and while attempting to call or drive it back, was enquired of if he was Robinson, and on being answered affirmatively, asked if he had any barley for sale; then said, "you have said that there are no honest Southern women," which he denied ever saying, and would prove his innocence if they would give him a chance. He got upon his knees, and for the sake of his wife and little children begged for his life. They told him to look down the barrel of the gun covering him and swear that he had never applied hard names to Southern women. He accordingly swore, and when he arose they told him they were going to kill him anyhow—that he was a d—d black Republican and should die, when the trigger was pulled and missed fire. He then started to run, when the other barrel discharged, the load taking effect in his shoulder, carrying it almost entirely away, and shattered one hand badly. Early in his attempt to run he fell, when the other human fiend approached, and with the two shots before spoken of, finished the work of hell....

More of the McClellan Raiders.—The third victim of Mason and Henry, the peace Democrats, who murdered Robinson and Hawthorne for not voting for their man, was a German, known as "Dutch Charley," and resided on the Joaquin river. The particulars of this case we have not been able to get at.

soldiers from Camp Babbitt tried to find the fast-moving outlaws and had no luck.

A San Bernardino sheriff's posse finally caught McCauley in that county and killed him on the morning of September 14, 1865. Mason holed up in the Tejon Pass area afterward and tried to form a new gang. When one of his prospects didn't bite, Mason threatened to kill him. The prospect reacted, after a strained conversation, by killing Mason one April night in 1866.

Gang violence in Fresno County subsided until the early 1870s, when Tiburcio Vasquez and his men appeared on the scene. Born in Monterey, California, on August 11, 1835 (by his own admission), Vasquez got his start in crime in his hometown during a raucous fandango one night. A scuffle broke out, a constable was shot and killed, and because he was somehow involved Vasquez fled. He became a horse thief in Los Angeles, Amador and Sonoma counties, which proved to be an unlucky profession for him. In each county he was caught, tried and sentenced to prison. Between incarcerations he was a professional gambler at New Idria (where he supposedly robbed and killed an Italian butcher) and was said to have associated with two other notable bandits: Juan Soto and Tomaso Redondo, the latter better known as Procopio and a nephew of Joaquin Murrieta.

In the fall of 1871, almost a year after his third prison stretch ended, Vasquez held up the Visalia stage near Hollister with Francisco Bercenas, Narcisso Rodriguez and others. Rodriguez was caught soon afterward by Monterey sheriff Tom Wasson, and Barcenas and Vasquez were tracked to the Santa Cruz mountains. A gunbattle with officers there ended in Barcenas' death, Vasquez's wounding of the local marshal, L. T. Roberts, and the remaining bandit fleeing to the Arroyo de Cantua. As in Murrieta's time, the Cantua remained a hideout for Mexican desperadoes. While there Vasquez reteamed with Cleovaro Chavez, Abdon Leiva, August de Bert, Romulo Gonzales and Teodoro Moreno, the last said to be Vasquez's cousin. They hatched a plan for a new, daring raid, and amid the plotting Vasquez managed to sneak in an affair with Leiva's wife. (To his dying day he had the reputation of being a ladies' man.)

The bandits had heard that $30,000 had been deposited at Firebaugh's Ferry to pay the men working on Henry Miller's nearby ranches. On the night of February 26, 1873, the men masked themselves and swept into George L. Hoffman's store there. The patrons were all forced to the floor, their hands tied, and robbed. Hoffman briefly escaped this fate, being in a back room when the excitement started, but he soon stumbled onto the crime scene and was forced to open his safe. While the bandits were in the store, a stage rolled up. The Wells, Fargo express box on it was

Reference 11:5

# THE KINGSTON RAID
## GEORGE BEERS

Emboldened, at length, at their continued success, a plan was finally laid to sack the little town of Kingston, about the centre of Fresno county, and near the southern boundary, and on the south bank of King's [sic] River. . . .

On the south side of the principal street in the main portion of the town, two stores and a hotel are clustered together, and the bridge directly fronts on these buildings, and also a stable owned by [O. H.] Bliss. The hotel is owned by L. Reichart, one of the stores by S. Sweet, and the other by Jacob & Einstein.

On Friday night, Dec. 26th, 1873—just five months after the terrible massacre at Tres Pinos, the little town was the scene of another of Vasquez's desperate exploits, and the whole southern country once more thrown into a fever of excitement, indignation, and speculation as to what the law-defying dare-devil would do next.

By appointment the members of the gang, numbering nine men, found their way, one by one, and by different routes, to a point about five miles north of the town, and soon after dark they approached the river and hid their horses in the thicket near the bank of the stream.

Shortly after seven o'clock they crossed the bridge on foot, and dividing, instantly took possession of the town. In less than five minutes they had bound thirty men, and then hurriedly proceeded to rifle the safes and money-drawers, and then robbed their victims of their watches, rings, and other valuables.

Mr. Bliss was the first person they encountered, and they compelled him to lie down, tied his hands and legs together, and took all his money, the pitiful sum of nine dollars—business not having been very lively with Bliss that day.

Complaining that his head was hurting him, one of the party considerately took a blanket from a wagon near the stable, placed it under his head, and left him in that blissful position to reflect on the uncertainty of mundane affairs.

Another delegation halted John Potts, M. Woods, and P. Bozeman near the stable-yard, and ordered them to lie down. Bozeman and Potts silently obeyed, and were relieved of their coin, Bozeman of $180, and Potts of a small amount.

Mr. Woods fastidiously objected, on the plea that it would "soil his good clothes." He was allowed to go to the hotel and lie down there.

One man was placed on guard in front of each of the business houses, while other portions of the band entered the bar of the hotel, and Jacob & Einstein's store.

In the saloon or bar there were ten or a dozen persons, and Vasquez ordering them to lie down, they obeyed, and were immediately relieved of their watches and money.

From the proprietor of the hotel they took $400 and a watch, and from the guests various amounts.

Ed. Douglas, a plucky gentleman from Visalia, whom Vasquez and Chavez discovered in the sitting-room, peremptorily refused to lie down, when [Cleovara] Chavez knocked him down with his revolver, and Vasquez took his money and watch.

Lance Gilroy, of Fresno, was eating his supper when these initiatory proceedings were transpiring. Blas Bicuna rudely entered the dining-room door, and Mrs. Reichart, terrified by the ominous glance of his eye, and the cocked revolver in his hand, emitted a piercing scream and fled from the apartment. Gilroy, startled by the shrill yell, sprang to his feet, and thinking it was some drunken loafer who had insulted the young lady, before Bicuna comprehended his design, the gallant Gilroy had felled the ruffian to the floor with a chair. But Gilroy's triumph was short-lived. The heavy thud of Bicuna's carcass on the floor was heard by Gomez, who was in the hall on his way to the dining-room, and springing through the doorway, he brought the belligerent gentle-

robbed, along with the passengers, and the robbers gained a $600 windfall.

Only two people were spared during the Firebaugh's Ferry raid. One was a Mexican named Parroda, who was acquainted with one of the gang members. The other was Hoffman's wife. Her husband was carrying her watch at the time of the raid. The robbers took it at first, but when they discovered its ownership, they dutifully returned it—not wishing to offend a woman.

After that foray Vasquez's gang retreated to the Cantua, venturing out long enough to rob a stage at Soap Lake (on the Visalia-Gilroy-San Jose route), the 21 Mile House at Gilroy and Snyder's store at Tres Pinos, San Benito County. The latter raid, on August 26, ended with $1,200 taken and three men killed.

A new manhunt, launched by the Santa Clara County sheriff, scoured the Cantua region with no results. Then the gang was traced to Little Rock Creek Canyon in Kern County, where they were nearly captured after a fierce gunbattle with the posse. Some accounts say that Leiva, having discovered his wife's infidelity, informed on Vasquez and was the real cause of the rout.

The fall of 1873 found Vasquez back at the Cantua,

where he induced new men to join him: Isador Padilla, Blas Bicuna, G. Gomes, T. Monteres and several others. One story, related by Lilbourne A. Winchell, has the gang visiting Fresno at this time, when posses were still searching for the men. The Vasquez gang put up its horses at Russell Fleming's stables, but refused to pay a nervous stable boy for the service. When Fleming, who had been away from his business, returned he found his boy cowering in a stall. Fleming found out what had happened, ran for his shotgun, and dashed for the corral where the outlaws were. Jamming the weapon through a protective fence, he yelled, "You damned bastards! Every man put four bits in that trough, and be quick as hell about it!" Winchell said the men "hastily bridled their horses, swung into their saddles, and as they whirled away shouted '*Bueno hombre!*' (good man)."

Not long afterward, on November 10, the Vasquez gang struck at Jones' Store just down the river from Millerton. Before the sunset raid John C. Hoxie saw the bandits atop their horses, waiting near the store. Not suspecting anything, he exchanged pleasantries with them and rode away. The band then descended on the store, splitting up into groups of three and block-

man to terms, by a strong blow over the head with a dragoon pistol.

At the store of Jacob & Einstein the robbers experienced no difficulty. The clerk, Ed. Ellinger, was first approached and ordered to lie down; but instead of complying, the young man sprang through the doorway, and flying as on the wings of the wind to Sweet's store, astonished the nerves of that individual by rushing up to the counter, with hair erect, and eyeballs protruding like those of a French manikin, exclaiming, in tones that froze the merchant's blood:

"The robbers have come!"

Sweet thrust his head out of the door to see, when it was instantly seized by the "guard" and he thrown down and tied.

When Ellinger left Jacob & Co.'s store so hurriedly, the other inmates were tied at once, and thrown to the floor, Lewis Epstein [Einstein] was seized and the key of his safe demanded. At first he evaded complying with the unpleasant demand by pretending the clerk Ellinger had carried it off. Vasquez made his appearance at that instant, and telling him he knew he had another key, and that if he did not willingly produce it he would blow his brains out, he produced it, and the safe was opened and robbed. $800 in coin was taken from the safe and the money drawers, and a considerable amount from the pockets of the customers and loungers present.

Sweet's store was next attacked, but now came an unlooked-for change in the scene. They had taken about $60, when the cheerful tones of a Henry rifle interrupted the game, a second shot was heard the next moment and the guard fell heavily against the door, ex-

claiming in Spanish,

"I am shot!"

While the wholesale work of robbery was going on J. W. Sutherland and James E. Flood had been informed what was in progress, and seizing their arms arrived in haste just as the attack was made at Sweet's, and fired the shots which stopped the robbers, and all of them made a precipitate rush for the bridge, firing right and left as they fled. When they started J. W. Sutherland, armed with a Henry rifle, tried to head them off, but was not in time. Springing across the bridge, the brave and determined man opened fire on them as they vaulted into their saddles, and one of his shots wounded [G.] Gomez slightly in the neck, and the other struck the redoubtable Chavez in the right leg, a little above the knee, inflicting a severe and intensely painful wound.

The robbers had obtained over $2,500 in hard coin, and a good deal of valuable jewelry. Vasquez, who took Reichart's watch and that of Douglas, promised to return them, but in his hurried exit from the town had no time to make his word good.

One of the new recruits, named Monteres, afraid to make the passage of the bridge, followed the river bank down a little ways and hid. His movement was unobserved by any of the citizens.

At a Mexican house, some eight miles from the scene of the robbery, the band halted, and the wound of Chavez was dressed, as well as the scratch on Gomez's neck, and the booty divided. . . .

Great excitement prevailed in Kingston, and a large crowd speedily collected, but no attempt was made to pursue the robbers

until the next day. Early in the morning J. W. Sutherland, taking two volunteers with him, followed the trail of the robbers for the purpose of getting a clue to their probable destination, and about four miles from Kingston captured Monteres, who had crossed the bridge a little after midnight, and brought him into town. He confessed to being with the gang when it entered the town, and to standing guard at the hotel, but claimed that he was not a member of the organization, and did not know a single one of the bandits.

His story was that he was on his way to Kingston to buy some clothes, when he was overtaken by the robbers, who took his money and then forced him to accompany them and act the part he did. When the shooting began he ran down the river instead of across the bridge, and the band carried off his horse. He was taken to Millerton on the following Sunday by Constables Blackburn and Andy Farley, and lodged in jail. He was tried soon after, convicted, and is now serving out a fourteen year's sentence in the State Prison.

The excitement was once more at fever heat throughout Fresno, Tulare, and Kern counties, when the news of the Kingston robbery was heard. Sheriff Glascock, of Tulare, at once organized a posse of men and started out to strike the trail of the bandits; Sheriff Ashmore [Ashman] of Fresno, also put scouts on their track.

SOURCE: *The California Outlaw*, ed. by Robert Greenwood. Los Gatos, California: The Talisman Press, 1960.

ing its doorways. As in the Firebaugh's Ferry holdup, store clerk Smith Norris was forced to open a safe, many goods were taken, and nearly a dozen men were forced onto the floor and robbed. One of the victims, John Bugg, recognized a gang member, Ignacio Ronquel, and shouted a foul Spanish epithet at him. He followed that with "If I had my six-shooter, I'd show you damned quick whether I'd be down or not!"

A posse under Sheriff J. Scott Ashman was hastily formed at Millerton after this robbery. It tracked the gang to Borden and scoured the Cantua area, having some interesting experiences along the way. While in the west side the men encountered some Mexicans who shared tortillas and beef with them; a posse member commented that "we were treated like gentlemen (nine of us, armed)." They also were said to have encountered Vasquez's sister, who told them no rope could hang her brother, that they were wasting their time and that they should hasten home. Early discouragement forced the posse to follow her advice. They were back at Millerton by November 20.

After several weeks of hiding, Vasquez and his men sallied out of the shadows in December. They rode to Kingsburg one Sunday morning, where store owner Simon Harris and his son, Jacob, spotted them coming from afar. Fearing that the bandits would steal a $5,000 delivery Wells, Fargo had just made to him, Harris whisked the money back to his nearby dwelling, had his wife hide it in their bedroom, and returned to the store to see what the Vasquez gang wanted. As it turned out, they wanted to eat.

Plates and silverware were brought from the Harris apartment and cheese, crackers, oysters and sundries from the store supplies made an appetizing spread. Whiskey bottles were filled from a liquor supply in the cellar and the bandits were given all they could eat and drink. They were given a final drink and a smoke to top it off with, and then came the crisis for the merchant. Would the bandits depart in peace? Vasquez and his men talked among themselves in Spanish and then, shaking hands all around, took their departure. (Account from the *Kingsburg Recorder*, August 18, 1954.)

Following this incident the gang made its last, and most important, raid in Fresno County—at Kingston (see 11:5). Afterward, the bandits secreted themselves on Chidester's Island in the San Joaquin River for three weeks. Despite the frantic searching of posses in the area, the gang's main members were not found. There was excellent tule and brush cover on the island and many lookouts were stationed around it. At the nearby California Ranch, the manhunters had better luck. The grave of Ramona, a wounded Kingston marauder, was found after a local Mexican "was stimulated by some judicious hanging." Then some other

Mexicans residing at the ranch, fearful of reprisals because of Vasquez's activities in the area, turned Ronquel over to the authorities. He was tried at Millerton and sentenced to ten years at San Quentin.

The Kingston robberies prompted state action against Vasquez. On January 24, 1874, Governor Newton Booth offered $3,000 for him if captured alive, and $2,000 for his corpse. Harry Morse, Alameda County sheriff, embarked on a sixty-day, 2,720-mile expedition on March 12 to find the gang. One of the members of his posse was Harry Thomas, a Fresno County deputy sheriff.

With this type of search being conducted, it was obvious Vasquez could not hold out for long. He was nearly captured when he tried to rob a San Gabriel rancher, Alex Repetto, on April 12. When the rancher sent out for a large bank draft to pay Vasquez, the bank became suspicious, lawmen were dispatched, and the badman effected another narrow escape.

Vasquez's luck ended on May 14 when a Los Angeles County sheriff's posse learned he was holed up at a confederate's cabin in the Cahuenga Mountains. He was captured there, but not until a fierce gunbattle broke out and Vasquez was severely wounded. Brazen to the last, he told his captors: "You dress my wounds and nurse me careful, you get $8,000! If you let me die, you only get six. [New reward money had increased the old figures.] You get $2,000 for being kind!" Although he was indulged, he was shipped back to San Jose for trial, was convicted and sentenced to hang. The gallows swung open for Vasquez on March 18, 1875, and California's epoch of large-scale gang violence was ended for more than a decade.

As Fresno County progressed into the latter nineteenth century, the number and variety of crimes increased dramatically. Some places on the map were dens of thievery, brawling and vice. After telling the story of an Indian shot dead for stealing a bottle of whiskey (and his white assailant's being acquitted), a Fresno Flats correspondent told the *Fresno Weekly Expositor* on October 1, 1879: "You remember I wrote you some time since concerning the rioting and drinking which was carried on here, and I thought that the Flats had an unjust reputation for such things. I withdraw that statement now. It is the worst place for such things . . . for its size and population."

Firebaugh, a rendezvous for hardened sheepmen and Mexican desperadoes of the west side, had a similar reputation. It was described as the "champion tough town of the San Joaquin" in the September 5, 1896, *Fresno Daily Evening Expositor*, which told of how three saloon owners there had just evaded convictions for keeping disorderly houses. No one would testify aginst them. The story also mentioned that Lady Godiva's ride had recently been re-enacted at the town and "the admiring populace did not rise up and slay a Peeping Tom, for no one was prepared to 'cast the first stone' . . . That [Firebaugh] is a tough town is amply evidenced by the fact that Justice of the Peace Crawford, under threats of great bodily harm, holds court in Mendota rather than in the modern Coventry."

Disputes had a way of erupting into gunbattles. When fishermen William Farrow and John Ballogh were robbed in November 1893—the former of a stove, the latter of his catch and some utensils, at gunpoint—they went to Fresno and obtained arrest warrants for two suspects. Accompanied by a Fresno deputy constable, they took a wagon south of town and started looking for the robbers. The officer tried to make an arrest after catching up with them on Fig Avenue, but was interrupted when one of the robbers fired his Winchester rifle at him. One of the men was wounded in an ensuing gunbattle. Farrow, who was paralyzed from the waist down, tried to crawl away from the scene and was shot and killed. The remaining robber fled north and disappeared. While on his deathbed the wounded robber, Charles Robinson, said, "Oh, it is about even. I sent Farrow to hell and he sent me. The only difference is he will get there a little ahead of me."

Law enforcement found it difficult to intervene in aggressive disagreements. In June 1896, when rancher Lee Blasingame's sheep began feeding in William Cloudsley Corlew's mountain pastures, the two men engaged in a fistfight at the latter's ranch. Corlew lost, and following the encounter Blasingame left on horseback to inspect his flocks on the upper Kings River. Corlew tagged behind him with a loaded shotgun, managing to wound Blasingame's horse and pepper Blasingame's jaw with shot. Despite the circumstances, Corlew somehow escaped indictment and justice. His name did not come up for trial when the county court convened its next session.

The unwillingness of witnesses to testify provided another problem. On October 21, 1899, a Chinese man ran out of a cellar in Fresno's Chinatown, pursued by another Chinese with a six-shooter. The armed man fired and hit his prey, who stumbled and fell down momentarily, then arose and scampered into another cellar. At least a dozen Chinese saw part of this incident, probably part of a gang feud (of which more later), but all professed ignorance when police arrived. "Me no see shooting," said one. "Me tink him alle same Fourth July. Chinee boy have little fun. Nobody kill."

Most of the time, the reasons for wielding guns were more obvious. Armed robberies occurred in every conceivable situation. Stages taking visitors to Yosemite were a common target. Two men named Prescott and Myers robbed two of them in 1885, taking $900 altogether. Captured by a posse headed by O. James Meade, Fresno County sheriff, they went through three trials and escaped prison through jury disagreements, although Prescott (true name: I. W. Hatch) was later incarcerated for assaulting his wife in Fresno with intent to murder.

Another conveyance, Fresno's streetcars, proved vulnerable to robbers. On the night of February 11, 1892, when one of the cars was coming into the city from the county fairgrounds, a man leaped out of the dark and stopped the horse pulling the vehicle. Another man jumped into the car, wrestled with the driver (and got five dollars for his trouble). An Armenian man was shot in the face during the scuffle and badly wounded. Both highwaymen got away.

Private travelers, expectably, were frequent robbery targets. Charles Burge, Gordon Myers, and brothers Edward and Andrew Rader, all of the Malaga area, slid into the profession in 1893–94 by stealing foodstuffs and petty items at first, then deciding to torment some Chinese near Sanger one day. "As we were going along we saw two Chinamen coming," said Myers later, "and the boys proposed we hold them up, just for fun, and to get a little money to have a good time in Sanger. I objected to it, but the boys insisted, and I finally agreed to go into it . . . We got 65 cents, not enough to pay for the trouble." Eventually the gang robbed traveling musician Dominic Imperatrice near Malaga, taking his watch, chain and revolver. When Andrew Rader attempted to fence these goods, Fresno police moved in and the ring was broken up. His brother and Burge were later tried and each sentenced to ten years at Folsom. At that time (March 23, 1894), the *Fresno Daily Evening Expositor* said: [As Rader] looks back he will no doubt wish that he had received a few sound whippings when they might have done him good and saved him from the punishment and disgrace which have now overtaken him."

The Fresno streets were no safer. On a single night—January 21, 1897—A. D. Michael's notions shop on Mariposa Street was robbed; R. B. Johnson was stuck up on J Street, clubbed, and relieved of $5.10; Thomas Richardson was divested of a gold watch, a chain and $41.00 in front of Norberto Tunzi's Hotel; John Bloomingdale was assaulted on K Street, wrestled with the robbers, and had his watch taken; and Antone Diaz, owner of the Circle Bar on Front Street, was beaten with a club and revolver near where Johnson had been robbed. Two reporters from the *Fresno Morning Republican*, Martin Madsen and R. M. Mappes, heard Diaz's cries and chased the robbers. A running gunbattle ensued around the Fresno Agricultural Works, Park Stables and Courthouse Park. Both sides traded shots in alleyways, shrubbery and open streets, with the criminals temporarily getting away.

Six men were eventually arrested for creating this miniature crime wave. Its ringleaders, James Wilson and Frank Hall, were not held for long. A smuggled saw allowed them to cut through the Fresno jail's iron bars on May 25, 1897. The night jailer heard noises and did not investigate them; it was up to patrolman H. C. Clifton to stop the criminals when he noticed them running down the street. They gave Clifton the slip and, judging from contemporary accounts, made their escape good.

Gang violence in Fresno County returned sporadically in the 1880s and afterward. In 1881 Billie Benton and Frank J. ("Tex") Kellett had the Fresno Flats area abuzz over their cattle-rustling activities. A posse raced eastward after the thieves; upon reaching the Mono Lake area, they found eight Fresno County cattle that had been palmed off on unsuspecting buyers. In the meantime, Kellett and Benton had returned to Fresno Flats where they got drunk, defied arrest, cursed the constable, shoved their pistols into faces at random, "and [paraded] the streets with a whoop, a threat and a wild halloo," according to the July 6, 1881, *Fresno Weekly Expositor.*

Kellett and Benton also made the mistake of disclosing their whereabouts to townsfolk. When the posse returned to Fresno Flats, the leaders were tipped off and led the lawmen into the high Sierra. There they surprised the rustlers in camp and engaged them in a gunbattle. The badmen got away and resumed operations in Nevada. Benton was killed there; Kellett eventually found his way back to Fresno County, where he stole a horse from Henry Clay Daulton and got Constable John M. Hensley hot on his trail again.

A new posse was formed that followed Kellett to a Sierra watering hole. Another gunbattle took place, in which Kellett was wounded twice in the leg. Unable to run, he was captured. Mountain residents wanted to lynch him, and Hensley had a terrible time quieting them down. Kellett was soon brought to justice in Fresno and served two terms in San Quentin.

The Cliff Regan gang, a band of occasional cattle rustlers and murderers, maintained a hideout near Stephenson Mountain in 1896–97. Although most of their thievery took place in Madera County and elsewhere, the locals were scared of the group's mere presence. Stage drivers Joseph House and Abner W. Petrea had to quit carrying money on their routes, and whenever Regan or a gang member entered a local tavern patrons were numbed with fright. Little is known of Regan gang activities after this time, although one member—Walter Low—was later apprehended for an 1898 train robbery near Cross Creek in Tulare County.

John Sontag and Christopher Evans made up the last great criminal gang—actually a duo, with occasional assists from accomplices—to occupy a place in pre-1900 Fresno County history. The men entered the crime annals for unusual reasons. Sontag was a brakeman for the Southern Pacific railroad in Fresno; he was injured one day when an iron rail from a moving flatcar flew off and punctured his back. While the Southern Pacific helped Sontag with medical expenses, it refused to find a less strenuous job for him after his recovery.

Sontag drifted down to the Tulare County area, where he met Evans, a farm laborer and warehouse superintendent. Evans was a man of surprisingly ethereal bent for that time and place. He was fond of quoting Shakespeare and the classics, and wanted to be buried in a redwood tree when he died, thus endowing his corpse with a new kind of life. Evans took a liking to Sontag, and Evans' daughter Eva became engaged to him. The two men began publicly cursing the Southern Pacific in a manner that started looking suspicious. When four trains were held up in the central valley, Evans and Sontag became prime suspects.

The first robbery happened south of Pixley, in Tulare County, on February 22, 1889. Two masked men stopped the train by crawling out of the tender and ordering the engineer to stop. The outlaws tried to get the safe open, dynamited the coach when that

---

Reference 11:6

## FOR THIS THEY NAMED A MOUNTAIN FOR HIM

Here is what [Fresno County Deputy Sheriff] Ed McCardle wrote about the Elwood ranch battle:

On the night of December 22, 1891, I was preparing for bed in the Treasurer's Office in the Fresno County Court House, when George Moore came to me and said, "I am going to take your place tonight, Ed; John [Hensley] wants to see you down in the sheriff's office."

It was just after several days of big collections at the Treasurer's office, and one of us unmarried deputies had been sleeping in the office during such times, as large amounts of money were held in the treasurer's vault.

I went down to Sheriff John Hensley's office and there met Sheriff Eugene W. Kay and Hensley. Kay had just got in from Visalia.

Hensley said, "Ed, go down to my barn and get your saddle horse and mine and take them to Centerville. You will meet Sheriff Kay's posse there. Wait there with them until Sheriff Kay and I get there with his buggy and team." I started out horseback, leading Hensley's horse. Kay and Hensley followed later in the buggy.

About the time I left Fresno it began to rain. It was as cold as I ever knew it to rain. Within a few hours it began to sleet, and kept it up every step of the way to Centerville. How I suffered! I was wet to the skin and my clothes and riding equipment were covered with sleet.

I arrived at the Caldwell Hotel at Centerville just as Kay's posse arrived. All eleven of us sat in front of a fireplace and a big oak fire for almost two hours, and partly dried out our clothes and recovered from the exposure we had suffered. Then we started out again on horseback.

With us was Joe Middleton from near Hanford. He had been scouting provisions for Riley Dean and Grat Dalton, whom he had secreted on what is now known as Dalton Mountain, near Kings River above the Judson Elwood home, now the Pierson Dude Ranch. He agreed with Sheriff Kay to guide us to the hide-out in return for a saddle horse and riding rig.

We rode through the hills toward the high mountains pointed out by Middleton. When we had finally arrived at a point a mile or two from where the camp was supposed to be, the whole party halted. Middleton described the hiding place, just over the brow of a ridge in our sight and under a big oak tree.

All of this time it was bitter cold and all of

us were chilled to the bone. It was about four o'clock in the afternoon of December 23.

Sheriff Kay and Hensley started out to reconnoiter and get the lay of the land, leaving the rest of us, eight in number.

About six p.m. Kay and Hensley came back. It was then too late to go to the camp and make an arrest. But plans had been laid for a return in the morning, and Kay and Hensley took us down to the Judson Elwood home to spend the night.

The Elwoods had no room to bed us for the night, so we all lay around on the living room floor in front of a big oak fire in the fireplace. But that floor was as cold as the ice on a pond of water. We rolled over and over, always freezing on one side. Mrs. Elwood did the best she could to feed us and make us comfortable.

About two o'clock in the morning we all piled out and made ready to climb the mountain to the place where the hide-out of Dalton and Dean was located. It was a bright moonlight night. The moon must have been full the evening before, because it was almost as bright as day as we made the climb up the mountain. Just after daylight we had arrived within one quarter of a mile of the camp. I can remember that we all halted for a rest while Kay and Hensley completed their instructions to us. We were to spread out and approach the ledge of rock from several angles.

I remember that I was as scared as a rabbit just then, but as I looked at the faces around me I could see that all of the rest were as badly scared as I was. Hensley told us, "Boys, those fellows are not going to be arrested without a fight. Some of us may not come back from this venture. If any of you do not feel that you want to go ahead, now is the time to drop out." Not one fell out of the procession as we started for that rock ledge.

Early as we were, fortune was against us. Dean and Dalton were starting out on a hog hunt. A yellowish-red bird dog was following them. As we came in sight on top of the rock ledge we could see them with their guns on their shoulders. There were perhaps twenty or thirty seconds when they could have been called upon to surrender and then be shot, for they would never have done anything but dive for cover.

Several of Kay's men wanted to shoot them at first sight, but Hensely and Kay would not allow it and in a few seconds they were out of sight. This action on the part of Kay and Hensley in not allowing the Visalia deputies to shoot Dalton and Dean down in cold blood was resented ever after by some of the party.

Well, it was about six-thirty on the morning of December 24, 1891, when Dalton and Dean disappeared into the brush and left our posse standing there in the cold. But none of us felt cold just then.

About ten o'clock we could see that they were drifting back toward camp. At eleven a.m. Hensley and I could see one of the men coming directly toward us. He was then about two hundred yards away. Hensley

said, "Keep out of sight and let him come as close as he will." Hensley hid behind a pile of rocks and I behind an oak tree a little apart, until he was within thirty feet of us. He was Riley Dean.

In a low, but determined voice, Hensley said, "Drop that rifle." Dean dropped the rifle. Hensley said, "Come here." Dean walked to within fifteen feet of us. Hensley said, "Unbuckle that revolver belt." Dean unbuckled the belt, and the revolver, cartridges, and belt all dropped to the ground.

During all of this time both Hensley and I had our rifles cocked and aimed directly at Dean's middle. If he had made a false motion of any kind we would have shot him instantly. When we had Dean safely separated from his guns, Hensley hurried over the brow of the ridge with Dean to get a pair of handcuffs from Kay.

Almost as soon as Hensley was out of sight I heard the sound of footsteps in the same direction from which Dean had approached. The dog was about ten feet ahead of Dalton and came into view at about the same time as Dalton did. The rest of it was over in two seconds. Dalton was carrying his winchester rifle over his shoulder. [When his dog barked] he threw it forward and to his shoulder in one quick motion, and fired instantly. I fired at almost the same instant. My bullet went over Dalton's head and whistled over the heads of the rest of the posse down the hill. The bullet from Dalton's rifle entered the oak tree about six inches from, and above, my face.

Dalton's action was the most instinctive, involuntary motion I have ever observed. From the time the dog barked until Dalton disappeared in the brush two seconds did not elapse. In one continuous motion he drew and fired the rifle, dropped flat on the ground and rolled into a gulch about ten feet away. Down that gulch he went like a frightened deer. . . .

When Hensley understood what had happened, he said, "Well, I am glad he didn't get you, Ed, but I am sorry you didn't get him." Soon the entire posse had assembled, but no trace of Dalton could be seen.

Judson Elwood was plowing with a six-horse team and gang plow in a field about two hundred yards above his house. While we were still on the mountain we saw Dalton approach the plow team. Elwood unhitched a white horse from the plow. Dalton jumped on it bareback and started along a trail over the side and brow of the hill in the distance. As he rode away he yelled and fired two shots from his revolver. The dog was still with him. They soon disappeared over the hill on the trail. That was the last we ever saw of Grat Dalton in Fresno County.

[For this Dalton had a mountain named for him.]

Soon after we reached the edge of the plains, Hensley and I proceeded to Fresno. Kay and his posse went south toward Visalia, taking Dean with them.

. . .

[Eugene W. Kay later said] during the time I was in the Sheriff's office there passed through my hands fifty-seven thousand dollars of money, all spent in tracking down and arresting the Daltons, Chris Evans, and the Sontag brothers, and in trying Grattan and Bill Dalton. In addition I spent $18,000 of my own money. I left Tulare County without a cent to my name.

[For this Sheriff Kay had no mountain named for him. Neither did the deputies who risked their lives and endured the cold on the day before Christmas.]

. . . .

There always has been deep mystery about the route taken by Grat Dalton after he escaped from the posse at the Elwood ranch, and about his "one hundred and seven" day ride from California to Indian Territory. It was a thrilling experience to hear Littleton Dalton tell in detail just what happened. According to Lit, Grat went direct from the Elwood ranch to the home of Charles Owen, a short distance west of the present town of Clovis. After a short stay there he rode eighty miles to the home of ex-supervisor W. W. Gray, seven miles south of Livingston, in Merced County. From there, almost a month later, the ride was begun to Indian Territory.

Charles Owen had passed away before material for *Dalton Gang Days* was being assembled . . . his son, Roy Owen, has furnished the following interesting account:

Yes, Grat Dalton stayed at our house a week or more just after his escape from the posse. Grat made his getaway on a grey plow-horse which he turned loose before he arrived at my father's house. Cole Dalton was working nearby for my uncle, Tom Owen. When Grat recovered sufficiently, my father outfitted him with a horse and an old saddle, and he and Cole started out [and] went north to Merced County.

It was from Littleton Dalton that the detailed story of the ride to Indian Territory was obtained:

After the battle with Kay's posse at the Elwood ranch, Grat came to Charlie Owen's. The officers were watching Cole Dalton at Tom Owen's, and me at Clovis Cole's, but they didn't think of watching the Charlie Owen ranch. Grat didn't come to me after the jail break, because I had told Bob and Emmett I wouldn't help any of them again; for them not to come to me for money, horses, riding rigs, ammunition, or guns.

[They then left California and a year later Grat was killed at Coffeeville, Kansas. Lit and Cole(man) Dalton were respected members of the Dalton family as were most of the twelve children. While the family lived in the Clovis area, the father bred race horses. Their close relationship with the Coles and Owens undoubtedly account in large part for their actions in this and other incidents in support of the criminal Daltons.

SOURCE: Excerpts from *Dalton Gang Days* by Frank F. Latta. Bear State Books, 1976.

233

failed, and wounded a railroad worker and deputy sheriff (the latter happening to be on the train) before leaving.

Another masked pair of robbers stopped a train two and a half miles south of Goshen on January 20, 1890. The engineer and fireman were marched to the express coach and made to throw down an express box containing $20,000 in gold.

A third robbery, a half-mile south of Alila on February 6, 1891, began like the Goshen holdup, but this time an irate express manager told off the bandits and chased them away with gunfire before any express loot was taken.

The fourth robbery, two miles south of Ceres on September 3, 1891, was also unsuccessful. The bandits slid out of the tender and got the train stopped, only to have another irate express manager shut the lights off on them. While the robbers were trying to enter the express coach by candlelight, railroad detectives Len Harris and A. B. Lawson engaged the bandits in a gun battle and drove them off.

If Evans was not a robbery participant at this time, he became an accessory of sorts after the Alila holdup. A friend of his and fellow warehouse employee, Gratton Dalton was arrested, tried at Visalia and convicted for the crime. Dalton, a former United States deputy marshal in Indian Territory (now Oklahoma), had taken up horse and cattle thievery there, gravitated to California, become known as a shady character at Tulare and other places, and had been tried mostly on his reputation. A poor alibi and disreputable defense witnesses doomed him. Though his brothers Bob and Emmett—fellow peace officers gone bad—were actually responsible for the robbery, Grat momentarily took the blame.

Evans may have known all this but, in any event, he supplied Dalton with everything he needed for a September 28, 1891, jailbreak. (Some said he furnished help because Dalton knew of Evans' involvement in the Goshen holdup.) Before the appointed night a hacksaw, rifle, ladder and horse were put into their appropriate places.

Dalton made his way out of Visalia's jail with two others, and the escape went undetected for some hours. He fled to Squaw Valley in Fresno County, where a friend of his named Joe Middleton holed him up, at a place three miles north of town. Before long Riley Dean—another friend, a suspect in the Ceres holdup (committed while Dalton was incarcerated) and also on the lam—arrived at the outlaw camp.

Tulare County Sheriff Eugene W. Kay knew of the Middleton-Dalton relationship, kept the former under watch, and leaned on him when it became obvious he was helping Dalton. The possessor of a criminal record, Middleton decided to avoid another prison term and inform on the two badmen. He led Kay and other officers to the hideout, known since then as Dalton

Mountain, where a gunbattle took place (see 11:6).

Once Dalton escaped this confrontation, he hid at the ranches of two friends—Charles Owen's, west of Clovis, and W. W. Gray's near Livingston. He headed east after a few weeks, reteamed with his brothers in their old haunts, and they launched a prairie crime wave. The Dalton Gang gained notoriety that endures today, yet their post-California career was short. When they tried to rob two banks in Coffeyville, Kansas, simultaneously on October 4, 1892, alert lawmen killed Grat, Bob and another brother, Bill. Emmett was crippled for life, and died on July 13, 1937.

To return to Sontag and Evans: On the night of August 3, 1892, it is almost certain they struck within Fresno County. Two men held up a train at the railroad stop then known as Collis, and now as Kerman. As in the Ceres job, two men came out of the tender and marched fireman Will Lewis and engineer Al Phipps to the express coach. To their surprise, the hostages were given cigars at this juncture, and Lewis was told to light a bomb fuse. When he protested, saying he knew nothing about bombs, one bandit barked: "What do you think I gave you that cigar for?"

Once Lewis complied, the bomb exploded but did little damage. A second try was more successful, hurling express manager George D. Roberts against a wall (the previous try had merely blown the shoes off his feet). After pistol-whipping Roberts, the bandits grabbed his keys and made off with three bags full of gold and silver, weighing approximately two hundred pounds altogether. Lewis and a brakeman loaded the loot onto a waiting wagon. Two men who had been running a threshing machine nearby, J. W. Kennedy and John Arnold, watched this scene with their rifles at the ready—yet never managed to draw a clear bead on either of the bandits. A railroad employee always managed unwittingly to shield one or the other!

Some of the physical descriptions of the disguised Collis robbers conflicted with those of Sontag and Evans, but their complicity looked rather obvious. Sontag was tall and Evans short, as the holdup men were. Worse yet, Sontag had rented a fast team of horses at Frank Bequette's Visalia stable before the robbery and returned it afterward. Evans claimed to be on a ranch near Selma when the holdup occurred, having visited Fresno earlier in the day to see a lawyer; yet no one had seen him during the hours most crucial to his alibi. Most damning of all, though discovered later, was the fact that part of the Collis loot had been buried in the yard of the Evans' home.

The evidence was convincing enough for railroad detective Will Smith and Deputy Sheriff George Witty, who tried to arrest Sontag and Evans at the latter's Visalia home on August 5. Shots rang out when they entered the house, and they fled from the scene, both wounded. Sontag and Evans left town but returned later that day to rescue Sontag's brother, George. An

*Sheriff Eugene W. Kay a few months before leading the posse after Grat Dalton.*

*Joaquin Murrieta as painted by early California artist Charles Nahl.*

*Grat Dalton a few months before he escaped jail in Visalia and fled into Fresno County.*

*Frank "Tex" Kellett, cattle rustler and horse thief.*

NOT TRANSFERABLE.

OFFICE OF THE SHERIFF
County of Fresno.                    FRESNO, CAL., Sept. 22nd, 1893.

Mr. *W. H. McKenzie*

You are respectfully invited to be present at the official execution of

## FRANK O. VINCENT

which will take place at the County Jail on the 27th day of October, 1893, at 12 o'clock NOON, SHARP.

*Jay Scott* Sheriff.

Present this Card at the Door.

*Fresno County Almanac*

*Those who accepted Sheriff Scott's invitation saw the only execution by hanging in Fresno County. The sheriff is on the left; his companion is not identified.*

## ONE THOUSAND DOLLARS REWARD.

THE SUM OF ONE THOUSAND DOLLARS IN Gold Coin of the United States, will be paid by the undersigned, for the apprehension and delivery to him in Millerton, Fresno county, California, of JOHN MASON, alias JOHN J. MONROE, and JAMES HENRY, the murderers of Charles Anderson, Joseph Hawthorne, and E. G. Robertson, on the 8th and 9th of November, 1864, in the county of Fresno. Or I will pay a

**Reward of Five Hundred Dollars**

in Gold Coin for the apprehension and delivery as above, of either of the murderers.

J. SCOTT ASHMAN, Sheriff.
Millerton, February 4, 1864.

### DESCRIPTION OF

**JOHN MASON and JAMES HENRY,**

the murderers of Charles Anderson and Joseph Hawthorne, who were killed on the night of Tuesday, November 8th, and E. G. Robertson, who was killed on Wednesday morning, November 9th, 1864, in Fresno county.

### JOHN MASON

is a heavy set man; about 5 feet 7 inches high; weighs about 165 pounds; about 30 years of age; light complexion; light colored hair, and very long, comes nearly to his shoulders, has it cut short underneath so that he can tuck the long hair under and give it the appearance of being short; light red-colored whiskers on the chin, and light mustaches, does not shave; high wide cheek bones; blue eyes, rather small and have rather a glassy appearance; front teeth black or decayed; has a very quick and restless motion, and a rocking walk; small scar on the face; (said Mason says that ''Mason'' is not his his true name; in the year 1860 went by the name of ''John J. Monroe;'' came from Fort Tejon in 1860, and reported killing a man at that place;) had on boots, overalls, check shirt, hat covered with coyote or badger skin, tail standing up in front, will probably remove the skin from his hat; had one six-shooter pistol, butcher knife with white handle, one double-barreled shot gun, one spy glass, when extended is about 18 inches long; riding rather small horse, of light grey color, branded with Hawthorne's brand; has two watches; one gold watch taken from Hawthorne, do not know what kind the other was; he took Hawthorne's saddle, (Spanish saddle) black leather, common Spanish bridle; said Mason has a small red-colered pointer or setter slut that follows him.

When last seen, there were four men in company, mounted on the following described horses, to wit: one grey horse, one black, and two bays or red-colored horses. They were at the head of what ir known as ''Moody Canon,'' and the San Burneto, traveling south.

### JAMES HENRY

is about 30 years old; height, about 6 feet 6 or 7 inches; weight, 145 or 150 pounds; light florid complexion, full prominent forehead, high wide cheek bones, chin rather sharp or peaked, dark hair, cut rather short, dark whiskers on the chin, but rather thin on the jaws or upper part of the face, may have very small mustaches, beard on all his face, but thin growth, does not shave; dark grey eyes, full and very prominent, rather popeyed, has a way of looking to either side without turning his head; stoop-shouldered and head thrown forward; went by the name of ''Spotty,'' at Watsonville; had one six-shooter pistol, and common butcher knife; riding a flea-bitten grey horse, branded something similar to an X on the right hip, has collar marks, and shod all round; Spanish saddle, known as ''Half Ranger,'' no macheros, small tapaderos, bridle, dragoon bit, small Spanish spurs; had on black hat, lopped down, had on boots and dark-colored coat.

*Reward offer for Mason and Henry. It appeared in each issue of the* Fresno Times *in 1865 when that was the only newspaper in the county (for all ten issues).*

*Chris Evans as he was pictured in an 1893 book by Hu Maxwell entitled* Evans and Sontag *(available in reprint).*

236

ex-con and drifter, he had been bragging of his involvement in the Collis holdup and had been picked up by the authorities. (Tried for robbery in Fresno, George was later sentenced to a term in Folsom state prison.) They failed to find him, but were spotted by a citizen's posse and another gunbattle broke out. Oscar Beaver, a member of the posse, was killed in the shootout. The men scampered away from this melee and headed for the nearby Sierra.

By September 6, Wells, Fargo and Company was offering a $10,000 reward for Sontag and Evans, or $5,000 for bringing in just one of them. U.S. Marshal Vernon "Vic" Wilson, with a new posse, and a team of expert Apache trackers began scouring eastern Tulare County for the men. According to historian Wallace Smith:

> The number of men deputized at one time or another to hunt Evans and Sontag finally reached the amazing total of more than 3,000. The woods were so full of man-hunters at times that at least eleven deputies were seriously wounded by other officers. Men who went deer hunting in the mountains during those days were in danger of being shot by over-zealous posses. A few such scrapes led otherwise righteous citizens to lose all respect for the representatives of law and order and to express sympathy for the fugitives trying to escape from the clutches of such fumbling minions of auth-

ority. On one occasion two clerks, Clarence Foin and Henry Minor, employed by the B. T. Scott grocery store of Fresno, were captured on their way to Yosemite to spend their annual vacation. Unfortunately for these two young men, they were riding in a cart drawn by a chestnut horse. According to the reports current at that time, Evans and Sontag were travelling along mountain roads with a similar horse and cart. So the poor boys were surrounded by a belligerent posse and held in custody for hours by some of its members while others rushed to Fresno to collect the reward. When the angry, agitated, and disheveled clerks were finally released, it may be assumed that they hoped that Evans and Sontag would thenceforth fight with resolution and shoot straight and often.

The Wilson posse found Sontag and Evans at Jim Young's Sierra cabin on September 13. In the gunfight that followed Wilson and one of his men, Andy McGinnis, were fatally wounded. Sontag and Evans raced from this bloody scene and began skipping between various hideaways in the Sierra. Reporter Henry D. Bigelow of the *San Francisco Examiner* caught up with the outlaws near Centerville and later wrote: "During the time I spent with them I was initiated into the custom of watchfulness which is observed by the fugitive who has a price of $10,000 put upon his head—alive or dead. While the two ate a [con-

Reference 11:7

## CHRIS EVANS ESCAPES FROM JAIL

The escape of Chris Evans from the county jail last evening at 6 o'clock was one of the most desperate achievements ever done in the desperate career of that famous bandit. In point of accurate planning and thorough execution it can scarcely find an equal anywhere. . . .

Evans arranged for confederates and arms, and then the supreme point was to get as many deputies out of town as possible. He did this with all the skill of Stonewall Jackson throwing his enemies off the track. The plan was to start the rumor that a gang intended to hold up the Porterville train last night, and thus call the officers down there. As the train was coming up yesterday morning a young man came to the conductor, who is also express agent, and told him that a band of robbers, of which he was a member, intended to hold up the train last evening just before reaching Porterville, giving as the reason for holding up a train on a small branch road, that it was holidays and a good deal of money would be coming up the line in return for poultry and other farm products shipped to the city.

"I have been roped into it," said the young man, "but I don't want to go through with it. I want to squeal on my partners, and undo the wrong I have done so far as I can. But I am into it now, and if I do not pretend to carry out my part of it, they will kill me. I will show up with them at the time for the robbery, but I will wear a white hat so the offi-

cers will not shoot me. Have the officers hid on the train, and when the men appear for the hold up, shoot them, but do not shoot me."

This was the young man's story and the conductor told it to railroad officials, and the sheriff's office was applied to for a special guard for the Porterville train . . . Deputy Sheriffs Peck, Timmins, Redford and White armed themselves and went off with the 5:30 train for Porterville, never dreaming that they were playing right into the hands of Chris Evans, and helping carry out his plan.

Last evening B. B. Scott was jailer, and when the hour of 6 arrived, he was the only officer about the building. This was a very unusual thing. There nearly always were others about the building at any hour, either day or night; but by some strange freak of fate which has always played to the hand of Evans, the coast was clear for the plot.

Shortly before six o'clock Mrs. Evans arrived at the jail and was admitted. Presently Ed Morrell came with a tray in which was a dinner for Evans. Many times Evans has been served with private dinners by his wife and other friends. So, nothing unusual was thought of it and Morrell was admitted unquestioned to the jail with the tray of dishes. To all appearances there was nothing in the tray but things to eat, but in fact, hidden in the bottom were . . . two large, new revolvers. . . .

Evans had been eating for a few minutes

when Morrell called to the jailer saying that he wanted to go, as Evans was done eating. Not suspecting anything, the jailer went up four or five steps, unlocked the door and went in. The next thing he knew Morrell thrust a pistol in his face and said: "Up with your hands!" The jailer was surprised, and was inclined to doubt the seriousness of the situation, although the pistol had nothing humorous looking about it. So his hands did not go up at once. But Evans was in it too, and he threw up a long, murderous pistol, and said in the calm but significant style of his, "That's right, Ben, hold 'em up." . . .

Morrell searched Jailer Scott and found no pistol on him. He and Evans then ordered Scott to lead the way to the door. He started toward the front exit, but Evans stopped him and ordered him to open the back door of the jail. But the jailer told Evans that the key to the back door was in the safe and he could not get it. "All right," said Evans, "go out the front way then."

The jailer locked the door and then the race began. As it happened, nobody was in front of the jail or court house, and they took the jailer with them at a brisk run across that corner of the park, and emerged on M street in front of the Christian church.

Just as they reached M street, they met ex-Mayor S. H. Cole, who was coming down town.

"Come on, we want you. Come with us; hurry, quick!" demanded one of the men.

237

federate] would keep watch with a shotgun resting on his legs. This was compulsory so far as I was concerned."

Throughout the 1892–93 winter the bandits were pursued across the Sierra, sometimes sheltered and fed by Southern Pacific-hating folks. A Squaw Valley rancher, Emil Tretten, gave them a meal one day—but more out of fear than resentment of the railroad. Much of Sontag and Evans' time was passed pleasurably in Sanger, Reedley, Dinuba and Visalia, visiting friends and saloons.

This fragile situation had to fall apart at some point. After months of stalemate yet another posse, headed by U.S. Marshal George Gard, learned that Evans and Sontag would be coming out of the mountains on June 11, 1893. They were going to visit Evans' wife, Molly, who had become increasingly distraught over her husband's fugitive ways. The two were intercepted near a place called Stone Corral, close to present-day Yettem in Tulare County, where a vicious gunbattle took place. Sontag suffered numerous wounds, was apprehended and trundled off to Visalia. He was later taken to Fresno, where he died on July 3. Evans somehow managed to escape the fracas, despite wounds in his back, head and right eye and a shattered left arm. He stumbled onto Elijah Perkins' cabin, some seven miles from the gunbattle's site, where he eventually was persuaded to surrender.

There was no money available for Evans' defense, so his wife and daughter, Eva, raised funds in an extraordinary manner. They accepted an offer to play themselves in a play based on the Sontag and Evans story, which had aroused great public interest by this time. The play—and its performers, though far from polished—were such a success that a sequel was mounted (*Evans and Sontag Up to Date*) and an expert defense team was hired, consisting of Fresno lawyer S. J. Hinds and State Senator G. G. Goucher. Evans' trial began on November 20, 1893, in Fresno and ended in a murder conviction on December 14.

In spite of his physical condition, Evans had no intention to spend more time in jail. Before he could be sentenced, a plot was hatched—and executed—to spring him (see 11:7). After it was pulled off, Fresno deputies tried to put a posse together at Sanger. Prospective members, remembering the other posses' misfortunes, demurred. In the meantime Evans and Ed Morrell, who brought Evans a gun on his dinner tray,

Mr. Cole was dazed and did not at first comprehend the situation, but supposed the men were officers and were arresting him by mistake for somebody else. He began to explain who he was. But the men waited for no explanations, and pointing their revolvers at him, from the distance of but a few inches, they ordered him to go along. . . .

When they reached O street, Evans remained behind with the two captives, while Morrell ran ahead to where a team was tied and in which they were to escape. [Molly Evans, three boys named Hutchinson and their sister, Rose, were later arrested for complicity in the jailbreak—Bill Hutchinson having procured the team mentioned here. The Hutchinsons were presumably convicted, but Evans' wife was released for lack of evidence.] The team was tied in front of the north side of the church, and it was undoubtedly the object of Morrell to have the team untied ready for Evans and himself to spring in when Evans should arrive. But here the unexpected happened, and had Evans not come to the rescue of Morrell, the latter would now have been in the jail.

Beside the team Morrell found W. M. Wyatt and City Marshal John D. Morgan standing talking. They had just met there, and Morrell ran up with his pistol drawn and said, "Up with your hands, and not a word out of you. Up with them!"

There was nothing left but to obey, and they held up their hands, and Morrell went through Marshal Morgan's pockets and took his pistol. Mr. Wyatt was standing partly behind Mr. Morgan, and Morrell turned to search Mr. Wyatt's pockets, and was just in the act, when Mr. Morgan glanced over his shoulder and seeing a chance to seize Morrell, wheeled and did so, catching him around the arms and body in a determined clasp. Mr. Wyatt at the same time clutched at the pistol in the hands of Morrell, and the man was about to be overpowered, when he called out, "Help! Shoot them! They have got me!"

It was all the work of a very few seconds. Evans left the jailer and Mr. Cole, and rushed forward to the assistance of his confederate, and exclaimed as he thrust his pistol forward, "Let go of him or I will shoot you." Marshal Morgan saw the pistol, and wheeled the body of Morrell around between himself and Evans, and still was grappling with Morrell. But Evans reached over Morrell's shoulder and shot Morgan in the side and called, "hands up!"

Marshal Morgan felt the bullet strike him, and he let go of Morrell and threw up his hands, saying, "I have my hands up."

Evans and Morrell then ran to the team which was tied within a few feet, to get in. But just as they had reached the horses, Evans wheeled and fired again at Mr. Morgan, but did not hit him.

The team was frightened at the shooting, and began to plunge. Before the outlaws could secure them the horses broke away and ran off, and Evans and his confederate ran down the alley between O and P streets. Mr. Morgan was taken to the doctor's house, and his wound was found to be severe, but will not prove fatal.

The excitement was tremendous in Fresno. As soon as Mr. Cole and Jailer Scott escaped from Evans they ran down town and spread the alarm. Jailer Scott, with his hat off, rushed along Mariposa street announcing that Chris Evans had broke jail. Almost at the same time the report became public that Marshal Morgan had been shot, but the two events were not connected for some time. But in a little while the full truth was known. Crowds gathered on the streets and citizens with guns were hurrying to and fro, and horses were hastily saddled for pursuit.

Not until about his time did it begin to dawn on anybody that the officers who had gone on the Porterville train had been led into a trap, and had been gotten out of the way.

Undersheriff Berry did everything in his power to capture Evans. He wired to every station in this and Tulare county and had the alarm sent to all the officers.

After the fight in front of the church Evans and Morrell ran down the alley to Tulare street, and a couple of minutes later appeared at the corner of Q and Mono streets, where they held up a boy named Benny Cochran and took his cart away from him.

The boy is a paper carrier for the Expositor, and was returning from delivering papers, and was near his home, when the two men ran out from under some trees and ordered him out. They presented pistols, and he jumped out of the cart and they jumped in, and headed west on Mono street. . . .

The boy set up a yell, and his brother and father came out, and joined in the chase to overtake the thieves, and were about to do so when Evans and Morrell fired twice at them, and they gave up the chase. . . .

SOURCE: *Fresno Daily Evening Expositor*, December 29, 1893.

wandered thoughout the Sierra for two months, staying at a place called Camp Manzanita and making occasional forays into the valley.

On January 11, 1894, while Evans and Morrell were at large, a holdup took place at Fowler. At the town train station, agent George A. Leon was robbed by a man masked with a red bandana. Pat Lahey and H. A. Mulligan, also inside the station, were robbed along with Howard A. Harris and A. A. Vincent. The latter pair had spied the goings-on from the outside and had attempted to report them, but the bandit snared the men before they could slip away. He then identified himself as Ed Morrell, and herded his victims across the street to the Kutner-Goldstein store. There Constable Ochs spotted the robber and engaged him in a gun battle—only to wound Lahey and Mulligan, and get shot in the hip himself. During the fracas, the bandit ran away.

The Fowler robber was always assumed to be Morrell, although there is evidence to the contrary. Fourteen years later A. G. Shoemaker, who had been in the store during the holdup, talked to a man while both were on a train bound for Southern California. The man—a drunk old miner, gabbing indiscriminately about his past, and definitely not Morrell—seemed like the Fowler bandit of years past. Shoemaker reported him to the authorities, who could do nothing. The statute of limitations for the crime had lapsed.

A short time later Evans and Morrell were chased out of their Camp Manzanita hideaway in the Sierra, and the place was burned by the deputies. Finally Evans was lured back to Visalia on the ruse that his young son was sick. Sheriff Kay descended on the Evans place on February 19, 1894, and after a few tense minutes when a messenger was taken hostage briefly, Evans and Morrell surrendered. There was considerable fear the men would be lynched, so they were taken to Fresno by the fastest team of horses available.

On February 20 Evans stood before Judge Milus King Harris and at last received his sentence: life imprisonment at Folsom. He was released, after several pardon petitions by his family and others, in 1911. Wracked by frequent headaches (due to the shot lodged in his head), palsy and paralysis, he died at his daughter's house in Portland, Oregon, in 1917. Morrell received a life sentence, which amounted to nine years' incarceration at San Quentin and Folsom. He went on to become a lecturer and crusader for a "new penology," and wrote of his outlaw days—in a book, *The Twenty-fifth Man.*

Burglary and thievery, as in the previous decades, were common scourges. The town of Fresno was a favored target. The December 27, 1882, *Fresno Weekly Expositor* noted that burglars had struck three homes in town the night before: W. T. Oden's (where they were frightened away by Mrs. Oden's screams), Mrs. Patterson's (where the grand sum of seventy-five cents was taken), and George Bernhard's (where they did not enter, apparently distracted or frightened by the housekeeper).

Criminals regarded almost every chattel as fair game. On the morning of October 3, 1883, the Fresno municipal court was beset with a diversity of theft complaints: stealing a roll of blankets from a drunk on I Street, a hat from George Rupert at the Palace Saloon, drying raisins from William Harris' vineyard and forging a bank draft to rent a team of horses. This type of problem became epidemic by 1888 (see 11:8)

Lawmen did much to keep the thieving part of the population in check. A large-scale burglary and fencing operation, headed by John Hern, W. H. Silvers and John Cooper, was broken up by Fresno County sheriff's deputies in April 1891. The men had preyed on households in and around Fresno and had accumulated hundreds of items, which the deputies had found cached at Merced Falls. Several years later, in 1896, a

Reference 11:8

## EVERY VARIETY OF THE LAW DEFIER

"Fresno never before contained as many hard cases as now," said a peace officer to an Expositor reporter. "The town seems to be a sort of central dumping ground for the ruffians who have found quarters in other parts of the State too hot for them. We have every variety of the law defier, from the sneak thief to the fellow who is ready to stop a train. If any one doubts that Fresno has more than its quota of drunk-rollers, burglars, so-called lovers, etc., let him take a stroll across the railroad track any night, or walk out on some of the back streets, and then refresh his memory with the mugs from any rogues' gallery in the State, and he will no longer doubt that this city is having more than its share of the undesirable element. You thought the toughs were being thinned out, which shows how mistaken you are.

Where two or three of them are pulled on a night, which is about the average, the ruffian stock is reinforced by an arrival of perhaps a half dozen.

"Then the vags have got on to the jury racket. Two of them, the worst and most notorious of their kind, were brought before one of our Justices yesterday, and each demanded a trial by jury, and handed in a list of witnesses for the defense as long as one's arm. Of course the fellow who demands a jury trial generally does it at the suggestion of his lawyer, and the latter looms up at the trial, pettifogs it from start to finish, and trusts to look for befogging the mind of at least one juror.

"'Where does the money come from to fee the lawyer with?' How simple you are. You might as well ask who clothes and feeds these

loafers, who furnishes them whisky and cigar money, or who gives them the stake with which to thow dice or play poker.

"The conviction of one of these vagabonds, as was the case yesterday, is creditable to the men who rendered the verdict, and will go far toward removing from this city the blackguard and generally vicious element. If the people will stand by the peace officers in their efforts to rid Fresno of its scoffers at law and morality, as they seem at last determined to do, we will clear Fresno of its thieves, loafers and wretches who live from the earnings of wantons."

SOURCE: Fresno County Scrapbook 1870-1899, taken from *Fresno Daily Evening Expositor*, April 6, 1888, p. 2, c. 2.

similar gang led by Ed Vanderzwiep and Frank Quintera was run aground. They were regularly shipping trunkfuls of stolen merchandise to San Francisco, but found themselves low on cash when the law became wise to their doings. In desperation the men held up A. A. Green and Harold Latter, Eisen Vineyard employees, near Martin Denicke's fig ranch. They obtained a fifty-dollar watch and no more than three dollars in coins. After this incident sheriff's deputies became overly suspicious of the two and apprehended them at William Degen's saloon in Fresno.

A surprising development of that year was the discovery of a latter-day Fagin in Fresno. The September 12, 1896, *Fresno Daily Evening Expositor* reported that Paul Baley, a Frenchman, had supervised gangs of youthful thieves in Fresno and Bakersfield. A wagonmaker by trade, Baley had skipped town by the time the article appeared. Left to stand trial for the looting of Antone le Mattos' home on Cherry Avenue were two of his assistants, Charles Hooper and Harry Owens.

A few attempts at theft were thwarted by wary citizens. When Mrs. Charles Berry found a burglar in her kitchen during the night of January 17, 1895—"a typical desperado, thick-set and ugly looking," according to one description—she grabbed a revolver, which she always kept near while her husband was away, and fired at the man. He made a hasty exit, and the undaunted Mrs. Berry chased him down P Street. She was composed enough to fire a final shot, although he got away.

A person equally intolerant—William Hill—was more successful (if that is the right word to use) than Mrs. Berry. During the early evening hours of January 24, 1897, a drunk named Fred Bowman or Bauman prowled around the door of Hill's house south of Fresno. When he refused to tell Hill why he was there, and started for a nearby barn where an axe was handy, Hill became wary. He went outside with his shotgun and exchanged some heated words with a cursing Bowman. When the prowler refused to leave, Hill fired. "We [have] been robbed twice in the past six months," said Hill later. "My wife, already alarmed by the footpad stories from Fresno, begged me to be careful, and I was. In fact, I . . . should have shot long before I did . . . I regret the death of the man, but I cannot see how I am in any way to blame. I certainly gave him every chance to get away and only shot when I believed my life was in danger."

In spite of discouragements like these, crime—as in any age—was not controlled entirely. If anything, its manifestations diversified toward the end of the century. Stable, tool and crop thefts were common in the county's rural areas in the late 1880s. Rancher Hank Hawn was relieved of four tons of hay in 1886, and the May 31, 1887, *Fresno Daily Evening Expositor* complained that "robbers go prepared with wagons to carry off their plunder, and several hundred pounds of barley and hay are carried off at a time."

Women shoplifters, a novel phenomenon for that era, were apprehended in Fresno on March 13, 1895. They were caught stealing items at A. J. Wiener's store and, it was found, had been shipping booty back to their Bakersfield homes. After their capture one of the women, Carrie Genrich, attempted suicide. The husband of the other woman, Annie Allen, was surprised to hear of his wife's arrest: "It is true, my suspicions were a little aroused last fall by seeing things around the house that we had no need of. But then she always handled the money and bought what she wanted. I will stand by her because she is the mother of my little girl." While no record is extant, the pair were likely convicted.

Burglars found ways to get around many obstacles. Despite the fact that Alfred Parker's Fresno store, located on Mariposa Street, was guarded by a policeman who walked by every fifteen minutes, and a private guard was kept posted at the store's rear, it was ransacked on September 15, 1898. Some "scientific" burglars got into the Mark Webster and R. M. Thompson stores, also in Fresno, on January 1, 1899. They gained entrance by sawing a hole through the Kutner Hall floor, the hall being located above the Webster drugstore. Once in the drugstore, the process was vertically repeated to enter Thompson's business. The burglars tried and failed to blow up Thompson's safe with gunpowder, after which "they ransacked the till in the drugstore and secured about $9 in change," according to the January 3 *Fresno Morning Republican*. As with many other crimes, the yield was disproportionate to the effort.

Fresno thievery did not lack an occasional humorous twist. When Fulton G. Berry's residence was burgled on February 10, 1895, the invaders first helped themselves to a set of silver-plated bowls, dishes and pitchers. (They probably thought the pieces were solid, coming from Berry's house, yet they were not.) Then, according to the *Fresno Daily Evening Expositor*, "the men got a meal for themselves. They finished two chickens, a large cake and several fresh eggs, with some choice wines for dessert. They recognized Mr. Berry's taste in the matter of wines, and helped themselves to several bottles . . . Mrs. Berry takes the matter very quietly."

Homicides, after the 1870s, became so frequent that only the more sensational cases can be discussed here. Under the headline of "It's Not So Bad," the December 30, 1890, *Fresno Daily Evening Expositor* came close to celebrating the fact that only eleven people had been killed in the county that year. Consolation could be had in the fact that some had been slain justifiably. Juan Dias had fatally stabbed Francis Estreda while they argued over "the moving of some furniture." John D. Smith killed Percy Williams at Fresno's Hughes

Hotel during "a game of cards." Centerville deputy constable William G. Lane had killed William Canfield for no apparent reason. Even in this period, which had brought some cultural sophistication to the county, lives were still being sacrificed for the most trivial provocations.

The 1880s proved to be a risky period for lawmen, and even for those who aspired to such positions. G. H. Vaughn killed sheriff candidate John Donahoo on September 6, 1880, in what was later ruled self-defense. They were bitter partisans (Donahoo a Republican, Vaughn a Democrat) and had been involved in an extended political feud. A Fresno Republican mob almost managed to lynch Vaughn afterward; justice managed to prevail, possibly because Vaughn was a local lawyer.

A feud in the eastern mountains claimed at least two lives during 1882-83. Two factions in the Pine Flat country—one headed by A. J. Lefevre, the other by Ephraim and James L. Musick—claimed a parcel of land there. Shooting incidents between the parties were common. One, on November 17, 1882, ended in the death of Henry Lefevre, A. J.'s brother. Jim Musick was tried in Fresno for the murder, but expert counselors S. J. Hinds and J. B. Campbell got him acquitted.

While Musick's trial was going on in Fresno, it gave rise to another murder. Seborn Lashley, a Pine Flat resident giving testimony in the case, voiced support for Musick while Lefevre was within earshot. According to the March 17, 1883, *Fresno Weekly Expositor*:

Lafever [sic] . . . took umbrage at the matter and hard words ensued and but for the interference of friends, serious results might have happened . . . They were parted, however, and Lashley was escorted to the hotel by Constable McCardle, and Lafever went on down the street. However, both were still excited and vowing vengeance against each other. Lashley soon returned to Mariposa street, and taking his station near the Acme Saloon, on the sidewalk, announced that he intended to kill old Lafever before he got to the Court House. Reputable witnesses state that Lafever made similar threats against Lashley . . . when near Ball's drug store the men seemed to have recognized each other and . . . Lashley drew his pistol and told Lafever to stop and take back what he had said about him. Lafever jumped into a hallway, drew his pistol, reappeared and fired, striking Lashley . . . [who] in a few minutes expired. Lafever was immediately taken into charge . . .

The reasons are unclear, but Lefevre was later acquitted.

The area remained a "dark and bloody ground." When a young man named Karl Peterson ventured into that neighborhood, vowing to locate some property despite the rivalry, he soon disappeared. Nothing more was heard of him until September 1896, when a skeleton was found near China Flat, one mile above Pine Flat. Then, as before, no faction bothered to identify the remains or say who was responsible for Peterson's presumed murder.

The 1890s opened with three of the most significant murders Fresno has ever seen. John D. Fiske's death at the hands of Joseph L. Stillman was the first. Fiske was a Fresno theater manager and developer (see Chapter 14) with a boorish, overbearing personality. An 1876 graduate of Harvard Law School, he was dismissed from the Massachusetts Bar six years later for committing various frauds, swindlings and misrepresentations. He moved to Fresno in 1887 with his wife, Amanda, and became embroiled in business controversies too numerous to repeat here. One of them proved fatal.

Fiske became covetous of a railroad car-coupling patent held by inventor Stillman, for which he offered an inadequate sum. When that failed Fiske demanded the patent, saying he would accuse Stillman of having an affair with his (Fiske's) French servant girl if it was not delivered. Before Stillman could consent, Fiske started the rumor-mill rolling. It was a situation that drove Stillman beyond sanity.

In the early evening of July 26, 1890, Stillman waited for Fiske outside the latter's building. When Fiske appeared, Stillman ran toward him and slapped his face. The two men began wrestling and Fiske began beating the furious inventor with his cane. Breaking away, Fiske ran diagonally across the Mariposa and J streets intersection, only to be stopped by a bullet from Stillman's revolver. Two more shots rang out, and Fiske slumped to the ground. Arrested and tried for the crime, Stillman was found guilty and sentenced to life imprisonment on October 29, 1890. "He had tried to ruin my poor wife and children, and I couldn't stand it any longer," said Stillman in explanation.

Another 1890 homicide arose from a domestic dispute and led to Fresno County's only legal hanging. Dr. Frank O. Vincent and his wife, Annie, had moved to Fresno in 1885, hoping to find contentment, but their marriage was not a happy one. Vincent lapsed into a despair of his own making, becoming a drunkard and all-around miscreant. His wife separated from him and instituted divorce proceedings. After the initial paperwork was served on Vincent, he snapped. On December 18 he drove a carriage to his wife's home, asked her if she still wanted the divorce, and tried to get her to take poison when she replied affirmatively. At that point Vincent drew a revolver, said, "Take that," and fired four shots into his wife. A nearby policeman heard the noise and arrived just before Vincent swallowed a fatal dose of the poison himself.

Hastily swept into the Fresno jail—a lynch mob was ready to move, since killing a woman was unthinkable in those days—Vincent languished there while awaiting and undergoing trial. His defense tried to prove insanity, but the doctor was convicted of murder and sentenced to hang on May 29, 1891. A series of appeals to the California and United States supreme courts followed, all for various technicalities.

All this postponed the execution process; in the event of a quick go-ahead, a scaffold that had already claimed four lives was brought in from San Bernardino. In mid-1893 the appeals process ran out for Vincent, and his execution was set for noon on October 27.

Vincent spent the last few hours of his life simply. He talked with his mother the night before, prayed with Mrs. T. H. B. Anderson, and discussed the afterlife with the Rev. J. H. Collins. On the morning of the twenty-seventh he ate breakfast—his last meal—while 600 people began jamming a special enclosure next to the jail, where the scaffold was waiting. Vincent was taken out two minutes before noon, led up to the platform, pinioned and asked to say his last words. "By the sheriff and his officers, I wish to thank you for the kind treatment I received at your hands. To my friends, God bless you. To my enemies, God forgive them." The trap was sprung on time and Vincent expired without a twitch, his neck broken cleanly.

"There seemed to be something of a relief when it was all over," said the *Fresno Daily Evening Expositor*. "Look at it in any light possible, it is not a pleasant thing to hang a human being, and the citizens all felt that it was an unpleasant necessity . . . The gallows had not a pleasing appearance after it had done its part. Perhaps it was a matter of imagination . . ."

Controversy surrounded the demise of Louis B. McWhirter, who died—either by his own hand, or by assassination—on the night of August 29, 1892, in Fresno. Whatever the cause, gunfire killed him as he stood outside the rear entrance to his home. It was claimed that McWhirter, a reform-minded Democrat, had offended more conservative members of the party (who happened to control the county offices). A lawyer and sometime journalist, McWhirter was known to have aroused some bad feelings with his crusading editorials in the *Daily Evening Expositor* and other local publications.

In time indictments were brought against Richard S. Heath, a so-called "barroom politician" of the traditional Democratic wing, and a carpet layer named Frederick S. Polley. Trials at Fresno and Tulare for Heath ended in hung juries, as did a Fresno trial for Polley. Their connections to the scene of McWhirter's death were proved too tenuous. There were those who believed the men were innocent all along and that McWhirter had committed suicide. He had failed as a lawyer, was turning to drink, had spent his wife's dowry, and had a large life insurance policy whose premiums he could no longer meet. Theorists vigorously debated these contentions until Heath was exonerated by default and interest lapsed.

The remaining part of the 1890s saw a notable increase in the west side's homicide rate. In the fall of 1893 Ramon Molina shot and killed Juan Para at Cantua Creek, while they were supposed to be celebrating the latter's birthday. A drunken quarrel led to a scuffle in which Molina drew his revolver and fired into Para's left eye. Molina fled the scene, and it was four years before he was apprehended and brought to justice.

On May 24, 1896, Firebaugh saloonkeeper John W. Lambert killed his former partner, Alexander Betbeder, after Betbeder defaulted on loans Lambert had made to him. Civil charges had been filed against Betbeder for the debts, and charges were even filed at the Knights of Pythias lodge to which both men belonged. Betbeder threatened to "pump hot lead" into Lambert, and he tried to do just that at Lambert's saloon one day. A patron named Murphy attempted to restrain Betbeder while Lambert hastily found a revolver, and shot his assailant. In a subsequent trial he was found not guilty of murder.

A few months after the Lambert-Betbeder incident, on August 23, another murder was committed at Firebaugh. This was the mistaken killing of Andreas Martinez by Hermesindo Arana. The night before Martinez's demise, Arana had quarreled with one Robles in a Firebaugh saloon. They contested the ownership of a dollar staked in a card game. After a few hot words were exchanged Arana let Robles keep the dollar, and made plans for retribution.

The next day, Arana went back to the saloon and fired three revolver shots in the ceiling, hoping to attract Robles—whom he had spotted outside and a short distance away. Instead of Robles, Martinez entered the saloon and was felled by a single shot.

A mob formed quickly after the shooting, and Arana had to run to the Firebaugh Hotel for safety. The mob was almost ready to pounce on the murderer when Deputy Constable Napoleon Galon arrived and interceded. Blocking the cellar door that hid Arana, Galon pulled out two pistols and barked at the mob: "You may kill me, but I'll take along with me just as many of you as I can." Galon and Arana holed up overnight at the hotel until reinforcements from Fresno could come in.

To get the prisoner out of Firebaugh, the men had to brave the mob—which had never really dissipated—again. Before the departure one of the mob members was heard to snarl: "Damn the officers, they're only boys. We'll take Arana away from them." Fortunately, Firebaugh resident Antone G. Laverone calmed the crowd enough to let the lawmen and Arana depart amid mere hoots and jeers. Arana was convicted of negligent manslaughter at Fresno the following November 24.

While hunting near White's Bridge on June 22, 1898, Frank G. Darby and one Beebe got drunk on a jug of red wine they had packed along for the trip. Darby invaded the camp of rancher E. Sanchez, threatening to fight three men there and rape Sanchez's wife. While chasing Mrs. Sanchez, Darby encountered Louis Berdini on the bridge's west end. Berdini pleaded for mercy, but Darby shot him anyway.

A constable at Mendota had been alerted and arrived to find Berdini mortally wounded and Darby asleep under some bushes. Darby was tried twice for the murder, the first trial ending in a hung jury and the second in a not guilty verdict. He came from a wealthy Northern California farming family and secured two of Fresno's top lawyers, Frank Hamilton Short and Raleigh E. Rhodes, who successfully battered the witnesses' credibility and the prosecution's use of that testimony.

Nearer to Fresno, there were other notable homicides during this period. One—assumed to have happened, for the body was never found—was the presumed murder of William Wooton. He disappeared from his farm near Kingsburg around February 1, 1894. No one knew what to suspect until Professor W. A. Sanders (see chapters 8 and 9), who lived near Wooton, tried to use a negotiable grain receipt in Wooton's name and displayed a deed to Wooton's property. According to Sanders, Wooton had left the county and had given Sanders his property for appropriate disposal. Since no body was available, no murder charges could be filed against Sanders. Instead, he was tried for forgery and convicted after four trials where, respectively, there was a jury disagreement, a guilty verdict overturned on appeal, another jury disagreement and a conviction. Sanders came out of the penitentiary after fourteen years, broken financially and spiritually, and died in the Fresno County poorhouse.

Another mystery came to light on June 5, 1896, when Stephen Shahamirian, his daughter, Queen, and son, Benjamin, were found shot to death in their vineyard two miles south of Fresno. "The old man's body was distorted, and his dead eyes were gazing blankly into the heavens as if his last conscious glance had been one of supplication to his Maker," said the *Fresno Daily Evening Expositor*. "The young woman lay near by prone upon the clods, and sixty yards away the body of the son and brother lay with his dead face to the earth."

Just what happened was never resolved. A powder mark was found on the elder Shahamirian's finger; some said he had gone mad, shot his children, and turned the gun on himself. But no weapon was found. Another theory was that Benjamin, who was mentally retarded, had insulted a prostitute on Fresno's west side and the killings were some kind of reprisal.

The same year witnessed a near-repeat of the Vincent case. W. W. Rockwell, suspecting his wife of infidelity, argued with her about it on August 1 and ended up brandishing a revolver. As she ran out of the house and into the street, Rockwell emptied all six chambers into his wife, severely wounding her. Rockwell turned himself in, and his wife died after enduring weeks of pain and paralysis in the hospital. Saved by a hung jury on his first trial, Rockwell later entered a guilty plea and was sentenced to life imprisonment.

Crimes of this later period sometimes had an interior or intra-racial character. The April 6, 1889, *Fresno Daily Evening Expositor* noted that open warfare had broken out between resident Armenians and Danes in Fresno's Clay Addition. The previous month had seen the groups hold a battle in a vacant lot with "brooms, pieces of scantling, shotguns, etc.," and they were constantly filing charges against each other for death threats, disturbing the peace and petty larceny.

Japanese farm workers, recent county arrivals at the century's turn, were frequently victimized. On February 16, 1899, a bunkhouse on the Mattei vineyard near Malaga, containing eleven of them, was held up. The yield was relatively low ($200 and two watches). Since the robbers were masked and the Japanese so frightened, they were able to give only rudimentary descriptions of their tormentors. One was big and bearded, with a gash over his eye, and the other was smaller.

The same night another Japanese bunkhouse on the Briscoe ranch was raided and sixty dollars taken. Ten days later, two Japanese working for the Southern Pacific at a station called Condo (Conejo?) were robbed of two watches and thirty dollars. The Japanese were probably singled out as targets because of their unfamiliarity with their surroundings, possible fears of reprisal, and the notion—prevalent among both races at the time—that whites could intimidate them however they pleased.

Warfare between Chinese gangs broke out in Fresno during the late 1890s. The growth of Chinatown had brought "tongs" into Fresno—benevolent societies that sometimes fronted for criminal activity. The tongs, loosely organized under two companies called the Sam Yups and See Yups, were often commanded by professional cutthroats known as "highbinders." Of the latter term *Fresno Morning Republican* reporter Henry Brickley said: "Strictly speaking, [highbinder] may be applied to any rough character, but it is used more specifically to designate a member of a Chinese secret society, which is composed of professional blackmailers." When the tongs quarreled over territorial and other rights to gambling, extortion, opium distribution, prostitution and other activities, body counts began mounting.

The Fresno tong war began in late 1898 when Chuck Hock, a member of the Suey On tong, was killed by Tai Choy, a half-Chinese, half-black Bing Kung tong member. Exact reasons for the killing that led to the dispute were not disclosed. They were enough, however, for an unofficial declaration of war to be made.

On April 19, 1899, a gun battle broke out in the area between F and G streets. Watchman Hiram Lee "Hi" Rapelje and policeman James D. Morss raced to the scene, hearing the shots from a short distance away. Rapelje found one Chinese on the ground, with a gunman pumping bullets into his body, and another holding the prostrate man down. Rapelje hit Leong Tung with his pistol, then shot and killed Tung when he ran, refusing Rapelje's command to stop. Another gunman, Ah Yung, ran out of the alley and was pursued by Morss down Tulare Street. There Yung shot and killed another Chinese named Ah Tai. Morss then ordered Yung to stop, but, like Tung, he failed to do so and was shot. Leong Gee, the man down in the alley, also died; that brought this incident's casualty count up to four. Contemporary accounts do not indicate which side won this battle, or if it was a draw.

Much better known than gang violence is the story of gambling in Fresno, almost exclusively a Chinese business. Serious crackdowns on the sport began in 1885, after incorporation and consequent municipal ability to confront the problem. The passage of anti-gambling and anti-opium regulations were among the city trustees' first acts. There were problems, however, in making raids effective.

When patrons were arrested at Lam Lee's gaming

Reference 11:9

# THE CHINESE LOTTERIES

The man who on Monday stopped his friend on the street corner and told him of the "ten strike" made in Chinatown on Sunday, when one of the lottery concerns lost $2000 on a single drawing, has been talking pretty freely to everyone in the same style since.

He has been a sort of walking advertisement for the seven lottery games in Chinatown, and the amount of the increase in the sale of Chinese lottery tickets in the city has been surprising. Everyone likes to get a chance of winning $2000 for 50 cents, especially when the chance is offered four times a day instead of once a month.

In Fresno there are four drawings a day in the Chinese lottery dens. It is perhaps scarcely fair to style them all dens, for one is a substantial building, a regular exchange, constructed expressly for the purpose at a cost of not less than $2000. Like all the other places of its kind, it has either iron doors or heavy iron bars to the doors of the chamber in which the drawing of the lottery is conducted.

Pretty nearly every one has seen a Chinese lottery ticket, for hundreds, maybe thousands, are sold in Fresno every day with scarcely any pretense of secrecy. The agents of the lottery dealers visit the hotels and do their business with only an affectation of disguise, in the back rooms of stores, saloons, etc. White men in Fresno, of good moral standing, do not hesitate to do business with the "little brown man" who peddles lottery tickets and cashes the chips for the lucky few who win.

The drawing is a mystery which only a favored few are permitted to witness. The selling of the tickets is a very simple procedure, scarcely if at all interfered with, though it is distinctly illegal, but the drawing is a more serious matter, and is guarded with the more watchfulness because it has necessarily to be conducted in a fixed place with a number of persons in attendance.

The four daily drawings take place at 2 p.m., 4 p.m., 8 p.m. and 10 p.m. Admission can be had by white men who "know the ropes," but they must be vouched for by some one known to the proprietor. Not more than six or eight persons are usually present at a drawing, nearly all Chinese.

The beauty of the whole Chinese lottery system is its simplicity. A child can play Chinese lottery, notwithstanding the "abracadabra" look of the characters and squares on the tickets.

The tickets are all of the same size and contain eighty Chinese characters set in little squares. The purchaser of a ten-cent ticket picks out at random ten of the eighty characters which he marks with a black spot. The seller marks a duplicate ticket and keeps it. At the hour of drawing all the duplicate tickets are turned in and laid in a pile beneath a perforating press.

The drawing is effected in an apartment at the rear of the lottery den, usually with a side exit to an alley, guarded with an iron door. The moment the parties to the drawing are assembled, every door and window in the place is closed as tight as wax.

The paraphernalia are simple. A small table and four china bowls about six inches in diameter are all. There is no excitement, no word or sign to indicate what is going on. A Chinese takes eighty tiny squares of paper, each bearing a character corresponding to those on the ticket, folds them into little balls and thoroughly mixes them and drops them into four bowls, twenty into each bowl. The bowls have special characters, and separate drawings take place, similar to drawing straws. The contents of the bowl so drawn represent the numbers for that drawing. The whole transaction is completed inside of fifteen minutes. As these numbers or characters are taken out of the bowl, a Chinese perforates the square with the corresponding character clear through the pile. All that remains is for the purchaser of the ticket to compare his ticket with another bearing the perforations, which the agent brings around as soon as the drawing is over. If the purchaser has spotted five out of the winning characters he gets 20 cents on his investment of 10 cents; less than five "don't count." For six spots he gets $2, which the agent will probably pay him. For seven spots he gets $20; for eight spots $100. If he has risked 50 cents and has by some almost inconceivable streak of luck made all the ten spots he gets $2000. The highest risk allowed is $1, and the gains are proportionate all through.

On the face of it the Chinese lottery looks a square proposition, but when the iron doors are opened and the bars let down the lottery men have always the comforting assurance that the odds are nineteen out of twenty in their favor.

To begin with, as five characters don't count, even if he draws them, and there are eighty characters in all, the purchaser starts in with sixteen to one against him. Then he has only ten of the twenty numbers down. Finally the doctrine of chances comes in and the algebraical rule of permutations and combinations will enable any one to calculate that if the odds are 500 to one against a man picking seven spots, they will be 10,000 to one against his picking eight; 500,000 to one against his picking nine, and several millions to one against his picking all the ten. In the Louisiana lottery the chances against winning a capital prize are about 10,000 to one; in the cases of the smaller fry—they vary from 100 to one up to 10,000.

The attraction of the Chinese lottery is that the investment is small and the opportunity constant. It has been estimated that $5000 is taken out of Fresno every month in this way that never finds its way back into circulation in this country.

The illegality of the lottery is established by sections 320, 321, 322, 323 and 326 of the Penal Code of the state. The offense is a misdemeanor with a penalty of six months imprisonment or a fine of $500 or both. There is no county or city ordinance covering the offense, the Penal Code being deemed sufficient. The enforcement of the law is presumed to be vested in the county officers, but seven of these lottery dens are openly run in Chinatown without any interference by the sheriff and under the protection of one of his deputies.

SOURCE: Fresno County Scrapbook 1870-1899, p. 525, taken from *Fresno Daily Evening Expositor*, September 14, 1894, p. 4, c. 4.

house in July 1885, they secured able legal counsel and beat their charges for lack of evidence. Raids in the fall of 1890 brought seventy-five fan tan players into Justice Samuel L. Hogue's court. They pleaded guilty, were fined ten dollars each, and no doubt returned to their previous business afterward.

Some years later, in 1898, the price of freedom went even lower. When police picked up thirty-six fan tan players on December 8, they were brought into court, allowed to plead guilty, and fined $3.50 apiece—for no one had actually seen them gamble. This sum had to be increased when it was discovered that, by statute, gambling fines could not be less than $100. Policeman Henry Russell, the raid leader, was disgusted to see his work so easily undone. Judge Clark, who had imposed the too-reasonable fines, countered by saying that a full-scale trial would cost taxpayers money and most likely end with a series of dismissals for lack of evidence.

There were other difficulties in breaking up the games. A contingent of policemen tried to raid a gambling den on March 4, 1899, by knocking down the guard posted outside its door and barging in. They were surprised, however, to find that there was an inner, well-locked door to the den. The next day's *Fresno Morning Republican* noted, "After trying vainly to kick it in they gave up the task and took the doorkeeper and another Chinaman to jail, where charges of vagrancy were lodged against them."

The following October 8, the *Republican* told of another failed raid that had taken place the night before. Gambling activity was suspected at the rear of the Tong Duck Company building, protected by two large steel-sheathed doors bolted from the inside. Constables John Dumas, W. H. Puleston and several private citizens tried working on the door with crowbars and a battering ram; "their efforts [were] answered by a volley of bullets, bricks, bottles and stones from the building opposite," said the *Republican*. "For a time it looked as if someone would be killed, but

Reference 11:10

## THE GAMBLING SCENE IN FRESNO, 1897

It has always been the theory that the Southern Pacific railroad track divided Fresno the good, and Fresno the bad; and that those who resided on "this side" of, and not "across" the track, are the good. Last night, however, the bad had evidently moved, and held sway on "this side." The Grand Central hotel, perhaps the first hotel in town, was their headquarters, while the several saloons in that neighborhood were sort of little off-shoots of this principal stamping ground of the crowd. For cappers and gamblers had possession of the town, and all night long the countryman's honest dollars and the grape-picker's hard-earned quarters flowed in a steady stream into the pockets of the sure-thing, be-diamonded gamblers who have come down upon this community like a swarm of locusts.

As has been stated their principal place of business last evening was the Grand Central hotel. The barroom had been cleared for the occasion, and it was packed with gamblers, cappers and suckers. No less than five games were running there with an openness of the "'49" gambling tent. Chucka-luck, craps, "Klondike" stud and straight poker and dice games filled the room...

About mid-night, for the Grand Central games ran from early yesterday evening, until the last sucker had been cleaned out this morning, an interesting and characteristic little scene was enacted at the chuck-a-luck table in the Grand Central. A "winner" was playing a given number. Dollars fairly rolled in upon him. He had a stack of them before him, which grew continually. He bet one, two, even five dollars at every turn of the wheel. He lost occasionally, but his pile continued to increase, and was watched hungrily by the crowd of suckers who were by this time drunk with the desire to gamble,

although many of them had been cleaned out earlier in the evening.

At the other end of the table from this successful gamee, was a thin, pale-faced little man who played the game as persistently, but he did not win. He had no stack of dollars in front of him—he played quarters. At every turn of the wheel his hungry eyes hunted the dice before the man at the wheel could pay the "winnings" or scoop in the hard-earned quarters. When this second player won, as he did occasionally, his lean, hard hand clutched the winnings. But at every loss the lines about his mouth became drawn and set. And the man at the other end of the table, who played dollars, kept on winning and winning. The man playing with quarters did not appear to be able to realize that those dollars were almost certainly owned by the man who was running the game....

The game "Klondike" as conducted in the Grand Central last evening, attracted a crowd.... The players bet on numbers up to six, dice are thrown, and bets are paid—when they are won—by the proprietors of the game. "Klondike" is nothing more nor less than a stupid old dice game. Players have no more chance of winning at it than they have to find twenty dollar pieces in the streets....

The "stud" poker game was one of the features of the Grand Central's gambling tournament last evening. This game is aristocratic and elevating when compared with the dice games that were running in their several variations. About this table were gathered a different set of men. It takes some skill to play the game. However, a vacant chair was noticeable at the table as a sort of standing invitation to the country youth, who might be in town to see the races, to

drop into.

The other games conducted by the Grand Central people last evening were cheaper variations of the eternal dice game.

The worst feature of it all at the Grand Central last evening was the large number of youths who were present. Many of them looked to be under 18 years of age. There was nothing to keep them away, and everything to attract them....

Over across the street from the Grand Central, at Harry Doble's Turf saloon, the same class of games as thrive in the rooms of the Grand Central, were having full swing, and, if anything, were conducted even more openly....

The White Fawn saloon was another establishment where gambling held full sway last evening. Here, openly, the "king of games," faro, was being played.... Quite a little knot of players were about the game, and the chips were stacked high in anticipation of the turn of the cards. It was a pretty good outfit. The proprietors of the game had nothing cheap nor simple about it. The dealer's box looked heavy and substantial, though no one was allowed to examine it closely, and the faces of the cards on the table, while a little worn, showed evidence of once having been "the thing."

Craps, chuck-a-luck and other dice games were running at the Fawn all night....

Marshal Woy was seen in regard to the matter of the gambling in town last evening, but declined to be interviewed.

SOURCE: *Fresno Daily Evening Expositor*, October 5, 1897.

thanks to poor marksmanship, the bullets flew wide of the mark and the bricks did nothing more than to skin a few shins." After a half-hour's work that had bashed only a small hole in the doors, Dumas had the sense to try to enter from the front. He succeeded, and found no gambling evidence anywhere. "The players, if there were any, had made good their escape."

In early 1895 City Marshal Martin Luther Woy led a series of Chinatown gambling raids, only to find them livelier than ever by August. The word was that a man, claiming to represent city officials, had told the Chinese their games could be safely reopened if his palm was greased—up to $400 per month per establishment. The games started again in earnest, and it was apparent that someone was being paid off. "Gambling tables are displayed before open doors, and prohibited games are run while the police pace up and down without molesting anybody," said the October 25, 1895, *Fresno Daily Evening Expositor*. "Stud poker is the game mostly played, but the Chinese lotteries and [fan] tan games also flourish in their accustomed haunts." Woy, in a display of naivete or insincerity, said, "I'll break [this] business up, or know the reason why."

Yet there was no unified drive against the gambling dens, along with disturbing signs that the police could not care less about them. Two *Expositor* reporters were miffed when they encountered a Chinatown policeman on February 13, 1897, and he asked them, "Well, when are you going to buy [lottery] tickets today?" The men said they would "keep a little money in circulation" and the policeman responded, "Yes, you're . . . enterprising men."

More disturbing was the allegation policeman J. E. Ragsdale made on August 21, 1896. He claimed that, several years earlier, the Chinese had tried to buy assurance from him that he would not disturb their games. They also wanted him to go into partnership with another officer already granting "protection"—Hi Rapelje. When Ragsdale complained about this and said Rapelje was in no position to defend the gamesters, one of them (Quong Chung) told him: "Hi Rapelje got the power. You no got the power. Hi Rapelje already fixed the district attorney, Sheriff [Jay] Scott and City Marshal Woy, and we have no trouble at all . . . I think you are very foolish not to accept Hi Rapelje as you partner."

Whatever the impediments, or lack thereof, gambling continued (see 11:9 and 10). There was outrage in 1897 when "spindle," or roulette, games were played on the streets and even had been licensed by Marshal Woy. More complaints were heard in 1899 when, according to the *Fresno Morning Republican*, "the grand jury found that boys, ranging in years from 14 and 15 to 18 and 19, had been making a practice of playing cards for money in Ball's cigar store and also in the cigar stand formerly kept by Al Harlan on J street." The article claimed that Woy "intends to keep a sharp look out to prevent persons under age from acquiring lessons in gambling," but, once again, there is no evidence suggesting his crusade was anything more than half-hearted and haphazard.

As Fresno made the transition from frontier village to commercial boomtown, the world's oldest profession began to gain a foothold (see 11:11). No one knows when the first prostitute or brothel began transacting business, and it is hard to obtain details. It is certain that, as with gambling, political and police payoffs kept the profession lively. Raids conducted against prostitution were even less frequent than those against gaming.

One of the earlier raids was made on September 24, 1891. Sweeping down on the area near the Tulare and F streets intersection, a group of police and sheriff's deputies "began operations on Fresno street," said the *Fresno Daily Evening Expositor*. "The houses of ill fame were surrounded and part of the contingent went inside and commanded the [pimps] to hurry up and dress and go outside, and on doing so they were corralled by the waiting officers . . . [The prostitutes] implored the officers to release them and promised

Reference 11:11

## VAGRANCY AND VICIOUS CONDUCT: THE FATE OF VIOLA DUNLAP

Viola Dunlap was committed to Whittier till she is 18 years of age this morning. That means for two years. A big sign reading: "Positively No Admittance. This case is being tried with closed doors," hung on the door of Judge Webb's courtroom this morning. It was evidence that the Judge was considering the case of the wayward girl.

Viola came home last night about 5 o'clock. Her mother sent for a policeman and the girl was taken to jail. She spent the night there and this morning was taken before Judge Webb.

She showed no signs of softening or repentance and told of her various escapades unblushingly.

The mother told of her trials and of her many endeavors to keep her daughter in the straight and narrow path. She blamed Rose Spinney for her daughter's downfall, saying that the former always had money and enticed her girl away in the hopes of having a good time. Her girl, she said, was only 16 years of age.

The girl's full name is Annie Viola Dunlap. It was so evident that she was not ashamed of her immoral and indecent behavior that the Judge did not hesitate in making out the commitment to Whittier. She goes south on the 5:20 train.

The commitment is something of a curiosity. It charges Annie Viola Dunlap, who is not quite 16 years of age, with the crime of vagrancy and vicious conduct. Her father, John Dunlap, is dead. A few of the answers given to the questions asked were:

"Have you attended school?"
"Very little."
"How long have you attended school?"
"One year."
"Do you smoke cigarettes?"
"No."
"In what have you been employed?"
"Bumming."
"Are you profane?"
"Yes, when indignant."
"Are you intemperate?"
"Only a very little."

SOURCE: *Fresno Daily Evening Expositor*, May 24, 1894.

anything and everything for a month's release. Every house in the quarter was taken in, and the occupants were hustled out and thrown into the corral."

In subsequent years the harassment was even less. When Marshal Woy was told of "Bacchanalian orgies" being held over the Gem Saloon in April 1895, he did not arrest the offending women. He merely told them to leave for the other side of the tracks, a request they were happy to honor. Such compliance did not continue, however. By 1897 there were more complaints that the "soiled doves" were soliciting on Fresno's respectable side. "A stranger, who has been accosted once or twice within a block by street walkers, is likely to make the mistake that every woman unattended is of the same ilk, and in this way a number of ladies have had very unpleasant encounters on the streets of late," said the April 27 *Fresno Daily Evening Expositor*.

Soon afterward the police told the women to relocate, and again in a manner not firm enough. The November 20 *Expositor* complained that "City Marshal Woy weakened too soon in his raiding of lodging houses on this side of the track inhabited by notorious women . . . Nearly every lodging house on the main streets are [*sic*] filled with these women."

Indeed, the only other significant raid of the decade was conducted on August 15, 1899, the *Fresno Morning Republican* admitting it "was the first of its kind" in years. Again the Tulare and F streets neighborhood was visited, with pimps, prostitutes and patrons swept up by three squads of police. While police were invading the Tulare Street cribs (small cubicles where prostitutes lived), "only one man was found," the *Republican* said, "—a young fellow named Arthur Bowen. He was more scared than grieved when the officers burst into the room, and heaved a sigh of relief when he saw who the invaders were. The fellow was as white as a sheet and thought he was about to be murdered. He was taken in tow."

During this period Fresno's criminal element preyed on prostitutes more than did the lawmen. There was talk of a "Fresno Ripper" at work in March 1891, when prostitutes Mattie Knox and Julia Derby were viciously attacked in the night. Knox was found dead in her cottage at Mariposa and E streets. Blood and brains were spread over the walls and there were deep gashes in her head. Despite an inquest among her acquaintances, no suspect emerged. Two days later Derby was attacked in her Tulare Street home, being knocked senseless first and later awakening to discover a four-inch gash in her head. Whoever was responsible for these crimes was never caught.

Another consistent problem in Fresno was arson. Though it was suspected as the cause of some of the city's more destructive fires (see chapters 7 and 14), little was done about it until August 15, 1889. Disgusted by a rash of blazes that had broken out since the previous June 9, a vigilante group of 200 invaded Fresno's west side and rounded up all the criminals, undesirables and shady operators in sight. The vigilantes and their captives then marched to the National Guard Armory. Lilbourne A. Winchell gives a harrowing version of what happened there:

Manacled and blanch-faced suspects were questioned; some cringingly told what they knew, and some truculently defied their questioners—arrogantly assuming innocence of complicity with the suspected criminals. Three of the defiant ringleaders were hoisted at intervals with ropes around their necks, to the heavy beams overhead. Let down when gasping, questions were renewed. One victim was drawn up three times before yielding. A final threat of death broke his nerve and he talked. After the desired confessions were secured, the ring leaders were triced up, their backs bared and lashed with black snakes. Others of the gang were also whipped, with a promise of worse if found in the city the next day.

The terror-stricken captives were then escorted across the track, with orders to leave Fresno before sundown of the following day, or be shot on sight.

. . . A reconnaissance of the west side saloons, opium dens and bawdy houses, the next night, revealed the absence of all the suspects. From that day the city suffered no midnight alarms of fire, during that season.

The ad hoc vigilante committee did not prove to be a panacea. On December 1, 1890, J. E. Williams was arrested for allegedly torching an undertaker's business on I Street the previous July 23. It was claimed that Williams had bought the establishment through a front man, James Chenowith, and sought to cash in on insurance by having C. Schillman and Fred Miller "fire" the place. When the case came up for trial Miller had fled the county and Schillman's testimony was doubted. Williams later became the recipient of a hung jury verdict.

Two groups were suspected of arson activities in 1893. An August 9 story in the *Fresno Daily Evening Expositor* claimed that some Fresno businesses had received letters, postmarked in San Francisco, from "anarchists" who promised to keep burning down buildings until certain offending whites stopped hiring Chinese labor. There was one problem: Unless the anarchists were truly demented, none of the businesses that had recently burned down employed Chinese.

A more reasonable accusation came to light the following October, when it was claimed that members of the "F.A.F." society had torched two houses on the fifth. The abbreviation stood for "Fresno and Fake"— a phrase whose meaning is now lost—and it was "composed of boys of respectable parentage who reside in the city, but are absolutely uncontrollable." A rundown of the group's membership list verified the former statement: Willie Grady, George Combs, Milton Hutchinson, Art Bradley, Porter Solomon, Frank Faymonville, Ed Hart and Johnnie Dunlap. Within a short time Solomon and Hutchinson were arrested for burglary, Dunlap confessed to a number of petty crimes, Grady was apprehended for assault, and the arson activities around town subsided.

Three years later, two boys no older than ten were caught trying to burn down some sheds on N Street. The *Fresno Daily Evening Expositor* of September 7, 1896, said the boys had tried to torch the Buckeye Grocery on Fresno Street twice and were suspected of setting other fires. Authorities did not prosecute the boys, instead warning "their parents to keep them under strict surveillance."

On June 20, 1897, Walter Furnish was caught trying to burn down the Pleasanton Hotel annex in the early morning hours. George Landrum, a worker at the Madary Planing Mill, had secretly seen Furnish light grass near the annex three times. The first two times the fire went out. The third attempt was successful, producing a large blaze. As Furnish ran away from the scene he collided with Landrum, was seized and turned over to the authorities.

Turn-of-the-century crimes in Fresno were not always commonplace. Clever fraud and bunco schemes were perpetrated on a wholesale basis. The April 6, 1894, *Fresno Daily Evening Expositor* told of a rancher, O. W. Jemison, who came to town with twenty-two dollars in his pocket. He was expecting to catch a train to San Francisco and see the Midwinter Fair there. A friend, Fred Rusher, told him where to obtain a cheap ticket and Jemison was interested. The two men then went to a saloon, where Rusher suggested Jemison join in a card game while he found the man with the bargain ticket. Time passed. Jemison, who had joined the game, found himself with four kings and was urged to bet all his money by a game partner. When the hands were laid down, someone else had four aces. Jemison walked out of the saloon downcast, then realized he had been taken. He swore out a court complaint but police could not find the cardsharps.

The strange case of Lizzie Lowell surfaced on September 7, 1896. The previous Saturday she had gained entrance to Mrs. M. T. Hertwick's home by asking for a glass of water. While inside she pretended to faint, at which time she cast a hypnotic spell on Mrs. Hertwick. "I have lost much money," Lowell told the woman. "You have money in your house, and with it you can and shall help me to regain mine." Hertwick then went from room to room, gathering money and valuables that were placed inside a pillow Lowell ripped open. She told Hertwick that as long as the pillow stayed closed for several weeks, her good fortune would return. She had the unsuspecting woman get a needle and thread for that purpose. When Hertwick came out of the trance and realized what had happened, she checked the pillow and found nothing. A switch had been made while she was looking for the needle and thread. Lowell was brought to trial because

of this affair and acquitted. The reason? There was no evidence suggesting that the valuables had been taken without the owner's consent!

James McHoguen, a bogus representative of the Fidelity Life Insurance Company of San Francisco, defrauded many Fresnans in 1899. By promising a $1,000 death benefit policy to his customers, after showing them legitimate-looking circulars, he persuaded many people to make an initial $1.50 to $15.00 "good faith" investment. The small sums he requested kept people from getting concerned when they had no further contact with McHoguen or the company. "Most of his work was confined to the outskirts among the poorer classes who he thought would be least likely to detect him," said the September 13 *Fresno Morning Republican*. One of his victims, a black man named Sam Shaver, eventually tried to contact the phony insurance company. When McHoguen learned this he knew the game was over and skipped town. His take was estimated in the $400 to $500 range.

McHoguen may not have been caught, but many other criminals were swept up by the long arm of the law in Fresno. Many went to jail, an institution first set up in the Courthouse in cramped, unsecured quarters. Breaks and break attempts were common. The first took place on November 14, 1875. While a deputy sheriff sought help for a wounded Mexican, four prisoners left in an exercise yard pried open a door and got away. Another escape was nearly made in November 1886. Inmates John Kelly and John Collins had filed off the bolt ends that held a lock assembly and replaced the heads with realistic soap substitutes somehow colored. Until this gambit was detected, the men could have pushed the assembly apart and fled their cell.

The situation got so bad that Sheriff Ezekiel Hall was told, "Sheriff, if you don't take care one of these days some prisoner will fall through the walls of that jail of yours and hurt himself." Before long the board of supervisors contracted for a new brick jail diagonally adjacent to the Courthouse, completed in 1888 at a cost of $24,782. This structure had dual advantages for prisoners. The accommodations were good (see 11:12) and it remained something less than escape-proof.

When convicted murderer Ah Gee Yung was incarcerated in the jail, awaiting appeal results that looked unpromising, he twice found ways to spring the doors and bolts holding him. The jail locks and bars were made of cheap iron that could be tampered with easily. Yung was caught both times, but decided to make a more sophisticated break in late 1890. Chinese friends furnished him with a potion that made his vital signs indistinguishable, along with cosmetics that allowed him to duplicate a dead man's outward appearance. One day, Yung was found in a very deep sleep by a jailer, with opium on his breath. Dr. Lewis Leach and

248

others tried to "revive" him for four hours, with no luck. Some Chinese claimed his body and came to the jail with two coffins in a wagon. One, empty, was taken to the Chinese cemetery and buried—to throw off the authorities. Yung was placed in the other and spirited to China, beyond the law's reach!

The jail did have its disadvantages. Prisoners' rations were cut from thirty-five to thirty cents a day in 1893, when the supervisors thought inmates were being fed too well. "Give them bread and beans for breakfast and potatoes and bread for dinner and a cup of coffee, and about twice a week give them meat," said Supervisor J. H. Sayre. Another problem was the "Kangaroo Court," which developed statewide notoriety. Vagrants who had a more or less permanent residence at the jail extorted money from new arrivals. When it was not paid they "beat a man about the body, using their fists and pieces of rubber hose," said the February 10, 1894, *Fresno Daily Evening Expositor*. "If the new prisoner remains obdurate he is likely to receive very severe punishment." Periodic laxity of the jailers was said to be the "Kangaroo Court's" cause.

To complete these annals of nineteenth-century crime in Fresno County, it is necessary to make an about-face here and look at a few sworn to uphold the law . . . who failed to do so. Corruption, viciousness and a lack of ethicality were sometimes found among the county's officials, lawyers, lawmen and even a few upstanding citizens.

Defalcations—misappropriations of county funds—were a recurrent problem. The first of note happened in August 1866 and began innocuously. County Treasurer Stephen A. Gaster informed his friends that he was leaving for San Francisco on the twelfth and expected to be gone for a week. Not long after his departure Charles Porter Converse, then building the Millerton Courthouse, became panicky. He said some money of his, entrusted to Gaster and in the county safe, was needed to pay his workers and only Gaster had a key. Converse hurried to San Francisco and made an unsuccessful search for the county treasurer. Soon officials became suspicious and had an arrest warrant put out for Gaster.

After two weeks went by with no sign of Gaster, Judge E. C. Winchell ordered the safe cut open on August 28. A big crowd gathered in William Faymonville's yard to watch the operation. When it was over, only a bag of gold dust belonging to stockraiser

Reference 11:12

## THE OTHER SIDE: WHAT A REPORTER SAW AT THE COUNTY JAIL

On Thursday evening the Expositor published a complaint from a prisoner incarcerated in the county jail. The prisoner stated that the inmates of the jail were starving; that they were lousy, and further, that they had no means of washing their clothes and no change of clothing. Yesterday afternoon a reporter of the Expositor was delegated to thoroughly inspect the management of the county jail and ascertain if possible the truth or falsity of these reports. He did so.

The first gentleman met was J. C. Collier, under sheriff. "Mr. Barker, the jailer," said he, "is out of town. He is at Madera and won't be home until late this evening. I know nothing about the management of the jail. I haven't been into it but two or three times since I was appointed to office. I believe the prisoners who do not work are fed twice a day, while those who labor get three meals. Concerning the squareness of those meals, I cannot say. The jail is open for inspection."

"How many hours do the prisoners work?"

"Eight hours, I believe. Those who are sick call for their drugs quite regularly. Dr. Leach is attending two or three of them now. Those in health take their rations very methodically."

"How many prisoners have you?"

"Well, the number varies from 40 to 60."

"How many do you put in a cell?"

"That, I couldn't tell."

"What about vermin?"

"Judging from the looks of some of the prisoners that come in here, there may be vermin in the recesses of their clothing."

Just as Mr. Collier concluded speaking, H. Smart, the courthouse jailer, entered the office. "Here's Mr. Smart. He may be able to give you some points about the jail management."

"Step this way," said Mr. Smart and the grate door was opened and the reporter entered the jail.

"Look here," said our representative, "I wish you would leave me, as I want to talk with the prisoners confidentially."

Mr. Smart did so. The first prisoner approached was J. C. Campbell, an emaciated-looking being, with small staring eyes and a close cropped mustache.

"I get all I want to eat," said Campbell, "and the man who would complain about grub here is a hog."

"How many meals do you get a day?"

"Two. Those who work get three."

"What do you get?"

"In the morning I get a good sized beef steak, a big hunk of bread, potatoes and coffee. We have breakfast from 7:30 to 8 o'clock."

"What do you get for supper or dinner?"

"A tin pan full of stew, bread and potatoes. Have enough to eat? I should say I did."

"What about bedding?"

"Before Hensley came in we were a little short of blankets. This was due to the large number of prisoners. Now every two prisoners gets from two to three pair of blankets and a mattress."

"Are you lousy?"

Campbell's face flushed up. He was surprised, no doubt, that such a question should be asked him.

"No, sir," he said emphatically. "Mr. Hensley gives me shirts as he does all the other prisoners, and I wash my dirty clothing."

Three other prisoners were interrogated, and Campbell's statements were fully corroborated by their testimony.

The reporter further inspected the jail. On the ground floor he found an immense stove, which furnished a volume of heat. On the second tier of cells was a big drum, which kept all the cells on the tier warm. He visited the kitchen and found it clean and neat. A Chinaman was cooking supper. Here he ascertained that the noonday meal for the prisoners that work consisted of stew, potatoes, beans and bread. The stew is served in one and a half pint pans. The amount of bread given at each meal is eight ounces, as the reporter took a piece from a large pile and had it weighed.

The statement made that the prisoners don't have an opportunity to wash their clothes is false in every particular, as the sheriff furnishes an abundance of soap and other appliances for the proper performance of the work.

From an inspection of many county jails in various parts of the State, the writer is convinced that the prisoners in the Fresno county jail are fed better, treated more humanely and have more liberty than any inmates of a like institution in California. . . .

SOURCE: *Fresno Daily Evening Expositor*, January 26, 1889, p. 1, c. 4.

Andrew M. Darwin (and entrusted to Gaster previously) was found. Some $6,603.06 in county funds was missing. Paul A. Vandor reported that "the Gaster estate later offered to compromise the shortage for $2,000, but it was declined and little was recovered by suit."

Many county residents believed Gaster had been victimized by Converse—somehow being forced to open the safe, after which he fled or was murdered. Converse's reputation had been damaged by a ballot-box stuffing incident in 1862 and was not improved later when he killed a man in the great Millerton shoot-'em-up of 1867 (see above). The following winter his ferry was destroyed in the big flood and he never adequately replaced it. Further damage was done when, after he and wife were divorced, he married Gaster's widow. Obviously, such suspicions were reasonable and he was hounded over this subject constantly. Years later he produced a letter from an American residing at Leon, Nicaragua, who said Gaster was operating a sawmill there. "He is generally esteemed for his honesty, industry and other good qualities . . . and leads a very laborious life," said the letter. But if it was true, why did Converse go into seclusion after the Gaster affair, become a drunk and vagrant in later years and drown himself in San Francisco Bay?

Eight years later, tragedy struck the county treasurer's office again. W. W. Hill, who had held the post since 1868, died on February 3, 1874. When the county safe, thought to hold $80,000 or more, was opened afterward, exactly $27,497.25 was there. It was learned that Hill had been making loans from the county till to friends and acquaintances, accounting for most of the deficit. A bond increase was effected to keep the county solvent, and actions were filed against the borrowers Hill had forced upon it. As with the Gaster incident, the total recovery was inadequate, covering somewhat more than half the deficit.

The county's last outstanding defalcation occurred in 1899. As before, the guilty party escaped justice. Fresno's city trustees found out that City Clerk John W. Shanklin had been accepting money for retail business, saloon, dog and other municipal licenses and was pocketing the fees. Though his account books were a mess, it was ascertained that Shanklin had taken $3,385 in this fashion and probably more than that. On April 2 he told City Marshal Woy—no angel himself—that he would refund the money at noon the following day. Instead he pulled a Stephen Gaster, leaving Fresno late on the second. He was subsequently spotted, or was said to have fled to, a number of places—the county's West Side, Ventura and Mexico among them.

"The story of the fall of Shanklin is similar to that of many men," said the April 4, 1899, *Fresno Morning Republican*. "He gambled considerably, but he also found other ways of spending the coin . . . [and] has been spending money with a lavish hand upon certain women. He did not drink to any great extent, but he had a weakness for playing the nickle [*sic*]-in-the-slot machine, although it is not likely he lost very heavily in this regard."

In time Shanklin was tracked to Oregon, where he was employed as a potato merchant. Extradited to Fresno for trial, he was let off on a legal loophole. The license money he had been collecting was actually due to the city license collector. Shanklin had been accepting the funds as a courtesy. Since the payers uniformly testified that they accepted Shanklin as the official fee receiver, it was said he had gained "legal" custody of the money, and he was under no "legal" obligation to turn it over to the license collector. In short, he was free to use the money as he wished. After acquittal on these grounds, he understandably left Fresno for good.

Members of the Fresno County legal profession often involved themselves in unethical, if not expressly

Reference 11:13

## THE GRADY-TERRY DUEL
### ERNESTINE WINCHELL

. . . While Fresno streets were straggling dustily and erratically about, and plank sidewalks rattled along the fronts of the business blocks so far as there were buildings, Walter D. Grady came to town, rented an office and entered the practice of law. Clever, fearless, and arrogant, he troubled himself but little with that elusive thing called ethics. Aghast, the conservative members of the local bar beheld witnesses confused by methods unheard-of, opponents abused, and even the judge on the bench defied.

Equally striking in a different way was Reel B. Terry, nephew of David S. Terry of pioneer note. Handsome, polished, a favorite in society, young Terry was also admired for his ability as a lawyer, even though

friends and enemies alike recognized the instability of his undisciplined character. He arrived in Fresno with the decade of the eighties, and immediately made felt the charm and power of his daring and magnetic personality.

Though Fresno Democrats were half delirious with delight over the nomination of Grover Cleveland for the presidential election of 1884, the local party had its differences, and there was burning contention as to whom should be given the honor of presiding at the meeting for formal ratification. W. D. Grady was prominently in favor of one candidate, and Reel Terry hotly supported a representative of the opposing faction.

On the appointed evening the Grady opera

house rapidly filled with Fresno county voters of both political parties. It was a primitive sort of structure, though adequate for its time; facing J street, it stood on ground adjoining the Fidelity Trust and Savings bank building of today. The lobby was one with the main auditorium, no partition nor draperies dividing that level space from the ranks of wooden seats descending to the orchestra pit. Members of the local band were in place and a few local dignitaries graced the stage together with the inevitable white crockery water pitcher and drinking glass.

Groups of excited men standing near the entrance exchanging warm opinions made of the lobby for the time being a substitute stage, with Grady, vitriolic, occupying the

illegal, activities. The most significant incident of this type was the Grady-Terry duel (see 11:13), whose participants were hard-pressed to stay out of trouble in subsequent years.

In 1893, Reel B. Terry was serving as defense counsel during Richard Heath's trial for the murder of McWhirter (see above). While drinking with reporter R. M. Mappes at the Bodega Saloon one day, Terry called the prosecution attorneys "dirty dogs." Mappes commented that McWhirter, while alive, had made a similar comment about Terry. "Do you endorse it?" asked Terry. "Every man is entitled to his own opinion," replied Mappes. "But do you endorse it?" "I am not compelled to say whether I do or not, but you can't scare me, and need not try it." A *Fresno Daily Evening Expositor* report described the scene that followed:

> The words were no more than spoken when Mappes let go a left hander on Terry's neck, and Terry went to the floor, while Mappes' spectacles struck the ceiling and dropped to the floor.
>
> The difference in the size of the two men was so great that it scarcely seemed possible that Terry should be defeated. He is fully 50 pounds heavier than Mappes, and Mappes is a cripple, having no use of his right hand.
>
> Terry regained his feet and the two men went together, and Terry went down with Mappes on top. They tumbled and floundered about the floor and worked their way near a pair of scales, and it looked as if they meant to use the iron weights upon each other, when the bystanders pulled them apart.
>
> But when they gained their feet, they went at each other again, and again Terry bumped the floor, with Mappes on top, and they tumbled through the doorway on to the sidewalk, where Mappes again knocked Terry down, and that ended the fight . . .

(Reel's uncle, David S. Terry, was a gadabout who led an incredibly varied life—as duelist, Confederate colonel, chief justice of the California State Supreme Court, attorney in a notable divorce case, and spur-of-the-moment pugilist. He practiced law in Fresno during 1888 and 1889, after—some think—being ostracized from Stockton for his boisterous conduct. David Terry's Fresno career was cut short when he got into an argument with Supreme Court justice Stephen J. Field at Lathrop, in San Joaquin County. A fight broke out and Field's bodyguard, David Neagle, shot and killed Terry. For more details on Terry's life, A. Russell Buchanan's *David S. Terry of California, Dueling Judge*, published by the Huntington Library in 1956, is an excellent source.)

Ordinarily respectable citizens disgraced themselves in diverse ways. In May of 1894 City Trustee Joseph Spinney's wayward daughter, Rose, disappeard after having been seen in the presence of two young men. Spinney decided to start searching possible hideaways of his daughter's, barging into private homes while waving what (he claimed) was a warrant. When asked about it later, Spinney admitted the "warrant" was a blank piece of paper. "Nobody didn't ask to look at it," he said. "I didn't break down no doors. I just went in."

Even the usually jovial Fulton G. Berry let his temper go out of control once. On September 2, 1898, a story appeared in the *San Francisco Examiner* stating that Berry's son (actually his nephew, Charles) had lost $1,000 in a poker game. Berry was livid at this incorrect reference and sought out John Danby, the *Examiner*'s local correspondent. He found the reporter in the Grand Central Hotel lobby. "Well, you played hell," bellowed Berry, and before he could protest that the mistake was not his, Danby was being punched in the face, with blood gushing from his nose and ears. Danby wasted no time in making a complaint, and Berry was eventually fined fifteen dollars for assault and battery.

center of attention. Terry came quietly in, stood a few minutes, and then went out, speaking to no one, but his progress noted as always, for he was a tall man carrying himself with a distinctive swagger in his stride.

Very soon Terry returned, swung directly up to Grady, addressed to him an insulting term and struck his face with a stinging palm, at the same instant reaching for his pistol. Fate had an open eye, however, for the fabric of the pistol pocket caught on the weapon and held it fast. From the first gesture Grady had drawn his own revolver and begun to shoot in his assailant's vicinity. Terry, meanwhile struggling with his entangled firearm, skipped and dodged this way and that to avoid the retributive bullets.

Stuart S. Wright, to whom Grady had been talking, seized his right arm to deflect his aim, but Grady exchanged to his left hand with the quickness of light and continued the fusillade. Others joined Wright and presently the shooting attorney was overpowered, but not before a bullet had found a mark in Terry's arm.

The wounded man was taken promptly to a surgeon, while the man with the smoking gun was hurried to the sheriff's office by his friends for his own protection. Unprovoked though the assault had seemed, much had gone before.

As tragedy turned the lobby into a stage, drama and comedy filled the rest of the room. The dignitaries vanished like magic. Through the orchestra doorways dived the band, wrecking expensive instruments in the frantic stampede. In the seats a few persons, turning at the first report, saw that the animated target drew the fire in a safe direction and stood to enjoy the spectacle, though tingling with apprehension as to the outcome.

Every window, open to the evening air, was darkened by forms of scrambling men. Too far away, too heavy for speed, or tripped by unknown impediments, others laid flat on the floor, craving immunity from bullets designed to stop the spirited footwork of an agile young Democrat.

In a few days Grady, freed from the sheriff, and Terry, released by the doctor, were walking Fresno streets once more, and though every chance meeting of the two caused near-by spines to chill, on no other occasion did they resort to firearms to express their mutual disregard.

SOURCE: Ernestine Winchell columns.

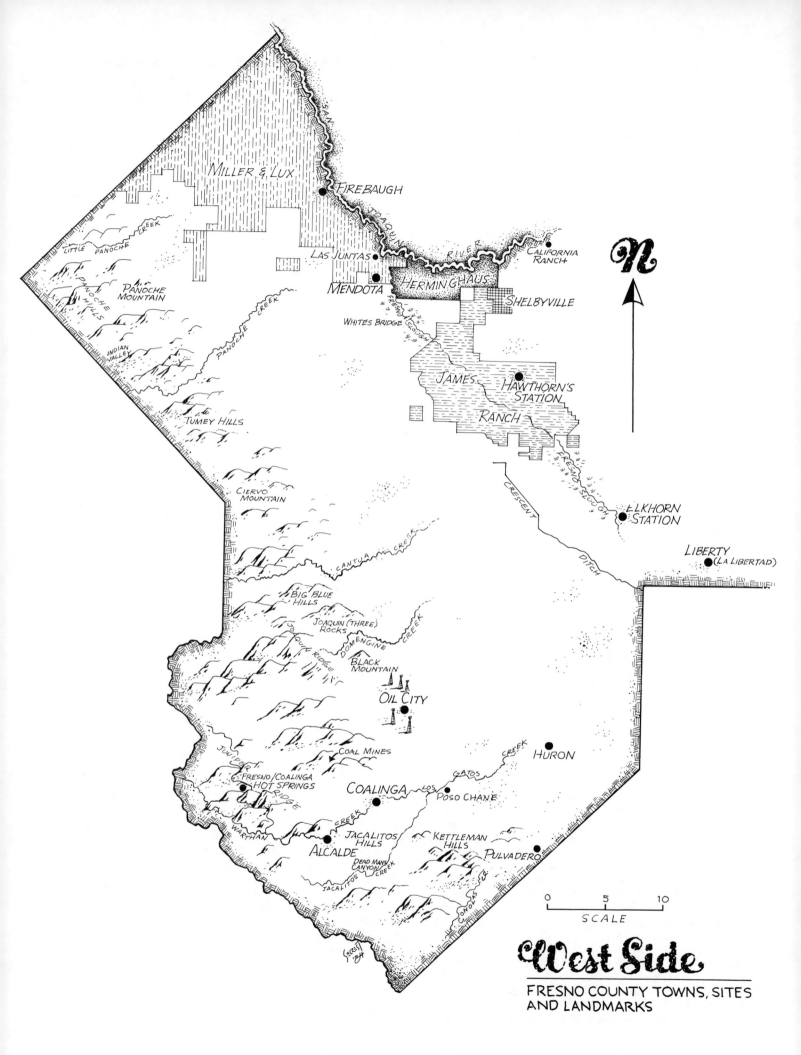

MILLER & LUX

LITTLE PANOCHE CREEK

FIREBAUGH

SAN JOAQUIN RIVER

PANOCHE MOUNTAIN

PANOCHE HILLS

LAS JUNTAS

HERMINGHAUS

CALIFORNIA RANCH

INDIAN VALLEY

MENDOTA

WHITES BRIDGE

FRESNO SLOUGH

SHELBYVILLE

PANOCHE CREEK

JAMES

HAWTHORN'S STATION

RANCH

TUMEY HILLS

𝕹

CIERVO MOUNTAIN

FRESNO SLOUGH

ELKHORN STATION

CRESCENT DITCH

LIBERTY
(LA LIBERTAD)

CANTUA CREEK

BIG BLUE HILLS

JOAQUIN (THREE) ROCKS

DOMENGINE CREEK

JOAQUIN RIDGE

BLACK MOUNTAIN

OIL CITY

COAL MINES

CREEK

HURON

JUNIPER R.

FRESNO/COALINGA HOT SPRINGS

LOS GATOS

COALINGA

POSO CHANE

KETTLEMAN HILLS

RIDGE

CREEK

JACALITOS HILLS

WARTHAN

ALCALDE

DEAD MANS CANYON CREEK

PULVADERO

JACALITOS CREEK

CONDAS CR.

SCALE
0     5     10

*West Side*

FRESNO COUNTY TOWNS, SITES
AND LANDMARKS

# Chapter 12
# The West Side

The road is over the barren plain, with no wood except upon the banks of the creeks . . . The soil is mostly alkali, and the taste of the water is much tinctured with it.

—Waterman L. Ormsby, *New York Herald* correspondent and first passenger on Overland Stage, 1858.

It was an open flat desert, and subject to the worst kind of windstorms, generally lasting three days. I remember one of these blows that was worse than all the rest . . . Cabins were actually blown and broken entirely to pieces and the side walls scattered across the plains.

—Horace McWhorter, Coalinga area pioneer, reminiscing circa 1943.

All the early accounts agree: Comfortable human habitation on Fresno County's west side prairie was difficult to achieve. Emigrants had no attractions such as farm land, timber or even sublime mountain scenery. The country's general isolation and desolation compound-ed these negative qualities.

There were notable exceptions which broad, general descriptions fail to include. The low overflow lands along the San Joaquin River in the Kerman area were described as a lush verdant refuge for thousands of birds and the other forms of wildlife found in the valley. The land along the river to the entrance of the Fresno Slough attracted and supported several Indian villages and the early Spanish-speaking vaqueros who established Las Juntas and Rancho de los Californianos. In the southern area the most conspicuous exception was Posa Chiné and the creeks that led into it. The white man's cutting of trees for shelter and firewood led to the early deterioration of these desirable areas.

Two outside factors, however, made settlement inevitable: the need for reliable intrastate transportation in California, and the dollar's undeniable lure.

As noted in Chapter 4, the gold rush in the southern mines and increased traffic between San Francisco and Los Angeles made it necessary for people to travel through Fresno County. Two men named Stone and Waters were apparently the first "west siders" to recog-

nize the potential profits. At the northern end of the San Joaquin River's great bend, they built a ferry—circa 1852—later obtained or purchased by Andrew Firebaugh. Four years later, Firebaugh built a toll road through Pacheco Pass to Monterey and San Francisco to service north-south travelers.

These improvements, together with L. A. Whitmore's Kings River ferry at Kingston (see Chapter 9), induced the Butterfield Overland Mail Company to plot its stage route through western Fresno County. When that road opened in 1858 it connected the two ferries. Between these points, two new stage stops flourished—C. A. Hawley and W. B. Cummings' Fresno City, or Casa Blanca, and John Barker's Elkhorn Station. Thus was created the earliest non-Indian settlement pattern on the West Side, and, in time, the first true communities.

The riverbend ferry's trading post and scow were operated by Stone, Waters and Firebaugh for only a few years each. Isolation and the country's bleakness may have caused these brief tenures, but a more likely reason was persistent danger. Mexican outlaws from the nearby California Ranch and Las Juntas (see Chapter 3) were always lurking around. One story says that Firebaugh, one of the few white men in the vicinity, went unmolested because he owned the ferry—a frequently-used getaway contrivance for the badmen. Firebaugh's involvement in the mountain road's construction may also have been responsible for his leaving the ferry business.

By 1856 or thereabouts ownership of the ferry and trading post had passed from Firebaugh's into other hands. Jacob Carman, Samuel McIntosh and John Iredell Wilson, known collectively as "Carman and Company," operated them sporadically from that time into the early 1860s. E. A. Wolcott and Company were the owners in 1857-58. In this period a hotel, bar, store and blacksmith shop were added to the complex; inexplicably, Carman and Company gave up the bar license in 1861. Four years later, on May 19, 1865, a post office was established at this hamlet. This replaced the earlier Firebaugh's Ferry post office, established on March 13, 1860, and discontinued on August

21, 1862. It is surprising that the post office lapsed, for Firebaugh was a busy place, with stages, individual travelers and steamboats regularly calling (see 12:1).

After Carman's death in 1866, Wilson maintained stables there and the hotel was sold or leased to Robert R. Burr and his wife. By 1875 the hotel, ferry and store had passed into the hands of Charles Kahn and Jacob Myer. Stages and mail service ran daily to the town (population twenty-five), since it was on the Gilroy-Berenda route. There were two homes, two saloons operated by Jesus Bernal and Joaquin Cabrera, and a private school operated by a Mr. Hadsell. Francisco Dubalos was justice of the peace and Jeremiah Noonan constable. For a town of twenty-five, it had an impressive array of services!

The late 1870s brought conspicuous changes to Firebaugh. In 1876 Myer bought out Kahn, leased the hotel to Sam Woldenburg, and moved the store to a warehouse overlooking the river. During the spring of that year, a sheep-shearing corral was built in town to service the nearby flocks of William Baxter, Perry Lay and Wade White. Some 150,000 sheep were sheared that year, 15,000 of them from the nearby Miller and Lux ranches (see Chapter 6).

Reference 12:1

# STEAMBOATING ON THE SAN JOAQUIN
## LILBOURNE A. WINCHELL

Navigation on the San Joaquin river began very early in the period of American immigration to California. The first vessel to penetrate the lower reaches was a small sloop which, in 1846, carried agricultural implements, seed grain and provisions for Samuel Brannan's Mormon Colony of thirty farmers. The little vessel made its way up the San Joaquin as far as the mouth of the Stanislaus river, and there in the midst of extensive, level and rich alluvial bottom lands, it discharged its cargo.

With the continuation of the labors connected with the erection of many substantial buildings at Fort Miller, there was constant need of supplies and materials, other than those at hand. Heavy rains and high water in the streams, while stopping the big wagons, provided excellent passageway for boats; so the light-draft, stern-wheel steamboats were employed to bring necessities. In the early summer rise of the San Joaquin waters, caused by rapidly melting snows of the Sierra, the first of these floating freighters nosed its pioneer way slowly through the windings of the river in the marsh lands, to a point where the bordering bluffs of the river merged with the flat lands. Tying up to sycamore trees, the little steamer was met by government wagons from Fort Miller. This embarcadero, located about three-fourths of a mile above Skaggs' Bridge, was called Sycamore Point, and is still so known.

Thus was inaugurated an important industry—a traffic which continued and grew in volume for many years, during the flood stages of the river. All these carriers were of very light draft—about two feet of water was necessary to clear; and with this advantage were enabled to carry cargoes through devious and shallow channels.

Not only supplies were carried for the military post, but freight for settlements on the Kings river, Four Creek regions [in Tulare County] and other growing communities. A regular freighting industry was developed by wagons hauling from the steamer landing to points south; the teamsters crossing Kings river during the earliest years at Poole's [sic] ferry—about twelve miles below what is now known as Centerville.

When the famous Overland Stage Company began operations in 1858, on a cross continent route from San Francisco, California, to St. Louis and Memphis, the steamboats found a new negotiable waterway—narrow, but deep. Up this lateral slough, which entered the San Joaquin above Firebaugh's ferry—now called Fresno Slough—the little steamers pushed to the end of the navigable channel. There a station was located, and the stage line supplied with immense tonnage of provender and other requisites, necessary for their relay stations through the southern San Joaquin valley. Later this landing place was known as Fresno City, when a townsite was surveyed and a map recorded, but commonly called "Casa Blanca," for the big, two-story white-painted hotel built there for the accommodation of travellers.

Of the large fleet of steamboats on the Sacramento and San Joaquin rivers (both side- and stern-wheelers), several were accustomed to visit the Fresno county regions. Among others, the more regular freighters were the Empire City, Fresno, Visalia, Esmeralda, Tulare, Clara Belle, Mary Ellen, Christine, Kate and Little Fawn.

The "Visalia" was launched at Sacramento in January, 1860, and in July brought in her cargo, 60,000 pounds of barley to Casa Blanca, for the use of the Overland Stage company.

The growing empire of Miller and Lux demanded great quantities of fencing, building, and other materials, and for many years—even after the competition of the railroad, solid loads of lumber and posts were brought in to the ranch landings on huge scows drawn by the little, snorting, splashing stern-wheelers.

The Fish Slough, or J. G. James, ranch, and the big Herminghaus stock ranges on the San Joaquin, were also enclosed by steamer loads of fencing materials.

When the Wm. H. Parker family were imprisoned in the second story of Casa Blanca, in January, 1868, by the unprecedented floods of the San Joaquin and Kings river [sic], they were, after several days' confinement, rescued with all their household goods (which had been carried upstairs when the floods poured into the lower floors) by the steamer "Empire City," which, upon arrival at the landing place, swung into position alongside the big house; tied up to the wall, by cables run through the windows and fastened inside, and took on board the family and all their belongings. The upper deck of the steamer was on a level with the upper story windows of the house.

Casting off, the steamer followed down the course of the slough, then outlined solely by the tops of bordering willows, till Four-tree slough was reached, into which submerged channel the steamer swung, and then cut across the open, but deeply flooded plain, to the San Joaquin river, and soon landed the family at a high knoll close to the stream, in the eastern part of the Herminghaus cattle range.

At this haven Parker built a store, which trading post became known as "Parker's," and was maintained for several years. All goods and merchandise for Parker were supplied at intervals by the steamboats. As late as 1875 steamers continued to run to this point. . . .

During this same flood season of 1867–68 Stone and Harvey, owners of the steamer "Alta," attempted to reach Tulare Lake by way of the Fresno and Fish Sloughs. They worked their way to a point near Elkhorn, where the marsh channel proved to be too shallow. All efforts to back out were unsuccessful, and the steamer was abandoned. There it remained for several years, an object of curious interest, till a great fire in the dry tules destroyed the hulk, and nothing remained to mark the scene of the adventure, but the iron works. The smoke stack was afterwards hauled away and used in a small sawmill in the mountains.

SOURCE: *History of Fresno County and the San Joaquin Valley* by Lilbourne A. Winchell. Original manuscript held by Fresno City and County Historical Society.

An 1877 drought, depression in wool and mutton prices, and consequent scarcity of pasturage wiped out many local sheepraisers. Henry Miller, as he had done before with cattle, put this adversity to work for him. He bought thousands of sheep at twenty-five to fifty cents a head, waited for prices to rise (which they did), and eclipsed his local competition within a short time. By 1878 his flocks numbered 75,000, and an April 2, 1897, *Fresno Daily Evening Expositor* report said he had 125,000.

Mr. Hadsell's 1875 school was replaced by the formation of the Firebaugh Joint School District on May 8, 1878. Its first trustees were Sam Woldenburg, R. B. Harris and Louis Ploeger. Other school districts operating nearby at the time were the Sycamore (formed on June 6, 1874), Cherry Hill (June 2, 1875) and Millardville (July 3, 1877). The Sycamore and Millardville districts were partially annexed to Firebaugh's on May 7, 1885.

Local school districts formed in the years after the Firebaugh's creation were the Oak Grove (September 6, 1884) and Sunnyside (March 6, 1893). Among the earlier teachers in the districts were Miss C. S. Richie (Cherry Hill, 1877), Louise Tuggy (Sunnyside, 1893), and Ludora Wheeler and Aurelia Gear (Firebaugh, 1898).

Firebaugh experienced a sudden population jump in 1879. The San Joaquin and Kings River Canal Company (see Chapter 6) had previously purchased the Las Juntas townsite, and it ordered the residents to vacate. Firebaugh merchant Myer began offering lots in his town for one dollar, which attracted almost all the people from Las Juntas. They swelled Firebaugh's population from (approximately) 50 to 250.

Although river traffic at Firebaugh had declined— except through the winters and early summers when the water ran high, the county built a steel drawbridge there in 1885. It cost more than $20,000 and forced the ferry into retirement. Myer quit the local mercantile and warehousing businesses around this time as well, selling his holdings to Miller and Lux. That act made Firebaugh a bona fide company town. Most of the Las Juntas refugees, who made up the bulk of the town's population, were Miller and Lux employees.

When the Southern Pacific railroad decided to build a branch south from Los Banos to Collis (Kerman) in 1889, Miller and Lux were quick to give the railroad land in Firebaugh. Tracks were soon placed through the town, and the first train rolled in on December 24, 1890. Townsfolk celebrated for three days, accompanied in their revelry by 100 Southern Pacific employees who had the holidays off. Another major improvement came in 1895, when Miller and Lux built an irrigation canal along N Street.

Turn-of-the-century Firebaugh experienced troubled prosperity. The sheep business, now dominated by Miller and Lux, made the town into a small commercial center—yet also attracted unruly elements. "During the shearing season the place is filled with Mexicans who have gathered from all points in the valley," said the August 2, 1898, *Fresno Morning Republican*. "Shooting scrapes, fights and bloody encounters are numerous . . . The herders and shearers scatter their earnings with total disregard of what may be the needs of the morrow . . . " An account of some of the lawless activity may be found in Chapter 11.

The free-flowing money, and the town's continued importance as a transporation center, made many willing to risk operating businesses there. During the 1890s Ciccarelli and Paccinelli, M. Caneras and James Finerty ran saloons; A. G. Laverone, the Mazziani House; Idiart and Son, the Firebaugh Hotel; D. Belli, the Garibaldi House; and A. Perrini, the Toscano Restaurant.

When the Los Banos-Armona railroad was constructed, the Southern Pacific decided it needed storage, switching and miscellaneous facilities near the route's midpoint. Firebaugh would have been a logical choice—except for its reputation for instability. To sidestep this problem, the Southern Pacific created its own town nine miles southeast of the raucous river burg. Christened Mendota, it was surveyed and platted in early 1891. As with a few other Fresno County towns, the reason for its naming has been lost. "Like many railroad stations, it was probably named after a town 'back home,'" comments Erwin G. Gudde in *California Place Names.* "There were a number of Mendotas in the Middle West at that time."

"Judging from the appearance of Mendota—our station—the Southern Pacific company must intend to do something generous towards our country here," said a correspondent in the October 14, 1891, *Fresno Daily Evening Expositor.* "A very handsome station, including warehouse, sitting-room, ticket-office and living-room grace the visitor. An artesian well, large tank, turntable and many sidetracks, besides considerable fencing, and a large deposit of coal, causes us to believe that in the dim and distant future, something shall have been done of decided benefit to our grand plains, and the people living thereon."

By late November, one report said, there were rarely less than three locomotives on hand at the railroad yard, and there were 200 cars on the sidetracks at one time. A saloon and hotel had been started by private hands, and town lots were costly. Corner lots were selling for $250 and inside lots for $150. Apparently everyone was too busy to get a post office started. Its coming was delayed until July 21, 1892.

At least the townsfolk had a good water and food supply. A Southern Pacific official regularly had the station's artesian well water shipped to him for bathing his feet; he said it provided "an unexcelled . . . cure for corns and rheumatism." Abundant local flora and wildlife inspired this March 11, 1895, *Fresno Daily*

*Evening Expositor* report: "During the early spring our table was graced with mushrooms in profusion. Now we must content ourselves with terrapin and salmon trout from the San Joaquin [River], while salad of salt grass and alfilaria, unobtainable elsewhere in such abundance, becomes part of our repast."

Mendota's population climbed to approximately two hundred by the mid-1890s, and its businesses and services multiplied proportionately (see 12:2). There was A. Joseph Arnaudon's combined hotel and general merchandise store, with P. Arripe as clerk. Separate hotels were kept by J. O. Doud and J. H. Harding, and another general store by Mrs. A. L. Rerat. D. J. Brown and J. E. Russell ran saloons, Mrs. W. P. Deardorff a boarding house, C. E. Rendell a Wells, Fargo express office, Billie Miller the town's Chinese restaurant, A. Adams a meat market (in addition to being town constable), E. J. Baker a barber shop, Frank Givens a blacksmith shop, and Mrs. M. Asher a confectionery store. E. Grunig was the town's contractor and builder, and Henry Hope its painter. Maintaining law and order were Adams, town marshal Walter Wyatt and Justice of the Peace A. L. Rerat.

Like Firebaugh, Mendota was a sheep-shearing center. The 1895 *Fresno Daily Evening Expositor* report quoted above mentioned that storekeeper Arnaudon "has erected a new sheep corral and will probably shear the great majority of sheep in this district. Already have arrived many 'Knights of the Golden Fleece.' ... Shearing commences on the 11th, and a new town suburban has sprung into existence, tho' it be of tents. For six weeks labor, life and luxury will be rampant in our Mendota, the City of Destiny."

Mendota's biggest employer remained the Southern Pacific. No fewer than twenty-eight men served at the station, including yardmen, switchmen, firemen, brakemen, car repairers, machinists, foremen and general laborers. Some of them must have been negligent in their jobs, for a bad section of track escaped their attention and caused tragedy on April 22, 1898. The rails gave way 300 yards north of the station as a train moved out, causing two engines and seventeen cars to crack up. The crews leaped from the cars to save their lives, but two hobos were believed to have perished. Goods were strewn all over the track, including a load of dynamite destined for use in the Spanish-American War. By some miracle, none of it exploded and the loss was kept to approximately $40,000.

A Mendota School District was formed on April 4, 1893. Its early teachers included J. I. Taylor (1894), L. West and Miss Harwood (1895) and Tillie Grunig (1898–99). Thirty-five students were attending in 1896. Local school districts predating Mendota's were the White's Ferry (formed on November 3, 1873), New Hope (May 9, 1888, with Ida M. Coyle the first teacher), and West Dry Creek (February 4, 1891). J. I. Taylor and Tillie Grunig of the Mendota School District also served the West Dry Creek at different times. As the Mendota area grew, two more school districts were added: the Artesia on March 5, 1895, and Herminghaus on March 8, 1898. Mary Barieau and W. R. Wilson were the first teachers, respectively.

Entertainments were many in the Mendota of yore, which was colloquially known as the "City of Constant Revelry." One was well-described in the May 6, 1896, *Fresno Daily Evening Expositor*:

The people and children of West Dry Creek school gave a picnic at Whites Bridge on Saturday which was the grandest affair of the kind ever attempted on the West Side. People attended from all directions, Mendota being represented largely. Music was furnished

Reference 12:2

## A STROLL THROUGH MENDOTA, 1896

Having an insane desire a few days ago to go slumming, we looked about for a field but found none, as our purse was too attenuated to allow us to visit some large city. As a compromise, we concluded to view the back yards of Mendota. Starting at the sheep shearing corral we proceeded south. The corral presented the appearance of being kept in good repair and were it not for the peculiar aroma arising to our delicate and extended nostrils, we would consider it a good place for a moonlight picnic. ...

Proceeding, we shortly were attracted by a perfume of loud size, and, on examination, discovered a pen in which were many hogs, some of great weight and fearful jowl. The disagreeable features of the smell were somewhat allayed by the pleasure in scratching the razor backs.

Proceeding we arrived back of the hotel, store, barn, etc. of Joe Arnaudon and learned of the abiding place of horses, cows, chickens, ducks, dogs, cats, pigeons, etc. However, as much business is done here, things are kept in good shape though a little crowded. Walking slowly along, we found ourselves in the environs of the Sunset hotel, which showed up great—if we except great hills of cans, papers, rags, dead soldiers [whiskey bottles], etc. However, these were there before the present management had charge. A few steps and we were in the rear of the first building in town. This has been occupied by many different ones, and all have left behind a reminder in untold quantities of battered cans. The building known as Cash Register, because before its fall it was a resort for unlimited credit, comes next. But a small business having been transacted during several months the back yard is in a condition fair to middling. Picking our way across a lot covered with cans, hoops, old clothes, etc.—the etcetera may be emphasized to suit imagination—scattered in a studied profusion, we plod, inhaling an increasing smell, to the back of the Chinese restaurant, where we found a pen of huge proportions and containing hogs of high and low degree, tout ensemble. One lazy mother lies deep in a muddy berth "as silent as a painted ship on a painted ocean." Nearby is an open cesspool which, truly, is cruel to witness, as on the coming of warm weather sickness is bound to be lavish. Proceeding, we come to the residences, all of which claim a back yard which needs embellishment. All are about on the same level and all deserve censure. We find too many chickens roosting in the space allowed and the pure air ordinance is abused. ...

In conclusion we beseech the people of Mendota to clean up their back yards. Let not the name of our town be changed from that of the City of Constant Revelry to that of the City of Accumulated Filth.

SOURCE: *Fresno Daily Evening Expositor*, May 6, 1896.

by the Grunig brothers. Miss Tillie Grunig, the efficient teacher, was the queen, her maids of honor being the Misses Evelyn, Ellen and Hilma Esbjornson and Daisy Barton. Jim Lowery, the duke of Whites Bridge, was pressed into service and showed the visitors cozy places for fishing and assisted in the boating exercises. In the afternoon all flocked to the loft of the great barn, where the floor, being as smooth as a fair lady's cheek, was polished by the soles of the peripatetic dancers. All kinds and conditions of good things to eat were in abundance while water of excessive coldness was the wash used. The money of the affair will enable the little ones to bear the next four months of hot weather with fortitude while in anticipation of the reopening of school. Adios! Adios!

The same issue also mentioned that

Word has arrived that Mrs. T. P. Fenelon, who has been away a few weeks, is anxiously awaiting the arrival of her husband so as to be enabled to present him with a girl baby. When the bold Tom heard the news he immediately procured untold gallons of Fresno port and right royally did he lay the foundation among the citizens for excessive mirth and frightful revelry. Tom deemed that, it being a girl, soft libations were alone allowed.

A town swimming tank, installed in late 1895, was a popular resort. Dances and hay rides were much the rage in the same year. Of them the *Expositor*'s correspondent, "Cdgn," said: "Let a strolling player enter town and he is immediately snapped up and a dance follows . . . The last [hay] ride ended at the river, where lines were cast and many huge fish landed. This, of course, more than pleased the [single] ladies of the party [which included several eligible men], who are now aware 'there are more fish in the sea.'" Surprisingly, there seems to have been only one organization in town during this period: Sunset Lodge No. 193, Knights of Pythias, which held regular Monday meetings in 1895.

The settlement referred to above—known as White's Bridge—deserves some comment. Located approximately one and a half miles southeast of Mendota on the Fresno Slough, it was the site of a ferry operated by one Watson prior to 1870. By that year it had been purchased by James R. White, who set up a hotel, store and warehouse there and replaced the ferry with a bridge eventually. A traveler writing in the July 6, 1870, *Fresno Weekly Expositor* remarked that "we took our departure for Jim White's (also known as Watson's Ferry) . . . On reaching that point we were ushered into a spacious hotel for no other purpose than to partake of the luxurious viands always to be found on the table at Jim White's."

Steamers frequently called at White's Bridge—which gave its name to the Fresno County road of today—and it became a notable sheep-shearing center. Inter-

estingly, White retained control of his enterprises there for a quarter-century or more. This is surprising, given the transience of Fresno County's other wayside innkeepers, ferrymen and storekeepers.

Transportation was a fickle force on Fresno County's west side. While it could bring towns like Firebaugh and Mendota into existence, a switch in emphasis—from steamboats to stages, or stages to rails—could kill a settlement. The former change spelled doom for Fresno City, located roughly eight miles southeast of Mendota. The latter caused Elkhorn Station, near present-day Burrel, to wither away over several decades. Both, in their heyday, were semi-important stops on the Butterfield Overland Mail route, as mentioned before. Albeit brief, their histories embody some interesting details.

Waterman L. Ormsby, the reporter whose remarks opened this chapter, visited Fresno City on October 9, 1858. Traveling on the Butterfield route just after its opening, he described the settlement—only a few weeks or months old—thus: "Frezeneau [Fresno] City is at the head of [the Fresno] slough . . . and consists of one finished house and one partly finished. The proprietor is boring an artesian well, for the purpose of obtaining good water. From this point to the Tulare Lake the course of a canal is marked by a furrow, which is, I believe, the only property of some anxious stockholders."

The "finished house and one partly finished" Ormsby refers to must have been the Casa Blanca, the store and hotel built at the hamlet, and a nearby warehouse. Both were situated on the east side of the Fresno Slough, and were regular calling places for steamboats operating in the area (see 12:1). The Casa Blanca (White House in Spanish, and probably dubbed as such by Mexican settlers in the area) was one of the few notable landmarks in western Fresno County. According to Lilbourne A. Winchell "it was moved [eventually] to [Jefferson] James' central headquarters near the present town of San Joaquin, and was, after some years, destroyed by fire.

It seems likely that Fresno City's "proprietor" in 1858 was Abner J. Downer, the man who became its first postmaster on January 4, 1860. He also filed a townsite map of the "city," as agent for C. A. Hawley and W. B. Cummings, on the following April 25. Hawley and Cummings were the Casa Blanca's owners, and Downer appears to have been its manager. All believed that Fresno City would become a significant transportation hub, and for three reasons: (1) its Butterfield route location, (2) the fact it was situated at the uppermost limit of easy navigation on the Fresno Slough, allowing for steamboat traffic, and (3) because Hawley and Cummings were building a ship canal southward to help extend their settlement's importance, as Ormsby notes.

For some reason—faulty finances, erratic Fresno

Slough water levels, or both—the Hawley and Cummings canal was never completed. Downer seems to have managed the Casa Blanca for no more than two years; he was succeeded as postmaster by Milton B. Holt on November 11, 1860. On March 17, 1862, George L. Gould took over from Holt and served until the post office's discontinuance on June 8, 1863. The Casa Blanca seems to have functioned for several more years, but its importance was waning. Steamboat traffic on the Fresno Slough continued to decrease, the location was prone to flooding, and William Hawthorne's stage stop to the southeast—away from the often-inundated slough region—seems to have become more popular.

Though records are sketchy, it is safe to assume that Fresno City was moribund by the time of the Fresno post office's institution. Nary a reference can be found to it in county newspapers after that date, unless it is mentioned in a purely historical context. Writing about the "city" in 1927–28, Lilbourne A. Winchell

said, "The Casa Blanca cellar, well hole, and willows which bear the mark of the steamboat hawsers [ropes or cables], are the only evidences remaining of the old time famous and active trading point."

Thanks to the reminiscences of John Barker, Elkhorn's founder, much more can be said about that stage stop's early days (see 12:3). It seems to have prospered until the Central Pacific railroad cut through Fresno County in 1872, making the stage route increasingly obsolete. Little happened there subsequently except for a telegraph line being strung through the village in 1885 and the creation of the Elkhorn School District on May 7, 1886. Always a small operation, it had only seventeen students in 1899 and one teacher, Mrs. Bessie Leavitt.

Although the railroad prompted Elkhorn's decline, it breathed life into a new settlement, twenty-two miles to the southwest, in 1877. Farming along the Kings River had been expanding on a westward course, and the Southern Pacific wanted to expand into—and

Reference 12:3

## HOW I FOUNDED THE FIRST SETTLEMENT ON THE FRESNO PLAIN

### JOHN BARKER

In the year 1856, about the last of August, I, in company with three other young men, went out on an elk hunt, following the eastern edge of the swamp that extends from where Kings River enters the Tulare Lake and down to the San Joaquin River, for a distance of about forty miles. I had been engaged exploring the lake and the swamp just previously, and while doing so had encountered several large bands of elk, which, on account of very little being known at that time about the locality described, had not been hunted or disturbed by man, and as a consequence were remarkably tame, and could be hunted without extraordinary labor.

We went equipped with a wagon, almost like a house on wheels, with a large cover. Each man had also a saddle horse, and the wagon was driven by four gentle oxen that were accustomed to camp life and would stay wherever camp was made without much herding. With the horses it was different; they had to be brought into camp every night, hobbled, and tied up short and grass gathered for their feeds in order to keep the bands of wild horses, of which there were thousands on the Fresno plains, from stampeding them and running off with the wild bands, and, if they once get away with them, they were apparently wilder than the wildest and fully as difficult to recapture.

We arrived at a point about midway between the Kings River and the San Joaquin and there found a convenient slough with water close to the edge of the plain. We made camp there. While the water was good enough for our animals, it was neither agreeable nor palatable for man. A fire had run along the banks of the slough in the heavy

growth of tules, and the burned tules had fallen into the water and made it look like weak-coffee and also gave it a very disagreeable and bitter taste. However, we made camp and prepared everything for the hunt to begin at daybreak the next morning. We carried out our program and it took us all that day to locate the feeding grounds of the elk and to kill a few antelope, of which there were thousands on the plains, for camp use.

That night there was great dissatisfaction expressed with the quality of the water, and during the afternoon, after my return from the hunt in the swamp, and while trailing antelope to get a shot, I noticed a depression in the plain in the form of a bowl. It was about fifteen or twenty feet below the level of the plain and in the bottom I noticed there were dead tule roots plainly indicating that tules had recently grown there and that water could not be far off. I told my party that I would stay in camp and sink a well at the point described, and that I thought I could get good water. They were not much impressed with my theory but consented to try it for one day more.

As soon as I had straightened up the camp, and while it was still cool, I took my tools and went to make a critical observation of the locality. I concluded to go up the sloping bank and sink a hole that would be at the surface, about four feet higher than the bottom of the depression. I started a hole about three feet wide by four feet in length, and after I had got down a couple of feet I struck a hardpan of yellow clay. This was a pretty solid formation and after I had sunk down in it two feet further it gave a sort of a hollow sound every time I struck the pick with it.

This made me watchful, as from the sound I feared I was going to strike a cavern below, and being there alone, if I did and fell into it before I could get any assistance, further proceedings in the case would not possess much interest for me.

However, remembering that "faint heart never won fair lady," I slammed away with the pick and shortly broke through. As soon as the crest was broken the water rushed in, and in short order there were four feet in the hole and it commenced running over the top, a stream as large as my arm, and running down to the bottom of the depression, where it formed a lake. The water was clear and cool, as fine as could be desired anywhere. It was also soft like rain water.

The plain all along the margin of the swamp for forty miles was covered with a heavy growth of grass that waved in the wind like a field of grain. The ground was thickly strewed with the horns of the elk where they annually shed them and a good many entire skulls with head or horns of bull elk that had been killed by hunters. Those were all bleached white as snow. I took my horse and riata and dragged up an immense pile and piled them up about eight feet high so that they could be readily seen a mile or more away. I established this mark so that the place could be easily and readily found again as there were no natural marks there and I then and there determined that I would locate there and would develop one of the best stock ranches in the valley.

When my party returned early in the afternoon they had the hind quarters of six elk packed on their three ponies, and were delighted to get a good cool drink of water.

We went on with our hunt and killed and

258

ahead of—that development. Accordingly, it began building a branch line from its Goshen station in Tulare County westward, toward Tres Pinos in San Benito County. This route led straight across the southwestern corner of Fresno County where, nine miles inside the border, a temporary terminus was built.

This new place, where a station was soon established, was called Huron. A manually-operated turntable was installed there so incoming trains could return to Goshen and the points in-between. A post office, also called Huron, was inaugurated on June 18, 1877. No authority seems certain why the name was selected, or by whom. Erwin G. Gudde, in *California Place Names*, mentions that the name "was given by the French to a group of four Iroquoian tribes in Ontario, and it became a popular place name in the United States."

Little happened around the station until 1884, when W. P. Kerr and J. M. Wells began farming in the nearby Pulvadero country. They soon were obtaining twenty-eight sacks of barley and five tons of hay an acre, probably through dry farming. Others learned of their success and, attracted by the cheap land prices of $6.50 to $15.00 an acre, began filtering into the area during 1887. (It is safe to assume that the increase in farm land prices in the better-established parts of Fresno County had driven many thrifty settlers to this region. See Chapter 8.)

dried the meat of a great many elk and antelope, and in about four weeks we had a load of dried meat which we took over to the San Joaquin river, followed it up forty miles to Fort Miller and sold out to miners and Indians for 50 cents per pound and realized $300 each the proceeds of our hunt.

I had a ranch on Kings River near Kingston that I sold and went down and settled on my Elkhorn property. The road from Visalia to Stockton was established so that it passed my house and all the supplies for Visalia had to come that way. A road was also opened through the Pacheco Pass to Gilroy. There was soon a string of teams on the road and Elkhorn became a noted point.

I was gradually developing my idea of a stock ranch, and at the same time keeping a road house, when along in the early summer of 1867 I got up one morning early, and looking down the road toward the west I saw an immense drove of horses being driven loose. Then, as they came nearer, I saw about twenty or thirty coaches, each with four horses attached, being driven along. When they arrived at my place I was introduced to the gentlemen in charge. One was the late A. O. Thomas, so well known in Bakersfield and Visalia, and the other was T. C. Kenyon. I learned that they represented the Butterfield Company... They were now stocking the road and establishing stations through to Los Angeles. The stage coaches were loaded with men, harness, grain, etc., and they were to meet a reinforcement of men, coaches, horses, etc., at Los Angeles that would have arrived by steamer by the time they reached that place. They made contracts with the farmers, whenever they could find any, for hay and barley, and the prices paid for such articles at that day would seem fabulous now. They contracted with me for hay. There was an abundance of grass growing near me to be got for the cutting—miles of it—but there were no mowing machines in those days and no men to be got to work with scythes, except Indian labor, and that was heart breaking to try to get any results from.

I will give a little of my experience here. I had a lot of scythes, handrakes and forks shipped up from San Francisco, also a couple of grind stones and a lot of scythe whitstones. I went to the rancheria on Kings river near the lake and made a contract with about twenty Indians to come to work. I was to pay them $1 per day and feed them on horse meat. This was not hard to do, as I employed a white man to shoot wild horses and made the Indians butcher them and pack in the meat. They preferred this to any other food.

I got started with about ten scythes. And such a start. They would mow a few yards, stop, look at their hands, and call on another one to take their place. When the sun got up warm they would all quit work, retire to the bank of the slough and plunge into the water, come out and stick their heads under the shade of a bunch of tules and go to sleep. At dinner time they were all on deck for grub, and so they went all day. About the third day when I got up in the morning, I was astounded to behold the arrival of the whole tribe which had trailed in during the night, and I was expected to feed the whole lot.

I gave them all the horse beef on hand and told them to all get up and get. Butterfield's whole million dollar mail contract could not have stood it. I was fortunate enough to meet with a company of Mormons, who were on their way from San Bernardino to the northern mines, with their teams and families, and I secured their services to cut and haul up a supply of hay for which the Overland Mail Company paid me $75 per ton and it retailed by the bale for $150 to $200 per ton. There was no alfalfa in those days—nothing but the wild swamp grass.

...The line was soon started and two stages a day, carrying from twelve to twenty-four passengers, were going night and day. They carried conductors like a railroad train and from eight to sixteen horses on a stage, all wild mustangs, and when the stage started from a station, every horse was standing on his heels and pawing the air and when they were let go they went like an avalanche on the dead run.

They had the most expert "whips" or drivers that could be found on the coast—I might safely say in the world. They paid them large wages and they earned it. They were the jolliest lot of fellows that ever cracked a whip and their memories still harbored and cherished by many an old pioneer throughout the San Joaquin Valley....

About 1858 a project was started to build a telegraph line through on the route of the overland mail from San Francisco by way of Los Angeles. The line was built as far as my house at Elkhorn. Winter coming on and all the poles having to be hauled by ox teams from the coast, the roads became too soft for heavy travel of that kind, so the end of the line from San Francisco was at my place. An operator was established there and when the stage arrived from the east the latest news was telegraphed from that point to San Francisco and in going east the stage got the last and latest news to be delivered somewhere in Missouri in like manner. The time between points was thus shortened very considerably....

As an illustration of the general honesty of the people who lived all along the line of the overland mail and the wild and untamed character of the country, it is a notorious fact that all the three years that the mail was in full operation large sums of money were carried by Wells-Fargo on it: that also during this time very rich mines were being worked in Arizona and vast amounts of gold bullion were transported by stages. I have seen as many as eight or ten heavy sacks made of sole leather, each one containing a gold brick of large size laying on the floor of the stage under the passengers' feet, and large amounts were also carried for merchants and for the payments at the military posts and this was generally known and no secret made of it; yet never in a single instance was a stage held up or was any attempt made to do so. In view of the frequent lawless robberies of railroad trains at the present day, this fact speaks well for the pioneers of [that period]....

SOURCE: *San Joaquin Vignettes, The Reminiscences of Captain John Barker*, ed. by William Harland Boyd and Glendon J. Rogers. Bakersfield: Kern County Historical Society and County of Kern, 1955.

*Madelene MacIntyre*

*Madelene MacIntyre*

*Madelene MacIntyre*

*Top: The riverboat J. R. McDonald at a festive event near Fresno. The date given was 1905 but it seems more likely it was the famous trip of 1911 to Sycamore Bend—the last. We never see the river like this now.*
*Middle: A riverboat loading grain at Firebaugh in the days of regular river traffic.*
*Bottom: Hotel at Firebaugh circa 1890 or earlier.*

*Andrew D. Firebaugh and wife, Susan B., in 1860, about the time they left Firebaugh.*

*The hotel and store built by A. J. Arnaudon in 1893 was Mendota's business center by 1900 when it also housed the water company, telephone exchange and post office.*

Fresno Bee Photo

F.C.C.H.S. Archives

*Erected by Fresno County Historical Society in 1952.*

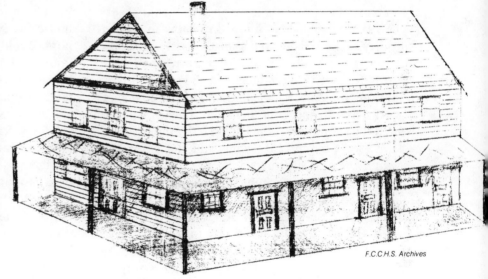

F.C.C.H.S. Archives

*Sketch of Casa Blanco, the stage stop at Fresno City. The 1860 plat of proposed Fresno City has it on the slough that they called the South Branch of San Joaquin River. On the south side of the river they show the Old Mail Route and station, and on the north the office of the Pacific and Atlantic Telegraph Line. They had great plans!*

Large fields of grain began pushing out the red clover and pepper grass that grew naturally in the area. "This part of the county is being settled very thickly," said a July 26, 1887, *Fresno Daily Evening Expositor* report, "cabins being on every 160 acres, which is very different to [*sic*] last year, there being about one cabin to every 23,000 acres last season." Artesian water wells could be dug for a more dependable water supply, at a cost of $700; the Humboldt Land Company purchased 3,000 acres and began dotting its holdings with wells. For those who needed water and were too busy—or lazy—to dig for it, the Fresno Artesian Well Company's digging services were available.

By 1890 Huron was a bustling commercial center. In the January 1–May 1, 1890, period alone, 51,608 sheep were moved out of the town, along with 905,523 pounds of wool. During the year 5,292 tons of wheat and 617 tons of barley left the station. The total outgoing freight was 17,250 tons—incoming, 3,111! Some 10,710 acres within a two-mile radius of the town had been planted; among the larger farms were those of S. Cosgrove, C. A. Landen, Joseph Mariott and R. M. Turner. Barley yields had jumped to between sixteen and thirty sacks an acre, and approximately 100 acres had been successfully set out in vineyards and fruit orchards. So much government land had been snapped up that the Southern Pacific had sold nearly 50,000 of its own acres to meet the demand. This prosperity inspired the formation of the Huron Irrigation District in 1892 (see Chapter 15), which did not enjoy the success of the area's farmers.

Turkey and chicken farming were also popular. Joel Smith started a turkey ranch near Huron in 1886, and not long after that Ransom Jones started chicken farming. He developed a novel way to feed his flock. Oyster shells, plentiful in the nearby hills, were brought by the thousands to his ranch. Once pulverized properly, the fossils became dinner for his birds!

In the first decade of its existence, Huron grew from a handful of people to a population of 250. George Schwinn was the first to start a business there, locating his general store on what he thought was a street corner (the town, apparently, had not been surveyed or platted) in 1886. By the next year there were stores operated by A. Dinkelspiel and Kutner-Goldstein; the Huron Hotel of George Beebee, and Taylorville House of William Taylor; the Taylorville livery stable of G. Barnes, and Huron Livery Stable of R. G. Tibbetts; B. M. Buckland's blacksmith shop; and Barnes and Meades' Palace Saloon. Beebee, Kerr and Jones conducted real estate businesses as well.

No wonder a Huronite took offense in 1888 when a *Tulare Register* correspondent noted that Huron had "four buildings, and a visible population of five men and one dog"; surely the town amounted to more than that. "Those four buildings he saw were four 'dead soldiers' [i.e., liquor bottles] lying near his head, and

his class of people surely knows what they are," said a June 28, 1888, retort in the *Fresno Daily Evening Expositor.*

Soon after, the Central Hotel was purchased by Joseph and Angela Mouren, emigrants from France who had been married in San Francisco in March 1889. Mouren had been in California for twenty years, traveling throughout the state working as a sheep buyer. Huron offered good prospects for growth so he also bought a livery stable and later raised sheep, operated a mercantile business and bought more land.

With his varied interests he prospered even though many of his customers, the early homesteaders, gave up in disgust as they discovered they couldn't make it on small acreages without water. By the 1920s the population of Huron had dropped below fifty, but the Mouren family stayed. A son, Joseph, now ninety, and a grandson continue in business in Huron although the hotel has long since been closed.

An 1891 report mentioned that two new stores, two lodging houses and a number of private homes had been built in town the year before. L. G. Kean built a house that year for $5,000. At that time, an adequate home could be had for $2,000, so it must have been an opulent structure. A setback to this mini-boom occurred on July 15, 1892, when the town's most important businesses burned. Included in the estimated $23,000 loss were Schwinn's store, Thomas Sirocco's saloon, George Arlin's butcher shop, Mrs. L. D. Copeland's restaurant and Dickey and Lindsay's general merchandise store. All but the last two businesses had been rebuilt by 1894, when a few new businesses had joined them: Thomas Arlin's blacksmith shop, George Arnold's general merchandise store, E. B. Martin's restaurant and livery stable, and N. L. Palmer's lumberyard.

The Huron School District was founded during the initial boom days, on May 5, 1887. For years it was a small, one-teacher school; R. McCourt was the first teacher to serve it. He was succeeded by a Mr. Ebsinger from Tulare later in the year. The nearby Burch School District also was formed on May 5, 1887, with Mrs. L. E. Drennan as its first teacher. Low attendance prompted its unification with the Huron school on April 15, 1889. Nearly two years later, on February 4, 1891, two new school districts were formed near Huron: the Idlewild and Lawn Tennis. Anna L. Burns was the first teacher in both districts. By 1899, she was succeeded by Mrs. M. J. Harriman in the Idlewild district. Lack of attendance eventually forced the Lawn Tennis school's closing and, as with the Burch, unification with Huron.

Close to Huron the only other area of concentrated settlement was Pulvadero (Pulvadera), roughly eight miles to the southwest. William and Robert Orr were the first to establish themselves there. A post office was created on April 5, 1880 (and merged with Lemoore's on October 9, 1882), but an October 23, 1894, *Fresno Daily Evening Expositor* article suggested that the community was thriving. "Thousands of acres of land are now being prepared for planting to grain," said correspondent "Double G." "The soil is excellent averaging, with irrigation, fifteen sacks per acre—last year being the first failure in years." The article also mentioned that a school, probably financed by area families, had opened the previous September 24 with Frank Green as its teacher. Existing records do not suggest it was part of the Fresno County school system, and the date this school ceased operating is unknown. Prominent farmers in the area included M. K. Jones, R. Smalley, and J. W. Gish and Sons.

Beyond the Huron and Pulvadero neighborhoods, the southwestern edge of Fresno County was enjoying a small-scale boom. Unlike the flatlands, the canyons and small valleys of this region—with small streams rippling through them—were conducive to habitation. Along the Canoas, Jacalitos, Warthan and Los Gatos creeks, tall oaks and expansive pasturage bloomed. Their elevation, several hundred feet above the valley floor in places, made for a cooler climate as well. The first homesteaders attracted to these settings first tried dry farming, then shifted to building small irrigation canals, dams and ditches for their crops. A few of them went into cattle- and sheep-raising, which remain profitable area businesses.

Pleasant Valley, watered by the Jacalitos, Warthan and Los Gatos creeks, was the first part of this region to be settled. Its first residents, in and around the watering hole there known as Poso Chané, were Yokuts Indians and Mexicans—the latter brought in via the El Camino Viejo road (see Chapter 3). White settlement came later, in 1869, and further up Warthan Creek, in the area known as Warthan Canyon. (Both were named, inaccurately, after another early resident named Albert Warthen.) The first settler there was Tolton Turner Barnes, accompanied by his children Zachary, James and Grace. Other families began filtering into this area and Pleasant Valley during the 1870s, notably the Gustave Kreyenhagens (see 12:4), John G. Crumps, S. M. Smoots, Mortimer Roundtrees, B. M. Colwells and Frames. On March 8, 1880, a Warthan post office was established. It was eventually (in 1902) merged with the one at Alcalde, of which more later.

The area became prosperous (see 12:5) and it remained so, making the formation of several school districts necessary. The Pleasant Valley was organized on March 4, 1872, followed by the Black Mountain on May 5, 1887, the Happy Canyon on February 12, 1890, the Rose on March 5, 1895, and Roundtree on March 7, 1899. The first teachers of the last three districts were G. P. Hatch, Ede Cutter and Clara Ochs.

One milestone in the area's development was the

Reference 12:4

## THE KREYENHAGENS
### VIOLA KREYENHAGEN VAN DYKE

Gustav Kreyenhagen, born October 14, 1821, in Vorden, Germany, was the son of a scholar and editor. His mother, an accomplished pianist, was from a well-to-do mercantile family in Hamburg. Gustav, the eldest of four children, graduated from the University in Berlin with a degree in mathematics and languages. It was while he was in college that he suffered, without benefit of anesthesia, the loss of a leg, and always thereafter used a wooden leg, which in later years in the San Joaquin Valley prompted the Mexicans to give him the sobriquet of "Pato Palo" [*sic*]. In 1848 he married Julia Hering, the daughter of a Lutheran minister. It was during this eventful year in German history that the couple left their "Fatherland," to make a new way in America.

After settling first in New Orleans, where Gustav Kreyenhagen taught in his own private academy and played the cathedral organ in the old French Quarter, they moved to St. Louis, Missouri. Here again he taught mathematics, Greek, Latin, and music in a school destined to become an outstanding institution of learning, Washington College. In St. Louis, the first two children born to the couple died of a disease so common to children in the Mississippi Valley of that era, known as "cholera infantum."

When Emil, the next child, was born

December 1, 1853, they decided to seek a more healthful climate. They came to San Francisco, where Gustav had two brothers, Edward and Julius. They traveled via the Isthmus of Panama, and in later years Mrs. Kreyenhagen frequently told her grandchildren of that trek; how they crossed the Isthmus on mules while she held the infant in her arms; and how they were carried on the backs of natives to the ship that was to convey them to California. She told of losing her hat in the stiff wind as their ship sailed through the Golden Gate, and how she entered San Francisco bareheaded, an impropriety in her day!

San Francisco! A magic city grown from the sleepy Spanish settlement of Yerba Buena into the metropolis the world knows today. It was not so when Mr. and Mrs. Kreyenhagen first knew it. In 1854 it was a town of tents and wooden buildings, with streets of mud, a town as raw and violent as any of the mining camps. Those were the days when the only law enforced was by means of the Vigilantes.

But, if life was cheap and primitive, it was softened by some refinements even then evident. Along with the outlaws and the flamboyant were many solid citizens. San Franciscans have always been lovers of music and the theater.

Upon arrival in San Francisco, Mr. Kreyenhagen established himself with his brother Julius in a general merchandise store, later in the Oriental tea importing business. They were to continue in business together after Gustav and his wife moved to Oak's Openings, later known as Oakland. Here another son, Hugo, was born November 2, 1858. Two years later Mr. Kreyenhagen started his sheep raising business near Gilroy. Soon two more children were born: Bertha, April 10, 1861, in Gilroy, and Adolf at Coyote, August 9, 1864. It was during the four years from 1860 to 1864 that he and Julius owned the historic Peachtree Grant near San Lucas. Julius was managing the San Francisco business and at the same time was in the diplomatic service in China. After the latter's untimely death, Gustav disposed of the Peachtree Ranch, and it was then that he decided to go to the San Joaquin.

For the next eleven years, Gustav operated a general store and stage station and raised sheep at what was known as "Kreyenhagen Corners." When nearby Los Banos began to grow he was one of its first settlers. He built a hotel and store and took his two older sons, Emil and Hugo, into the business. A fourth son, Charles, was born here on January 14, 1867.

Los Banos became the center for freight-

*Central Hotel in Huron in the early 1890s.*

*Huron Station of the Southern Pacific during the five or six years before the town developed.*

*A typical homesteaders house on the West Side built before they learned they couldn't make it dry farming on forty acres.*

*Pleasant Valley Store, one of the earliest businesses in Coalinga.*

*Mr. and Mrs. Gustav Kreyenhagen, probably in the 1860s before they moved to Posa Chiné.*

The main thoroughfare of Coalinga in the oil rush 1890s. Sometimes lower portion
was called Whiskey Row but in the center is a barber shop and at right is obviously
a general store.

By 1900 trees and more businesses were in Coalinga. On left is the Arthur P. May
store, behind two trees is the Comet Saloon and then a meat market and Pleasant
Valley market. There are at least two hotels in remaining buildings.

*R.C. Baker Museum*

*R.C. Baker Museum*

Arthur P. May's first store building was also post office,
telephone exchange, first oil well supply center, and bank.

Drinking water was in short supply in early Coalinga
because of underground alkalies. John J. Jackson solved
this problem by delivering water in a small tank and then
in a water wagon. For years the community drank water
brought in by train.

formation of the Pleasant Valley Farming Company in 1887. While traveling from his Santa Margarita, San Luis Obispo County, home about this time, William Sloan is said to have spied the valley and recognized its agricultural potential. Sloan and land developer J. W. Morshead, who wanted a place to raise horses for a livery he owned, formed the company with a few other local families. They began buying as much local acreage as they could.

Gravity ditches from the hillside creeks and artesian wells were put into service for the company, whose main lands were located near present-day Coalinga. "Old-timers remember the miracle of the gushing water [and] the lush green growth around the resulting stream," said a March 31, 1963, *Fresno Bee* article. "To the parched early homesteaders, the spot was like a Garden of Eden."

Warthan Creek's upper reaches featured another attraction outside of farming and stock-raising possibilities. It became known in the 1860s when, one story says, James Rogers was hunting in the area. He shot a bear, inspected his quarry, paused to wash his hands in a spring and noticed a strong sulfurous smell. Rogers' discovery was soon turned into a small resort, known as Rogers' Sulphur Springs, Fresno Hot Springs (later) and Coalinga Mineral Springs today.

Rogers built a hotel and bathhouse at the site. He sold both to Colonel Henry Burrough of Burrough Valley in the Sierra (see Chapter 5) during the 1870s. The hotel was destroyed by fire and Burrough borrowed money from Gustave Kreyenhagen to rebuild it.

Lack of business volume, mismanagement, or both caused Burrough to default. Kreyenhagen foreclosed on the property, which his family owned until 1926. He filed a homestead claim on the springs to affirm his title, and furnished the hotel with his family's linen, silver, library and square piano—most of which had been brought from Germany. All these possessions were lost in an 1884 fire. A makeshift hotel and some cottages had to suffice until a more elaborate hotel was built in 1896. Beginning in the late 1880s other locals— the S. Barker family, Mrs. Floy Hays Forbes, James T. Barnes and the Sing Vaughns—leased and operated the property. A Rogers post office was inaugurated there on August 28, 1897, its name commemorating the springs' discoverer. It was discontinued August 14, 1909.

Guests were brought to the springs by stages that ran from Alcalde several times a week. By the turn of the century, the site had become a popular resort. There was a dance hall in the hotel, barbecues, band concerts, a separate Men's Club (with a bar and card and billiard tables), hiking and mountain climbing—in addition to bathing in the fifteen springs. Viola Kreyenhagen Van Dyke relates some interesting stories of these years:

Some highly individual persons were guests at the Springs. There was the vivacious Florence Canfield, the teenage daughter of Charles Canfield, the well known California oil promoter, who gave her chaperone "Mrs. Emil" [Kreyenhagen] some anxious moments; for instance the time when Florence was ready

ers hauling supplies from San Francisco to the San Joaquin Valley before the coming of the railroad. Emil drove teams over the old Pacheco Pass; he made the trip from San Jose to Los Banos in four days—Gilroy the first stop-over, Bell Station the second, and San Luis de Gonzaga Rancho, the third. By maintaining several establishments, Mr. Kreyenhagen recouped his losses suffered in the early 1860s, contributed toward the development of the San Joaquin Valley, and became a man of modest means. It was he who is credited with planting and growing the first grain on the West Side.

In fact, he was doing so well in Los Banos that it is not quite clear why he sold out in 1875, and moved farther south in the San Joaquin, inhabited sparely by Mexicans and a few hardy whites. Clearly defined were the causes for former moves—revolution in Germany, search for a better climate, loss of his brother and livestock. Always a man of vision, it might have been a desire to spread out.

At any rate, he sent son Emil ahead the previous year to start constructing a store and small hotel. Here he also established public sheep shearing facilities where as many as 150,000 sheep would be shorn in one season. The wool from 1875 to 1878 was

freighted by teams to Banta near Stockton on the San Joaquin River, and from there by boat to San Francisco. Son Emil was in charge of the freighting, and on the return trips would haul supplies for the store. When the Southern Pacific Railroad extended its line to Huron in 1878, the wool was hauled there for shipment....

During the shearing season, son Adolf was in charge of the crews composed mostly of Chinese, Indians, and Mexicans. Never would Adolf enter the shearing corrals without his gun strapped on his hip. Frequently he was forced to quell fierce quarrels among the shearers. Although Adolf always said the Chinese were the most dependable and industrious workers, they were especially troublesome when opposite tongs erupted into violence.

Adolf often told his children of those early days at the Posa Chene. Life was primitive and hard, and it took a woman of hardy courageous spirit to live there. Such a woman was his mother, Julia, for she could face robbers without fear, and endure the hot dry summers and fierce windstorms which swept in clouds of dust. Once when all the men were absent from the store except Charles and Bertha and Julia, two suspicious looking men rode up. Suspecting they might be

robbers, Julia hastily buried all the money on hand in a flour barrel. When the two robbers entered the store, and securely tied the three of them, Julia never ceased berating them in Spanish as cowards and thieves, and that she knew who they were even though they were masked. Charles and Bertha were at the same time pleading with her in German to keep quiet. Although much merchandise was stolen, the hidden money was never found.

About 1880, Gustav Kreyenhagen purchased the Fresno Hot Springs, later known as the Coalinga Mineral Springs....[See text, Chapter 12.] [Seven years later] the four sons had taken over the business. The older couple had retired to live in Oakland where brother Edward and his wife lived. Gustav died in February 1890 while on a visit to his son Emil's home on the Polvadero [Pulvadero] and was buried in the family vault in Mountain View Cemetery in Oakland. His widow survived him until August of 1906 when she died at the Fresno Hot Springs where she was visiting her widowed daughter. Dr. Tiffany, Coalinga's first pioneer physician, attended her last illness.

SOURCE: *Ash Tree Echo*, Volume III, No. 1, pp. 11-15.

to take the stage which was to start her on her journey back to her home in Los Angeles. Some one had roped her trunk in a tall pine tree. Finally "Mrs. Emil" said, "Boys, you have had your fun. Remember, you are holding up the U.S. mail."

Most historical places have their exciting moments of murders and fights and the Springs were no exception. Attending one of the dances were two young men from Warthan Canyon, both suitors for the hand of the same woman. After the dance, on their way down the canyon and not far below the Springs, one jealous lover waylaid the other, and shot and killed him. As for fights, they usually occurred in the kitchen of the hotel. In that era, the best and most available cooks were Chinese and as was common at the time, the Chinese belonged to different Tongs [see Chapter 11]. Several times when Kreyenhagens operated the Springs Tong wars would break out among the cooks. Butcher knives, cleavers, wooden potato mashers; any available utensil—would fly through the kitchen domain to the accompaniment of Chinese shouts and curses, and it would become necessary for some of the Kreyenhagens to stop the battle.

Northwest of Pleasant Valley was the Los Gatos Creek area, said to have been first settled by a man named Hays and other English-speaking people in 1872 or 1874. When Emil Kreyenhagen arrived in 1874 he said there were many Spanish-speaking families "in the mountains," meaning along the Three Creeks flowing into Pleasant Valley. Little is known of this area before 1900. It did obtain a sizable-enough population to form two school districts, the Lewis Creek on May 7, 1886, and the Los Gatos on February 4, 1891. The latter district was annexed to the Alcalde on April 5, 1899.

Eleven miles due north of Los Gatos Creek lies the Cantua Creek region, first made famous by Joaquin Murrieta's exploits, soothsayer/religious revivalist Mariana La Loca, and the discovery of the Cantua Creek Petrified Man (see Chapter 10 and 12:6, 12:7). The first permanent settlers in the area were John and Pedro Etchegoin, Frenchmen who raised sheep on Etchegoin Creek as early as 1868–70. The other early settler of note, Adolph Domengine, arrived a few years later. French by descent, he got his start in the sheep business by working for Miller and Lux. He eventually struck out on his own, running a large sheep ranch on Domengine Creek that passed to his children and still exists today.

Reference 12:5

## PLEASANT VALLEY, 1877

To Thomas H. Slaven, the efficient teacher of the Pleasant Valley school, we are indebted for the following facts relative to that vicinity, for which he will accept our thanks:

Warthen's Canyon (often erroneously spelled Walton and Waltham) is about twenty miles long, and lies nearly in a southeastern and northwesterly direction. It is situated in the southwestern part of Fresno county, and in the Coast Range mountains. The bottom lands of the valley in no place exceed a quarter of a mile in width. These lands are exceedingly fertile and are finely watered by the Alcalde creek which courses the entire length of this little valley, although in a few places it sinks, as is usually the case with most mountain streams.

The foothills on either side of the Canyon produce in abundance fine, nutritious, natural grasses, which afford valuable ranges for stock. They are also very well timbered with oak, especially in the upper portion of the canyon. Many of the settlers utilize the waters of the creek for irrigation purposes, only, however, on a small scale, simply for the nourishment of garden vegetables, fruit trees, vines, etc., raising stock, which consists mostly of cattle, sheep, swine and Angora goats, being their principal pursuits.

The climate of this part of the State is all that could be desired, especially for those having weak or diseased lungs, or suffering from rheumatic affections, and for the cure of the latter malady Rogers' Sulphur Springs, which are conveniently located, are unsurpassed.

Warthen's Canyon comprises a portion of the Pleasant Valley school district, and in it is located the school house, which is a neat and substantial little building, pleasantly situated on the east bank of the Alcalde, at the confluence therewith of one of its main tributaries. The schoolhouse is well furnished with maps, globes, blackboards, etc., and for the number of its volumes the district has the finest library of standard works in the county. Although the district numbers nearly a hundred census children, the attendance at school is not large (about 20) owing to the sparseness of the population. For the last half year the school has been under the charge of T. H. Slaven. The following is a statement of the aggregate percentage made by the pupils at the quarterly written examination, held on January 31st and February 1st and 2d, 1877. Owing to the patrons of the school being busily engaged in seeding, several of the larger boys were kept out of school to assist: Nannie Crump, 81; Marinda Smoot, 95; Jennie Barnes, 94; Dixie Smoot, 83; Nannie Rogers, 82; Fannie Barnes, 82; Lizzie Crump, 86; Mollie Smoot, 80; Victor Crump, 74; Robert Smoot, 83; Richard Rogers, 82.

The head of the Canyon, just over the Priest Valley mountain, is occupied as a stock range, which has been enclosed by the Vaughn Bros. These young men appear to be doing well, having large bands of cattle, swine and a few horses. The brother Sing., is however, like a good many others, becoming a little scared, and it is said he is, Christian like, now and then, soliloquizing a few prayers for rain. It is certainly much needed.

The range adjoining the Vaughn Bros., is occupied by J. G. Crump, Cox and Son. These settlers also have their range mostly substantially enclosed with good picket fences, and are thrifty and well doing stock men. Their herds consist chiefly of cattle, and a few sheep. This deserving, but unpretending firm, have been long in the stock business, formerly on King's River, and rumor has it that they have made not a little. The elder Cox is almost an octogenarian; still he reads intelligently his Bible and newspapers without the aid of spectacles. He is a good man and a consistent Democrat, having cast his first vote for General Andrew Jackson, and has been voting a "straight ticket" ever since.

To the southeast of the ranch of the last named persons, in that connection, lies that of the Smoot Bros.—now entirely owned by S. M. Smoot—his brother Wm. H. having disposed of his interest therein to him. . . .

The good people of this neighborhood had a grand Christmas assembly at the school house during the holidays, which was largely attended by the elite from a radius of miles and miles. The occasion will long be remembered as one of the pleasantest and happiest of the kind that ever took place in the Canyon.

SOURCE: *Fresno Weekly Expositor*, March 7, 1877.

*The only picture of Mariana in existence, this was taken on a tintype in 1860 and copied in 1976. (Copyrighted by Ruth Lucy Parra and L. R. Johnston, used with their permission.)*

By 1886 the Cantua region had grown enough to support a school district, organized on May 7; a post office of the same name was created on March 7, 1888. Unfortunately, the school district was merged with Lewis Creek's on May 9, 1888 (probably for low attendance), and the post office was decommissioned the following June 15. A new post office with the same name opened on March 19, 1890, but was merged with Huron's on January 25, 1892.

Additional residents of southwestern Fresno County, by 1870, were sheepmen Daniel Bartlett and Albion Baker; stock raisers Juan Zubiri and Pedro Idiart; Frenchmen Juan Legliese and Jacques Treshou, who lived on Zapato Creek; and the William B. Kell family of Canoas Creek.

Over a period of three decades, the economy of this region underwent a major shift. Although the traditional livelihoods of farming and stock raising remained, increasing numbers of businessmen, laborers and profiteers were attracted to the area's natural resources. Oil deposits in the Pleasant Valley area had long been known and utilized (see Chapter 3). Later pioneers used the substance for greasing cart and wagon wheels and building campfires.

By 1862 several men were mining petroleum in the area roughly nine miles north of Coalinga's site—where Oil City or Oilfields was later to rise. No drilling or derrick equipment was available, so "Coal Oil Tommy," Thomas Harvey, was reduced to digging pits and scooping out the substance. He claimed that the oil could be used as a good substitute for coal oil, hence his name. This was borne out in later years when some

Reference 12:6

## MARIANA LA LOCA

*A remarkable religious phenomenon occurred in the mid 1880s at Las Tres Piedras (Three Rocks) about twenty-five miles north of Coalinga. The event was described in a booklet, "Mariana La Loca, Prophetess of the Cantua and Alleged Spouse of Joaquin Murietta [sic]", published in 1970 by the Fresno City and County Historical Society. The following is a condensation of that book plus a previously unpublished incident in the later life of Mariana.*

Mariana Andrada was probably her true name when she arrived in California from Sonora, Mexico, at the age of 22 in late 1852 or 1853. She was known by many names but Mariana La Loca (Crazy Mariana) is the name she is best known by today.

An attractive girl, she was quickly caught up in a loose, fast life. Joaquin Murrieta was a popular figure around the dance halls that catered to Spanish-speaking customers, and she claimed to have wooed and won him as her husband in the later days of his career. There is no evidence to support this and it is known that later she offered to pay friends to confirm not only the story of her marriage,

but also that she had borne a son by Murrieta. The details of her life are sketchy, but it was believed that she worked in a fandango house in New Idria where many Spanish-speaking men were hired in the quicksilver mines, and in several communities in west Fresno County. Some were inclined to simply classify her as a prostitute while others called her a "housekeeper" for some of the sheepherders in the foothills around Coalinga.

In 1874, a posse searching for a criminal, Tiburcio Vasquez, south of Coalinga, was accompanied by a reporter for the *San Francisco Chronicle*. He met Mariana and after a drink or two of whiskey she confided to him the story of her life with Joaquin Murrieta. In a jealous rage, Joaquin had slashed her across the face, leaving a scar which she carried the rest of her life.

Although her "marriage" apparently was known within the Spanish-speaking community, the reporter's story in the *Chronicle* was the first public report of her involvement.

By 1879, Mariana was working near

Three Rocks, also known as Joaquin Rocks because it was near there that Murrieta supposedly engaged in his last gun battle with the rangers who claimed to have killed him. Mariana's life had taken a turn toward religion at that point, and it is believed that she began some type of revival preaching with a Catholic undertone in that year. Later she had the support of probably four people, Theodora Arredondo, Manual Amara, Juan Salgado or Silva, and one only known as Guadalupe. Her success during this period is not known but in 1882 she received an assist from an unusual source who certainly had no intention of helping her.

In the late fall of 1882, the fathers at Santa Clara College decided that information should be gathered about one of their former associates, Father Magin Catala, who was known as the holy man of Santa Clara. They petitioned the archbishop to appoint someone to compile testimony as to the sanctity of Father Magin's life, while witnesses were still living. The archbishop agreed and an investigator started interviewing all possible informants throughout Northern Califor-

268

nia, thereby making the name of Father Magin well known again. For Mariana, this revival of the memory of the departed holy man was perfectly timed. All she had to do to enhance her position as a powerful prophetess was to pretend that she was in touch with the spirit of Father Magin.

News of her preaching and prophesying and of her impersonation of Father Magin soon spread throughout the Spanish-speaking communities of the central valley. She was apparently well enough known so that "by May [1883] the Mexican section of nearly every town in the valley was deserted; people had all gone to Cantua to hear Mariana preach!"

The first public notice appeared in the *Fresno Daily Expositor* of April 30, 1883:

## THE END APPROACHING
## "LET THEM THAT BE IN JUDEA FLEE TO THE MOUNTAINS"

## AN IMMORTAL SPIRIT, 866 YEARS OLD, LABORED FOR THE GOOD OF HUMANITY

## PADRE MAHIN
## "I AM HE THAT LIVETH AND WAS DEAD: AND BEHOLD I AM ALIVE FOR EVERMORE"

*("Magin" is the correct spelling; "Mahin" is a phonetic spelling adopted by the* Expositor.*)*

The wonderful stories that are wafted here from the Coast Mountains, relative to the venerable priest who holds forth in a lonely valley near the Cantua, continue to excite attention, especially among the Mexican population, and many families of that nationality, as well as a number of Frenchmen and Portuguese, are abandoning their property and repairing thither, as they say, to remain until the end of time. A number of those who went over at the first bidding have returned, and have packed up their household goods, or are now doing so, preparatory to returning.

Pedro Lascelle, an intelligent Basque Frenchman, who was over with his wife to investigate matters, returned home last week, and packed up and started back last Saturday.

Wishing to gain some facts relative to the mysterious man of the mountains, an Expositor reporter interviewed Mr. Lascelle, but was unable, in consequence of the difficulty of conversing with him, he speaking very broken English, to gain as full particulars as desired. However, he ascertained that Mr. Lascelle had seen and conversed with the unknown being. He describes him as a wonderful man, possessing the power to call all who come by their proper names at sight; to heal the sick, and relieve the distressed. He has sent out word to all who want to be saved to go and see him, and if they believe on him they shall not die.

Who this wonderful being is Mr. Lascelle does not pretend to say, but he says others claim that his name is Father Mahin, a priest who was venerated for his righteousness, and who passed away from this earthly life and became an immortal spirit 866 years ago, and that he before visited the same section some 46 years ago.

He announces to the faithful that all mankind who do not respond to his invitation to locate in the Coast Mountains, and obey the commands of God, will be destroyed by fire and flood within three years. He says for them to abandon everything and come there and he will provide for them and take care of them. He has with him tablets of stone containing the laws of God engraved on them. These he brought from the shores of Galilee, they having been engraved by immortal hands. He asks no money, nor worldly goods. They are as mere dross to him. His wants are supplied by hands unseen. One of the young Mexican ladies who went over declares she saw the Virgin Mary pass from the presence of the holy man, and disappear in the solid rock.

It is related by Mr. Lascelle that a Portuguese who did not at first believe, has, on further investigation, become so thoroughly convinced that the padre is a supernatural being, and that he truthfully foretells the end of time, that he has sent for all of his relatives, now residing in Portugal, to come there and be saved. A bedridden woman has by his magic touch been restored to health and youthfulness.

We have tried not to elaborate on this story, but have given the plain statements of those who have been over there. Who the man is that is pretending to be immortal, and what is his real object, is not for us to say, but certain it is, someone has stirred up quite a commotion. Were the distance not so great, we would endeavor to give a more elaborate statement of the matter, by sending a reporter there, but the cost would be too great.

Mr. Lascelle says that people call him a fool, but he has seen enough to satisfy him that it is good to be in the presence of the great prophet. He has left his home and property here in town, and says he has confidence that it will be protected by a higher power during his absence.

On May 2 the paper reported:

About ten wagon loads of people have left this section (Fresno County) during the past week, for the purpose of seeing the Cantua Saint, and more will start today.

Two days later another brief notice said:

We learn that the Cantua Prophet has announced to his hearers that a certain mountain in the neighborhood of where he is will soon be transformed into a grand cathedral, with minarets, spires, etc., and that the rock is already hollowed out for the purpose.

From a reading of the above articles it is evident that Mariana was successfully maintaining her position as the "voice" of the deceased Father Magin, and either by ventriloquism, or by making use of the voices of one or more of the men who were her accomplices, she was able to persuade her deluded followers that "Father Magin," or the "Cantua Prophet," was actually still alive within the hollow parts of the Three Rocks, and would and could communicate with them, at least through Mariana.

Lascelle returned a week later and reported that on May 16 they were going to have a great feast and "upon that occasion he will be visible to all who believe and invisible to those that do not. The apostles, the Virgin Mary, and other celebrities are honored to be present."

On May 13 it was reported that the town of Borden was almost deserted as 60 of the Spanish population had left to attend the feast. One man "had sold his house for $10; another a watch worth $64 for $20; all were perfectly wild on the subject."

The newspaper changed its mind and sent a reporter for the event of the 16th but the presence of him and other "unbelievers" was given by the prophet as an excuse for an indefinite postponement of the great festival. The reporter was told when seeking admittance that only members of the Latin race were eligible for salvation by the venerable padre. He found about 500 men, women and children encamped in a secluded valley along a creek that flows past what is known as Joaquin's Lookout. They were living in a primitive style in tents, in brush houses and in the open air as best they could. His report continued:

The Prophet himself is invisible to all save a few of the elect, and he makes all communications to them through his priest or from the rocks—his voice appearing to come forth from the solid stone. The priest who conducts the worship is described as a man of small stature, who dresses in priestly robes, whose hair and beard are very long, and as white as snow. . . . Joaquin's widow— old Mariana—is one of the leaders, and seems to be a trusted representative of the immortal Padre.

. . . Mariana, Joaquin's widow, received every one with open arms, crying and praying alternately; she said, "brothers and sisters, I am here to receive you all with my arms open, by the order of Padre Mahin and the power of the Almighty. Sisters and brothers, this world is coming to an end, and I am here to save you all from the blazes of hell." The men and women gathered around her, begging and crying, praying to be saved. She said, "Brothers and sisters, all those who have appeared before me this 16th day of May shall see the new and coming world. And you shall have salvation after death, but that will be hundreds of years after you enter the new and coming world. You shall never grow any older, nor can you estimate the great length of time that you will live in the new world."

She then said that the San Joaquin River and Buena Vista lake would flood this valley and drown all that are in it. She said that the Pope of Rome was hid in the temple with Father Mahin.

[The reporter described some of the rituals and concluded:]

Early next morning Mariana was out again, crying and praying, and announced that the Almighty had called upon her and she was going to heaven at once. The others begged her not to go, but she said when she was called she had to obey. But when I left she was still there, waiting for her wings to grow so she could fly to heaven, but I am afraid she will never get there. She is better suited for the Stockton Asylum than for heaven.

Subsequent reports from Cantua indicated that life continued much as it had in the past after the May 16th postponement.

A reader of the *Expositor* who lived in Nevada sent a copy of the first article to the archbishop and asked him for guidance. The archbishop responded in a letter in the diocesan newspaper, the *Monitor*, on May 30 branding the whole affair as a "fraud, an imposition and a witchcraft." The *Expositor* quickly picked up the story and reprinted his condemnation but if it had any impact on the Spanish-speaking population is not known. However, on July 10 the *Expositor* reported that things were not going as smoothly as they had previously and that Mariana had burned down the building that had been reserved for counseling and prophetic utterances and had "lit out" with some $1,500 of community funds. She soon returned, however, and rallied those who still remained faithful to her preaching and retained a nucleus of devoted followers for a period of nearly two more years. She consistently reminded them that Father Magin had predicted the end of the world "within the next three years" and that only those who remained faithful would be saved.

Among the remaining families, the Chevoya family was one of the most loyal. A neighbor, Anderson Akers, told newsmen the senior Chevoya had a nice herd of cattle until he fell under the spell of the Loca Mariana. Then for about three months he killed a beef every day to feed the people at the rocks and sold nearly all the rest of his herd to get money for Mariana. One of Chevoya's daughters married a Delfino Corona who lived nearby and was skeptical of Mariana and her preaching. Mariana apparently felt threatened and prophesied that one of the family would die within a few days. She offered to allow Senora Chevoya to make a choice of which of the three would die. The old lady, torn between her loyalties, finally decided that the grandchild could "go to the angels."

Corona had to make a trip to Fresno on business and when he returned on July 5 he insisted that his wife and child leave the encampment and return to their home a few miles to the north. Mariana reminded him of her prophecy. As they departed, Mariana called out to them that they could start for home but would come back crying. They had been on the road only about a half an hour when the baby became violently ill and

died before they could get back to the camp. The family concluded that Mariana had in some way managed to poison the child before their departure and therefore could predict his death.

The coroner considered the circumstances of the child's death sufficient grounds for issuance of a warrant for Mariana's arrest. Deputy sheriffs arrested Mariana and also brought back the child's stomach for further chemical analysis. Mariana remained in jail and the case was set for hearing three times with the prosecution each time asking that it be postponed because of lack of evidence. No report was ever released as to the contents of the stomach and other details of the investigation were not revealed, but the district attorney released Mariana, apparently for lack of evidence.

There is no further record of her ever again preaching and she returned to Coalinga to continue a life such as she had lived prior to 1879.

Source of preceding: Wood, Dr. Raymund F., "Mariana La Loca, Prophetess of the Cantua and Alleged Spouse of Joaquin Murrieta," Fresno City and County Historical Society, 1970. ($2.50)

It was in the Coalinga area that an episode occurred which has not been previously reported. Mariana La Loca also worked as a cook in large camps of farmworkers and maintained a friendly relationship with the local citizens.

In 1899 she was reportedly living with a sheepherder south of Coalinga, just as she had often done in her younger years. As they drank together one evening, talk turned to an acquaintance who owned a large herd of sheep and who was scheduled to receive a substantial payment for a recent sale. They decided that they should go up and celebrate his good fortune with him.

Details are lacking, but before long the visit was cut short when the sheep owner was murdered, hacked up by a common kitchen knife.

When neighbors heard of his death, they got together to go search for his murderers. The trail led to Mariana and her unnamed companion, who were found in Los Jacalitos Canyon. Being law-abiding people, the "posse" members decided that a proper trial should be held before a jury, which they thereupon appointed from among their members. Needless to say, no report of the trial was kept but one member of the jury was impressed by the fact that Mariana several times leaned over and told her companion, in Spanish, "Be a man, die for the woman you love."

She must have prevailed because she went free and he was hanged from a convenient cottonwood tree at the foot of a canyon known thereafter as Deadman Canyon.

In October 1899, a body was discovered by a Juan Camino who reported it to the authorities. Deputy sheriffs J. N. Atkisson, H. G. McCuetchen, and F. R. Newcome went out to pick up the remains. The coro-

ner, G. L. Long, empaneled a jury on October 20 to examine the case of the unknown dead man. The jury was told that the body had been there for about four months and was that of a man of fifty or more who was about five feet ten inches tall. The back had separated in two places and the head was some distance from the body and the body was separated at the waist. The victim's purse was twenty feet from the body with $5.05 in it, and his personal effects, a knife, a book, toothbrush, soap and a water can, were scattered over a wide area. The jury held that the deceased was two miles from water and had obviously died of thirst.

This account has been constructed of the known facts plus local accepted knowledge in the absence of likely alternatives. Although the coroner's records are available for that period, the record of the crimes is not and the murdered man has not been identified. It is possible that he could have been killed in nearby Monterey or Kings County which is only two to three miles from the place where the murderer was captured.

Mariana later lived in Hanford, and in April of 1902 was known to be living with a woodcutter by the name of Gabriel near Laton on the Kings River.

On Saturday, April 12, 1902, she was struck and killed by a Santa Fe train, the California Limited, on its way to Los Angeles. The story of the circumstances of her death vary somewhat. The newspaper and Dr. Wood's book say simply that she was crossing the railroad tracks. At the coroner's inquest, the report says "the engineer said that he had no idea that the woman would try to cross the track, hence he made no attempt to stop or slacken the speed of the train; but to his surprise, when the train was near the crossing, she stepped on the track and in a moment the train struck her."

Friends in Coalinga received the story that she had been drinking heavily and went up the railroad track with a bottle in one hand and with her other fist clenched, challenging the train engine to a duel, which she obviously lost. The coroner's report also said that a bottle of wine was found near her and it was supposed that she was intoxicated.

The jurors found "that her true name was Ana Andrada, a native of Mexico, aged about 70 years; that she came to her death on the 12th of April 1902 from being struck by engine Number 4 on the Santa Fe Railroad and that the cause was unavoidable on the part of the railroad officials."

Gabriel was apparently a devoted companion of Mariana. The newspaper reported when they got to Hanford with the body he was "in great distress of mind, so much so that he could be heard for a block." People who knew them said that she was deranged in mind but was able to cook the old man's meals.

wells produced oil of such a low viscosity it could be used, unrefined, as gasoline. Near the Oil City site, and between Warthan and White creeks, the brothers Josiah, John and William Worswick dug for oil along with "Coal Oil Tommy." Virtually unusable at the time, the substance was sold locally as axle grease.

As the 1860s progressed and more uses were developed for petroleum—to make dyes and artificial flowers, among other things—more Fresno County pioneers entered the business. When Frank Dusy, John Clark and Charles Strivens hunted for antelope near Vallecitos Canyon in 1864, they found large oil seepages and decided to file homestead claims there on December 21. Soon afterward Dusy and Clark, along with W. A. Porter, helped form the San Joaquin Petroleum Company and transferred their oil rights to that corporation. (What happened to Strivens at this point is unknown. He most likely sold out to the company.)

The San Joaquin, created by late January 1865, was soon joined by several others. February 18 notices in the *Mariposa Gazette* indicated that the Pacific and Occidental petroleum companies had been formed, with Howard A. Martin and Fred M. Bennett as their respective secretaries. The Pacific company had its headquarters in Fresno County, while the Occidental's bases were at Princeton and Mount Bullion, both in

Mariposa County, at different times. The February 4, 1865, issue of the *Fresno Times* noted that another company had come into existence. Known as the Elk Horn, it was capitalized at $160,000 (1,600 shares offered at $100 each), with its main offices located at Mariposa. Ralph T. Williams, S. B. Alison and J. R. Coats were elected as its first trustees.

Corporate claims were supplemented by individual and homestead filings on the most desirable oil properties. The title and ownership situation changed daily, which led to arguments and claim jumping. A few unfortunates were chased off their lands altogether. It became necessary to form an Elk Horn district on January 13, 1865, "for the purpose of forming mining rules and regulations," although it seems to have had little impact on the over-excitement of the times. Meeting at John Chidester's California Ranch, oilmen Ralph Williams, Galen Clark (famed Yosemite pioneer), M. T. Brady, Cuthbert Burrell and others adopted the following resolutions:

1. This district shall commence at the Cantour [Cantua] Canon, and running in an easterly direction to the line of Tulare County, a distance of about forty miles in length, and about thirty in width, including the Pacheco Range of mountains in this District...
2. A claim on a Petroleum vein or lode shall be one thousand feet in length, and four hundred and fifty feet

Reference 12:7

# FRESNO COUNTY'S PETRIFIED PEOPLE
## WILLIAM RINTOUL

Some three years after the San Joaquin mine began, a mind-boggling discovery occurred on the bank of Cantua Creek, twenty miles to the north. It provided coal miners, as well as others, with an engrossing topic of conversation. Two farmers, S. L. Packwood and R. L. Barrett, discovered a petrified man. Not a normal-sized man, but a giant one, whose petrified remains seemingly lent credence to the oft-pronounced theory of the day that giants had once walked the land.

The *Fresno [Daily Evening] Expositor* of Dec. 17, 1890, after asking in its headline, "Is It Genuine?", went on to make a strong case for the petrified man, stating, "We are ready to accept theories when there is foundation to sustain them."

The newspaper explained that the Cantua man, as the petrified man quickly became known, was not an actual petrification, but a "calcareous deposit formed in a cavity which previously contained human remains." The newspaper explained that the body had been buried thousands of years before in a dry sand place over which water flowed, packing the sand tightly around the body. "Then there followed a long dry spell of perhaps hundreds of years. This dessicated the body, which crumbled to dust. And after the cavity was formed, the rain came and washed in a

quantity of lime and sand which became a kind of cement which hardened into the perfect likeness of the man whose body was buried."

And what a man he had been. The stone man was seven feet tall, weighed 500 pounds and had, according to the newspaper, "the classic features of a Greek god."

Peter and M. J. Donahoo, Fresno business men, purchased the stone man from Packwood and Barrett for an undisclosed sum, intending, the newspaper said, to exhibit "Cantua man" on the Pacific Coast and in the east.

Before the Donahoos could cash in on their purchase, they were threatened by competition. Soon after the first find, there was another discovery. This one was a petrified woman, found by Presley Bozeman, Jr., and J. W. Livermore in Jacalitos Canyon, only a few miles south of [Coalinga]. The petrified body was placed on the train for shipment to Fresno. A one-column advertisement appeared in the *Expositor*, preparing Fresno for the arrival of the Petrified Woman, whom, the advertisement stated, would be exhibited for only a few days. Critics and scientists, in that order, were especially invited to the showing. Bozeman and Livermore, apparently having no desire to enter the show world themselves, quickly

traded the Petrified Woman to a Selma man for a livery stable. The Selma man, it was reported, planned to take the Petrified Woman east for exhibition. Before he could cash in, he too was undercut by the discovery of yet another petrified specimen, this one a petrified boy who was found at Los Gatos Creek, between the discovery sites of the Cantua man and the Petrified Woman. This discovery completed the family trio of giants who had once roamed the land, but it also ruined the business. The leg of the boy, roughly handled in shipment, broke off, and it was abundantly evident that the boy had been molded of plaster of Paris. The accident brought the Petrified Woman under investigation with a hammer and chisel, and she was found to be made of the same substance. The Selma livery owner turned show business entrepreneur demanded, and got back, his livery stable, and the rash of discoveries of petrified giants ceased as abruptly as it had begun, allowing men to get on with more productive pursuits, such as the development of the coal industry and the building of the community of Coaling A, also known as Coalinga.

271

on each side of the vein or lode. The discoverer being entitled to two claims.

3. A claim on gold, silver, quicksilver, copper or other mineral veins shall be five hundred feet in length, and one hundred and fifty on each side.

4. All persons shall hold one claim on as many different springs or holes as they may locate.

5. All persons holding claims in this District, shall be entitled to wood and water necessary for working their claims.

6. All claims shall be recorded in this District within thirty days after discovery, and a written notice shall be posted on said claim at the time of discovery or location.

7. All parties holding claims in this District shall do three days' work on each vein every six months.

[Resolutions 8 and 9 concerned the appointment of the district's recorder, and publication of the resolutions.]

Notable among the claims filed at this time were those of Frederick Law Olmsted, Talleyrand Choisser (who sold his to a New York company for $20,000), William Ashburner, E. O. Darling, J. P. Ostrom and Frank P. Bennett, brother of Fred M. Bennett. A report from Firebaugh's Ferry in the March 22, 1865, *Fresno Times* described the scene:

People flock thither by hundreds. Even now, while I am indicting this epistle, a swarm is passing by the house, like unto a battalion of soldiers—some in wagons, some on horse and muleback, and many on foot, all bound for the land of petroleum. Looking up the San Joaquin River, toward Fresno City, at any time of the day, you can see squads of two, four and six, who come from thk [sic] remote counties . . . That part of Fresno County will shortly be thickly populated, and I am fearful that if the oil excitement does not soon abute [sic], there will be ere long a great many applications for admittance to the insane asylum at Stockton.

The writer's fears were groundless. Lack of transportation facilities discouraged these pioneers from advancing far into their schemes. With no railroad, and river transportation hampered by low water (1865, like many years, was dry), no great quantities of oil could be taken out of Fresno County profitably. The largest known shipment was a mere fifteen casks to San Francisco, according to the *Los Angeles Tri-Weekly News* of August 15.

Before good transportation finally came to southwestern Fresno County, some other hands tried their luck in the oil business there. The Pacific Development Company drilled a 400-foot test well at the Oil City site—the first county oil well—in 1867, under Caleb Strong Merrill's direction. Presumably manufactured for use in the east, the rig used to drill the well had come around Cape Horn and was brought down from Stockton in three wagons.

Reference 12:8

# ABC'S AND OIL
### From Letters of Dora McWhorter Banta

The earliest recollections I have of my father are of his many experiments with petroleum in seeking the best way to refine the heavy oils produced here in the San Joaquin Valley. We were then living on a large wheat ranch on what is known as the West Side. We were located a considerable distance west of Selma, and our nearest neighbor was *miles* away. We were pioneers in the fullest sense of the word.

I can still remember the long, winding road leading up to our ranch. It seemed to stretch for miles and miles, one end was at our ranch and the other seemed to finally end in a bright, golden sea. Wagons and horses coming in from a distance appeared to be suspended in the air, or floating along on water. This was my first experience with a "mirage," which mother fully explained to me. Even today, whenever I see a mirage, my mind goes back to that old ranch and to my father's experiments there. . . .

My father and brother, Horace, made trips to the vicinity of Coalinga, bringing back barrels and five gallon oil cans full of very thick, black crude oil. Soon there were cans and cans of it stored under the house, that being the only place, except the barn, where there was a storage place. The idea seemed to be that oil and hay in close prox-

imity would constitute a too serious fire hazard.

I began to hear talk of some of the things for which this ugly black stuff might be good. There were several vehicles on the place: two or three wagons for heavy hauling, a "spring" wagon for hauling lighter loads from town, a "buck board," two buggies, a cart or two, and a windmill, all needing grease—and town forty-five miles away. However, thick as this heavy black stuff was, it was too thin for the purpose. It must be boiled down to a proper consistency—there was the answer!

A two-burner kerosene stove was just the thing. Next a nice cool spot. Being July, it was a little too hot for comfort in the sun, besides a stray breeze might come along and put out the fire. The living room seemed a likely location. The stove was placed in the middle of the room in front of a nice big window and with all the doors open for comfort who could ask for a more pleasant laboratory.

A five gallon oil can about one fourth full of the crude was soon bubbling away on top of the stove with vapors floating away on the desert air. It was fascinating. I watched father's beaming face as he noted the mixture really was boiling down thicker and

thicker. But not thick enough. The vapors had about stopped coming. If he could only keep it boiling a little longer, he would surely have axle-grease! Ah! A little water might help.

I had been sitting in a little willow rocking chair before the open door, undressing my little brother for bed. When I saw that water go in, I grabbed that baby tight in my arms and fled by the front door, not a second too soon. A flame the size of the door followed us out, and the window seemed to shoot out an equal blaze. I shrieked to father to come. With relief I found him not more than a step behind me.

Mother had been in the kitchen just back of the living room washing up the "milk" things. She took in the situation, grabbed her dishcloth, and made a speedy getaway out the back door. The two little girls were outside playing and big brother was feeding the stock, so all the family were safe. Mother hugged her baby to her breast. The dishcloth was all we saved from our little six-room ranch house.

At the time of the fire we were told to go behind the barn for safety and protection, as we had a number of loaded guns in the house and the heat was causing them to explode the cartridges and the bullets were flying in

More than a decade later "Coal Oil Tommy," still plying the fields in 1878, dug a new well near Merrill's location. His partners in this venture were Thomas Creighton and Hugh Mooney of Tulare County. Hugo Kreyenhagen, who transported the drilling equipment for the men, later said that "[oil] was either all on the surface or so deep they couldn't reach it. They could only go about ninety feet deep. It was a light, horse-powered rig with a derrick about thirty feet high."

Almost everyone forgot about west side oil until 1890, when Milton McWhorter (see 12:8) began developing the Oil City area. A founder of the Sunset Irrigation District (see Chapter 15), McWhorter needed an inexpensive fuel to run the proposed district's pumps. Learning that crude oil was readily available in the southwestern county hills, he began exploratory drilling in the summer of 1890. "I adapted a hand-operated water [well-drilling] rig to a horsepower," he said later. " . . . My drilling rig operated with an old stationary thresher 'horse-power' which I had rigged up with a tumbler and gears to operate a rotary head, turning 2-inch pipe on top of a kind of auger, like a posthole auger. I did not have the present idea of running water down into the hole [while drilling], but

there was water in the well, and I occasionally worked the auger up and down to make a thin batter of the tailings. Then I bailed it out."

McWhorter's first well, on Salt Creek in the Cantua country, produced nothing. A little later, he was told that a Los Angeles company had drilled a producing well on the Oil City site about 1888. The only problem was that more salt water than oil gushed out of it. McWhorter decided to try the site anyway. He brought in a fifteen-barrel-a-day well after drilling to 300 feet—apparently without the water problem. McWhorter was so encouraged that he set up a $5,000 refinery to make kerosene. Unfortunately, it did not work ("it would smoke like fury and the candle power was low," he said later). He was soon balancing his time between the oil fields and the University of California, studying chemistry and trying to make the oil stop smoldering.

In the meantime, a host of newcomers began Oil City's formal development. William Youle (who named the place) started drilling for the Puente Oil Company of Los Angeles soon after McWhorter's discovery. A Fresno Oil Company was incorporated in 1890 with a capital stock of $3 million, with George Schwinn, Moritz Simon, Edward Vogelsang of Huron, and

all directions. However, we all escaped injury. Mother's sewing machine was burned, along with everything we had. As it could not be replaced, mother did all of our family sewing by hand for several years. . . .

About a month later we were again living at the ranch. In those short thirty days father had bought and moved three little cabins from the claims of settlers who had "proved up" and no longer needed the buildings. . . .

Again there were cans and barrels of crude oil on hand—this time stored in a shed a safe distance from the house.

Now, in addition to axle-grease, we needed light and fuel, and of course, many other things. Necessity being the mother of invention, a collection of pipes, bolts, wire, and what have you, made its appearance in the shed. The shed was now the laboratory. The men hardly took time to eat. Gradually their excitement was communicated to mother and us girls, busy as we were, settling in the new home. At a supposedly safe distance, we also watched and waited with bated breath as that evil smelling black stuff poured into the little still and came out miraculously clear.

There was a general family rejoicing when the first lampful of kerosene gave forth a light that seemed to us brighter than the sun, moon, and stars, all rolled into one. I shall have to admit that this first "vintage" smoked a little, but it did not cloud our ardor. . . .

Fire or possible accidents were of course our chief concern. Sure enough, that summer the little refinery did burn down, destroying the equipment which had been so laboriously assembled. Courageously another was built. And another and another, down through the years.

My youthful mind could not comprehend all of these things. All I knew was the toil, the sleepless nights, the privations suffered by our family in order that father might put the slender means at our disposal into this business and his experiments, so that these discoveries could be made which would mean so much to the commercial and scientific world. Later I learned how important and valuable his discoveries were to science and to the oil business in general. . . .

In addition to experimenting with oil, father drilled a number of oil wells. I can remember the period of "spudding in" and setting up the derrick and getting the standard tools to working. The drillers would, now and then, let me put my hands on the cable as it worked the bit up and down, and this made me feel grown-up. Sometimes I rode a horse round and round the rig, to furnish power for the drilling. Those were the days before gas engines were very much in use. Now it would be quite a sight anywhere to see horse-power used in connection with drilling.

My sister and I rode our horses to school every day. We had to travel several miles to Coalinga. On these trips we often saw wildcats and coyotes. Badgers would peek out of their holes on the sides of the canyon as we passed. My sister and I could ride any of the horses we had. Father would say that he could scarcely tell that anyone was on the horse until we came quite near, for I was so small.

We would mount and dismount by catching hold of the tail of the horse, stepping up on the joint of the hind leg, then scramble up the rear. We often ran home by holding to the tails of the horses and letting them pull

us. Often we saw large tarantulas and lizards by the way, but we were never afraid unless we saw a rattlesnake. Sometimes a skunk would come quite close to us and circle around, getting a little closer each time, until we could stand it no longer, then we would get onto our horses and scurry home.

The house we lived in after the fire, was built near the natural asphaltum deposits, and as I look back at it now, it seems that there were great stretches of this oil seepage which had become hardened with the heat of a blistering summer sun. It did not seem to melt very much. My dolls and toys had all been burned, so I used my ingenuity and fashioned my dolls of this asphaltum. I would mold and shape them when the material was warm and somewhat pliable, and then put them in a cool place to harden. They served their purpose, and I was very happy with them and with the animals and things I made to amuse myself.

Prospectors had dug many holes and pits over this oil territory, and the black, thick, viscuous oil would seep in until they were filled and running over. We never knew just how deep these places were, and we children had a fear that we might fall into them and not be able to get out again. We were not very strong, and the men and grownups were not always near enough to be called upon for help. Sheep herders would often bring their flocks by that way and did not seem to mind the dangers of these pits.

SOURCE: Edited by Frank F. Latta in *Black Gold in the Joaquin*. Caldwell, Idaho: The Caxton Printers, Ltd., 1949, pp. 154–59.

D. A. McDougald, Charles Parisot and Edward Lynch of Fresno as directors. After drilling a well ten miles north of Huron, this company hit oil at a mere eight feet. "Samples were brought to this city and pronounced by experts to be of first class quality," said the *Fresno Morning Republican*.

The San Francisco firm of Dietz and Company located several claims in this new territory, and commenced exploration activities. Joining them in July 1891 were two Los Angeles oilmen named Pierce and Tauber, who drilled a 267-foot well that outproduced McWhorter's. The Standard Oil Company was also busy drilling wells, and before the end of 1891 the Union and Coast Range oil companies of Los Angeles had set up shop. By November the Puente company had embarked on a particularly ambitious project. A steam engine and boiler rig was being used to go down deep, as much as 2,000 feet when necessary. In the next year the company had three wells in production, yielding ten to forty barrels of oil daily.

Most of the early companies did not overwhelm McWhorter's initial success. The Coast Range had a well with a windmill pump that yielded ten barrels a day, and a 400-foot Puente company well was slightly less productive at nine barrels a day. This lack of sensational production, together with the refinery problems McWhorter was trying to resolve, stymied Oil City's progress. Five oil wells were capped in 1893; the Puente company pulled out at about the same time, and reports of new discoveries and ventures virtually ceased until 1895.

Everything changed in that year. Plans were made to drill deeper wells, which would yield more pressure and output. McWhorter eliminated the smoking problem by boiling sulphur out of the oil and filtering the residue through water and soda ash lye. The resulting fuel was good enough to use in the Fresno Gas Company's gas-generating system. (A previous try with unrefined, sooty crude left customers up in arms, and had to be discontinued hastily!) McWhorter also had managed to make good axle grease from oil deposits two miles west of Coalinga (as A. Barieau of Selma was doing at the time), and was manufacturing lacquers and paints from petroleum by-products. Now Oil City was ready for an unrestrained boom.

The Producers and Consumers Oil Company of Selma, which began drilling in October 1895, sank two 695- and 700-foot wells for a fifteen- to twenty-barrel daily output. Frank Barrett, James McClurg and H. H. Welsh of Selma founded this company, with the help of a rig brought in by Los Angeles oilmen Charles A. Canfield and Joseph H. Chanslor. The latter two men, who had been down on their luck, resuscitated their fortunes by staying at Oil City and starting their own operations there in 1896. At different times their partners there were a Dr. H. Hayward, a man named Cannon and E. L. Doheny, the last eventually becoming Southern California's most noted oilman. A. J. Waltman, later of Bakersfield, reminisced that "there was no trouble in bringing in the Chanslor and Canfield well. I put in the pump, got everything under control and at almost the first revolution it began flowing."

Within a short time Chanslor and Canfield had wells 500 and 600 feet deep and a new concern, the Home Oil Company of Selma, had an 890-foot producing well. By July eight wells were in production, approximately forty men were working at Oil City, and the combined daily output of the wells was 6,500 gallons. "No pumping is necessary, an agitator—simply a rod run down into the well to stir up the gas—is all that is needed to cause the well to spout and force the oil into the [storage] tanks, which stand from ten to sixteen feet above the surface of the ground," said the October 21, 1896, *Fresno Daily Evening Expositor*.

New oil companies were sprouting at almost a daily rate. On March 13, 1896, the San Joaquin Oil and Fuel Company was incorporated. Among its directors were ex-Ohio governor James E. Campbell and James L. McLean, "a well-known journalist of Winfield, West Virginia," along with Frank Barrett and James McClurg of Selma and Judge Milus King Harris of Fresno. The Pleasant Valley Oil Company, whose main holdings were three miles west of Alcalde, was also formed about this time with Judge William D. Crichton as its president.

McWhorter was encouraged enough to start a new refinery, the Sunset Oil Refining Company, in Fresno. He described it thus:

> Our refinery . . . stands on an acre of ground and cost $1000 to build. The machinery and plant will cost another $2000. Our capacity will be about $1500 worth of crude oil per day, which will be more than half the product of the oil fields at the present time. The refinery is ready to begin business. We have on the spot one 6000-gallon tank, one 5000, one 3000 and one 2500 for both crude and refined oil . . . We propose to make kerosene that will stand the 120-degree fire test. Gasoline is about 10 per cent of the distillate. The residuum consists of lubricating oils of different grades. Nothing is lost.

Amid the great good fortune, disaster hit in August. Secretary of the Interior David R. Francis declared all previous petroleum claims in the country invalid, and threw the lands open to homesteaders. Many area landowners were ruined as hordes of legitimate claim jumpers flocked to Oil City. Amazingly, little or no violence resulted. "People are still coming into the district land office in Visalia for the purpose of filing homesteads on oil lands," said the November 2 *Fresno Daily Evening Expositor*. "Some of the persons are the original locators of the claims, but a majority are interlopers."

The Producers and Consumers company lost all but 160 acres of its holdings, which were leased subsequently to Chanslor and Canfield. A civil engineer for the San Francisco and San Joaquin Valley Railroad, W. J. Weems, lost several of his claims but "proceeded to the oilfields and located my most valuable claims on a homestead . . . I am out $700, which sum I can ill afford to lose." McWhorter's best claims were eaten up by greedy others as well, yet he did not lose his enthusiasm. In December he, Creighton, McClurg and J. Miner of Fresno formed a new company, which purchased 1,600 acres for oil development in the Alcalde area.

In 1897 Chanslor and Canfield were the dominant forces at Oil City. By July the men had opened eleven wells on their property, one of which had a 900-foot depth. "The first day, the natural flow[of the well] was eighty barrels," said the July 13, 1897, *Fresno Daily Evening Expositor*. "This has increased until it is now 120 barrels a day. By pumping, 160 barrels can be obtained from the well." Twenty miles of pipeline, which had been laid to Coalinga and a railroad junction east of it, made oil transfer easy—and inexpensive. Before long the men were making $1,000 a day apiece. It was a far cry from the time they first entered Oil City, flat broke.

The magic touch held for Chanslor and Canfield in 1898. On April 24 they made their best strike ever, a 300-barrel-a-day well. "When the flow was struck the oil came rushing up with such force that it spurted 100 feet into the air," said the *Fresno Morning Republican*. "On Friday and Saturday persons from miles around came to see the gusher. Workmen endeavored to control the stream, but were only partially successful . . . This is the fifteenth flowing well in the district, and until it was struck the[district] output was between 400 and 500 barrels a day." Incredibly, this single-well figure was superseded later in the year, when the Canfield Well No. 2 began producing 700 barrels a day at a 1,500-foot depth. The Home Oil Company's Blue Goose well, after its initial strike on January 21, 1899, chalked up a startling 1,000 barrels a day.

It was during these times of high excitement that Chanslor and Canfield (now operating as the Coalinga Oil Company), along with the Producers and Consumers and Home oil companies, formed a cartel to control crude prices. A board of representatives from each company was set up to fix a uniform price and modify it when needed, with all sales to be made through a single agent. The cartel was formed in April 1898, and the next month a new oil company—the New York—was incorporated, as a venture of Selma oilman Frank Barrett, with L. L. Cory of Fresno as its president.

Some other companies were having less luck. A group of Fresno investors formed the Commercial

Reference 12:9

## THE WEALTHIEST TOWN PER CAPITA IN FRESNO COUNTY: OIL CITY, 1899
### ORLANDO BARTON

Sixty miles west and seven miles south of Visalia is Oil City. It is situated on a point where a spur of the Coast Range runs down to the plains to the southeast. This spur belongs to the same upheaval as the Kettleman Hills. The Pulvidero [*sic*] and the Los Gatos Creeks cut it at right angles and prevent it from forming a continuous ridge to the latter.

The entrance to the canyon in which the town is situated is from the south. The first thing to attract the traveler's attention is the white cliff that at that distance looks like a cloud, where Marcus Lavelle many years ago commenced to mine for gypsum, and so laid the foundation for the town.

Above the line of the gypsum the road follows a narrow, tortuous canyon, barely wide enough for wagons to pass each other. A strong odor of kerosene is wafted on the wind long before the town is reached. Rivulets of oil and water run down the side canyons or tumble over the bluffs into the road. They are the pumping of the 6 wells that are being bored.

A steep pull and the traveler comes out on a mesa covered with the soft purple soil so characteristic of the oil belt. Around is the town. Not many houses, perhaps two dozen. Twenty four derricks are in sight, mostly standing over yielding wells, for the derrick is not removed from a yielding well. The roar of a gusher, 30 rods to the southeast, sounds like a violent rainstorm. Close to the gusher is another flowing well of almost equal capacity.

Five or six wells flow, from the remainder oil is pumped. A huge eccentric wheel, high above the ground, run by a 25 horsepower gasoline engine, whirls continually round. To the periphery of a loose rim of this wheel are hooked the steel cables that run the pumps of all the wells. The gas for the engine is furnished by the wells themselves.

The gusher is southeast of the other wells. Further in that direction runs a row of derricks, showing where new wells are being bored. The derricks are mostly 64 feet high. Their timbers are saturated with oil. It was shot against them when oil was first struck in the well beneath.

Notices on every hand warn the public against smoking in the vicinity. This is a necessary regulation. A few months past one of the derricks caught fire and burned to death a man who was up in the rigging.

The most violent Socialist could not find fault with the regulations existing between laborer and employer in this town. The employer no doubt pays his help well. The employees appear to be willing to do everything with their hands or their mouths that the interest of their employers requires.

Now it is the interest of the well owner to keep from the public a knowledge of how deep the well is, the amount of the flow, and more particularly the depth of any new well he may be sinking. An impertinent public is always asking questions on these very points. The manner in which owners and laborers parry these questions, while it may strain the decalogue almost to the breaking point, is excusable on the ground that it is none of the public business. But it is very vexatious to a newspaper man in quest of information for the benefit of the readers he represents.

Counting the oil tanks that come out of Coalinga on the railroad every day, I concluded that the daily average is about 12. An oil tank holds 155 barrels. This would show the daily output of oil to be 1,860 barrels. I have heard that the oil sells for $1.25 per barrel at the wells. Is there any other town of 40 inhabitants in this or any other state that can show a money making record like this?

SOURCE: Edited by Frank F. Latta in *Black Gold in the Joaquin*. Caldwell, Idaho: The Caxton Printers, Ltd., 1949, pp. 217–18.

*The hotel and bath house at Fresno Hot Springs in the late 1890s—a social center as well as a spa. (See page 267.)*

*"Old Betsy" rail car carried people, supplies and coal between Coaling Station A and San Joaquin Valley Coal Mine (note S.J.V. C.M. Co. on the side of the car).*

*Oil City in the 1890s—the richest community per capita.*

Petroleum Company in mid-1897; repeated well failures and unproductive drilling expenditures put it out of business by the century's turn. The Home Oil Company had embarked on a frenzy of exploratory drillings, each at a reputed cost of $25,000 and going as far down as 1,700 feet, only to end up with thirty dry holes.

In the century's last year, production reached unparalleled heights (see 12:9). Some eighty-seven cars of oil, each holding 6,500 gallons, left Oil City in January. By May, the single-month figure ascended to 271. On July 14 the Coalinga Oil Company struck a new gusher that spewed oil 155 feet into the air until scurrying workmen stopped it. The well's record soon eclipsed that of the Blue Goose. A day later, on the fifteenth, a Home Oil well brought in a respectable flow—not as large as the new well's, but bigger than the Blue Goose's.

Fire hit the new Home Oil producer nearly two weeks later, the first serious incident of its kind at Oil City. It was tough to get the blaze under control. "The well gushes twice an hour and several times when the workingmen thought they had the fire under control a sheet of liquid flame would shoot into the air undoing all their work," said the July 30, 1899, *Fresno Morning Republican*. "... The feat was finally accomplished by running a steam pipe from one of the engine houses, several hundred feet away. While the oil in the burning well was receding the pipe was taken up to the casing and the steam turned into the well."

A more persistent difficulty of this year was the lack of water at Oil City. Drought had plagued the west side for two seasons, and increased drilling activities nearly wiped out the available supply. To remedy this potentially disastrous situation, the Los Gatos and Oil City Water Company was formed on September 11, 1899. It built a reservoir 800 feet above nearby White Creek, filling it with water pumped from the stream via pipeline. Leading down from the reservoir was another pipeline. It worked on the gravity-flow principle, stretching down to the lower elevations—and Oil City.

While this system did not go into service immediately, its coming must have reassured the oil companies then operating in and around Oil City. They included the Aetna, Coast Range, Cosmus, Clarfield, Central California, Crescent, Eagle, Easton & Eldridge, El Dorado, Fresno Company of Fresno, Fresno Company of Los Angeles, Fresno Oil Tank, Gold State, Home, Homestake, Hanford, Investment, Kern Valley, Kreyenhagen Land, Keystone, Los Angeles Petroleum Smelting and Mining, Mutual of Selma, McKittrick, Nevada Sierra, New York, Old Keystone, Olaly, Oil City, Producers and Consumers, Pleasant Valley, Parkfield, Pioneer, Polverdero [sic] Queen, Selma, Stanley, State, Sunnyside, Sunset, Utica, Western and West Side.

Despite the competition, strikes were being made all

the time. New-found wealth seemed boundless. "Three years ago, the owners of this section were poor men, whose assets consisted of a string of second-hand tools, a few dollars in cash and a large fund of pluck," said H. T. Compton, Stockton's city engineer, in the October 21, 1899, *Fresno Morning Republican*. "Today they are millionaires and have a steady income of $1500 a day."

The overriding importance of Oil City and oil has caused most historians to overlook other natural resource developments of the early west side. Coal was mined, at varying times between 1873 and 1898 and in varying quantities, in an area roughly three miles northeast of Coalinga. The *Fresno Weekly Expositor* of October 29, 1873, gave the first report of mining in the region: "One or two claims have been located by wealthy men, and enough work done on them to hold them; but, beyond this, nothing has as yet been done toward developing this vast dormant wealth."

Four years later David Seacord started the first systematic coal mining operation. After Tom Beatty of Grangeville told him of the deposits, Seacord was sure a quick, easy fortune could be made by working them. This may have been the coal mine referred to in Wallace W. Elliott's *History of Fresno County*, which states that a coal vein was opened in 1878 on the Posa Chiné to a depth of 600 feet. The vein is about forty inches wide and is considered of good quality ... The coal has been tested as fuel at the Lemoore flour-mill with satisfactory results."

Hard work and high freight costs discouraged Seacord fast. Much expensive wagon shipping was still necessary, since the railroad stopped at Huron. Realizing that the profit, if any, was not worth the effort, Seacord withdrew from the business. He became a pioneer apiarist and storekeeper of the Pleasant Valley area.

The most important coal mine in the area, the San Joaquin, was started in 1881 by county merchants Louis Einstein and Elias Jacob, along with some other investors. A controlling interest in the property was sold to some English businessmen soon after. It was, in turn, purchased by two Englishmen named Robinson and Rawlins. Placing a countryman of theirs named Joseph (Jodie) Fearon in charge of the place, tunneling began that eventually extended a half-mile underground. Water and oil seepages were constant, and a Cornish water pump had to be run for twenty minutes every four hours to keep the tunnels clear. Initially fifteen men or so worked on this site, and lived there in a bunkhouse (since Coalinga and Alcalde had not come into existence yet). Fearon's wife served as the company cook.

In the first seven years of operation, Robinson and Rawlins were reduced to hauling their coal out by wagon, like their predecessor Seacord. Then the news came, in 1888, that the Southern Pacific Railroad was extending its line to Alcalde. At last there could be a convenient transportation outlet. For $20,000 a spur line was built from the mine to a junction with the rails. Coaling stations B and C were established on the spur, with Coaling Station A (hence, Coaling A or Coalinga) at the intersection.

The shortened name stuck when a post office was created at the station on July 22, 1889. Though settlers had been in the area for some time—M. L. Curtis was the first to homestead on the Coalinga site, in 1882—about all there was in "town" was a loading platform. The 1890s passed without the nicety of a station house. If one wanted to visit Coaling A at first, passage had to be paid to Alcalde and the train would hurriedly leave passengers off at the loading platform.

The railway innovation allowed miners to load an engine and car, nicknamed "Old Betsy," with coal at the mine site. It was a steady downgrade to Coaling Station A, so Betsy made the three-and-a-half mile trip there in a brisk eight minutes. In the early days, though, there was no turntable at Coaling A, and Betsy had to be backed up for an hour to reach the mine again.

By the early 1890s a Hanford man named Moor had opened a new coal mine a mile east of the San Joaquin. Known as the California, it employed fifteen men, produced six tons of coal a day, and had a main tunnel which eventually extended to 525 feet.

The San Joaquin was even more productive in this era, sending out 200 tons a month in 1892 and 300 in 1894; in the latter year, its work force reached a peak of forty men.

As promising as this outlook seemed, both mines were closed by 1898. A number of different factors worked against the mines ever succeeding. The biggest problem was the coal itself. "[It] was never any good, as it was just shale soaked in oil, and you took out more ashes than you put in coal," recollected W. J. Kilby of Coalinga. A report in the September 8, 1886, *Fresno Weekly Expositor* confirmed this, saying that the "coals do not coke, and are too highly volatile and inflammatory for railroad engines, but for stationary engines, domestic use and purposes where a quick hot fire is needed at a small expenditure of fuel they are unsurpassed."

Despite the *Expositor*'s critique, Robinson and Rawlins almost interested the Los Angeles Cable Car Company in purchasing the product for its use. When the Englishmen admitted they could not mine the coal as fast as the company desired—300 tons in twenty days—the deal fell through. In the meantime, virtually no one else wanted the coal and the San Joaquin mine languished.

Other problems stemmed from the fact that Robinson and Rawlins had a tendency to gamble away their earnings at Coalinga's Whiskey Row, causing production to falter and stop. Eventually they lost control of

the mine after losing a high-stake poker game! To complicate matters, "Old Betsy" periodically jumped her track or it was washed out from underneath her. Worst of all, the latter 1890s saw vast amounts of cheap Utah coal dumped on the marketplace. That signaled the demise of the Coalinga mines, and their more expensively-produced article, by 1898.

In 1892 gypsum was discovered on the San Joaquin Canal mine property and was sent to professor Ernest W. Hilgard of the University of California, who said it was of excellent quality. A rock-crushing apparatus was set up at the company property and production commenced. About the same time the Eureka Gypsum Company, which Milton McWhorter was involved in, began extracting the material from the Coalinga and Cantua areas. Eight miles north of Coalinga, Mark M. Lavelle and two partners named Hall and Doverall opened another gypsum mine in November 1892. It was described thus in the February 3, 1896, *Fresno Daily Evening Expositor*:

> The Southern Pacific company have made him [Lavelle] a very low rate, viz. $1.84 per ton, on gypsum from Coalinga to Fresno and neighboring stations where the vineyardists are troubled with alkali in the soil. [Gypsum was then widely used as a soil rejuvenator.] Mr. Lavelle has done considerable work on his property. He has erected buildings and a 2000-gallon tank near the mine, and in two shafts, which he sank to a depth of twenty-two and thirty-one feet respectively, he has struck a constant flow of both water and oil. Heretofore water and fuel for [his] engine had to be hauled in. Now they are furnished in the ground with only the nominal expense of pumping.

Natural gas also was prevalent in the area. One tale has it that "Coal Oil Tommy" heard it hissing from a crack one day, lit the leak with a match, and it continued to burn for a number of years! While this resource was not developed in the nineteenth century, some local limestone deposits were. "A vast deposit of limestone only a quarter of a mile distant [from Alcalde] will soon be operated by Fresno capitalists," said the August 8, 1896, *Fresno Daily Evening Expositor*. "Lime shipped from the north costs the consumer in the neighborhood of $3 a barrel. The Alcalde lime can be put to the consumer at Fresno, Stockton, Merced, Bakersfield and other inland places at from 75 cents to $1.25 per barrel." Even gold was discovered on the west side, though little seems to have happened with it.

The towns that prospered, thanks to the oil, coal, gypsum and limestone discoveries—Alcalde and Coalinga—have been mentioned fleetingly and will now be dealt with at length. Alcalde, located roughly five miles southwest of Coalinga, represented the farthest extent of the Southern Pacific's Goshen to Tres Pinos route. A projected lack of business induced the railroad to stop there. The agricultural, coal and oil traffic in the

Pleasant Valley area, however, must have made the completed section of track profitable.

The Alcalde terminus, reached by building west of Huron and through the site of Coalinga, came into being during 1888. A two-story depot was built, and a post office established on October 29 of the same year. The year before an Alcalde School District had been formed, with Karl A. Floden as its first teacher. Area historian Lula Grigsby claimed that the name derived from the reputation of early settler Tolton Turner Barnes. He served as a doctor, lawyer, constable and justice of the peace to the local folks—many of whom were Mexican—and was given the unofficial title of "alcalde" (see Chapter 11) for the lower Pleasant Valley region. The name was eventually applied to the town. "The Barnes home [near] Alcalde was always a sort of frontier hospitality house, where travelers could eat and stay all night," Grigsby once wrote. "After the railroad came through, the family frequently fed and lodged people waiting for the twice-a-week trains across the valley."

Once the natural resource developments were under way, Alcalde thrived. An August 8, 1896, *Fresno Daily Evening Expositor* report said: "Two months ago there was only a small cabin [at Alcalde], this cabin being the shelter of the section boss of the railroad company. Large stores are now going up, a hotel is being built and numerous dwellings are in progress of construction." A year later, James Barnes was building another hotel, daily train service had been established, and two stages departed every day upon the train's arrival. One went to the Coalinga Mineral Springs and the other to Barnesville, Priest Valley and King City in Monterey County.

The coal and oil excitement brought a host of businessmen to the town of Coalinga, whose genesis is explained earlier in this chapter. Frederick R. Tibbets opened a saloon, and Louis O'Neil a store, very early in its history. Following them closely were S. Barker and his family, who opened the Pleasant Valley Hotel; W. H. Childers and T. C. Johnson, who built the two-story, $4,000 Coalinga Hotel and a butcher shop in 1890; and Arthur P. May, another storekeeper who became Coalinga's leading businessman.

Born in England in 1863, May came to Pleasant Valley in 1888, settling on Los Gatos Creek. He opened his first general merchandise store in 1894 to which he soon added the first oil well supply business, the post office, Wells Fargo express agency and installation of the first telephone in Coalinga.

Mining and oil workers entrusted their savings to him until the money could be transported to banks in Fresno and elsewhere. As this service grew in popularity, May was obligated to purchase a small safe, and his operation was the precursor of the Bank of Coalinga. May remained a leader in the community until his death in 1940.

The protection May gave was necessary. A town correspondent, writing in the August 20, 1890, *Fresno Daily Evening Expositor*, remarked: "If we don't get an officer in Coalinga soon we will be obliged to call in the sheriff, as professional drunks and petty thieves are getting too numerous." To combat this problem, Jack Atkinson soon became the first village constable and W. J. Kilby the first justice of the peace. When his case load was not demanding, he also served as postmaster.

Toward the century's end Coalinga was a collection of two dozen or so frame buildings, dominated by a "Whiskey Row" of thirteen saloons and gambling dens. The row bred a good number of drunken brawls, fisticuffs and shoot-'em-ups. Fortunately, from a cultural standpoint—unfortunately, from an historical—these violent encounters are now vague memories, with the specifics long forgotten.

Water was scarce in town and had to be brought in by a train, known as "Old Sixbits," from Armona in Tulare County. John J. Jackson brought the precious fluid in and sold it by the barrel, plying the town's dusty streets in a horse-drawn wagon.

Besides the saloons, more substantial businesses were now operating in town. William Kinney and J. N. Jackson were the town's new hotelkeepers, Joe Dalton's and W. J. Kinney's blacksmith shops had been set up, along with D. and G. Forbes' livery stable, Frank Cleary's insurance office, and the Webb and May store. In addition oilmen Frank Barrett, Mark M. Lavelle, Milton McWhorter, H. G. Posten and Chanslor and Canfield maintained Coalinga offices.

It was still a rough-and-tumble frontier town, but edges of sophistication were in evidence. There being no respectable town hall, a great ball was held at one of the nearby coal mines in 1890. No churches were organized before 1900; however, a few traveling ministers, such as Elder Coffin of the Methodist Episcopal Church, held services in 1898. Unbelievably enough, there was a town literary society functioning in that year. It discussed momentous issues of the day, such as the wane of American patriotism and the annexation of Cuba.

From steamboats and stages to farming, oil-drilling and mining, Fresno County's West Side had witnessed profound changes in a half-century. Had Andrew Firebaugh, Abner Downer and John Barker remained to witness the transformations, they doubtless would have been astounded. At first the region had attracted only a few, to service the needs of those passing through it. By the century's turn it was drawing settlers, on its own merits, to exploit the wealth lying about the land. Just as that latter phase of development was starting, a *Fresno Daily Evening Expositor* reporter made an accurate prediction that applies today: "With this large acreage [under development,] Fresno County will put on an air of pride she has never before felt."

# Towns

## OF THE EAST SIDE

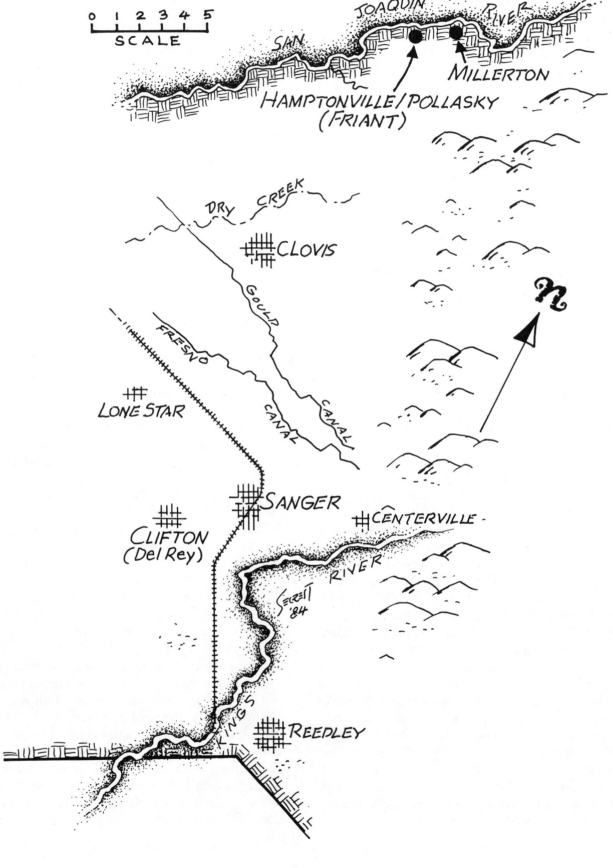

0 1 2 3 4 5
SCALE

SAN    JOAQUIN    RIVER

Millerton

HAMPTONVILLE/POLLASKY
(FRIANT)

DRY CREEK

Clovis

GOULD CANAL

FRESNO CANAL

Lone Star

Sanger

Centerville

Clifton
(Del Rey)

SECREST '84

RIVER

KINGS

Reedley

n

280

# Chapter 13
# The East Side

Perhaps no Fresno County town has endured a longer infancy, or identity crisis, as the one situated two miles downstream from Millerton. It was unofficially founded sometime around 1854, when Charles Porter Converse and W. W. Worland opened a ferry on the site (see Chapter 4). In 1868, after the previous year's flood, Converse sold the damaged property and business—now exclusively his—to James Richardson Jones, who operated a store and hotel on the north bank. So many travelers passed by the road-stop that a fair number died there; Jones was obligated to start a cemetery.

After Jones' death in March 1877 the businesses at Jonesville—as it was then known—were run for a time by his nephew, Phillip. Soon afterward store clerk William R. Hampton leased and operated them. The name then changed to Hamptonville, and operations were transferred to the south bank where the new lessee and his son-in-law, Edward McKenzie, built a new hotel next to Converse's adobe.

The Jenny Lind bridge, built in 1884 near Hamptonville, eliminated the need for a ferry. With Millerton nearly dead and commercial activity concentrated on the Southern Pacific tracks, little happened for nearly a decade. The situation changed in 1891, though. A promoter named Marcus Pollasky proposed building a railroad from Fresno to Hamptonville, and to the Sierra later, with an eye toward opening the Hamptonville area for settlement.

With some Fresno businessmen, Pollasky organized the San Joaquin Valley Railroad Company, purchasing rights-of-way for $100,000 and extensive property near and in Hamptonville for $17,000. The investors intended turning that hamlet into a major metropolis, as an August 17, 1891, *Fresno Daily Evening Expositor* report attests. A hydroelectric plant was to be built nearby that would bring electricity to all of Fresno County. A flouring mill, ice factory, woodworking factory and broomhandle factory were to go up, and a tunnel was to be bored through a nearby mountain, allowing water to flow onto the plains below. This was a new version of the old Upper San Joaquin Canal scheme (see Chapter 8).

Excitement ran high in early 1892, when Pollasky's railroad was completed to its temporary terminus—now rechristened Pollasky. A celebratory excursion via train to the "new" town and a barbecue there, were attended by many. Soon afterward a brick depot, wooden hotel and D. Berry's saloon opened, and a school was organized on May 8, 1892.

Unfortunately, the grandiose improvements proposed for the town never materialized. Once the railroad had been partially completed, Pollasky—who had little of his own money in the scheme—quietly left Fresno County. His befuddled cohorts disposed of their interests to the Southern Pacific. Rumor had it that the sellout had been engineered long before. Equipment for building the railroad often arrived in cars and crates suspiciously marked "S.P." Pollasky's claimed the initials were those of his brother, Simon!

In the meantime, Pollasky's town enjoyed the fruits of modest progress (see 13:1). A First Baptist Church was established there on August 17, 1894, and there was a population of approximately one hundred fifty the following year. An October 11, 1898, report in the *Fresno Morning Republican* noted that "Our little burg is very busy these days. We are making quite a showing in the lumber business. There is about a million feet from the Cascadel mill piled up along the south side of the track . . . The town fills up occasionally with mules and donkeys and jennies with their pack saddles, giving it quite the appearance of a mining camp headquarters for supplies." This activity had made a town general store, run by a Mr. Morrisey, and some slaughtering houses prosperous. A train arrived from Fresno every day, and stages departed for Madera County communities on the same basis. Later the village was renamed Friant for Thomas Friant of the White-Friant Lumber Company.

In 1886 another loosely-knit community came into being on Fresno County's eastern plains. Called Clifton for reasons now unclear, its first enterprise was a general repair and manufacturing shop operated by A. T. and J. R. Wilkinson. The men, brothers from Ohio, had been the first to settle in the neighborhood two years before, purchasing land for $12.50 an acre. At their carpentry, coppersmithing and tinning shop the Wilkinsons located a post office on January 28, 1885, and formed a Good Templars lodge on February 1, 1886, with nineteen charter members. A planing mill, barley crusher, and even a cemetery district were added about this time.

When the Santa Fe Railroad constructed a branch line through Clifton in 1896, a station was built there and named Del Rey for the nearby 600-acre Del Rio Rey Raisin and Fig Company property. The town adopted this new name soon afterward. By this time a Baptist church had been established; Methodist Episcopal services had been held in the town's Good Templars lodge as early as 1887. By the late 1890s Mrs. A. T. Wilkinson was postmistress, and Charles Clark operated a general store and there were few other noteworthy civic improvements. Small wonder that on July 14, 1897, the *Fresno Daily Evening Expositor* remarked that the station "looks like it will swallow up Clifton, and who knows but that it may." The only

other noteworthy enterprise built before the century's turn was the Smiley Brothers packing house.

The Lone Star district southeast of Fresno owes its name to (1) early settlers from Texas, or (2) three school children who, when a small school was built in 1882, decided "the little lone schoolhouse set in the midst of grain fields reminded them of a lone star," and the name was accepted. The first is offered by a postal reference book, the writer of which probably jumped to an easy conclusion. The latter is by Robert M. Wash, local historian whose family was among the first in the district.

The first school was built by local residents, Wash continues:

> The next year the Lone Star School District was formed, a tax levied, and a larger school built on the same site. This was used until 1898 when a grand new two-story school was built a mile and a half away on Fowler Avenue between North and Jensen. With new settlers pouring in, the great grain ranches being cut up, a village grew up around the school. It had its own

Reference 13:1

## FOURTH AT POLLASKY

There was no special celebration in Fresno yesterday, and a large number of the patriotic people went elsewhere to spend the Fourth.

The nearest attraction was at the town of Pollasky, and those who did not care to stay at home, and did not go somewhere else, had a very pleasant day on the banks of the placid San Joaquin, where the new city is destined to crown the bluffs at some future time.

The attraction was mainly fishing, although it cannot be ascertained that a solitary flounder of the flood was lifted from the cavernous depths of the sunlit river and landed on the immutable rocks of terra firma.

But this did not in the least deter the people from trying their fortunes at the old and time-honored pastime. There was no scarcity of fish of every conceivable size and shape. They swam in proud defiance to and fro, and dodged the hooks with great success.

There were many innocent anglers on the banks of the river, who meant no harm, and who did no harm; but about the most innocent and harmless were two. He was about 19 years old and she was some four years less.

They sat in the shade of a willow, on the bank above a deep, dark eddy, and each had a pole, hook and line, and there they sat, so wrapped in conversation that they did not notice that neither one of their fish hooks was within a yard of the water, but had been dangling in the air for half an hour.

"Hello, there," said a person approaching, "you are fishing, I suppose?"

"Yes," they replied, "we are trying to catch a few trout."

When told that they could probably have better success if they would drop their hooks in the water, they did so amid some embarrassment, but they talked so much that no fish would venture near enough to be caught. . . .

There is a skiff at Pollasky in the San Joaquin. The river is nice for riding, and it is said that very frequently people in the boat are lucky in catching large strings of fish, more so than when fishing from the bank.

Yesterday the boat was very much in demand. There were not very many minutes when it was not in the possession of someone.

Finally the young man and his girl came along. They were the same who had been fishing with their hooks dangling a foot above the water. They saw the boat and at once made up their minds that it was just what they were looking for, and in it they got and pushed it from the shore.

It was evident they never had been in a skiff before. The young man took up an oar and began to pull. The skiff whirled round and round. The more it whirled the harder he pulled. The harder he pulled the faster it whirled. And in a short time it was spinning round like a whirligig on the water and was slowly drifting down stream.

The young lady became excited and helped pull on the oar, which of course improved the predicament, as it whirled the boat a little more rapidly than before. When it had drifted down stream 200 yards the current beat it to the shore and the young sailors lost no time in getting out and chaining the boat to a stump.

Among the principal attractions at Pollasky yesterday was the dancing. The new pavilion there is really a fine one, clean, cool

and convenient. A bracing breeze from the river blows across it, and no better place for dancing could be desired. Scott's family band went out from Fresno and furnished music for the dancers, while lemonade and other refreshments were at hand.

The old house where Mr. Hampton formerly lived is now vacant and lonesome. A sense of decay and dilapidation exists. "Latchless doors on creaking hinges swing unceasing day and night."

A gang of Indians of all ages and descriptions sit on the edges of the porches around the old, empty house, and seem to mourn for departed glory. They remember the good old times which are passing away with the coming of the railroad and attendant civilization. The old adobe house is also vacant and haunted with foreboding stillness. Its cracked and yawning walls tell that its days are about numbered and that it will soon go down in a mass of ruins.

The people who went to Pollasky did not all return at one time. They came back on every train; but the majority came in on the train that left at 4 o'clock. The only thing that attracted special attention on the return was the lacerated and mangled skeleton of a watermelon under the shade of a fig tree. A tramp had plunged his savage knife in it, and after gorging himself to his full satisfaction, he lay down to sleep by the ruins he had wrought, and there he lay in slumber as the train passed.

SOURCE: *Fresno Daily Evening Expositor,* July 5, 1892, p. 3, c. 1-2.

*Pollasky in 1891, when the branch railroad line there was completed (note crowd to left and in center). On the left is W. R. Hampton's hotel and on the right is his son-in-law's store. In the distance is what had been the hotel and store of Jonesville, which prospered as the northern landing of the Converse Ferry.*

*1891 station at Pollasky, formerly Hamptonville and destined to be changed again to Friant.*

*The Charles P. Converse adobe, built in 1852, is shown in 1894. Standing in front are its later owner, W. R. Hampton, his wife, their daughter, Clara McKenzie, and her sons, William and Edward. Cracks in the building were caused by the flood of 1867.*

*This early picture of Centerville is believed to date prior to 1890 in one of the town's less active periods.*

*Centerville Hotel, circa 1880.*

*Lone Star school, built in 1898, was one of the most attractive rural school buildings in the county.*

Lone Star post office, a general store, blacksmith shop, community hall and depot on the recently arrived Santa Fe Railroad.

The Lone Star Community Hall was built in 1899 by volunteer contributions which included the land upon which is was built, given by J. B. Hancock, a farmer who was that year elected county treasurer. The *Fresno County Almanac* says "for many years it was the social center of all the large area southeast of Fresno. It saw many a wedding, dance, 'Literary' and other social event."

The post office, given the name Lonestar, was established in 1891, discontinued in 1895, reestablished in 1900 and discontinued in 1910.

Fresno County's east side contains two communities that have undergone five name changes apiece. The first is the one which started as Converse's Ferry and ended up as Friant, described above. The second lies twelve miles due east-southeast of Clovis, on the Kings River. When a post office was established there on December 3, 1856, the designation was "Scottsburgh" —after a town restaurateur and saloonkeeper, William Y. ("Monte") Scott. (No early references preserve this spelling; the name is uniformly given as Scottsburg.) The post office used the "h" spelling until it was discontinued on December 1, 1858, and during a June 30, 1859, to January 19, 1864, revival.

After a two-year lapse, the post office was reborn as the "Kings River" station on December 4, 1866. This appellation endured, but was never popular. People began calling the town "Centerville" circa 1869 because of its central location on the Kings, and that name survives today. Inexplicably, the "Kings River" designation was retained by the post office even after the Centerville name became generally accepted, and was further modified on February 20, 1895, to "Kingriver." It retained that name until final discontinuance and merger with Sanger's post office, on April 30, 1905.

Scottsburgh(h)/Kings River/Centerville/Kingriver was unofficially founded circa 1853, when William J. Campbell and his brother, Ed, operated a ferry there (see Chapter 4). Business was good since the ferry was on the upper detour of the Stockton-Visalia stage road, and the Campbells were soon joined by other wayside fortune-seekers. J. B. Sweem opened a grist mill there, "Widow" Flanagan a hotel called the Falcon, and Scott his restaurant/saloon.

Scott is worth a few incidental comments, courtesy of Lilbourne A. Winchell. "'Monte' was elected sheriff of Fresno County in 1858. He had led a life of adventure—Mexican fighter, Indian fighter, guerrilla, gambler and duelist—but withal a likable and dependable citizen. An old companion of the miners related to this author that when Scott was naked his body revealed more wound scars—bullets, knife and arrow—than any human being he had ever known."

Progress was slow in the first few years of Scottsburg's existence. After its school district was organized on February 3, 1860—one of the first three in the county, Millerton and Kingsburg being the other two—County School Superintendent E. C. Winchell visited there and reported that a groggery (saloon), hotel, store, post office and postmaster's residence were the sole buildings in town.

"Most of the residents in this part of the valley are in good circumstances and many families of children are springing up—yet no school has ever been opened here," he wrote in his diary. "I quickly selected three substantial men of the neighborhood; took them into the post office—the aforesaid groggery—and on a round table used only by gamblers, and on which lay the dirty greasy pack of cards in use by the unwashed public, wrote out the [school board] appointments and other documents. Administering the constitutional oath under the same imposing and auspicious circumstances, I gave the necessary directions to the new officials and left them to the enjoyment of their freshly blown honors and the discharge of their monotonous duties."

The 1861–62 floods on the Kings River caused considerable damage to the town. Situated on the river's south side, Scottsburg was inundated and its Falcon Hotel undermined and destroyed. Debris jammed the river farther upstream, causing it to cut a new northern channel—and wiping out Sweem's mill and William J. Campbell's residence, which lay opposite Scottsburg. Alexander Moody and his family, who had been staying at the Falcon, found themselves trapped by the raging waters: "Moody hastily built a platform on the top of some willow posts that had been used for a hog pen, and placed his wife and four children thereon," wrote John C. McCubbin. "He then managed to get ashore where he hoped to get a boat with which to rescue his family. The wife and children were compelled to remain on the platform two nights and a day before a boat could be secured . . ."

During the remainder of the 1860s, little happened at Scottsburg—now removed to a point three-quarters of a mile below the present town of Centerville, on higher land thought to be safe from flooding. Like the rest of Fresno County, the town was a hotbed of Southern sympathy during the Civil War. Paul A. Vandor said that, at one time, "the [American] flag was torn down, trampled upon, tobacco juice spit upon it as one version has it, defiled with human ordure according to another. The offender was a Confederate veteran, but later a loyal man, who deeply repented his act." Another semi-noteworthy development was the 1864 sale of Widow Flanagan's hotel, resurrected after the flood, to William C. Caldwell and his wife, Pelina.

Educational progress continued throughout the decade: in 1865 a $250, eighteen- by twenty-four-foot schoolhouse was built for the Scottsburg district to house the community's students. Increased settlement around the town led to the formation of the nearby Hazelton district on February 9, 1865, and the Centerville on December 14, 1869. In time the Centerville district absorbed the Scottsburg (on May 10, 1877) and the Hazelton (on May 5, 1887), but the Hazelton district was reorganized separately on February 15, 1895.

The most memorable event of this period was another flood, in 1867. Early rains that year had caused all the waterways flowing out of the Sierra to rise; the San Joaquin raged out of control, devastating Millerton (see Chapter 4), and the Kings behaved similarly. Despite its new, higher-elevation location, Scottsburg was wrecked again and had to establish itself on its present-day, even-higher site. With the rebuilding of the town, the Centerville name began to take hold. More substantial buildings and businesses appeared.

The use of the Centerville name began in the following manner, as related by an "Old Timer" in the *Fresno Republican* of October 24, 1926:

M. R. Anderson, who opened the store in the new town, went to San Francisco to purchase a stock of goods. When asked for his address he suddenly remembered that the town was as yet nameless. "Call it Midway or Centerville," he replied to the inquiry, and the city man marked the cases and bundles "Centerville," and thus the town was christened.

Caldwell's hotel was rebuilt as a handsome, two-story structure; Samuel A. Frankenau and Elias Jacob opened stores, with the former possessing a Wells, Fargo agency; William J. Hutchison and one Campbell (William? Ed?) started a blacksmith shop, and a Mr. Ayres a connected, wagon-making concern; and Leonard Farrar built another two-story building, with a well-stocked saloon on the lower floor and a dance hall on the upper. The village was bustling, and excitement of all kinds abounded.

At this juncture another early settler in the area, Gabriel Bibbard Moore, deserves mention. An Arkansas native who arrived with the Akers wagon train in 1853 (see Chapter 4), Moore was one of the first blacks to live in Fresno County. Not long after he arrived he became the victim of prejudice, as recorded in Wallace W. Elliott's *History of Fresno County*:

... At that time there was an Indian Agency on Kings River, near Centerville, under the control of one [William J.] Campbell, who had inaugurated among the squaws the patriarchal customs of Brigham Young, and had, without law, though possibly with the license of their fathers, taken unto himself several of the most presentable of the dusky maidens. He was a man of consequence accordingly, outside his large possession in calico, and withal a fellow of ferocity and determination. It seems that Gabe cast some longing eyes upon some of these possessions, and having a watermelon patch in the near "bottoms" was quite popular with the dusky maidens—only when they wanted melons—greatly to his exasperation. Finally one of them with grievous lamentations reported to her lord that in her case the incident of the Sabine woman [i.e., rape] had been re-enacted and that Gabe was the actor. Campbell swore dire vengeance in Gabe's instant death. Learning his peril, Gabe flew for protection to his former masters [Richard and William Glenn, fellow Akers party members]. They gave it. In those days courts were as little respected as needed. Each man according to his manhood was generally a law unto himself, the executive officer of which was carried at his hip in the shape of a navy revolver. Campbell at last consented to submit the matter to judicial determination.

Old Squire — [*sic*] was Justice of the Peace. There was no lawyer within twenty miles. The whole community assembled at the Justice's cabin. An indictment of some sort was framed, not a complaint for commitment, but to begin an action for the final determination of the guilt or innocence of the prisoner.

Counsel was assigned him; the late W. W. Hill, a man of great humor, and strong sense, who had married into the family of Gabe's former masters. Campbell prosecuted. A jury was impanelled and the trial proceeded. There were no books of course. Had there been there would have been no use for them. There were, however, some old volumes of statutes in the hands of the squire. These were brought forth with great ostentation. Gabe pleaded not guilty, in fear and trembling, and to the end of his days ever refused to admit that his plea was untrue, although the belief there was and continued to be that he was guilty, whether as charged or not. The witnesses for the prosecution were all Indian women. Neither the prosecution, the defense, nor the court could extract anything intelligible from them; but enough evidence was adduced to cause the court to submit the case to the jury. The trial was extended far into the night, and in order that "all hands" might better endure the labors incident to it, a jug of whisky was of course on hand, and "all hands" availed themselves frequently of its support, and so frequently that by the time the arguments of counsel opened the atmosphere was more clouded than was consistent with judicial clearness. The arguments were long, if not learned. Counsel for defendant read decisions of the Supreme Court in full sustaining his position *from the old statute books*. It is unnecessary to say that under these circumstances, respect for the law required that Gabe should be, and that he was unanimously acquitted by the jury.

The trial was once rehearsed to the writer in Gabe's presence. I asked him: "Gabe, why did you commit such a cowardly crime?" He replied with a chuckle and grin peculiar to his race: "Ah! Massa, 'oman war a scarce article in dem days!"

Moore eventually became accepted in the community, marrying a black woman named Mary and siring a son, Ephraim. Any clouds the rape incident cast upon him were soon forgotten. By 1857 he was a full-fledged county taxpayer, was farming in the Kings River bottomlands and had become a stock raiser. Local white families respected him, allowed their sons to work for him, and saw nothing demeaning in such labor.

On May 25, 1880, Moore was killed while driving some cattle across the Kings River. He was found drowned in the river, still clutching a bush; it was assumed he had been thrown from his horse, and was overwhelmed by the current before he could reach land. The *Fresno Weekly Expositor* of the following June 2 mentioned that "he accumulated quite a property—worth at this time probably $15,000." If the estimate was accurate, Moore must have been one of the richest black men in California when he died.

A correspondent in the February 22, 1872, *Fresno Weekly Expositor* wrote that "[the] little town of Centerville had improved and grown so rapidly since I was last here that I scarcely knew where I was when I first drove into town..." He noted that two new "large and magnificent" stores had been opened by Dr. S. R. Cockrill and J. D. Silverman and Company, two doctors named Graves and Grover had initiated practices ("and deal out their delicious medicines when it is required to relieve disease"), and a Mr. Higby had opened a "male and female institute." The latter may have been a counterpart of the Big Dry Creek Academy, founded in the same year (see Chapter 4).

To a large extent, increased farming and stock-raising activities were responsible for Centerville's progress. W. D. Perry, A. A. Burrough, Peter William Fink, John H. Byrd, J. B. Craven and Newton Phillips were cultivating large grain and flax fields, and John A. Patterson, William Hazelton and William Deakin were important stockmen. They all needed the services of a commercial center, and helped build Centerville to provide themselves with one. Many business deals were made in the town; freighting teams, grain shipments and cattle drives were constantly parading from or through it.

The older Centerville businesses prospered in the early seventies. An earlier *Expositor* notice, dated October 5, 1870, said, "we noticed that all of [William] Caldwell's boarders looked remarkably healthy, but were unable to determine whether it was on account of the wholesome food he placed before them or the excellent quality of Len Farrar's whiskey, as we noticed they partook equally of each; but we think that perhaps it was owing to their combining the two." Dances, balls, organization socials and other festivities were held at the hotel for many years afterward. Caldwell died in 1873, and all subsequent references give his wife as the sole proprietor.

Ernestine Winchell described the heyday of Farrar's saloon well:

To the big balls on the Fourth of July, Christmas, New Year's and Odd Fellows' Day everybody came. The young bloods rode in with clanking spurs and creaking leather, prepared to sleep on their coats and saddles whenever weariness might overtake them. Couples came on horseback or in buggies, the families in wagons, and many of them planned on all day to come, all night to dance, and all day to return home.

For these important affairs a regular string band was employed—Minkler and Myers, violins, and Winter, guitar, with sometimes Roc Rockefeller, the Fresno barber, to help out. But for the little neighborhood parties the favorite fiddler was Uncle Billy Hutchison—and when even now the notes of Money Musk, the Arkansas Traveler and Turkey in the Straw have power to stir the pulse, what then must have been the thrill! For still other occasions Nigger John, a local farmer of color, was ready to draw a compelling bow.

Farrar's prosperity did not last. After a slow business streak in 1872 he sold out to Millerton saloonkeeper Fritz Friedman, who did not do much better. J. A. Blasingame obtained the property three years later, had it torn down, carted to Fresno and reassembled (with some modifications) as the town's Metropolitan Hall.

To coordinate activities with his Kingston store, and connect Centerville with the outside world, Elias Jacob had a telegraph line strung from his store in mid-1873. The wires, which were stretched out across the county by then, allowed connections to remote Firebaugh's Ferry when necessary. The year before, Jacob had diversified his holdings by purchasing a half-interest in Jesse Morrow's three-story, $22,000 flour mill. It had been built on the edge of town to replace the old Sweem mill, washed out in 1867, and utilized some of its predecessor's parts. "A canal from Kings River supplies the turbine wheel which runs the mill," said Wallace W. Elliott's 1882 Fresno County history. "This canal alone cost $6,000. Four run of stone [are] used in manufacturing flour, and one for corn and barley."

Most authorities give this mill's construction date as 1872, but a September 20, 1871, *Fresno Weekly Expositor* notice tells of two men named Farris and Van Tassel who were operating a two-story, thirty-by-sixty-foot, water-powered flouring mill near Centerville. It seems likely that this enterprise was purchased and expanded by Morrow; flour mills were uncommon in those days, no community could support more than one, and no nineteenth-century Fresno County town in known to have had more than one.

Other businesses operating in the seventies were Jesse Morrow's four-horse stage line, which ran daily between Centerville and Fresno; Pete Donahoo's blacksmith shop, which replaced Hutchison's; a new hotel, started by a Mr. Bernhard from Visalia; and another saloon, presided over by Putnam and Stevens.

Added to these was a butcher shop and a drugstore whose proprietors are now unknown.

In 1877 Professor William A. Sanders conducted the "Scottsburg and Centerville Union School," which had an enrollment of fifty-seven and average attendance of forty-five. In a January 24, 1877, *Fresno Weekly Expositor* article, he related some details about the school:

> ... The principal room of this building is one of the finest in the country, size 30x50 feet; height, 14; area of blackboard, 320 feet. The room is furnished with the best of hard wood, iron framed, patent Peerless seats and desks, best of ink wells, with Gilbert and Moore's patent settees for recitation sheets ...
>
> ... The conscientious teacher cannot let any pupil have less than four daily recitations, while here, very many of them have eight daily lessons. Every pupil, however small, must be taught to read, spell and print, or draw. All in the Second Reader must also be taught arithmetic, while above that grade, they must also be taught geography, history, grammar, composition, physiology, etc. How to get time to do this every day, is a harder problem than any in geometry. We have so far had all lessons daily, except history and physiology which we alternate ...
>
> During something over twelve years' experience in the highest schools of the interior of our State, I've never enjoyed such immunity from viciousness, have never seen so many students so perfectly free from falsehood, unkindness to each other, and all other school vices, as the school is here: nor have I ever been so perfectly free from the querulousness and irritability of flaw-hunting, fault-finding grandmothers, both male and female, as I have been here in Centerville.

Sanders mentioned also that his high school students from the Big Dry Creek Academy had been transferred to this school, after the demotion of the former institution to an elementary school. Accompanying the ex-academy students were "four students who were attending college at Washington" (?).

Additional touches of civilization were supplied by the Masons, who organized a Centerville lodge in 1870, and the Independent Order of Odd Fellows, who followed suit in 1872. During the same year a grange organization for local farmers was founded, as was a Centerville Literary Society. Among this latter group's usual activities were readings of humorous stories and parodies, and debates on subjects relevant today: "Should Capital Punishment Be Abolished?," "Who Was the Greater Man—Columbus or Washington?," and "Does the Newspaper Press Exert a Greater Influence than the Ministry?" The town was also home to the county's second church. Built in mid-1871, it housed a Methodist Episcopal Church South congregation and was built through private donations.

The groups held celebrations of all kinds at Centerville. A memorable May Day outing, hosted by the church and grange association, was described in the May 6, 1874, *Fresno Weekly Expositor*:

> [As] for eatables, when we say that the ladies of Centerville cannot be surpassed in the cooking line, and on this occasion their liberality had no limits, we think it will be quite sufficient ... The gathering, after having partaken of a most beautiful lunch, were entertained by a march and grand display by the Grangers. After witnessing their force and grand maneuvers in the field, we were convinced that they could harvest what little grain we have growing in the vicinity before breakfast, and not have it very early either. As for the female portion of the Grangers, we concluded that if we were going into the dairy or chicken business we should say: "Give us a Granger!" The evening entertainment was adjourned to Caldwell Hall, where the "light fantastic toe" was tripped to music by Charley Moore's band. After dancing until half past 11 o'clock, some discreet person remarked that to-morrow was Sabbath. A Georgiaville girl was heard to remark that "she hoped the next dance they had, they would commence day before yesterday," but such was fate, the dance had to close—and thus ended May-Day.

By 1879 Centerville, with a population of 300 or so, was the second largest town in Fresno County—surpassed by Fresno alone. In the ensuing decade it continued to grow, adding hotels operated by Payton Blevins, Mrs. Simpson and Philip Weihe, blacksmith shops owned by A. A. Henry, Simeon Evinger, Benjamin Royal and John Lindsey, saloons kept by A. G. Anderson and M. E. Blade, a drugstore presided over by Dr. L. T. Davis, a carpentry shop whose proprietor is unknown, a newspaper (the *Kings River News*; no copies seem to have survived), and the medical practices of S. A. Young, J. B. Pressley, B. E. Stevenson and one Wadsworth. A new town hall (Haddon's) had been built, and Clark Stevens had taken over the stage line to Fresno—since Jesse Morrow had relocated to that town and was running the Morrow House.

Morrow's old flour mill, now wholly owned by Jacob, was remodeled in 1880 so it could grind forty barrels of flour a day. Later on, its capacity was increased to fifty-five barrels daily. A host of different people managed this enterprise (a Mr. Tulloch in 1880, Kidd and Keran in 1881, and John H. Danielson circa 1883 and afterward) until it burned in 1887.

The Centerville school's enrollment averaged thirty-five to forty pupils, and was taught by Minnie Bassham in 1883. By that year there were a few more organizations functioning in town: a Social and Glee Club (formed on April 17, 1880), an Ancient Order of United Workmen chapter (circa 1880), and a Good Templars lodge (circa 1883). Roman Catholic church members were served by Father Valentine Aguilers, who visited from Fresno, and the Methodist Episcopal Church South had the Reverend C. H. Cooper as its resident pastor.

A new form of entertainment came into town circa 1880, when some citizens built a race track. It does not seem to have been popular among horse owners, compared to the other county tracks of the day. The June 5, 1881, *Fresno Weekly Expositor* noted that, despite good attendance, only two horses ran there on one race day—E. T. Lowery's "Maggie Early" and C. C. Baer's "Robert Lee," for a purse of $100. "As usual with the races the sporting fraternity was well represented," said the newspaper's correspondent. "Dancing commenced in the schoolhouse promptly at 7 o'clock, and continued till four o'clock in the morning." Other popular diversions of this period included Fourth of July festivals, temperance picnics, cotillion balls, corn-parching socials and candy-pulling parties.

Local grain farming and stock raising began to wane in the 1880s, and Centerville's economy was correspondingly slowed. Further misfortune occurred later in that decade, when the Fresno to Porterville railroad line was built nearby. Squabbles between railroad officials and townsfolk over rights-of-way and property grants prevented a station from being built in Centerville, so in 1888 facilities were located at Sanger instead (see below). This sent Centerville into a rapid decline. For nearly four years it was a virtual ghost town, although prosperity returned—just why is not clear—in the late nineties. Mrs. O. Brown opened a new hotel, J. N. Kilgore initiated a town hall and storage facilities in an old two-story building, John Lindsey and Orie Oliver started new saloons, the Muller brothers and one Allison set up general merchandise stores (along with two others), and men named Bacon, Matson and Mateisen rejuvenated the blacksmith trade. There also were two feed yards in town and two doctors, and after 1891 telephone lines were strung out to Sanger and neighboring hamlets.

Agricultural activities in the area were now dominated by vineyard and citrus production. John Carey became a prominent lemon grower, and Thomas Yost, Frank Lillient and A. H. Powers were noted for their bountiful orange groves. Considerable crop experimentation was taking place as well. The November 5, 1891, *Fresno Morning Republican* said that sorghum and Egyptian corn were being grown close to town, and the June 21, 1899, issue of the same newspaper mentioned that "[the] potato crop is being dug. The acreage is small on account of the frost killing the early crop in the [river] bottom land."

One of the town's prized institutions, the Methodist Episcopal Church South, was subjected to considerable ignominy in 1891. When a sister Methodist congregation was formed at Sanger, parishioners there asked the Centerville church—whose membership was declining—for the loan of a dozen pews. This was agreed to, but the greedy Sangerites came back later and extracted all the remaining pews, plus the church bell! "Only last week the *Sanger Herald* told boast-

fully that its Methodist church was truly progressive since it was the first church [there] to get a bell," said a Centerville correspondent in the April 17, 1891, *Fresno Daily Evening Expositor*. "But since this is the congregation indebted to us for their seats, it would hardly seem possible that they would be destitute of every moral obligation as to rob its benefactors of that which we still most decidedly need."

In spite of the correspondent's sentiments, the church disappeared completely by 1896. Religious services were still being held in town, by the Reverend Williams, but they were being held at the schoolhouse. A Sunday school and Christian Endeavor Society also were functioning in town. Accompanying them was a Centerville Improvement Association, devoted to keeping the town's cemeteries, streets and businesses spruced up; the literary and debating society, whose meetings were still well-attended; and the Odd Fellows lodge, reorganized in 1898 after an apparent period of inactivity.

Though these were Centerville's twilight years—little was left of the town after 1900—its citizens still managed to indulge in occasional entertainments. Baseball games and picnics were held frequently, and the holidays continued to bring festivities universally enjoyed and remembered fondly. The December 30, 1890, *Fresno Daily Evening Expositor* described a special Christmas Eve celebration:

Wednesday night the school house was ablaze with light. Here assembled all the neighbors with their little ones—those who had no little ones bringing someone else's little one whose age varied from sixteen to thirty-nine. The Christmas tree, tastefully decked with its lovely fruit by fair fingers, amply repaid the large audience for their wade through the dense fog that had rolled up from Fresno.

Many were the "Ohs!" and "Ahs!" that burst from little lips as they viewed the great tree, whose branches had but a few days before nodded a farewell to its near snow-clad neighbors, the Sierras[sic]. Strings of white popcorn, bunches of yellow oranges and bright colored books, and toys vied with each other in making the bending boughs, with their mass of bright green needles, a picture that would be a "joy forever" to many a childish heart.

At 8 o'clock a programme, consisting of Christmas carols and Christmas readings and recitations, was rendered by the school children, and its excellence was attested by the loud and frequent applause that greeted the little performers. As the words of the last carol, "Peace on earth, good will to men," were dying away, in at the door burst Santa Claus with happy words and a pleasant nod of his gay, old head, for each of his friends, the acquaintance of many of whom he had made in the "long ago." After a song and a story for the little ones Santa Claus saw to it that each boy and girl had a full supply of toys, candy, nuts, and the happiness that comes only with the Christmas time. And then, his work being done, with a cheery "Good night" to all the little ones whose hearts he had helped to brighten, he started again on his journey to see that other boys and girls should be made happier by his presence.

As agricultural interests began fanning out toward the eastern San Joaquin Valley, Southern Pacific officials began wondering if a Fresno-to-Porterville branch line might be profitable. In 1887 the railroad began building such a route, spawning two new towns on Fresno County's eastern flatlands: Reedley and Sanger. Both towns were founded the following year, and at about the same time. Beginnings of civilized

Reference 13:2

# THOMAS LAW REED

### J. C. McCUBBIN

T. L. Reed (by which name he was generally known) was born at Chester, Ohio, on Nov. 13, 1847, and died in Reedley, California, on Sept. 11, 1911, at the age of 64 years plus.

During the early days of the gold rush, T. L. Reed's father joined the great trek to California. After his arrival in California, his family received two letters from him, via Pony Express. In these letters Mr. Reed expressed great loneliness for his family, and a fear of the rough frontiersmen surrounding him in his mining operations. It is supposed that tragedy must have befallen him, at least his family never heard from him again.

T. L. Reed's two oldest brothers were then in the Civil War, which left young T. L. to take care of his mother. In order to provide some money for her, at the age of 16, young Thomas accepted $300 from a doctor to go to war in place of the doctor's son. This "selling of one's services" was common practice at that time, though the price paid was usually much greater than he received. Thomas served in the Civil War until peace was declared, two years later. He was wounded in the shoulder during the battle of Shiloh.

On November 5, 1863, Reed was married to Miss Amantha Ann Smith. Shortly after their marriage they moved to Michigan where he took charge of a cheese factory.

Leaving his family in Michigan, he spent the summer of 1876 working in Yolo County, California. He decided to settle in California, so he sent for his wife and children. They arrived in Woodland, California, on Nov. 16, 1876.

The following year Reed rented the Yolo County Allen ranch of 400 acres and farmed it to wheat. Soon his farming in the Sacramento valley became quite extensive.

By this time the 76 country's canal system was well along toward covering the district, 20,000 acres of which the 76 Company owned. They were in need of men who would come in and farm their lands. Some of the 76 stockholders had T. L. Reed as a tenant on their Yolo County lands, so when his leases expired in the north, they induced him to come down to Fresno County and farm portions of their 76 Company lands . . .

Reed moved from Yolo County to the 76 country in 1884. They lived in the old Smith Hotel building for a little over two years while their house was being built. . . .

Other families with children were settling in the locality which was known then as "Smith's Ferry." T. L. Reed headed a local group that organized the Smith's Ferry school district. Reed donated a corner of his land for school use and soon a school house was erected thereon. Miss Edith Hatch of Selma was the first teacher. Reed was elected clerk of the school board. . . .

In 1888 Mr. Reed sold the first [Reedley] town lots. He had a clause in the first contracts and deeds prohibiting the sale of intoxicants. These clauses were later discontinued because bottled liquor was being brought in and consumed in the homes. Mr. Reed considered this a worse evil than the saloon, where often the bartender curtailed their drinking to a certain extent. . . .

Following the idea of the Fresno County Colony system, Reed divided his land surrounding the new townsite into 5 and 10 acre colony lots. Among the first buyers were: William McCreary, J. B. Moomaw, John Fairweather, J. L. Gilbert, Harry Winnes, Samuel Reed, and Rev. T. J. Bauder, Minister of the United Brethren Church, the first church in Reedley.

On July 12, 1888 Reed purchased 1,259 acres of land from the 76 Company. The purchase price was $51,341.25, which averaged about $40 per acre. This land adjoined the original townsite of Reedley on the north, east, and west sides. This increased his local holdings to approximately 3,000 acres in one solid body. He also owned other detached acreage in the 76 country. . . .

At the peak of Reed's farming activities he was known as one of the wheat growing barons of California. He was farming 15,000 acres in the 76 country and 14,000 acres on the Chowchilla ranch in Merced County, a total of 29,000 acres. In 1886 he introduced the first Houser combine into this territory.

Speaking in the vernacular of that day, Reed was considered an exceptionally good judge of "horse flesh." He owned and worked 516 head of mules and horses. Of these, 214 were used on the home ranch, 132 at the Smith Mountain ranch, and 170 on the Chowchilla ranch. He used twelve animals in each team, and in one of these teams, not a mule weighed less than 1650 pounds. His buggy animals were considered the finest in the country. Reed raised many head of horses for himself and other people. Once he was severely wounded when kicked in the stomach by a horse. It was thought the kick

caused the cancer from which he passed away in September, 1911. . . .

A slump in wheat prices broke Reed financially, and he was forced into bankruptcy. But Reed was not a man to give up. He went to Bakersfield where he made a fortune in oil. He returned to Reedley and paid every cent he owed, which amounted to about $100,000.

In either 1902 or 1903 the Reedley Chamber of Commerce was organized. T. L. Reed was elected its first president. The Chamber of Commerce was not incorporated until Jan. 23, 1914.

About January 7, 1904 the Reedley Co-operative Packing Co. was incorporated, which was a real forward step in the packing industry. The directors were T. L. Reed, T. M. Lane, W. H. Graham, A. E. McClanahan, and J. C. McCubbin.

T. L. Reed had great foresight. No doubt he was the first man to advocate the construction of a dam on the Kings River for irrigation purposes, the approximate location to be where Pine Flat Dam is located. He boosted for that project as long as he lived.

It was Mr. Reed who first promoted the building of the present Sand Creek road that leads into the mountains from Orange Cove. The contract for its construction was granted to him, but he passed away before its construction. His two sons, Horace and Edmond, fulfilled the contract, but due to changes in prices, the road was built at a great financial loss to them.

It was said that Mr. Reed always took time to speak to the lowliest person, even though Reed was a very busy man. When any of his neighbors needed seed, feed, or provisions they would go to T. L. Reed, who never refused them. He never made a book account of such loans, but depended upon their honesty for repayment. Some took advantage of his generosity, but the honest ones appreciated his kindness. He never took a cent of interest, even though their payments might have been low, and extended over quite a period of time.

Reedley can proudly call T. L. Reed "The Father of Reedley."

SOURCE: McCubbin Papers, Reedley Public Library.

settlement appeared around Reedley first, so its history will be described before Sanger's.

The need for Reedley was obvious long before its founding. Its townsite stood in the middle of a huge wheat belt, near the northern tip of the 76 Land and Water Company's holdings. As early as 1883 the company had recognized the importance of the area, building a town called Wahtoke several miles east of what became Reedley. A post office was established there and soon one Jacobsen was running a store, John S. Cole had a blacksmith shop and David Bowman was operating a hotel.

The founding of nearby Traver in 1884, and the establishment of the 76's headquarters there, caused Wahtoke to die out. A replacement settlement, however, became necessary three years later. More farmers had located in and around the 76's northern lands. Knowing that the Southern Pacific was coming through, that a convenient shipping place was needed and that the founding of a new town was inevitable, the farmers decided to form two neighborhood schools— the Smith's Ferry and Wahtoke, on May 7, 1886. Edith Hatch and Nellie Baird, respectively, were their first teachers.

Eager for the Southern Pacific to build a convenient depot, local wheat farmer Thomas Law Reed (see 13:2) gave the railroad a one-half interest in a 360-acre townsite. It was adjacent to the east bank of the Kings River and near the Fresno-Tulare county line. Not only did the railroad opt to build a depot there, it named the site after Reed. According to one report, he accepted the gesture grudgingly.

In May 1888 L. D. Norton surveyed Reedley, and later in the month Reed began selling lots inside and outside of town. Mr. and Mrs. F. S. Knauer built the town's first house in June, and began operating a post office (transferred from Wahtoke) from their home on October 31. This substantial two-story home was far better than what the Knauers had had before: a cabin with walls made of warehouse doors and a roof made of quilts and held down with lumber scraps.

Late in 1888 the Southern Pacific began building a depot—a caboose had been used as such before. Next to it Reed set up a storage facility, half of a 500-foot grain warehouse moved from Traver. It was a welcome arrival. The previous July, farmers had had to stack their sacked wheat next to the railroad tracks without any protection.

Reedley's first businesses, set up before 1888 was over, were William McCreary's livery stable and the E. Hirschfield general merchandise store, the latter opening on December 13. Reed moved a portable cook house from his ranch down to the north side of town, the dining room offering family-style meals at twenty-five cents apiece. A justice court was opened, with Fresno County's youngest judge presiding: twenty-two-year-old Charles A. Parlier.

The Reverend E. F. Austin began conducting United Brethren services in mid-1888, with the Reverend T. J. Bauder succeeding him in the fall and presiding over a permanent congregation organized on November 17. The Harmony Baptist Church was founded in the same year, holding its first services in the Wahtoke School.

A February 8, 1889, *Fresno Daily Evening Expositor* report said that "the town of Reedly [*sic*] is improving gradually, and it is thought that when the railroad puts the town lots on sale there will be a rapid growth..." When the railroad got around to it, starting on April 25, it found a fair number of buyers. On the final sales day, $16,000 worth of property was sold.

New businesses continued opening up: a drugstore owned by L. A. Rockwell of Traver and operated by his clerk, W. W. Green; Harry Winnes' tobacco, candy and notion store; and another grain warehouse—similar in size to the first, and constructed by the Grangers' Bank of San Francisco. Not to be outdone by these entrepreneurs, Reed built and began operating a hotel (the Reedley) managed by H. E. Barnum, a blacksmith shop rented to Charles Gummow, and a livery stable. Mr. and Mrs. Robert Simpson purchased the hotel in 1892 and ran it for several years afterward. The town passed another milestone in March 1889, when John C. McCubbin installed a telephone in the Hirschfield store.

Reedley's United Brethren congregation raised an $1,800 subscription to build a church in 1889. Not completed until 1892, it was used for a variety of functions; an amusing tale is connected with one. At the 1889 Christmas celebration all the children were given presents save for T. L. Reed's seventeen-year-old son, Horace. When the boy's despair seemed complete, he was told to follow a rope tied to the church Christmas tree and leading somewhere outside. At the rope's other end Horace found a shiny new single-seat buggy... the nineteenth-century equivalent of a sports car. Overjoyed, he spent the rest of the celebration taking everyone present for a ride.

In 1890 Reedley counted a population of about one hundred seventy-five and had developed into a major grain-shipping center. One McNear was building a third warehouse, there were fifteen commercial buildings in town, and fifteen brick masons were hard at work building more. The San Joaquin Lumber Company established an outlet that year, L. C. Reed (not a known relative to T. L. Reed) built a livery stable that was leased to Miller and Bourland, and L. N. Thomas opened another store.

Following the lead of nearby Kingsburg, Reedley businessmen formed an improvement company in 1890 to erect commercial buildings. Its first venture was a 150- by 35-foot, two-story brick store topped with a tower. To guard against the persistent menace of that era, it was built with seven-foot fire walls. A Good

Templars lodge with 100 members was founded at this time, as was a Methodist Episcopal congregation that met at the town depot; its first minister, who arrived later in the year, was T. E. Tippet.

One measure of Reedley's growing significance was the removal of the Smith's Ferry School (see 13:3) to a site in the town on February 5, 1890. The structure mysteriously caught fire on the night of February 14 and was destroyed. Classes met at the United Brethren church until September 14, 1891, when a new $15,000 two-story brick school was opened. Miss C. A. Boyer and Carrie Weaver were its first teachers.

Not long after Reedley's founding a noticeable Chinese population moved into the town. Jim Ah Chung, who worked as a cook in Traver, was one of these early residents and made substantial property investments. Arriving soon afterward were the Sam Hing Yoong, Walter Lee and Lee Sam families, the last of which opened a restaurant. White townsfolk behaved toward these people in a manner purely schizophrenic. When Chung went to San Francisco to claim his bride, Anna, the couple was greeted by a large multi-racial celebration on their return. Likewise, when their son, Charlie, was born, many local whites went to see the new Chinese baby and bring him gifts. Yet when Fresno bricklayer Joseph Spinney brought a Chinese crew to work on the new Reedley Hotel in April 1891, he was solemnly told to remove his workmen. When he demurred, a mob of fifty citizens marched to the hotel site, made a more insistent demand to the Chinese, and trundled most of them away in a wagon.

The Reedley hotel, another Reedley Improvement Company project, was a $30,000 three-story brick showplace with forty bedrooms. It was the most important building erected in 1891, and stands on the town's main street today. Another enduring Reedley institution started on March 26 of the same year—the *Exponent* newspaper, published by A. S. Jones. Issued every Thursday, an initial year's subscription was $1.50. By the end of the *Exponent*'s first month of existence, 450 subscribers had signed up. Jones continued as editor until September 22, 1892, when W. W. Holland took over. John Fairweather bought the *Exponent* from Jones in June 1895, serving as its proprietor down to the century's end.

By the early 1890s Reedley's importance as a commercial center was indisputable. In 1891 alone, 12,000 tons of grain and 1,031,957 feet of lumber left the town via teams and trains. The individual volume of some of these shipments was staggering. On a July day in 1892, L. C. Reed brought a team of eight horses to Reedley pulling 34,390 pounds of wheat in a wagon, or an average of 4,299 pounds *per horse*. This massive traffic had necessitated enlargement of the Grangers' Warehouse the previous May, and the opening of the Eppinger and Company warehouse about the same time.

Other businesses thrived amid this bustle of 1892,

Reference 13:3
# LIFE AT SMITH FERRY SCHOOL
### CARMI DIEUDONNE
### DECEMBER 5, 1959

As to the Smith's Ferry school desks, they were the kind typical to schools of those days. Underneath the top was the shelf for books, slates, pencils, etc. On the right side at the top of the desk was the inset ink well. Woe be to the girl with long hair if she sat in front of a teenage boy. He saw to it that the cover was off the ink well. There were benches without backs where classes sat to recite their lessons.

For spelling we stood in a row. For punishment we paid the usual penalty, such as sitting on a bench, staying in at recess or after school, writing words or sentences on the board, cleaning erasers, etc.

I remember there was one big blackboard, and we studied the three R's, grammar, and geography. The teacher's desk was not modern like the teacher's desks are of today. It was plain with a few drawers. One drawer held various things taken away from the children playing with them during study period. Of course, they were returned to the owners later.

As to games, there was ante-over. We chose sides and threw the ball over the schoolhouse to each other, a game known to all pupils those days. Then there were the games of dare base, steal sticks, marbles, spin the top, and mumble [*sic*] peg.

The Christmas program was much the same as today. We had the decorated Christmas tree, we sang Christmas carols, the children gave their recitations, presented tableaus, and so on. The big excitement came when the bags of candy and nuts, an apple, and an orange were first handed out to the children. And there was excitement also for the grown-ups. Families and friends brought gifts for each other, and there was a large pile of them under the Christmas tree. There were no electric lights, of course.

The school was built of lumber and painted white inside and out. The wall was neither plaster nor papered, it was a ceiling wall. There were shutters on the windows.

Miss Hatch and Miss Wallace were there before my day. We arrived at Reedley in 1888. I feel sure the school house burned down in Feb., 1890.

The first name of Mr. Simon was William. When the school house burned we youngsters wept, but at the same time kidded ourselves into thinking there would be no more school for the rest of the term. But the schoolboard acted quickly and set up desks for us in the new, unfinished U.B. Church in Reedley, and school was held as usual. Some things had been salvaged from the burned school. The unfinished walls were completed at the end of the term.

The three first teachers of the new brick school in Reedley were Miss Weaver, Miss Boyer, and Mr. Barthel, teaching the lower, the middle, and the upper grades in that order. (Mr. Barthel came the second year.)

One night there was an entertainment in the new school house. Mr. Joe Moomaw had the first jewelry and sports goods store in town. He could play most any musical instrument made. His number on the program was "Jack of All Trades." Horns, violins, mouth organs, and so on, were laid out on the platform, and he played all of them.

Also wonderful entertainments were put on by home talent. The pageant "Queen Esther" was beautiful, and the different parts were enacted by local persons. It was played on several successive nights to accommodate all the people.

SOURCE: Katherine Nickel, *Beginnings in the Reedley Area*. Reedley, California, 1961, pp. 92–93.

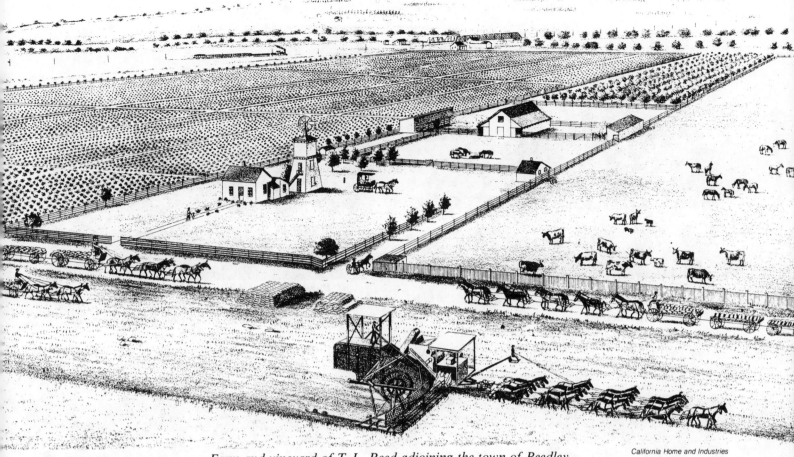

*Farm and vineyard of T. L. Reed adjoining the town of Reedley.*

California Home and Industries

Fresno Bee Photo

*The first Reedley post office was in the F. S. Knauer home built in 1888 at F and Eleventh streets. Mrs. Flora Knauer was the first postmaster and is second from left.*

Reedley Historical Society Archives

*T. L. Reed and family in early days of Reedley.*

293

*Reedley's Hotel Grand was called the Arlington when built in 1891–92 by the Pacific Improvement Company. The top floor was destroyed in a late 1920s fire but the remaining two floors are still in use, though not as a hotel.*

*One of Reedley's early businesses was the Drake Wagon Making Company of John Drake. He made this wagon circa 1895 to carry sacked wheat—about eight tons per load. It was later used to carry building materials in Kern County and lumber between Millwood and Sanger. It is now a part of the exhibit in the Reedley Museum.*

*A surge in the economy of both Reedley and Sanger resulted from the arrival of the Southern Pacific Railroad. The first train is arriving at the Reedley depot. The Sanger depot is pictured to the right.*

*The Sanger Lumber Company brought much of its lumber from the mountains by its famous flume. The workers seem to like posing to emphasize that work on the flume was sometimes precarious.*

*General view of the Kings River/ Sanger Lumber Company's finishing plant outside of Sanger. Even during slow periods, as much as 50,000 board feet were processed in a single day. Shingles, boxes and boards were the major items produced at the plant.*

*Sanger's Seventh Street in 1890, looking east. On left are the J. S. Filloon residence, black-smith shop, water tower and livery stable, and on the right is the popular French Hotel.*

*By 1900, Sanger's Seventh Street looked like this, looking west from Academy.*

notably the general merchandise stores of Kutner and Company and the Goslinger Brothers; the real estate businesses of C. A. Parlier and J. G. Wright, and T. L. Reed and A. E. McClanahan; J. B. Moomaw's jewelry store; J. N. Thomas and W. B. Rice's confectionery stores; Ollie and Theo England's millinery stores; and R. F. Crooks' construction company. Riley Monroe Wilson moved a flour mill from Traver to the Kennedy Slough near Reedley in this year. It was such a success that it ran day and night for several years following its relocation.

Also in Reedley were three saloons, a barbershop, a meat market, a brickyard, a shoe shop, two ministers and two doctors. Telephone service was expanded to fifteen other towns in the summer of 1892, with the costs of calls ranging from thirty-five to sixty cents. Important businesses established a few years later included the D. C. Smith and Sons Cash Store (circa 1893), Christopher Dennis' saddle and harness-making shop (1894), the Long Brothers packing house (around 1895), and J. W. Shipe's livery stable (1898).

The town's economic climate continued to be favorable, helped partially by the fact that no significant fires occurred before 1900. Perhaps the worst happened on June 5, 1892, when O'Brien's saloon, Potter's tin shop and the *Exponent* building were destroyed, and the Green drug store damaged, at a loss of $3,300. Compared to what most other Fresno County towns suffered in their early history, this damage was negligible.

As in any other frontier town, Reedley's streets were unpaved. Rains turned them into mudwallows, and in the summers freight teams, trains and people stirred up dust clouds constantly. When the air was clear, an unusual sight often greeted the eyes of Reedleyites. "Among my boyhood memories," said longtime resident L. C. "Clay" Milton, "were the wonderful images [mirages] of those days. It was a puzzling sight in the early morning to see the town of Traver, about twelve miles south rise up out of what looked like water. The buildings looked as if they were four or five stories high, and the people seemed to be walking around on stilts. One could also see cattle and horses at times and a man on horseback with a dog following, all having long legs and walking high in the air. I would like to see it all over again."

At points surrounding the town, educational progress continued throughout the 1890s. The Riverside School District was formed on February 16, 1891, and a schoolhouse was built at Dinuba and Lac Jac avenues later that year. The first teacher was Mrs. Kate Burford, followed by a Mr. Traber, a Miss Collins, a Mrs. Milton, a Mrs. Zumwalt and a Miss Kirsch. Created on that same 1891 day was the Fink School District, which hired Alice J. Heath as its first teacher and expanded its staff no further until 1917. In October 1892 another local school, the Windsor, opened with

William L. Worth teaching a class in a twenty-seven-by-twenty-nine-foot building. Worth was succeeded by Maud P. Howlet in 1895 and a succession of other teachers conducted the school before 1900: Carrie Weaver, Jennie Espey, James M. Brooks and Elizabeth Spencer.

Inside the town itself, the Reedley School District was organized from the Smith's Ferry School District on February 8, 1898. W. A. Adamson was named the new district's teacher. Nearly four months later, on June 3, voters approved the formation of the Alta Joint Union High School 111-37. It was established subsequently on the upper floor of Reedley's other school, which housed a 296-seat auditorium and community meeting hall. Granville F. Foster was hired as the first principal.

The two homeless religious congregations in Reedley built permanent churches for themselves in the early 1890s. With the help of ministers I. N. Woods of Kern County and W. E. Adams of Oakland, the Baptists built a $2,000 thirty- by fifty-foot structure on Main Street in mid-1891. Something apparently happened to this building; a January 31, 1893, *Fresno Daily Evening Expositor* report mentions that the Baptists were again meeting in the United Brethren Church. The first pastors to serve the Baptists, on a visiting basis, were J. N. Lacy (1893 and perhaps before) and J. E. Barnes (after 1894). Auxiliary groups also were formed in these years: a ladies' aid society on November 30, 1893, and a Baptist Young People's Christian Association on March 22, 1893. The former group was initially headed by Mrs. H. E. Barnum. It solicited "plain sewing" work to raise money for missionary causes.

Joining the other churches in mid-1892 was the Methodist Episcopal, built and organized by the tireless efforts of the Reverend Oliver Frambes of Hanford. Sent originally to minister to a congregation of five, Frambes canvassed the area, found more members, and collected funds for a $1,200 church. Opened for use on June 19, 1892, it was dedicated the following September 11. A home mission society was organized at the church in late 1893, and Frambes was replaced by the Reverend T. L. Bradley about that time. He returned after a while and served until 1898, when William Dunwiddie was appointed pastor.

Along with the churches, Reedley had a strong complement of clubs and organizations in its early years. A Masonic lodge was founded in 1891, the same year in which the town was said to have a "wide-awake" Woman's Christian Temperance Union of nineteen members. The Independent Order of Odd Fellows, Mount Campbell Lodge, was doing so well by 1892 that it organized a Rebekah lodge (women's auxiliary) on December 20. A Masonic women's equivalent (Eastern Star) and an Independent Order of Foresters lodge started about the same time.

The next significant club to come along was the Reedley Lyceum, organized at the town depot on November 24, 1899, with Mrs. Joel U. Smith as president. Its pledge: "Our aim is Intilectual [?] Improvement and to work for the best interests of the Lyceum." For one dollar a year its members—limited to twenty-five—studied and discussed the English language and classical literature. In late 1899, the club ordered some books, charging each member a special assessment of eighty cents each, and began assembling Reedley's first public library.

According to an uncorroborated story, the Southern Pacific founded Sanger because landowners in the Centerville area declined to cooperate with the railroad and give it the rights-of-way and property necessary to establish a station there. Whatever the reason, railroad officials had decided on Sanger's creation by 1887, naming it in honor of Joseph Sanger, Jr., secretary of the national Railroad Yardmaster's Association. As with the founding of Reedley, there were good reasons for the railroad's decision: farming activities in the immediate area had intensified, and there was talk of building a branch line to lumber flume terminuses east of the prospective town.

Actual settlement began in early 1888, with Sanger's first residents being J. B. Daniels and W. B. Miller.

Reference 13:4

# SANGER THROUGH A YOUNG BOY'S EYES
## AL C. JOY

Perhaps because I knew him best of all and because he was an influence of considerable importance in my own life, I shall always regard the late E. P. Dewey as Sanger's leading citizen of those long-ago days. Some of the old timers may disagree. I am sure, however, there will be no disagreement from the Herald staff. Ed Dewey—of course, I never called him anything but Mr. Dewey—started the Herald. I think previously he had been at Porterville, where he started the old Porterville Enterprise. He came of an old-time family of country newspaper folk. When I knew him he had two brothers in the newspaper business in the San Joaquin Valley—Fred Dewey running the Hanford Journal, and Wilbur Dewey running the Lemoore Advance. Their father had once operated a paper in Visalia; their uncle was the publisher of the Pacific Rural Press.

People liked Ed Dewey. He was a quiet man, a good family man, with a kindly disposition and a keen sense of humor. Each week the Herald carried a column of jokes headed "Efforts at Wit." Many people thought Dewey wrote the jokes, but it was common for some of the citizens to come guffawing into the office to repeat his latest funny ones. Of course, he didn't write the jokes; he clipped them. In fact, clipped items occupied a lot of the Herald's space. I must admit that the office shears did yeoman editorial service.

I think I was about thirteen or fourteen years old when Dewey proposed I should come into his shop to learn the printing trade.... Everybody in Sanger was poor then. We had gone through the depression of the early nineties and had by no means recovered. Wages in the mill were small, men getting from $1.50 to $2.00 a day for ten hours' work. Farmers were paid starvation prices for their crops. And nearly every man in business along Main Street had suffered from disastrous fires.

The Herald had been burned out twice. Each time a new plant had to be bought. When I went to work for Dewey, his equipment was about as meager as could be expected. I doubt if it represented more than $1,200 in complete cost, brand new, and included a Washington hand press, a 10x15 Chandler & Price Gordon job press, a Paragon paper cutter, about 2000 pounds of eight-point body type and between thirty and forty fonts of display type for job work and advertising and the necessary stones, rules and furniture.

Until I went to work for him Dewey had for a year or so done all the work himself—gathering and editing the news, setting the type, soliciting advertising and job work, setting up jobs and "kicking" the job press. On press day he had to get somebody to help him and Peter Hoy, the jeweler had been a sort of volunteer assistant. I took over the running of the big ink roller over the face of the forms. During the time I worked for Dewey I think I climbed up to the munificent stipend of three dollars a week. I wonder if I was worth it?

The old-time joke about the country publisher who was paid off in butter and eggs is rarely heard these days. It was common enough then and it was not entirely an exaggeration. For instance, there was old Farmer Brown from out Centerville way. He was but one of several farmers who came to the Herald office regularly with melons and fruits and vegetables. This is the way they paid their subscriptions. Besides they rather liked to see that little item which appeared regularly: "Our good friend, Elmer Brown, dropped in on Ye Editor during the week with a basket of luscious peaches from his thriving orchard at Centerville. Come again."...

Somebody tells me Brehler's is one of the two oldest business institutions in town! Well, back in those first days of Sanger's existence, the Elmore Drug Store had a monopoly. It was run by A. J. Elmore, known to everybody as "Dick" probably because that wasn't his name. Equally as well known as Dick was his brother, Al. The The Elmores represent my own experience in the drug business. I washed bottles, swept out the store, occasionally wiped off the two big window jars of colored water which every drug store displayed in those days and helped make soda water. My pay was chiefly soda water. Because of my interest in the soda fountain, which worked overtime when I was left alone in the store, I didn't last long on the job. Nor did I hold on to one other job very long, although while I had it I was the envy of all the other twelve-year-olds in town. That was being the village bootblack.

The principal barber shop was run by a negro. He was a big, fat fellow, good natured as I recall him, and he needed two employees. One was another barber, and at the time I recall, this second barber was also a negro, very light colored and also little and skinny. He played an accordion, and being the only individual along Main street with such an accomplishment he loomed as quite a person in young Sanger's eyes. The other employee looked after the four or five bath tubs which were a part of the establishment and which masculine Sanger patronized liberally every Saturday, and also had the shine concession. This was, of course, merely a week-end job. An enterprising boy might make as much as a dollar and a half on Saturday, but a dollar and a half was terrific money. So I got the job. And the first week-end went along alright. One trifling detail, however, about my connection with the job disturbed me. I overlooked entirely mentioning it at home. But somebody told his mother and she told one of her neighbors, and eventually it got around to the ears of my mother. She was the daughter of a Virginian. The news that her son was shining shoes in a barber shop run by a colored man was virtually as heartbreaking as if it had been news that that same son was laid out cold at the morgue. Business was proceeding briskly on the second Saturday when the young man's father suddenly appeared, took him by the back of the neck and moved him out of there. My first venture into business was not really successful....

SOURCE: Golden Anniversary Edition, *Sanger Herald*, 1888–1938.

For several months the sole signs of habitation were their dwellings, a store Miller was operating, and a water tank built by the railroad.

Settlement in earnest began on May 23, 1888, when the Southern Pacific auctioned some of the 800 acres it owned in and around Sanger. Construction of a depot had begun about a month before, and a section house, tool house and lodging house, all built by the railroad, were finished the following November. A post office was established by Lee McLaughlin on June 26, 1888; five days later (July 1) the Fresno-to-Porterville line formally opened. Demand for property became so brisk that the railroad withdrew its little remaining for-sale land by mid-September.

By mid-1888 D. C. Blevins was building a hotel in Sanger, as were Matthew Rogallo and Augustin Sicre; A. D. Young was running a restaurant and rooming house; J. S. Filloon and Frank Lindsay were operating livery stables; Daniel S. Evinger and D. A. Swain had opened up blacksmith shops; L. W. Hobler was serving drinks in his saloon; Prescott and Pierce had a lumberyard in town; Costigan, Cohen and Company were erecting a warehouse near the railroad tracks; L. W. Hanke was serving as the town butcher; I. Brownstone had opened another store (and Max Frankenau was building another); and J. T. Walton was selling real estate and insurance. Along with this comprehensive array of businesses, there were three doctors practicing in town (Helm, Watson and Porterfield), and A. A. Hill, R. Jones, Hanke and Filloon had built substantial homes for themselves. In a mere six months Sanger had undergone a metamorphosis from vacant tract to fully-functioning small town—a feat unparalleled in Fresno County history.

Sanger's progress continued pace in 1889, when townsmen I. N. Pattison, W. B. Miller and F. S. Douty induced the Kings River Lumber Company to locate a flume terminus and large lumber finishing plant there. J. T. Walton installed the first pay phone in the Weiner Building, E. P. Dewey began publishing the *Sanger Herald* in May (see 13:4), William N. Barr founded the Barr Insurance Agency, and Charles and Emma Gailey opened a new rooming house.

Perhaps the most notable 1889 development was the

Reference 13:5

## SANGER AND ITS BUSINESSES AND INDUSTRIES

. . . A year or so ago Sanger only existed on a railway map, unless a few rough board shanties could be looked upon as a town. But its splendid location for manufacturing, packing, brick making, lumbering, etc. could not long remain unutilized, and to-day several hundred people are taking advantage of these golden opportunities and rapidly building what will soon be a handsome and substantial town. Prices for real estate have increased over 500 per cent. within the last twelve months; but this proves no drawback to those who are enterprising and really see the bright future in store for this pushing town; but land is purchased and buildings are being erected on every side. At present there are seven in course of construction, and many more are contemplated. . . .

In less than a year, the town will have several beautiful and substantial churches. The Methodists and Presbyterians have begun negotiations for houses of worship, but at present the Baptist church is the only one that has made a start. The building, which will be completed in a few weeks, will be quite a handsome structure and an ornament to the town.

Rev. A. D. Smith of Fresno has accepted a call extended to him a few weeks ago, and will henceforth act as pastor and preach regularly.

Sanger's citizens show their culture and taste in surrounding themselves with many of those things that go to make up the comforts of life. There are many very pretty residences in town, but that of Mr. Wm. Hanke is worthy of special notice. It was built last year, and is of the Italian villa style of architecture.

### HOTEL DE FRANCE.

This is a large and commodious building, situated in the center of town. Here at all times the delicacies of the season can be found, and the cellar is supplied with the best wines of California and Europe. All the rooms are commodious and clean; in fact, all conveniences can be found here. The building was put up 18 months ago by A. Sicre. A. M. Rogalla is manager.

A bowling alley is now being built in the rear of the building; and in less than a year other alterations will be made. Then it is the intention of the proprietors to make it one of the most popular resorts in this part of the country.

### VALLEY LUMBER COMPANY.

This concern, which has its headquarters at Fresno, established the Sanger agency in June, 1889, with George Wendling manager. The present buildings were put up in 1889. A complete stock of lumber can always be found here, and also a full assortment of sash, doors, blinds and builders' hardware. The company have always furnished the surrounding country with all the raisin trays, sweat boxes, etc., used. The outlook for the future is very bright. The business in the past has averaged between $5000 and $6000 a month.

### FRANKENAU BROS.

Their Sanger stores were built and ready for occupancy about one year ago. It is a branch of the oldest store in the county, the original house being located in Centerville and under the supervision of Max Frankenau. If an ingenious writer gave scope to his imagination, columns might be written about the earlier experiences of this firm. It is, however, best to contain one's self to facts and avoid predicating. The brothers have been subscribers of the Expositor since its first issue some 21 years ago, and their business has grown with the county until now it requires two separate stores, the larger of which is the Sanger establishment under the care of Sig Frankenau. The building is fire proof and 40 feet wide by 100 feet deep. A leading feature of this establishment is the spacious cellar, 10 feet deep, with brick walls and floor, stocked with general merchandise.

### I. BROWNSTONE & SONS.

I. Brownstone & Sons began a general merchandise business in Sanger November 1888, in a small wooden shanty. They have now established a trade throughout this section of the county commensurate with the importance of the community in which they are located. Their fine brick store in Sanger is 50x100 feet. It is a branch of the Selma store. H. P. Brownstone is the youngest business man in Sanger, and handles the cash of this establishment and is referred to as the mascotte of this enterprising firm.

### PETER HOY.

The leading jeweler and watchmaker in Sanger is Peter Hoy, who has had years of experience in practical watch work in the old country. He is thoroughly qualified to repair the most complicated watches and clocks, and his prices are reasonable and satisfactory. Mr. Hoy is a new comer in Sanger and brings with him the best of references. Watches and jewelry bought here can be relied upon as represented.

### W. B. HAZLETON.

Prominent among the many firms en-

February 26 founding of the Sanger School District. John Evans, its first teacher, presided over a class of eighty-four that grew to 158 the next year, when he was joined by A. Allen and Mrs. C. P. Walton. By then a $10,000 brick schoolhouse with a three-cornered steeple had been built and was in use. The steeple, recalled Sanger old-timer Al Joy, eventually had to be dismantled for fear it would blow off and crush anyone standing outside. He also remembered Evans as being "a somewhat stern man of that old schoolmaster type who believe[d] in discipline maintained with the aid of a good whip." Students sat at tables and benches which, Joy said, allowed Evans to "whale three or four of us consecutively without any of us having to move from our seats." In 1895 Dr. E. E. Baird was installed as principal of the school, and was succeeded in 1899 by a Mr. Thom.

Sanger's explosive growth showed no signs of slowing down in 1890. After more than a year's work the Kings River Lumber Company's fifty-four-mile flume was completed in early September. Its planing mill, box, window, sash and door factories and shingle, lathe and resawing mills were already operating on sixty-five acres near Sanger, employing 125 men. This was the largest lumberyard in California, and the flume servicing it was the longest in the state. The town celebrated in a grand way when the latter was completed. Hundreds of people, many of whom came on a special train from Fresno, listened to speakers and feasted on three whole bulls, ten sheep and 300 loaves of bread.

Knowledge of the lumber company's coming had made many town businesses prosper, and had caused a myriad of others to spring up (see 13:4 and 13:5)). A number of specialized enterprises came to the fore around this time: the Babby sisters' dressmaking shop, the Sanger Home Bakery, Elliot's jewelry store, Deming and Edgar's billiard parlor, J. M. Reese's bicycle

gaged in business in Sanger is the meat market of W. B. Hazleton. He is enterprising and industrious, and furnishes meat to the leading, and, in fact, nearly all the families in his portion of the town. He launched out for himself on the 17th of January, 1890, and to-day is supplying a large territory in the county by a wagon. His market is located on the east side of the track.

### DENING & EDGAR.

This well-known and popular resort, located on the principal business street in Sanger, is conducted by Dening & Edgar. It is the only place in Sanger where a glass of Welland's refreshing lager beer can be had for five cents. Their personal popularity has added friend to friend from day to day, and nobody ever goes through Sanger without stopping to see Dening & Edgar. They soon expect to put in a number of billiard tables, and they are reckoned among the most prosperous citizens of the town, and keep only the finest assortment of wines, liquors and cigars, they are at the service of any guest at any hour of the day.

### SANGER HERALD.

On the 11th day of May, 1890, the Sanger *Herald* first made its appearance. The paper was established by E. P. Dewey as a seven-column weekly, and is issued every Saturday at the modest sum of $2 per year. The advertising columns present a good healthy appearance, and proves that the people of Sanger are enterprising and possessed of considerable push. The *Herald* has done much toward advertising Sanger and its advantages, and we sincerely hope that brother Dewey will continue the good work and reap a well-deserved reward.

### SANGER'S BRICKYARD.

One of Sanger's most important industries is the brickyard owned by Renfro & Betteridge. It is situated about three-quarters of a mile from the center of town and employs about 30 men most of the time.

They keep two kilns running now with a combined capacity of 100,000 brick a week. A kiln for burning press brick has just been built.

The clay in this vicinity is very good and soil scarce, so it is an assured fact that Sanger will make its own brick for years to come.

The yards have been established 15 months, and in all that time the company has had to work hard to fill orders....

### KINGS RIVER LUMBER COMPANY.

This is a joint stock company organized within the last few years. Messrs. Moore & Smith of Frenso being the principal shareholders.

The box factory which is now in successful operation has just been completed. The engine house is as perfect as can be found anywhere. It contains a 150-horse power compound Atlas engine built expressly for the work. The steam for which is generated in three 50-foot return flue boilers. The entire building is constructed of brick and iron, and the floors are made of hard concrete.

The box factory is a building 75x150 feet, lying about 100 feet back of the engine houses, to which power is communicated by a strong steel cable. The main floor, which is devoted entirely to the manufacture of boxes and trays for raisins, contains two planers; four circular saws; one large rip saw; one groover, one labeler, and all the other necessaries for the business. The factory, when in good running order, has a capacity of 10,000 boxes a day.

The planing-mill is still in course of erection, but that will not be needed until the big flume, which the company is constructing, is finished.

The flume, which is still 20 miles from Sanger, taps Kings river at the mouth of Mill Flat creek and hugs the canyon all the way to its mouth.

This is one of the most gigantic undertakings for many years, and when completed the flume will be 54 miles long, without the feeders, of which there are five, and it will require 250 inches of water to run it.

A reservoir of stone is built at the head of the flume and covers 120 acres at a depth of 20 feet.

The first survey for this work was made about two years ago, and the work of construction commenced the 20th day of July, last year. The first 27 miles of the work lay in the wildest part of the Sierra Nevadas, and all the materials used had to be carried on the shoulders of the men. This took over 5,000,000 feet of lumber. It is estimated that over 9,000,000 will be used before the work is finished.

When the first 27 miles were finished the river had to be crossed, which necessitated the construction of a suspension bridge 454 feet long. The bridge is supported by two piers, to which are attached 14 1½ inch steel cables which carry the flume. A wooden truss is also placed under the center of the bridge, which prevents the flume from sagging or springing, according to the quantity of water.

In many places the trestle on which the flume is carried is over 100 feet high, but so far the work has been accomplished without serious injury to any of the 150 men that are kept constantly at work.

When completed the flume will be the largest in the State. It is V-shaped, with 42-inch sides, and can carry down to Sanger all the lumber cut by two mills which have a capacity of 150,000 feet a day each.

All this work has been under the supervision of Charles B. Eads, an engineer of good ability, as is shown by the way he has handled this enormous undertaking.

SOURCE: *Fresno Daily Evening Expositor*, July 7, 1890, p. 2, p. 3 c. 1–2.

shop, and Joy's tinshop. Merchants Frankenau and Kutner and Goldstein even saw fit to incorporate the Bank of Sanger on October 4, 1890.

There were 100 structures in town, thirteen of which contained saloons, and a population of 300. Every hotel and rooming house in town was cramped with people, and some had to live in tents. As a result, additions to the town (South Villa and Sanger Heights) had been plotted and were being occupied rapidly.

A nearby school was gained on February 12, 1890, when the Frankwood School District was organized—supposedly named for Sanger businessman Frankenau and R. M. Wood, who made heavy contributions toward building the district's first schoolhouse.

Community spiritual development had begun early, with the founding of a Presbyterian Sunday School on January 3, 1890. Its successor, the First Presbyterian Church, was organized the following May 4, with the Reverend George C. Giffen called as its minister in October. Sanger's first church congregation, however, was the Baptist, organized on January 6, 1890, at Dr. J. H. Hudspeth's home. Members built a $2,000 house of worship that summer and dedicated it the next September 7; J. N. Lacy was the first pastor. A Methodist Episcopal Church South organization built a $2,500 structure for itself at the same time, and Catholic services were being conducted in a number of private homes.

J. S. Filloon built a water works for Sanger in 1890–91, consisting of a boiler room, pump house and water tower. Some time afterward C. Small purchased this enterprise, and he was bought out by Frank Kummeth in 1896 for $4,000 and three city lots. Shavings from the nearby lumber mill were used to fire the works' boiler. The service had been inaugurated at the behest of local businessmen who wanted it to help fight the fires that had begun to strike the town.

A particularly destructive blaze hit on August 25, 1890, before the water works could be completed. A. J. Elmore's drugstore, the *Sanger Herald*, and Dr. M. C. Hoag were burned out of their places of busi-ness. *Herald* proprietor Dewey raced to San Francisco via train after the disaster, scampered back with new printing supplies, and managed to resume publication without missing an issue.

Businesses coming into existence at this time included the Sanger Electric Light and Power Company, incorporated by A. W. Chase and E. de Reynier after a similar scheme had failed the year before. The Edison Electric Light and Power Company supplied the generating equipment and service began sometime in 1892. A one-man operation, the company was purchased by Anton Borel around 1896 and managed by John T. Chick. During day hours, Chick serviced lighting fixtures and transacted business. By night, he ran the plant steam engine and dynamo.

The 1890s were not a particularly prosperous time for Sanger. Its economy was closely tied to that of the Kings River Lumber Company, which did not weather the decade well. In September of the depression year of 1893 the company came close to failing, and was paying its workers on an irregular basis. This led to a strike on June 22, 1894 (which was quickly settled) and a corporate reorganization, with an increase in capital stock, the following October. Now known as the Sanger Lumber Company, its work force was cut to 125 because of increased mechanization and other factors. The rapid depletion of county timber lands, together with competition from the coastal lumber mills, restricted production to approximately 50,000 finished feet of lumber a day.

Thus, only ten years after its founding, Sanger experienced a commercial slump. A hotel and several rooming houses went out of business, and many buildings were vacant. Its population, around 1,500 by 1895, began moving into the Parkhurst West and other town additions at a slower rate. Few major businesses opened in town during this era. Among those that did were the Burton Brothers saloon, William Barton's boarding house, and William Basler's hotel, all in early 1891; and, later in the decade, the Sanger Sanitarium, Shell-enbarger and Ingels' grocery store, D. R. Evinger's plumbing shop, and the Boysen and Williams grocery and hardware store.

A fair number of town businesses were housed in large brick commercial blocks, notably the Simmons-Tiles, Gray, and Pattison East and West blocks. The two-story Pattison West Block alone contained A. J. Elmore's drug store, W. A. Hurry's grocery store, Daniels and Parkhurst's real estate office, R. Ellis and W. S. Harvey's wine and liquor stores, P. Hoy's jewelry store, the *Sanger Herald*, R. McEwen's confectionary and the Blood and Sons market, along with forty-five lodging suites on its upper floor. Some of these concerns were serviced by Sanger's infant telephone company, whose switchboard was first located in the J. C. Pottle grocery store and later moved to Redfield's Pharmacy. At the latter location a Miss Ries served as store clerk and operator for the telephone company's subscribers—all twenty or so of them.

Fire continued to plague Sanger. A November 2, 1891, blaze consumed fourteen businesses and caused an $11,000 loss. Another on June 25, 1892, destroyed the Commercial Hotel and a smaller building, together worth $8,000. The Pattison West Block was hit on two separate occasions (February 5, 1894, and June 26, 1897), with the first conflagration causing $35,000 worth of damage, and the second—due to an explosion of undetermined cause—destroying the building. A veritable tinderbox, the Sanger Lumber Company was hit by flames on December 20, 1897. Its $15,000 box factory burned down, and had winds been blowing the loss would have been greater.

So many fires happened in these days that Sanger

businessmen often muttered, "I wonder who'll burn out tonight." Arsonists were suspected, and one named Jack Schoolie was caught one day setting a blaze under the Frankenau store. Despite the fact he was retarded, he was sent to the penitentiary for his deed. A carpenter named Gibson was also thought responsible for some of the fires, though no charge was ever proven against him. It was observed that when he was half-finished with a job, it would burn down. He would then begin anew, at a higher price. Local insurers soon refused to cover his work, and Gibson had to leave town. Before departing, he claimed that jealous competitors had really caused the havoc.

There were only two significant educational developments in Sanger during the 1890s. The first was the opening of a private kindergarten, with Florence Burns McAllister as teacher, in 1894. The second was the formation of the Sanger Union High School District on June 27, 1899. Classes started later that year and were first conducted in the Sanger Opera House. First-year students took courses in English literature, algebra, Latin and English history, with plane geometry and examination of Caesar's Gallic Wars reserved for the second year. The school drew pupils not only from the Sanger and Frankwood schools but from seven other long-established districts as well: the Georgiaville (founded on May 6, 1872), Round Mountain (August 4, 1873), Fairview (November 3, 1873), Bethel (May 15, 1879), Rosedale (February 29, 1881), Lone Star and Eureka (December 12, 1886).

Churches continued to be established, notably the Methodist Episcopal in 1891 and the Christian in 1893. The Methodist Episcopal, under the leadership of the Reverend George A. Miller, built a house of worship in 1892. The Presbyterians dedicated theirs on January 10 of the same year with the Reverend James L. Wood as its pastor. Visiting ministers serviced the Christian congregation (which apparently erected a church in the year of its founding) until 1895, when the Reverend Shields was installed there.

About this time, auxiliary organizations were beginning to flourish in Sanger's churches. The Baptists had a Ladies' Home Mission Circle, and the Methodist Episcopal Church South a similar group, by 1894. A Women's Home and Foreign Missionary Society was founded at the Presbyterian Church in 1895; a Christian Church ladies' club, by 1898; and a Christian Endeavor Society at the Presbyterian Church in 1899.

Fraternal and other organizations were also attracting attention—and members—in these days. By 1892 Sanger had Forester and Odd Fellows lodges, along with a miscellany of clubs: Knights of Hoppergrass, Sanger Harmonic Association, Theosophical Literary,

Reference 13:6

## ARTHUR CHEDISTER'S CLOVIS MEMORIES

The little town of Clovis in the years of 1893, 1894, was completely dominated by the lumber company. This was true for many years, although to a lesser degree each year, as the agriculture area expanded.

The Company never interfered in the affairs of the town. It was only that the living of every man, woman and child depended upon the welfare of the lumber industry, not only for their monthly pay checks, but for the fuel used in cooking and heating as well.

The "mill," as the whole plant was referred to locally, dominated the whole area physically as well as mentally. The view from town toward the east was completely blocked off by the forty acres of lumber piles, all about forty feet high. The big V-shaped flume, about twenty-five feet in height, stretched away towards Academy as far as the eye could see. The two eighty-foot water towers looked as high as a mountain on the flat plain, and the two big smokestacks belched forth huge columns of black smoke all day long, and the big brick sawdust burner, located 150 yards south of the engine house, burned fiercely day and night. It gave off a big red beautiful glow at night, when seen from a distance; up close it looked and smelled like a small Hades.

The big steam whistle at the engine house awakened Clovis, and a very considerable area of Fresno County, at exactly 5:30 a.m.

Monday to Saturday, inclusive, all the year around. The working hours were from 6:30 a.m. until 11:30 a.m. Then from 12:30 p.m. until 5:30 p.m. The big whistle tooted . . . at these hours, and also accommodatingly gave a five-minute-warning blast at 6:25 a.m. and again at 12:25 p.m.

Any young husband who was a good runner could wait until that warning whistle for one last kiss and then make it to the box factory in time to start work.

People in lumber towns had small use for alarm clocks as the big steam whistle solved all time problems, except on Sunday.

In Clovis in those early years the whistle at the lumber company engine house served as the local fire alarm. At night it seemed loud and eerie enough to wake the dead. Anyhow, when it started to toot a number of short ones, then a long one, and so on in the middle of the night everyone woke up, started to dress and looked out to see where the fire was.

You could hear people all over town talking and yelling while they tried to find their clothes in a hurry. All the men and boys hurried to the fire; the women and children mostly stayed at home.

The burning house or store usually burned down, taking the adjacent buildings with them, but the people worked furiously to save what they could. Bucket lines were run from all nearby wells. It was a thrilling sight to see men sitting up on the roofs of buildings next to the one burning, pouring water over the roof as fast as [it] was handed to them.

Anyhow, that's the only way fire was fought in Clovis or any other early town, before they put in their own water systems . . .

There was something weird or perhaps I should say "screwy" about the old stores, saloons and other shops on Front Street as Clovis Avenue was then known. This was the fact that no two adjacent buildings had their floors at the same height. They sometimes varied as much as two feet. Also each one had its own front porch and wooden sidewalks the same level as the floor. For this reason a person's progress down Front Street was never boring. You had to look where you were going or break a leg or worse. It was positively dangerous for an inebriated person or a very small child.

The streets were nothing but wagon and buggy tracks. They were inches in dust in the summer and likewise in mud in the winter. Those were the days when women wore a lot of skirts and underskirts which dragged the floor, and they wore them down the dusty and muddy streets of this town, too. It took one hand to hold up the skirts alone. I've forgotten how they used to hold up the skirts

301

Progressive Euchre, and Nights at the Green Cloth—the last presumably composed of card players. The Literary Club, founded by Mrs. Emma Miller, was successful enough to form a spinoff Shakespearean Club. In 1893 a Masonic lodge was founded, with Henry Bascom Rogers as its first master; after it had met in a number of places for three years, a generous member (William Benning Depew) built a hall for the group. A Rebekah lodge was initiated on January 5, 1894, and a Farmers' Alliance was operating by that date. Just before the century's end a Woman's Christian Temperance Union lodge was started (in 1897, with Mrs. M. L. Clark as president), along with a Woodmen of the World lodge and a Sanger Social Club, which hosted balls and other community events.

The amusements and entertainments available in young Sanger were as varied as its social groups. Tamale socials, May Day parades, barbecues, and picnics along the banks of the nearby Kings were the most common. At first, the Episcopal Church's Guild Hall presented regular Thursday-night musical and dramatic shows. It was supplanted eventually by the Odd Fellows' Depew Opera House, said to have "the smoothest dance floor in Fresno County." This building, which served as the Sanger Union High School's first home, held another distinction—it was the town's first motion picture theater. A February 5, 1897, report in the *Fresno Daily Evening Expositor* noted that the "Edison projecting kinetoscope is to be at the Depew Opera House tonight."

Athletic events were also popular. In 1894 Sanger had a baseball team that played the Centerville and Fowler teams on the same day, beating both; and wrestling matches were being held in one of the Pattison blocks. Tennis became popular among townsfolk in 1896–97, so much so that a court was put in northeast of Sanger. Winter rains, unfortunately, made it unusable: " . . . if they would just put it into a refrigerator and freeze it over it would make a fine skating rink," said a contemporary newspaper correspondent. Another favored sport, held on an improvised track south of town, was horse racing.

In addition to the foregoing there was a less conventional, and more imaginative, side to early Sanger's social and recreational life. "The Ladies' Aid Society [its affiliation was not specified] gave a very pleasant entertainment at Tucker Hall Monday evening," said the February 11, 1892, *Fresno Daily Evening Expositor*. "It was called a weight social. The ladies deposited their cards in a basket, and the gentlemen drew one each, escorted his lady to a pair of scales and paid her half a cent per pound for their supper."

Another story, in the June 25, 1894, issue of the same newspaper, told of a social the Methodist Episcopal Church South ladies had given the previous Friday. Some fifty or sixty young women were placed behind a

and lead two or three children, but they did it.

There were no street lamps. The only illumination was by kerosene lamps, which were a continual fire hazard . . .

The livery stable was the gathering place of all people interested in horses, and there were lots of people who owned horses, raised horses or broke and trained them to driving and riding. There were usually several of these expert drivers and mule skinners spending their time between jobs at the livery stable, "chewing the rag" on the benches in front . . .

For the benefit of the younger generation, I will try to explain how this place operated.

Suppose for some reason at any time of the day or night, I wanted to get to Fresno with my wife or best girl. Well, I'd just meander down to the livery stable and rent a horse and buggy. If I had the cash I could be on my way in about ten minutes or less.

It would take probably an hour or hour and a half to drive to Fresno, where, if I was to stay for several hours, I would put the horse and buggy in another livery stable, where the horse would be fed while I shopped or went to a show, or what have you.

In all honesty I must here state that for the purpose of courting a gal, no other vehicle ever made now or before could ever equal a good little old horse and buggy . . .

Well, in the early days of 1893 and 1894, people more or less made up their own diversions.

The first dance held in the town was in the lumber company boarding house in the Company Row which normally boarded the lumber company office workers and executives the first few years of the job.

I believe dances were held there for several years until James M. McCord built his dance hall on Clovis Avenue, about [March] 1897.

These dances were held about twice a month during the fall, winter and spring months. They were organized by Mr. J. G. Ferguson and his charming wife. These two always led the Grand March which started these dances. They were still doing the same as late as 1901, which is where I came into the picture; that is, my parents started taking me to dances, baby sitters being unknown at the time.

A town dance of those days was quite a social affair. Everyone that could dance went to them, richer or poorer. However, once in the dance hall, good manners prevailed. Any man even slightly inebriated was politely taken outside by the floor manager, who was usually a pretty husky individual.

No gentleman, as any decent man of those days called himself, would ever think of asking a strange young lady to dance. If none of his friends could introduce him, he would seek the services of the floor manager. The latter would then go to the young lady, point out the interested man. If the lady said, "Yes, I'd like to meet him," all right, it was done. If she said "no," why that ended it.

When a man took a woman to a dance in those days, unless it was a program dance, he would dance the first dance with her, one along in the middle, and always the last one. In between, he saw that she had plenty of good dances and that she met decent men that she did not know.

Furthermore, when a man wanted to dance with a gal, he walked over to her, bowed and politely asked her for the next dance, or whichever one she could give him. If she said "no" he said "thank you," and tried another.

It may seem to people of this generation that with all this politeness their grandparents or fathers and mothers never had much fun at dances.

But the writer has been around dances as a spectator and participant for more years than he cares to admit, and I must say that I've never seen people have as much decent fun as they used to have in the early days of Clovis.

SOURCE: *The Story of Clovis*, by Arthur W. Chedister. Typescript taken from 1953 and 1954 issues of the *Clovis Independent*, at Clovis Branch of the Fresno County Free Library. Extracts given here from pages 5, 8–9, 22, and 28.

*Wheat, early backbone of the economy of Clovis-Big Dry Creek as well as most of the county, was harvested by horse or mule drawn harvesters like the above, owned by Clyde Bissel and Albert P. Smith and being used on the Potter place east of Clovis circa 1900. Clovis Cole operated four of these to cut, thresh and sack wheat from 210 acres in a day. The four units required twenty men and 108 mules.*

*Lumber assumed primary importance in the 1890s when the flume brought lumber from Pine Ridge to Clovis. The yard in the lower left later became site of the Clovis Union High School.*

*Clovis mill of the Fresno Flume and Lumber Company in the early 1890s. It operated all year, usually in ten-hour day and night shifts.*

*Clovis Hotel, on the northwest corner of Fourth Street and Clovis Avenue, 1913.*

*In the 1890s this was the central business district of Clovis. From the left the businesses are: R. E. Sunderland and Company, post office and meat market; unknown; barbershop; unknown; Clovis Stables and Clovis, Madera and Fresno Stageline; Clovis House; S. L. Herring Drugs and Dry Goods; and R. E. L. Good, general merchandise.*

*J. W. Cate and his son had high hopes for their flouring mill but in 1896, after only a few years in business, it burned and was not rebuilt.*

curtain with only their bare feet sticking out. A man was then taken into the room, where he could "buy" a pair that suited his fancy. This transaction "entitled him to the lady and a dainty box of luncheon." It was said that the crowd attending this function was large, and the women cleared a large sum of money.

When the San Joaquin Valley Railroad built its first—and last—leg in 1891, three stations were established alongside it: Pollasky at one end, Tarpey (approximately six miles northeast of Fresno) and, between the two, Clovis. Situated on land donated by wheat farmer Clovis Cole (hence the name), it seemed

like a bad location at first. The terrain was dotted with "hog wallows," or depressions amid low-lying hills. Flooding from Big Dry Creek regularly soaked the ground and brought hordes of mosquitoes and bullfrogs. After the town was laid out by Ingvart Teilman in late 1891 or early 1892, though, settlers began filtering in. Agricultural development, which had fanned out to the southeastern parts of Fresno County, had now moved to the northeast sections and a regional commercial center was needed.

A grain warehouse, built by M. W. Muller, was the second structure to be erected in town—after the railroad's "chicken-coop" depot. It soon acquired a sizable clientele, causing other business ventures to spring up in its wake. Aggressive promotions by local real estate salesman H. G. DeWitt and the Shepherd and Teague company also attracted town lot buyers.

It took only three or four years for Clovis to reach relative sophistication. By the mid-1890s the town had James Turner's livery stable, A. F. McAfee's blacksmith shop, Tom Coddington's barbershop, Jacob Swartz's drayage and hauling business, a Chinese laundry, and R. E. L. Good's general merchandise store and grain warehouse. (According to historian Arthur Chedister, "Bob Good could and did sell everything from a needle to a combined harvester.") There was a newspaper, operated by A. C. Wren, of which the name and all files appear to be lost. A Mr. Foulke operated the Clovis Hotel, Mr. and Mrs. B. K. Smith were proprietors of the Smith Hotel, and Maude, Hannah and Minnie Clifford ran a boarding house.

Indications of progress continued to proliferate. A post office was established—in of all places, the Turner stable—on February 1, 1893. E. S. McClung and E. Coberly were serving, respectively, as the first town constable and justice of the peace. Even those two bitterly opposed institutions of that day, churches and saloons, made their appearance. John W. Potter and James Cate established the Clovis Methodist Church as a branch of the Academy church in 1893, with the Reverend Joel Hedgpeth as its first minister. The O K Saloon came into being at about the same time.

The most important enterprise in town was the Fresno Flume and Irrigation Company. Like Sanger's Kings River/Sanger Lumber Company, its headquarters were placed in the flatlands. Original plans called for its manufacturing facilities and flume terminus to be built at Fresno, but owners L. P. Swift and C. B. Shaver balked at the county seat's high real estate prices. They decided to purchase a sixty-acre lot from Clovis Cole instead, and this move greatly benefited his namesake town.

By 1895, the second year of its operation, $1 million had been spent on the Fresno Flume plant. It employed between 300 and 500 people and had a monthly payroll that exceeded $10,000. Workers processed twenty million feet of lumber annually and five finished carloads daily. The plant's main features were a box factory, planing mill, drying kiln, warehouse, restaurant and rooming house for employees, six cottage homes for company executives, and even a five-acre pasturage for the company's horses. (Today this site is occupied by the Clark Intermediate School and Clovis rodeo grounds.)

Without the Fresno Flume enterprise it is certain that Clovis' early growth would have been less robust. The company attracted men from all over, including a number of Italian, German, Scandinavian and Greek immigrants. Many of them increased their stake in Fresno County by saving money and forsaking lumber for farming. This type of agricultural growth, coupled with a demand for lumber products, pushed Clovis into a mid-1890s boom. "Hard as the times are one can step off the train here any morning and hear the sound of the hammer in all directions," said an October 19, 1895, *Fresno Daily Evening Expositor* report. Nearly a month later the same newspaper commented that thirty homes and four business blocks had been built in the town in less than that many days.

Fire visited early Clovis a few times, taking with it the Southern Pacific depot in 1896, the J. W. Cate and Son flour mill in 1897, and the Fresno Flume planing mill on June 7, 1898 (see 13-6). A $16,000 loss resulted from the flour mill blaze (the facility, only a few years old, had been expanded shortly before), and it was only the work of a bucket brigade that kept the rest of the town from going up in flames.

Infrequent disasters, luckily, did not daunt the town's progressive spirit. Around 1895 storekeeper Good installed a telephone line to Fresno in his place of business; an assistant postmistress (Miss Ida Dawson) had to be hired, at six dollars a week, in 1897; and there was a privately-funded town library functioning by 1899, the same year in which local merchant Al E. Sunderland spearheaded an unsuccessful incorporation drive.

An impressive array of businesses were established in Clovis during the late 1890s. Sunderland opened the town's first meat market in 1896; three years later his wife opened the Home Bakery and Lunch Parlors, which sold bread, pies, cakes, ice cream and tobacco. "Believe me, the ice cream or milkshakes sure felt good in those days before electric fans or refrigerators were available," commented Chedister in later years.

Joining Good on the retail front were Billy Hurry's general merchandise store in 1899, Dr. S. L. Herring's dry goods, drug and notions store, William MacCabe's grocery store, a jeweler, the Clovis Cash Store, and Mrs. M. E. Kelly's Economy Dressmaking and Millinery Parlors. Charles Belden, W. M. and C. B. Beare, W. S. Judkins and Dominic Imperatrice all opened saloons, William Shortridge started a blacksmithing business, A. D. Petee began plying his trade as a barber, and Turner sold his livery stable to Ovid and James Ingmire.

The town's economy, allied to that of the Fresno Flume company, suffered a few reverses just before 1900. Although the company added a night shift in February 1897 and was shipping out twenty-five carloads of lumber a day (quintuple its 1895 rate), twenty men were laid off in January 1899 and production went down to five carloads daily. The factors that caused the Sanger Lumber Company's business to drop off at the same time were also at work here. The remaining work force, pared to 100, staged a strike on August 25 of that year and shut down the plant for a half-day. Management quickly acceded to demands of a ten-hour workday (rather than eleven) and a 10 percent pay raise; average daily salaries then ranged from $1.35 to $1.50.

Fewer men at the plant meant less business at Clovis hotels. There were only two in town by 1898—F. M. Husted's Mountain View and E. A. Doody's Byron, along with R. E. L. Good's boarding house. The Fresno Flume labor cutbacks may have also caused Wren's newspaper to expire at about the same time, although a replacement (the *Clovis Bee*) may have been started in early 1899 by two men named Gentry and Childs.

For all the setbacks, Clovis kept moving ahead in its first decade. A Clovis School District was formed on March 5, 1895. Miss Elizabeth Kanstrup was its first teacher and conducted classes at the town depot. The following August 10 a $5,000 bond issue was passed and a permanent schoolhouse built. The staff was changed in 1896 when B. M. Trautwein was appointed principal and Miss Birdie Lester his assistant.

"Teaching was formal, stern and strict with physical punishment not uncommon," according to one recollection, and a February 11, 1897, *Fresno Daily Evening Expositor* report mentioned that many students had been held back in their grades "as the teacher believes in thoroughness before making promotions." In that year the school moved to a new two-story structure on Pollasky and Second avenues. It accommodated some eighty students at first, but enrollment slipped to fifty-seven after the Fresno Flume cutbacks. There was another staff change in 1899, when a Miss Lewis began teaching and C. A. McCourt became the school's new principal.

Despite the Clovis School's decline, there was great community interest in establishing a high school. Following a mass meeting in Clovis on April 23, 1899, interested residents of nearby school districts began circulating petitions for such a formation. The county schools superintendent soon recognized these efforts and the Clovis Union High School came into being on June 27. Students were drawn from the Clovis, Jefferson (organized May 6, 1884), Red Banks (August 3, 1874), Garfield (May 14, 1883) and Wolters school districts.

Louis K. Webb was appointed as Clovis High School's first teacher and principal. He opened classes in the grammar school's second floor on September 11, 1899, with an average attendance of twelve. Webb, a well-qualified teacher for his day—he had studied at the University of Michigan and Stanford—drew a $120 monthly salary. "Those who studied under him are unanimous in their praise of Mr. Webb, not only as a most excellent teacher, but also as a very fine man," said one contemporary newspaper report.

Compared to other Fresno County towns, Clovis' spiritual development was somewhat laggard. Only three congregations were established before the century's turn: the Methodists, the Baptists (about 1895) and the Presbyterians (about 1898). The Baptists apparently worshipped in a temporary edifice before 1897, when they built a church at Woodworth and Fourth avenues and installed the Reverend T. C. Rush as their pastor. In 1899 the Presbyterians erected a modest structure between Sixth and Seventh avenues on Woodworth. They had held services in the parlor of Burt Smith's home previously.

Entertainments and organizations were many in these days—in fact, they were disproportionate to the town's size. Clovis residents could join a literary club, Good Templars lodge, Epworth League, Anti-Saloon League, Flume City Social Club, Clovis Cotillion Club, and Clovis Amateur Orchestra, the last formed in 1899. Merchant Al Sunderland organized a town dramatic club in February 1897; among its early productions were "The Spy of Gettysburg," "Finnegan's Fortune," and "Among the Breakers." (Note of interest: This enthusiasm for theatrics passed on to Sunderland's daughter, Nan, who became a minor stage and film actress and later married actor Walter Huston.) For Fresno Flume employees there was a Woodmen of the World chapter, and for their wives, a Women of Woodcraft auxiliary known as the Pine Burr Circle.

At first some of these groups held their functions—dances, ice cream socials, benefit dances and other entertainment—at the Fresno Flume plant. This changed in February 1897, when James McCord built a public hall after the Woodmen guaranteed him twelve dollars in monthly rentals. This establishment played host to events conventional and unconventional. The Woodmen liked to have socials with songs, recitations and speeches—and plenty of cakes, pies, sandwiches, coffee and doughnuts afterward.

Other groups, including the Woodmen's auxiliary, were fond of giving "sheet and pillowcase" balls. At these, participants would dress up Ku Klux Klan-style and, apparently, unmask themselves at an appropriate time. Traditional-style balls also were held. One of these, given by the Woodmen in January 1899, attracted sixty couples who danced to the music of Reitz's orchestra. It did not break up until 3:30 a.m., an exceedingly late hour for those hard-working times and an obvious measure of the event's success.

There also were opportunities for the athletically inclined. A November 18, 1895, *Fresno Daily Evening Expositor* report mentioned that Clovis had *two* baseball teams, the "Mill Boys" and the "Flumes." By 1897 a football team also had been organized. Contemporary reports suggest these teams did not fare well on diamond or gridiron. When a Clovis-Sanger football game was anticipated in March 1897, an *Expositor* reporter said: "Only a few of our boys have had experience at all and we predict a walkover for the Sangerites." A July 1898 Clovis-Fresno baseball game, begun although the Clovis team was three men short, ended in a 10 to 1 defeat. "Practice is what we need, and then we are willing to try any team—even those 'swellheads' of Fresno again," whimpered a Clovis *Fresno Morning Republican* correspondent. The team was vindicated, at least partially, when it beat Sanger in May 1899.

If team sports proved unappealing, there were alternatives. "The sporty games here Christmas day," said a December 30, 1896, *Fresno Daily Evening Expositor* story, "were sack races, a potato race, long jump, foot race, horse race and fat man's race. It was a jolly day for the boys."

# Chapter 14
# From Town to City, 1885-1900

The 1887 boom in agriculture and land values brought a simultaneous boom to Fresno that lasted for some time. In 1889, on Mariposa Street alone, new buildings worth $1 million were erected. "It is remarkable how the town continues to grow," said a February 18, 1895, report in the *Fresno Daily Evening Expositor*. "It is gradually spreading and now nearly all the original townsite is occupied"—the area bounded roughly by today's Divisadero, California, Thorne and First streets.

Even the 1893 depression hardly touched Fresno's economy, probably because of its agricultural base. The *Fresno Morning Republican*, in 1894, noted there had been no bank failures the previous year "and consequently no weeping depositors."

The business climate continued favorable into 1897, when the November 15 *Fresno Daily Evening Expositor* mentioned that "the city is growing and there are fine inducements held out to investors. The field is as yet not half occupied . . . " and fifteen commercial activities unknown or under-represented in Fresno were then named. Indeed, it is hard to find business failure notices in the newspapers of this era.

The housing demand continued strong into the 1890s. The April 16, 1890, *Fresno Daily Evening Expositor* noted that a good home, which sold for $2,000 to $3,000, would soon be selling for $3,000 to $4,000. This projection soon became a reality. In the July 1891–June 1892 period 130 homes were built in Fresno for $306,550, and better homes were selling within the predicted range—two-story brick dwellings with ten rooms or thereabouts. Large frame houses with eight rooms went for about $3,000, with four rooms at about $1,000, and with three rooms at about $600. While many of these residences were not substantial, some were (see 14:1). Demand remained constant, too. The November 8, 1895, *Fresno Daily Evening Expositor* reported that, as in times past, there were no vacant houses in Fresno.

During the boom period, opulent business blocks continued to go up. Notable among them were the Olcese and Garibaldi Block, built *circa* 1885; the three-story Hughes Block of Thomas E. Hughes (1887); the Phillips Block (1888); the Asa Shinn Edgerly, Henry Voorman, A. F. Baker, Temple Bar, Kutner-Goldstein, Louis Einstein Pioneer and John D. Fiske blocks (all

Reference 14:1
## "A HANDSOME FRESNO RESIDENCE"

The residence of Mr. and Mrs. J. O. Herrington, on J street, a short distance from the new City Hall, which an Expositor reporter visited on Saturday last, is a beautiful and commodious home throughout.. It is near the business center and yet in a neighborhood of that bevy of beautiful residences lining J street on the north. The plans of this residence were drawn by J. Haffell, and the building was erected by A. Jackson. It consists of thirteen living rooms, all necessary closets and bathrooms, is two stories in height, and is of the Roman style of architecture. On opening the gate one finds his or her feet resting upon a walk of artificial stone pavement, which leads up to the front steps. Mounting the steps the large front doors are thrown open and a sight of gorgeous colors greets the eye that for a time leads one's mind back to the tales of the

fairies. The main hall is decorated in Moorish style of paper, the ceiling being of sky-blue tinsel, interspersed with colors of gold. On the right and left of the hall is the double parlor and sitting-room, decorated in the highest taste of the decorator's art, the ceiling and walls being in embossed gilt, with what is known as the one-band border. The sitting room is in granite, ingrained with tinsel ceiling of beautiful pattern, set off by Japanese border to the depth of eighteen inches. Next we come to the family Blue-room, and here Mr. Widner has shown himself a true blender of beautiful contrasts and colors. Facing the north and to the rear of the sitting-room it commands a fine view. The carpet, which is of heavy Brussels, is of light sky-blue color, and the furniture of a similar hue. The bedrooms, which, in themselves, are one mass of comfort, are all con-

nected with bathrooms. Gas is used in all the rooms, and the gas fixtures are of a high grade. The double doors to the entrance are additionally improved by large stained-glass fronts. The residence as a whole will compare, for finish and fineness of work, with the most elegant in the San Joaquin Valley, and as Mr. Herrington states, it is all due to that prince of paper-hangers, W. H. Widner of Stockton, whose work speaks volumes as to his ability. Mr. Widner is a resident of Stockton, but at present will remain in Fresno, having the contract to redecorate the well-known Joss-house saloon.

SOURCE: Fresno County Scrapbook 1870-1899, p. 1050, taken from *Fresno Daily Evening Expositor*, April 2, 1888.

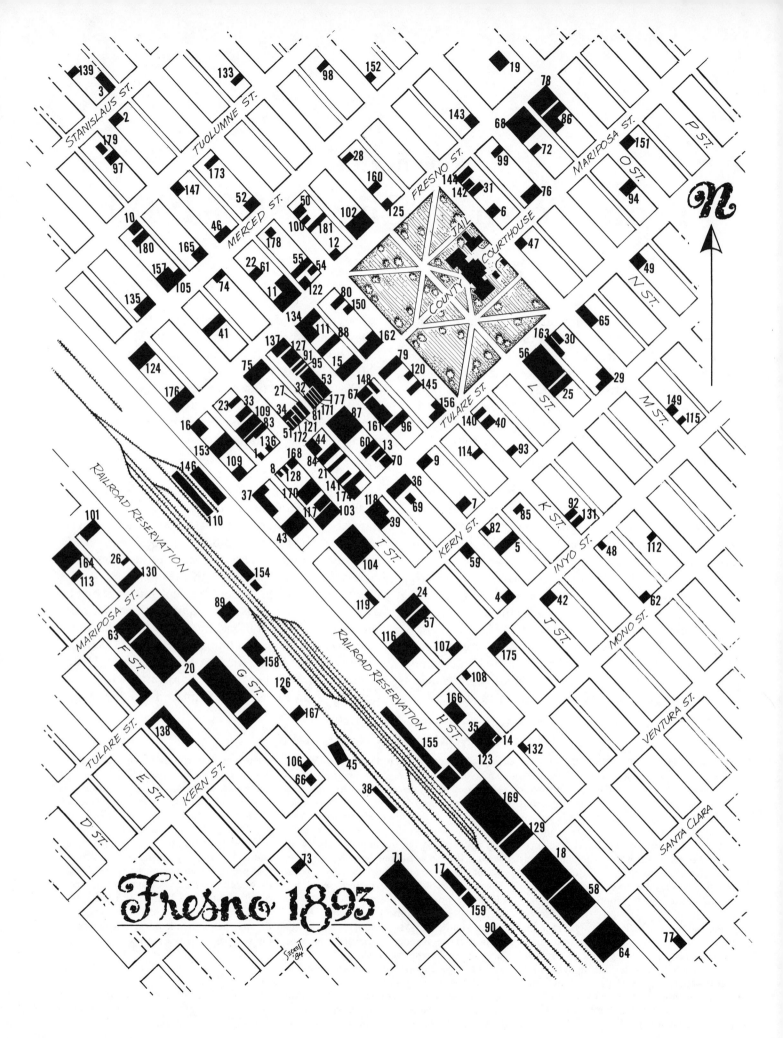

Fresno 1893

308

*Barton Opera House and Armory Hall, one of the most "beautifully decorated," as it appeared shortly after completion in 1890.*

## Key to Map of Fresno in 1893

1. Taylor Albin's Grocery Store
2. Arcade Hotel
3. Arcade Hotel Warehouse
4. Arlington Hotel
5. Armory Livery and Stables
6. Gillum Baley Residence
7. Frank H. Ball Residence
8. Bank of Central California Building
9. Gustavus A. Baron's Comice Works
10. Barton Electric Works
11. Barton Opera House/Armory Hall
12. Blachly and Woods Blacksmith Shop
13. Bohemian Saloon
14. G. W. Bond's Machine Shop
15. Bradley Block
16. George Brainard's Blacksmith Shop
17. Burleigh Grain Warehouse
18. California Raisin and Fruit Packing Company
19. Central (White, Hawthorne) School
20. Chinatown
21. City Bakery and Restaurant
22. City Hall
23. City Market
24. Taswell V. Clowdi's Feed Yard
25. Club Livery Stables
26. Colombo Hotel
27. Commercial Saloon
28. Corlew and Barton Boarding House
29. Oliver H. Curtis' Livery Stables
30. David W. Cutten's Blacksmith Shop
31. James H. Daly Residence and Boarding House
32. Denicke Building
33. DeWitt Block
34. Donahoo, Emmons and Company Hardware Store
35. Earl Fruit Packing Company
36. Edgerly Block
37. Louis Einstein and Company's Pioneer Block
38. Louis Einstein and Company's Pioneer Warehouse
39. Louis Einstein Block
40. Louis Einstein Residence
41. Excelsior Livery and Feed Stables
42. Exchange Livery and Sale Stables
43. Fahey's Hotel
44. Farmers' Bank Building
45. Farmers' Warehouse Company
46. First Baptist Church
47. First Christian Church
48. First Congregational Church
49. First Cumberland Prebyterian Church
50. First Methodist Episcopal Church
51. First National Bank
52. First Presbyterian Church
53. Fiske Block
54. Mrs. V. A. Foye's Lodging House
55. William Fraser's Boarding House
56. Fresno Agricultural Works
57. Fresno Blacksmith and Carriage Shop
58. Fresno Cannery
59. Fresno County Chamber of Commerce
60. *Fresno Daily Evening Expositor* Building
61. Fresno Fire Department, Station No. 1

62. Fresno Fire Department, Station No. 2
63. Fresno Gas Light Company Plant
64. Fresno Home Packing Company
65. Fresno House
66. Fresno Infirmary Veterinary Hospital
67. Fresno Loan and Savings Bank Building
68. Fresno Milling Company/Sperry Flour Company
69. *Fresno Morning Republican* Print Shop
70. Fresno National Bank Building
71. Fresno Raisin and Fruit Packing Company
72. Fresno Sanitarium
73. Fresno Soap Works
74. Fresno Soda Works
75. Fresno Street Improvement Company Building
76. Fresno Swimming Baths
77. Fresno Warehouse Company
78. Fresno Water Works Plant
79. Garibaldi Block
80. John F. Garver's Junk Yard
81. Gilmour Building
82. Golden Gate Institute (Liquor, Morphine, Opium, Cocaine and Tobacco Cures)
83. Gonzalez Block
84. Grady/Fiske Opera House and Beer Hall
85. Walter Drane Grady Residence
86. Grain Warehouses
87. Grand Central Hotel
88. Grand Central Livery Stables
89. Granger's Warehouse
90. Griffin, Skelley and Company Packing House
91. Griffith Building
92. Leopold Gundelfinger Residence
93. Louis Gundelfinger Residence
94. Milus K. Harris Residence
95. Helm Building
96. Simon W. Henry's Livery Stables
97. Mrs. Laura Hicks' Boarding House
98. E. R. Higgins Residence
99. Fred T. Hilton's Blacksmith Shop
100. Edward W. Hollenbeck's Blacksmith Shop
101. Hotel de France
102. Joseph H. House's Feed Stable and Wood Yard
103. Hughes Block
104. Hughes Hotel
105. Independent Order of Odd Fellows Hall
106. John A. Klee and Philip Horn's Blacksmith Shop
107. Kohler House
108. Jens J. Krog's Blacksmith Shop
109. Kutner-Goldstein Stores
110. Kutner-Goldstein Warehouses
111. Kutner Hall
112. Mrs. Virginia P. Lander's Boarding House
113. George Larsen's Blacksmith Shop
114. Dr. Lewis Leach Residence
115. W. Parker Lyon Residence
116. M. R. Madary's Planing Mill
117. Martin Block
118. Masonic Temple Block
119. Mayer's Lodging House
120. Thomas M. May's Blacksmith Shop
121. Meade Building

122. Mecartea Brothers Blacksmith Shop
123. Mechanics' Planing Mill
124. Merced Street Wood Yard
125. Methodist Episcopal Church South
126. National Ice Company
127. Nichols Hall
128. Alexander Noble's Saloon
129. Pacific Fruit Company
130. Palace Swimming Baths
131. I. H. Patterson's Boarding House
132. Charles C. Pease's Foundry
133. Dr. A. J. Pedlar Residence
134. Pleasant View Boarding and Lodging House
135. Pleasanton Hotel
136. Police Headquarters
137. Post Office
138. Prostitutes' Dwellings and Cribs
139. Frank Rehorn Residence
140. Dr. Chester Rowell Residence
141. Sachs and Heringhi Grocery Store
142. Saint Augustine's Academy
143. Saint James' Episcopal Church
144. Saint John's Catholic Cathedral
145. Salvation Army
146. San Joaquin Lumber Company
147. Claudius Golon Sayles Residence
148. Charles A. Schweizer's Harness and Saddle Shop
149. Jay Scott Residence
150. Frank Serpa's Restaurant
151. Seventh-day Adventist Church
152. J. W. Shanklin Residence
153. William A. Shepherd's Livery Stables
154. Southern Pacific Railroad Depot
155. Southern Pacific Railroad Freight Depot
156. Southern Pacific Railroad Hotel
157. Spinney Block
158. Stock Yards
159. W. R. Strong Packing House
160. Mrs. Emma D. Swanson's Boarding House
161. Taylor Block
162. Temple Bar Building
163. Mrs. Ida Tilton's Lodging House
164. Tippecanoe Stables
165. Tombs Hotel
166. Truman, Hooker and Company Agricultural Implements
167. Union Ice Company
168. United States Hotel
169. Valley Lumber Company
170. Voorman Block (Radin and Kamp Store)
171. Walker Building
172. Henry C. Warner's Jewelry Company
173. James R. Webb Residence
174. A. J. Wiener's Store
175. Williams and Perry Livery Stables
176. John T. Williams' Hay Barn and Feed Yard
177. Winchell Block
178. Elisha C. Winchell Residence
179. Martin L. Woy Residence
180. Young Men's Christian Association Building
181. George W. Young's Junk Yard

erected in 1889); and the Woodward-Chance Block (1890).

Some buildings of this type were merely functional, while others strived to bring architectural sophistication to Fresno. Einstein's block, fashioned of brick, iron and French plate glass, was built in French Renaissance style with a fifteen-foot mansard roof. The Fiske Block was the most imposing of them all. It was a 50- by 150-foot, three-story rectangle covered with bay windows on its upper floors, gables, and extensive gingerbread, and topped with a neo-Gothic clock tower—the highest point in Fresno. The building's cost was $100,000, which allowed for amenities such as speaking tubes (instead of telephones), a private water works, and ground-glass folding doors in every room.

The depression and subsequent stabilization of Fresno's growth and population (10,890 in 1890, 12,470 in 1900) put an end to this dazzling era of construction.

Most of these buildings have been torn down. Fresno would have an incredible architectural heritage today had progress not had its way.

The boom era kept two clerks at Fresno's Grand Central Hotel (Am Hays and Jean Lacour) so busy that they are said to have gone prematurely bald, trying to put 250 people or so into the eighty available beds day after day. In the mid-1880s the Grand Central, Morrow and Ogle hotels remained Fresno's primary lodging houses, although the competition continued to increase. Jerry Ryan (see Chapter 7) was operating yet another hotel, the Arlington House, by 1886. Two years later, Thomas E. Hughes opened his three-story Hughes Hotel at I and Tulare streets. The poshest establishment in Fresno at the time, nothing short of a full description would do it justice (see 14:2).

Joining the Hughes in 1889 was Arthur Tombs' handsome Tombs Hotel at J and Merced streets, and in 1890 the 115-room Pleasanton Hotel at I and

Reference 14:2
## "A MODEL HOTEL"

A Republican reporter was loitering around the Hughes hotel last evening alert for a news item when Fred Dodd, the genial proprietor of the place, invited him to take a look through the big establishment. A pleasant hour was spent in admiring the several departments of this great enterprise which represents an investment of $300,000.

Leaving the commodious office, where every convenience for writing and reading is afforded, the reporter was taken to the tastefully decorated and spacious parlors on the second floor. The luxurious reception rooms are always open to the many guests of the hotel and a fine piano makes the place a pleasant resort for social gatherings. The parlors are carpeted and otherwise furnished in an elegant manner.

A trip to the fourth floor impresses one with the size of the hotel. There are two hundred large, airy, well furnished rooms in the place. The hallways are all spacious and airy. Cold and hot-water pipes run throughout the building, affording water for baths, etc. Each room is an outside room owing to the splendid architectural design of the building. Several large air shafts keep the building well ventilated and also a current of cool air constantly passing through the building.

The hotel is built around a large court, perhaps 100x100 feet square. Orange trees and flowers growing in the court create a pleasant impression. A beautiful peacock makes his home in the court. The bird was named "Admiral Dewey" recently in honor of the hero of Manila. A pretty view of the court is afforded from the balconies around the second, third and fourth stories.

A trip to the fourth floor in the elevator is accomplished with ease, being a great improvement over the tiresome climbing of stairs necessary in other buildings in the city.

Electric lights in all parts of the house make it brilliant during the evening hours, and it is a favorite resort for the best class of people. Prominent citizens locally and the most notable persons from a distance who visit the city congregate in the lobby and pass the hours pleasantly.

A visit to the dining room and kitchen was interesting. The dining room is large, light and cool, making a delightful place in which to appease the inner man.

"As to the cuisine, ask any guest who has been entertained under the present management," remarked Mr. Dodd.

It is unequalled at any hotel in the state outside of San Francisco or Los Angeles. The kitchen is a model cookery. There are four 6-foot ranges and a charcoal broiler, a refrigerator, storehouse, etc. are features of the kitchen that do not escape notice. The refrigerator takes a ton of ice at a time, and Proprietor Dodd smiles quite complacently over the ice war. The kitchen is supplied with every convenience in the way of steam, heating and cooking appliances.

The hotel has its own water works and this is no small matter, as will be seen by a visit to the engine room. A twenty-five horse power engine is run during the greater portion of the day, requiring two cords of wood per diem. The engine pumps water from a well 300 feet deep at the rate of 8000 gallons an hour. The greater portion of the water is used in the laundry in connection with the hotel.

The laundry is a very complete affair, consisting of the latest apparatus for washing, drying and ironing clothes. The dirty clothes first go into one of these large revolving washing machines, thence they pass into what is called an extractor. The extractor revolves very rapidly, throwing the water out of the cleansed clothes. The clothes are

then placed in dryers heated by steam pipes. When dry they are ready for ironing and pass into another room of the building where apparatus for this purpose is located. Six persons stand at the large 100-inch mangle and feed the clothes in for ironing. It is a busy scene. At other machines shirt bosoms are starched and then ironed in a surprisingly quick time.

The reporter was marveling at the extent of the business and was about to depart when he was informed that the Hughes block across the street is also under the management of Mr. Dodd. He took charge of the place two years ago and has made it one of the most popular rooming houses in Fresno. Every room is fitted up in splendid style and is lighted with electricity.

"By the way," remarked Mr. Dodd, "we must not forget the bar. Come in and have a cigar."

The invitation was accepted and while noticing other departments it may be well to add that the bar would be a credit to any city. It is the finest place in the city and the liquors and cigars furnished its patrons are of the best.

Mr. Dodd's success is due to his splendid management. Whatever he does he believes in doing well. Only the best class of people are catered to and he emphatically insists upon the respectability of his patrons. It requires no small amount of ability to successfully manage two such large establishments as will be readily seen when it is considered that they give employment to about sixty persons whose weekly payroll amounts to a large sum.

SOURCE: *Fresno Morning Republican*, May 6, 1898, p. 8, c. 4.

*Temple Bar Building at K (Van Ness) and Mariposa in Fresno, 1889. Typical of the buildings of the late 1880s, it was planned and promoted by S. N. Griffith and owned by O. J. Woodward.*

*The Hughes Hotel, Fresno's finest for many years, was built in 1888.*

*View of downtown Fresno from Courthouse Park, circa 1890. In less than twenty years Fresno had acquired a fine array of large buildings. Intersection of Mariposa and K (Van Ness) streets is in bottom right of photo.*

*China Town in Fresno west of the railroad, 1880s, as photographed by E. R. Higgins.*

*Clubhouse and grandstand at the Fresno Fairgrounds, 1890. A small octagonal display building was added later in the year. Horse racing has continued to be an important part of the fair.*

*Water tower and San Joaquin Electric Company, circa 1890, at Fresno and O streets.*

*Masonic Temple built by Jefferson James at I and Tulare streets about 1888. It was later known as the James building.*

*Drill team of the Lodge of the Ancient Order of United Workmen, Fresno, 1895.*

312

Merced streets. A November 15, 1897, blurb in the *Fresno Daily Evening Expositor* mentioned that the Pleasanton gave "one of the best 25-cent meals to be had in the city," and pridefully noted that its manager, Al. Baker, "employs nothing but white help. His [room] prices are $1.00 to $1.25 per day, but he makes special rates for families or theatrical people."

The only other hotel of consequence to open during the 1890s was the Fresno Depot Hotel of Simpson, Whittaker and Ray, located at the Southern Pacific depot. It featured an elegant parlor, bath rooms, and meals served quickly for the benefit of passing railway patrons. Prices were fifty cents per meal in 1897 "but [they made] good rates by the week," according to one report. Lesser hotels of this period included the Arcade, Commercial, Flores, Germania, Hotel de France, Kohler and Pleasant View House. Boarding houses also were doing a lively trade (see 14:3).

The 1894 Fresno County Directory lists fifty-two saloons in Fresno—roughly one for every 200 people living in town. Under the sanitized heading of "Liquors-Retail," establishments such as the Acme, Bohemian, Buffalo Brewing Company, Cosmopolitan, New Palm Garden, Tivoli, Turf and White Fawn saloons are listed, along with popular establishments run by J. R. Austin, William Davison, William Degen, Nick Justy, Fritz Paatsch and George Schorling. Drinking remained a popular pastime in Fresno, and it

Reference 14:3

## "LIFE IN FRESNO LODGING HOUSES, 1896"

It is an old saying that poverty makes men acquainted with strange bedfellows. In no way can the truth of this proposition be more convincingly demonstrated than by a temporary sojourn in a lodging house which does business at rates from 50 cents a night down to a dollar a week. But while the visitor would be prepared for a curious commingling of the waifs and strays of society under such conditions, he will not be slow to find out that the features of lodging-house life differ only in degree, whether the roomer pays $20 a month for a suite, or 25 cents a day for a "sky parlor." It is an easily demonstrable case of all sorts and conditions of men, and women.

In the average lodging house of Fresno there are certain characters the visitor is sure to meet with. The man whose wife has run away with another man. The wife whose husband has gone off with another woman. The gentleman without any means of subsistence, who may have been an actor, a teacher, a preacher, an artist, a journalist, or what not, but who is always—like Micawber—waiting for something to turn up. The dressmaker, the beauty doctor, the chiropodist, the manicure, the trance medium, the gifted healer, the fakir, the professional gambler, the fruit packer, the "shyster" lawyer, the quack doctor, the old soldier, all meet in the corridor of the lodging house or pass each other on the stairway.

The first floor tenants are, of course, the aristocracy of the lodging house, and the nearer the roof the lower the grade of goods, socially speaking. But honesty and virtue are quite as often found in the garret as knavery and vice on the carpeted floors of the rooms en suite. The lodging house keeper who undertakes to ask questions of lodgers opens a veritable Pandora's box of troubles. If she is self-possessed and discreet, as she usually is, she will not even pretend to see the empty beer bottles left on the floor by the two ladies who occupy the first floor room and pay $10 a month each. Both of them have given her every assurance of respectability and both pay their rent regularly. Both have registered their names.

And, by the way this register is one of the funniest features of lodging house-life. If any person could be so credulous as to believe that lodgers invariably give their real names, a glance at the pages would be all-convincing. Next to the name of Fairfax Farquier Fitzhugh of Virginia (who is careful to state that he belongs to the E.F.V.'s) will be seen the signature "Old Sausage, Grub Gulch." The one name is doubtless as mythical as the other. So are the Irenes, the Daisies, the Floras, the Myrtles, the "Birdies," who sign their names with something of a flourish of the pen, and whose stay varies from a day to a week.

Women are quite as liberal patrons of lodging houses as men are. The increasing love of independence and, it may be added, an increasing aversion to household toil, causes the number of widows who do not care to marry again and unmarried women who prefer single-blessedness to attain a representation that the average domesticated man and woman would deem possible. A woman who earns $8 a week can live comfortably on $4, taking her meals in a restaurant at a rate of about 40 cents a day. Many women, by doing light cooking with an alcohol stove, make two ends meet on $3 a week and have a comfortable room to receive their friends.

It is only when children and pets (birds, cats or dogs) are imported into the lodging house that the landlady enters a protest and the lodger begins to realize that there is no place like home. It is hard to restrain children; and dogs and cats have a way of wandering into the rooms of other lodgers that is certain to provoke war. The young man who practices cornet solos from 7 p.m. to 3 a.m. then wakes up at 5 a.m. and begins over again, is bearable compared with the unhappy mother of little children. This is why the general surroundings of lodging-house life tend to make men and women selfish, moody and misanthropic. When sickness overtakes the tenant of a lodging house there may be some temporary demonstration of sympathy but, in the long run, the sooner the patient is removed to a hospital the better everyone is pleased.

Lodging house business is conducted on as nearly a cash basis as circumstances will permit. Rent daily or weekly in advance is the rule, credit the exception. Once in a while the lodging house keeper is beaten out of a bill but not often.

It is a paying business, decidedly. One Fresno lodging house keeper recently admitted clearing $250 in a single month out of his venture in a house of forty rooms. It will frequently happen in the case of transients that the same room may be occupied twice or even thrice in the same day.

On the other hand the lodging house keeper leads an anxious, toilsome life, with no rest night or day. Undesirable tenants have to be watched and ejected. Now and then a morphine fiend gets in and the circumstance is not discovered till a coroner's inquest is in order. To keep forty rooms clean will require costly help. But on the whole, the lodging house keeper does pretty well, and the owner of the place—whose name is seldom known—does better. But of the ultimate effects of lodging house life, on women particularly, no doubt can be entertained. It breaks up every home instinct. It makes men and women reckless, self-indulgent and indifferent to the opinion of society. There are many cases where the wives of well-to-do merchants and professional men leave town to escape the summer heat, and their husbands take to lodging house life with the result that on the wife's return she finds the man's whole nature changed. He has probably rented a snug little room furnished according to his own taste; he has acquired bachelor companions and bachelor tastes, and it is odds if he ever gets back into the beaten track of docile, patient hubbyism again. A tour through the lodging houses of this city would be a revelation to absent wives in this line. It would banish a thousand pet illusions forever.

SOURCE: Fresno County Scrapbook 1870-1899, p. 1083-84, taken from *Fresno Daily Evening Expositor*, July 7, 1896.

became even more popular when influenza hit the town and whiskey was rumored to cure it. "This I know, I am taking it and as yet I am free from any symptoms of the Russian influenza," said a bartender in the January 17, 1890, *Fresno Daily Evening Expositor.*

This behavior, of course, did not sit well with the town's temperance elements. They had persuaded the city council to close the saloons at midnight in November 1888, and hoped to go further than that. The year 1892 saw many anti-saloon lectures and meetings. At one an orator, Lou J. Beauchamp, claimed that $657,-000 was spent annually in Fresno saloons, that they should be outlawed, and suggested the following punishment for defiers of such a measure: "Put them in jail and feed them on dried apples for breakfast, let them drink warm water for dinner, and swell up for supper. They will soon become tired of the saloon business."

At another meeting the Reverend E. O. McIntire lamented that there were nearly 100 saloons in the city "and in conjunction with every saloon there is a pool room, and a brothel not far away. The three go together." Apparently this agitation worked to some extent. On October 12, 1893, the supervisors voted to close saloons on Sundays.

Down to the turn of the century, Fresno's two most important general stores continued to prosper. Adolph Kutner and Samuel Goldstein expanded their 1131 I Street store greatly in 1890. Before then they had diversified by setting up clothing, dry goods, grocery, shoe, household and hardware departments under separate managers. When visiting Kutner-Goldstein "jewelry, cutlery, fancy cases, marble clocks, and other handsome articles will demand a large part of your time," read a December 20, 1894 *Fresno Daily Evening Expositor* promotional announcement. "In fact... when you get home, you will find it is supper time." Louis Einstein's store, where the assortment of goods was virtually as wide, made a specialty of carrying crockery, glassware and carpets and boasted that these departments had comprehensive selections.

Joining these establishments, and gaining a similar significance, was Henry Radin and Aaron Kamp's store. Opened in 1889, and later renamed the White Front, this store began in a twelve- by twenty-foot space and expanded to a 7,500-square-foot facility on I Street soon afterward. These merchants attributed their success to this sales philosophy: "To treat all patrons alike, to sell goods as cheaply to small children as to grown buyers, to never misrepresent and to always give satisfaction to [our] customers at whatever cost or trouble to [ourselves]."

Other mercantile businesses of this period included the Armen Sachs and Louis Heringhi store, another store operated by Heringhi called "The Leader," the Boston Cash Store (see 14:4), William McCallum's store at Mariposa and J streets, and J. E. Brown's store.

Grocery stores became increasingly popular as business ventures. H. D. McLane, George Kohler, Witham and Nourse, George A. Smith's Temple Bar Grocery (in the building of the same name), and H. Graff and Company were all operating by the late 1880s. Other entrants in the field included B. T. Scott, the Sims brothers, Taylor Albin, the Berbora brothers, Holland and Holland, Henry Hansberger, and W. T. Rice. Like Louis Einstein's store, most of these carried a wide range of goods while carrying a few unique items. The November 15, 1897, *Fresno Daily Evening Expositor* noted that Albin made "a specialty of imported sausages and cheese," and the Sims brothers carried "a full assortment of tinware and agateware."

With patent medicines and remedies so common, it was inevitable that Fresno would get some drugstores. Fred Smith began operating one in 1888, and a year later H. O. Buker and W. C. Colson began another that became renowned for its "Buker's 974 Cough Syrup." Dr. John Bassian's Golden Rule Drug Store made a specialty of imported medicines, and at one time featured "French Fever and Acne Cure" and "German Bitter Tonic," said to be popular. Also prominent among Fresno druggists were George H. Monroe who operated the Yellow Front store; J. A. and E. E. Webster, who opened the Webster Brothers Drugstore in 1884; Henry Michaels; Lefonso Burks; and E. A. Cutler.

Reference 14:4

## PRICES AT THE BOSTON CASH STORE, 1893

The Boston Cash Store, corner N and Mariposa, is now offering special rates to parties going to the mountains, particularly to holiday people, and to the public generally. All staples are going at unprecedented prices and imported goods at European rates. Banks may fail, but prices, never.

The wise and the prudent are requested to deposit their United States gold coin at the Boston Cash Store and get the luxuries and necessaries of life at San Francisco prices. There is no "Man's inhumanity to man" at the Boston Cash Store. It is fair play and

special privileges to none. Read our hand bills. Give us a call and here are our prices.

9 cans Salmon $1
9 cans Oysters $1
7 cans Sardines $1
10 cans Potted Ham $1
12 packages Corn-starch $1
5 cans Peaches, Apricots, White Cherries or Corn $1

13 pounds of Sugar $1
16 pounds of Rice $1
Flour at 95¢
Vegetables cheaper than the China-man
5 pounds finest Japan Tea $1.50
1 pound famous

5 glasses of fine Jellies $1
3 pounds finest Java or Mocha Coffee $1

"Giant Spider Leg" 60¢
6 gallon can Coal Oil $1

Everything else in proportion.

The place where such prices rule supreme as "The Monarch of all it surveys" is on the corner of N and Mariposa streets.

SOURCE: Fresno County Scrapbook 1870-1899, p. 446, taken from *Fresno Daily Evening Expositor*, September 1, 1893.

Furniture stores, a spinoff from a product line that general stores in town had carried before, began opening in this era. The pioneers of this business were W. A. Foster and D. H. Williams, who opened stores in 1885 and 1890, respectively, and W. Parker Lyon, a New York native who got his start in 1892. His establishment was described in 1897 as being stocked with "high class furniture. No cheap goods in this store." A man unacquainted with subtlety, Lyon deserves to be remembered for an advertisement that once ran in the *Fresno Daily Evening Expositor*:

> Attention! Sinners!
> Hot Stuff Coffins
> Asbestos Coffins
>
> My factory . . . is turning out a line of Asbestos Coffins that are rapidly going out of sight. No one need fear the hereafter, as I guarantee to see a corpse through without singeing a hair.
>
> W. Parker Lyon
> Philanthropist and Furniture King

Other dealers, who presumably had a calmer sales approach, were W. F. McVey, D. H. Williams and D. R. Bowling.

Livery, blacksmith and related businesses were still flourishing, since the horse had yet to be outmoded as a means of transportation. The Hart brothers and W. S. Lane served as draymen, and C. A. Schweizer, A. Weilheimer and Edward Emery ran harness and saddlery shops. Numbered among the stables in town were C. W. Cutten's Exchange, the Excelsior, the Fashion, J. H. House's, O. W. Mennett's Tippecanoe, the Park, the Stage, the Fresno City Livery Company, the Fresno Hack and Carriage Company, George Pickford's Armory, William Shields and Martin L. Woy's Grand Central, and Smith and Fullington's.

Owing, probably, to the wheat production decline, only Church's Champion Mills continued to operate in Fresno, but under different ownership. Harry Sherwood of the Capital Flouring Mills in Los Angeles purchased the property from Church in 1885. He enlarged the building and canal adjoining it for greater flour-grinding capacity, and was able to produce 200 barrels of flour daily in 1887 and 275 in 1890. Demand was heavy enough for this single mill to run day and night, and a warehouse was added to the premises in 1887. Eventually a steam plant was installed to power the mills and the Sperry Company took over the property. W. D. Coates was then installed as its manager.

While the mill benefitted Fresno in many ways, it created one big, ugly problem. The adjoining Fresno Canal and Irrigation Company ditch, once used to power it, accumulated trash, dead animals and sewage constantly. Bridges had to be built over this open cesspool at different locations; they were narrow and

hard to negotiate in a wagon or buggy, especially at night. Several public officials protested this situation before the city trustees on March 27, 1886, but nothing happened until the trustees decided the ditch was a nuisance on June 12, 1890 and ordered its abatement. Judge Milus King Harris upheld this action the following October 1, after the company protested it, but its officials continued to obtain injunctions against any action being taken.

When County Road Supervisor John Letcher ordered some workmen to fill in part of the Mill Ditch (as it was known) on October 28, 1891, they were all arrested since an injunction was in force. Attorney H. H. Welsh had given Letcher the go-ahead, claiming it was a public nuisance that deserved obliteration. He was arrested as well. When an injunction expired on March 19, 1892, and before another could be sought, City Health Officer W. T. Maupin and others began filling in the ditch. The work continued for two days. Since no injunction could be granted to protect an abated nuisance, it remained filled in.

Banks enjoyed varying fortunes in this era. Under the leadership of a former shoe merchant from DeWitt County, Illinois, named Oscar J. Woodward, the First National Bank enjoyed an unusual period of prosperity. After becoming its president in 1888, Woodward erected an opulent headquarters for his bank, "being a three-story brick, with sandstone trimmings, Scotch granite pillars guarding either side of the main entrance. The interior arrangements are exceedingly convenient and effective—everything being substantial and rich," according to an 1891 description of the place. Deposits in the bank were $602,217.87 in 1895, and capital stock $100,000. Following this lead, the Farmers' Bank moved into a handsome new edifice at Mariposa and I streets in 1888–89. It had assets and liabilities of $554,984.43 in 1895, and Adolph Kutner of the Kutner-Goldstein store served as its president.

Although some feared a Fresno bank failure in the panic year of 1893, all stayed open and afloat. During the worst part of the crisis, they were inspected by state officials and declared solvent. It was two years before a bank failure occurred, on April 12, 1895. The Fresno Loan and Savings Bank had overextended itself on loans and a raisin market slump had caused its deposits to taper off. It took more than two years for the bank to pay off its creditors and depositors. A few of them started legal proceedings against the bank, but a sympathetic court decision later put an end to such actions.

The boom era saw the creation of three new banks in Fresno. The first was the Bank of Central California, founded on February 21, 1887, with merchant Louis Einstein as its president. A mere three years after its founding, the bank's volume of annual transactions was $5 million and deposits had increased by 55 percent. The Fresno National Bank was organized on

May 1, 1888, and had a paid-up capital stock of $200,000 and deposits of $300,000 two years later. J. H. Hamilton was its first president, succeeded by H. D. Colson in July 1888 and John McMullin in February 1895. Located at Tulare and J streets, this bank was unusual because most of its investors and capital transactions were local.

The People's Savings Bank of Fresno, exclusively a savings bank, was organized on December 10, 1890, with a capital stock of $100,000. Woodward and Kutner invested in it, and Chester Rowell served as its president. Its management was conservative; only real estate loans were made and it was necessary to make only six foreclosures in the bank's first five years of existence. Its headquarters were in the Hughes Block.

The newspaper field saw several births, deaths and mergers in this era. The *Expositor* started the boom years well enough, increasing its size from a seven- to an eight-column format on January 26, 1887, and to a six-column format of eight, rather than four, pages on April 4, 1887. A new two-story building, later equipped with a modern Cottrell press, was erected for the newspaper in 1888 and occupied the same year. The editorial offices were hit by fire on June 9, 1890, creating a $7,000 loss, but the *Expositor* kept publishing and did not miss an issue. After numerous ownership changes, a syndicate called the Fresno Publishing Company took over the newspaper in 1897. Financial difficulties intervened and the *Expositor* published its last edition on September 1, 1898.

The *Republican* continued its ascent at this time— and partially at the aging, over-politicized *Expositor*'s expense. John W. Short and J. W. Shanklin, who had bought out S. A. Miller, began daily publication (as the *Fresno Morning Republican*) on October 1, 1887 and began experimental home deliveries to the Fresno and Central California colonies in 1889. The newspaper was sold again, to T. L. Judkins, in 1890. Fiscal ineptitude on Judkins' part caused Chester Rowell to reclaim his brainchild after a year or two, after which the *Republican* began prospering again.

By 1886 the population and business growth together with the mounting volume of property transfers prompted an enterprising publisher to launch a newspaper devoted to legal notices and news. In 1886 he sold to Morris B. Webster and the paper has continued publication under family ownership ever since. Today it is known as the *Daily Real Estate Report*.

The *Fresno Weekly Democrat* appeared as a daily in 1886, was issued as the *Weekly Inquirer* in March 1889, and was later consolidated with the *Weekly Budget*, which had started in 1888. This merger resulted in the weekly *Central Californian*, which started publication in February 1891. The *Evening Democrat*, a new newspaper, was started in 1898 and consolidated with another weekly, the *Keystone*, the following September. The weekly *Watchman* combined with the

*Democrat* in August 1899.

Other newspapers were printed, for brief periods of time, in these days. During the early 1890s, at a time of municipal corruption, a satirical publication called the *Roaster* appeared. An article in the June 5, 1891, *Fresno Daily Evening Expositor* said that J. G. Rhodes was the proprietor of the newspaper, which had yet to appear, and was intended to "roast a few of Fresno's people, and prepare them for the roasting they will get in the next world." At the same time the *Roaster* was to appear, said the article, two other newspapers were to commence publication. One was a commercial sheet called the *Fresno Home-Seeker* by T. D. Calkins, the other a literary sheet called the *Sunday Sayings*, edited by former Expositor reporter R. M. Mappes. Some *Roaster* issues have survived, but no copies of the other two newpapers are known to exist.

Business organizations became quite popular in post-incorporation Fresno. They were of three types— civic betterment, commercial and labor.

The first civic betterment organization was the Fresno Board of Trade, formed in 1885 with John Hyde Braly as its president. It is mentioned briefly in Chapter 7. Ultimately the board merged with the Fresno Chamber of Commerce, created on February 5, 1895, with Alexander Goldstein as its first president. Its headquarters were in the Taylor Block, where exhibits pertaining to Fresno County agriculture and other enterprises were set up. A competitor of the chamber of commerce was the Hundred Thousand Club, organized in April 1895. Its members wanted to build Fresno's population to 100,000 through sustained business growth, hence its name. The group's activities were similar to those conducted by the chamber of commerce.

Commercial organizations were created to address distinctive business needs. A real estate exchange was opened in 1887, and in 1890 the I (Broadway) Street Improvement Company was formed for the purpose of erecting and maintaining commercial buildings on that thoroughfare. The Fresno County Abstract Company was organized on January 21, 1891, with William H. McKenzie as its president—to maintain and check data on property within the county—and on April 6, 1892, the Fresno Branch of the Merchants' Retail Commercial Agency was formed as the county's first retail credit bureau. Its duty was to maintain a "black list" of county bad-debtors and make it available to local businesses and nationwide branch agencies. Finally, a Business Men's Association of Fresno was formed in 1894. Its goal was to build a canal from Fresno to the San Joaquin River, a project that has never been realized.

The beginnings of labor organizations in Fresno are hazy. A Retail Clerk's Association was formed in 1890 to protest the operation of retail stores after 6 p.m. It eventually won out and the group's president, H. Burton, requested a boycott of several stores that refused to observe earlier closing times. A Fresno Cooks and Waiters League also was organized, sometime around 1894.

When the twenty-four bed county hospital began holding as many as sixty-two patients, the board of supervisors decided it was time to erect a new building. A $25,240 contract was given to J. L. Smith in February 1888 for this purpose, with the new edifice to be built near the county fairgrounds on Ventura Avenue. When completed it had five wards of seventeen beds each and its own grain farm on the premises. The county paid for most maintenance expenses, but the state gave a daily 27½-cent allowance for keeping patients over sixty years of age.

Dr. Lewis Leach, the hospital's head physician, operated the facility at a minimal profit to himself. He paid drug bills for outpatients who had no money and the traveling costs for transferring inpatients to other institutions. "I think the tax-payers know how I conduct [this] institution," he told a reporter in the December 18, 1889, Fresno Daily Evening Expositor. "I run it exactly as I do my own family." Eventually the hosptial expanded to ten wards with twenty beds apiece. One was named "Q" and in it were put "all the old victims of the institution and all the old cripples, cranks and fossils," according to one 1891 report.

With Fresno's doctors increasing in number from twelve to twenty-one between 1885 and 1890, the County Medical Society continued active, with its members delivering papers such as "Fractures of the Elbow" and "Artificial Feeding of Infants" at its meetings. Joining this organization on March 23, 1897, was a San Joaquin Medical Society, organized at Spinney Hall in Fresno. A similar group was formed for valley dentists in the same year.

Health care services began diversifying and not just for humans. Two men named Wicks and Mills set up a hospital "for the treatment of maimed and crippled horses, and also those suffering from overwork and disease" in 1887, according to the Fresno Morning Republican.

For the regular population Doctors George A. and Jessie Hare opened a private sanitarium in Fresno in 1891, and in 1894-95 a county orphanage was created. It was first situated in a residence behind Saint James' Episcopal Church. Later, the operation was moved to the former residence of Judge G. A. Nourse on Ventura Avenue, near the county hospital.

Like all other municipal services, education had to expand during these times. In addition to the Central ("White," "Hawthorne") School, the C Street (later known as Columbia) and K Street (later known as Emerson) schools opened in 1889. The Ward (later Lowell) School, on Park and Poplar streets, opened in 1894 and a free kindergarten was founded by some Fresno women in 1891.

Other private schools also were formed at this time. The Sisters of the Holy Cross opened Saint Augustine's Academy on M Street in 1894. An even more important development was the opening of William Carey Jones' Fresno Normal Academy in 1885. It was Fresno's first true high school. A few secondary classes had been taught in the town by H. A. Kenyon, Mrs. John Walton and others before, but no comprehensive curriculum had been offered.

With the support of some community leaders, Jones induced the city school trustees to form a public high school in 1889. It opened its doors on September 16 of that year in the K Street School. Thomas L. Heaton was appointed the first principal of the school, which started with three teachers and fifty students. Its opening was marred by the death of one of its prospective students, Henry Church. While playing around with other boys in the school's belfry, waiting for classes to start, he fell two stories below to his death.

Reference 14:5

## FRESNO HIGH SCHOOL MEMORIES, 1893–94

By the merest chance, a manuscript came into the hands of an Expositor reporter the other day. It was labeled "Reminiscences of the past year's school." This was not encouraging. A glance into the contents, however, revealed a knowledge of humanity and its failings (from a high school girl's point of view) that was decidedly interesting. The paper was written in a girlish hand. It is as follows:

At last the Fresno High School is closed.

With a new born sense of freedom, we linger idly under the trees planted by our four (more or less) fathers, and after gathering together our scattered thoughts, we take note of the many little things that have happened during last year's school. We came as Sub-Juniors, with a look of K Street Eighth-Grade hauteur. But our pride was short lived. We were scorned by the Seniors, scoffed by the Middlers, and buffetted by the Juniors. At last we became Seniors and were able to render miserable the lives of the lower class boys and girls who now sit by in silent subjection, waiting their turn to squelch the gushy Eighth graders of next year.

Their silence is painful; and, as William Nye says, "one can hear them cut their eye teeth in the hazy hours of the afternoon."

Like all other good organizations, our school has had its trials and tribulations in the way of fads. Among these the memory cards are the most distressing. These cards were dealt out impartially to all who were seen whispering. Then on Friday afternoons, we had to listen for hours to pages from Shakespeare, Byron or the United States history. The time came, however, when many of the scholars had three or four cards charged up to their name. Then our professors gave up in despair.

We were free from any extra burdens for some time. But all at once a "sporty" feeling filled the minds of the young ladies, and a rousing football team of about twenty-five members was organized. A ball the size of a bushel basket was obtained, and during the recess and noon hours very exciting games were played. This pastime, too, was short lived.

Again the school breathed a breath of freedom. The breathing-time was very short-lived. Once more a dark cloud appeared upon the horizon in the form of the Athletic Club. Promptly a Fresno High School Girls' Athletic Club was organized with a constitu-

While there were only seven graduates when Fresno High School held its first commencement, in June 1891, its growth was so rapid that it soon moved into new quarters in the Central School. The high school continued there (see 14:5) until contractor F. W. Hickox could finish an imposing new building on O Street specifically for the school's use. Made of brick and costing $53,100, the building was equipped with the latest facilities: a gymnasium, a theater-style lecture room, a chemical laboratory and a library. The total student capacity was 400, and the building was first occupied—with far fewer students than that—in September 1896.

"Manual Training" was established by teacher Walter A. Tenney at Fresno High School in 1897, a combination of industrial arts and drafting courses. Girls were allowed to take these classes at first, but when increasing enrollment began excluding some boys, the school trustees took out the girls. Course offerings were otherwise rather standard, although the *Fresno Morning Republican* of October 11, 1898, said some were complaining because fad courses such as "drawing music," nature study, and modeling were being taught. In 1897 C. L. McLane was appointed the new principal of Fresno High School, and in 1899 a student body organization was formed with George Hodges as its first chairman. Enrollment at the high school was 170 in 1899; at the White School 343; at the Lowell 329; at the Emerson 313; and at the Columbia 239.

Sometime during the boom era, Fresno's privately-owned library appears to have ceased functioning. There were periodic cries for a new public library in its absence, and *circa* 1892 a public board of trustees was formed to establish one. Eventually a new library was opened, in rooms at the Woodward Building, in February 1893. Mrs. E. J. Latimer was appointed the first city librarian. She helped increase the holdings to 3,210 volumes by July 1895, with 1,411 library cards issued and a total circulation of 16,000.

Mrs. Latimer resigned on June 1, 1896, and was replaced by Mrs. Katherine Bingham. Her tenure was brief. She was discovered to be a Swedenborgian and a suffragist—considered reprehensible behavior for a woman in the 1890s—and was fired. Miss Alice Armstrong was appointed as her replacement.

The library was moved to the upper part of Judge E. W. Risley's K Street building in March 1898. Its holdings went up to 5,418 volumes the next year, with a 34,636 circulation. Some of the titles at this time were "Celebrated Tommy," "Young Mistley" and "When Knighthood Was in Flower."

Nathan W. Moodey turned over the Fresno Post Office to Wesley W. Hughes in April 1886. Hughes died not long afterward and his wife, Mary, took over the office—moving it to the new Winchell Building on Fresno and J streets. The major improvement during her tenure was free delivery to letter boxes, starting on July 1, 1889. Moodey became postmaster again in March 1890 and removed the office to the Edgerly Block on Tulare Street. On May 5, 1894, he was succeeded by William L. Hedrick; under his administration the office had six letter carriers and eight clerks, increased the home delivery area in town to six square miles, and set up letter drop boxes all over Fresno.

A scandal of sorts broke out when a government postal inspector, according to the *Fresno Daily Evening Expositor* of July 23, 1896, claimed that "carriers have idled while on duty... and have indulged in pleasant conversation when they ought to have been paying strict attention to their employment." This problem appears to have been solved through discipline rather than a personnel shakedown. In May 1898 John W. Short succeeded Hedrick and continued in that post until the century's turn.

---

tion stronger and greater than that of any of the girls. As the warm weather drew on the ladies gradually drew out until finally the club was disbanded.

The mighty Senate was an organization which absorbed the minds of the young gentlemen. All the weighty subjects of the day were discussed. On Friday nights they would congregate in the school building and after talking over subjects of national interest, they would come down to the more common topics of the day—say, the latest acrobatic feats performed by the young ladies, or maybe comment on the latest invention, which was Mr. Sones' electric clock.

That clock, by the way, was irrepressible. It was warrented to go off at the wrong time, and was never known to go off when expected to. It had a worse effect on our nerves than our lunches.

The next fad struck the teachers. It struck 'em hard, too. I'd say "you bet" if it was proper.

It was a "dancing club," very exclusive, and for teachers only.

While some of the older and more sedate people shook their heads and said the influence wasn't just the right thing, and so on, we of the young fry considered it a source of great amusement. We were one composite High School giggle whenever we thought of the ten or fifteen gentlemen teachers dancing with the forty or fifty ladies.

Although the pious folks found fault with the teachers for dancing it was nothing to the storm raised by the patriotic people over the desecration of Memorial day. Again, we young folks had something else to think of, namely how awful it was for the men's athletic club to "swipe" our bathing suits for their "Kalamazoo" friends.

Now, if there is one thing in the world a member of the F.H.S.G.A.C. doted on it was her bathing suit. The very thought of a suit belonging to a maiden of ninety (pounds, not summers), being used to deck the fat, muscular form of an athlete of 250 pounds, struck dumb even the most courageous heart.

But now our high school fun is over.

No more will we have occasion to play hookey, to visit wonderful red, white and blue triplets or to attend Forester's picnics. No more will the harsh voice of the teacher break in upon our slumbers on a warm afternoon. And now when we whisper, no more will we have to write the "Comparative Advantages of a Good Classical and Scientific Education," for, alas, school is closed.

As we sat in the box last Friday night at the Barton, surrounded by the wealth and culture of Fresno, our hearts swelled with pride for the graduating class of '94, and we looked forward with anxious anticipation to the time, a year hence, when we will graduate and be admired thusly.

SOURCE: *Fresno Daily Evening Expositor*, August 17, 1894, p. 1, c. 3.

With incorporation in 1885 street grades and town lot numbers were established, and four years later the first street paving was accomplished. The Pacific Paving Company handled the work, laying down a cement foundation at first, then covering it with steamed and crushed bituminous rock. W. C. Road, the superintendent of this work, said these streets would be a good advertisement for the city of Fresno. Portions of I, J and Mariposa streets were given this treatment, and at the same time Louis Einstein put bituminous rock sidewalks in front of his store. The same was done for the Glenn Building one year later.

By 1890 the total cost of curbing, grading and paving in Fresno had reached $290,000. The paved streets were kept clean under a $109.90 private monthly contract. For unpaved streets the city maintained a public well off K Street for sprinkling water. In 1899 an experimental sprinkling of crude oil, rather than water, was used on dirt streets. It created such a terrible stench that it was never attempted again.

Despite the improvements, Fresno's streets remained in a deplorable condition. After complaining about filthy alleys and stagnant pools of water "Miss Terious" wrote in the April 19, 1887, *Fresno Daily Evening Expositor* that "Fresno might offer better inducements to Eastern tourists with long purses" if it accepted the "Cleanliness is next to Godliness" idea.

As always there was much talk, yet nothing effective seemed to have been done (see 14:6). Even after many streets had been paved John Hinrichs, their custodian in 1895, allowed several to get caked with mud several inches deep. This made water collect, just as in pre-pavement days, and hindered travel greatly.

Fresno's throughways and byways were much improved on January 25, 1892, when streetcars finally arrived in town. Investors had tried to bring them in before, but had always experienced financial frustration in their efforts. In 1887 six franchises for serving certain areas of the city with horse-drawn cars were granted, yet two were later given up and one repealed. This induced city trustees to require a $500 performance bond of anyone requesting a municipal franchise.

Although it took several years to pull financing together, the remaining franchise holders had better luck. The streetcar lines eventually set up were Fulton G. Berry's Fresno Street Railroad Company, whose main line went from Mariposa to K to Tulare streets out to the city limits, and whose sideline traversed H Street; Thomas E. Hughes' Fresno Railroad Company, which went from Tulare to I to Ventura streets and out to the county fairgrounds; and the Fresno, Belmont and Yosemite Railroad, owned by a stock company with E. C. Winchell as president. Its first line

Reference 14:6

# "A BAPTISM OF DUST ON THE FRESNO STREETS"

**WHITED SEPULCHERS**
An Eastern Visitor On
Fresno's Streets

---

Picturesque But Untidy Alleys
And Back Yards

---

A Broad Hint to Clean Up and Put
Our City in Order for Midwinter
Fair Guests, Which We Hope Will
be Promptly Acted Upon.

Among the strangers who recently passed through this city on the way to the Midwinter fair was a gentleman from one of the middle Atlantic States. He was accompanied by his wife and had stopped off to have a look at Fresno county's raisin colonies, and incidentally to speculate in land and make his home here.

"I spent a week quietly taking in the sights," said the visitor to the Expositor reporter, "and if you will promise to take everything in good part I will give you my impressions. I want to say right at the start that I did not come in a carping or fault finding spirit. I am in hopes that in the near future I may call myself one of Fresno's citizens, and I don't want to get unpopular with them before I have even got my baptism of dust on the streets. . . .

"Won't you let one of your men bring a pencil and tablet to make a sketch or two as we walk along?"

The stranger appeared to have used his eyes to good effect during the few days of his stay. As soon as the sad-eyed pencil sharpener announced himself in readiness, his attention was directed to a vacant lot in the very heart of the city, between I and J and Fresno and Mariposa streets.

The swill barrel, running over; the tramp's discarded shoes, the abandoned broom and the bottle were the nucleus of a collection which included scores of damaged articles of household furniture, chucked right out on the vacant lot, old stoves, broken crockery and enough scrap iron to start a foundry.

"Did you ever read the Scripture story of the 'whited sepulcher'?" said the stranger with a smile.

The reporter confessed that, as one of a class commonly regarded as social pariahs, he had not, like Timothy, read scripture

from his youth, but he had an idea of what the metaphor meant.

"What I mean," said the stranger, "is that it would simply never be tolerated in any eastern town calling itself a city, that two of the best and cleanest thoroughfares, like those (pointing to I and Mariposa streets) should have such a background as this. Verily, I would say to your city fathers, 'Ye make clean the outside of the cup and platter,' but within is what?" . . .

"What remedy would you suggest," asked the reporter when the artist had finished his sketch.

"Reform it altogether," replied the visitor, this time quoting from Hamlet.

"The artist might take that little ruin," siad the observant one, pointing to the ruins of the Goldberg and Einstein building on I street between Kern and Tulare.

"That was an accident—the city fathers are not responsible for ruins caused by fire," put in the reporter.

"I don't say anyone is responsible," replied the stranger. "But don't you think a fire-blackened ruin on a leading business street of a city is a very bad advertisement? I do. To begin with, every such ruin is a reflection on the fire department and in Fresno's case it is the more unjust, because the department is wonderfully well handled and prompt in turning out to a fire. But if you go around your city with your eyes open, as a

319

went from Mariposa Street to J Street and out to the city limits, and its second out J to Tuolumne, to O, to Stanislaus, and then to Blackstone Avenue. Berry's line was served by antiquated cars that, before they were whitewashed, had "To the Ferries" and "To the Cliff House" painted on them; they had been purchased in San Francisco. Marcus Pollasky, of the ill-fated San Joaquin Valley Railroad (see Chapter 13), formed a company to buy out these lines in late 1891. His railroad enterprise folded soon after that, and nothing came of the idea.

Railroad activity in Fresno during this time was intense, save for when the great Pullman strike occurred in 1894 and the city was cut off from food supplies. Teaming between Fresno and San Francisco via Pacheco Pass had to be revived, and mail was relayed by teams of bicyclists. Otherwise, traffic was lively enough for the Southern Pacific to erect a new, larger depot in 1889. Some 106,351,450 pounds of freight moved out of this building the following year.

When the Valley Railroad (see Chapter 15) sent its first trains through Fresno on October 5, 1896, the town welcomed them with militia drills, band music and congratulatory addresses. The streets were lit up with 3,800 incandescent and 145 arc lights as well. Soon afterward, this railroad built its own depot at Inyo and Q streets, and a roundhouse was constructed about two miles south of the depot.

Once incorporation had been achieved, Fresno needed more efficient sewage disposal facilities. In December 1887 voters approved a $175,000 bond issue for such a system, $100,000 of which was to be spent on sewers alone. The California Sewer Pipe Company of Los Angeles won an installation bid, which it gave up. The contract was then given to Alexander McBean and C. D. Vincent in September 1888. Two hundred men worked on the project, which involved hacking through hardpan and pumping water out from ditches the previous company had dug and abandoned. Property owners had to install lateral pipes extending to their houses and businesses from the mains—because the city balked at a $1.20-a-foot price the company planned to charge for this. The price was still reasonable, since a high water table and many existing pipes made this a difficult job. A twenty-four-inch trunk pipe conducted the city's sewage from the edge of Merced Street to a 320-acre sewer farm southwest of town, the city's first. The mains were flushed daily by the Fresno Canal and Irrigation Company, under a $4,800 yearly contract, and major construction work for the system was completed in late 1889.

The boom period encouraged the Fresno Gaslight Company to go into electrical production while expanding its gas facilities. In July 1886 the city granted the company an electricity franchise. Soon after, electric lights were rigged by the company on an experi-

stranger would, you will see not one, but nearly a score of such blackened ruins. Of course they are mostly frame buildings, but the effect on the visitor's mind is that they have all been recently destroyed, while in a number of cases the fire occurred months ago. It makes a stranger feel that his home and his belongings are not likely to be safe, and you cannot create a worse impression than that in any man's mind. Wherever a fire occurs the wreck should be removed just as quick as possible."

The artist having finished sketch two was given a respite until the corner of J and Kern streets was reached. Here a frame building, evidently only a few years old, but utterly abandoned to decay, attracted the stranger's attention, and the pencil was set to work while the moral was drawn.

"Not a good advertisement for Fresno real estate," remarked the visitor, pointing to the structure which occupied a corner lot in what appeared to be a very desirable location.

"Here," said he, "is a fine corner lot, quite close to the business section of the city, but I do not think you could call that shanty in its present condition an "improvement." It has been quite a nice little place in its time, but 'why this business,' as the poet says."...

"Right here I want to say that nothing looks worse in a city than tumbledown fences. On the corner of Fresno and J street, right opposite the postoffice, is a fine corner

**AT E AND TULARE STREETS**

lot, with the fence all down and pools of stagnant water all over it. And this is but one of many.

"I notice you have quite a large colored population," said the visitor as the way was taken in the direction of K and Tulare streets. Now I like niggers—I beg pardon, 'colored people.' They remind me of home and old times. Fresno is, in this respect, more like a Maryland or Virginia town than any place in California that I have yet seen.

"But here again I am forced to say that your colored people are not as neat and tidy as they might be. I notice the same dirty

backyards, full of waste and refuse, that I have seen in other parts of this city. I will venture to say that there is as much kindling wood in the back yards and vacant lots of Fresno as would warm up every humble home in it for the entire winter, yet no one seems to have the energy to gather it up and clean up the yard. As for the broken household furniture, I never saw anything like it. Do you have any earthquakes here, or what is the matter?"...

"You asked me what I would suggest as a remedy. First of all give the city a thorough cleaning up—back as well as front. Set your tramps at work, a hundred or more, to cleaning up every vacant lot and every back yard, especially those in the heart of the city. Let the refuse be carted and dumped well outside the town. When you have once got the yards and lots clean it will be easy to keep them clean by individual effort."...

The artist was here shown a couple of bits for his pencil, the stranger suggesting that Oscar Wilde had evidently lived and preached in vain so far as window decorations are concerned. "The broom makes a support for the frame, it is true," said he, "but an unkempt and disheveled maiden, inhaling the morning air, ought to find a frame in a more secluded spot."

SOURCE: *Fresno Daily Evening Expositor*, December 14, 1893, p. 4, c. 1–2.

mental basis. By mid-1887 a new gasholding tank, capable of supplying 50,000 cubic feet of gas daily, and two electrical dynamos powered by an eighty horsepower engine had been built and installed in separate buildings. In September 1887 four sixty-foot electric light masts were placed in Courthouse Park—the first public use of electricity in Fresno—and other businesses were soon wired to use this then-novel commodity.

Business was good enough for the gas and electric company to reorganize in 1889. It was recapitalized at $50,000 and the company retained many of its previous shareholders. The Edison Electric Light Company established a competing plant at about the same time. The Fresno Gas and Electric Company (as it was then known) bought out the latter company in 1893, taking over its I and Tuolumne streets plant. The following year, these consolidated works were shut down. In March, the city had cut back on its electricity use, had deducted $100 from one bill it thought too high, and began fussing about the service. As a result the company lost its franchise, restricted itself to gas production, and allowed room for a new competitor to enter.

The concern that entered this void was the San Joaquin Electric Company. It was formed on April 2, 1895, by civil engineer John J. Eastwood and some other businessmen, with $800,000 in capital stock. The company immediately began building a diversion ditch from the San Joaquin River, high up in the mountains, which later led to a reservoir and dam. Below this was built a granite powerhouse capable of generating 200 horsepower. The San Joaquin Electric Company obtained a new contract to light Fresno streets with 100 or more incandescent lights on March 7, 1896. By the middle of that year service was under way.

Like its predecessor, this company had its share of problems. Lack of city money caused the lights to be shut off again during the summer of 1898, and a drought that year idled the company's generating plant. The directors decided to build a new dam, reservoir and power plant for reserve use, but ended up overextending the company before improvements could be made. It was in receivership by August 22, 1899, and lasted only a few years beyond that.

Sensing a good business opportunity, W. S. McMurtry of San Jose bought the Fresno City Water Works in 1887. To augment the existing system, he proceeded to bore two 200-foot wells, built a pumping plant with a two million-gallon daily capacity and set up two 500-ton tanks. These new features were put into operation on July 16, 1887.

Nearly three years later, in April 1890, the Municipal Investment Company of Chicago bought out McMurtry. J. J. Seymour, later associated with the San Joaquin Electric Company, became the new water works president. The new owners made further improvements. By 1892 eight eight-inch wells and a Holly Gaskill pump capable of lifting 6 million gallons per day were in use, and mains were constantly being extended to service Fresno's additions.

The greatest achievement of the private water company came in 1894. It decided to replace the ugly black tanks built seven years before at O and Fresno streets with a new, $20,000 water tower. Designed by Chicago architect George W. Meyer, the tower contained a 250,000-gallon tank, which increased the company's storage capacity threefold. It also featured a Roman arch doorway, wrought iron railings and a conical roof with a weathervane to give it a distinctive appearance. Now that the old county Courthouse is long gone, Fresno's water tower—still standing today—rates as the city's best-known landmark.

After the pioneering effort of S. A. Miller ran its course, several others kept telephone service going in Fresno. George C. and Herman Eggers bought out Miller's interests in 1886, obtained a municipal franchise on May 2, 1887, and began erecting poles and stringing lines throughout town for vastly expanded service. A total of 135 subscribers were soon signed up.

Direct dialing was still a thing of the future. When customers wanted to make a call they had to contact the main office, hang up, allow time for the operator to make a connection, and wait for her callback. At that time she would say, "Here's your party, go ahead." In the exchange set up by the Eggerses, sleeping quarters were maintained for a male night operator who took over for the female day operator. After this innovation Fresno had twenty-four-hour telephone service.

In 1890 the Sunset Telephone Company, then building a long-distance line from San Francisco to Los Angeles, thought it would be useful to obtain the Fresno franchise—which intercepted its proposed route. The sale was completed on October 25 of that year. It made possible, for the first time, long-distance calls to Modesto and Tulare for the local exchange customers. They now numbered approximately two hundred and kept the main switchboards *very* busy (see 14:7). Despite early promises of opening a Fresno to San Francisco long-distance line—which should not have been difficult to accomplish—it took until March 1893 for the Sunset Company to inaugurate one. Service to Los Angeles appears to have begun not long afterward.

The expansion of municipal and county services heralded an increase in governmental functions, and it became necessary to expand Fresno's relatively new county Courthouse. The hall of records, then located inside the building, was badly cramped by 1890 and described as " . . . low, dark and uninviting. The dampness, added to the poisonous gas [?], nearly takes one's breath," said a report in the November 13 *Fresno Daily Evening Expositor.*

To alleviate the situation, plans were drawn for extensive interior remodeling, with north and south wings to be added to the existing building. It also was planned, as a final cosmetic touch, to sheath the Courthouse dome in copper. The Smilie brothers of Oakland, building contractors, were engaged to do this work in 1892–93. The original contract price was $99,387 but unforeseen delays caused this sum to increase. The county balked at paying additional money, and while the "new" Courthouse was finished on schedule it took five years for the Smilies to obtain a satisfactory settlement.

Fresno County enjoyed its expanded Courthouse for only a short while. Fire struck it the night of July 29, 1895, with practically all its rooms suffering some kind of damage—from water, smoke and falling debris, if not flames. The great copper dome melted, perspiring red metal rivulets until it crashed through the upper floors. Despite the damage, most county records were saved and the board of supervisors rebuilt the ravaged structure. Plans by John M. Curtis of San Francisco were accepted to improve the previous building. A third story, a large front room and a wider, fireproof dome were added. The total repair cost was $46,700.

Churches in Fresno survived several important vicissitudes in the 1890s. The first involved the town's Congregational Church, which had a large Armenian membership. A missionary of that sect had served this ethnic group soon after its members started arriving in Fresno, causing the initial influx to the church. Claims were made that the church's pastor, J. H. Collins, was refusing to receive additional Armenians into membership, was charging higher tithes to the ones already there, and was seating them exclusively on the right side of the church.

When an Armenian named Masrap Sinanian tried to defy the seating rule one Sunday he was forcibly ejected from the church. The Armenians protested this discrimination and lost their case. They were all expelled from the church, an action later upheld by a state Congregational tribunal. "No longer will the worshippers . . . have their olfactory nerves shocked by the odors of garlic," snickered the May 24, 1894, *Fresno Daily Evening Expositor*. It is sad to see that the spirit of Christian brotherhood was so lacking in early Fresno.

Another incident upset all of Fresno two years later. The Reverend I. T. Johnson, a visiting evangelist, startled the town by claiming that "three-fourths of the

Reference 14:7

## "THE HELLO GIRLS"

Good morning. I am an Expos—
Hello, there!
I'm a newspaper—
Hello, say? hello! Hel—all right.

"Something you wish?" said a handsome, light haired young lady in accents as soft as the mellow notes of a guitar. This occurred in the Telephone Exchange where the reporter had to wait and watch his chance to make his mission known between "hellos."

The Exchange is one of the busiest places in Fresno, and the operators have but little time for newspaper reporters or for anybody else. There are two lady operators engaged at the Exchange during the day and one at night. No, that will have to be taken back. They are not "engaged" so far as any one knows, they are employed there. That's it. Big difference in these words. After the volley of hellos and the clatter of bells had momentarily ceased, the reporter asked:

"How many wires have you here, Miss Walters?"

"We have, hello! two hundred and hello! twenty."

"Well, what are those big grape vines that extend from the window east, that resemble the main roots of a distant vineyard?"

"O, those are, hello! our—what is it? hello! cables that we will—hello, use to San Francisco."

"When do you expect to have the long distance telephone in operation?"

"Well, we think we can be ready for the first of March. Mr. Gray has just arrived in San Francisco over the route via Hollister and through the mountains, and will return

through the mountains by an entirely different route, and whichever is selected will be put into operation at once. When we get the long distance line into working order," continued Miss Walters, "we will have booths erected in here, so that nothing whatever can be heard except by those who are talking. This will make all messages strictly private. You see there are three cables that come into that window. One of them forms our trunk line to Hanford and Visalia, while the other, the cowbell line, takes in Sanger and Reedley."

"How long has this exchange been in operation?"

"Well, I can't tell you. It was first built and controlled by Mr. Herman Eggers. This company purchased it from him about three years ago. I have been in this office for a year."

Miss Walters was asked what, if any, the effect was upon her hearing. She replied that constant work for more than a year had not had the least effect upon her hearing. She likes the work but when on duty there is hardly a moment she can call her own. When questioned about uniforms, Miss Walters said it was a universal rule now with all telephone companies that the operators wear uniforms, although nothing had ever been said about it in this office.

Miss Mae Holmes, a pretty little brunette, spoke up at this juncture and registered her objection to all ugly, black uniforms like the hello girls have to wear in Chicago. Miss Walters didn't like black nor gray and everybody else wore blue, who had uniforms, and

she didn't know just what she would do in the event that a uniform edict was issued.

Miss Emily Kellet is the third operator and is on duty at night. The work time is not so very long but requires incessant attention. The girls change shifts every nine hours just as they do in a telegraph office or in other places where the work goes on continuously. Miss Walters is on duty most of the time from 7 a.m. to 6 p.m. Miss Holmes goes off duty at 3 o'clock in the afternoon and goes back on again at 6 and remains till 9 in the evening. Miss Kellet then takes charge and remains on duty until 7 o'clock in the morning. By this arrangement each girl works nine hours.

The young ladies say that there are often unpleasant things connected with the business. "People are so cross and impatient sometimes," said Miss Holmes, "that they seem to think we can answer everybody at the same time."

The great network of wires in the Exchange is something wonderful, while the intricate switchboard is a veritable 13-14-15 puzzle to the uninitiated. The wires handled by the operators in switching, are incased in colored hose that look like so many garter snakes coiled up on the desk.

Well, good day.
Hello, there!

SOURCE: Fresno County Scrapbook 1870-1899, pp. 932–33, taken from *Fresno Daily Evening Expositor*, December 15, 1892.

*Fulton G. Berry, owner of the Grand Central Hotel, real estate developer, and Fresno booster. Through the last two decades of the nineteenth century, this colorful Fresnan owned and operated Fresno's plushest hotel, the Grand Central at Mariposa and Fulton streets. Dressed as pictured here, Berry would ride in San Francisco parades on a white horse. According to his wishes, Berry's funeral in 1910 included a parade down J Street complete with brass band. J Street was later renamed Fulton Street in his honor.*

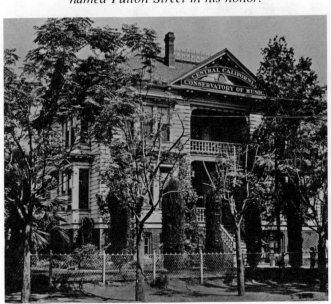

*Hook and ladder company of Fresno Volunteer Fire Department, looking east on Fresno Street (near J Street), 1896. Note the Barton Opera House in left foreground and the new water tower in background.*

*Among the many social-cultural groups was Fresno's Query Club. The ladies' club, organized in 1894, explored topics of antiquity and subjects of current interest. This photo was taken in 1896.*

*The cultural life of Fresno was enriched in 1896 when Paul Fast established the Central California Conservatory of Music at Mariposa and O streets. In 1897 it had 36 students studying piano; 11 violin; 18 voice culture; 5 harmony; and 33 in a choral class.*

*Home of attorney Henry Tupper on K Street. A typical size home in 1890.*

*The first bicycle mail stamp was issued in Fresno during the railroad strike of 1894. The twenty-five-cent stamp was issued for a relay mail service from Fresno to San Francisco established by Arthur C. Banta, a Fresno bicycle dealer. Gene Banta of Fresno identifies the route as follows: "On July 7, at 4:30 a.m., the first rider left Fresno with some 4 pounds of mail, doing 20 fast miles to Kerman. The next rider took it to Firebaugh, 20 miles farther, then on to Los Banos 35 miles farther. Next relay was to Bells Station, just over the Pacheco Pass summit. The next four relays were to Gilroy, San Jose, Redwood City and finally, San Francisco. There was a total of seven relays. The time was just short of the estimated 18 hours. Mail and packages were thus transmitted, including letters to Europe, the Northern states, and the Eastern seaboard." Some 380 pieces of mail were handled.*

*Camp meetings were common in the smaller towns, but apparently pictures were seldom taken. Below is one meeting of the Adventists, at Mariposa and O streets in 1888. It appears they didn't depend on hotels.*

*Central Drug Store on Mariposa Street in Fresno in 1892. Pictured are the pharmacy's owners, Sam Colson (left) and H. O. Buker (right).*

girls in this city had been ruined before they reached the age of 14 years." Although supported by the Methodist Episcopal Church where he had been preaching, Johnson had to leave town briefly—escorted by a sheriff's deputy. It was feared that the candid minister would be assassinated in the street.

Whatever their problems, Fresno's churches were still basically prospering. The oldest church, the Methodist Episcopal South, had a membership of 300 by 1892 and was in dire need of a new building. It was eventually constructed in 1897–98. The church also boasted a large Sunday school, Junior Epworth League, Wesleyan Epworth League and ladies' aid and missionary societies.

By 1895 Saint James' Episcopal Church recorded a membership of 177. Over the years, and up to that point, it had seen 268 baptisms, 172 burials, 119 marriages and 143 confirmations. It had two guilds, known as Saint James' and Saint Agnes', and a young men's association known as the Brotherhood of Saint Andrew.

The town's First Methodist Episcopal Church had added a Christian Endeavor society, Junior Epworth League and ladies' aid, foreign missionary, and home missionary societies by the 1890s. The First Baptist Church had an identical complement of societies with the exception of the Epworth League. The latter church also maintained a mission Sunday school for blacks and had survived a split in its congregation. Some members had formed an Emmanuel Baptist Church in 1892, but the divisions were overcome three years later and the churches reunited.

The Presbyterians built a $10,000 church in 1888, and boasted ladies' aid and missionary societies, along with Christian Endeavor societies for all age groups, by 1895. The Christian Church also completed a house of worship during this period. It was dedicated in October 1885. "The dedicatory sermon was delivered by Elder J. W. Ingram," said the February 18, 1888, *Fresno Daily Evening Expositor*, "[whose] sermons were noted for their depth and power, and through them all runs a golden thread of beauty and sweetness, giving food for the philosopher and poet, while they bring joy to the most obscure and lowly of God's children."

The establishment of new churches in Fresno was proceeding apace as well. In 1885 the Disciples of Christ built a church at M and Mariposa streets. Its first pastor was the Reverend James Logan. Three years later, three other churches got their start in town. The Cumberland Presbyterian Church, organized by settlers from Kentucky and Tennessee (where that sect was strong) was formed on June 10, 1888 by the Reverend W. N. Cunningham. The Reverend B. D. Austin was the first permanent minister. A $2,000 permanent structure, said to be the smallest church in Fresno, was built for the congregation in late 1892. About this time

missionary, young peoples' and aid societies were formed within the church, which had eighty members in 1895.

The two other churches formed in 1888 were the Second Baptist Church (for blacks), by the Reverend Edward Lindsey, and the Seventh-day Adventist, formally organized that year after sporadic meetings in and around Fresno. Moses J. Church built a $40,000 church for the congregation, a handsome brick structure with a clock tower and seating capacity of 800. This building was used by the congregation for many years afterward.

Other notable church foundings of these years included the Emmanuel Lutheran Church (1890, with a church later constructed at Ventura and L streets), the Holy Trinity Armenian Apostolic Church (1894), the First Armenian Presbyterian Church (1897, formed as a result of the Congregational Church dispute mentioned earlier), and the First Church of Christ, Scientist (organized by twelve people in 1897).

A host of other churches were organized in this same era, but details of their histories seem all but lost. The Reverend J. F. Gilberg organized a Swedish congregation in Fresno sometime before 1894, when the Reverend J. Johnson was serving a Danish Lutheran Church in town and the Reverend Karl Meckel a German Evangelical Church.

Club and fraternal organizations continued to grow, just like the churches. The year 1886 alone saw the formation of another Knights of Pythias lodge, the Raisina Chapter of the Order of the Eastern Star, and the Young Men's Christian Association. The latter organization was formed on August 20 with sixteen members and grew rapidly. First established in rooms in the Grand Central Hotel, it moved into sumptuous I Street quarters of its own in early 1890. The new building had a main hall that seated 600, a gymnasium, plunge bath, reading room and parlors. Association membership was 437 at this time, and continued to rise for years afterward.

Two years later, the Fresno Commandry was organized by Captain J. R. Williams, along with the Central California Lodge of the Odd Fellows and the Fresno Gun Club, with Andrew D. Ferguson as its first president. The only other clubs known to have been formed in the late 1880s were the 89-90 Social Club (which held regular monthly dances for a number of years) and the Wednesday Club, one of the preeminent women's groups in early Fresno. Limited to a membership of twenty-five, the club was devoted to a wide range of literary, artistic and social activities.

The 1890s dawned with the establishment of the Rebekah Degree Lodge, with thirty charter members; the Hermann Sons, a German-American association; the Mono Tribe of the Improved Order of Red Men, a fraternal organization that did not admit Indians into its membership; and the Forest Grove Chapter of the

Ancient Order of Druids. Following this spate of club formations was the founding of the Star of Bethlehem Lodge in January 1891 and the Wawona Division of the Uniformed Knights of Pythias in July 1892.

Women's clubs suddenly became popular in 1894 with the formation of the Parlor Lecture Club (a lecture and discussion group) and the Leisure Hour Club, a twenty-member society devoted to studying literature and the arts. Also created in this year were a German Order of Foresters and the Kindergarten Dancing Club, a popular group that started out with fifty couples.

In the latter 1890s few clubs were started in Fresno. Among the more important that did emerge were the Woodmen of the World (1895), Benevolent and Protective Order of Elks (1898), and the Sequoia Club (1899). The latter association was formed as Fresno's answer to the Bohemian Club of San Francisco and Jonathan Club of Los Angeles—a small group restricted to the town's male elite. Membership dues were fifty dollars initially, and even at that then-high price there were forty charter members. Nor was this the only exclusive men's club in early Fresno. A similar group known as the Alfalfa Club, which met at secret times and places unbeknownst to wives and girlfriends, had been organized earlier.

Other groups that existed during this era, but whose founding dates appear to have been lost, were the Fortnightly Cotillion Club, the Hawthorne Literary and Social Club, the Native Daughters of the Golden West, the Saint Andrews' Society (devoted to Scottish culture), the Cotton Club (a social group for men and women), the Thimble and Query clubs, the Knights of Honor, and the Sunday Afternoon Society. The Merry-Go-Round and North Side whist clubs also enjoyed great popularity during these times.

Baseball's popularity in Fresno varied widely in these days. The Fresno Stars were succeeded by the Fresno Baseball Club, which had its own playing field at Blackstone and Belmont avenues, and a later sponsored team known as the Fresno Republican Tigers. Rivalries between teams were taken seriously in those days. One person commented that "if a game pulls off without bloodshed [in Fresno] there is little interest taken in the contest." Indeed, on October 30, 1898, a match between local teams concluded with fisticuffs rather than a gracious concession by the losing team.

The Fresno Athletic Club fielded a football team by 1894 and Fresno High School went to the gridiron as early as 1897, but these early games and teams appear to have been incidental. There was also the Fresno Lawn Tennis Club, organized on June 18, 1891 and

Reference 14:8
## FRESNO FRIVOLITIES, 1887–1899

Mr. and Mrs. Frank Bedford have returned from their bridal tour and taken refuge in their permanent home on North L street. They slipped in very quietly on us, but some few of their numerous friends concluded not to let them escape. Last night about 11 o'clock, when the favored couple were sound asleep, fifteen young men, headed by Professors Smith and Baume, piled into the Grand Central 'bus and were driven to the newly wedded couple's home, and as the moon smiled gently down upon them called the happy couple back from dreamland by music sweet, the dulcet serenade. Professor Smith had his cornet, mellowed and sweet; Professor Baume his violin, with Mr. Riley as second, and a bass viol and clarinet made up the orchestra, and it is not to be wondered at that the young couple on awakening thought they had been wafted into the confines of Elysium. It was not long, however, before the doors were opened, and a most hearty welcome was extended and an invitation to "come in" given by the flattered couple. A table was mysteriously and rapidly prepared with delicacies called forth from fairy land, and the music was resumed in the parlors. To everyone's pleasure Professor Baume came armed with "Dream of My Heart," and it was prettily rendered.

Sometime or other they sat down to a table loaded with delicacies, and sometime during the night they got up from that same table and with congratulations bade adieu to the young family.

As the wine went round toasts were responded to by nearly all. If any young couple so popular as Mr. and Mrs. Bedford think they can slip home and not let their friends welcome them they are mistaken. It isn't in the nature of Fresno's young people to lose the opportunity to wish their companions joy in every venture in life.

Mr. and Mrs. Bedford, here's to you! May Mr. Bedford love his wife forever; may she never grow less beautiful; may the wrinkles keep from her fair face, and the gray from her hair, and when the time comes to answer the call we all have to obey, to cross that mysterious river and go down into the dark and mysterious grave, may you hand in hand united, as in life, cross to that bourne together, leaving behind a life well spent in usefulness and well doing. May you be happy.

### AMUSEMENTS
FRESNO OPERA HOUSE—Chassagnon, the world renowned mesmerist and mind reader, promises to give an interesting performance tonight. Mr. Chassagnon says he has seen a number of people in his rambles about town who are highly susceptible, and he says they are attracted to him like a needle to a magnet. They come determined to resist, but they come. He says he sometimes gets his match at the first trials, but after they have once been there they are bound to return, and he says when they do return after having left once without yielding, then he is sure of them in spite of all

determination on their part to resist his will. The entertainment promises some amusing and strange developments of the mysterious power he claims to possess.

RIGGS' THEATER—The peerless Carleton Opera Company, the best operatic organization in this country, appear at Riggs' theatre next Friday and Saturday, presenting the first night the latest successful operatic novelty by the composers of Erminie, entitled "Mynheer Jan;" the music is of the bright and catchy order and the libretto uproariously funny, and said to be superior to Erminie, same composers. Incidental to the second act is a grand march of Amazons by the ladies of the company attired in gold and silver armor. The costumes will be gorgeous and historically correct. Saturday night, Strauss' masterpiece, the Queen's Lace Handkerchief, will be given on a spectacular scale. The finale of the second act of this opera is the best ever composed for light opera, and the Carleton company have received as high as eight encores for their admirable rendering of the same. Prices will be $1.50, $1.00 and 50 cents. Sale of seats begins Monday morning at Thompson's drug store.

All Fresno was out to hear Sousa's Band and "Maud Berry" last night. The lower part of the house was filled. The balcony was crowded and the gods were on hand in large numbers to vent their appreciation of the splendid programme presented with prolonged howls of ecstatic delight. The swag-

possessing its own courts at Tulare and N streets; the Fresno Wheel Club, which participated in many bicycle races; and several other organizations that participated in track and boxing events.

For the more musically inclined, it was possible to enjoy the Fresno Band under the baton of Nick Justy, as well as the Drach and Reitz orchestras that played at socials. There was a wide assortment of other entertainments besides (see 14:8).

In addition to the Riggs establishment mentioned in 14:8, Fresno gained its first true theater in 1890. It was the Barton Opera House, built in 1889-90 by Fresno vineyardist Robert Barton at the corner of Fresno and J streets. The Barton was "beautifully decorated," said the December 25, 1895, *Fresno Daily Evening Expositor*, "presenting shades and tints of the most delicate colors, gold, pink and drab . . . lending a soothing influence to the eye under the electric lights . . . Its acoustic properties are excellent . . . "

Seating for 1,600 was provided in the building, which played host to some of the most celebrated actors and actresses of its time. Numbered among them were Lillie Langtry, Helena Modjeska, and Eddie Foy. "Located as this city is midway between San Francisco and Los Angeles, the most popular companies that visit this coast find it both profitable and convenient to present the best they have [at the Barton]," concluded the *Expositor* article.

After incorporation, Fresno's city government took over the existing fire department in February 1886. The department's equipment consisted of a new hook and ladder truck, an old hand engine and hose cart, a small chemical fire extinguisher, its station house and two reserve cisterns. Soon afterward the city purchased a new $2,750 Silsby steam fire engine for the department and built a combination brick city hall and fire house to replace the old frame station. More improvements followed—a team of horses was purchased for the engine in 1887, a modern Ahrens fire engine in 1888, a chemical fire engine in 1891 and a comprehensive alarm system in the 1890s—but there were still problems.

The department remained a volunteer effort, and money was often lacking. Firemen frequently paid operating expenses out of their own pockets, resorting to fund-raising balls and similar activities to keep afloat. "Most of the members are young men who have little or no property interests, and it cannot be expected that they will always continue to pay for the privilege of saving other peoples' property," commented a *Fresno Weekly Republican* reporter in 1885.

After the tremendously destructive 1885 blazes no serious fire struck until August 12, 1888, when the blocks bounded by Fresno, Tulare, J and K streets were hit. The loss was $160,000. There were several serious conflagrations during the summer of 1889, the

ger set were out in great force, the name of Mrs. Maud Berry-Fisher being a strong drawing card for Sousa.

When the curtain rolled up shortly after 8 o'clock, it disclosed the orchestra in place. Then Sousa, with a little bow, took his place on an improvised platform and struck an attitude. He led with a Deleartean grace. He is a handsome, well-built man, and has evidently studied to get the best scenic effects from his theatrical position by making the most of his physical excellencies.

The audience waited breathless for the appearance of Mrs. Maud Berry-Fisher. She appeared a picture of youthful loveliness. She wore a beautiful white satin dress on which was pinned a great bunch of red roses while another red rose nestled in her abundant blonde hair.

Her appearance was the signal for a thunder of delighted applause, which was as much a greeting as a mere mark of pleasure. She sang Tours' "Because of Thee," and at its close was greeted with tremendous applause while great masses of flowers, the gifts of her many appreciative admirers, were sent over the footlights. As an encore she sang a pretty little ballad and was obliged to come out and bow again and again, by the delighted audience.

A Hallowe'en party was given at 845 P street last evening by the Misses Hamilton and Miss Hall, a large number of invited guests being present. The customs observed

in "ye olden tyme" characterized the evening's amusement, and it is said that the reflections of intendeds were exceedingly vivid, the married gentlemen of the party not accepted.

The early part of the evening was spent in various social amusements in which games, singing, etc., abounded. At 12 o'clock the gentlemen of the party were provided with mirrors, and after gazing into them intently for a few moments, the lights were turned up. Behind each one stood a white robed figure of a most spine-creeping presence and the inquisitive mirror-gazers forthwith proceeded to efforts of identification which were finally successful. The programme was well carried out and all united in declaring the occasion an exceedingly enjoyable one.

Those who composed the party were: Misses Margaret Kennedy, Maud Pierce, Carrie Hall, Lillian Laverty, Jessie Kennedy, Mae Pierce, Mr. and Mrs. George L. Hoxie, Mr. and Mrs. W. C. Colson; Messrs. S. S. Parsons, Professor C. T. Elliott, Roy Chaddock, Frank Helm, George Freman, Albert Munger, Howard Parish, William Conn, G. R. Andrews, Ed L. and Bert Hamilton.

At the Barton tonight the wonderful Projectoscope will be seen for the first time in this city. The machine, which is Edison's latest and most wonderful invention, and which, by the way, cost Jim Corbett the championship of the world, is the only one west of the Rocky Mountains. It projects

life-sized figures upon a screen thirty feet square.

Those who attend tonight and see the reproduction of the great Corbett-Courtney fight want to closely watch it. The program tonight is as follows:

The great Corbett fight with knockout. Runaway at Central park, showing horse and carriage running away. The boxing cats. Dentist scene, showing Dr. Colton administering laughing gas. Mounted police charge a mob—city of Dublin during riot. The hurdle race—taken in England. Cissy Fitzgerald's wink and dance. May Irwin and John Rice in their famous kissing scene, showing the only proper and correct way how to kiss. Major McKinley taking the oath as president of the United States, in front of the White House. The fire alarm—starting for the fire, showing the entire fire department led by the chief. Fighting the fire, representing the fire engine in full action. The Santa Fe limited express. The scene represents the eastern flyer emerging from the woods in the distance at full speed, going at the rate of sixty miles an hour.

With all the paraphernalia of special scenery, gorgeous costumes and a famous name which seem necessary to make a Shakesperian play "go" before a modern audience, "Macbeth" was produced by the Modjeska company at the Barton opera house last night before an audience that filled every seat and box and overflowed into the stand-

worst of which occurred on July 12 and 17. A hastily assembled committee suspected that arsonists were responsible for these blazes, rounded up a number of likely candidates on the west side, and questioned them at length at Armory Hall. According to historian Lilbourne A. Winchell, "After the desired confessions were secured, the ring-leaders were triced up, their backs bared and lashed with black snakes. Others of the gang were also whipped, with a promise of worse if found in the city the next day . . . A reconnaissance of the west side saloons, opium-dens and bawdy houses the next night, revealed the absence of all the suspects."

These drastic measures still failed to rid Fresno of the fire nemesis. It was still a frontier town full of wood and other highly flammable construction materials. A $50,000 blaze struck on September 2, 1890, and thirteen days later the Fresno Milling Company warehouse went up in smoke. Nearly three years later, on July 15, 1893, the milling company itself burned. The loss was $139,500 and insurance covered less than half that amount. Four days later the Valley Lumber Company's warehouse and offices were destroyed, and the following August 7 a blaze took out the large Masonic temple and many adjacent buildings worth $115,000 altogether. Jack Picconi's boarding house and the Portuguese Hotel, an establishment for sheepherders, went up on January 16 and June 14, 1895, respectively, and on October 18 the E. G. Chaddock and Company packing house burned to the ground.

Arsonists were back at work in Fresno during 1896–97, with a preference for practicing their trade around churches. The First Baptist Church was lost to fire on August 2, 1896, as was the Presbyterian Church on September 12. Emboldened by these strikes, the arsonist or arsonists struck at the African Methodist Episcopal Church on September 20, 1896 (though unsuccessfully), but caused serious damage to a structure being used by the burned-out Presbyterians on January 17, 1897.

Although the arson fad seemed to die out, the unintentional fire menace did not. Three of them hit various sections of town on August 25, 1897 and five separate areas were burned the next November 2.

Terrible as these blazes were, they were insignificant compared to an August 13, 1898 fire that wiped out two packing houses, two warehouses, and some Southern Pacific property. The loss was $400,000, the highest recorded for any Fresno fire up to that time. Destructive fires continued right up to the century's turn, wiping out the Radin and Kamp store (worth $150,000) on December 16, 1898, two large Standard Oil tanks on Front Street on May 13, 1899, and the First Baptist Church (once again) on July 4, 1899.

Nor were these the only disasters to hit Fresno in its post-incorporation period. As in 1884, the town was visited by floods in 1885, 1886, 1888 and 1893. In all these instances crews of volunteers raced out to build levees and diverting ditches, hoping to spare the main parts of town from the deluge, but their success was never complete. The March 22, 1893, *Fresno Daily Evening Expositor* graphically demonstrated how bad the situation was:

> John H. Nelson, who lives a mile this side of the Toll House, was in town with an anxious face and a distressed countenance.
>
> When asked what the matter was, he said he was hunting for his farm. It had come down Dry Creek in chunks of about an acre each, and he was trying to find enough of these chunks for identification. So far as[is] known he was unsuccessful, but he was still on the look out, thinking any moment he would see a piece of his farm coming down Inyo street. If it should come, he was ready to file a homestead on it.

It seems odd that a Fresno reporter wrote this anecdote in the face of disaster, but there was a reason for his jocularity. He knew the debris would be cleared away, the wreckage repaired and the city—if anything—rebuilt better than before. Fresno's importance to commerce, agriculture and industry ensured that any ruination could be only temporary. It was a smug, simplistic—and appropriate—attitude, because this type of confidence makes a city great. And, although it was tempered by problems like any other city's, no one disputed turn-of-the-century Fresno's greatness.

ing room. It was a finished and adequate presentation of a great play, and was evidently well appreciated by the large audience. The only thing that marred the pleasure of the evening was an annoying amount of stir in the back part of the house, and the indecent interruptions of sundry gallery gods, who evidently imagined that it was highly humorous to interrupt the most serious scenes with cat-calls. There was nothing which was strictly disorderly, or which would have been intolerable on ordinary occasions, but on such exceptional occasions there ought to be some means of enforcing the external semblance of good taste on those to whom nature has denied the reality.

The company was adequate and the staging—barring some slight hitches in the mechanical department—more than adequate. The few leading parts might have been in stronger hands, but the subordinate parts might easily have been, and usually are, in much weaker ones. John E. Kellerd, as Macbeth, was unfortunate in his voice and stage presence, and was unconvincing in the mystic and introspective scenes of the earlier acts, but rose to the occasion in the more dramatic scenes later and won the favor of the audience. Wadsworth Harris, as Banquo, was a favorite from the beginning, and regret at the early retirement of the actor was added to the regret at the untimely death

of Banquo which occasioned it. Frederick Mosley was a robust and eloquent Macduff and succeeded in rising to the melo-drama of the part without being ridiculous, even to the irreverent gallery gods.

SOURCES: (in order of presentation) *Fresno Daily Evening Expositor*, November 5, 1887; January 26, 1889; April 28, 1894; May 27, 1895; November 1, 1895; November 12, 1895; May 14, 1897. *Fresno Morning Republican*, September 21, 1899.

# Chapter 15

# Mixed Harvest: Agriculture, 1888-1890

If Fresno County's 1887 boom certified agriculture as the county's economic mainstay, one question remained. After that giddy era, what new heights could farm activities reach? The answer was obvious by the century's end. In the value of its agricultural output, Fresno County ranked twenty-fifth among all United States counties in 1889 and *fourth* in 1899. Irrigated acres, vineyard acres and the number of fruit trees roughly tripled. The county's gross agricultural income topped $10 million for the first time. Signs of progress there were, but difficulties—a national depression, commodity market collapses, and labor troubles among them—abounded as well.

A continued demand for land, and consequent increase in farming activities, helped keep the county's agricultural output growing throughout the 1888–99 period. In actuality, the "boom" did not end until the 1893 nationwide depression. In 1888 the county recorder's office was still logging $500,000 worth of land transfers during a good week. Four years later, Emil Bretzner sold his forty-three-acre vineyard southwest of Fresno for $1,000 an acre. Alternatively a good, if not prime, twenty-acre tract could be had for $400 an acre ($2,000 down, with payments over four to six years at 8 to 10 percent interest).

In the post-depression years, values depreciated greatly. A January 16, 1894, *Fresno Daily Evening Expositor* article noted this, while insisting property remained a good investment ("It is simply like buying twenty-dollar gold pieces for ten dollars"). While sales did taper off in this period, deflated prices brought some buyers back by 1899. In that year Fresno realtors E. F. Bernhard, Haber Brothers and Company, and Easton, Eldridge and Company were doing well, selling land for anything between $50 and $150 an acre.

Extensive settlement on easily farmed lands and the depression brought a virtual end to colony development in the mid-1890s. Notable among the subdivisions begun in this era were the 6,000-acre New England Colony, started in 1888; the Fairview Colony, begun on 3,000 acres of Laguna de Tache river bottom land in 1890; Alexander Gordon and John Reichman's

Caledonia Colony, also opened for settlement in 1890; and two tracts opened by the Pacific Agricultural and Colonization Company around 1895—one 2,560 acres and located near the Eggers Ranch, the other northwest of Fresno and known as the Victoria Colony.

Near Reedley several colonies were prospering by 1891: the 2,800-acre Curtis and Shoemaker tract (where land sold for seventy-five dollars an acre), the Reed Colony consisting of T. L. Reed's subdivided farming lands, the Matthews Colony and D. T. Curtis' Level Orchard Colony. The last derived its name from the fact that its lands needed no leveling. Nearer to Fowler Philip W. Hastie opened a large tract for settlement around 1895. As before, people came from all over the United States and some foreign countries to shop for farm lands, with many of them buying and staying. The number of farms in Fresno County went from 2,350 in 1890 to 3,813 by the century's end.

Entranced by board of trade, newspaper and other promotional literature, many Fresno County landowners expected to find vast riches in the soil—only to harvest discontent. When the depression hit and Fruit Vale Estate farmers could not make payments on their property, original owner M. Theodore Kearney was ruthless in foreclosing on loans he had made and repossessed much of the estate.

Another colonization scheme, the Holland, caused its investors much grief although for different reasons. It was formed around 1890 when one Koch in the Netherlands and one Mack in California decided to buy the Perrin Colony No. 2, due north of Fresno, and offer the land bounded by present-day First, Blackstone, Shaw and Herndon avenues to Dutch settlers. The developers failed to mention that most of the land was desolate, sun-baked hardpan. When about thirty colonists arrived in December 1890 "words of dismay, of question, of explanation were showered in two languages upon the crisp air, but nothing came of them," according to historian Ernestine Winchell.

Encouraged, perhaps, by local examples of successful farming under poor conditions, many of the immigrants stayed. A thousand acres were being cultivated in the Holland Colony by May 1891. Dutch common- ers such as Marten and Peter Van Wyhe, G. Crans, Carlier Van Dissell and A. H. Hartwelt tilled the soil with noblemen Baron Van Heekeren-Brockhuyzen Van Bransenburg and Freiheer de Casembroot. A few farmers managed to get decent lots, but the generally poor soil caused Van Dissell, Peter Van Wyhe and others to leave eventually. The fact that the land is now covered by urban sprawl bears some testimony to its agricultural worth.

Older, well-established colonies and their colonizers were doing much better than the hapless Dutch (see 15:1). A few, like the Washington and Central Califor- nia colonies, were little communities in their own right. The Temperance Colony had a social club, tri-monthly literary society, and regular entertainments for its resi- dents. In 1895 the West Park Colony boasted a school, Methodist Episcopal Church and Sunday school, Ep- worth League, Good Templars Lodge, Farmers' Alli- ance, Haymakers' Club and—as one report proudly noted—"no saloon." The only colony that sank into a decline at this time was the Washington. Well-drilling caused alkali to rise to the surface in some areas around it, rendering the land useless. After the passage of some years only eucalyptus and acacia trees marked the homes of farmers evicted by the sterilized soil.

Irrigation systems were expanded, improved and inaugurated constantly in this period. The county had approximately 300 miles of main canals, 1,000 miles of branch canals and 5,000 miles of distributing ditches in 1897. The Fresno Canal and Irrigation system alone went from serving 500 settlers on 5,000 acres to 20,000 on 200,000 acres, and its main canal was extended to a forty-mile length. In the late 1880s and early 1890s it was joined by three other irrigation works: the Enter- prise Canal; the small Roundtree Ditch, draining Murphy Slough below the Reed Ditch; and the Stim- son Canal, with its headgate on Bogg Slough. Ap- proximately nine miles long without branches, the Stimson was built for $23,000 and watered 14,000 West Side acres. The nearby Hite Ditch also was owned by the Stimson Canal Company, but was later taken over by independent management.

Most canals built in the 1890s were relatively small. Only two large-scale operations, the James West Side and Outside canals, came into being at the time. The first of these was actually two canals, one built in 1892–93 and the other in 1899. Both were about forty feet wide, three feet deep, and ten miles long. Rancher Jefferson James built these canals to raise wheat and corn on his lands, and—in exchange for periodic repair work—allowed farmers living adjacent to his property to tap into them.

The Outside Canal system, another 1890s develop- ment, was considerably larger. It ran parallel to the San Joaquin and Kings River Canal for thirty-seven miles, cutting through Miller & Lux land, and was used to water wheat and corn patches, like the James canals. This waterway drew from the San Joaquin and Kings River Canal's supply as did the Parallel Canal,

Reference 15:1
## "TWO FRESNO COUNTY FARMING TESTIMONIALS"

George Boyde, Lot 150, Washington Col- ony, said: I came here six years ago [1879] from old Ireland. When I landed in Fresno my capital amounted to $1300. After I had been here a few days I bought this 20-acre lot and built this house and barn. The lumber for buildings cost me $450. Most of the labor I did myself. With the balance of my capital I purchased horses, cows and farm imple- ments, and made the first payment on my land. I have now on this 20 acres, 16 acres of raisin vines. My wife, with her cows and chickens, always adds $15 to $25 a month to our income, according to the number of cows we have in milk. We invested our savings in a second 20-acre lot, which I have planted to vines. I calculate that I shall this year have an income from my 40 acres of about $4000. For the first five years I did all the work myself, and very hard work indeed I found it. Let all men coming to Fresno County with a small capital, expecting to make money, be prepared to work hard. The land is so rich that if it is not constantly plowed and cultivated the weeds begin to grow, and fruit and weeds will not grow together. Now I hire the greater part of my work done, and content myself with superin- tending and seeing that it is done properly.

In reply to the question if he was not a happy and satisfied man, Mr. Boyde said:

Why, happy? certainly. Satisfied? yes. But when my last 20 acres are in full bearing I mean to sell both farms and buy 160 acres. I shall then have sufficient capital to enable me to hire all the hard, laborious work to be done for me. As you know, the profits on 160 acres are enough to make an Irishman very well satisfied. . . .

W. Kanserup, who resides in the Scandi- navian Colony, five miles from Fresno City, was next interviewed:

Q. When did you first come to this coun- try?

A. In 1879.

Q. What capital did you bring with you?

A. Well, very little. I paid $160 as a first installment on my twenty acres, and then borrowed $200 with which to erect a little shanty, and went to work on my land, planting it out in vines, alfalfa and fruit trees. I filled in my time by working out, and by that means, with the help of my cows and chickens, kept the family going until the vineyard began to bear.

Q. Is your ranch all paid for, Mr. Kan- serup?

A. Yes; I am happy to say it is all paid for.

I have no mortgage on it at all. I have a nice eight-roomed house, large barn, two horses and two cows, and money in the bank. I do all the work in the vineyard myself, except picking the grapes, for which I have to hire assistance. My wine grapes produce, when dried, about two tons to the acre, which I sell to be shipped East and made into wine. They bring me about $100 an acre on an average, sometimes more, and my raisin vines about the same.

Q. What about alfalfa?

A. I have four acres in alfalfa, and that keeps and feeds all my stock, cows, horses, etc., and enables me to make a little by selling it when cut.

Q. Are you and your family healthy here?

A. Yes, we are always healthy. I believe Fresno to be a great place.

SOURCE: [Fresno County Board of Trade.] *Fresno County, California, where can be found climate, soil and water, the only sure combination for the vineyardist, fruit grow- er, cattle raiser and farmer.* Fresno, Cali- fornia: *Fresno Evening Expositor* print, 1893.

whose headgate was located four miles below Firebaugh. Abutting the Fresno Slough, and only one and a half miles above the San Joaquin and Kings River intake, a fourth canal—the China Slough—was added in 1897–98.

In the Kings River sloughs a number of ditches were built to expand irrigation coverage. Among them were the Burrell and Turner ditches (constructed in 1890), which tied into Murphy Slough, and the $1,000 Calamity Ditch built four years later with its headgate on Fish Slough. Toward the northeast, and near the main canal intakes, another group of small ditches were developed: the Dunnigan-Boyd (1892), Hanke (1895), Carmelita (1896, built to service the nearby Carmelita Vineyard), and New Jack (1898). As period maps show, these additions gave central California a comprehensive grid of irrigation waterways by 1899.

With all these canals dependent on irregular river flows, it was natural that farmers would look for a more dependable irrigation method. Some found it in the ground, where the water table had risen dramatically—thanks to surface irrigation. Well-drilling for agricultural purposes was thus made feasible. When frustrated Selma farmer William De La Grange discovered that his lands were left dry by day, due to overuse of the Centerville and Kingsburg Canal, and flooded by underuse at night, he decided to use an underground water source. By digging a hole eighty feet deep and pumping out sand and clay at that level, he formed a subterranean reservoir that could be easily tapped with a three-inch, steam-driven centrifugal pump.

De La Grange, who had dug the well for twenty-two dollars, was soon the envy of his neighbors because he had a consistent water supply. One of them, Thomas G. Martin, copied his scheme with a slight variation: he used a five-horsepower gasoline pump. These were among the first irrigation pumping stations in the world, and were joined in 1898–99 by four units that lined Fresno Slough's lower reaches. They ranged from 40 to 150 horsepower and conveyed water at a cost averaging three cents per acre. Artesian (deepwell) drilling also had found infrequent use. In the June 25, 1889, *Fresno Daily Evening Expositor* Gustav Eisen reported that between 200 and 300 such wells were functioning in the San Joaquin Valley. Some could furnish a 175,000-gallon daily flow.

When the Wright Act's passage made the establishment of public irrigation districts possible (see Chapter 7), a new era in water rights had begun, but its start in Fresno County was sluggish. Private canal building, maintenance and ownership had worked—in most instances—making farmers uninterested in changing the status quo. Only one public irrigation district was created in the county before 1900: the Alta, consisting of the 76 Land and Water Company's canal and ditch holdings. It was formed, in part, to help stockholders

of the latter enterprise save face. The boom years had caused the "76" to get greedy and boost land lease prices. One of its directors, P. Y. Baker, defected and formed a citizens' group in 1888 whose objective was to buy out the old company and form a new public irrigation district. The Tulare County Board of Supervisors approved this scheme on July 10 of the same year, and the district was voted into existence on August 14. ("Alta" was adopted as the district's name because its proposed boundaries included the Kings River's highest diversion point.) District headquarters was first located at Dinuba, and was moved to Reedley in 1893.

In the August 14 election T. L. Reed, E. E. Giddings, J. E. Toler, J. D. Vannoy and Baker were elected directors of the Alta. They began negotiating for purchasing the "76" immediately. The district was asked to pay $500,000 at first, although the canals it contained had been built for $100,000. After some haggling a $410,000 price was agreed upon in February 1890. Bonds were issued and assessments were approved to finance the deal, along with the construction of 150 more miles of canals for $133,000. (When some Smith Mountain farmers protested the first assessment, district lines were redrawn to exclude them.)

These massive expenditures, coupled with the depression, almost ruined the district. It had to cancel a January 1895 bond issue and was then paying only seventy-five cents on the dollar for previously issued bonds. Refinancing and tight management averted disaster, however. Annual operating expenses were pared to about $16,000 by 1899.

Attempts to form other irrigation districts in Fresno County made the Alta look like a resounding success. A Selma Irrigation District was approved by voters of that area on April 19, 1890. It was to serve 600,000 acres by buying $500,000 worth of existing canals and building $500,000 worth of new ones. A bond issue providing for this scheme was defeated the following July 12—the prices involved were generally thought to be excessive. Similar measures were voted down on December 17, 1890, and November 16, 1891. Although the district never accomplished anything, it survived a dissolution suit and election to continue functioning until 1907.

Also unsuccessful was the Sunset Irrigation District, formed in March 1891. Its engineers planned to divert water into a $1.5 million diversion dam and reservoir near Summit Lake, raise it to a higher elevation via Krough centrifugal pumps, and thereby irrigate a 400,000-acre area northeast of Coalinga. Steam and hydro-generated power sources were considered, but the former was too inefficient and the latter too wasteful. This, coupled with the fact that the Southern Pacific owned most of the district's land—and had no interest in irrigating it, or being assessed to do so— spelled doom for the scheme. The Southern Pacific induced a judge to declare a construction bond election for the district illegal, and it lapsed into obscurity. Even a lesser project, started in 1892 and actually built—the $25,000 Huron Irrigation District—had to be abandoned after faulty design made it inefficient and ineffective to use.

Squabbles over water rights, so prevalent during agriculture's infancy in Fresno County, continued up to the century's end. Riparian claimants, who wanted an undiminished, unblemished flow of water past their property, took irrigation appropriators to court and were winning—as happened in 1899, when riparianists Miller and Lux obtained a cease-and-desist judgment against the Enterprise Canal Company. The canal company had been draining the San Joaquin River above the Miller and Lux ranch lands, clearly prohibited by the 1886 *Lux v. Haggin* decision (see Chapter 6). Similar judgments—one in 1888 against the Fowler Switch Canal, one the following year against the Alta Irrigation District—shut down these appropriating water systems.

In apparent contradiction, water rights also were being doled out to appropriators. An 1892 decision gave the Lower Kings River Canal Company a guaranteed flow of water, as did 1898 rulings for the Stimson and Crescent canal companies. Engineer Carl Ewald Grunsky, in a 1901 report, gave the probable reason for this tangled state of affairs. The courts did not wish to indulge or antagonize either side, he said, and saw fit to vacillate freely on individual water issues.

A series of irrigation controversies began in 1887 when land speculator E. B. Perrin acquired the Fresno Canal and Irrigation Company. The system could handle only 100 cubic feet of water per second, while Perrin needed 1,200 feet to fulfill sub-contracts. Consequently, he filed suit to obtain additional irrigation rights. Perrin thought he could win by liquoring up an engineer, having him inspect the canals while inebriated, and declare later in court that the Fresno Canal system could handle the increased flow. Unfortunately, the engineer's testimony was picked to pieces under cross-examination.

Perrin then tried bribing expert witnesses and inebriating the judges involved on a canal inspection tour. Again he failed. Then he decided to try a different tactic. Under riparian law, the Kings River water flow mostly belonged to the Laguna de Tache land grant owners, Poly, Heilbron and Company and Sinon C. Lillis. If they could be persuaded to sell, a virtually unlimited water supply could be obtained. Perrin commenced negotiations, obtained a loan from a consortium of English insurance companies, and ended up buying the grant for $800,000 in mid-1891.

This move, if self-serving on Perrin's part, was fortunate in one respect: it kept the irrigation waters flowing around Fresno. Had it continued under ap-propriation status, the Fresno Canal system might have been shut off by a capricious court decree. New problems arose, unfortunately. Perrin neglected to improve or maintain the canals, defaulted on his loan and the English companies took over the grant and insurance companies.

In the resulting confusion one appropriator, the Alta Irrigation District, tried to extract more water from the Kings by enlarging its intake facilities. A team of Fresno Canal workmen under Ingvart Teilman tried to correct this situation surreptitiously (trying to repair the damage Perrin had caused), and was chased away with bullets. At this point the English interests' superintendent, Llewellyn A. Nares, went to court over the issue and won. Not wanting to antagonize the Alta and other water interests further, he asked them to "sit around the table without the attorneys" and adopt a schedule for the use of Kings River water. This led to a comprehensive agreement among the major irrigation companies in 1897 and the land grant, Reed, Turner, Millrace, Riverdale and Burrell ditches in 1899.

Nares' conciliatory gesture ended much of the trouble along the Kings, but low water conditions in 1898 caused some old problems to crop up again. When T. C. White, J. C. Moore and W. H. Shafer tried to turn on the Fowler and Emigrant Ditch Company's headgate in April, Frank Shannon of the Lower Kings River Ditch Company threatened the men with a gun and was arrested. Shannon claimed that his company, whose intake was far down on the Kings, was getting scarcely any water. By July 2 threats to blow up the Fresno Canal headgate were being heard. A sheriff's deputy named Cash Thomas had to defend that property until early October.

Irrigation difficulties were not the only problem Fresno County farmers faced in this era. As always, their crops were threatened by a variety of pests which seemed to be increasing in diversity. Perhaps the worst was the jackrabbit, which thrived and multiplied on the sudden increase of roots, seeds and alfalfa. Vineyards afforded them good cover, making it difficult for farmers to find and kill them. About the only way they could be controlled was by a "rabbit drive." In vehicles and on foot, hundreds of people would fan out over a large stretch of countryside. By making noises and waving sticks, they frightened the rabbits into a massive V-shaped enclosure built for the drive. If not caught during the drive itself, the rabbits were killed once forced inside the enclosure.

Of a March 8, 1888, drive near Wildflower, the *Fresno Daily Evening Expositor* remarked that "sticks were flying in the air like black thorns at Donnybrook, hi-yis pierced the ears of spectators and participants; men and boys ran over each other in their eagerness to hurry up the slaughtering work, and many a luckless one got a rap intended for a rabbit." Some 1,500 people participated in the drive, and 5,000 took part in an even bigger drive on February 29, 1896. The latter event netted so many carcasses that they could not be counted, although a typical yield was 5,000 to 10,000. A fair number of these were sent to San Francisco meat packers where, suggested Ernestine Winchell, they were probably processed as "chicken tamales" or "potted chicken."

Thrips, or vine-hoppers, created constant problems during the 1890s. "They will lay all winter in frost and ice and when spring opens bob up serenely with constitution unimpaired and excellent optics," said a May 4, 1894, *Fresno Daily Evening Expositor* report. In an effort to wipe out a thrip plague in 1897–98, vines were sprayed with a whale oil-sulphur mix and flooded. This method failed, and only a cyanide-sulphuric acid spray, used on the Eshleman and Gordon vineyards, was said to have worked. Whatever its effectiveness, thrips were still attacking vineyards east of Fresno in the spring of 1899.

Grasshoppers swept down the Dry Creek area in July 1891 and June 1895, and were so thick in the latter instance that they blacked out the sky at times. One farmer, W. R. Birmingham, had to cover his trees with sacks and plow earth around them to keep them from being defoliated.

Other pests of note were the San Jose scale (which attacked 336,669 out of 759,454 fruit trees in Fresno County in 1895), cottony cushion scales (decimated by the introduction of Australian ladybugs in 1895), cutworms, red-headed linnets and red spiders. They were all periodically blamed for crop losses, although other forces may have been responsible by 1899. In that year Alexander Gordon addressed the county Farmers Club and asked, "Why is it that the raisin crop has decreased from 5,000 carloads to less than 3,000? We say one year it is caused by hoppers, another by frost, another that it is high wind that caused it; but we shall soon have to face the fact that our rich farms are gone if we do not fertilize." Few farmers, possibly none, were bothering to replenish their soil, some of which had been worked for a quarter-century or more with no relief. There was probably appreciable truth to Gordon's remarks.

Different difficulties—those posed by the Southern Pacific and its high freight charges—began lessening after 1895. Farmers and other businessmen were tired of paying sixty-five cents to ship 100 pounds of freight from San Francisco to New York, and eighty-two cents to send the same cargo from the Bay Area to Bakersfield, so they decided to build a competing railroad that year. With the slowly-gotten financial backing of some millionaires, corporations and municipal governments, a San Francisco and San Joaquin Valley Railroad was inaugurated. Construction began in "The City" and reached Fresno on October 5, 1896. Immediately the Southern Pacific started to offer freight reductions and the elimination of switching charges at Stockton.

Dubbed the "People's" or "Valley" railroad by some, the new enterprise was said to have been partially financed by the Southern Pacific's rival—the Atchison, Topeka and Santa Fe. Tool shipments for the Valley Railroad came in boxes marked "A.T.S.F." and even though the railroad appeared to have been built by San Joaquin interests for their own use, it quietly slipped into Santa Fe control in December 1898.

In the boom era's wake, when it seemed inevitable that a Southern Pacific alternative would be developed, farmers began focusing their scorn on a new object: Chinese labor. With Fresno County continuing to increase its agricultural output, and whites desiring to become foremen and managers rather than menials, the Chinese controlled the lower end of the agricultural labor market by 1891 and were resented for it.

Because of low prices (approximately $1.75 a day for each worker, with a substantial percentage withheld) labor contractors in Fresno's Chinatown were supplying 7,000 men, many from San Francisco, to work in the fields and packing houses. Whites did not live in large numbers in the rural areas and wanted higher wages, so isolated farmers could use only Chinese help. This situation created much white resentment. Because of their sometime involvement in gang warfare, secret societies and vice, the Chinese were regarded with prejudice and/or suspicion by most whites.

As realization of the Chinese labor dominance took hold, whites began combatting it with measures that became increasingly ugly. County packing houses began refusing Chinese help; raisin grower A. B. Butler explicitly fired his Chinese workers and replaced them with white women and girls. He was so anxious to retain his new work force that he chartered a train to bring them to his estate in the morning and take them back to Fresno in the evening. With economic conditions worsening by 1892, farmers also began cutting the wages of the Chinese to as little as $1.15 per day. T. C. White even suggested that grapes be sold cheaply to wineries or be left to rot on the vines, rather than pay the Chinese to pick them.

The outright depression of 1893 caused even greater hostilities. Many whites were unemployed while Chinese toiled at sub-standard rates. On August 14, 500 unemployed men came close to running the Chinese out of Fresno's Chinatown. They were stopped only when local businessmen agreed to open an employment agency for them. An Anti-Chinese League had been formed in Selma two days before that incident, when the Earl Fruit Company fired its white female packers in favor of Chinese men. A riot the following September 1, led by a group of hobos, came close to driving Selma's Chinese population away for good.

Eight days later a Chinese bunkhouse on the Metzler Vineyard was attacked by a group of whites. They pounded on the door, demanded to be let in, and were

*View of the "barbecue" in Fresno on October 5, 1896, to celebrate the arrival of the first passenger train of the San Francisco and San Joaquin Valley Railroad (forerunner of Santa Fe Railroad), as photographed by H. H. Alexander. With a crowd estimated at 15,000 to 20,000 people, the day-long festivities also included a parade led by Fulton G. Berry, a military review, banquet, and illuminated bicycle parade. This railway was known as "The People's Railroad" and was developed largely through public subscription.*

*Seropian Brothers Packing House, Fresno, circa 1897. In 1881, John Seropian was one of the first Armenian residents of Fresno. He and his brother, George, pioneered in the packaging and shipping of dried fruits. They conducted "The Shippers' Revolt," and the* San Francisco Examiner *chronicled the progress of the caravan's 210-mile trek. The Seropians' challenge undoubtedly encouraged the construction of the San Joaquin Railroad, which was later sold to the Santa Fe Railroad Company.*

*Rabbit Drive conducted by the Grand Army of the Republic, 1892. Everyone joined to protect the crops from the over-population of jackrabbits.*

*"This is a picture of my brother J. P. Cull's ranch five miles north of Kerman taken around 1900. The one on the right is J. P. Cull, the other his hired man, H. C. Morton."—Mrs. D. O. Hill. Cull was one of the many who wrested a living from the land.*

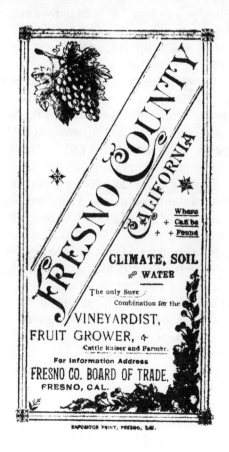

*Above is part of the cover of a book giving all possible information to encourage people to come to Fresno. On right the Board of Trade joins the effort.*

refused. At that point they peppered the front door with bullets and began tearing the structure down. Eleven of the Chinese ran away and three were captured, robbed and marched back to Fresno. There also was much agitation in the Kingsburg area. The effigy of a Chinese laborer, labeled "Wun Wing," was hanged from a telegraph pole near the depot there, and a boycott of the Earl Fruit Company (the lone packer using Chinese help) was organized.

Tensions began to ease as the economy's recovery progressed. Although menial wages had declined to one dollar a day there was work for almost everyone, regardless of race, by 1896. Japanese workers started joining the Chinese in the fields about this time, along with whites who found it impossible to obtain better work. "The men are of all ages, from saucy-looking little 16-year-old boys to men of many years, whose hapless look tells of ambitions departed and their resignation to circumstances which have turned them out on the highway during old age," said a report in the August 28, 1897, *Fresno Daily Evening Expositor*. "At frequent intervals during the day wagons drive up to [Courthouse] Park and load up with twenty or thirty of the eager laborers."

Things improved enough by 1898 for the farmers to employ large numbers of Chinese and Japanese— white labor could be had, but was scarce—and even menial wages increased to $1.50-$1.75. Prosperity had returned and even the lowest-status agricultural laborers began demanding a share of it. Women working at the Las Palmas packing house were emboldened enough to strike for a twenty-five cent daily wage increase and all but three walked off their jobs when it was refused.

Wheat, the crop responsible for starting Fresno County's agricultural development, sank into a decline after the boom years. Two factors were responsible: the depression and the expansion of fruit acreages, which were more profitable. Until the wheat market fell apart in 1891-92 (sixty-three cents was offered per 100 pounds, compared to $1.65 in 1889), it had been quite strong; E. P. Hammers of Selma reported an excellent yield of eleven sacks per acre in 1890. When early rains damaged much of the San Joaquin Valley crop that year, Fresno County's was somehow spared, its yield going to 6.5 million bushels. Some 650,000 bushels were shipped from the Reedley area alone, and the Southern Pacific could have used several hundred more cars to carry out the crop.

All kinds of disasters befell the industry in 1892 and after. T. L. Reed, who had accumulated 150,000 sacks of wheat on speculation (and had borrowed heavily to get them), held out too long and found himself bankrupt. Early 1893 rains wiped out much of the county crop, and more than half of the losses were on the West Side—an area where wheat planting had recently begun. Bankers refused to allow advances on warehoused wheat, and farmers thought the money lenders were plotting with shippers and buyers to ruin the grain market. The total county acreage in wheat slid from 156,145 to 78,967 in the 1895-96 period alone, a startling decline from the earlier years.

Production began rallying by 1897. By May of that year the county had received 10½ inches of rain, non-irrigated fields had done well, and export demand had risen in Argentina, Australia and Europe. Prices had recovered, to $1.50 per 100 pounds. The only problem was that too little was being produced within the county—approximately seven million pounds each year during this time. Wheat growing was still being undertaken in all areas, but the increase in vineyard acreage had limited production severely. Perhaps this situation was fortuitous, though. While crop quality remained good, prices fell below one dollar per 100 pounds in 1899, when a grower had to make a cent a pound to break even. By that time only one major wheat grower remained in Fresno County: Clovis Cole, who harvested 20,000 acres in a typical turn-of-the-century year.

While wheat became less significant, orchard and non-raisin fruit crops were enjoying an unbelievable growth rate. In 1889 Fresno County produced 4,632,-200 pounds of dried and 713,650 pounds of green fruit. One year later, the respective figures swelled to 7,490,-135 and 7,942,572 pounds. When the wheat market began falling apart in 1891, dry fruits commanded the wondrous sum of 6¼ cents a pound. Some contended it was more profitable to grow raisins; this is not borne out by available records. Fresno orchardists Page and Morton obtained $430 an acre for pears in 1890, and a mere $240 an acre return for raisins. "Taken all around, perhaps those that suggest a mixed crop, both fruit and grapes, is the most profitable, are nearest the truth," remarked a writer in the June 19, 1891, *Fresno Daily Evening Expositor*.

Throughout this era there were periodic fears of overproduction (there were 2,035 county orchards and 1,575,323 trees in 1896); but they were never realized. Population and consumption, here and abroad, were on the rise and California fruits were always held in high regard (see 15:2).

Heat waves in 1891 and 1894 baked apricots on the trees, an 1897 drought damaged the county crop and 1899 frosts made them even more scarce. They remained a moderately profitable fruit, bringing six and a half cents a pound in 1894 and twelve cents a pound in 1898, and were grown extensively on the colony lots. Nectarines began as a lucrative item, commanding ten cents a pound in 1889; unfortunately, one atypical grower received only $100 an acre for his crop in 1891. In the Fowler area one peach orchard realized a $500 an acre gross in 1891, with average growers obtaining $250 to $300 less for the same crop. The 1897 drought hit peaches hard in the county, reducing the yield to one-third its yearly average.

Pears, as noted above, could be immensely profitable, although the market fluctuated wildly. D. W. Lewis of Malaga received fifteen cents a pound of dried pears in 1891, while two years later a grower obtained one cent for two boxes of the fruit. Bartlett and Winter Nellis were the most popular varieties, the Bartlett commanding a higher price. The county pear crop did not do well in 1899, being ravaged by blight and improper cultivation, and it sank to a quarter of its normal yield.

French prunes were, perhaps, the most profitable crop produced during this period, gaining a $1,200 an acre return for one owner. A $400 to $500 return was more common. W. S. Staley of Selma, A. C. Bryan of Oleander and F. R. Stone of the Washington Colony were the primary growers of this crop.

Around this time it was recognized that citrus fruits thrived in the foothill "thermal belt" of eastern Fresno County. That area, high enough to avoid fogs and frosts and temperate during much of the year, had attracted several important orange and lemon growers by 1889. Among them were Fulton G. Berry, Wesley Hazelton and Frank Locan. The groves Locan planted yielded $600 an acre that year—he said, "I wish now I had set out ten thousand trees, as nothing on my ranch has done better in proportion than my orange trees." One of his trees had a two-and-a-half-foot limb loaded with fifty-seven oranges, all in perfect shape and condition.

Three years later, the January 1, 1891, *Fresno Daily Evening Expositor* noted that "an orchard of five-year-old [orange] trees yielded to its proprietor $1000 worth of fruit, an amount per acre equal to that produced by the very best raisin vines in the county." Soon afterward John Rayson and T. L. Reed began planting orange trees near Reedley, and Sanger nurseryman D. W. Lewis was doing a brisk trade.

Lemon growers such as William Hazelton, a Mr. Lowrey and Berry were raising fine products (one of Lowrey's lemons was 13¼ inches in circumference) but were not realizing great profits. Berry made only $100 an acre, from his three-acre crop, in 1894.

In 1895 approximately 140 citrus fruit acres came into bearing, and thirty carloads of the fruit were shipped out of the county. Since the "thermal belt" crop ripened several weeks earlier than those in other areas of the state, it was thought that Fresno County would assume importance in the industry. In anticipation, a "Citrus Fair" was held in Fresno in January 1896. Records of the occasion note that a few valley growers (A. B. Butler, Minnie Eshleman, George Malter and the Eisens) were experimenting with oranges, T. Crockett Douglas of Centerville was growing grapefruit, the Williams brothers of Reedley were growing limes, and Mrs. William Helm and William G. Uridge were experimenting with lemons, with their results on display. This fair, which featured musical entertainment, dances, comic songs and recitations, was covered by many California newspapers and generated much interest.

Freak frosts in the "Citrus Fair" year set the county citrus industry back—but only temporarily. Some of the crop reached London the following year, and 4,000 boxes of lemons left Sanger alone. Uridge was operating a citrus tree nursery near the "Orangedale" orchard of Berry and R. B. Wallace, and one of the Hazeltons realized a $560-an-acre yield. In 1898 county output amounted to 300 carloads of oranges and more than 6,000 boxes of lemons.

Packing of the crop was undertaken at the Earl Fruit Company and Farmers' Warehouse of Sanger; because of the early maturity advantage it was always picked early, usually in November and December. Oddly enough, some dealers were reluctant to handle the huge, succulent oranges that came from Fresno County. Because of their size, two or three of them had to be sold for a nickel when five or six "normal" ones could be had for the same price. Many felt gypped and refused to buy them!

Among Fresno, Oleander, Selma, Fowler and Malaga there were twenty-three packing houses in 1888. They concentrated on preparing raisins for market although the Earl, Williams, Brown and Company (of Fresno), Olivet (of Malaga), Curtis (of Oleander) and Fowler Fruit and Raisin Packing Company packed most of the fruit varieties mentioned above.

Reference 15:2
## GOOD FRUIT

THE FRESNO ARTICLE RECEIVED WITH RAPTURE IN ENGLAND.
[London *Evening Star*, August 22, 1892.]

At Covent-garden market Messrs. W. N. White & Co. have been selling consignments of fruit from the California colonies. There can no longer be any doubt as to the complete success of the experiment. A very interesting fact told to a *Star* man by Mr. White is worth remembering. In very many instances the men who are making money by fruit-growing in California are the same men who failed to sustain a profitable business of the same character in Kent. Fifteen or twenty years ago the Fresno Valley would scarcely grow grass enough to feed sheep. Then a system of irrigation was carried out, with the result that the products of the once desert land were the pick of the world's finest at Covent-garden during the latest sale. Peaches a half a pound in weight, with the bloom on them as though just plucked; pears such as would fill the hot-house producer of England with envy, and plums the size of duck-eggs, all found quick sale at good prices. "French fruit," said Mr. White, "will not be in it with this stuff, and we can get thousands of tons of it. Fourteen thousand dollars was the offer to one of the growers for his season's crop of pears only."

SOURCE: [Kearney, Martin Theodore.] Fresno County, a wonderfully prosperous district in California, the land of sunshine, fruits and flowers . . . Chicago: Donahue and Henneberry, circa 1893.

During the 1890s two fruit canneries were established in Fresno. The first was set up as a stockholding venture by fruit dealers A. Lusk and Company, based in San Francisco, with financing obtained from that city and from Fresno sources. It was christened the Fresno Fruit and Canning Company, built and put into operation in 1891, and had a wildly successful first season: 4,290,000 pounds canned, 600 people employed, and a 20 percent dividend handed out to stockholders. Apricots, peaches, Bartlett pears, plums, grapes, nectarines, blackberries, figs and tomatoes all rolled out of the plant. Unfortunately, the cannery's output slid to 2,324,000 pounds in 1892, and it got into financial trouble the next year when it attempted to borrow on goods it had received.

By 1896 a new operation, financed like the Lusk venture, was being managed by the A. F. Tenney canning company of San Francisco (see 15:3). Competing with the Tenney plant was Charles G. Bonner's California Fruit and Raisin Company, C. B. Jeffries, Hobbs and Hoyt and the Castle Brothers.

Fig growing and packing became an important Fresno County industry in the post-boom years. The first important variety grown was the White Adriatic,

cultivated and packed by Emil Bretzner and Martin Denicke in 1888. Since these early figs had to be exposed to sulphur fumes, sun-dried, dipped in salt water and packed by hand, they commanded a high price (about twenty cents a pound).

Joining these pioneers the following year were Melcon G. Markarian, his son Henry, and shortly after that Serbian immigrant Samuel N. Mitrovich and John Seropian. Markarian and Seropian were part of a miniature immigration wave from Armenia which had brought 327 of their countrymen to Fresno County by 1897. Some of Mitrovich's figs were displayed at the 1893 Columbian Exposition in Chicago.

Seropian soon established himself as the county's pre-eminent fig packer, employing 250 people by 1899. To emphasize his disgust with the Southern Pacific's freight rates in 1894, he hired C. A. Campbell's mule teams—idled by the off-season in the lumber mills—to haul his figs to San Francisco. This method, which proved to be cheaper than railway service, did not catch on but made Seropian a temporary folk hero.

The expansion of the fig business brought some difficulties. Prices declined markedly, from a thirty-cents-per-pound high in 1894, to around a nickel by the

Reference 15:3

## A HUMMING BEE-HIVE OF INDUSTRY: THE TENNEY CANNING COMPANY

One of the foremost of Fresno's business enterprises is the Tenney Canning Company's establishment on South Front street. It is a veritable bee-hive. The hum of industry pervades the whole institution.

An Expositor reporter was this morning introduced to the working of the various departments of the cannery.

The whole of the machinery is run by a 12-horse-power engine, driven by a boiler sixteen feet by five feet. This boiler also furnishes steam to run twelve cooking tanks, into which are lifted the cans of fruit after they have been filled and capped.

The sugar room is reached by a flight of steps which are just inside the door of communication between the office and canning rooms. The sugar is made into syrup of fifty degrees and upwards, and this again is reduced by water to the consistency needed for the various qualities of fruit canned.

Three syrup machines are used in this process, and the juice is hoisted up to the syrup tanks. There are four of these tanks, each having a capacity of 1000 gallons.

The syrup is made from the finest quality of dry granulated sugar, and afterward put into the galvanized iron tanks.

The fruit is first taken into the receiving room and immediately goes over the scales and is put through the grading machine, and is separated into five grades. The best of these grades is called 3-pound extras; second, 2½ extra standard; third, 2½ regular standard; fourth, seconds, and fifth, pie fruit, the last grade packed without syrup.

After being graded, the fruit next goes on to the table, is cut and the pits are taken out. From here it goes into the hands of the canners, after having been inspected.

The cannery is at present turning out from 2000 to 2500 cans per day. The full capacity of the cannery has not as yet been tested, as the busiest season has not commenced.

Apricots is the only fruit canned at the present time, the season for this brand of fruit lasting till about the 12th of July. After that comes peaches and pears. Mr. Tenney expects them to double the number of hands employed.

White labor is employed in every department of the cannery except the tinning and cooking departments, and in these only are Chinese employed. This is the rule that obtains in every cannery in California. This work has been offered to white help, but they have refused it as the work is too hot.

At present there are about 250 or 300 white people employed at the cannery, and the weekly rent roll of this little army of workers amounts to somewhere in the neighborhood of $1200. This will be greatly increased when the peach and pear season is on, when it will reach some $1800 or $2200.

In regard to the statements recently made by certain parties in regard to the price paid for fruit by this cannery, as compared with that paid by other canneries in the state, Mr. Tenney says he will pay $40 a ton for 3-pound extras, for which other concerns are paying $25 per ton. He says also that he will pay $20 a ton for peaches of this class.

The fact is that peaches of this grade are not presented at the cannery. The experienced growers of this fruit will not allow their peaches to grow closer than five or six inches on the trees, but keep them continually pruned out, so that the remaining ones have a chance to attain to this quality. The trouble with most peaches is that they are left to remain so thick together on the trees, and in consequence they attain numbers rather than quality.

In speaking to one of the other partners of the Tenney cannery, your reporter was informed that the former had just made a trip to San Francisco and learned that the prices paid for fruit by the canneries there does not compare favorably with those paid here, with freight and everything else taken into consideration.

For the edification of the discontented element, the company advises that the growers ship a carload of fruit to San Francisco and see what the result is when the returns come in.

The value of canned fruit is based on the value of the dried article. If this were not the case it is hard to account for the immense quantities of fruit being secured every day at this cannery.

SOURCE: *Fresno Daily Evening Expositor,* June 22, 1896, p. 1, c. 3.

next year, and a correspondent in the June 5, 1895, *Fresno Daily Evening Expositor* claimed that dishonesty and the incompetence of "a crowd of foreigners, partly Armenians," had caused this situation. The Seropian concern later expanded its business, however. The October 26, 1897, issue of the same newspaper commented on "the neat and attractive package" that Seropian produced; how he expected to pack sixty carloads that season; and how his figs were being shipped to diverse points all over the United States. Thus one wonders how valid the 1895 accusations were. The loss of foreign crops to frost in the following year boosted Seropian's sales further. Sadly, the destruction of his packing house by fire at the same time slashed his output and profit margin.

Other than monetary setbacks, Fresno County's early fig growers had but one regret. They were restricted to cultivating the White Adriatic variety because the more flavorful Smyrna, native to the Mediterranean region, would not grow in California. After Martin Denicke set out some Smyrna trees in the 1880s, he reported that the fruit reached the size of a hickory nut and then dropped off the branches. Curious as to why this occurred, Fresno nurseryman George C. Roeding sent W. C. West to Turkey in an effort to learn the answer. West's findings of 1886, confirmed by the research of Gustav Eisen at about the same time, were startling. The female Smyrna trees had to be pollinated by a wasp, or blastophaga, that frequented Capri (wild) fig trees. For years people in the Mediterranean had facilitated this process—as part of a folk tradition, and with no scientific knowledge—by placing Capri cuttings in Smyrna groves at particular times of the year. When Roeding announced this discovery, few believed him and his efforts to grow the Smyrna fig were fraught with difficulty (see 15:4). When success was achieved, it was obvious that the Smyrna would replace the White Adriatic as a production favorite.

The Smyrna fig type Roeding experimented with most intensively, and adjudged to be the best, was the Lop Injir. When large-scale growing began, Roeding felt uncomfortable with that Turkish name and selected "Calimyrna" as a replacement for its more pleasing sound—and apt meaning. The name remains familiar to most Fresno County residents of today.

Roeding also deserves credit for another pioneering agricultural venture. He was the first substantial olive

Reference 15:4

# HOW THE FIG WASP CAME TO CALIFORNIA

### GEORGE C. ROEDING

From letters written by Mr. West, and from what meagre [*sic*] information I had succeeded in obtaining from reports made by the leading scientists, who had been investigating the subject of caprification, I was fully aware . . . that Smyrna Figs could not be produced without the fig wasp, Blastophaga grossorum. In the year 1890, a few of the Smyrna Figs as well as the Capri Figs having produced fruit, I determined to try an experiment of artificial fertilization, although I was extremely doubtful of success. On June 15, quite a number of the Capri Figs were opened; the stamens or male blossoms at that time were matured and covered with pollen, which when shaken into the palm of the hand, and then transferred by means of a wooden tooth-pick into the orifice of the fig, fertilized the female flowers. Of the half dozen figs thus treated, every one matured, while all the others on the tree, when one-third grown, shriveled up and dropped to the ground. When the fertilized fruits were dried, they were carefully examined and to my surprise, were found to contain a large number of fertile seeds, with a flavor very similar to the imported fig, but not equal to it, as only a portion of the female flowers had developed seeds, due to the crude manner of fertilization.

To my mind this experiment proved conclusively that although other varieties of figs grown in California would mature their fruit, the Smyrna would not do so unless the flowers were fertilized, either by artificial means or by the fig wasp. . . .

Experiments of artificial fertilization were carried on for a number of years in the absence of the insect. In the year 1891, the old method was improved upon by using a glass tube, drawn to a fine point at one end for introducing the pollen. After gathering a small quantity of the pollen in the tube, it was inserted in the orifice of the fig, and by blowing through the other end, the pollen was more evenly distributed than by the method followed the previous year; 150 fruits represented the results of this experiment and when dried, they were sent to a number of the leading horticulturists and fruit growers of the state, all of whom made most favorable comments, and the concensus of opinion was that they were the finest figs ever produced in California, and were equal in flavor to the Smyrna Fig. In spite of these experiments, the fruit growers and the public at large were loath to believe in the subject of caprification, and I, as well as others, who had interested themselves in this subject, were regarded as cranks with some ulterior object in view. . . .

Having become fully satisfied of the genuineness of my trees, all that now seemed necessary in order to produce the Smyrna Fig on a commercial scale was to introduce the fig insect, in which no difficulty was anticipated. That expectations in this direction were not to be very promptly fulfilled, the following will show.

In the fall of 1891, in corresponding with Mr. Thos. Hall of Smyrna, who had assisted Mr. West in obtaining the fig cuttings, arrangements were made with him to send several consignments of Capri Figs containing insects, the first of which was received June 30, 1892, in very fair condition. Those which followed, however, arriving in July, were mostly rotten and the insects dead. The first figs were cut open and placed in glass jars, and thousands of insects were seen to emerge from them. These were then taken to the orchard and hung in branches in which young figs were growing, the same having been previously covered with cloth in order to prevent the insects from escaping.

In the same year, during the months of April and May, a number of consignments of Capri Figs with insects were received by Mr. E. W. Maslin, the same having been forwarded to him from Mexico, by Dr. Gustav Eisen, who was there at that time making investigations in the interest of the California Academy of Sciences. These figs, like the others, were given every attention, but the Blastophaga evidently objected to making Fresno its abode, for it failed to establish itself.

No further consignments of insects were received until April, 1895, when a package containing half a dozen specimens of Capri Figs in an excellent state of preservation, arrived from Smyrna, the same having been forwarded to me by Mr. M. Denotovich, a resident of that place. These figs were green and hard, and upon cutting them open were found to be full of galls, the insects being in the pupae state.

Following out these deductions the writer

grower in Fresno County and was cultivating sixty acres of the crop by 1890. Eight years later he opened a pickling and drying facility on Front Street in Fresno that processed thirty-five to forty tons of olives annually. They had to be stemmed by hand, dipped in lye, washed, salted, pickled and finally packed into barrels, and were said to have an excellent taste. Frank Locan, whose property was not far from Roeding's, was another early olive experimenter as were James Jameson and E. W. Gower of the Fowler area.

The crops mentioned above (with the exception of grapes, to be dealt with later) were the principal types grown in Fresno County at this time. Produced in more sparing amounts were apples, mostly in the foothill and mountain regions; bananas, which periodically bore fruit on the William Hazelton ranch near Sanger; melons, grown principally by M. M. Parsons and S. Z. Ickes; pomegranates, grown in small quantities near Sanger; and berries, beans, chestnuts and corn.

A few experimental crop plantings were highly unusual. Charles F. Crocker of the Southern Pacific brought 1,000 Arabian coffee plants for cultivation in 1895. It was thought that Fresno County's warm

in the year 1896 planted a number of Capri trees in a cañon in the foothills in a place known to be almost entirely free from frost. Several of these trees are now in full bearing and producing regular crops. In addition, two old fig trees at this place had been grafted, one of which is now completely worked over, and many of the grafts are 4 inches in diameter, and from 12 to 15 feet long.

In the year 1896, another series of consignments were received from Dr. Francis Eschauzier, of the State of San Luis Potosi, Mexico, which were also failures.

Learning that Mr. Koebele was in Mexico in the employ of the Hawaiian Government, another attempt was made, with his assistance, to establish the insect, but as usual nothing materialized. Finally Mr. Koebele wrote that he was satisfied that each species of Ficus had its own species of Blastophaga, and in his opinion it would be necessary to import the insect from the locality from which the fig cuttings were taken, to succeed.

A Capri Fig tree had been previously covered with sheeting so that immediately upon receiving the figs, they were cut open, placed in jars and suspended by strings on the branches of this tree. However, none of the insects became established.

In the year 1899 another attempt was made by Mr. Swingle, each fig being wrapped in tin foil and packed in cotton in a wooden case. A series of consignments were forwarded by him to Dr. Howard at Washington, and the same were remailed from there, arriving in Fresno between the 6th and 15th of April. The figs arrived in excellent condition, due to Mr. Swingle's painstaking method of packing. They were quite firm, plump and green, and looked as if they had just been picked. On cutting them open it was found that they contained many live and fully developed insects.

So many experiments had been made in former years to establish the insects in a similar manner, without success, that the writer foresaw no better prospects in this instance, and the following is an extract from a letter written to Dr. Howard at about that time:

"I will cut the figs open and place them under the Capri trees, which I have covered, but anticipate no results, nor do I think a success will be made of this matter until fig trees with fruit on them are sent out here during the winter months. If this is done, the insects will have a chance to develop in a natural way, and, being full of vitality, will enter our Wild Figs, just as they do in their nativity, passing from one crop of Capri figs to the following one."

While one of my employés was engaged in artificial fertilization, in the latter part of June, 1899, he informed me he had found seeds in some of the Capri figs, and to him it was a singular fact, as he had performed this same work of artificial caprification before, and had never found any seeds. On making an examination of one of the figs which had been left for the writer's inspection, what were apparently seeds were found to be in reality galls, and the writer's elation after so many years of work and experimenting can be well understood. A careful inspection of the tented tree revealed that there were fully forty figs which were still green, but badly shriveled, and on opening a few it was found that the female wasps had already made their exit, and those that remained were the wingless males. The figs under the covered tree had reached maturity much earlier than they would have done ordinarily, because of the higher temperature maintained by the tree being enclosed. Fortunately, for the success of the experiment, the tree adjoining was also a Capri fig tree, and some of the insects having escaped through an opening in the cover, caprified about twenty-five figs on this tree. These figs were picked and taken to the other Capri trees in the orchard, which at that time had a few figs, most of which were so small, however, that it seemed impossible for the insects to enter, none of them being larger than two peas. A few figs were also taken to the foothill ranch, but no fruits were to be found on the Capri trees growing there.

The Capri trees in the orchard were carefully watched, and on July 19, 1899, for the first time, a marked change in the development of some of the young figs was noticed; they being of a dark green color, plump and hard, an indication that they contained something; the metamorphosis in the appearance of the fruit being the same as in the Smyrna Fig when artificially pollinated.

On August 12, the first Capri Fig matured on one of these trees, and on examination it was found to contain pulp, a few galls containing female insects, as well as fertile seeds. This was a great disappointment, and the writer in his letter to Dr. Howard said that he was convinced that if all the figs then developing in the trees should, on ripening, be like the first one, a new and difficult problem had arisen, and it was feared the insect would be lost, as it would be smothered in the pulp of the fig before it could make its escape. Between the 20th and 26th of August, ten Capri Figs came to maturity, resembling very closely the June crop, except that the staminate flowers were absent, and the figs were much smaller. About the same time a new crop of figs made its appearance, and the insect entered them. When this crop began to mature, from the 15th of October to the 10th of November, nothing but pulpy figs were to be found. On the last date named and during a visit of Mr. Walter T. Swingle for the purpose of observing the workings of the insect, thousands of them were found to be emerging from the figs . . . This was a new phase in the matter, for all writers on this subject had described only three generations of the insect, but in the salubrious climate of California a fourth generation had developed.

Not knowing how low a temperature the Mamme or fall crop of figs would stand, it was deemed advisable to protect those remaining on the trees during the winter months, and over three of the trees, those in which this crop was the most abundant, a cloth house was built, 28 feet wide, 75 feet long and 16 feet high. This covering served its purpose admirably, and on March 5, 1900, when Mr. E. A. Schwarz, the special agent from the Division of Entomology at Washington, arrived, he found fully 400 or more of the Mamme crop, in fine condition, all of which, from their general appearance, indicated that they contained the insect in the hibernating state. Quite a few figs on the Capri Fig trees, which were not covered, were also found to be in fine shape, although the temperature during the winter on several occasions had been as low as 29 deg. Fahrenheit. . . .

SOURCE: Roeding, George C. *The Smyrna Fig at Home and Abroad . . . Fresno, California*: Published by the author for general circulation, 1903.

340

climate and moist soil would prove ideal for this crop, but the experiment seems to have failed. Another tropical plant, sugar cane, enjoyed greater success in the county. James Boyd of Lone Star produced several excellent crops in the early 1890s. Cuttings from his farm were used to start an experimental station on the San Joaquin River in 1894. This enterprise, inaugurated by E. J. Wickson at the behest of the Department of Agriculture, appears to have gone the way of Crocker's coffee plants.

Tobacco was successfully grown in the county at this time. J. C. Allen of the West Park Colony brought in a handsome crop in 1895, and A. D. Michael, an Armenian immigrant, ventured even further in this area by 1899. According to an article in the August 30 *Fresno Morning Republican*, Michael was producing superb Cuban and Turkish tobaccos on a foothill farm. The leaves were able to reach their proper delicacy there—something that was impossible in the valley. In addition, Michael used a curing method he had learned as a boy in Armenia to ensure his product's excellence.

As farming activities broadened in Fresno County, related industries continued a parallel expansion. In 1890 Roeding's Fancher Creek Nurseries was the home of 350,000 fruit trees, 30,000 palms and ever greens, 500,000 grape vines, 60,000 rose bushes and many other plants and trees. It was the largest nursery in Fresno County—and perhaps the state. The only serious competition it received was from the Fresno City Nursery of J. H. Wilson, C. W. Nicklin and S. W. Marshall, located near Centerville and specializing in citrus trees. In 1897 this concern had 97,000 trees, of which 45,000 were orange and 25,000 lemon.

Dairy enterprises continued to flourish under the direction of Minnie Eshleman (see 15:5) and A. T. Johns, who built the county's first creamery near Riverdale in 1890. Johns' establishment boasted a centrifugal-force, steam-powered cream separator that "[enabled] the production of the very finest grades of butter... It leaves the skim milk sweet and clean, making a most excellent feed for calves and pigs. The cream... is allowed to ripen before churning," according to an August 22, 1890, *Fresno Daily Evening Expositor* report.

No other creameries were started in the county until 1895; then there was one established in Selma, one by J. C. Vaughan, John Baird, J. C. Collyer and F. C. Burris, and another formed by a group of Danish farmers. Known as the Danish Creamery Association, it began with a 1,000-cow capacity and $6,150 plant and continues to operate today. The Holstein-Frisian cow breed, which remains the most popular among local dairy farmers, was brought by the Danes to Fresno County.

Important as these facets of agriculture were, they paled into insignificance compared to the grape. The great farming estates developed in this period were largely given over to its cultivation, indisputably profitable in the non-depression years (a $350 or more an acre yield). Prime among these estates was the Oothout Vineyard, which grew most of the major varieties (along with alfalfa, peaches, apricots, oranges and figs) and was surrounded by a four-mile-long rabbit-proof fence. Like most other important vineyards, it had complete carpentry and blacksmith's shops, worker housing, vegetable gardens, a main residence, and a large poultry operation. It even boasted a tennis court.

Also significant was the 800-acre Carmelita Vineyard, laid out by a San Francisco syndicate in 1890 near the Kings River and Reedley; the Estrella Vineyard, organized by settlers from Shelbyville, Indiana, in the same year; the 320-acre Fairview Vineyard of

Reference 15:5

## MINNIE ESHLEMAN
### ERNESTINE WINCHELL

The Eshleman family in the early '80s did not feel particularly optimistic about the future. Troubled by a serious bronchial affection, Dr. Isaac S. Eshelman had come to the Pacific coast [from Pennsylvania] in 1877, establishing a new residence in Oakland....

In this decade [a Comstock mine interest he owned] had ceased to pay dividends and its stock was now deemed worthless. Looking over some papers one day, Dr. Eshelman came to his certificate of stock, commented upon his disappointment in it, and flung it toward the open [fireplace] grate. It fell short and his daughter Minnie, then in her twenties, picked it up; instead of continuing it on its way she asked her father if she might keep it.

Like a story-book tale the prospects of the silver mine changed, and shortly the Eshelmans were able to sell the stock at par. With the $50,000 as resource, 640 acres of land [in Fresno County] was purchased in 1886, at the time when all the world was looking toward Fresno.

A beautiful and spacious home was created, and also everything necessary in the way of farm buildings. Thirty-five acres were set to Emperor grapes and from the Minnewawa vineyard in due time went the first Fresno County consignment of this variety to the market. Olives, peaches, prunes, Muscat vines, and many other of both experimental and staple plantings were made....

So long as Dr. Isaac Eshelman lived he and his younger daughter, Minnie, worked happily together in the efficient management of Minnewawa vineyard. For a period of 16 years they reveled in the creation and enjoyment of a beautiful and valuable property, and generously shared the results of their research and experiment with the Fresno community.

The doctor wrote helpful articles for the *Republican* of his day, and joined with Col. Trevelian and other vineyardists in discussion of frost prevention practices. Soil analysis also interested him.

While her father's attention was held mostly by the plantings, the livestock appealed to Minnie Eshelman herself. She loved her high-bred Holsteins and Jerseys and bred a strain the fame of which brought buyers from afar.

During the '80s butter was of uncertain quality in the Fresno markets. Scarcity of ice, carelessness and ignorance resulted in a production having all degrees and sorts of imperfection. In consideration of their own fastidious tastes, Miss Eshelman undertook to make butter for their own table, and entered into scientific study of the process.

Norman Parrish, Martin O'Connor, Oscar Lewis and E. J. Root, set out in 1889; the La Favorita and Paragon vineyards of Captain W. A. Nevills; the 270-acre Richland tract; the large Hogue and Sesnon Vineyard near Selma; and the Posa Rica, Ten Broeck, Place, Nestell and Patrol vineyards west of Fresno.

Most of the older large vineyards were still in business before the depression and doing well. A. B. Butler's vineyard, covering a square mile, was California's largest in 1892. Although it produced more than 1,000 tons annually, Butler was unable to supply his clients' demands and opened a raisin brokerage in Fresno's Masonic Building. William Forsyth's raisins, pronounced better than those grown in Spain's Malaga district, brought a $200-an-acre profit for their owner (good in those days) in 1888. Kearney's subdivided Fruit Vale Estate, where the Alexander Goldstein and Fruit Vale vineyards had been established, also produced a superb product. Fewer than 1 percent of the vines planted within the tract failed to grow.

Since wine grapes commanded less money than raisins (there was often a one to two cent a pound difference when raisins brought five cents a pound), many vineyards switched their cultivation to the raisin grape in the 1890s. Yet the important Fresno County vintners did not abandon their specialty, and a few newcomers entered the field during the 1890s. Total production hit 2.5 million gallons in 1890, according to the *New York Daily Tribune*. Individual wineries produced enormous vintages: 250,000 gallons from the Margherita Vineyard in 1888 (it burned down the following year), 300,000 from the Malter Vineyard in 1891, 220,000 from the Barton Vineyard in 1895, and 300,000 from the Eisen Vineyard in 1896. George Malter's operation expanded to 1,280 acres in this period, and he installed vast wine tanks—one with an 82,000-gallon capacity, the world's largest—on his estate.

Major wine vineyards and wineries established in this era were the Scandinavian Colony (1889), Andrew Mattei's (1890), Fred Roessler's Estella Blanca (1890) and Louis Rusconi's (1893). Several enterprises stood out particularly.

A syndicate of San Francisco investors formed the California Fruit and Wine Land Company in late 1887 purchasing 6,640 acres near Reedley and wasting no time in developing the tract. By 1892 much of it was leased to wheat farmers, with sizable acreages devoted to wine grapes and other fruits. W. C. West, who had been involved in other county agricultural ventures, developed the land and F. T. Briggs served as its superintendent.

In 1896 the California Wine Association began building a $2.5 million winery and distillery southeast of Fresno. It featured two fermenting cellars 160 feet in diameter, ten 50,000-gallon and twenty 20,000-gallon storage tanks, and was the largest facility of its type in California at the time. This enterprise absorbed the Eggers Vineyard in 1897 and produced 2.5 million gallons of wine the next year, along with 60,000 gallons of brandy. A small community eventually developed around the enterprise. Taking a cue from the *California Wine A*ssociation name, its founders christened the town "Calwa."

Like wine-making, raisin-packing became a notable Fresno County industry in the post-boom years. Gustav Eisen's authoritative 1890 treatise on *The Raisin Industry* noted twenty-two such establishments operating in Fresno County the previous year: the American Raisin Company, A. D. Barling, Barton Estate Company, A. B. Butler, California Fruit and Raisin Company, Cook and Langley, H. E. Cook, Fresno

---

Producing more than was required for the place, appreciative customers were supplied, and presently a wagon and driver were required to deliver butter, cream and other superior products from the Minnewawa dairy.

At that time the practical means of controlling milk temperature were limited to thick-walled dairy houses provided with ventilation, protection from the sun, and cooling by evaporation of sprinkled water. All these this clever woman reduced to standard, taking the deepest interest in the subject. Of her workers she required the utmost of cleanliness in every stage of operation.

When the Farmers' Institute came into being in Fresno Minnie Eshleman became active in its field. In 1897 she prepared a competent paper on "The Present Dairy Situation in California" and this was read by Nellie Boyd at the meeting held that year in Malaga.

For a number of years contributions under the name of M. D. Eshelman in the *Pacific Rural Press* did much for the dairy business, and that agricultural journal also carried her advertisements all over the state. She made numerous trips with the Institute, filling important places on the programs and lending valuable aid to the work.

But her aristocratic Holsteins and the dairy interests held only a part of Miss Eshelman's activity. Not at all a society woman, she was yet of a social disposition and was identified with the Wednesday club and the Parlor Lecture club, both of which, during her time, she served as president.

The beautiful vineyard home was several times the setting for club meetings, with almost royal entertainment by its mistress. There is still a charming picture of the Wednesday club with the stylish ladies of the nineties, huge of sleeve, tiny of waist, wide of flowing skirt, grouped about the fountain in the spacious and lovely grounds....

About 1899 Minnie Eshelman was married to Dr. [H. D.] Sherman, a man much older than herself, with a nearly grown son and daughter. Dr. Sherman had the traditional idea that women knew nothing of affairs and essayed to take the management of Minnewawa from his wife's hands.... Unwise and autocratic interference in administration increased the complications of an unfortunate situation.

As if disillusionment, exasperation and anxiety were not enough to overwhelm this brilliant and generous women, the dread malady of cancer attacked her body. For years she suffered indescribable agonies of the flesh as well as of the heart.

The vine-draped mansion that had been an ideal home became a place of torture and fear; finally she came into town for better medical attention and nursing, and in hope of some measure of peace. In April of 1918 she passed away, tenderly cared for at the last by a faithful and loving friend.

SOURCE: Ernestine Winchell, two articles, "Minnie Eshleman" and "The Minnewawa Vineyard."

Fruit and Raisin Company, Griffin and Skelley, Charles Leslie, James Miller, Meu, Sadler and Company, J. W. Reese, and Schact, Lemke and Steiner in Fresno; the Curtis Fruit Company and Fresno Raisin Company in Oleander; the Fowler Fruit and Raisin Packing Company and Rodda and Nobmann in Fowler; S. B. Holton in Selma; and E. H. Gould and N. and S. P. Viau in Malaga.

The Oleander packing houses were cooperative ventures, as was the Fowler Fruit and Raisin Packing Company and several others. Most of them had been started by local farmers and businessmen, although Griffin and Skelley had been based in Riverside before taking over T. C. White's packing house, and their ranks increased over the years. An operation in Covell, the Fresno Home Packing Company, and a house run by the Noble Brothers of Boston were added in 1890 and the Earl Fruit Company, Williams, Brown and Company, and the Olivet Packing Company of Malaga about the same time; Charles G. Bonner's packing house (still in business today) in 1892; George B. Otis' Selma packing house in 1893; C. B. Jeffries, Hobbs and Parsons, the Porter Brothers, and Producers Packing Company in 1894; and the Golden West, Phoenix, Castle Brothers and Co-operative houses by 1899. Two additional firms, E. G. Chaddock and Company and Brooks and Company, failed in 1897; the former concern had operations in Fresno, Fowler, Selma, Kingsburg and Armona in Kings County.

The packing houses produced boxed raisins with fascinating names—"Butler's Cluster," "Forget-me-not," "Parrot" and "Cartoons" among them—and their processing methods became increasingly sophisticated. An October 10, 1890, *Fresno Daily Evening Expositor* story explained that at Barling's "El Modelo" plant raisins were steamed by a boiler for up to forty-eight hours, then taken by conveyor belt to a room where they were stemmed and cleaned, graded and sacked if not top-quality. The best raisins were then weighed into five-pound trays, steam-blown clean, packed into layers, pressed and boxed.

Seeding operations were simplified for some packers after 1896, when William Forsyth began offering the services of a raisin-seeding machine invented by George Pettit, Jr. and John D. Spomer. Forsyth was later bought out by A. Gartenlaub, who formed the Pacific Coast Seeded Raisin and Packing Company with five other packing houses in 1897–98. Even with these improvements, packing required immense labor. A typical house employed 200 to 300 people, and county-wide they employed more than 2,000 people as early as 1890. Seldom did any worker earn more than three dollars a day. An average wage for this period was half that sum.

During the 1890s no Fresno County agricultural crop was upset by more adverse forces, natural and man-made, than the raisin. Prosperous in the post-boom era (see 15:6), a variety of conditions reduced profits in the years that immediately followed it. Just as in the present day, bad weather took its toll on the raisins: slight losses to rain in late 1889, to heat in the summer of 1891, to frosts in April 1896, again to rains in the early autumns of 1896 and 1897, and again to frost in April 1899. The last four instances were par-

Reference 15:6

## FRESNO'S RAISIN INDUSTRY: 1889

### GUSTAV A. EISEN

Fresno, as seen from the railroad station, is not as inviting as it might be, and the thousands of travelers who pass by on the cars, headed farther south, can judge but little of the town and the district behind it. The country is so level, that the only way to get a good view of the country is to ascend some elevated building, the courthouse being the highest, and through its location the best suited building for the purpose. . . .

For a mile in every direction the town stretches out, the center thickly built, the outskirts with sparsely scattered houses. Adjoining these the country begins—vineyards as far as we can trace, groups of houses shaded by trees in different tints of green, while broken rows of endless poplars traverse the verdant plains and lose themselves in the distant horizon. . . .

The street-car lines of Fresno do not run very far out in the country, and to see the latter we must procure a team. The colonies or settlements of small farms immediately join the town limits; we are thus with one step out in the country. On either side we see continuous rows of vineyards,—the leaves green and brilliant, the vines planted in squares and pruned low, with the branches trailing on the ground. To begin with, the houses stand closely, almost as in a village. As we get farther out there is a house on every twenty-acre farm, or every one-eighth of a mile. The cottages are neat and tasty, surrounded by shade trees, while rose-trees and shrubbery adorn the yard, and climbers shelter the verandas from the sun. At every step, almost, we pass teams going in various directions,—teams loaded with raisin boxes, teams with raisin trays, teams crowded with raisin-pickers or colonists generally, who rush to and from town to transact business connected with their one great industry. Everywhere is bustle and life; every one is in a hurry, as the grape-picking has begun, and the weather is favorable; no one has any time to lose. Some of the avenues are lined with elm-trees, others with fig-trees, with their luscious, drooping fruit, others again are bordered with evergreen and towering gums, with weeping branches and silvery bark.

Every acre is carefully cultivated; there is room for only a few weeds. . . .

The raisin harvest has just begun; the vineyards are full of workers, grape-pickers are stooping by every vine, and are arranging the grapes on small square or oblong trays, large enough to be easily handled; teams with trucks are passing between the vines distributing the trays or piling them up in small, square stacks at every row. Some trays with their amber grapes lie flat on the ground in long continuous rows between the vines, others again are slightly raised so as to catch as much of the sun as possible. In some vineyards the laborers are turning the partially cured and dried raisins by placing one tray on top of another, and then turning them quickly over. In other places, again, the trays with the raisins already cured are stacked in low piles, so as to exclude the sun and air, and at other stacks a couple of men at each are busy assorting the grapes, and placing the various grades in different sweat-boxes, large enough to hold one hundred pounds each.

ticularly destructive, with as much as one-third of the county crop wiped out.

An even bigger problem was posed by raisin marketing. When Fresno County raisins began reaching London and the East Coast in large quantities, in 1888 and 1889 respectively, they found buyers aplenty. Unfortunately, the method by which they were sold nearly wrecked the industry. A packer named E. L. Chaddock had devised the "commission" system of selling raisins, by which growers sold directly to packers, who extracted a 5 per cent commission and sold in turn to brokers in the East and elsewhere. To create less financial risk the last-mentioned transaction was made on a consignment basis. Although they were given advances, growers got all their money only after the brokers had disposed of their crops. With two middlemen in place (packers and brokers) and a cash-flow pattern that allowed growers to be held off, this situation was ready-made for exploitation. Soon brokers were refusing to enter the market until late in the

In every vineyard, large and small, we find the hands at work, and every one able and willing to do a day's work is engaged to harvest the large crop. [Most] of the pickers are Chinese, at least in the larger vineyards, while in the smaller vineyards, where large gangs of men are not absolutely necessary, white men and boys are generally employed. The fame of the raisin section and the harvest has spread far and wide, and at picking time laborers gather from all parts of the State to take part in the work, and find remunerative wages at from $1.25 to $1.50 a day. The country now swarms with pickers of all nationalities,—Germans, Armenians, Chinese, Americans, Scandinavians, etc., and as the schools have closed in order to allow the children to take part in the work, boys of all sizes are frequently seen kneeling at the vines....

The aroma from the drying berries is noticeable, and the breeze is laden with the spicy and pronounced odor of the Muscatel raisins.

The average size of a colony lot is twenty acres. Many settlers own two or three lots, a few owning four or five. But it must not be understood that the whole of these lots are planted to raisin grapes. While most of the larger tracts are almost exclusively planted to raisin grapes, the smaller farms of twenty acres contain as a rule only a few acres of vines, the balance being occupied by alfalfa, berries, garden, fruit trees, and yard for houses and barns. From three to fifteen acres of raisin-vines are found on every twenty-acre farm; none is without its patch of raisin-vines. We step off and inspect many of the places, large as well as small....

We pass by the large vineyard of Frank Ball, containing about 120 acres, all in vines except a small reserve for house, barn and alfalfa field. Adjoining on the same road is the Bretzner vineyard of forty odd acres, the vines loaded with grapes. We turn to the left and, passing the vineyards of Merriam and Reed, see on our left the magnificent Cory vineyard of eighty acres, bordered by a wonderfully beautiful row of umbrella trees, with crowns as even as veritable-gigantic umbrellas, and through the foliage of which not a ray of light can penetrate. A little farther on, also to the left, is the Gordon vineyard, lined by fan palms and fig trees. A large sign across the main road announces that we now enter the Butler vineyard, the largest and most famous vineyard in the State, with its six hundred acres nearly all in vines,—the largest vineyard in one body and owned by one man in the world....

The four hundred acres owned by the Fresno Vineyard Company are devoted to wine grapes, and large wineries and cellars built of adobe show the wealth and extensive business of the place.... Farther to the north lies in an unbroken row the well-known Eisen vineyard, where the first raisins were made in this district, but where now principally wine is produced; the Nevada and Temperance Colonies, devoted mostly to raisins; the Pew, the Kennedy, the Forsyth, Woodworth's, Duncan's, Goodman's and Backman's raisin vineyards, all splendidly cared for and lined by fig trees.

Of these the Forsyth vineyard deserves more than a passing notice, as it is more inviting to an hour's rest than any other. Containing 160 acres, nearly all in vines, it is one of the best properties in the county. The place shows an uncommon taste and refinement, and is beautified by avenues of poplars and magnolias, by groves of acacia and umbrella trees, by palms and flowers, and by roses and climbing plants. A pond with its lilies, overhung by weeping willows and shaded by stately elms, is an unusual sight even in this county of abundant irrigation. The packing-houses and dryer all display a taste and practical arrangement hardly seen elsewhere.... The courteous owner conducts us through his packing-house and shows us how the bunches are placed in layers and carefully made to fit every corner in the box, how the boxes are covered with papers and artistic labels and finally made ready for the market.... As we turn again towards town, we pass the well-kept Goodman vineyard, after which we enter the large Barton vineyard, now partly owned by an English syndicate. The old 640 acres are nearly all in wine grapes, while several hundred acres of young raisin grapes have lately been added....

When we return to town, a visit to the packing-houses is one of the most interesting that can be made. Of these packing establishments Fresno has four or five, besides several in the colonies or in the larger vineyards. Three of these packing-houses are the largest in the State. The building of each one of them, though large, is full and overcrowded. Women at long tables pack the raisins in boxes, at other tables men weigh and assort raisins and take them out of the large sweat-boxes in which they left the field. At some tables fancy packing is done, and women "face" the boxes by placing large selected raisins in rows on the top layers. At another table the raisin-boxes are covered with fine colored labels, then nailed and made ready for shipment. Some four hundred men and women are busy with this work under one roof, all earning wages of from one to two dollars a day each.

We catch a glimpse of the equalizing room, where fifty tons of raisins are stored at one time for a week or more in order to become of even moisture, the floor being sometimes sprinkled with water to make the air sufficiently moist. As we go out we see the raisin-boxes already packed being loaded on cars and shipped east by the train-load, from four to six such raisin trains leaving every week, each train of from ten to twenty cars. On the other side of the packing-house is a continuous row of teams from the country, all loaded with raisins, brought by the country growers to the packers in town. It takes a gang of men to receive, weigh and unload them. In another department we see the large stemmer and grader, which runs by steam, and stems and assorts from thirty to forty tons per day, the clean and uniform raisins running out in a continuous stream, each grade in separate boxes. There is restless activity on every side. The large raisin crop this year is very large; it must be handled in a few months, and every grower and packer is pushing the work to his utmost ability.

When we consider that most of the crop, which this year will reach five hundred thousand boxes, comes from the country immediately surrounding Fresno City, and that the San Joaquin valley is 250 miles long by 75 miles wide, almost all of the land capable of being highly cultivated and of producing abundant crops of one thing or another, then alone can we realize what the future has in store for this wonderful valley, an agricultural empire in the very center of California.

SOURCE: Eisen, Gustav. *The Raisin Industry*. San Francisco: H. S. Crocker and Company, 1890.

Ground-breaking at Chateau Fresno Park in February 1892.

The Kearney Cash Store and stable building on the Fruit Vale Estate, 1902. Note M. Theo Kearney standing at right in foreground.

Load of pumpkins (average weight 120 pounds) at Chateau Fresno Park on M. Theo Kearney's Fruit Vale Estate, 1897.

345

season, when a raisin glut had occurred. Growers had to sell out for less and packers ended up with a bigger cut from the brokers.

The 1891 crop, because of this situation, ended up as a total loss to the growers. The next year they began supplying packers with as many poor-quality raisins as they could find (grades were unknown) and asking for six cents per pound when four- and five-cent prices had held for years. This decline in product quality spelled a decline in demand. Coupled with the 1893 depression and subsequent over-production (35,000 tons produced in the county during 1894 and 32,000 in 1896, always at least two-thirds of the state crop), ruination for all seemed imminent. By 1897 one desperate Fresno farmer was using raisins to feed his stock animals!

Appeals to the middlemen for mercy, and to state and federal governments, proved useless. In the late 1890s it was obvious that the growers could look only to themselves for help. Everyone knew what to do—get the growers to form a cooperative, pack the raisins themselves, and sell to brokers at a fixed price—yet this scheme went unrealized. When county farmer O. B. Olufs suggested this approach in 1890, before the situation fell apart, he was ignored. Two years later, when the growers' six-cent-per-pound price seemed unreachable, a California State Raisin Growers Association was formed with a more modest 4½-cent goal

in mind. The packers agreed to this, and 95 percent of all Fresno County crops were signed up, but withdrawals of growers who wanted five cents or more sank the market price to 1¼ cents and the organization as a whole.

This same fate befell another organization, the California Raisin Growers' and Packers' Company, in 1894. Although the cooperative was willing to accept a 3¾-cent price for its members, it could control only 80 percent of the crop. The remainder was sold low enough to make the rest of the cooperative fall apart.

As 1898 began, over-production continued, malcontent heightened and growers were itching to form a sturdy cooperative. Up to this year, though, Fresno County had seen few effective agricultural organizations created or maintained. Fruit cooperatives—the California Dried Fruit Association in 1888, an 1892 local group, and the 1894 California Fruit Exchange and California Fruit Growers and Shippers Organization—all expired quickly, probably because the orchardists did not have to deal with the destructive commission system. A county horticultural society was formed in 1896, a Poultry, Pigeon and Pet Stock Association the next year, and farmer's institutes were periodically held. These groups were more educational and social in nature, although the Horticultural Socirty tried to start its own Central Fruit Exchange

Reference 15:7

# M. THEO KEARNEY, THE MAN

Martin Theodore Kearney was one of Fresno's significant early developers and also its most enigmatic. Little is known of Kearney's pre-California life: it is suspected he was a native of Ireland; he had at least one sibling (Thomas); he was living in Boston in 1866; and by 1870 he had migrated to San Francisco. Kearney's early business interests were divided between commercial and real estate speculation in the West (primarily in the San Joaquin Valley but also in Nevada mines). This gave way by the late 1870s to his ever more exclusive involvement in agricultural development—raisins and the Fresno Winery.

From the early 1880s until his death in 1906 M. Theo. Kearney's life was devoted to the activities of the California Raisin Growers Association and the creation of his 5,000 acre Fruit Vale Estate. Located seven miles west of the city, Kearney's estate was a composite vision of farm, ranch, vineyard and garden home which was designed on a scale unprecedented for California's interior.

Kearney's lifestyle pattern of long annual European sojourns, residence in San Francisco hotels, and temporary visits to his "home place" in Fresno projected an image of a man who was coldly removed from the concerns of most Valley residents. He was seen as an outsider—an absentee landlord who was capitalizing on Fresno's potential without participating in the daily life of the

community. When present on the local scene Kearney restricted his social intercourse to overseeing the business affairs of the Fruit Vale Estate. The closest Kearney came to enjoying personal contact in Fresno was with the family of his ranch manager, Ralph Frisselle, and with Colonel and Mrs. William Forsyth.

In contrast with his reserved manner in Fresno (or pose as the singular member of San Joaquin landed gentry) Kearney maintained a full range of social pursuits beyond Fresno. Perhaps some of the zeal with which Kearney approached life outside the Valley was due to a probable period of self-education in the 1860s when he sought to acquire genuinely the tastes and manners of genteel society. In whatever cosmopolitan environment Kearney moved—San Francisco, New York, Saratoga, London, Paris, or the great German spas of Baden-Baden and Nauheim—he was surrounded by friends of both sexes, formed close relationships with several women and a San Francisco family, and eagerly sought out what was new and exciting. Kearney studied French, took dancing lessons, visited museums and artists' studios, had a refined and expensive sense of sartorial style, and enjoyed bicycle and horseback riding.

An avid traveler, Kearney collected numerous books, photographs, postcards and prints of the places he visited. He viewed

every major world exposition between 1876 and 1900. Not only did the expositions provide Kearney with a venue for promoting his valley real estate holdings, but they also furnished him with a pervasive enthusiasm for the latest developments in the world of art, communication, transportation, agriculture, horticulture and mechanics.

Kearney was a man of the moment and sought from 1890 onward the finest available resources to incorporate into his valley oasis. The Fruit Vale Estate was a synthesis of European style in a San Joaquin Valley context. It was made possible by that unique end-of-century flowering when technological progress became allied to the humanist concerns of design, craftsmanship and environment. When Kearney died in 1906 his long-planned French chateau was still a dream. Yet where once there was no water, Kearney left as his Valley legacy a carefully tended garden in full bloom to the University of California as a working ranch to advance the science of agriculture.

SOURCE: Compiled by the Fresno City and County Historical Society; information derived from the Kearney Manuscript Collection, F.C.C.H.S. Archives and diaries and correspondence in the Kearney Collection at the Bancroft Library.

cooperative (unsuccessfully) in May 1896. Now, two years later, the raisin industry was on the verge of collapse. Its sole hope for survival was a cooperative. Desperate growers were doubtlessly wondering if one could be organized and, after that, if it could survive.

To this end a meeting was held at the Fresno Farmers' Club on May 7, 1898. Fresno developer and vineyardist Martin Theodore Kearney (see 15:7) reported that San Francisco packers were becoming reluctant to deal with individual growers because of past losses, so an organization was temporarily formed. Its intent was to seek a 3¼-cent a pound raisin price.

A week later, at Fresno's Armory Hall, the farmers formally banded together as the California Raisin Growers' Association. T. C. White proposed that ten wealthy Fresno businessmen buy the association's capital stock and, in turn, buy the growers' crops and negotiate for them. Kearney proposed an issue of 100,000 shares of stock, available to growers, and the appointment of a board of trustees. Shares would be purchased through a 10 percent assessment on all crops, and the money would be used to "buy all the packing houses in the country and have plenty of money left to loan at interest to any of our members who might need it," according to Kearney. Not surprisingly, the growers accepted Kearney's organization option. Trustees were elected: T. C. White, Louis Einstein, L. S. Chittenden, A. L. Sayre, W. S. Porter, Robert Boot and Kearney. Kearney was chosen president as well.

Now came the next hurdle: signing up the growers. Association canvassers and members began spreading out across California, asking other vineyardists to join. Illustrious local names were soon taken into the fold: the Fresno Vineyard, J. W. Pew, August Weihe and others. The trustees asked that members consign their crops to the cooperative, while all nervously hoped that at least 75 percent of the state growers would sign up. When the first official association meeting was held on June 4, the 50 percent mark had been reached and Kearney was hoping for 90. During the summer Kearney managed to get packers to accept association raisins only, T. C. White and others began combing all corners of California for additional members, and the cooperative's success became virtually assured. By September Kearney's goal of 90 percent membership was realized—along with a solid 4½-cent-per-pound raisin price.

The association survived into the next year, when it succeeded in re-enlisting most of its members and obtained an unparalleled 6½-cent-a-pound price. It had proved itself, although it did not function altogether smoothly.

This view may have been correct, but in retrospect it seems unfair. Agriculture had become the economic mainstay of Fresno County, and the raisin industry its backbone. Through truly democratic organization and effective management, it had been saved from comprehensive disaster. Kearney deserved much of the credit for this feat; one can only wonder why his contemporaries remained so vehemently contemptuous of him. There is no wondering why he wrote the following obituary for himself, sometime after his raisin association's eventual failure:

### WARNING

Here lies the body of M. Theo Kearney, a visionary who thought he could teach the average farmer, and, particularly, the raisin grower, some of the rudiments of sound business management. For eight years he worked strenuously at his task, and at the end of that time, he was no farther ahead than at the beginning. The effort killed him.

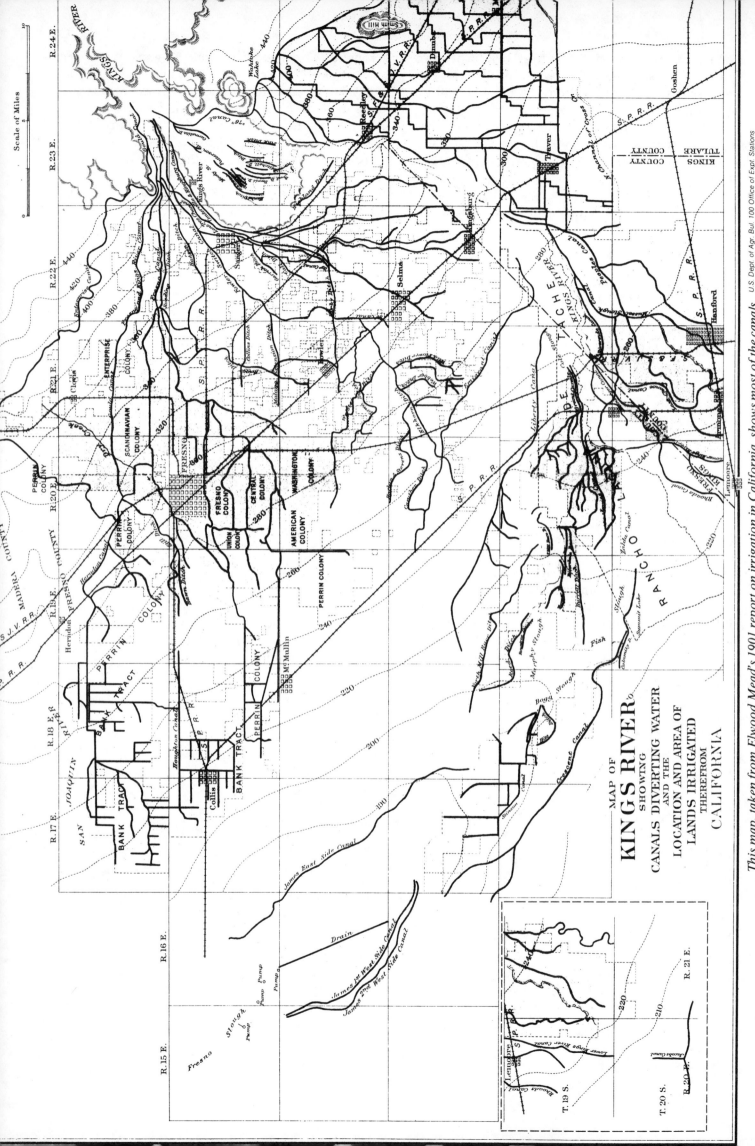

MAP OF
KINGS RIVER
SHOWING
CANALS DIVERTING WATER
AND THE
LOCATION AND AREA OF
LANDS IRRIGATED
THEREFROM
CALIFORNIA

*This map, taken from Elwood Mead's 1901 report on irrigation in California shows most of the canals and ditches built in Fresno County up to the turn of the century. Although works stemming from the San Joaquin River are not depicted, they were not so important as those spreading out from the Kings.*

# Bibliography

The following bibliographical guide to sources is offered in lieu of conventional footnotes. It enumerates and comments on the important sources used in writing this history. Works of a lesser character, which yielded only a fact or two, are omitted; references to them will be occasionally found in the text.

Bancroft, Hubert Howe. *History of California, 1542-1890*, 7 volumes. San Francisco: The History Company, 1886-90. By now a classic reference.

Barker, John. *San Joaquin Vignettes: The Reminiscences of Captain John Barker.* Edited by William Harland Boyd and Glendon J. Rogers. Bakersfield, California: Kern County Historical Society and County of Kern, 1955. The proprietor of the Elkhorn stage station, Barker presents in his account practically everything known about this subject. Said to be erroneous in its non-Fresno County sections.

Boyd, William Harland. *Stagecoach Heyday in the San Joaquin Valley, 1853-1876.* Bakersfield, California: Kern County Historical Society, Inc., 1983. An excellent survey of the subject.

Brewer, William Henry. *Up and Down California in 1860-64.* Third edition. Edited by Francis P. Farquhar. Berkeley and Los Angeles: University of California Press, 1965.

Brown, J[ames] L[orin]. *The Mussel Slough Tragedy.* N.p., c1958. The standard, and probably definitive, work on the subject.

*California Homes and Industries and representative citizens. A serial showing the improvements and progress of the state . . . This number is exclusively devoted to Fresno County.* San Francisco and New York: Elliott Publishing Company, 1891. Contains a few interesting items on agricultural estates and production.

California State Mining Bureau. *State Mineralogist's Reports.* Sacramento, 1888, 1890, 1916 and others.

Carson, James H. *Recollections of the California Mines.* Reprinted from the Stockton edition of 1852. Oakland, California: Biobooks, 1950. This volume's greatest contribution to Fresno County history is its remarks on the Garner expedition (see Chapter 4).

Catlin, Anne F. *The Kingsburg Saga.* Typescript at Fresno County Free Library; most of it reprinted in the *Kingsburg Recorder* Golden Anniversary Edition. Has a few interesting anecdotes about the early town, and is generally accurate.

Cearley, C. T., compiler and publisher. *Fresno City and County Directory . . . .* Fresno: Fresno Republican Print, 1898. Many useful details here concerning early residents, doctors, lawyers, businessmen and businesses, etc. The advertisements are a historical education in themselves. (See also Husted, F. M. and *Fresno Republican.*)

Chedister, William L. *The History of Clovis.* Typescript at Clovis Branch, Fresno County Free Library. The only useful survey of the subject that has yet appeared.

Cook, Sherburne F. *The Conflict between the California Indian and White Civilization.* Berkeley and Los Angeles: University of California Press, 1976. A most useful study of demographic trends among the California Indians.

Davidian, Nectar. *The Seropians, first Armenian settlers in Fresno County, California.* Berkeley, 1965. An interesting and reliable account of this family, pioneers in the county fig business.

Derbec, Etienne. *A French Journalist in the California Gold Rush: The Letters of Etienne Derbec.* Edited by A. P. Nasatir. Georgetown, California: The Talisman Press, 1964.

Dow, John Allan. "History of Public School Organization and Administration in Fresno County, California." Ph.D. dissertation, University of Southern California, June 1967. Takes up the background of every school district formed in Fresno County, and relates a wealth of details in the process—most of them unavailable anywhere else. An accurate, behemoth study of its subject (more than 600 pages) and a valuable research tool.

Dunn, Viola Jean. "Miller and Lux, a contribution toward a history." M.A. thesis, San Jose State University, January 1970. Has a few anecdotes and facts not to be found elsewhere, and can be regarded as accurate.

Eaton, Edwin M. *Vintage Fresno: Pictorial Recollections of a Western City.* Fresno: The Huntington Press, 1965. The sections concerning Fresno business buildings have some new and interesting information. The many historical photographs are excellent.

Eccleston, Robert. *The Mariposa Indian War, 1850-1851.* Edited by C. Gregory Crampton. Salt Lake City: University of Utah Press, 1957. Together with Crampton's incisive annotations, this eyewitness diary is a prime sourcebook. Not to be missed by anyone interested in the subject.

Edgar, William F., M.D. *Historical Notes of Old Land Marks in California: Old Fort Miller.* Los Angeles: Historical Society of Southern California, Annual Publication, Volume 3 (1893).

Eisen, Gustav. *The Raisin Industry.* San Francisco: H. S. Crocker, 1890.

Elliott, Wallace W., publisher. *History of Fresno County, California. With illustrations descriptive of its scenery, farms, residences, public buildings, factories, hotels, business houses, schools, churches, etc., from original drawings . . . .* San Francisco: 1881. A somewhat useful account that is generally accurate.

English, June. Articles in *Ash Tree Echo*. Mrs. English is a prodigious researcher and the ultimate authority on any historical matter relative to Fresno County. Her contributions to this periodical are without peer. Those that proved most helpful to this study were: "Chinese Pioneers in Fresno County" (Vol. 8, No. 1), "Andrew D. Firebaugh and Firebaugh's Ferry" (Vol. 10, No. 2), "Foreigners in Fresno County" (Vol. 7, No. 3), "Fresno County's Black Pioneers" (Vol. 4, No. 1), "Fresno County's Six Courthouses" (Vol. 6, Nos. 1, 2, 3, Vol. 7, No. 1), "Gold Miners of Fresno County" (Vol 4, No. 2), "The Inhabitants of Fort Miller" (Vol. 5, No. 3), "Kingston on the Kings River" (Vol. 9, No. 3), "Leaves from the Past" (Vol. 3, No. 4), "McKinley Grove of Big Trees" (Vol. 17, No. 3), "Major James D. Savage: Villain or Hero?" (Vol. 9, No. 2), "Obscure Pioneers of Fresno County" (Vol 5, No. 1), "A Place Now Called Friant" (Vol. 16, No. 3), "The Place of the Ash Trees" (Vol. 9, No. 1).

Farquhar, Francis P. *History of the Sierra Nevada.* Berkeley and Los Angeles: University of California Press, in collaboration with the Sierra Club, 1966.

Faymonville, William. "Reminiscences of Fresno County." *Fresno Weekly Expositor*, January 1, 1879. The granddaddy of all Fresno County histories; mercilessly plagiarized and paraphrased by later writers, and a good chunk of it has found its way into this volume. It is substantially accurate and interesting.

Fresno County Board of Trade. *Fresno County, California, where can be found climate, soil and water, the only sure combination for the vineyardist, fruit grower, cattle raiser and farmer.* Fresno: Fresno Evening Expositor Print, 1893.

*Fresno County Centennial Almanac.* Fresno, 1956. While most of this book is a repetition of the standard county histories, the vignettes it contains about county communities and specialized historical subjects are sometimes informative, presenting information not seen elsewhere. A good source of information about past county officials.

*Fresno Republican*, compiler and publisher. *General Directory of Fresno County, California, for 1881 . . . .* Fresno, [1881?]. The first county directory, containing much useful data on the earlier residents and businesses.

*Fresno Times*, January 28–April 5, 1865. Published at Millerton by Samuel J. Garrison. See Chapter 5 for additional comments. More a curiosity than historical source.

"Fresno's Yesteryears." Set of file boxes at the Fresno City and County Historical Society. Contains historical retrospective articles from the *Fresno Bee* and *Fresno Republican* files, most of them dating back to the 1920s and 1930s although the subject matter is pre-1900. Some excellent material pertaining to agriculture, irrigation, and the early history of Fresno is to be found here; noticeably weaker on other subjects.

Frickstad, Walter E. *A Century of California Post Offices, 1848 to 1954.* Oakland, California: Philatelic Research Society, 1955. A collection of data regarding the formation, suspension, merger and disbandment of post offices statewide, including Fresno County's. Most valuable for the dates it gives.

Gardiner, Howard C. *In Pursuit of the Golden Dream: Reminiscences of San Francisco and the Northern and Southern Mines, 1849–1857.* Edited by Dale L. Morgan. Stoughton, Massachusetts: Western Hemisphere, Inc., 1970. Has some information on Chowchilla River mining during 1855; see Chapter 4.

Greenwood, Robert, comp. *The California Outlaw, Tiburcio Vasquez, Including the Rare Contemporary Account by George Beers, with Numerous Photographs and Excerpts from Contemporary Newspapers.* Los Gatos, California: The Talisman Press, 1960. A reliable account, and valuable because of the inclusion of Beers' narrative.

Gudde, Erwin G. *California Place Names: The Origin and Etymology of Current Geographical Names.* Third edition, revised and enlarged. Berkeley and Los Angeles: University of California Press, 1969.

———. *California Gold Camps: A Geographical and Historical Dictionary of Camps, Towns and Localities Where Gold Was Found and Mined; Wayside Stations and Trading Centers.* Berkeley and Los Angeles: University of California Press, 1974.

Heizer, Robert F., ed. *The Destruction of California Indians.* Salt Lake City and Santa Barbara: Peregrine Smith, Inc., 1974. A fair amount of the material here pertains to the mistreatment, subjugation, and reservation lifestyle of the Fresno County Indians. This book is especially valuable because it contains little other than primary accounts and documents.

———. *Handbook of North American Indians. Volume 8, California.* Washington, D.C.: Smithsonian Institution, 1978. While this book does not replace Kroeber's classic account (q.v.), it is nevertheless informative and accurate.

———. *They Were Only Diggers: A Collection of Articles from California Newspapers, 1851–1866, on Indian and White Relations.* Ramona, California: Ballena Press, 1974. Contains two good items on Indian women as wives of white men and Indian slavery.

Hull, Donna M. *And Then There Were Three Thousand.* Fresno, California: privately published, 1975. The saga of the Akers family, prominent in early Fresno County history. A meticulously researched genealogy, containing a useful blend of biographical and general information.

Hurt, Bert. *The Sawmill History of the Sierra National Forest, 1852–1940.* Washington, D.C.: U.S. Government Printing Office, 1941. The sole source for information on many sawmills and lumbering activities. Its value is marred by the fact that much of its data cannot be verified.

James, David Bice. *Reminiscences of Early Days in the "Southern Mines."* Typescript, Fresno City and County Historical Society and Fresno County Free Library. One of the few firsthand accounts available; somewhat garbled in places, and lacking a narrative structure, but of indisputable worth nevertheless.

Johnston, Hank. *They Felled the Redwoods: A Saga of Flumes and Rails in the High Sierra.* Corona del Mar, California: Trans-Anglo Books, 1966.

Kearney, Martin Theodore. Series of pamphlets in the Kearney Papers, Fresno City and County Historical Society, published at his behest. *The Anglo-Californian Vineyard, Limited. Complete reports, with maps and illustrations,* on the Fresno Vineyard and Fruit Vale Estates. English and American press opinions on California. Unprecedented emigration. Remarkable development. Great prosperity. N.p., 1887. Fresno, the raisin district of California . . . San Francisco: H. S. Crocker, [1888]. Fresno, California, subdivision of the Fruit Vale Estate. San Francisco: H. S. Crocker, [1888]. Fresno County, California, the center of the raisin and dried fruit industries. Subdivision of the Fruit Vale Estate . . . . N.p., [1892?]. Fresno County, a wonderfully prosperous district in California, the land of sunshine, fruits and flowers. Chicago: Donohue and Henneberry, [1893?]. To promote his real estate business Kearney was remarkably adept at clipping and circulating items pertaining to Fresno County agriculture from New York, San Francisco, Chicago and London newspapers. Published in the aforementioned booklets, they are a bonanza for the historian.

————. Newspaper clippings and notes regarding the formation of the California Raisin Growers' Association. Kearney Papers, Fresno City and County Historical Society. The items in this collection mostly come from the Fresno Morning Republican and are helpful in understanding the early history of the growers' organization.

Keyes, E. D. Fifty Years' Observation of Men and Events, Civil and Military. New York: Charles Scribner's Sons, 1884. Has some material on Fort Miller and the Indians.

Kingsburg Recorder. Golden Anniversary Edition, November 18, 1954. While only moderately complete, this special edition newspaper still ranks as the most thorough history of the town. It incorporates significant portions of Catlin (q.v.). Churches, education, recreation, businesses and similar subjects are dealt with.

Kip, William Ingraham. Early Days of My Episcopate. New York: Thomas Whittaker, 1892. Contains data on Bishop Kip's trip to Fort Miller and Millerton. See Chapter 5.

Kroeber, A[lfred] L[ouis]. Handbook of the Indians of California. Bulletin 78, Bureau of American Ethnology, Smithsonian Institution. Washington, D.C.: U.S. Government Printing Office, 1925.

Latta, Frank F[orrest]. Black Gold in the Joaquin. Caldwell Idaho: The Caxton Printers, Inc., 1949. The most complete account of early oil development in the Coalinga area although some information is questionable.

————. Dalton Gang Days. Santa Cruz, California: Bear State Books, 1976. Accurate and the best of Latta's last few books.

————. Handbook of Yokuts Indians. Second edition. Santa Cruz, California: Bear State Books, 1978. Much like the Heizer and Kroeber handbooks in terms of subjects explored but far more detailed owing to its length and treatment of only one tribal group.

————. Joaquin Murrieta and His Horse Gangs. Santa Cruz, California: Bear State Books, 1980. For now, the best single account available, although it is hampered by a garbled narrative and uncertain chronological arrangement.

————. Tailholt Tales. Santa Cruz, California: Bear State Books, 1976. Useful for a few details concerning early mining on the San Joaquin River.

Lawrence, William David. "Henry Miller and the San Joaquin Valley." M.A. thesis, University of California, Berkeley, 1933.

McCubbin, John C. Papers on the History of the San Joaquin Valley. Typescripts at the California State University, Fresno Library, Special Collections, and at the Reedley Branch, Fresno County Free Library. An early resident of the Reedley area, McCubbin was responsible for preserving much of its history through these writings. The prominent subjects are early stage and travel routes, Smith's Ferry, the 76 Land and Water Company, the rise and fall of Traver, and the beginnings of Reedley. All of McCubbin's material is accurate and interesting.

McFarland, J[on] Randall. Centennial Selma: Biography of a California Community's First 100 Years. Selma, California: the author and the Selma Enterprise, c1980. Thus far, the best comprehensive study of a Fresno County town. No subject pertaining to Selma's history has been neglected in this book, which is an indispensible reference.

————. Village on the Prairie: The Story of Fowler's First 100 Years. [Fowler, California], c1972. Like the author's Centennial Selma, well-researched, well-written and highly accurate, with all important subjects given their due.

McKee, Irving. Historic Fresno County Winegrowers. N.p., 1947. Typescript at California State University, Fresno Library, Special Collections. A basic account, with a few facts and figures lacking in other sources.

Mahakian, Charles. "History of the Armenians in California." M.A. thesis, University of California, Berkeley, 1935. Factually solid, with a good amount of space devoted to Fresno County's early Armenian population.

Mansfield, Joseph King Fenno. Mansfield on the Condition of the Western Forts. Edited by Robert W. Frazer. Norman, Oklahoma: University of Oklahoma Press, c1963. The description of Fort Miller here, reproduced in Chapter 5, is one of the best.

Marten, Effie Elfreda. "The Development of Wheat Culture in the San Joaquin Valley, 1846–1900." M.A. thesis, University of California, Berkeley, 1923. Has much valuable data on climatological and marketing conditions, together with planting and harvesting technology notes.

Mead, Elwood, director. Report of Irrigation Investigations in California. United States Department of Agriculture, Office of Experimental Stations, Bulletin No. 100. Washington: U.S. Government Printing Office, 1901. A little-known work, but indispensable to an understanding of Fresno County's irrigation systems: their inauguration, their technical specifications, and the battles (legal and otherwise) over them.

A Memorial and Biographical History of the Counties of Fresno, Tulare, and Kern, California . . . Pen pictures from the garden of the world. Chicago: Lewis Publishing Company, [1891].

Meyer, Edith Catharine. "The Development of the Raisin Industry in Fresno County, California." M.A. thesis, University of California, Berkeley, December 1931. A few facts, unique to this source, are given; however, the bulk of its information is in the standard county histories.

Mitchell, Annie R. Jim Savage and the Tulareño Indians. Los Angeles: Westernlore Press, c1957. A superlative account of this Fresno County frontiersman. Intriguing, accurate, and a fundamental source that contains all the important available data on Savage.

Muir, John. John of the Mountains: The Unpublished Journals of John Muir. Edited by Linnie Marsh Wolfe. Boston: Houghton Mifflin, 1938. Some material on Muir's Fresno County sojourn is presented here.

351

Newspaper Articles. The bulk of information in this history has been gleaned from individual articles in the *Fresno Weekly Expositor*, 1870–1886; the *Fresno Daily Evening Expositor*, 1887–1897; and the *Fresno Morning Republican*, 1898–1899. While the information they supply is sometimes fallible, it is still relatively accurate, was recorded contemporarily with the events described (which often leads to a reduced error factor) and can frequently be checked against other sources. In addition, the newspaper files have yielded a fair amount of information that other writers have overlooked—or failed to utilize. Hence our heavy reliance on them. The newspaper references used for this book are given below, listed by subject so that inquisitive readers may go back to our sources for pleasure or profit. Note the three periods within which the above three newspapers were published; the date of each entry determines the newspaper in which it appeared.

**Agricultural Colonies**—July 5, 1871; Feb. 25, 1872; May 14, Aug. 13, 1873; Sept. 15, Oct. 6, 1875; Mar. 8, 1876; Feb. 14, Mar. 7, Nov. 28, 1877; Feb. 28, 1878; June 25, Nov. 5, 1879; Dec. 8, 22, 1880; Aug. 3, 1881; Apr. 26, Sept. 6, 1882; Feb. 3, 1886; Feb. 8, 1889; May 29, 1891; Mar. 30, 1892; Mar. 15, Apr. 20, 1893; Mar. 3, 28, 1894; Dec. 25, 1895; May 4, 1897; Jan. 26, 1899.

**Agricultural Enterprises**—Aug. 23, 30, 1882; June 27, July 18, Aug. 16, 1883; Oct. 7, 1885; July 13, 1889; July 30, Oct. 10, 1890; Feb. 3, 11, June 5, Oct. 12, 1891; Apr. 1, July 15, DEc. 25, 1895.

**Agricultural Exhibitions**—Jan. 4, Dec. 16, 1896.

**Agricultural Organizations**—Sept. 1, 1875; July 23, 1879; Nov. 7, 1883; Aug. 18, 1886; May 6, 1891; Feb. 23, June 8, 1892; Feb. 2, 1893; Jan. 23, Mar. 7, May 2, 1896; Jan. 27, 1897; Jan. 30, 1898; Aug. 6, 1899.

**Agricultural Labor**—Aug. 19, Sept. 3, 28, Oct. 15, 1891; July 28, Aug. 15, 17, Sept. 9, 1893; Aug. 31, 1899.

**Agricultural Statistics**—Aug. 18, 1875; July 16, 1879; July 21, 1880; July 6, 1881; July 19, 1882; July 6, 1888; July 12, 1890; Dec. 25, 1895; Aug. 5, 1896.

**Auberry**— Jan. 3, 1877; Oct. 8, 1884; Apr. 29, 1885; July 19, Aug. 4, 1888; Feb. 27, 1889; Apr. 25, 1893; Apr. 17, 1894; May 1, 1898.

**Big Dry Creek**— Nov. 29, 1871; July 24, Sept. 4, Nov. 20, 1872; Feb. 16, 23, May 24, 1876; Jan. 3, 24, Feb. 14, May 2, 1877.

**Burrough Valley**—Jan. 29, Feb. 28, 1887; Aug. 19, 1890; July 23, Dec. 14, 1892.

**Centerville**—Feb. 22, Mar. 1, Sept. 20, Nov. 29, 1871; Oct. 23, 1872; May 21, 1873; May 6, 1874; Jan. 24; Feb. 28, 1877; Apr. 21, June 2, 23, July 7, Dec. 29, 1880; Feb. 9, June 5, 22, Sept. 14, 1881; Feb. 7, 21, Mar. 14, 1883; Feb. 20, Apr. 16, 1884; Feb. 23, 1887; Jan. 28, Dec. 30, 1890; Mar. 20, Apr. 17, 1891; Apr. 23, 1894; Feb. 26, Apr. 27, 1896; Feb. 15, Nov. 5, 1898; June 21, Sept. 16, 1899.

**Clifton/Del Rey**—Feb. 10, 1886; Apr. 27, 1887; July 14, 1897.

**Clovis**—June 7, 28, 1894; Oct. 19, Nov. 18, Dec. 25, 1895; Sept. 19, 29, Oct. 20, Nov. 3, Dec. 30, 1896; Feb. 11, 26, Mar. 13, Sept. 18, Dec. 30, 1897; Feb. 15, June 8, July 15, 1898; Jan. 31, Apr. 23, May 11, Aug. 6, Sept. 8, Oct. 15, Nov. 23, 1899.

**Coal**—May 14, Oct. 29, 1873; Nov. 18, 1885; Sept. 8, 1886.

**Coalinga**—Aug. 20, Sept. 24, 1890; Jan. 27, 1898.

**Coalinga Area: Natural Resources**— Sept. 11, 1891; Apr. 23, 1892; Mar. 23, 1893; Mar. 13, 14, 18, 25, Apr. 20, July 13, 28, 31, Oct. 21, 27, 28, 30, Nov. 2, Dec. 12, 1876; Mar. 6, July 13, 1897; Jan. 27, Mar. 27, Apr. 13, July 14, Oct. 8, 21, 27, 1898; Jan. 6, 26, Mar. 11, 15, Apr. 28, June 1, 21, 24, 25, July 16, 19, 30, Aug. 29, Sept. 9, Oct. 28, Nov. 22, Dec. 20, 1899.

**Cotton Cultivation**—Nov. 2, 1870; Apr. 17, Sept. 25, Oct. 23, 30, 1872; Mar. 5, June 18, 1873.

**Crops, unusual**—Nov. 22, 1871; Aug. 25, 1880; Feb. 21, 1883; Mar. 4, May 19, 1892; Mar. 22, 1894; Dec. 14, 25, 1895; Aug. 30, 1899.

**Easton**—July 24, 1891; Jan. 2, Feb. 15, Dec. 20, 1892; Apr. 25, Oct. 31, 1893; Apr. 17, 1894; Jan. 28, 1897.

**Elkhorn**—Oct. 31, 1883; Sept. 26, 1887.

**Fig Cultivation**—Aug. 16, Oct. 30, 1888; May 19, 1892; Oct. 26, 1897; July 14, 1899.

**Firebaugh**—Mar. 12, 1873; June 6, 1883; Apr. 2, 1887; Sept. 5, 1896; Aug. 2, 1898.

**Food Processing**—July 9, Dec. 17, 1879; May 17, 31, Sept. 6, Oct. 11, 1882; Dec. 8, 1886; June 7, July 28, Dec. 29, 1887; June 2, Sept. 3, 8, 1890; May 9, Oct. 29, 1891; Jan. 16, June 28, 1893; Apr. 13, Sept. 2, 1896; Sept. 25, Oct. 15, Nov. 15, 1897; Oct. 6, 1899.

**Fowler**—Oct. 8, 1884; Feb. 3, 17, Mar. 3, Nov. 17, 1886; Nov. 22, Dec. 5, 1889; Jan. 1, Apr. 27, Sept. 3, Nov. 7, 1891; Feb. 16, 23, Dec. 16, 1892; Mar. 22, Apr. 25, May 25, July 24, Nov. 15, 1893; June 25, 1894; July 29, 1895; Dec. 22, 1896; Sept. 27, 1898.

**Fresno: Business Buildings**—July 15, 1874; Mar. 29, 1882; Nov. 7, 14, 1883; Jan. 3, Feb. 25, Oct. 11, 1889; Feb. 1, Apr. 9, Oct. 23, 1890; Dec. 25, 1895; Jan. 22, 1898.

**Fresno: Businesses**—July 9, 1879; Apr. 6, Oct. 26, 1881; Feb. 8, Mar. 1, Apr. 26, Aug. 16, 23, Sept. 6, Dec. 8, 22, 1882; Jan. 16, Apr. 9, 30, Oct. 8, 1884; Feb. 18, Mar. 4, 1885; Mar. 10, 1886; Feb. 1, 23, 28, 1887; Apr. 10, Oct. 11, 1888; Feb. 8, June 24, July 10, Oct. 9, 1889. Mar. 6, 1890; Jan. 1, Nov. 19, 1891; Mar. 24, Dec. 9, 1892; Apr. 27, June 26, 28, 1893; Oct. 17, Dec. 20, 1894; Mar. 22, Apr. 12, 13, Dec. 25, 1895; Jan. 19, June 9, Nov. 15, 1897.

**Fresno: Churches**—Nov. 5, 26, 1887; Feb. 18, 1888; Jan. 1, 1889; June 21, 1890; Sept. 7, 1891; Dec. 25, 1895; Aug. 3, Sept. 14, 22, 1896; Jan. 18, Mar. 30, 1897; Feb. 22, 1898.

**Fresno: County Courthouse**—Sept. 22, Nov. 17, 1875; Jan. 23, Dec. 28, 1892; Nov. 2, 8, Dec. 19, 1893; July 13, 30, 31, Aug. 3, Oct. 14, 18, 19, 1895; May 17, 1898.

**Fresno: County Library**—Dec. 6, 1882; Jan. 3, 1883; Dec. 5, 1892; Feb. 11, 1893; Nov. 17, 1894; July 2, Dec. 25, 1895; May 27, 28, Oct. 12, 1896; Apr. 1, 1898; June 7, 1899.

**Fresno: County Orphanage**—Dec. 25, 1895; May 24, 1897.

**Fresno: Crime and Law Enforcement**—Aug. 23, Dec. 27, 1882; Oct. 3, 1883; Jan. 9, Feb. 27, Mar. 19, Apr. 16, May 7, July 16, Oct. 8, Dec. 17, 1884; Apr. 29, July 1, Dec. 30, 1885; Feb. 17, Mar. 3, 31, Aug. 4, Nov. 3, 24, 1886; Mar. 17, 21, 29, Apr. 6, July 6, Aug. 6, 1888; Jan. 26, Mar. 18, Oct. 2, Dec. 11, 1889; Jan. 13, 15, 16, Feb. 1, June 30, Oct. 29, Nov. 14, 1890; Mar. 23, 24, 25, Apr. 13, 23, 1891; Feb. 11, Mar. 16, Dec. 14, 15, 16, 17, 21, 1892; Jan. 25, Feb. 2, Apr. 17, Sept. 26, Oct. 27, Nov. 6, 14, 22, 1893; Mar. 20, 21, 23, 28, 30, May 24, 1894; Jan. 19, 26, Mar. 11, 14, 16, 26, Apr. 24, June 27, Aug. 9, 21, 22, Sept. 14, 20, 30, Oct. 2, Dec. 5, 1895; Apr. 15, Sept. 7, 12, Oct. 13, Nov. 9, Dec. 4, 1896; Jan. 22, 26, Feb. 10, 11, 12, 13, 15, 16, 17, 18, 19, 22, 24, 27, Mar. 3, 6, 23, 25, Apr. 27, 29, May 26, 29, Aug. 2, 26, Sept. 6, Oct. 5, 6, 9, 1897; July 14, Aug. 17, 30, Sept. 3, 7, 16, 22, Nov. 8, 12, 13, 19, Dec. 8, 9, 1898; Jan. 3, 20, Feb. 2, 18, 25, Mar. 5, Apr. 20, 21, 22, 23, 27, May 19, June 3, Aug. 4, 16, Sept. 13, 20, Oct. 8, 22, Dec. 3, 1899.

**Fresno: Electrical Utilities**—June 6, July 16, 1887; Mar. 27, 1889; Aug. 17, 1894; Apr. 2, July 13, 23, Oct. 18, Nov. 23, Dec. 25, 1895; Feb. 24, Mar. 7, Apr. 4, 15, June 25, 1896; Nov. 15, 1897; July 20, 22, Aug. 9, Dec. 13, 1898; Aug. 23, Sept. 5, 1899.

**Fresno: Entertainments and Recreation**—Dec. 13, 1876; Nov. 5, 1879; May 31, 1882; Jan. 9, May 7, June 18, 1884; Feb. 10, Mar. 3, 1886; Nov. 11, 1887; Jan. 1, 1889; Mar. 24, July 16, Sept. 30, 1890; Jan. 27, 1892; Jan. 28, Feb. 11, 1893; Mar. 24, May 10, Oct. 15, Dec. 24, 1894; Jan. 29, Oct. 14, Dec. 25, 1895; May 20, July 10, 1896; June 25, May 26, 1897; Feb. 1, Apr. 28, July 3, 21, Aug. 25, 1898; Feb. 25, Apr. 4, 12, 1899.

**Fresno: Fires and Firefighters**—Jan. 12, July 19, 1876; Oct. 1, 1879; July 26, Aug. 2, 30, 1882; Feb. 21, June 27, 1883; Mar. 4, Sept. 9, 1885; Aug. 13, 22, Oct. 6, 1888; July 12, 13, 17, 1889; Mar. 28, May 2, June 9, Sept. 2, 15, 1890; July 15, 19, Aug. 7, 9, Oct. 9, 11, 1893; June 15, Oct. 19, 1895; Nov. 9, 1896; Aug. 26, Nov. 3, 1897; Aug. 14, 16, Dec. 17, 25, 1898; May 14, July 5, 1899.

**Fresno: Gas Utility**—April 6, 1881; Dec. 20, 27, 1882; June 16, 1887; Dec. 25, 1895.

**Fresno: Health Care and Doctors**—Jan. 10, 1877; July 11, 1888; Apr. 3, Dec. 18, 1889; June 9, 1891; Dec. 25, 1896; Mar. 23, Sept. 7, 1896.

**Fresno: Housing**—Dec. 6, 1882; July 8, 1892; Nov. 8, 1895.

**Fresno: Natural Disasters**—Feb. 7, Mar. 27, Oct. 23, Dec. 18, 1872; July 15, 1874; July 24, 1896.

**Fresno: Newspapers**—July 26, 1888; Apr. 12, June 9, 1890; Sept. 2, 1898.

**Fresno: Post Office**—Dec. 25, 1895; July 23, 1896.

**Fresno: Schools**—Mar. 19, 1879; July 6, 1888; Sept. 16, 1889; Feb. 18, Sept. 14, 1891; Oct. 3, 1892; June 27, Dec. 25, 1895; Aug. 28, 1896; Aug. 19, Sept. 17, Oct. 5, Nov. 17, 1897; Jan. 4, Feb. 1, Oct. 11, 1898; Oct. 28, 1899.

**Fresno: Water Works**—Jan. 19, July 19, 1876; Apr. 16, 1884; Apr. 23, July 27, Dec. 15, 1897; May 19, 1892; Dec. 25, 1895.

**Fresno County: Crime and Law Enforcement**—Feb. 1, 1871; Apr. 6, 1889; July 16, 28, Oct. 27, Dec. 30, 1890; June 15, 27, 1891; Oct. 27, 1893; Jan. 30, Mar. 23, 1894; May 25, 26, June 6, 9, 30, Aug. 3, 4, 6, 15, 24, 28, Sept. 23, Nov. 24, 1896; Jan. 25, 26, Feb. 1, Apr. 26, 1897; June 24, Sept. 27, 1898; Feb. 17, 22, 27, 1899.

**Fresno County: Description and Travel**—July 6, Oct. 5, 1870; Aug. 28, Sept. 4, 11, 18, Oct. 16, Dec. 11, 18, 1872; July 30, 1873; Mar. 21, 1877; Apr. 14, 28, May 19, 1880; June 15, 22, Sept. 14, 1881; Feb. 21, 1883; Feb. 3, 1886; Mar. 25, June 25, 1889; July 14, 29, 1890; July 1, 20, 1891; May 10, 19, 1892; June 26, Sept. 1, 1893; Feb. 10, 1895; Aug. 26, Sept. 16, 1898.

**Fruit Cultivation**—July 24, 1872; Dec. 8, 1880; Sept. 21, 1881; Feb. 1, 1887; Mar. 9, 1888; Jan. 1, Mar. 11, Dec. 18, 1889; Jan. 1, 1891; Apr. 15, May 19, Dec. 1, 1892; Oct. 31, 1893; Jan. 9, Apr. 10, 1894; Mar. 4, Apr. 1, Nov. 9, Dec. 25, 1895; Oct. 10, 1896; Jan. 30, Feb. 27, Mar. 20, Nov. 8, 1898; Mar. 1, July 26, Nov. 15, 1899.

**Grain Cultivation**—Sept. 6, Oct. 25, 1871; July 3, Aug. 7, Sept. 4, 1872; Feb. 26, Mar. 12, May 21, June 18, 1873; May 6, 1874; July 23, 1879; Aug. 30, 1882; June 24, Sept. 3, 1890; Mar. 16, May 5, 19, Sept. 2, 8, 1893; May 8, July 21, 1897; July 17, 1898; July 16, Aug. 5, 1899.

**Hamptonville/Pollasky**—Aug. 17, 1891; Jan. 4, July 5, 1892; Jan. 16, Mar. 15, 1893; Aug. 17, 1894; Jan. 4, 1897; Oct. 11, 1898.

**Huron**—Feb. 24, June 22, July 26, 30, Sept. 15, Oct. 31, 1887; June 28, 1888; May 3, 1890; Apr. 12, July 15, Dec. 25, 1895; Feb. 3, 1896.

**Indians**—Aug. 20, 31, Sept. 14, Nov. 2, 1870; May 15, 22, 1872; Aug. 4, 1890; Mar. 5, 1892; Sept. 7, 1893; Jan. 9, Mar. 12, 15, 1898.

**Irrigation**—July 13, 1870; Sept. 20, Nov. 22, Dec. 13, 1871; June 5, July 31, Dec. 11, 1872; Jan. 15, Feb. 26, June 18, July 30, 1873; Aug. 4, 1875; Mar. 8, 1876; Feb. 28, Mar. 14, Apr. 25, 1877; Mar. 20, July 21, Aug. 4, Nov. 17, 1880; Aug. 17, 1881; May 31, July 19, Aug. 30, Oct. 11, Dec. 6, 1882; Feb. 7, Apr. 25, 1883; Apr. 16, Dec. 10, 1884; Jan. 1, June 25, 1889; May 5, 19, 1892; Dec. 25, 1895; Nov. 26, 1896; Feb. 6, 1897; Apr. 6, 1898.

**Kingsburg/Wheatville**—July 15, 1874; July 2, 1879; June 2, 23, July 7, 21, Aug. 4, Dec. 8, 22, 29, 1880; Jan. 12, Mar. 23, Sept. 7, 1881; Jan. 25, Apr. 26, May 3, Aug. 23, 1882; Mar. 7, 1883; Dec. 8, 1886; Apr. 2, Sept. 7, Nov. 23, 1887; Jan. 1, 1891; June 26, Aug. 3, 21, Sept. 16, Oct. 9, Nov. 15, 1893; Mar. 20, Oct. 17, 30, 1894; Feb. 12, Mar. 29, Apr. 30, May 14, Sept. 3, 1895; Dec. 22, 1896; Jan. 27, Aug. 13, 1897; Feb. 5, Mar. 27, May 4, 26, July 24, 1898; June 2, Sept. 17, 29, 1899.

**Kingston**—Aug. 30, 1871; May 15, June 25, Sept. 4, 1872; Mar. 12, May 7, Aug. 20, 1873; Jan. 14, 1874; Jan. 31, 1877.

**Liberty/Riverdale**—Jan. 3, 17, 1877; Jan. 25, Aug. 2, 1882; Feb. 21, Apr. 25, Oct. 31, 1883; Apr. 23, 1884; Feb. 1, Dec. 29, 1887.

**Lumber Industry**—June 4, 18, Aug. 13, Dec. 3, 1873; Jan. 21, 1890; Jan. 1, May 30, 1891; Jan. 15, May 19, Dec. 27, 1892; Sept. 16, 18, 1893; Mar. 14, 1894; Dec. 25, 1895; Aug. 26, 1899.

**Malaga**—Aug. 25, 1890; Sept. 20, 1892; Jan. 17, Apr. 19, 1893.

**Mendota**—Jan. 16, Mar. 11, Oct. 14, Nov. 8, 1895; May 6, 1896; Apr. 23, Oct. 6, 1898; June 20, 1899.

**Mill Creek/Dunlap**—Mar. 23, Oct. 26, 1881; Mar. 6, Apr. 29, June 17, 1889.

**Millerton**—June 15, July 6, 13, 1870; Apr. 26, 1871; Mar. 20, July 31, 1872; Jan. 23, 1878; July 18, 1891.

**Millwood**—May 13, 1899.

**Mining**—June 21, 1871; Feb. 21, July 10, Aug. 7, Dec. 11, 1872; Aug. 13, 1873; Feb. 23, Mar. 29, May 24, 1876; May 26, June 2, July 7, 21, Sept. 15, Dec. 8, 29, 1880; May 31, Aug. 16, 1882; Jan. 3, 1883; June 25, 1890; Jan. 1, May 23, Aug. 8, Nov. 11, 1891; Feb. 17, 1893; Jan. 24, Mar. 9, Aug. 1, 1894; Jan. 11, Dec. 25, 1895; June 8, 12, Sept. 9, Oct. 16, 20, 1896; Feb. 6, July 24, Aug. 17, 28, 1897; Jan. 20, June 1, Dec. 15, 1898.

**Ockenden**—July 16, 23, Aug. 6, Sept. 3, 1899.

**Oleander**—Jan. 16, 1884; May 31, Sept. 10, 25, Dec. 11, 1889; Jan. 22, May 20, Nov. 19, Dec. 3, 1890; Mar. 16, June 28, Sept. 18, Dec. 3, 1893; Mar. 31, Oct. 17, Dec. 1, 17, 1894; Jan. 8, 17, Oct. 19, Nov. 18, 1895; Mar. 30, Apr. 13, Dec. 22, 1896; Apr. 5, 1897; Sept. 2, 1899.

**Olive Cultivation**—Feb. 13, Oct. 9, 1898; Jan. 6, 1899.

**Pine Ridge**—June 21, 1882; June 18, 29, July 20, 22, Aug. 2, 10, 13, 1892; July 11, 1893; Aug. 18, 1894; Dec. 14, 1895; July 18, Aug. 11, 17, 1896; July 12, 26, 1898; June 2, 1899.

**Rabbit Drives**—Mar. 10, 1888; Feb. 29, 1896.

**Raisin Cultivation**—Oct. 15, 1879; May 26, 1880; Jan. 12, Apr. 30, 1881; Oct. 3, 1883; Sept. 2, 1885; Sept. 28, Oct. 27, Nov. 24, Dec. 8, 1886; July 13, 1887; May 10, Nov. 8, 1888; Sept. 13, 1889; June 19, Sept. 9, 1891; Jan. 23, May 7, 19, 1892; May 19, 1893; Aug. 1, 22, 1894; Dec. 25, 1895; Apr. 17, June 15, 1896; Aug. 28, Oct. 26, 1897; Aug. 27, Sept. 3, 27, 1898; Apr. 30, Aug. 6, 1899.

**Reedley**—Feb. 8, 1889; June 10, Dec. 8, 20, 1890; Jan. 1, Feb. 18, Mar. 20, Apr. 21, 28, May 6, 1891; Apr. 19, June 18, July 5, 22, Dec. 20, 1892; Jan. 31, Apr. 25, 1893; June 10, Dec. 25, 1895.

**Sanger**—Apr. 26, May 23, Sept. 15, Nov. 26, 1888; June 24, 1889; Feb. 17, July 7, 29, Aug. 14, 1 , 25, Sept. 4, 9, 22, 29, 1890; Jan. 1, Feb. 7, Oct. 16, Nov. 2, 28, 1891; Feb. 11, June 25, July 16, 1892; Nov. 2, 1893; Feb. 5, June 2, 25, oct. 29, 1894; Jan. 16, 19, Feb. 5, May 4, June 26, Dec. 20, 1897; Feb. 13, Mar. 28, 1898.

**Selma**—Dec. 29, 1880; Sept. 21, Oct. 26, 1881; Mar. 29, Aug. 23, Dec. 27, 1882; July 4, 1883; Jan. 16, Feb. 20, 1884; Dec. 30, 1885; Mar. 31, 1886; Apr. 7, 1887; Mar. 11, Sept. 12, 1899.

**Sentinel**—Jan. 17, 1877.

**Sheep Raising**—Nov. 2, 1870; June 21, 1871; June 5, July 10, Oct. 23, 1872; Aug. 13, 1873; July 10, 1890; Dec. 15, 1896; June 21, July 7, 28, 1898; Aug. 29, 1899.

**Squaw Valley**—Jan. 11, May 3, 1882; Feb. 25, May 6, July 1, 1885; Feb. 3, 1897.

**Toll House**—June 24, July 1, 8, 1885; Jan. 29, Apr. 2, 19, July 26, 1887; Mar. 4, 1889; Feb. 1, 1890; Oct. 31, 1891; Apr. 23, Aug. 6, 1892; Mar. 16, 1893; Nov. 1, 1899.

**Watts Valley**—Mar. 23, Apr. 15, 1892; June 10, 1895.

**West Side**—June 17, 1889; Feb. 25, Oct. 14, Nov. 7, 28, 1891; Apr. 9, Sept. 9, 1892; Jan. 17, 1895; Nov. 30, 1898.

**Wildflower**—Feb. 12, Mar. 19, May 21, 1879; Apr. 25, 1883; Jan. 16, 1891; Mar. 15, 1893.

**Wine Production**—Aug. 18, Sept. 22, 1896; Dec. 25, 1895; June 10, 15, July 18, 1896; Nov. 2, 1898.

Nickel, Katharine, ed. *Beginnings in the Reedley Area. A Treasury of Historical Accounts 'Till 1913. Written by Pioneers of the Reedley Area.* [Reedley, California]: December 1961. Just what the title promises, and much more. Although the reminiscences get choppy and over-anecdotal at times, virtually all aspects of the area's development are discussed—and, thanks to the recollecting, in a more entertaining way than in most history books.

Oakeshott, Gordon B., *California's Changing Landscapes: A Guide to the Geology of the State.* New York: McGraw-Hill, 1971. An excellent introduction to the subject.

Ormsby, Waterman L. *The Butterfield Overland Mail.* Edited by Lyle H. Wright and Josephine M. Bynum. San Marino, California: The Huntington Library, 1962. One of the first to travel the route, Ormsby left behind a good capsule description of Fresno County's west side in 1858.

Otis, George B. *Reminiscences of Early Days. The Pioneer Days of Selma and the Surrounding Country.* Selma, California: Press of the Selma Irrigator, July 1911.

Powers, Stephen. *Tribes of California*, with an introduction and notes by Robert F. Heizer. Berkeley and Los Angeles: University of California Press, 1976 (reprinted from *Contributions to North American Ethnology*, Volume III, U.S. Government Printing Office, 1877).

Roeding, George C[hristian]. *The Smyrna Fig at Home and Abroad. A treatise on practical Smyrna fig culture, together with an account of the introduction of the Wild or Capri fig, and the establishment of the Fig Wasp (Blastophaga grossorum) in America.* Fresno: published by the author for general circulation, 1903.

*Sanger Herald. Golden Jubilee Edition, 1888-1938. Fifty years of progress . . . from a desert wasteland to one of California's outstanding diversified agricultural districts.* Sanger, California: *Sanger Herald*, April 29, 1938. Many articles and photographs of historical interest are here, and despite the disjointed quality this work ranks as the best available history of Sanger.

———. *Diamond Jubilee Progress Edition. Celebrating the 75th Anniversary of the Founding of Sanger (1888-1963). Progress Through Community Effort.* Sanger, California: *Sanger Herald*, September 1963. The emphasis here is more on progress than history, although a few tidbits missing from the golden anniversary issue are present.

Secrest, William B. [Sr.] *Joaquin: Bloody Bandit of the Mother Lode.* Fresno, California: Saga-West Publishing Company, 1967. A brief, but accurate, account containing some details Latta (q.v.) missed or ignored.

———. *When the Great Spirit Died. The California Indian Wars, 1850–1860.* Manuscript in possession of author, Fresno, California. As the title suggests, the statewide field is covered within the given time frame but there is still much on all the Fresno County disturbances of the period. Many details, other than those concerning the Mariposa Indian War, are new and have been gleaned from previously untouched state and federal records.

Shallat, Todd A. *Water and the Rise of Public Ownership on the Fresno Plain, 1850 to 1978.* Fresno: City of Fresno Public Works Department, October 1978. An excellent, accurate survey, with many interesting details about the Fresno Water Works and early utilities in town.

Shaw, John Andrew, Jr. "Commercialization in an agricultural economy: Fresno County, California 1856–1900." Ph.D. dissertation, Purdue University, August 1969.

Sinclair, Laura Wickham. *Early History of Caruthers.* Typescript, Fresno City and County Historical Society. Useful and trustworthy; aside from a few newspaper clippings and the Dow dissertation listed above, the sole source on the subject.

*Smith, Jedediah S., the Southwest Expedition of: His Personal Account of the Journey to California, 1826–1827.* Edited by George R. Brooks. Glendale, California: The Arthur H. Clark Co., 1966. Good resource.

Smith, Wallace [Paul Victor]. *Garden of the Sun.* Los Angeles: Lymanhouse, 1939, and subsequent reprintings. An informative work that has much to say about every aspect of the San Joaquin Valley's early history. Smith writes of the Indians, early towns and agriculture in great detail. The only problem is that some of his facts are in error.

Sweet, Nathan E. "Early Traders and Trading Posts Along the Fresno River." *Ash Tree Echo*, Vol. 8, No. 3.

Teilman, I[ngvart] and Shafer, W[illiam] H. *The Historical Story of Irrigation in Fresno and Kings Counties in Central California.* Fresno: Williams and Son, 1943. A useful, accurate, albeit small narrative, with interesting stories about Dr. E. B. Perrin and the irrigation controversies.

Thickens, Virginia Emily. "Pioneer Colonies of Fresno County." M.A. thesis, University of California, Berkeley, 1942. Does not contain much new material; mainly useful for some details on obscure Fresno County colonies.

Thompson, Thomas H. *Official Historical Atlas Map of Fresno County.* Tulare: Thos. H. Thompson, 1891. Excellent maps of the county and towns, with a condensed history by C. O. Ziegenfuss.

*Those Were the Days: Early Days in Clovis.* [Clovis, California:] Clovis Adult Education, 1976. An informative, generally accurate compendium of recollections pertaining to Clovis. A good complement (and balance) to Chedister, q.v.

Vandor, Paul E. *History of Fresno County, California, with biographical sketches of the leading men and women of the county who have been identified with its growth and development from the early days to the present.* Los Angeles, California: Historic Record Company, 1919. The historical narrative in this book has many inaccuracies, inconsistencies and oversights. It should be used with caution. Lack of an index seriously reduces its value.

Van Dyke, Viola Kreyenhagen. *Coalinga Mineral Springs.* Typescript, Coalinga Library. A brief, accurate history.

Walker, Ben Randal. *Fresno Community Book.* Fresno: Arthur H. Cawston, 1946. A miscellany of facts and figures relating to Fresno County agriculture and Fresno proper.

———. *Fresno County Blue Book, containing facts and impressions for the better understanding of Fresno County . . . with biographies of representative Fresno County people.* Fresno, California: Arthur H. Cawston, 1941. Basically a somewhat larger version of *Community Book*.

———. *Formative Years of the Alta District.* Manuscript dated November 11, 1938, in Fresno City and County Historical Society Archives.

Walker, J. N. Letter in Fresno City and County Historical Society Archives concerning the Ghost Dance of 1870 in Fresno County.

Wardlaw, Muriel E. "The Big Dry Creek District." *Ash Tree Echo*, Vol. 9, No. 3. A basic account with some useful information.

Winchell, Ernestine. *Fresno Memories.* Manuscripts in possession of Thelma Carpenter, who made copies available for this book and the archives of Fresno City and County Historical Society. During the 1920s and 1930s Ernestine Winchell, wife of historian Lilbourne Alsip Winchell, wrote a regular historical column for the *Fresno Morning Republican* entitled "Fresno Memories." She dealt with a myriad of historical subjects and obtained much of her data from firsthand observers of events; as a result, her columns have much original information. The only defect of Mrs. Winchell's writing is that she consistently paraphrased the recollections of old-timers and rarely wrote stories told in their own words. Despite this, the contributions of Ernestine Winchell to Fresno County history are enormous. Even if indirectly, she preserved much that would otherwise have been lost.

Winchell, Lilbourne Alsip. *History of Fresno County and the San Joaquin Valley; narrative and biographical.* Fresno: Arthur H. Cawston, 1933. The best, most accurate history of Fresno County published thus far. Save for a few instances, all its facts and figures can be used with confidence. Its only defect is that, other than Fresno itself, county towns are treated in an exceedingly summary fashion. Fortunately, the data on early agriculture is rather substantial, as is that concerning the first years of Fresno.

Zierer, Paul A. "Sanger, California: A Study of Industry in a Small City." M.A. thesis, University of California, Los Angeles, 1966. A few details concerning early Sanger businesses are given; the emphasis is on the twentieth century, however.

# Index

357

360